UNITED STATES CONGRESSIONAL DISTRICTS 1788–1841

☆ ☆ ☆ UNITED STATES CONGRESSIONAL DISTRICTS 1788–1841

Stanley B. Parsons
William W. Beach
Dan Hermann

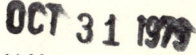

GREENWOOD PRESS
WESTPORT, CONNECTICUT • LONDON, ENGLAND

Library of Congress Cataloging in Publication Data

Parsons, Stanley B

  United States congressional districts, 1788-1841.

  Bibliography: p.
  Includes index.
  1. United States. Congress. House—Election
Districts—History. I. Beach, William W., joint
author. II. Hermann, Dan, joint author. III. Title.
JK1341.P37   328.73'07'345   77-83897
ISBN 0-8371-9828-3

Library of Congress Catalog Card Number: 77-83897
ISBN: 0-8371-9828-3

First published in 1978

Greenwood Press, Inc.
51 Riverside Avenue, Westport, Connecticut 06880

Printed in the United States of America

10 9 8 7 6 5 4 3 2 1

FOR
THOMAS B. ALEXANDER
AND
ALLAN G. BOGUE

PIONEERS IN THE STUDY
OF AMERICAN CONGRESSES

CONTENTS

Acknowledgments

United States Congressional Districts, 1788-1841, was conceived as a joint project of its editor-compilers, but many students, staff, and faculty members at the University of Missouri-Kansas City have made contributions toward its completion. The entire project would have been impossible had it not been for the Federal Work-Study Program at the university. Ms. Linda Lawrence, work-study administrator, displayed consistent interest and was most helpful in securing the fine student assistants who helped in all phases of the project. The Faculty Research Council of the University of Missouri-Kansas City, under the leadership of Dean Herwig Zauchenberger, provided a generous grant that made possible the collection of maps, necessary travel expenses, and the preparation of the final copy. The staff of the University Library, particularly Ms. Shirley Mickelson of Inter-Library Loans and Ms. Bernice Miller of Government Documents, proved unfailingly helpful and tolerant of our many minute problems. Dale Neuman, campus ICPSR representative, acted with his usual efficiency in helping secure the ICPSR tapes used in checking the party affiliations and district numbers of all congressmen.

Outside our university other scholars proved most helpful and encouraging. Andrew Modelski of the Map Division of the Library of Congress helped fit the task of locating early national maps with distinct county boundaries into a manageable length of time. Professor Perry Howard of Louisiana State University contributed his expertise toward at least a partial solution of the enigmatic official description of district boundaries in Louisiana after 1822. We also acknowledge the timely assistance of the Harvard Law Library, New York State Library, Kentucky Law School Library, and the State Historical Society of Missouri. A special note of gratitude goes to Steven Demaree of the University of Missouri-Columbia for his assistance on Maryland's congressional districts and to Annabelle Corrick for her assistance in preparing many of our maps. Janet Vavra of ICPSR proved most helpful in shortening our turnaround time for information requested from Ann Arbor, while George Dahlgren, Dean of UMKC's College of Arts and Sciences, receives our special gratitude for recommending and supporting our continuing membership in the ICPSR.

The greatest debt we must acknowledge is to those who helped in the actual preparation of this work. Four work-study research assistants—Greg Frisbie, Brooke Heagerty, Bonnie Moxley, and Greg Aubrey—adopted the project as their own and with enthusiasm and dedication helped us order our masses of detail into its final form. Elizabeth Bailey typed the entire manuscript in camera-ready form. Her attention to detail and her help in proofing have greatly increased both the accuracy and logical presentation of the work. The editor-compilers accept the responsibility for any remaining errors or omissions.

In a project involving as many separate operations as *United States Congressional Districts,* we believe it appropriate to indicate the areas of responsibility assumed by each of the editor-compilers. The nature and sequence of these steps is indicated in the section on methodology.

Stanley B. Parsons assumed the general direction of the project, secured the original maps of counties and districts, and participated actively in all other phases of the project.

William W. Beach assumed responsibility for the appendix and index and participated actively in all of the other phases of the project.

Dan Hermann helped with the location of districts in the early state records and with the drawing of the maps.

Michael J. Dubin generously reviewed many of the maps presented in this volume. His suggestions, based on his own extensive research on the location of congressional districts, proved most helpful. We are most appreciative of his help.

Introduction

The editor-compilers of *United States Congressional Districts, 1788-1841,* believe this atlas fulfills a long-standing need for students of American political and legislative behavior. Presented here for the first time are the county compositions, boundaries, and selected statistical information relating to all of the congressional districts in the United States during the early national period. With its projected companion volumes covering the years from 1842 to 1942, we envision that this work will be particularly valuable for two areas of contemporary scholarly concern: legislative behavior and aggregate election analysis.

LEGISLATIVE BEHAVIOR

When *United States Congressional Districts, 1788-1841,* is used in conjunction with the Congressional Quarterly's *Guide to U. S. Elections* (1976) and the congressional roll-call data available from the Inter-University Consortium for Social and Political Research (ICPSR), scholars will find it possible to relate the legislative behavior of individual congressmen to the economic, social, and political characteristics of their respective constituencies. By using these new resources we believe that the House of Representatives will become a more useful focus for the study of American politics. The more homogeneous nature of the congressional district, as compared to the heterogeneity of the typical state, will make possible a more precise analysis than has previously been possible of the relationship between constituency characteristics and policy positions of legislators.

AGGREGATE ELECTORAL BEHAVIOR

We also believe that *United States Congressional Districts, 1788-1841,* will prove useful in aggregate voting analysis. In analyzing political developments at the national level, the utility of votes aggregated at the district level is greater than county-level aggregate data. Many districts are sufficiently homogeneous socially and economically to be treated as a reliable observation over time; the voters' policy concerns are often similar to those of their representatives; and, most importantly, districts are not as numerically overwhelming as are counties. For these reasons, the two-year sequence for congressional elections, when related to constituency characteristics, may reveal significant information about changing patterns in the American political experience.

Finally, we hope that by putting district information in an easily accessible form, we will stimulate both new and more comprehensive explanations of traditional historical problems as well as present material that will lead to new insights about American political life.

The descriptive information about congressional districts presented here is meager when compared to that presented in the two recent decennial publications of the Census Bureau, *United States Congressional Districts.* The earliest censes were devoted solely to their original intent of enumerating the population for congressional reapportionment. They enumerated only the males and females of the white, free-black, and slave-black populations and contained no economic or other demographic material. Although these early enumerations are admittedly inadequate by modern standards, we believe they can yield useful insights into the composition and nature of the antebellum districts. The following data is presented in this volume:

1. The population of the district. Early districts varied greatly in population. There are probably many explanations for this variance, but certainly political

conflict between older and newer sections of a state is an important factor during the era covered by this volume. The political and economic ramifications of this variance played an important part in shaping American society. In this regard, such differences in population undoubtedly influenced both the perceptions of voters and those people who represented them.

2. The population of counties can indicate the degree of uniformity within the district—was the district totally or only partially rural in its county composition? The population per square mile by county would also indicate the demographic homogeneity of the district.

3. The slave population and its relative size serve as indicators of counties or districts influenced by the psychological, sociological, and economic implications of slavery.

4. The area in square miles and the population per square mile serve as rough urban-rural and commercial-noncommercial indices for both districts and counties.

The following descriptive information about early congressmen is also presented:

1. Party affiliation.
2. Post office and county address.
3. Number of terms served (index).
4. Listing of congressmen by state delegations (index).

Methodology

The assembly of the different types of data presented in *United States Congressional Districts, 1788-1841*, has involved many procedures, assumptions, and practical decisions. These problems arose because of the uneven quality of specific information about early districts, counties, and congressmen. We hope that our solutions to these problems have produced the greatest possible accuracy; if we have failed in this regard, then we believe that an explicit description of our methods will aid those who will improve the quality of our data. We explain our procedures in the order of the specific steps used in producing the work.

IDENTIFICATION OF DISTRICTS

The county composition of each congressional district between 1788 and 1841 was usually secured from the session laws of the respective state. Each volume of session laws was arranged chronologically as the laws were enacted, so it was usually possible to find the act that districted the state during the third year of each decade. Roughly, the process of creating districts involved the Census Bureau enumerating the population during the first year of the decade (−00); congressional legislation for apportioning representation according to the census toward the end of the second year (−01); and finally the state legislatures districting their states during the early months of the third year of the decade (−02). There were, of course, many exceptions to this procedure, so we found it necessary to look at each page of all the session laws enacted during the period. We double-checked our findings by referring to the combined statutes of the states. These are noted in the bibliography. When we found major off-year rearrangement of the districts, we treated them as distinct from our regular decennial sequence of district

presentations, for example, the New York apportionment of 1798, and placed them after the usual third-year districting. In instances where successive districting acts within a decade effected only minor changes in district composition, we have noted these changes in preceding or succeeding acts. Finally, we have included in our regular sequence of presentation some districts created in the fourth year of the decade. These have been noted.

Between 1788 and 1841, Massachusetts used two methods of identifying its congressional districts in the session laws: Districts were identified by the name of the principal county contained within them or by a number and letter combination, such as 1 W and 2 N. Inasmuch as we wished to maintain continuity in the designation of districts, we adopted the policy of numbering the districts in Massachusetts. Our wholly arbitrary numbering system for districts in that state usually begins with the eastern-most district and ends with the western-most district. By following this practice districts tend to maintain their same numerical designation from decade to decade. However, this practice has made our numerical designations inconsistent with those districts in Massachusetts given by ICPSR. The consortium's district numbers for Massachusetts would have served our purposes had they met the criterion of geographical consistency from decade to decade. This not being the case, we chose to take an independent stance on numbering the districts of that state.

IDENTIFICATION OF DISTRICT AND COUNTY BOUNDARIES

The county boundaries of the districts presented in this work were taken from atlases and maps cited in the bibliography. These maps were secured from various sources. The largest number came from the Cartographic Section of the Library of Congress. Others were located in the Virginia Historical Society, the State Historical Society of Missouri, and, in a few instances, modern retrospective atlases published by a few states.

Cartography prior to the 1820s was not an exact science, and in many cases several maps of the same year show different boundaries for the same counties. Cross-checking for accuracy was effected by referring to the data on county creations that we assembled for the appendix. This enabled us to determine if new county boundaries were similar or were derived wholly or partially from older, "parent" counties in the same area. Most of the difficulty in estimating accurate boundaries occurred during the early years of the settlement of an area. During that time some counties often approached 50 percent of the land area of a given state. When boundaries consisted of obvious physical features, assigning a boundary was relatively precise. More difficulty was experienced when cartographers simply circumscribed areas by using crude, straight-line representations of county boundaries. When such maps were obviously incorrect, we had to rely on later, more accurate maps, on the printed material relating to county creations and, in a few cases, on rough descriptions of county boundaries found in state session laws.

COUNTY CREATION DATES

During the course of identifying the county composition of the congressional districts, it became necessary to determine when a specific county was created. We needed this information for two reasons. First, we found counties listed in the state-districting acts that did not appear in the published census closest to the districting legislation. When this discrepancy was discovered, we used the county creation date to ascertain whether the census had committed an error of omission or whether the county had been created between the time of the federal enumeration and the time of the statute that districted the state. We always found the latter explanation for the discrepancy to be true. Second, creation of the county did not necessarily mean that the new county had achieved administrative and electoral powers separate from the parent county or counties. In nearly all cases autonomy was achieved simultaneously with creation, but in a few instances a statute subsequent to the statute of creation was enacted by the legislature organizing the county for these purposes. Created but unorganized counties are so noted in the list of county creations.

On a more general level, we assembled this listing to facilitate the work of scholars interested in data sets of continuous observations. With this listing in hand, counties subject to creations can be excluded in any data set in which time is a factor. For example, any statement comparing the population per square mile of a county existing in both 1800 and 1810 when that county was reduced in size by a division would need to be adjusted for the creation or stand meaningless.

In preparing the list of county creations (the appendix), we worked from a listing of county creation dates taken from Kane's *American Counties* and *The Handy Book for Genealogists.* The data taken from these two sources was then compared to the statutes creating the counties. When this comparison was made, a number of inaccuracies in the spelling of the county names and the dates of creation were found to exist in both *The Handy Book* and *American Counties.* In addition, both sources often failed to include creation information on bona fide counties. We see these errors, however, as insufficient grounds for dismissing the usefulness of these two monumental compilations. Rather, we offer our table as a corrective addendum to the pioneering efforts of both Joseph Kane and the genealogists of the *Handy Book.*

We used the Library of Congress's *Records of the States of the United States of America* microfilm series as our principal source on county creations. Unfortunately, this excellent collection ends its legislative series with the early 1830s. For the purpose of interpreting census data and constructing both district tables and maps, the end of the microfilm series in 1832 did not present us with great problems. The few questions that could not be answered by looking at the *Records of the States* were referred to gracious law librarians throughout the country. When it became apparent, however, that our listing might be of some help to scholars using county-level data, we attempted to bring the listing up to 1841, the terminal date of this volume. This attempt presented us with logistical and budgetary problems we could not overcome. Therefore, we decided to present our original table with the hope that our next listing of creation dates will bridge the gap from 1831 to 1841.

AREA OF COUNTIES AND DISTRICTS

After locating county boundaries, we then determined the number of square miles in each county and congressional district. Since no census information concerning land area is available prior to 1881, our basic source for these data was the most recent edition of the *City and County Fact Book,* which contains the land area of every present-day county in the United States. For those countries whose boundaries have remained unchanged, we assigned the contemporary land area. For those counties that today are obviously portions of earlier, larger counties, we derived the area of the earlier, larger county simply by adding the area of the contemporary, smaller counties. The greatest number of earlier counties, however, was not simply divided into smaller and smaller segments to make modern counties. These often had irregular boundaries and land areas unrelated to contemporary counties. For this category of counties we estimated the land area by using two complementary methods: (1) by estimating the percent of a known portion of a state occupied by an unknown county land area (this would then be multiplied to give an explicit land area); (2) by roughly calculating the area of the county using the scale of distances on our original map. The result of the two methods would then be compared. A final check of the land area assigned to each county was achieved by summing the area of all the counties within the state. If the sum came within 5 percent of the current area, we accepted our figures as being within a reasonable range of error.

The land area in each district was determined by summing the land areas of the constituent counties.

POPULATION ESTIMATES OF COUNTIES AND DISTRICTS

Population statistics are, of course, the *raison d'être* for the census, and our use of them requires little explanation.

We did not think the usefulness of this work would be greatly enhanced by using the "free negroes" category, so our "slave" category includes "free negroes" in the South. Free negroes are included in the aggregate population in the North.

In cases in which counties were divided after the census had been taken, we often pro-rated the population to each of the newly created counties on the basis of the population per square mile of the original county. This was especially true if the newly created counties were placed in different districts. In other instances in which county boundaries were interdistrict and did not affect district figures, we listed the newly created county but did not attempt to calculate its area or population.

CORRELATION OF REPRESENTATIVES WITH DISTRICTS

A major problem encountered in this work was that of identifying the congressional district represented by each congressman. District-congressman correlation poses no problem after ICPSR data becomes available and relatively complete with the Nineteenth Congress (1825), but before that date there is no single source for this information. Until 1807 the congressional rosters in the *Biographical Directory of the American Congress* do not even list the post office, let alone the district designation, of any congressman. In most of the early congresses we were able to determine a congressman's district by finding his post office address in his biographical sketch in the *Biographical Directory of the American Congress,* in another reference work, or in a scholarly monograph. Then by locating the post office within a county, we were able to place the congressman within a district. In most cases this procedure worked adequately; in some, however, we were unable to locate the congressman's residence. We then made an educated guess about the district he represented. This determination was made in several ways. In some instances sources mentioned the congressman's county or general area of residence. In others, when we had no residential information at all, we assigned districts when the number of terms the congressman served would only "fit" one district in the state. Finally we checked our district designations with available ICPSR congressional elections data. All uncertain district designations are identified in the text by an asterisk after the name of the congressman.

REPRESENTATIVES AND PARTY AFFILIATION

The party affiliation of congressmen often proved difficult to ascertain. To obtain this information we checked the sources listed in the bibliography. Particularly helpful for the more difficult earlier congresses were Rudolph Bell, *Party and Faction in American Politics,* and Manning Dauer, *The Adams Federalists,* and, of course, the *Biographical Directory of the American Congress.* Because of the detail of the Bell and Dauer works, we were able to identify the party affiliation of most of the congressmen who sat in the First through the Seventh congresses. The greatest number of unidentified congressmen are those who sat in the Eighth, Ninth, Tenth, Eleventh, Fifteenth, and Sixteenth Congresses. Thereafter the *Biographical Directory* supplied more detailed information on party affiliation. For the period after 1824 Congressional Quarterly's *Guide to U. S. Elections,* derived from the ICPSR collection of election data, is the most useful work.

The assignment of uniform party labels presented us with a major problem because of the numerous names used to identify the same political group in different localities. No uniformity exists between states; individuals frequently invented their own subparty to signify deviation from a major party, and modern historians attach party labels according to their own interpretation of the era. For the sake of uniformity as well as our belief that our system probably represents a rough consensus among those familiar with the era, we devised the nomenclature seen in the table of party abbreviations.

DISTRICT AND CONGRESSIONAL DATING

Some confusion may arise from misunderstanding the relationship between district dating and congressional dating. For example, when the congressional districts of Maryland between 1802 and 1811 appear with the Eighth through Twelfth Congresses, this does not mean that the Twelfth Congress ended in 1811. Unless otherwise noted, all dates refer to districts. Thus, Maryland's representatives to the Twelfth Congress were elected in 1810 under districts created in 1802. The Twelfth Congress ceased its deliberations in 1813.

ADMISSION DATES FOR THE STATES

Delaware	Dec. 7, 1787
Pennsylvania	Dec. 12, 1787
New Jersey	Dec. 18, 1787
Georgia	Jan. 2, 1788
Connecticut	Jan. 9, 1788
Massachusetts	Feb. 6, 1788
Maryland	Apr. 28, 1788
South Carolina	May 23, 1788
New Hampshire	June 21, 1788
Virginia	June 25, 1788
New York	July 26, 1788
North Carolina	Nov. 21, 1789
Rhode Island	May 29, 1790
Vermont	Mar. 4, 1791
Kentucky	June 1, 1792
Tennessee	June 1, 1796
Ohio	Mar. 1, 1803
Louisiana	Apr. 30, 1812
Indiana	Dec. 11, 1816
Mississippi	Dec. 10, 1817
Illinois	Dec. 3, 1818
Alabama	Dec. 14, 1819
Maine	Mar. 15, 1820
Missouri	Aug. 10, 1821
Arkansas	June 15, 1836

PARTY ABBREVIATIONS

Ad	=	Administration
A-Ad	=	Anti-Administration
AB	=	Anti-Bank
AM	=	Anti-Mason
AR	=	Adams Republican
CR	=	Clay Republican
D	=	Democrat
F	=	Federalist
I	=	Independent
JD	=	Jacksonian Democrat
JR	=	Jeffersonian Republican
N	=	Nullification
ND	=	Nullification Democrat
NR	=	National Republican
OR	=	Old Republican
PT	=	Protectionist
R	=	Republican
SFT	=	States Rights Free Trader
SRD	=	States Rights Democrat
SRN	=	States Rights Nullification
SRR	=	States Rights Republican
SRW	=	States Rights Whig
SWD	=	States Rights War Democrat
UD	=	Union Democrat
W	=	Whig
WR	=	War Republican

SYMBOLS

†	=	Died
r	=	Resigned
ce	=	Contested Election
*	=	Educated Guess
----	=	No Data
e	=	Estimated Data
**	=	Date available, but too unreliable to be included

1

Congressional Districts of the Constitutional Apportionment

1788–1791
1st and 2nd Congresses

| County | COUNTIES | | | | | REPRESENTATIVES | | | | |
	Aggregate	Slave	%S	sq.mi.	P/sq.mi.	Representative	Cong.	Pty.	Address	County
						AT LARGE				
Fairfield	36,250	797	2.19	626	57.9	Benjamin Huntington	1	Ad	Norwich	New London
Hartford	38,029	263	0.69	739	51.5	Roger Sherman	1	Ad	New Haven	New Haven
Litchfield	38,755	233	0.6	925	41.9	Jonathan Sturges	1	Ad	Fairfield	Fairfield
Middlesex	18,855	221	1.1	372	50.7	Jonathan Trumbull	1	Ad	Lebanon	New London
New Haven	30,830	433	1.4	604	51.0	Jeremiah Wadsworth	1	Ad	Hartford	Hartford
New London	33,200	586	1.7	667	49.8	James Hillhouse	2	Ad	New Haven	New Haven
Tolland	13,106	47	0.3	416	31.5	Amasa Learned	2	Ad	New London	New London
Windham	28,921	184	0.6	514	56.3	Jonathan Sturges	2	Ad	Fairfield	Fairfield
TOTALS	237,946	2,764	1.1	4,863	48.9	Jonathan Trumbull	2	Ad	Lebanon	New London
						Jeremiah Wadsworth	2	Ad	Hartford	Hartford

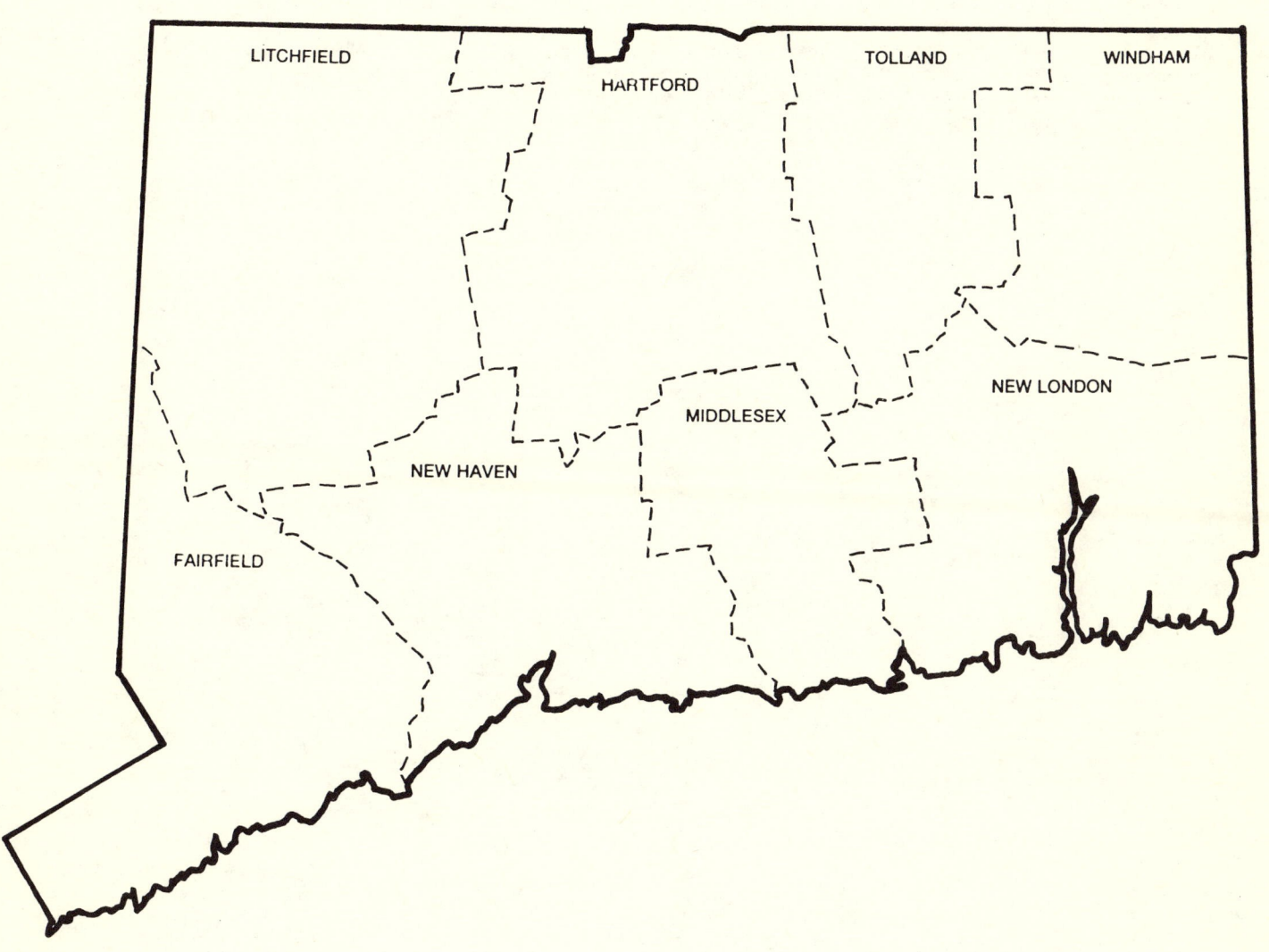

COUNTIES						REPRESENTATIVES				
County	Aggregate	Slave	%S	sq.mi.	P/sq.mi.	Representative	Cong.	Pty.	Address	County
Kent	18,920	2,300	12.1	594	31.8	John Vining	1	Ad	Dover	Kent
Newcastle	19,680	2,562	13.0	438	44.9	John Vining	2	Ad	Dover	Kent
Sussex	20,488	4,025	19.6	950	21.6					
TOTALS	59,088	8,887	15.0	1,982	29.8					

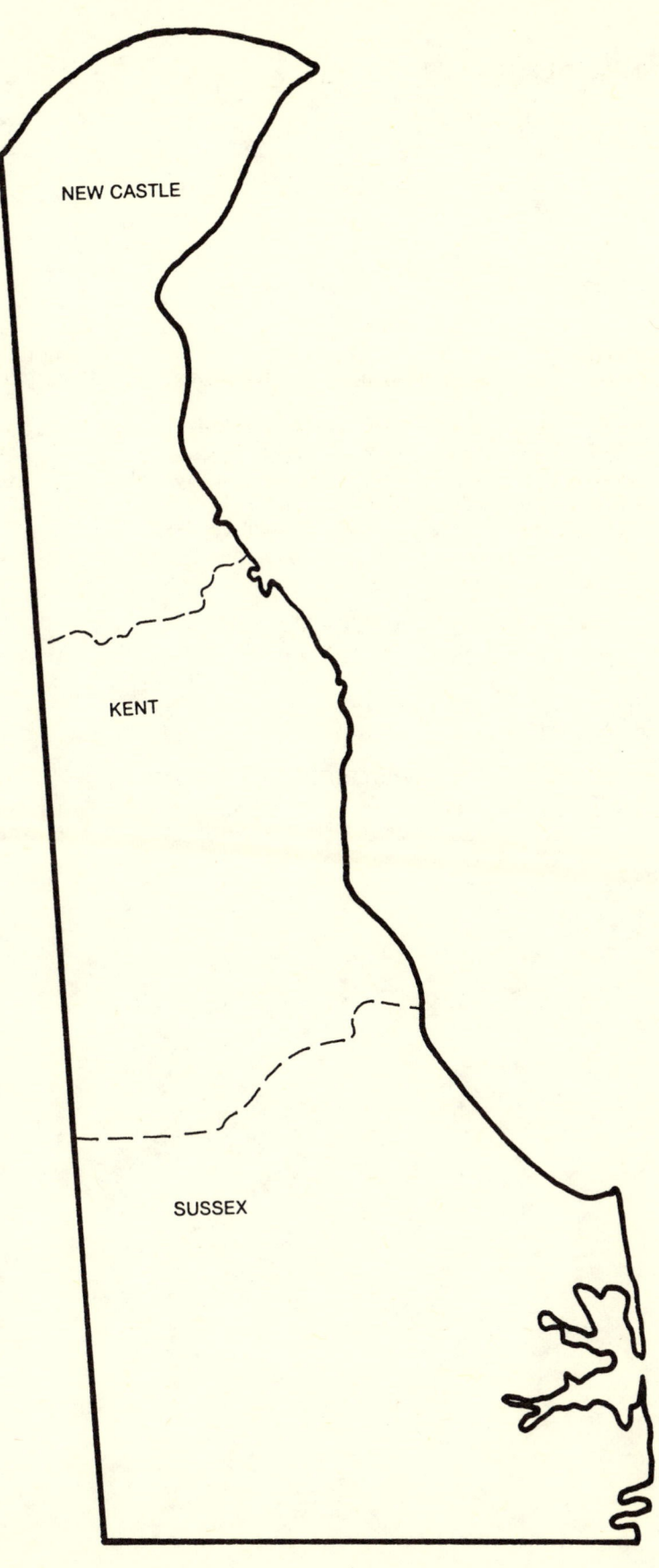

NEW CASTLE

KENT

SUSSEX

| | COUNTIES | | | | | REPRESENTATIVES | | | | |
County	Aggregate	Slave	%S	sq.mi.	P/sq.mi.	Representative	Cong.	Pty.	Address	County
						DISTRICT 1 (LOWER)				
Camden	305	70	22.9	1,187	0.3	James Jackson	1	A-Ad	Savannah	Chatham
Chatham	10,769	8,201	76.1	445	24.2	Anthony Wayne[ce]	2	Ad	Savannah	Chatham
Effingham	2,424	750	30.9	1,131	2.1	John Milledge	2	A-Ad	Savannah	Chatham
Glynn	413	215	52.0	412	1.0	(Replaced Wayne)				
Liberty	5,355	4,025	75.1	1,342	4.0					
TOTALS	19,274	13,261	68.8	4,517	4.3					
						DISTRICT 2 (UPPER)				
Franklin	1,041	156	14.9	2,175	0.5	George Mathews	1	A-Ad	----	Wilkes
Greene	5,405	1,377	25.4	881	6.1	Francis Willis	2	A-Ad	----	Wilkes
Wilkes	31,500	7,268	23.0	2,155	14.6					
TOTALS	37,946	8,801	23.2	5,211	7.3					
						DISTRICT 3 (MIDDLE)				
Burke	9,467	2,392	25.2	1,612	5.9	Abraham Baldwin	1	Ad	Augusta	Richmond
Richmond	11,317	4,116	36.3	423	26.8	Abraham Baldwin	2	Ad	Augusta	Richmond
Washington	4,552	694	15.2	4,526	1.0					
TOTALS	25,336	7,202	28.4	6,561	3.8					

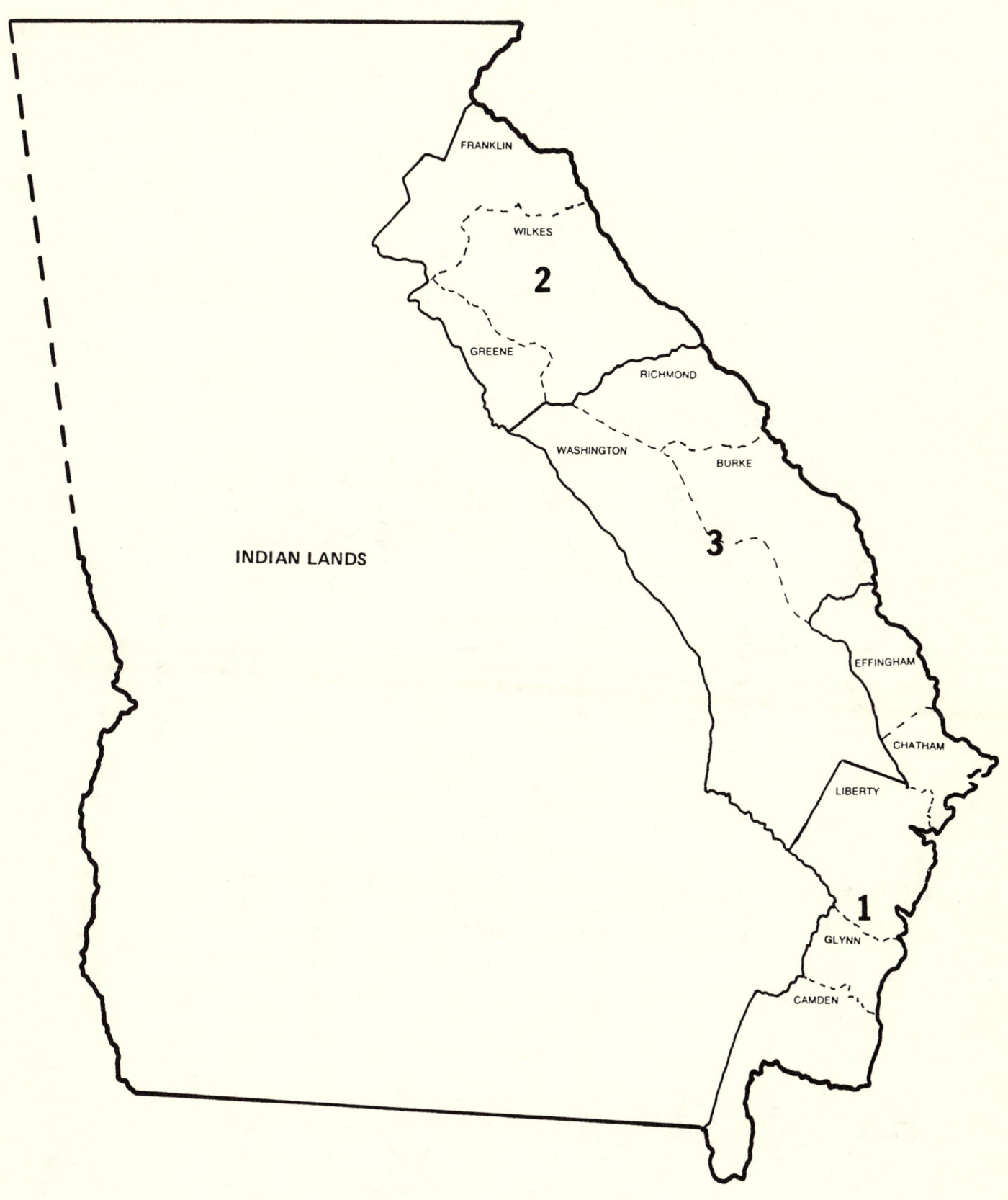

INDIAN LANDS

FRANKLIN

WILKES

2

GREENE

RICHMOND

WASHINGTON

BURKE

3

EFFINGHAM

CHATHAM

LIBERTY

1

GLYNN

CAMDEN

	COUNTIES					REPRESENTATIVES				
County	Aggregate	Slave	%S	sq.mi.	P/sq.mi.	Representative	Cong.	Pty	Address	County
DISTRICT 1										
Calvert	8,652	4,305	49.7	217	39.9	Michael Jenifer	1	Ad	Port Tobacco	Charles
Charleston	20,613	10,085	48.9	459	44.9					
St. Marys	15,544	6,985	44.9	373	41.7	Philip Key	2	Ad	Leonard-town	St. Marys
TOTALS	44,809	21,375	47.7	1,049	42.7					
DISTRICT 2										
Caecil	13,625	3,407	25.0	363	37.5	Joshua Seney	1	Ad	Church Hill	Queen Annes
Kent	12,836	5,433	42.3	281	45.6	Joshua Seney	2	Ad	Church Hill	Queen Annes
Queen						(Resigned May 1, 1792)				
Annes	15,463	6,674	43.1	375	41.2	William Hindman	2	Ad	----	Talbot
Talbot	13,084	4,777	36.5	261	50.1	(Replaced Seney)				
TOTALS	55,008	20,287	36.80	1,280	42.2					
DISTRICT 3										
City of Annapolis (no data)						Benjamin Contee	1	Ad	Brooke-field	Prince Georges
Anne-Arundel	22,598	10,130	44.8	674	33.5	Samuel Sterett	2	A-Ad	----	----
Prince Georges	21,344	11,176	52.3	505	42.3					
TOTALS	43,942	21,306	48.3	1,179	37.3					
DISTRICT 4										
Baltimore	25,434	5,877	23.1	598	42.6	William Smith	1	Ad	Town of Baltimore	
Town of Baltimore	13,503	1,255	9.2	78	173.1	William Pinkney	2	Ad	----	Hartford
Harford	14,976	3,417	22.8	453	33.1	(Resigned November, 1791)				
TOTALS	53,913	10,549	19.5	1,129	47.8	John Francis Mercer	2	A-Ad	----	----
						(Replaced Pinkney)				
DISTRICT 5										
Caroline	9,506	2,057	21.6	321	29.6	George Gale	1	Ad	"Brook-land" (estate)	Caecil
Dorchester	15,875	5,337	33.6	594	26.7					
Somerset	15,610	7,070	45.2	339	46.0	William Vans Murray	2	Ad	Cambridge	Dorchester
Worcester	11,640	3,836	32.9	479	24.3					
TOTALS	52,631	18,300	34.7	1,733	30.4					
DISTRICT 6										
Frederick	30,791	3,641	11.8	765	40.3	Daniel Carroll	1	Ad	Forest Glen	Montgomery
Montgomery	18,003	6,030	33.4	515	34.9	Upton Sheridine	2	A-Ad	Liberty	Frederick
Washington	15,822	10,957	16.9	2,677	24.1					
TOTALS	64,616	10,957	16.9	2,677	24.1					

[1] The First Congress elected at large, but representatives were required to be residents of districts.

8

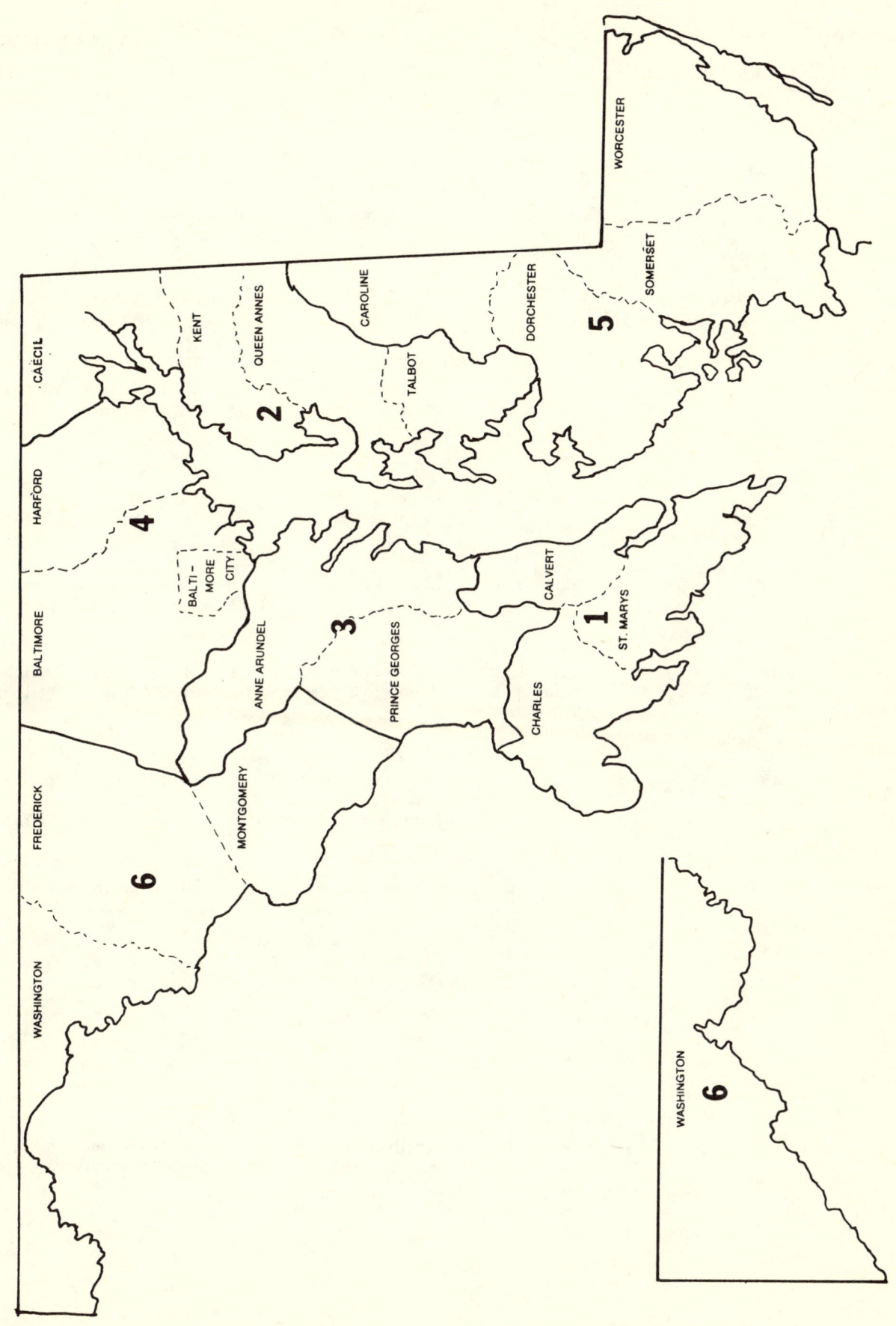

	COUNTIES						REPRESENTATIVES			
County	Aggregate	Slave	%S	sq.mi.	P/sq.mi.	Representative	Cong.	Pty.	Address	County
DISTRICT 1										
Suffolk	44,875	----	----	450	99.7	Fisher Ames	1	Ad	Dedham	Suffolk
						Fisher Ames	2	Ad	Dedham	Suffolk
DISTRICT 2										
Essex	57,913	----	----	494	117.2	Benjamin Goodhue	1	Ad	Salem	Essex
						Benjamin Goodhue	2	Ad	Salem	Essex
DISTRICT 3										
Middlesex	42,737	----	----	825	51.8	Elbridge Gerry	1	A-Ad	Marblehead	Essex
						Elbridge Gerry	2	A-Ad	Marblehead	Essex
DISTRICT 4										
Berkshire	30,291	----	----	941	32.2	Theodore Sedgwick	1	Ad	Sheffield	Berkshire
Hampshire	59,681	----	----	1,856	32.2	Theodore Sedgwick	2	Ad	Sheffield	Berkshire
TOTALS	89,972	----	----	2,797	32.2					
DISTRICT 5										
Barnstable	17,354	----	----	393	44.2	George Partridge[r]	1	Ad	Duxbury	Plymouth
Plymouth	29,535	----	----	654	45.2	(Resigned August 1790)				
TOTALS	46,889	----	----	1,047	44.8	Shearjashub Bourne	2	(----)	Boston	Suffolk
DISTRICT 6										
Cumberland	25,450	----	----	3,669	6.9	George Thacher	1	Ad	Biddeford	York
Lincoln	29,962	----	----	24,832	1.2	George Thacher	2	Ad	Biddeford	York
York	28,821	----	----	2,937	9.8					
TOTALS	84,233	----	----	31,438	2.6					
DISTRICT 7										
Bristol	31,709	----	----	554	57.2	George Leonard	1	Ad	Norton	Bristol
Dukes	3,265	----	----	104	31.4	George Leonard	2	Ad	Norton	Bristol
Nantucket	4,620	----	----	46	100.4					
TOTALS	39,594	----	----	709	55.8					
DISTRICT 8										
Worcester	56,807	----	----	1,509	37.6	Jonathan Grout	1	Ad	Petersham	Worcester
						Artemas Ward	2	Ad	Shrewsbury	Worcester

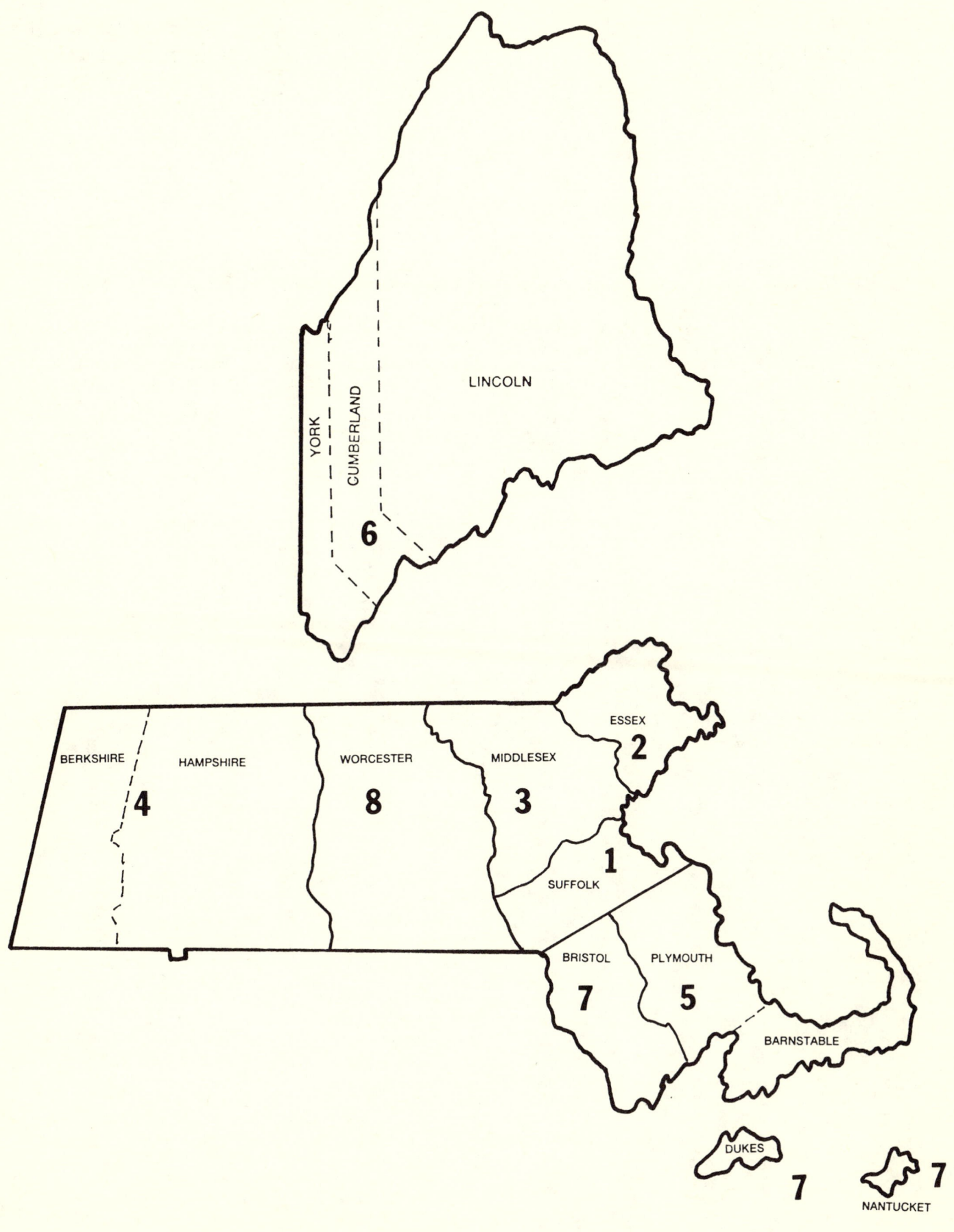

COUNTIES						REPRESENTATIVES				
County	Aggregate	Slave	%S	sq.mi.	P/sq.mi.	Representative	Cong.	Pty.	Address	County

AT LARGE

County	Aggregate	Slave	%S	sq.mi.	P/sq.mi.	Representative	Cong.	Pty.	Address	County
Cheshire	28,772	16	0.005	1,174	24.5	Abiel Foster	1	Ad	Canterbury	Rockingham
Grafton	13,472	21	0.15	3,852	3.5	Nicholas Gilman	1	Ad	Exeter	Rockingham
Hillsborough	32,871	----	----	1,477	22.3	Samuel Livermore	1	A-Ad	Holderness	Grafton
Rockingham	43,169	98	0.2	1,041	41.5	Nicholas Gilman	2	Ad	Exeter	Rockingham
Strafford	23,601	23	0.09	1,414	16.7	Samuel Livermore	2	A-Ad	Holderness	Grafton
TOTALS	141,885	157	0.5	8,958	15.8	Jeremiah Smith	2	Ad	Peterboro	Hillsborough

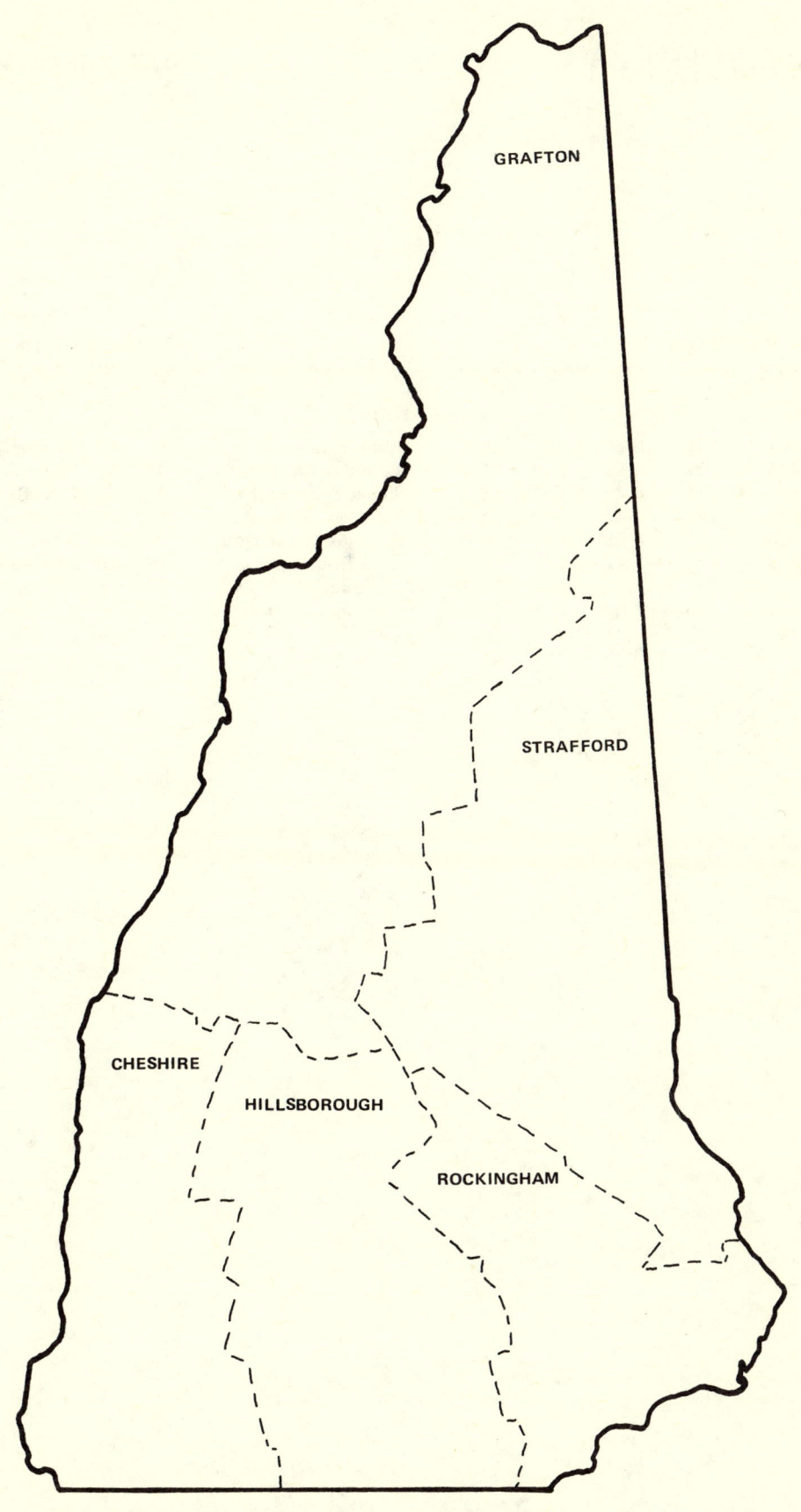

COUNTIES						REPRESENTATIVES				
County	Aggregate	Slave	%S	sq.mi.	P/sq.mi.	Representative	Cong.	Pty.	Address	County
						AT LARGE				
Bergen	12,601	2,301	18.26	426	29.5	Elias Boudinot	1	Ad	Elizabeth	Essex
Burlington	18,095	227	1.25	819	22.0	Lambert Cadwalader	1	Ad	Trenton	Hunterdon
Cape May	2,571	141	5.48	267	9.6	James Schureman	1	Ad	New Bruns-	Middlesex
Cumberland	8,248	120	1.45	500	16.4				wick	
Essex	17,785	1,171	6.58	233	76.3	Thomas Sinnickson	1	Ad	Salem	Salem
Gloucester	13,363	191	1.42	1,119	11.9	Elias Boudinot	2	Ad	Elizabeth	Essex
Hunterdon	20,253	1,301	6.42	651	31.1	Abraham Clark	2	Ad	Raway	Essex
Middlesex	15,596	1,218	7.80	312	49.9	Jonathan Dayton	2	Ad	Elizabeth	Essex
Monmouth	16,918	1,596	9.43	1,118	15.1	Aaron Kitchell	2	Ad	Hanover	Morris
Morris	16,216	636	3.92	468	34.6					
Salem	10,437	172	1.64	365	28.5					
Somerset	12,296	1,810	14.72	307	40.0					
TOTALS	183,879	11,323	80.62	7,474	24.6					

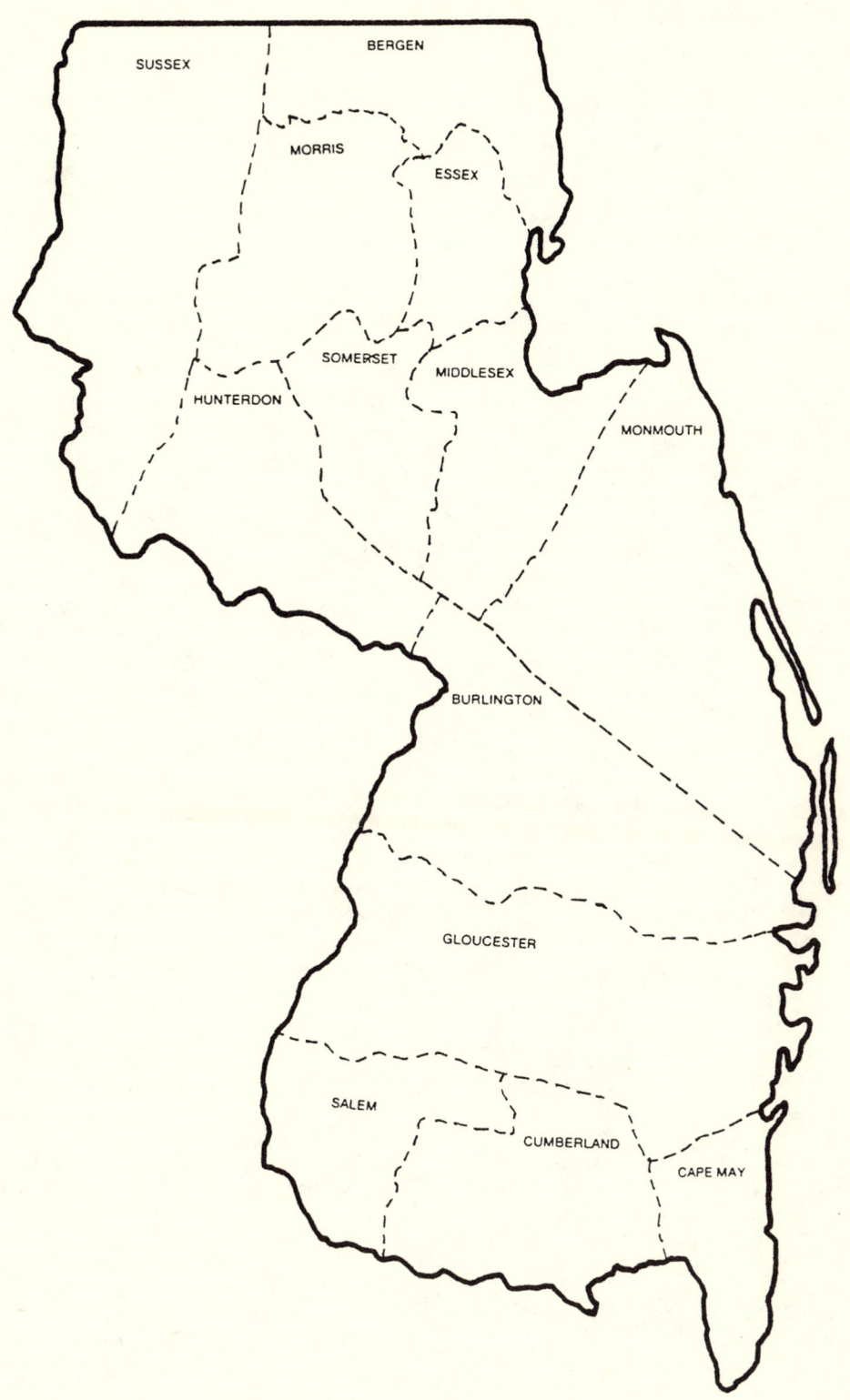

COUNTIES						REPRESENTATIVES				
County	Aggregate	Slave	%S	sq.mi.	P/sq.mi.	Representative	Cong.	Pty.	Address	County

DISTRICT 1

County	Aggregate	Slave	%S	sq.mi.	P/sq.mi.	Representative	Cong.	Pty.	Address	County
Kings	4,495	1,432	31.8	70	64.2	William Floyd	1	A-Ad	Brookhaven	Suffolk
Queens	16,014	2,309	14.4	108	148.2	Thomas Tredwell	2	A-Ad	Smithtown	Suffolk
Richmond	3,835	759	19.7	58	66.1					
Suffolk	16,440	1,098	6.6	1,218	13.4					
TOTALS	40,784	5,598	13.7	1,454	28.1					

DISTRICT 2

County	Aggregate	Slave	%S	sq.mi.	P/sq.mi.	Representative	Cong.	Pty.	Address	County
City of New York	33,131	2,369	7.1	64	517.7	Egbert Benson	1	Ad	City of New York	
Westchester	16,654	1,228	7.3	474	35.1	Egbert Benson	2	Ad	City of New York	
Except towns of:										
Salem										
North Salem										
Cortlandt										
Yorktown										
Stephentown										
TOTALS	49,785	3,597	7.2	538	92.5					

DISTRICT 3

County	Aggregate	Slave	%S	sq.mi.	P/sq.mi.	Representative	Cong.	Pty.	Address	County
Dutchess	45,266	1,856	4.18	813	55.6	John Laurence	1	Ad	----	Dutchess
Towns (in Westchester County) of:						John Laurence	2	Ad	----	Dutchess
Salem										
North Salem										
Cortlandt										
Yorktown										
Stephentown										
Total, towns	7,349	191	2.5	200	36.7					
TOTALS	52,615	2,047	3.8	1,013	51.9					

DISTRICT 4

County	Aggregate	Slave	%S	sq.mi.	P/sq.mi.	Representative	Cong.	Pty.	Address	County
Orange	18,492	966	5.2	1,009	18.3	John Hathorn	1	Ad	Warwick	Orange
Ulster	29,397	2,906	9.8	2,774	10.5	Cornelius Schoomaker	2	A-Ad	Shawangunk	Ulster
TOTALS	47,889	3,872	8.0	3,783	12.6					

DISTRICT 5

County	Aggregate	Slave	%S	sq.mi.	P/sq.mi.	Representative	Cong.	Pty.	Address	County
Clinton	1,614	17	1.0	7,324	0.2	Peter Silvester	1	Ad	Kinderhook	Columbia
(includes remaining part of the state lying on the east side of the Hudson River)						(Took seat April 22, 1789)				
						Peter Silvester	2	Ad	Kinderhook	Columbia
Columbia	27,732	1,623	5.8	645	42.9					
Washington	14,042	47	0.3	1,729	8.1					
TOTALS	43,388	1,687	3.8	9,698	4.4					

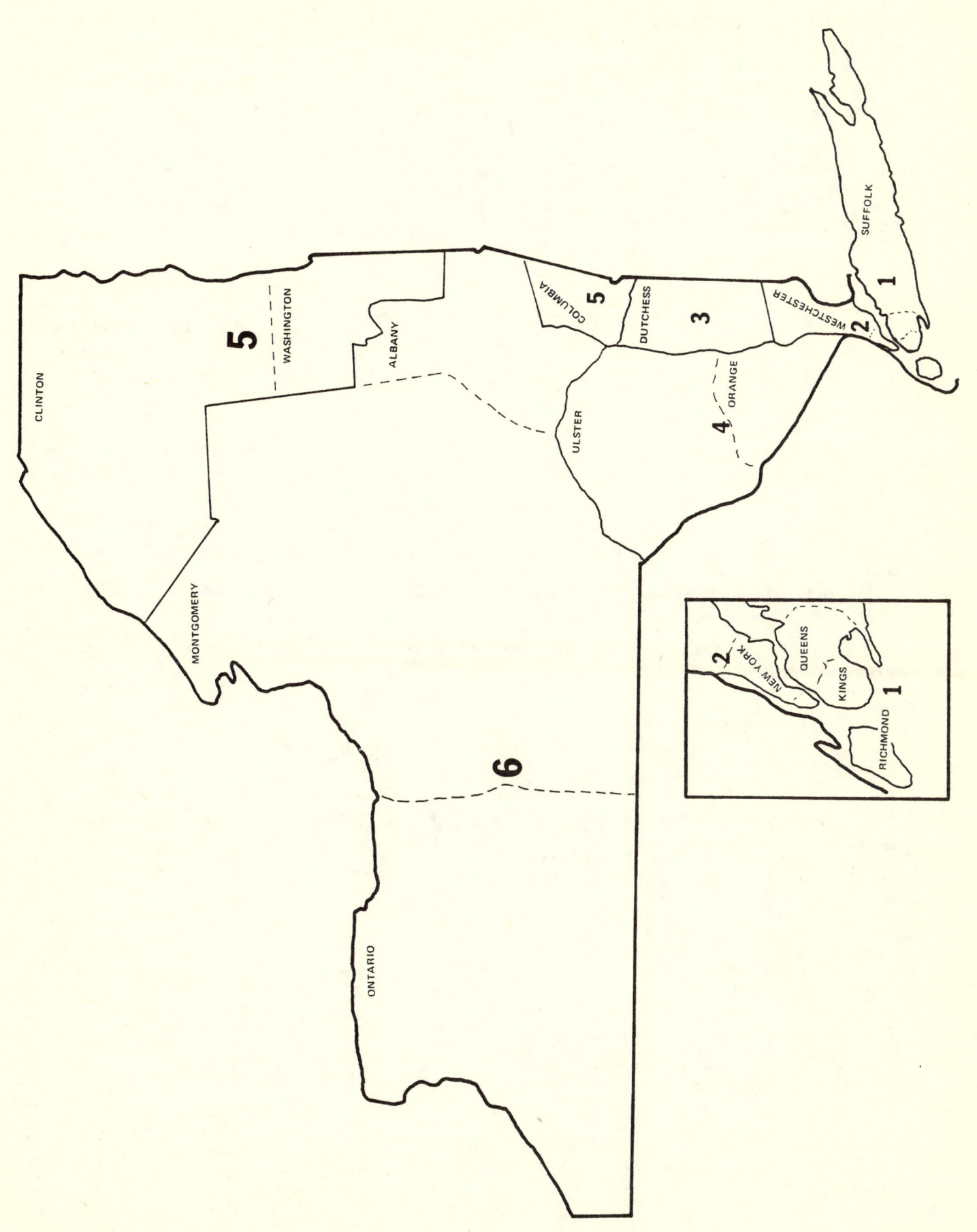

| COUNTIES | | | | | | REPRESENTATIVES | | | | |
| County | Aggregate | Slave | %S | sq.mi. | P/sq.mi. | Representative | Cong. | Pty. | Address | County |

DISTRICT 6

County	Aggregate	Slave	%S	sq.mi.	P/sq.mi.	Representative	Cong.	Pty.	Address	County
Albany	75,736	3,924	16.3	3,016	25.1	Jeremiah Van				
Montgomery	28,848	588	2.0	19,117	1.5	Rensselaer	1	A-Ad	Albany	Albany
Ontario	1,075	11	1.0	10,754	0.09	James Gordon	2	Ad	Ballston Spa	Albany
TOTALS	105,659	4,523	4.2	32,887	3.2					

NORTH CAROLINA[2]
5 DISTRICTS
5 CONGRESSMEN

| COUNTIES | | | | | | REPRESENTATIVES | | | | |
| County | Aggregate | Slave | %S | sq.mi. | P/sq.mi. | Representative | Cong. | Pty. | Address | County |

DISTRICT 1 (YADKIN)

County	Aggregate	Slave	%S	sq.mi.	P/sq.mi.	Representative	Cong.	Pty.	Address	County
Morgan	----	----	----	----	----	John Steele	1	Ad	Salisbury	Salisbury
Salisbury[1]	----	----	----	----	----	John Steele	2	Ad	Salisbury	Salisbury
TOTALS	86,400	11,957	13.8	16,699	5.2					

[1]Estimated to comprise the western one-third of the state, west of the boundaries of present-day Guilford, Moore, and Anson Counties.

DISTRICT 2 (CENTRE)

County	Aggregate	Slave	%S	sq.mi.	P/sq.mi.	Representative	Cong.	Pty.	Address	County
Franklin	----	----	----	----	----					
Hillsborough[2]	----	----	----	----	----	Nathaniel Macon	2	Ad	Warrenton	Warren
Warren	----	----	----	----	----					
TOTALS	81,317	22,289	27.4	7,269	11.2					

[2]Estimated to comprise the counties in the north central third of the state, from Warren through Rockingham and from Wake through Randolph.

DISTRICT 3 (ROANOKE)

County	Aggregate	Slave	%S	sq.mi.	P/sq.mi.	Representative	Cong.	Pty.	Address	County
Craven	10,469	3,658	34.9	1,037	10.1	John B. Ashe	1	A-Ad	Halifax	Halifax
Dobbs (became Lenoir and Greene Counties)						John B. Ashe	2	A-Ad	Halifax	Halifax
Edgecomb	10,255	3,152	30.7	510	20.1					
Halifax	13,965	6,506	46.5	737	19.0					
Jones	4,822	1,681	34.8	467	10.3					
Martin	6,080	1,889	31.0	455	13.4					
Nash	7,393	2,009	27.1	544	13.6					
Northampton	9,981	4,409	44.1	536	18.6					
Wayne	6,133	1,557	25.3	557	11.0					
TOTALS	72,668	24,861	34.2	4,843	15.0					

[2]Districts in the First Congress were somewhat different due to the inclusion of the present state of Tennessee. John Sevier served as representative from Tennessee in the First Congress.

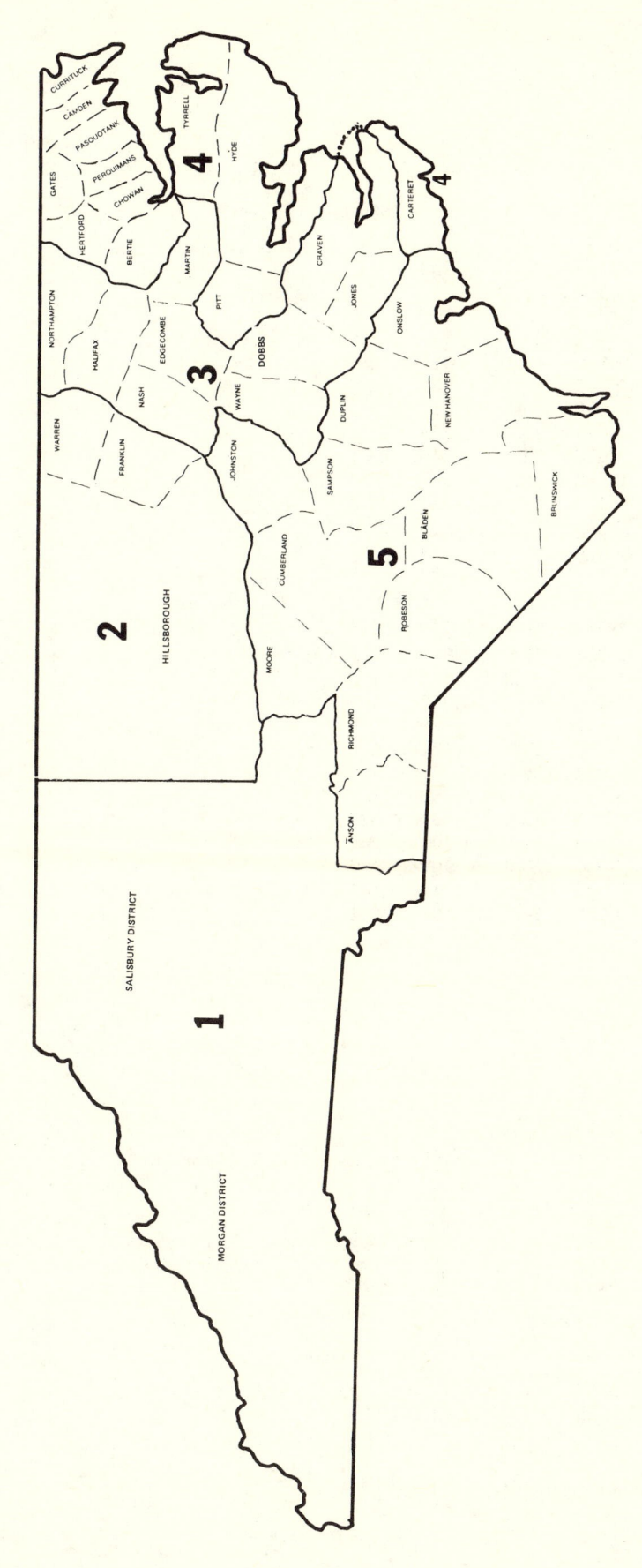

CURRITUCK

CAMDEN

PASQUOTANK

PERQUIMANS

GATES

CHOWAN

HERTFORD

TYRRELL

BERTIE

HYDE

NORTHAMPTON

MARTIN

4

HALIFAX

EDGECOMBE

PITT

CRAVEN

CARTERET

NASH

3

WAYNE

DOBBS

JONES

4

WARREN

FRANKLIN

ONSLOW

DUPLIN

NEW HANOVER

JOHNSTON

SAMPSON

2

HILLSBOROUGH

MOORE

CUMBERLAND

BLADEN

BRUNSWICK

5

ROBESON

RICHMOND

1

SALISBURY DISTRICT

ANSON

MORGAN DISTRICT

COUNTIES						REPRESENTATIVES				
County	Aggregate	Slave	%S	sq.mi.	P/sq.mi.	Representative	Cong.	Pty.	Address	County

DISTRICT 4 (ALBEMARLE)

County	Aggregate	Slave	%S	sq.mi.	P/sq.mi.	Representative	Cong.	Pty.	Address	County
Bertie	12,606	5,141	40.7	698	18.0	Hugh Williamson	1	Ad	Edenton	Chowan
Camden	4,033	1,038	25.7	239	16.8	Hugh Williamson	2	Ad	Edenton	Chowan
Cataret	3,732	713	34.8	467	7.9					
Chowan	----	----	----	173	----					
Currituck	5,219	1,103	21.1	246	21.2					
Gates	5,392	2,219	41.1	337	16.0					
Hertford	5,828	2,442	41.9	353	16.5					
Hyde	4,120	1,048	25.4	613	6.7					
Pasquotank	5,497	1,623	29.5	228	24.1					
Perquimans	5,440	1,878	34.5	246	22.1					
Pitt	8,275	2,367	28.6	655	12.6					
Tyrrell	4,744	1,166	24.5	781	6.0					
Chowan	5,011	2,588	51.6	173	29.0					
TOTALS	69,897	23,326	33.4	5,036	13.9					

DISTRICT 5 (CAPE FEAR)

County	Aggregate	Slave	%S	sq.mi.	P/sq.mi.	Representative	Cong.	Pty.	Address	County
Anson	5,133	828	16.1	633e	8.1	Timothy Bloodworth	1	A-Ad	Wilmington	New Hanover
Bladen	5,084	1,676	32.9	1,828	2.8	William B. Grove	2	A-Ad	Fayetteville	Cumberland
Brunswick	3,071	1,511	49.2	856	6.9					
Cumberland	8,671	2,181	25.1	1,093e	7.9					
Duplin	5,662	1,676	32.9	1,828	2.8					
Johnston	5,634	1,329	23.5	797	7.0					
Moore	3,770	371	9.8	704	5.4					
New Hanover	6,831	3,738	54.7	1,056	6.5					
Onslow	5,387	1,748	32.4	756	7.0					
Richmond	5,055	583	11.5	794	6.4					
Robeson	5,326	533	10.0	900e	5.9					
Sampson	6,065	1,183	19.5	945	6.4					
TOTALS	65,689	17,357	26.4	12,190	5.4					

PENNSYLVANIA[1]

8 DISTRICTS
8 CONGRESSMEN

COUNTIES						REPRESENTATIVES				
County	Aggregate	Slave	%S	sq.mi.	P/sq.mi.	Representative	Cong.	Pty.	Address	County

DISTRICT 1

County	Aggregate	Slave	%S	sq.mi.	P/sq.mi.	Representative	Cong.	Pty.	Address	County
Delaware	9,483	50	0.5	184	51.5	Thomas Fitzsimons	1	Ad	City of Philadelphia	
City of Philadelphia	42,520	273	0.6	29	1466.0	Thomas Fitzsimons	2	Ad	City of Philadelphia	
TOTALS	52,003	323	0.6	213	244.0					

DISTRICT 2

County	Aggregate	Slave	%S	sq.mi.	P/sq.mi.	Representative	Cong.	Pty.	Address	County
Bucks	25,401	261	1.0	614	41.0	Henry Wynkoop	1	Ad	Northampton Township	Bucks
Philadelphia	11,871	114	0.96	100	118.0					
TOTALS	37,272	375	1.0	714	52.2	Andrew Gregg	2	A-Ad	----	Bucks

[1] The First Congress was elected at large.

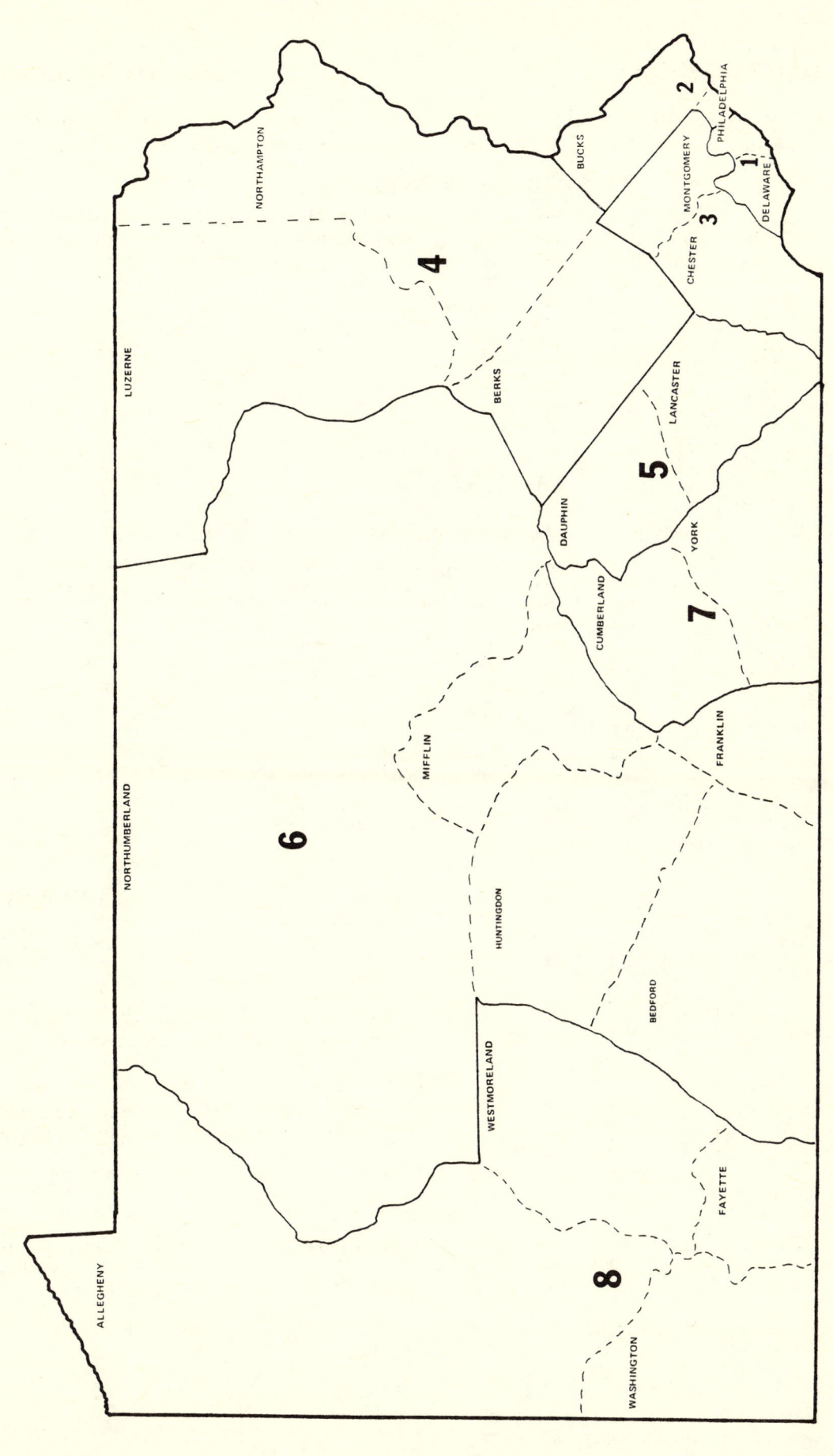

| | COUNTIES | | | | | REPRESENTATIVES | | | | |
County	Aggregate	Slave	%S	sq.mi.	P/sq.mi.	Representative	Cong.	Pty.	Address	County
DISTRICT 3										
Chester	27,931	145	0.5	761	36.0	John Peter Muhlenberg	1	A-Ad	Providence	Montgomery
Montgomery	22,929	114	0.5	496	46.0	Israel Jacobs	2	Ad	Providence	Montgomery
TOTALS	50,860	259	0.5	1,257	40.0					
DISTRICT 4										
Berks	30,179	65	0.2	1,486	20.0	Daniel Hiester	1	A-Ad	----	Berks
Luzerne	4,904	11	0.2	3,512	1.3	Daniel Hiester	2	Ad	----	Berks
North-ampton	24,250	23	0.1	3,182	7.6					
TOTALS	59,333	99	0.2	8,180	7.2					
DISTRICT 5										
Dauphin	18,177	212	1.1	881	20.6	George Clymer	1	Ad	----	----
Lancaster	36,147	348	1.0	946	38.2	John W. Kittera	2	Ad	Lancaster	Lancaster
TOTALS	54,324	560	1.0	1,827	29.0					
DISTRICT 6										
Bedford	13,124	46	0.3	2,787	4.7	Frederick Muhlenberg	1	Ad	----	Northum-berland
Franklin	15,655	330	2.1	754	220.7					
Huntingdon	7,565	43	0.6	2,264	3.3	Frederick Muhlenberg	2	Ad	----	Northum-berland
Mifflin	7,362	59	0.8	1,432	5.1					
Northum-berland	17,161	89	0.5	12,792	7.3					
TOTALS	60,867	567	0.9	20,029	3.0					
DISTRICT 7										
Cumberland	18,243	223	1.2	1,106	16.0	Thomas Hartley	1	Ad	Yorktown	York
York	37,747	499	1.3	1,435	26.0	Thomas Hartley	2	Ad	Yorktown	York
TOTALS	55,990	722	1.2	2,541	22.0					
DISTRICT 8										
Allegheny	10,300	159	1.5	5,902	1.7	Thomas Scott	1	Ad	Washington	Washington
Fayette	13,325	282	2.1	802	16.6	William Findley	2	Ad	Youngstown	Westmoreland
Washington	23,866	263	1.1	1,435	16.6					
West-moreland	16,018	188	0.8	2,072	7.7					
TOTALS	63,509	892	1.4	10,211	6.2					

COUNTIES							REPRESENTATIVES			
County	Aggregate	Slave	%S	sq.mi.	P/sq.mi.	Representative	Cong.	Pty.	Address	County
						AT LARGE				
Bristol	3,211	98	3.0	25	128.4	Benjamin Bourn	1	Ad	Providence	Providence
Kent	8,848	63	0.7	173	51.1	Benjamin Bourn	2	Ad	Providence	Providence
Newport	14,300	366	2.5	115	124.3					
Providence	24,391	82	0.4	416	58.6					
Washington	18,075	339	1.8	321	56.3					
TOTALS	68,825	948	1.3	1,050	65.5					

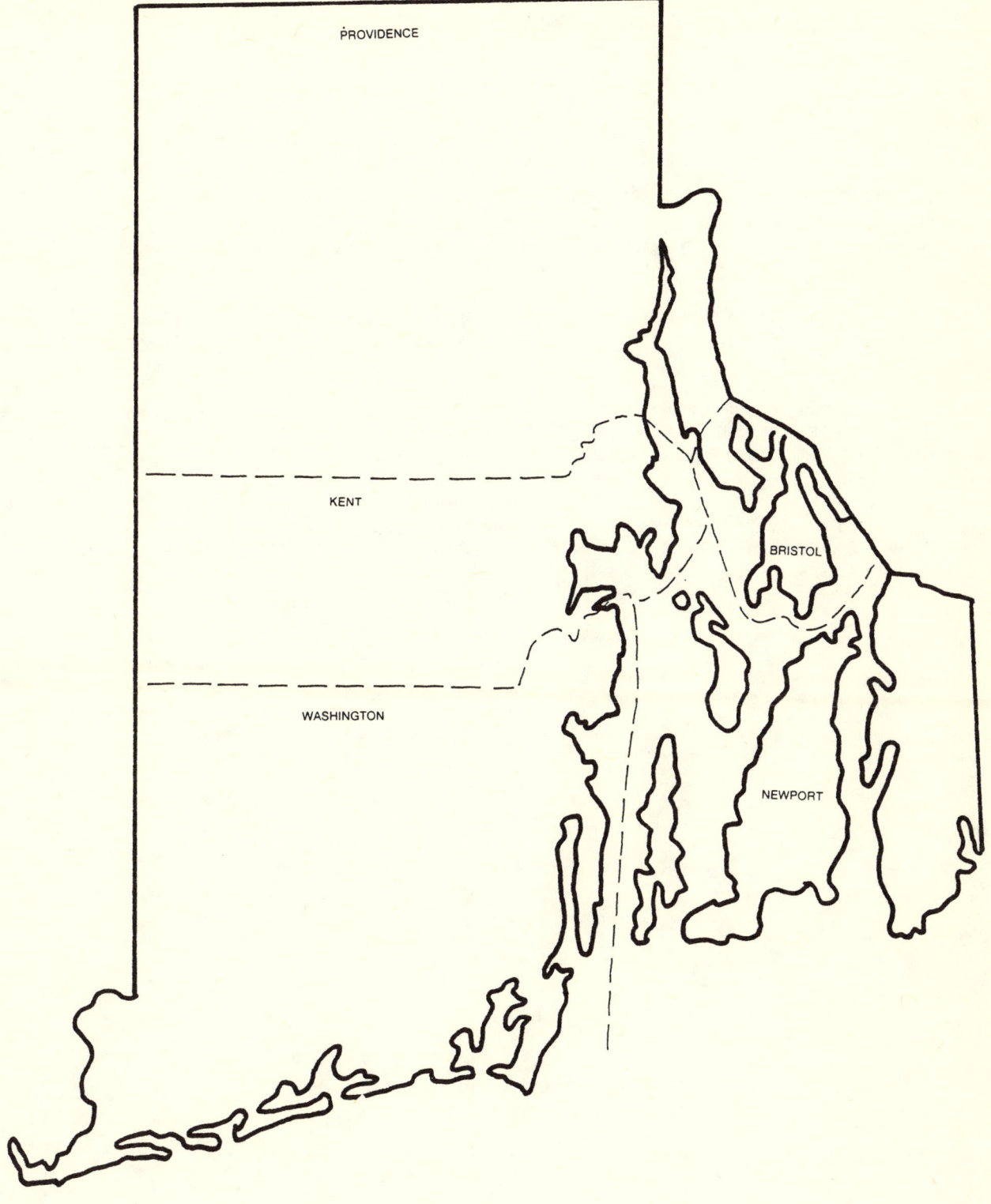

PROVIDENCE

KENT

WASHINGTON

BRISTOL

NEWPORT

| | COUNTIES | | | | | | | REPRESENTATIVES | | | |
County	Aggregate	Slave	%S	sq.mi.	P/sq.mi.	Representative	Cong.	Pty.	Address	County
DISTRICT 1										
Charlestown	66,990	50,633	75.58	3,246	20.6	William L. Smith	1	Ad	Charlestown	Charlestown
						William L. Smith	2	Ad	Charlestown	Charlestown
DISTRICT 2										
Beaufort	18,753	14,236	75.9	1,793	10.4	Aedanus Burke	1	A-Ad	----	----
Orangeburgh	18,513	5,931	32.0	4,345	4.2	Robert Barnwell	2	Ad	Beaufort	Beaufort
TOTALS	37,266	20,167	54.1	6,138	6.0					
DISTRICT 3										
Cheraw	10,706	3,229	30.1	6,837	4.8	Daniel Huger	1	A-Ad	Georgetown	Georgetown
Georgetown	22,122	13,131	59.3	4,715	4.6	Daniel Huger	2	A-Ad	Georgetown	Georgetown
TOTALS	32,828	16,360	49.8	6,837	4.8					
DISTRICT 4										
Camden	38,265	8,965	23.4	5,675	6.7	Thomas Sumter	1	A-Ad	Statesburg	Camden
						Thomas Sumter	2	A-Ad	Statesburg	Camden
DISTRICT 5										
Ninety-Six	73,729	11,069	15.0	8,350	8.8	Thomas Tucker	1	Ad	----	----
						Thomas Tucker	2	Ad	----	----

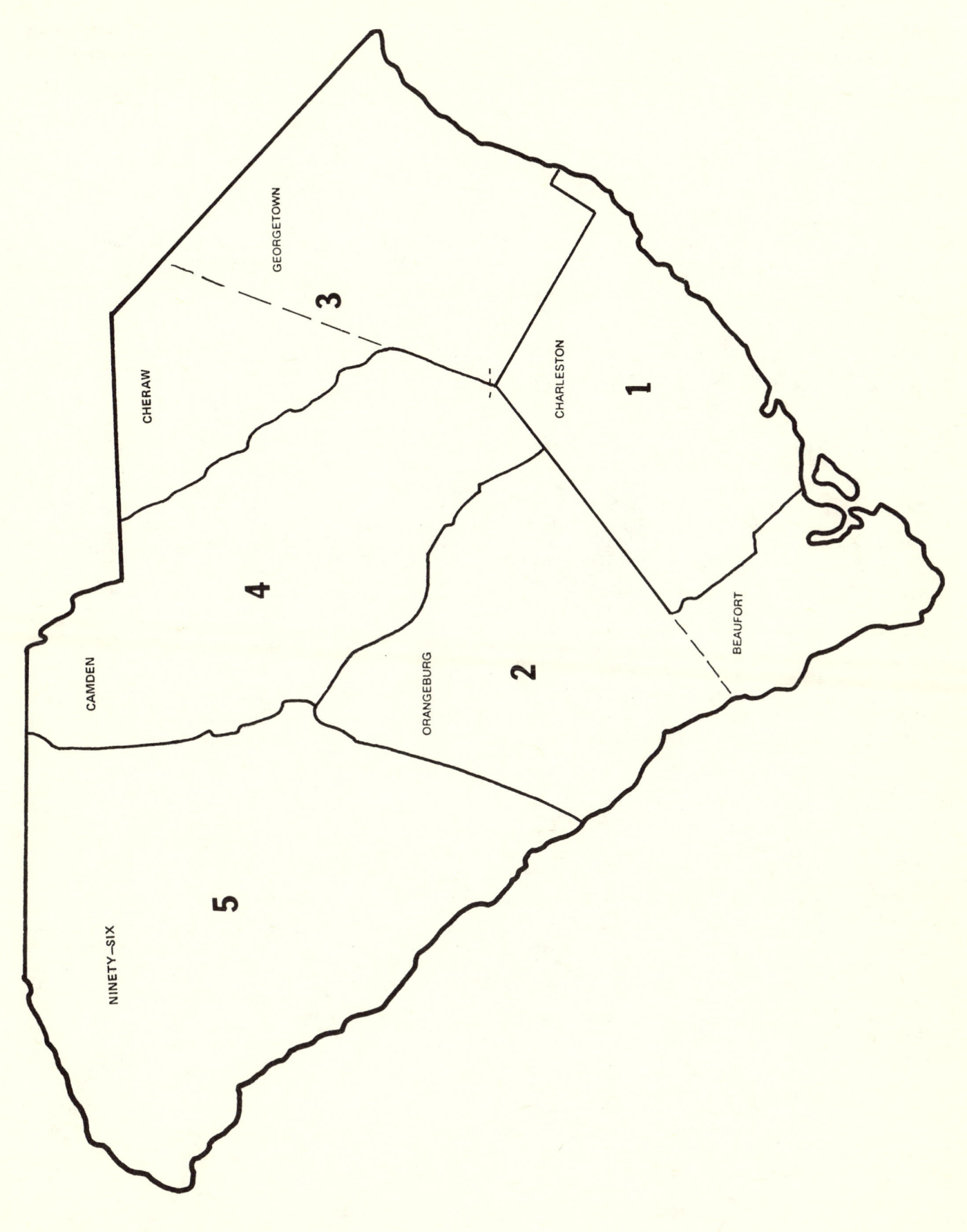

	COUNTIES						REPRESENTATIVES				
County	Aggregate	Slave	%S	sq.mi.	P/sq.mi.	Representative	Cong.	Pty.	Address	County

DISTRICT 1

County	Aggregate	Slave	%S	sq.mi.	P/sq.mi.	Representative	Cong.	Pty.	Address	County
Berkeley	19,713	2,932	14.8	760	25.9	Alexander White	1	A-Ad	"Woodville"	Frederick
Frederick	19,681	4,250	21.6	729	27.0	Alexander White	2	A-Ad	"Woodville"	Frederick
Hampshire	7,326	454	6.1	969	7.6					
Hardy	7,336	369	5.0	1,063	6.9					
Harrison	2,080	67	3.2	3,099	0.7					
Monongalia	4,768	154	3.2	8,154	0.6					
Ohio	5,212	281	5.3	1,331	3.9					
Randolph	951	19	1.9	2,429	0.4					
Shenandoah	10,510	512	4.8	823	12.8					
TOTALS	77,577	9,038	11.7	19,357	4.0					

DISTRICT 2 (KENTUCKY)

County	Aggregate	Slave	%S	sq.mi.	P/sq.mi.	Representative	Cong.	Pty.	Address	County
Bourbon	7,837	908	11.5	3,828	8.6	John Brown	1	A-Ad	Frankfurt	Mercer
Fayette	12,576	3,152	20.9	650	27.0	John Brown	2	A-Ad	Frankfurt	Mercer
Jefferson	4,765	903	19.1	1,746	2.6					
Lincoln	6,548	1,094	16.7	16,214	0.4					
Madison	5,772	737	12.7	2,607	2.2					
Mason	2,729	229	9.1	6,428	0.4					
Mercer	7,091	1,339	18.9	519	13.4					
Nelson	11,315	1,248	12.0	4,280	2.4					
Woodford	9,210	2,220	24.1	2,106	4.4					
TOTALS	67,843	11,830	17.4	38,378	1.8					

DISTRICT 3

County	Aggregate	Slave	%S	sq.mi.	P/sq.mi.	Representative	Cong.	Pty.	Address	County
Augusta	10,866	1,222	11.2	1,942	5.6	Andrew Moore	1	A-Ad	Lexington	Rockbridge
Botetourt	10,524	1,259	11.9	1,590	6.6	Andrew Moore	2	A-Ad	Lexington	Rockbridge
Greenbrier	6,015	319	5.3	11,793	0.5					
Montgomery	13,228	828	6.2	4,200	3.1					
Pendleton	2,452	73	2.9	695	3.5					
Rockbridge	6,548	682	10.4	601	10.9					
Rockingham	7,449	772	10.3	865	8.6					
Russell	3,338	190	5.6	5,324	0.6					
Washington	5,625	480	8.0	624	9.0					
TOTALS	66,045	5,825	8.8	27,634	2.4					

DISTRICT 4

County	Aggregate	Slave	%S	sq.mi.	P/sq.mi.	Representative	Cong.	Pty.	Address	County
Fairfax	12,320	4,574	37.1	425	28.9	Richard Bland Lee	1	Ad	Leesylvania	Prince William
Fauquier	17,892	6,642	37.1	660	27.1	Richard Bland Lee	2	Ad	Leesylvania	Prince William
King George	7,366	4,157	56.0	176	41.9					
Loudoun	18,962	4,030	21.2	527	35.9					
Prince William	11,615	4,704	40.4	347	33.5					
Stafford	9,588	4,036	42.0	270	35.5					
TOTALS	77,743	28,143	36.2	2,405	32.2					

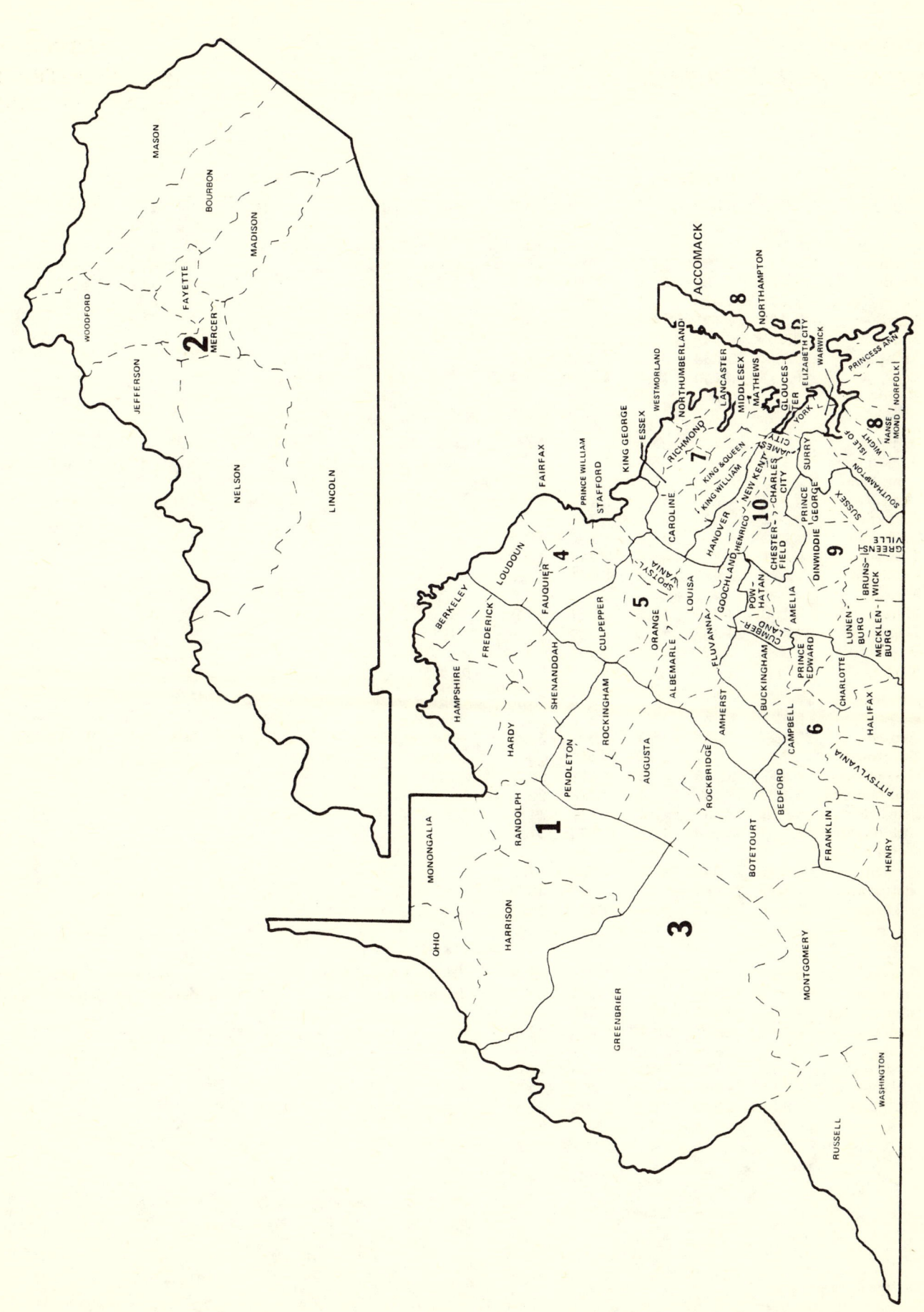

	COUNTIES						REPRESENTATIVES				
County	Aggregate	Slave	%S	sq.mi.	P/sq.mi.	Representative	Cong.	Pty.	Address	County

DISTRICT 5

County	Aggregate	Slave	%S	sq.mi.	P/sq.mi.	Representative	Cong.	Pty.	Address	County
Albemarle	12,585	5,579	44.3	740	17.0	James Madison	1	A-Ad	"Mont-pelier"	Orange
Amherst	13,703	5,296	38.6	941	14.6					
Culpepper	22,105	8,226	37.2	983	22.5	James Madison	2	A-Ad	"Mont-pelier"	Orange
Fluvanna	3,921	1,466	37.3	288	13.6					
Goochland	9,053	4,656	51.4	289	31.3					
Louisa	8,467	4,573	54.0	517	16.4					
Orange	9,921	4,421	44.5	508	19.5					
Spott-sylvania	11,252	5,933	52.7	545	20.6					
TOTALS	91,007	40,150	44.1	4,811	18.9					

DISTRICT 6

County	Aggregate	Slave	%S	sq.mi.	P/sq.mi.	Representative	Cong.	Pty.	Address	County
Bedford	10,531	2,754	26.1	727	14.5	Isaac Coles	1	A-Ad	Coles Ferry	Halifax
Buckingham	9,779	4,168	46.2	737	13.2	Abraham B. Venable	2	A-Ad	Prince Edward Court House	Prince Edward
Campbell	7,685	2,488	32.3	669	11.5					
Charlotte	10,078	4,816	47.7	470	21.4					
Franklin	6,842	1,073	15.6	716	9.6					
Halifax	14,722	5,565	37.8	796	18.5					
Henry	8,479	1,551	18.2	845	10.0					
Pittsylvania	11,579	2,979	25.7	1,001	11.6					
Prince Edward	8,100	3,986	49.2	407	19.9					
TOTALS	87,795	29,380	33.4	6,368	13.8					

DISTRICT 7

County	Aggregate	Slave	%S	sq.mi.	P/sq.mi.	Representative	Cong.	Pty.	Address	County
Caroline	17,489	10,292	58.8	545	32.0	John Page	1	A-Ad	"Rosewell"	Gloucester
Essex	9,122	5,440	59.6	250	36.5	John Page	2	A-Ad	"Rosewell"	Gloucester
Gloucester	13,498	7,063	52.3	228	59.2					
King and Queen	9,377	5,743	61.2	318	29.5					
King William	8,128	5,151	63.3	278	29.2					
Lancaster	5,638	3,236	57.3	137	41.2					
Middlesex	4,140	2,558	61.7	130	31.8					
Northumberland	9,163	4,460	48.6	190	48.2					
Richmond	6,985	3,984	57.0	190	36.7					
Westmorland	7,722	4,465	57.8	229	33.7					
TOTALS	91,262	52,392	57.4	2,495	36.6					

DISTRICT 8

County	Aggregate	Slave	%S	sq.mi.	P/sq.mi.	Representative	Cong.	Pty.	Address	County
Accomack	13,959	4,262	30.5	476	29.3	Josiah Parker	1	A-Ad	Maccles Field	Isle of Wight
Isle of Wight	9,028	1,551	17.1	317	28.5					
Nansemond	9,010	3,817	42.3	408	22.0	Josiah Parker	2	A-Ad	Maccles Field	Isle of Wight
Norfolk	14,524	5,345	36.8	394	36.8					
Northampton	9,153	4,460	48.7	220	41.6					
Princess Ann	7,793	3,202	41.2	259	30.0					
Southampton	12,864	559	4.3	602	21.4					
Surrey	6,227	368	5.9	277	22.5					
TOTALS	82,558	23,564	28.5	2,953	27.9					

	COUNTIES					REPRESENTATIVES				
County	Aggregate	Slave	%S	sq.mi.	P/sq.mi.	Representative	Cong.	Pty.	Address	County

DISTRICT 9

County	Aggregate	Slave	%S	sq.mi.	P/sq.mi.	Representative	Cong.	Pty.	Address	County
Amelia	18,097	11,307	62.4	674	26.8	Theodoric Bland†	1	A-Ad	Petersburg	Prince George
Brunswick	12,827	6,776	52.8	579	22.1	(Died June 1, 1790)				
Cumberland	8,153	4,434	54.3	291	28.0	William B. Giles	1	A-Ad	Amelia	Amelia
Dinwiddie	13,934	7.334	52.6	507	27.5	(Replaced Bland)			Court House	
Greensville	6,382	3,620	56.7	299	21.3	William B. Giles	2	A-Ad	Amelia	Amelia
Lunenburg	8,959	4,332	48.3	442	20.3				Court House	
Mecklenburg	14,733	6,762	45.8	612	24.0					
Powhatan	6,822	4,325	63.3	269	25.4					
Prince										
George	8,173	4,519	55.2	276	29.6					
Sussex	10,554	5,387	51.0	494	21.4					
TOTALS	108,634	58,796	54.1	4,443	24.4					

DISTRICT 10

County	Aggregate	Slave	%S	sq.mi.	P/sq.mi.	Representative	Cong.	Pty.	Address	County
Chesterfield	5,588	3,141	56.2	442	12.6	Samuel Griffin	1	A-Ad	----	James City
Elizabeth						Samuel Griffin	2	A-Ad	----	James City
City	3,450	1,876	54.3	69	50.0					
Hanover	14,754	8,223	55.7	465	31.7					
Henrico	12,000	5,819	48.4	229	52.4					
James City	4,070	2,405	59.0	152	26.8					
New Kent	6,239	3,700	59.3	210	29.7					
Warwick	1,690	990	58.5	75	22.5					
York	5,233	2,760	52.7	129	40.6					
TOTALS	53,024	28,914	54.5	1,771	29.9					

2

Congressional Districts

1792–1801
3rd–7th Congresses

COUNTIES						REPRESENTATIVES				
County	Aggregate	Slave	%S	sq.mi.	P/sq.mi.	Representative	Cong.	Pty.	Address	County

AT LARGE

County	Aggregate	Slave	%S	sq.mi.	P/sq.mi.	Representative	Cong.	Pty.	Address	County
Fairfield	36,250	797	2.19	626	57.9	Joshua Coit	3	Ad	New London	New London
Hartford	38,029	263	0.69	729	51.5	James Hillhouse	3	Ad	New Haven	New Haven
Litchfield	38,755	233	0.6	925	41.9	Amasa Learned	3	Ad	New London	New London
Middlesex	18,855	221	1.1	372	50.7	Jepheniah Swift	3	Ad	Windham	Windham
New Haven	30,830	433	1.4	604	51.0	Uriah Tracy	3	Ad	Litchfield	Litchfield
New London	33,200	586	1.7	667	49.8	Jonathan Trumbull	3	Ad	Lebanon	New London
Tolland	13,106	47	0.3	416	31.5	Jeremiah Wadsworth	3	Ad	Hartford	Hartford
Windham	28,921	184	0.6	514	56.3					
TOTALS	237,946	2,764	1.1	4,853	48.9	Joshua Coit	4	Ad	New London	New London
						Chauncey Goodrich	4	Ad	Hartford	Hartford
						Roger Griswold	4	Ad	Lyme	Middlesex
						James Hillhouse[r]	4	Ad	New Haven	New Haven
						James Davenport (Replaced Hillhouse)	4	Ad	Stamford	Fairfield
						Nathaniel Smith	4	Ad	Woodbury	Woodbury
						Zephaniah Swift	4	Ad	Windham	Windham
						Uriah Tracy[r] (Resigned October 13, 1796)	4	Ad	Litchfield	Litchfield
						Samuel Dana (Replaced Tracy)	4	Ad	Middletown	Middlesex
						John Allen	5	F	Litchfield	Litchfield
						Joshua Coit[†] (Died September 5, 1798)	5	F	New London	New London
						Jonathan Brace (Replaced Coit)	5	F	Hartford	Hartford
						Samuel W. Dana	5	F	Middletown	Middlesex
						Nathaniel Smith	5	F	Woodbury	Woodbury
						James Davenport[†] (Died August 3, 1797)	5	F	Stamford	Fairfield
						William Edmond (Replaced Davenport)	5	F	Newtown	Fairfield
						Chauncey Goodrich	5	F	Hartford	Hartford
						Roger Griswold	5	F	Lyme	Middlesex
						Jonathan Brace[r] (Resigned in 1800)	6	F	Hartford	Hartford
						John C. Smith (Replaced Brace)	6	F	Sharon	Litchfield
						Samuel Dana	6	F	Middletown	Middlesex
						John Davenport	6	F	Stamford	Fairfax
						William Edmond	6	F	Newton	Fairfield
						Chauncey Goodrich	6	F	Hartford	Hartford
						Elizur Goodrich	6	F	New Haven	New Haven
						Roger Griswold	6	F	Lyme	Middlesex

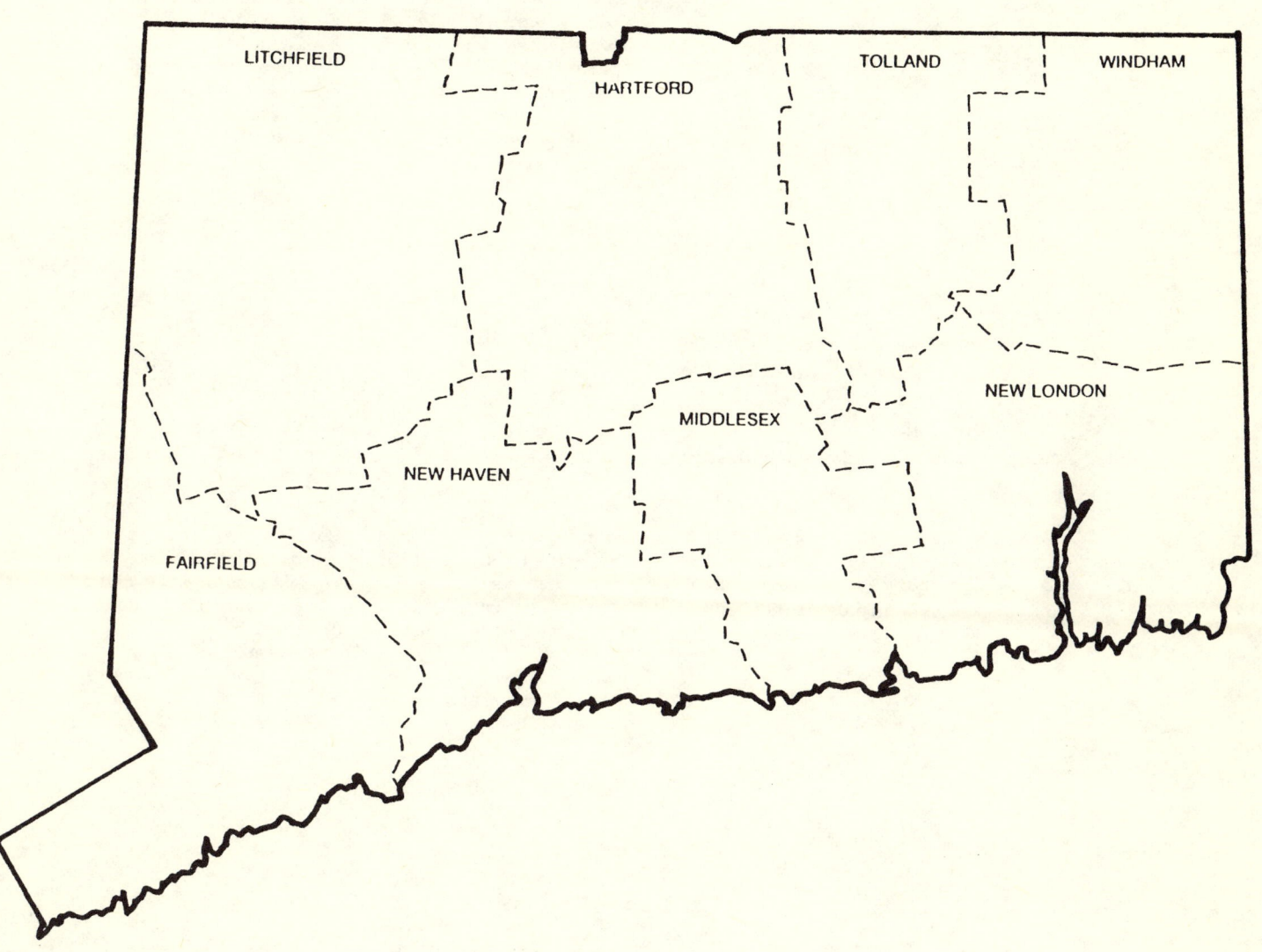

COUNTIES						REPRESENTATIVES				
County	Aggregate	Slave	%S	sq.mi.	P/sq.mi.	Representative	Cong.	Pty.	Address	County
						Samuel Dana	7	F	Middletown	Middlesex
						John Davenport	7	F	Stamford	Fairfield
						Roger Griswold	7	F	Lyme	Middlesex
						Calvin Goddard	7	F	Plainville	Windham
						Elias Perkins	7	F	New London	New London
						John C. Smith	7	F	Sharon	Litchfield
						Benjamin Tallmadge	7	F	Litchfield	Litchfield

DELAWARE
1 CONGRESSMAN

COUNTIES						REPRESENTATIVES				
County	Aggregate	Slave	%S	sq.mi.	P/sq.mi.	Representative	Cong.	Pty.	Address	County
						AT LARGE				
Kent	18,920	2,300	12.1	594	31.6	John Patten[r]	3	A-Ad	Dover	Kent
						(Resigned February 1794)				
Newcastle	19,680	2,562	13.0	438	44.9	Henry Latimer	3	Ad	Wilmington	Newcastle
Sussex	20,488	4,025	19.6	950	21.6	(Succeeded Patten. Took seat in February 1795, then				
TOTALS	59,088	8,887	15.0	1,982	29.8	resigned, having been elected Senator.)				
						John Patten	4	A-Ad	Dover	Kent
						James A. Bayard	5	F	Wilmington	Newcastle
						James A. Bayard	6	F	Wilmington	Newcastle
						James A. Bayard	7	F	Wilmington	Newcastle

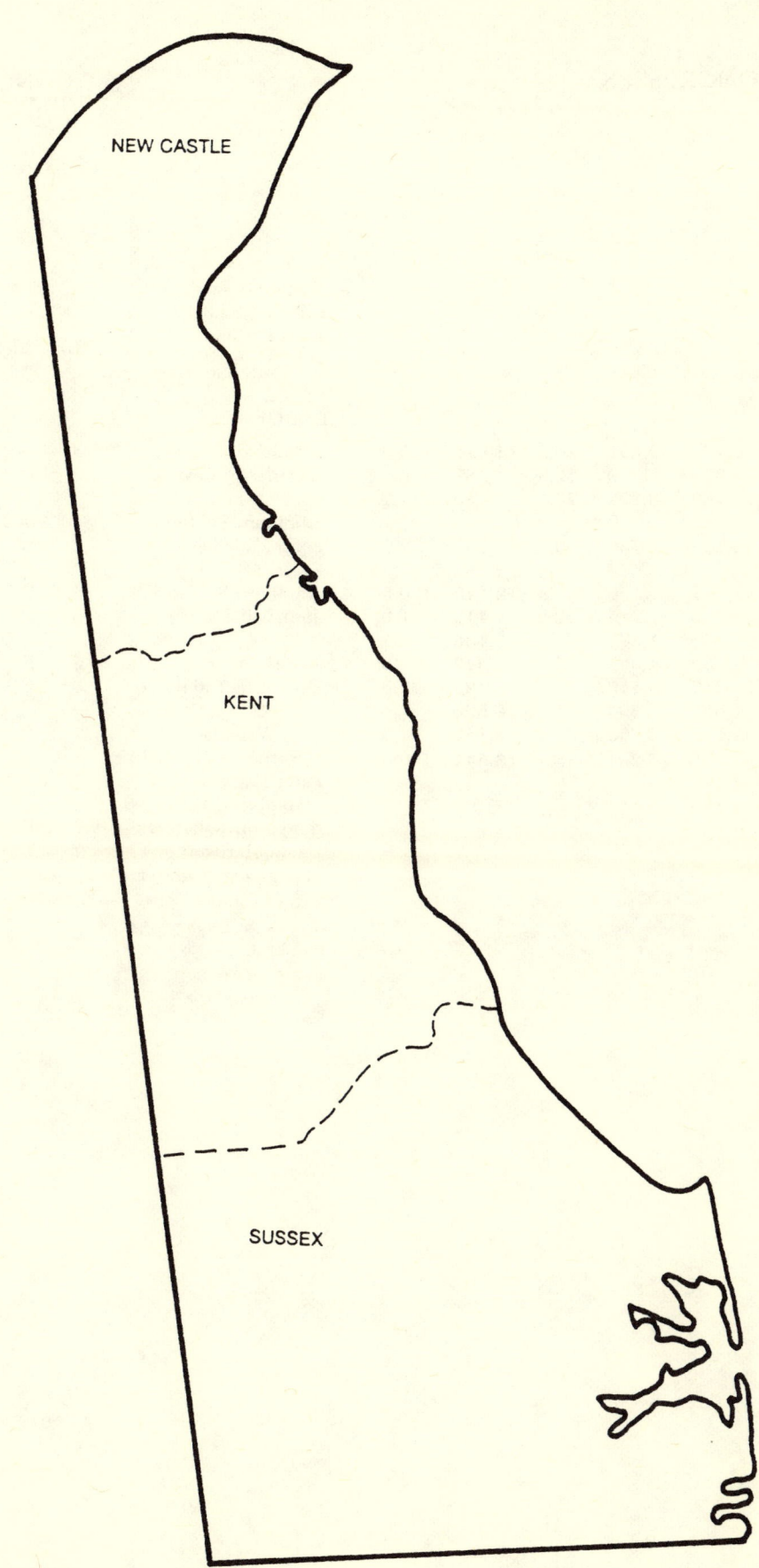

County	Aggregate	Slave	%S	sq.mi.	P/sq.mi.	Representative	Cong.	Pty.	Address	County
		COUNTIES					REPRESENTATIVES			

AT LARGE

County	Aggregate	Slave	%S	sq.mi.	P/sq.mi.	Representative	Cong.	Pty.	Address	County
Burke	9,467	2,392	25.2	1,612	5.9	Abraham Baldwin	3	A-Ad	Augusta	Richmond
Camden	305	70	22.9	1,187	0.2	Thomas F. Carnes	3	A-Ad	----	Franklin
Chatham	10,769	8,201	76.1	445	24.2					
Columbia						Abraham Baldwin	4	A-Ad	Augusta	Richmond
Effingham	2,424	750	30.9	1,131	2.1	John Milledge	4	Ad	Savannah	Chatham
Elbert										
Franklin	1,041	156	14.9	2,175	0.5	Abraham Baldwin	5	R	Augusta	Richmond
Glyn	413	215	52.0	412	1.0	John Milledge	5	R	Savannah	Chatham
Greene	5,405	1,377	25.4	1,136	6.1					
Liberty	5,355	4,025	75.1	1,342	4.0	James Jones	6	F	Savannah	Chatham
Richmond	11,317	4,116	36.3	423	26.8	Benjamin Taliaferro	6	F	----	Wilkes
Washington	4,552	694	15.2	4,526	1.0					
Wilkes	31,560	7,268	23.0	2,155	14.6	John Milledge[r]	7	R	Savannah	Chatham
						(Resigned May 1802)				
TOTALS	82,608	29,264	35.4	16,544	5.0	Peter Early	7	(----)	Scull Shoals	Greene
						(Replaced Milledge)				
						Benjamin Taliaferro[r]	7	F	----	Wilkes
						David Meriwether	7	R	----	Wilkes
						(Replaced Taliaferro)				

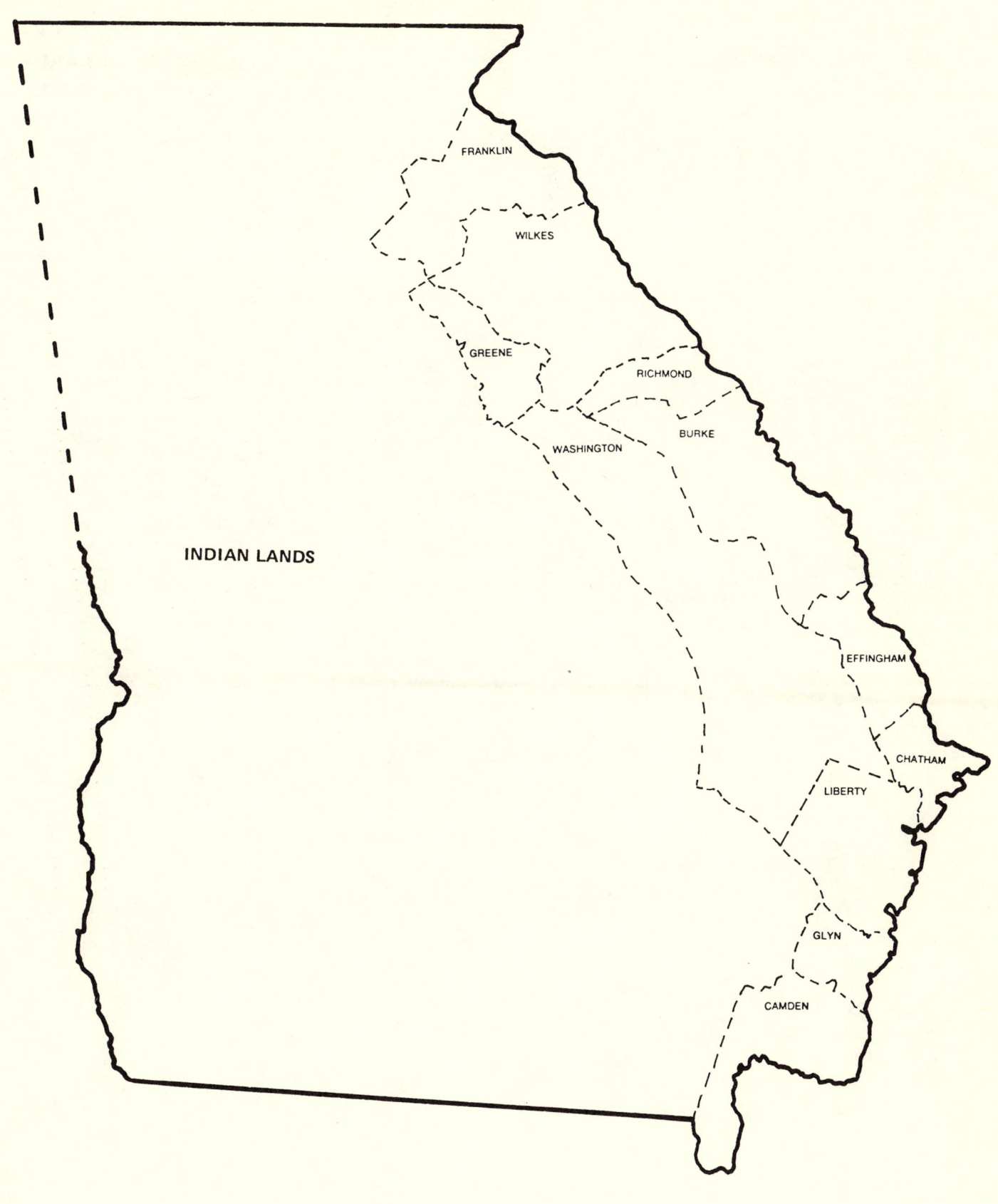

INDIAN LANDS

FRANKLIN

WILKES

GREENE

RICHMOND

BURKE

WASHINGTON

EFFINGHAM

CHATHAM

LIBERTY

GLYN

CAMDEN

	COUNTIES						REPRESENTATIVES				
County	Aggregate	Slave	%S	sq.mi.	P/sq.mi.	Representative	Cong.	Pty.	Address	County

DISTRICT 1

County	Aggregate	Slave	%S	sq.mi.	P/sq.mi.	Representative	Cong.	Pty.	Address	County
Jefferson	4,565	876	19.1	1,746	2.6	Christopher Greenup	3	A-Ad	Harrodsburg	Mercer
Lincoln	6,548	1,094	16.7	16,214	0.4	Christopher Greenup	4	A-Ad	Harrodsburg	Mercer
Madison	5,772	737	12.7	2,607	2.2	Thomas T. Davis	5	R	----	Mercer
Mercer	6,941	1,317	18.9	519	13.4	Thomas T. Davis	6	R	----	Mercer
Nelson	10,099	1,219	12.0	4,280	2.4	Thomas T. Davis	7	R	----	Mercer
TOTALS	33,925	5,243	15.4	25,366	1.3					

DISTRICT 2

County	Aggregate	Slave	%S	sq.mi.	P/sq.mi.	Representative	Cong.	Pty.	Address	County
Bourbon	7,837	908	11.5	3,828	8.6	Alexander D. Orr	3	A-Ad	Maysville	Mason
Fayette	17,576	3,689	20.9	650	27.0	Alexander D. Orr	4	A-Ad	Maysville	Mason
Mason	2,267	208	9.1	6,428	0.4	John Fowler	5	R	Lexington	Fayette
Woodford	9,210	2,220	24.1	2,106	4.4	John Fowler	6	R	Lexington	Fayette
TOTALS	36,890	7,025	19.0	13,012	2.8	John Fowler	7	R	Lexington	Fayette

[1]Kentucky was listed as the second district of Virginia in 1788.

[2]Elections were held at large for the fourth through sixth Congresses, and by districts for the Third and Seventh Congresses. Data are presented by district.

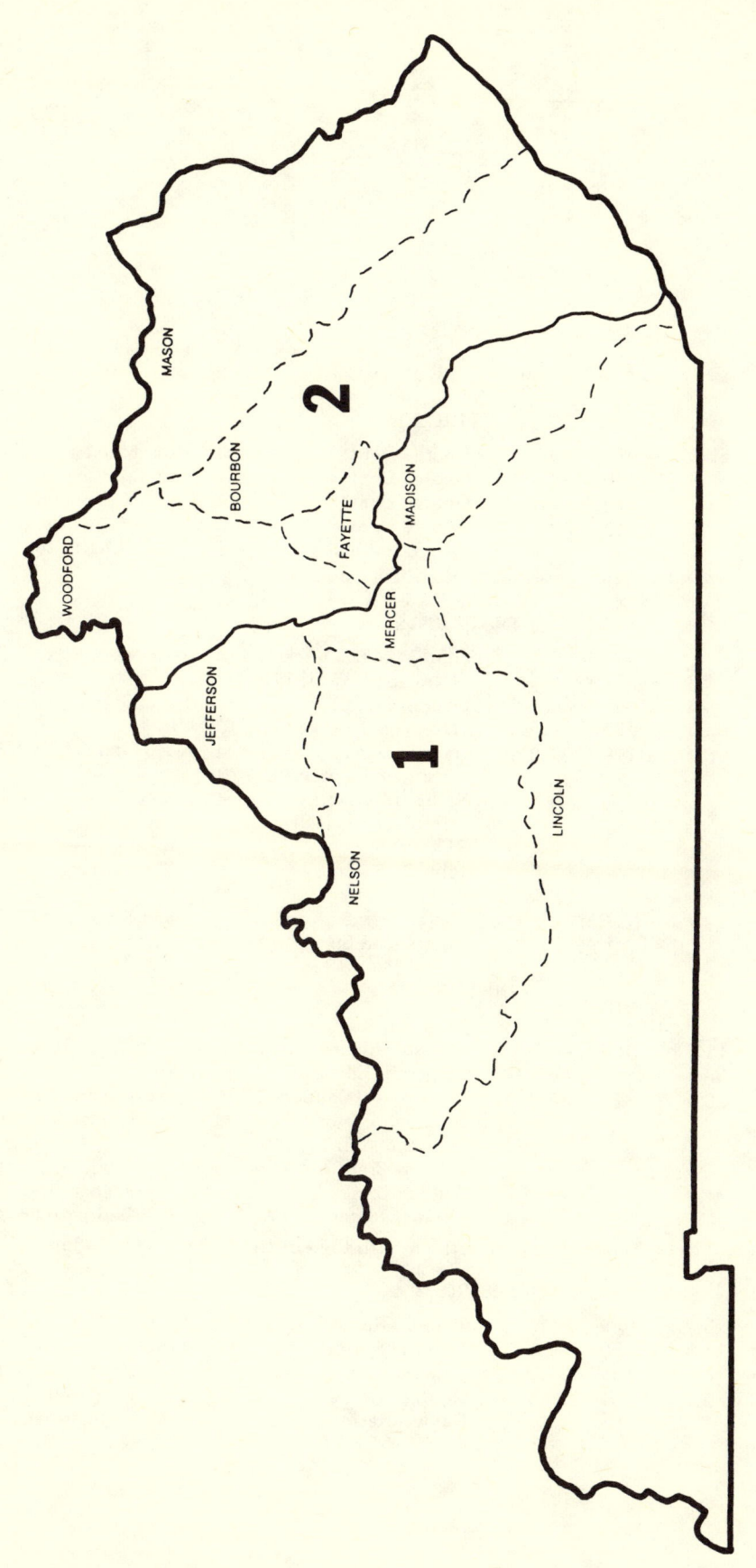

MASON

BOURBON

WOODFORD

2

FAYETTE

MADISON

MERCER

JEFFERSON

1

NELSON

LINCOLN

COUNTIES						REPRESENTATIVES				
County	Aggregate	Slave	%S	sq.mi.	P/sq.mi.	Representative	Cong.	Pty.	Address	County

DISTRICT 1

County	Aggregate	Slave	%S	sq.mi.	P/sq.mi.	Representative	Cong.	Pty.	Address	County
Calvert	8,652	4,505	52.0	217	39.9	George Dent	3	Ad	Mattawoman	Charles
Charles	20,613	10,085	48.9	459	44.9	George Dent	4	Ad	Mattawoman	Charles
St. Marys	15,544	6,985	44.9	373	41.7	George Dent[a]	5	F	Mattawoman	Charles
TOTALS	44,809	21,375	47.7	1,049	42.7	George Dent	6	F	Mattawoman	Charles
						John Campbell	7	F	"Charleston"	Charles

[a]Served as speaker during the second and third sessions of the Fifth Congress.

DISTRICT 2

County	Aggregate	Slave	%S	sq.mi.	P/sq.mi.	Representative	Cong.	Pty.	Address	County
Anne-Arundel	22,598	10,130	44.8	674	42.3	John Francis Mercer[r] (Resigned April, 1794)	3	A-Ad	West River	Anne-Arundel
Prince Georges	21,344	11,176	52.3	505e	33.5	Gabriel Duvall (Replaced Mercer)	3	A-Ad	Glenn Dale	Prince Georges
TOTALS	43,942	21,306	48.3	1,179	37.3	Gabriel Duvall[r] (Resigned March 28, 1796)	4	A-Ad	Glenn Dale	Prince Georges
						Richard Sprigg (Replaced Duvall)	4	R	----	Prince Georges
						Richard Sprigg	5	R	----	Prince Georges
						John C. Thomas	6	F	Fairland	Anne-Arundel
						Richard Sprigg[r]	7	R	----	Prince Georges
						Walter Bowie (Replaced Sprigg)	7	R	Collington	Prince Georges

DISTRICT 3

County	Aggregate	Slave	%S	sq.mi.	P/sq.mi.	Representative	Cong.	Pty.	Address	County
Frederick (portion)[a]	15,395	1,820	11.8	380	40.5	Uriah Forrest[r] (Resigned November, 1794)	3	Ad	----	----
Montgomery	18,003	6,030	33.4	495	36.4	Benjamin Edwards (Took seat January 1795; replaced Forrest)	3	Ad	----	Montgomery
TOTALS	33,398	7,850	23.5	875	38.2	Jeremiah Crabb[r] (Resigned in 1796)	4	Ad	Rockville	Montgomery
						William Craik	5	F	Frederick	Frederick
						William Craik	6	F	Frederick	Frederick
						Thomas Plater	7	F	Georgetown	Montgomery

[a]That part of Frederick adjacent as far as Monocacy from the mouth thereof to the Pennsylvania line.

DISTRICT 4

County	Aggregate	Slave	%S	sq.mi.	P/sq.mi.	Representative	Cong.	Pty.	Address	County
Alleghany	4,809	258	5.3	959	5.0	Thomas Sprigg	3	A-Ad	----	Washington
Frederick[a]	15,395	1,820	11.8	380	40.5	Thomas Sprigg	4	A-Ad	----	Washington
Washington	15,822	1,286	8.1	428	37.0	George Baer, Jr.	5	F	Frederick	Frederick
TOTALS	36,026	3,364	9.3	1,767	20.4	George Baer, Jr.	6	F	Frederick	Frederick
						Daniel Hiester	7	R	Hagerstown	Washington

[a]The remainder of Frederick.

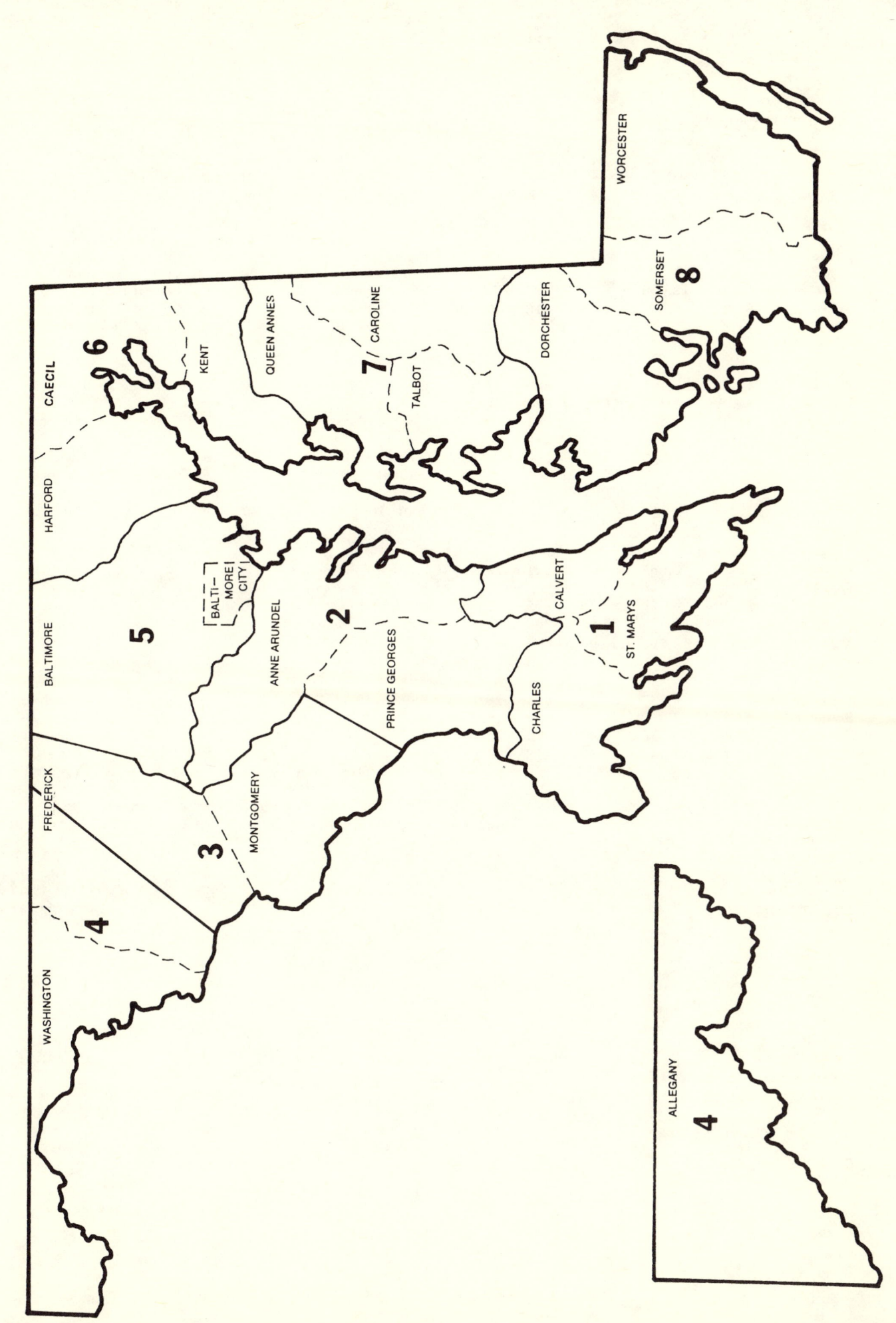

COUNTIES						REPRESENTATIVES				
County	Aggregate	Slave	%S	sq.mi.	P/sq.mi.	Representative	Cong.	Pty.	Address	County

DISTRICT 5

County	Aggregate	Slave	%S	sq.mi.	P/sq.mi.	Representative	Cong.	Pty.	Address	County
Baltimore	25,434	5,877	23.1	598	42.6	Samuel Smith	3	A-Ad	City of Baltimore	
City of						Samuel Smith	4	A-Ad	City of Baltimore	
Baltimore	13,503	12,555	9.2	78	173.1	Samuel Smith	5	R	City of Baltimore	
TOTALS	38,937	18,432	47.3	676	57.6	Samuel Smith	6	R	City of Baltimore	
						Samuel Smith	7	R	City of Baltimore	

DISTRICT 6

County	Aggregate	Slave	%S	sq.mi.	P/sq.mi.	Representative	Cong.	Pty.	Address	County
Caecil	13,625	3,407	25.0	362	37.5	Gabriel Christie	3	A-Ad	Havre de Grace	Harford
Harford	14,976	3,417	18.3	676	22.2					
Kent	12,836	5,433	42.3	281	45.1	Gabriel Christie	4	A-Ad	Havre de Grace	Harford
TOTALS	41,437	12,257	29.5	1,319	31.4					
						William Mathews	5	F	----	Coecil
						Gabriel Christie	6	R	Havre de Grace	Harford
						John Archer	7	R	Churchville	Harford

DISTRICT 7

County	Aggregate	Slave	%S	sq.mi.	P/sq.mi.	Representative	Cong.	Pty.	Address	County
Caroline	9,506	2,057	21.6	321	29.6	William Hindman	3	Ad	----	Talbot
Queen						William Hindman	4	Ad	----	Talbot
Annes	15,463	6,674	43.1	375	41.2	William Hindman	5	F	----	Talbot
Talbot	13,084	4,777	36.5	261	50.1	Joseph H. Nicholson	6	R	Easton	Talbot
TOTALS	38,053	13,508	35.5	957	39.8	Joseph H. Nicholson	7	R	Easton	Talbot

DISTRICT 8

County	Aggregate	Slave	%S	sq.mi.	P/sq.mi.	Representative	Cong.	Pty.	Address	County
Dorchester	15,875	5,337	33.6	594	26.7	William Vans Murray	3	Ad	Cambridge	Dorchester
Somerset	15,610	7,070	45.2	339	46.0	William Vans Murray	4	Ad	Cambridge	Dorchester
Worcester	11,640	3,836	32.9	479	24.3	John Dennis	5	F	----	Somerset
TOTALS	43,125	16,243	37.6	1,412	30.5	John Dennis	6	F	----	Somerset
						John Dennis	7	F	----	Somerset

SPECIAL NOTE: Most Maryland district information for 1792-1816 was secured from Dorothy M. Brown, "Party Battles and Beginnings in Maryland," unpublished Ph.D. dissertation, Georgetown University, 1961.

COUNTIES						REPRESENTATIVES				
County	Aggregate	Slave	%S	sq.mi.	P/sq.mi.	Representative	Cong.	Pty.	Address	County

DISTRICT 1

County	Aggregate	Slave	%S	sq.mi.	P/sq.mi.	Representative	Cong.	Pty.	Address	County
Essex	57,913	----	----	494	117.2	Fisher Ames	3[1]	Ad	Dedham	Suffolk
Middlesex	42,737	----	----	825	51.8	Benjamin Goodhue	3	Ad	Salem	Essex
Suffolk	44,875	----	----	450	99.7	Samuel Holton	3	A-Ad	Danvers	Essex
TOTALS	145,525	----	----	1,769	82.3					

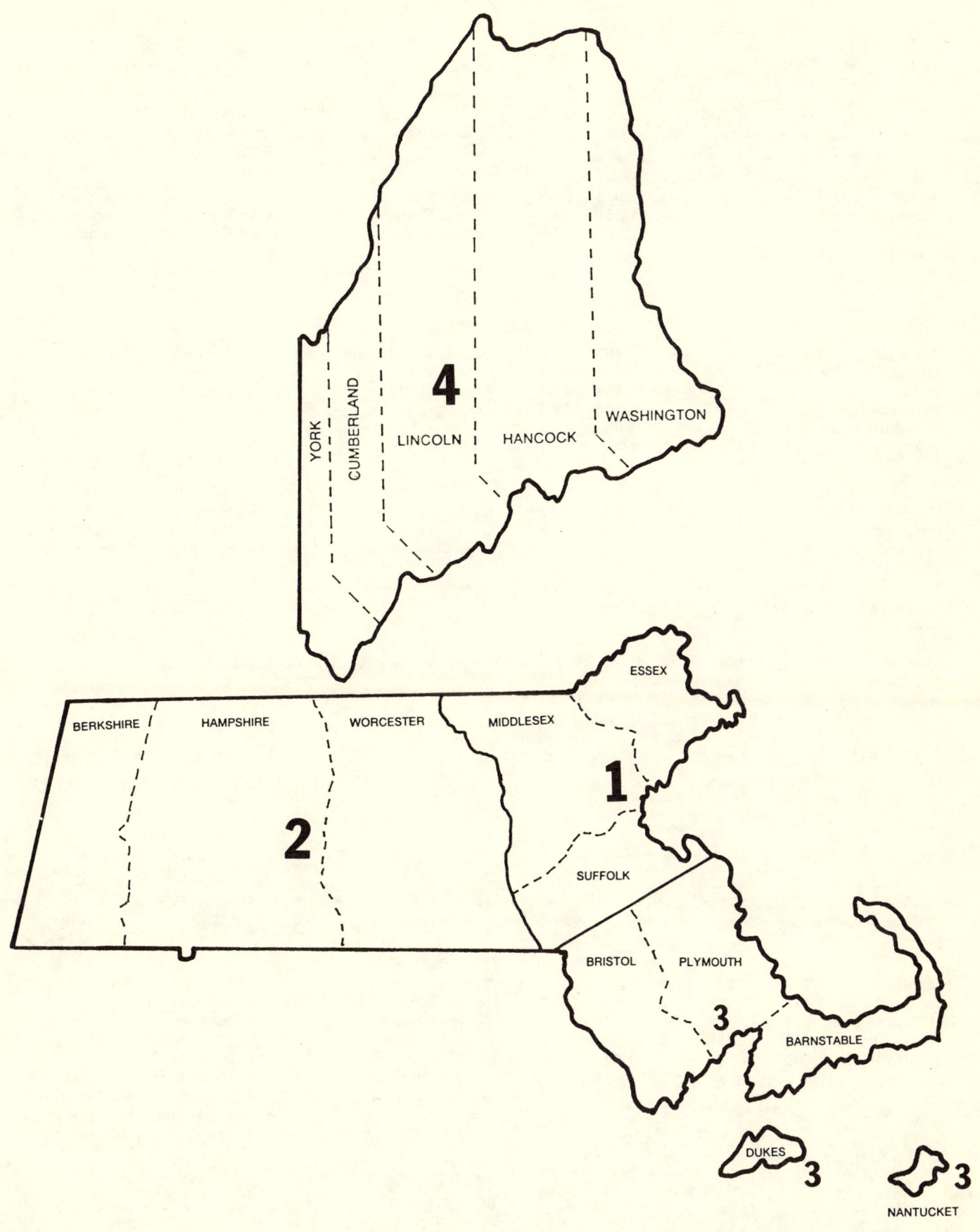

County	Aggregate	Slave	%S	sq.mi.	P/sq.mi.	Representative	Cong.	Pty.	Address	County
COUNTIES						**REPRESENTATIVES**				
DISTRICT 2										
Berkshire	30,291	----	----	941	32.2	Samuel Dexter	3	Ad	Lunenburg	Worcester
Hampshire	59,681	----	----	1,856	32.2	Dwight Foster	3	A-Ad	Brookfield	Worcester
Worcester	56,807	----	----	1,509	37.6	William Lyman	3	A-Ad	North-ampton	Hampshire
TOTALS	146,779	----	----	4,306	34.1					
						Theodore Sedgewick	3	Ad	Sheffield	Berkshire
						Artemas Ward	3	Ad	Shrewsbury	Worcester
DISTRICT 3										
Barnstable	17,354	----	----	393	44.2	Shearjashub Bourne	3	Ad	Boston	Suffolk
Bristol	31,709	----	----	554	57.2	David Cobb	3	Ad	Taunton	Bristol
Dukes	3,265	----	----	104	31.4	Pelig Coffin, Jr.	3	Ad	Nantucket	Nantucket
Nantucket	4,620	----	----	46	100.4					
Plymouth	29,535	----	----	654	45.2					
TOTALS	86,483	----	----	1,751	49.4					
DISTRICT 4										
Cumberland	25,450	----	----	3,669	6.9	Henry Dearborn	3	A-Ad	Monmouth	Lincoln
Hancock	9,549	----	----	12,030	0.7	George Thacher	3	Ad	Biddleford	York
Lincoln	29,962	----	----	9,198	3.2	Peleg Wadsworth	3	Ad	Portland	Cumberland
Washington	2,758	----	----	3,504	0.8					
York	28,821	----	----	2,937	9.8					
TOTALS	96,540	----	----	31,343	3.0					

[1]Congressmen for the Fourth, Fifth, Sixth, and Seventh Congresses are given in the apportionment of 1794.

County	Aggregate	Slave	%S	sq.mi.	P/sq.mi.	Representative	Cong.	Pty.	Address	County
COUNTIES						**REPRESENTATIVES**				
AT LARGE										
Cheshire	28,772	16	0.06	1,174	24.5	Nicholas Gilman	3	Ad	Exeter	Rockingham
Grafton	13,472	21	0.16	3,852	3.5	John S. Sherburn	3	A-Ad	Portsmouth	Rockingham
Hillsborough	32,871	0	----	1,477	22.3	Jeremiah Smith	3	Ad	Peterboro	Hillsborough
Rockingham	43,169	98	0.23	1,041	41.5	Paine Wiengate	3	A-Ad	Stratham	Rockingham
Strafford	23,601	23	----	1,414	16.7					
TOTALS	141,885	158	0.5	8,958	15.8	Abiel Foster	4	Ad	Canterbury	Rockingham
						Nicholas Gilman	4	Ad	Exeter	Rockingham
						John S. Sherburn	4	A-Ad	Portsmouth	Rockingham
						Jeremiah Smith	4	Ad	Peterboro	Hillsborough

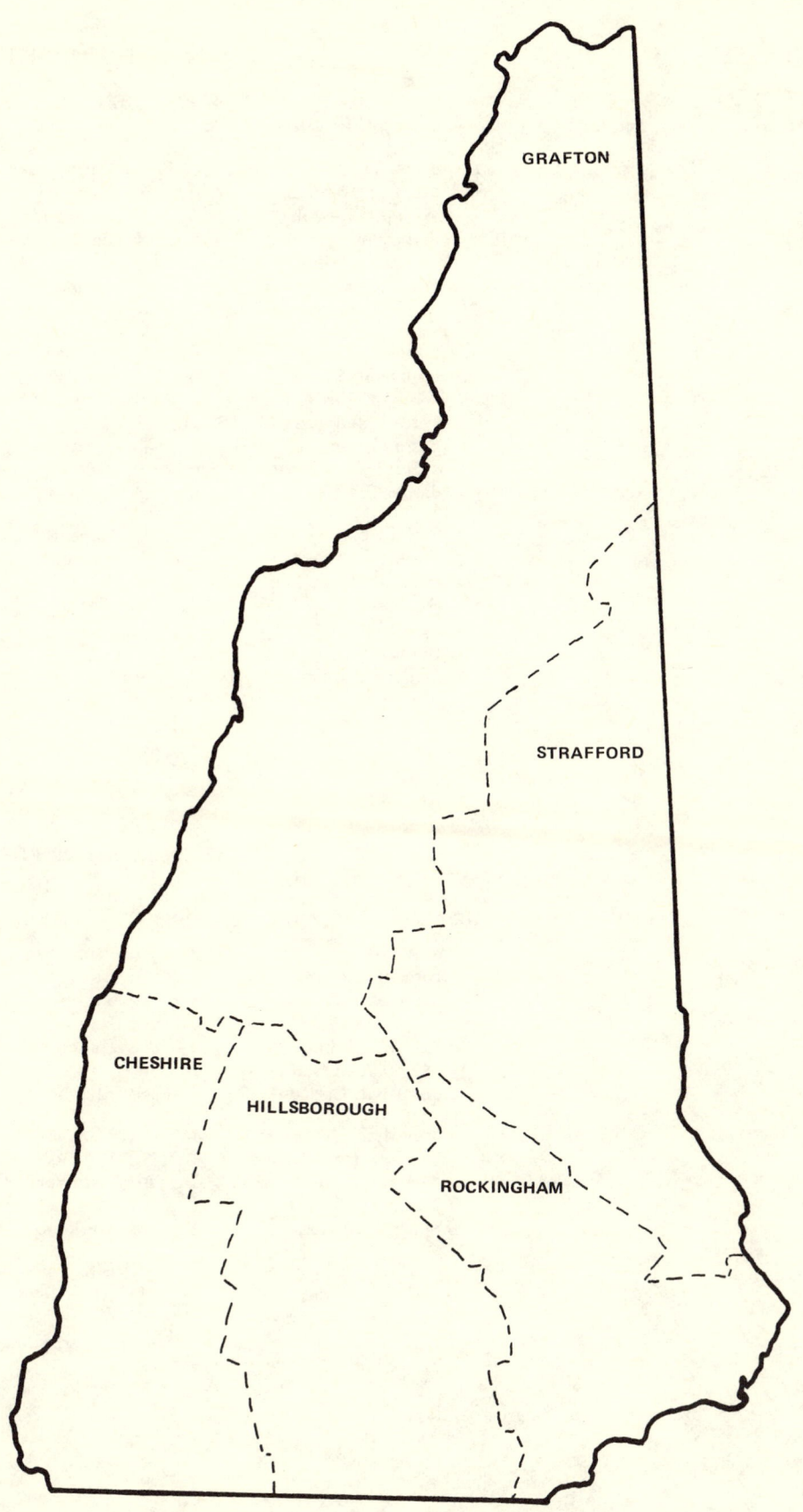

COUNTIES						REPRESENTATIVES				
County	Aggregate	Slave	%S	sq.mi.	P/sq.mi.	Representative	Cong.	Pty.	Address	County
						Abiel Foster	5	F	Canterbury	Rockingham
						Jonathan Freeman	5	F	Hanover	Grafton
						William Gordon	5	F	Amburst	Hillsborough
						Jeremiah Smith[r]	5	F	Peterboro	Hillsborough
						(Resigned July, 1797)				
						Peleg Sprague	5	F	Keene	Cheshire
						(Replaced Smith December 15, 1797)				
						Abiel Foster	6	F	Canterbury	Rockingham
						Jonathan Freeman	6	F	Hanover	Grafton
						William Gordon[r]	6	F	Amburst	Hillsborough
						(Resigned June 12, 1800)				
						Samuel Tenney	6	F	Exeter	Rockingham
						(Replaced Gordon December 8, 1800)				
						James Sheafe	6	F	Portsmouth	Rockingham
						Abiel Foster	7	F	Canterbury	Rockingham
						Joseph Pierce[r]	7	(----)	Alton	Strafford
						(Resigned in 1802)				
						Samuel Hunt	7	(----)	Keene	Cheshire
						(Replaced Pierce December 6, 1802)				
						Samuel Tenney	7	F	Exeter	Rockingham
						George Upham	7	(----)	Claremont	Cheshire

NEW JERSEY
5 DISTRICTS/AT LARGE[1]
5 CONGRESSMEN

COUNTIES						REPRESENTATIVES				
County	Aggregate	Slave	%S	sq.mi.	P/sq.mi.	Representative	Cong.	Pty.	Address	County

AT LARGE: THIRD, FOURTH, AND FIFTH CONGRESSES

						Representative	Cong.	Pty.	Address	County
						John Beatty	3	Ad	Princeton	Somerset
						Elias Boudinot	3	Ad	Elizabeth	Essex
						Lambert Cadwalader	3	Ad	Trenton	Hunterdon
						Abraham Clark[†]	3	Ad	Raway	Essex
						Aaron Kitchell	3	Ad	Hanover	Morris
						(Replaced Clark)				
						Jonathan Dayton	3	Ad	Elizabeth	Essex
						Jonathan Dayton[a]	4	Ad	Elizabeth	Essex
						Thomas Henderson	4	Ad	Freehold	Monmouth
						Aaron Kitchell	4	Ad	Hanover	Morris
						Isaac Smith	4	Ad	Trenton	Hunterdon
						Mark Thomson	4	Ad	Marksboro	Sussex
						Jonathan Dayton[a]	5	F	Elizabeth	Essex
						James H. Imlay	5	F	Allentown	Monmouth
						James Schureman	5	F	New Brunswick	Middlesex
						Thomas Sinnickson	5	F	Salem	Salem
						Mark Thomson	5	F	Marksboro	Sussex

[a]Served as Speaker for the Fourth and Fifth Congresses.

	COUNTIES						REPRESENTATIVES			
County	Aggregate	Slave	%S	sq.mi.	P/sq.mi.	Representative	Cong.	Pty.	Address	County
DISTRICT 1 (EASTERN)										
Bergen	12,601	2,301	18.2	420	29.6	John Condit	6	R	Orange	Essex
Essex	17,785	1,171	6.5	233	76.3	John Condit	7[2]	R	Orange	Essex
Middlesex	15,956	1,278	8.0	312	51.1					
TOTALS	46,342	4,750	12.4	965	48.0					
DISTRICT 2 (NORTHERN)										
Morris	16,216	636	3.9	468	34.6	Aaron Kitchell	6	R	Hanover	Morris
Sussex	19,500	439	2.2	889	83.6	William Helmes	7	R	Hacketts-town	Sussex
TOTALS	35,716	1,075	3.0	1,357	26.3					
DISTRICT 3 (WESTERN)										
Hunterdon	20,253	1,101	5.4	651	310.8	James Linn	6	R	Princeton	Hunterdon
Somerset	12,296	1,810	14.7	307	40.0	Henry Southard	7	R	Basking Ridge	Somerset
TOTALS	32,549	2,911	8.9	958	33.9					
DISTRICT 4 (MIDDLE)										
Burlington	18,095	227	1.2	819	22.0	James H. Imlay	6	F	Allentown	Monmouth
Monmouth	16,918	1,196	7.0	1,118	15.1	James Mott	7	R	Middletown	Monmouth
TOTALS	35,013	1,423	4.0	1,937	18.0					
DISTRICT 5 (SOUTHERN)										
Cape May	2,571	141	5.4	267	9.6	Franklin Davenport	6	F	Woodbury	Gloucester
Cumberland	8,248	120	1.4	500	16.4	Ebenezer Elmer	7	R	Bridgetown	Cumberland
Gloucester	13,363	91	0.7	1,119	11.9					
Salem	10,437	172	1.6	365	28.5					
TOTALS	34,619	524	1.5	2,251	16.3					

[1]Elections were held at large for the Third through Fifth Congresses, and by districts for the Sixth and Seventh Congresses.

[2]Although representatives to the Seventh Congress were elected at large, they were actually elected from the districts created for the Sixth Congress.

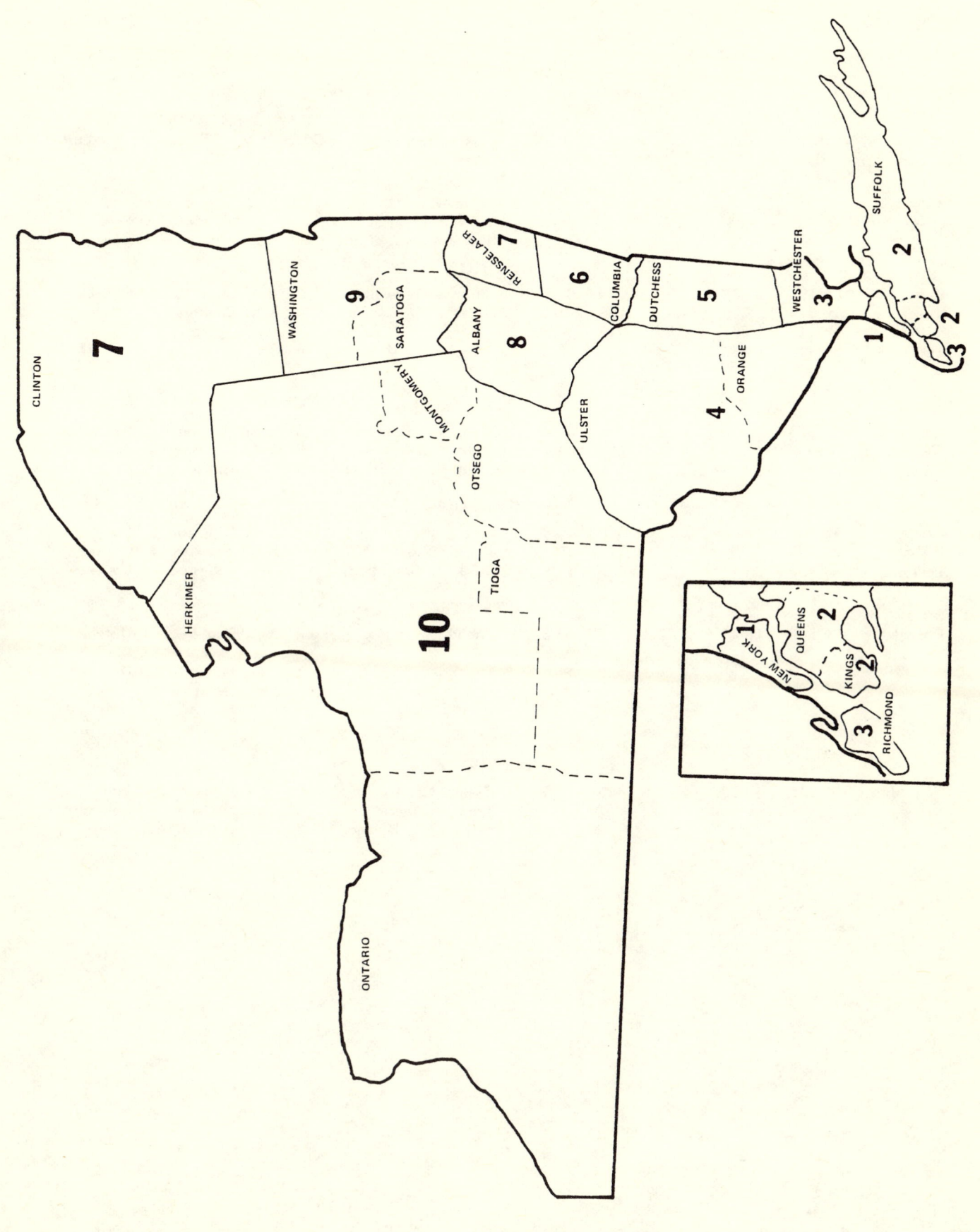

	COUNTIES					REPRESENTATIVES				
County	Aggregate	Slave	%S	sq.mi.	P/sq.mi.	Representative	Cong.	Pty.	Address	County

DISTRICT 1

City of						John Watts	3[1]	Ad	City of New York	
New York	33,131	2,369	7.1	64	517.6	Edward Livingston	4	A-Ad	City of New York	
						Edward Livingston	5	R	City of New York	

DISTRICT 2

Kings	4,495	1,432	31.8	70	64.2	Thomas Tredwell	3	A-Ad	Smithtown	Suffolk
Queens	16,014	2,309	14.4	108	148.2	Jonathan N. Havens	4	A-Ad	Shelter	Suffolk
Suffolk	16,440	1,098	6.6	1,218	13.4				Island	
TOTALS	36,949	4,839	13.0	1,396	26.4	Jonathan N. Havens	5	R	Shelter	Suffolk
									Island	

DISTRICT 3

Richmond	3,855	759	19.6	58	66.4	Philip Van Cortlandt	3	A-Ad	Hudson	Westchester
Westchester	24,003	1,419	5.9	443	54.1	Philip Van Cortlandt	4	A-Ad	Hudson	Westchester
TOTALS	27,858	2,178	7.8	501	55.6	Philip Van Cortlandt	5	R	Hudson	Westchester

DISTRICT 4

Orange	18,492	966	5.2	1,009	18.3	Peter Van Gaasbeck	3	A-Ad	Kingston	Ulster
Ulster	29,397	2,906	9.8	2,774	10.5	John Hathorn	4	A-Ad	Warwick	Orange
TOTALS	47,889	3,872	8.0	3,783	12.6	Lucas C. Elmendorf	5	R	Kingston	Ulster

DISTRICT 5

Dutchess	45,266	1,856	4.1	1,044	43.3	Theodorus Bailey	3	A-Ad	Pough-	Dutchess
									keepsie	
						Theodorus Bailey	4	A-Ad	Pough-	Dutchess
									keepsie	
						David Brooks	5	F	Pough-	Dutchess
									keepsie	

DISTRICT 6

Columbia	27,732	1,623	5.8	645	42.9	Ezekiel Gilbert	3	Ad	Hudson	Columbia
						Ezekiel Gilbert	4	Ad	Hudson	Columbia
						Hezekiah L. Hosmer	5	F	Hudson	Columbia

| | COUNTIES | | | | | | REPRESENTATIVES | | | |
| County | Aggregate | Slave | %S | sq.mi. | P/sq.mi. | Representative | Cong. | Pty. | Address | County |

DISTRICT 7

County	Aggregate	Slave	%S	sq.mi.	P/sq.mi.	Representative	Cong.	Pty.	Address	County
Clinton	1,614	17	1.0	4,556	0.3	John E. Van Alen	3	Ad	----	Rensselaer
Rensselaer	37,868	299	----	665	56.9	John E. Van Alen	4	Ad	----	Rensselaer
TOTALS	39,482	316	----	5,221	7.6	John E. Van Alen	5	F	----	Rensselaer

DISTRICT 8

County	Aggregate	Slave	%S	sq.mi.	P/sq.mi.	Representative	Cong.	Pty.	Address	County
Albany	37,868	1,962	5.1	1,388	27.3	Silas Talbot	3	Ad	City of Albany	
City of						Henry Glen	4	Ad	Schenectady	Albany
Albany	3,498	572	16.3	20	174.9	Henry Glen	5	F	Schenectady	Albany
TOTALS	41,366	2,534	6.1	1,408	29.4					

DISTRICT 9

County	Aggregate	Slave	%S	sq.mi.	P/sq.mi.	Representative	Cong.	Pty.	Address	County
Saratoga	3,071	53	1.7	818	3.7	James Gordon	3	Ad	Ballston Spa	Saratoga
Washington	14,042	47	0.3	1,729	8.1	John Williams	4	Ad	Salem	Washington
TOTALS	17,113	100	0.5	2,547	6.7	John Williams	5	F	Salem	Washington

DISTRICT 10

County	Aggregate	Slave	%S	sq.mi.	P/sq.mi.	Representative	Cong.	Pty.	Address	County
Herkemer	1,525	8	0.5	14,325	0.1	----	3	(----)	----	----
Ontario	1,075	11	1.0	10,754	0.09	William Cooper	4	Ad	Cooperstown	Otsego
Otsego	1,702	8	0.47	1,043	1.6	James Cochran	5	F	Oswego	Tioga
Montgomery	28,848	588	2.0	906	31.8					
Tioga[a]	----	----	----	2,843	----					
TOTALS	33,150	615	1.8	29,871	1.1					

[1]Congressmen for the Sixth and Seventh Congresses are given in the apportionment of 1798.

[a]Created after 1790 census.

COUNTIES						REPRESENTATIVES				
County	Aggregate	Slave	%S	sq.mi.	P/sq.mi.	Representative	Cong.	Pty.	Address	County

DISTRICT 1

County	Aggregate	Slave	%S	sq.mi.	P/sq.mi.	Representative	Cong.	Pty.	Address	County
Buncomb[a]						Joseph McDowell	3	A-Ad	Morganton	Burke
Burke	8,118	595	7.3	**	**	James Holland	4	A-Ad	Ruther-fordton	Rutherford
Lincoln	9,224	935	10.1	**	**					
Rutherford	7,808	614	7.8	**	**	Joseph McDowell	5	R	Morganton	Burke
Wilkes	8,143	549	6.7	**	**	Joseph Dickson	6	F	----	Lincoln
TOTALS	33,293	2,693	8.0	11,388	2.9	James Holland	7	R	Ruther-fordton	Rutherford

[a]Included in Burke County and Rutherford County statistics; created in 1791.
**Rapidly changing boundaries preclude individual county statistics.

DISTRICT 2

County	Aggregate	Slave	%S	sq.mi.	P/sq.mi.	Representative	Cong.	Pty.	Address	County
Cabarrus[a]						Matthew Locke	3	A-Ad	----	Rowan
Iredell	5,435	858	15.7	572	9.5	Matthew Locke	4	A-Ad	----	Rowan
Mecklenberg	11,395	1,603	14.0	893	12.8	Matthew Locke	5	R	----	Rowan
Montgomery	4,725	834	17.6	761	6.2	Archibald Henderson	6	F	Salisbury	Rowan
Rowan	15,828	1,742	11.0	1,337	11.8	Archibald Henderson	7	F	Salisbury	Rowan
TOTALS	37,383	5,037	13.4	3,563	10.5					

[a]Included in Mecklenberg County statistics; created in 1792.

DISTRICT 3

County	Aggregate	Slave	%S	sq.mi.	P/sq.mi.	Representative	Cong.	Pty.	Address	County
Caswell[a]	5,048	1,368	27.0	428	11.7	Joseph Winston	3	A-Ad	Germantown	Stokes
Guilford	7,191	516	7.1	655	11.0	Jesse Franklin	4	A-Ad	----	Surrey
Rockingham	6,187	1,100	17.7	569	10.8	Robert Williams	5	R	----	Rockingham
Stokes	8,528	787	9.2	876	9.7	Robert Williams	6	R	----	Rockingham
Surrey	7,191	698	9.7	872	8.3	Robert Williams	7	R	----	Rockingham
TOTALS	34,145	4,469	13.0	3,400	10.0					

[a]One-half of the population became part of Person County (District 4).

DISTRICT 4

County	Aggregate	Slave	%S	sq.mi.	P/sq.mi.	Representative	Cong.	Pty.	Address	County
Chatham	9,221	1,632	17.6	709	13.0	Alexander Mebane	3	A-Ad	Hawfields	Orange
Orange	12,216	2,060	16.8	1,123	10.9	Absalom Tatom[r]	4	A-Ad	Hillsborough	Randolph
Person[a]	5,048	1,368	27.0	401	12.6	(Resigned June 1, 1796)				
Randolph	7,276	452	6.2	798	9.1	William F. Strudwick	4	Ad	----	Orange
TOTALS	33,761	5,512	16.3	3,031	11.1	(Replaced Tatom)				
						Richard Stanford	5	R	Hawsfield	Chatham
						Richard Stanford	6	R	Hawsfield	Chatham
						Richard Stanford	7	R	Hawsfield	Chatham

[a]Created from Caswell (District 3) in 1791.

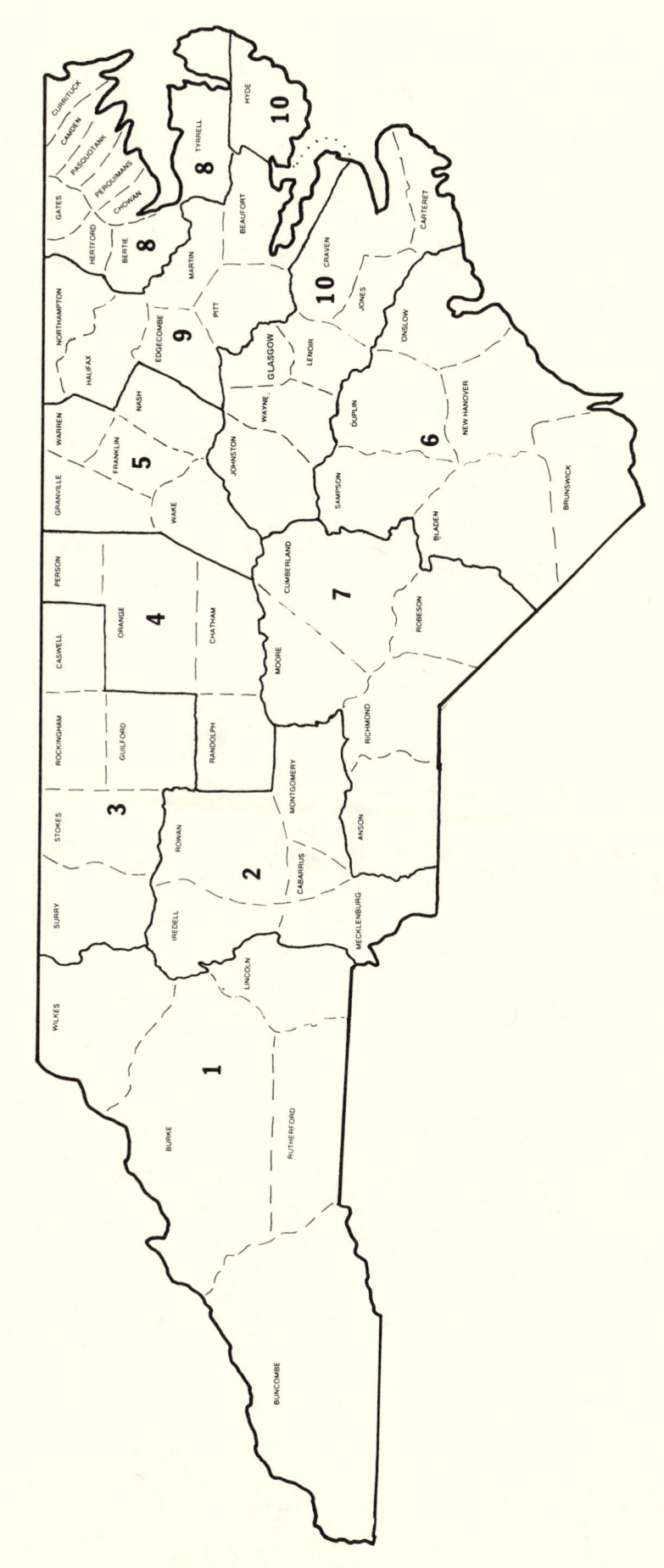

	COUNTIES						REPRESENTATIVES			
County	Aggregate	Slave	%S	sq.mi.	P/sq.mi.	Representative	Cong.	Pty.	Address	County

DISTRICT 5

County	Aggregate	Slave	%S	sq.mi.	P/sq.mi.	Representative	Cong.	Pty.	Address	County
Franklin	7,559	2,717	35.9	491	15.4	Nathaniel Macon	3	A-Ad	Warrenton	Warren
Granville	10,982	4,163	37.9	686	16.0	Nathaniel Macon	4	A-Ad	Warrenton	Warren
Nash	7,393	2,009	27.1	544	13.6	Nathaniel Macon	5	R	Warrenton	Warren
Wake	10,192	2,463	24.1	858	11.8	Nathaniel Macon	6	R	Warrenton	Warren
Warren	9,397	4,720	50.2	524	17.8	Nathaniel Macon[a]	7	R	Warrenton	Warren
TOTALS	45,452	16,072	35.3	3,103	14.6					

[a]Served as Speaker during the Seventh Congress.

DISTRICT 6

County	Aggregate	Slave	%S	sq.mi.	P/sq.mi.	Representative	Cong.	Pty.	Address	County
Bladen	5,084	1,676	32.9	1,828	2.8	James Gillespie	3	A-Ad	Kenamsville	Duplin
Brunswick	3,071	1,511	49.2	856	3.6	James Gillespie	4	A-Ad	Kenamsville	Duplin
Duplin	5,662	1,383	24.4	815	6.9	James Gillespie	5	R	Kenamsville	Duplin
New Hanover	6,831	3,738	54.7	1,056	6.5	William H. Hill	6	F	Wilmington	Brunswick
Onslow	5,387	1,748	32.4	765	7.0	William H. Hill	7	F	Wilmington	Brunswick
Sampson	6,065	1,183	19.5	945	6.4					
TOTALS	32,100	11,239	35.0	6,265	5.1					

DISTRICT 7

County	Aggregate	Slave	%S	sq.mi.	P/sq.mi.	Representative	Cong.	Pty.	Address	County
Anson	5,133	828	16.1	633e	8.1	William B. Grove	3	Ad	Fayetteville	Cumberland
Cumberland	8,671	2,181	25.1	1,093e	7.9	William B. Grove	4	Ad	Fayetteville	Cumberland
Moore	3,770	371	9.8	704	5.4	William B. Grove	5	F	Fayetteville	Cumberland
Richmond	5,055	583	11.5	794	6.4	William B. Grove	6	F	Fayetteville	Cumberland
Robeson	5,326	533	10.0	900e	5.9	William B. Grove	7	F	Fayetteville	Cumberland
TOTALS	27,955	4,496	16.1	4,124	6.8					

DISTRICT 8

County	Aggregate	Slave	%S	sq.mi.	P/sq.mi.	Representative	Cong.	Pty.	Address	County
Bertie	12,606	5,141	40.7	698	18.1	William J. Dawson	3	A-Ad	Edenton	Bertie
Camden	4,033	1,038	25.7	239	16.9	Dempsey Burgess	4	A-Ad	Shiloh	Camden
Chowan	5,011	2,588	51.6	173	29.0	Dempsey Burgess	5	R	Shiloh	Camden
Currituck	5,219	1,103	21.1	246	21.2	David Stone	6	R	Hope	Bertie
Gates	5,392	2,219	41.1	337	16.0	Charles Johnson†	7	R	Edenton	Chowan
Hertford	5,828	2,442	41.9	353	14.2	Thomas Wynns	7	F	Winton	Hertford
Pasquotank	5,497	1,623	29.5	228	24.1	(Replaced Johnson)				
Perquimans	5,440	1,878	34.5	246	22.1					
Tyrrel	4,744	1,166	24.5	781	6.0					
TOTALS	53,770	19,198	35.7	3,301	16.3					

DISTRICT 9

County	Aggregate	Slave	%S	sq.mi.	P/sq.mi.	Representative	Cong.	Pty.	Address	County
Beaufort	5,462	1,632	29.8	826	6.6	Thomas Blount	3	A-Ad	Tarboro	Edgecombe
Edgecombe	10,255	3,152	30.7	510	20.1	Thomas Blount	4	A-Ad	Tarboro	Edgecombe
Halifax	13,965	6,506	46.5	734	19.0	Thomas Blount	5	R	Tarboro	Edgecombe
Martin	6,080	1,889	31.0	455	13.4	Willis Alston	6	R	Littleton	Halifax
Northampton	9,981	4,409	44.1	536	18.6	Willis Alston	7	R	Littleton	Halifax
Pitt	8,275	2,367	28.6	655	12.6					
TOTALS	54,018	19.995	36.9	3,716	14.5					

| | COUNTIES | | | | | REPRESENTATIVES | | | | |
| County | Aggregate | Slave | %S | sq.mi. | P/sq.mi. | Representative | Cong. | Pty. | Address | County |

DISTRICT 10

Cateret	3,732	713	19.1	536	7.0	Benjamin Williams	3	A-Ad	Smithfield	Johnston
Craven	10,469	3,658	34.9	1,037	10.1	Nathan Bryan	4	A-Ad	----	Craven
Glasgow	6,893	1,915	27.7	267	25.8	Nathan Bryan[†]	5	R	----	Craven
Hyde	4,120	1,048	25.4	613	6.7	Richard D. Spaight	5	F	New Bern	Craven
Johnston	5,634	1,329	23.5	797	7.1	(Replaced Bryan)				
Jones	4,822	1,681	34.8	467	10.3	Richard D. Spaight[†]	6	R	New Bern	Craven
Lenoir[a]	----	----	----	400	----	John Stanley	7	R	New Bern	Craven
Wayne	6,133	1,557	25.3	557	11.0	(Killed Spaight in a duel)				
TOTALS	41,803	11,901	28.5	4,674	8.9					

[a]Created after the 1790 census.

COUNTIES						REPRESENTATIVES				
County	Aggregate	Slave	%S	sq.mi.	P/sq.mi.	Representative	Cong.	Pty.	Address	County

DISTRICT 1

City of Philadelphia	42,520	273	0.06	29	1466.0	Thomas Fitzsimons	3	Ad	City of Philadelphia	
						John Swanwick	4	A-Ad	City of Philadelphia	
						John Swanwick[†]	5	R	City of Philadelphia	
						Robert Waln (Replaced Swanwick)	5	F	City of Philadelphia	
						Robert Waln	6	F	City of Philadelphia	
						William Jones	7	R	City of Philadelphia	

DISTRICT 2

Philadelphia[a]	11,871	114	0.1	100	118.0	Frederick Muhlenberg	3	A-Ad	City of Philadelphia	
						Frederick Muhlenberg	4	A-Ad	City of Philadelphia	
						Blair McClenchan	5	R	City of Philadelphia	
						Michael Leib	6	R	City of Philadelphia	
						Michael Leib	7	R	City of Philadelphia	

[a]Persons from the city of Philadelphia probably were eligible to hold this seat.

DISTRICT 3

Chester	27,937	145	0.5	761	36.0	William Irvine	3	Ad	----	----
Delaware	9,483	50	0.5	184	51.0	Richard Thomas	4	Ad	----	Chester*
TOTALS	37,420	195	0.5	945	39.5	Richard Thomas	5	F	----	Chester*
						Richard Thomas	6	F	----	Chester*
						Joseph Hemphill	7	F	Westchester	Chester

DISTRICT 4

Bucks	25,401	261	1.0	614	41.4	John P. G. Muhlenberg	3	A-Ad	Providence	Montgomery
Montgomery	24,250	23	0.1	3,182	7.6					
Northampton	22,929	114	0.5	496	46.2	John Richards	4	A-Ad	----	----
TOTALS	72,580	398	0.5	4,292	16.9	Samuel Sitgreaves	4	Ad	Easton	Northampton
						Samuel Sitgreaves[r]	5	F	Easton	Northampton
						Robert Brown	5	R	Weaversville	Northampton
						John Chapman	5	F	Wrightstown	Bucks
						Robert Brown	6	R	Weaversville	Northampton
						John P. G. Muhlenberg	6	R	Providence	Montgomery
						Robert Brown	7	R	Weaversville	Northampton
						Issac Van Horn	7	R	----	Bucks

[1] The Third Congress was elected at large.

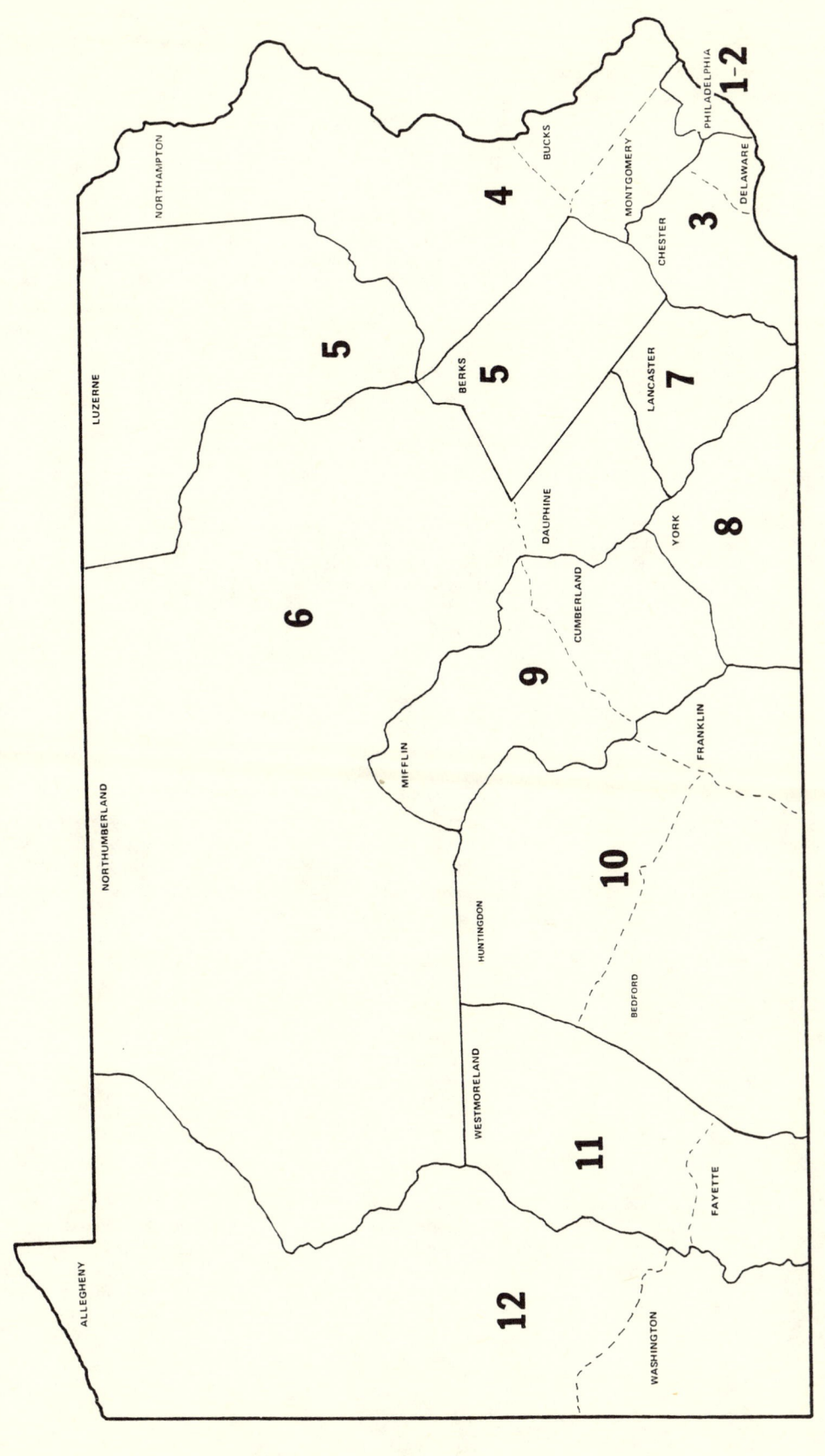

	COUNTIES					REPRESENTATIVES				
County	Aggregate	Slave	%S	sq.mi.	P/sq.mi.	Representative	Cong.	Pty.	Address	County

DISTRICT 5

	COUNTIES					REPRESENTATIVES				
Berks	30,179	65	0.2	1,486	20.3	Daniel Hiester	3	A-Ad	----	----
Luzerne	4,904	11	0.2	3,512	1.3	Daniel Hiester[r]	4	A-Ad	----	----
TOTALS	35,083	76	0.2	4,998	7.0	George Ege (Replaced Hiester)	4	Ad	Marion Township	Berks
						George Ege[r]	5	F	Marion Township	Berks
						Joseph Hiester (Replaced Ege)	5	F	Reading	Berks
						Joseph Hiester	6	F	Reading	Berks
						Joseph Hiester	7	F	Reading	Berks

DISTRICT 6

	COUNTIES					REPRESENTATIVES				
Dauphin	18,177	212	1.1	881	20.6	WilliamMontgomery	3	(----)	----	Northumberland
Northumberland	17,161	89	0.5	12,792	1.3	Samuel Maclay	4	A-Ad	----	----
TOTALS	35,338	301	0.8	13,673	2.5	John A. Hanna	5	R	Harrisburg	Dauphin
						John A. Hanna	6	R	Harrisburg	Dauphin
						John A. Hanna	7	R	Harrisburg	Dauphin

DISTRICT 7

	COUNTIES					REPRESENTATIVES				
Lancaster	36,147	348	0.96	946	38.2	John Wilkes Kittera	3	Ad	----	Lancaster
						John Wilkes Kittera	4	Ad	----	Lancaster
						John Wilkes Kittera	5	F	----	Lancaster
						John Wilkes Kittera	6	F	----	Lancaster
						Thomas Boude	7	F	Columbia	Lancaster

DISTRICT 8

	COUNTIES					REPRESENTATIVES				
York	37,747	499	1.3	1,435	26.3	Thomas Hartley	3	Ad	York	York
						Thomas Hartley	4	Ad	York	York
						Thomas Hartley	5	F	York	York
						Thomas Hartley[†]	6	F	York	York
						John Stewart (Replaced Hartley)	6	R	York[*]	York
						John Stewart	7	R	York[*]	York

DISTRICT 9

	COUNTIES					REPRESENTATIVES				
Cumberland	18,243	223	1.2	1,106	16.4	Andrew Gregg	3	A-Ad	----	----
Mifflin	7,562	59	0.8	1,432	5.2	Andrew Gregg	4	A-Ad	----	----
TOTALS	25,805	282	1.0	2,538	10.1	Andrew Gregg	5	R	----	----
						Andrew Gregg	6	R	----	----
						Andrew Gregg	7	R	----	----

DISTRICT 10

	COUNTIES					REPRESENTATIVES				
Bedford	13,124	46	0.3	2,787	4.7	James Armstrong	3	Ad	----	----
Franklin	15,655	330	2.1	754	20.7	David Bard	4	A-Ad	Frankstown	Blair
Huntingdon	7,565	43	0.6	2,264	3.3	David Bard	5	R	Frankstown	Blair
TOTALS	36,344	419	1.1	5,805	6.2	Henry Woods	6	F	Bedford	Bedford
						Henry Woods	7	F	Bedford	Bedford

| | COUNTIES | | | | | REPRESENTATIVES | | | | |
| County | Aggregate | Slave | %S | sq.mi. | P/sq.mi. | Representative | Cong. | Pty. | Address | County |

DISTRICT 11

Fayette	13,325	282	2.1	802	16.6	William Findley	3	A-Ad	Youngstown	Westmoreland
West-						John Smilie	3	A-Ad	Fayette	Fayette
moreland	16,018	128	0.8	2,072	7.7	William Findley	4	A-Ad	Youngstown	Westmoreland
TOTALS	29,343	410	1.3	2,874	10.2	William Findley	5	R	Youngstown	Westmoreland
						John Smilie	6	R	Fayette	Fayette
						John Smilie	7	R	Fayette	Fayette

DISTRICT 12

Allegheny	10,300	159	1.5	5,902	1.7	Thomas Scott	3	A-Ad	Washington	Washington
Washington	23,866	263	1.1	1,435	16.6	Albert Gallatin	4	A-Ad	New Geneva	Fayette
TOTALS	34,166	422	1.2	7,337	4.6	Albert Gallatin	5	R	New Geneva	Fayette
						Albert Gallatin[r]	6	R	New Geneva	Fayette
						William Hoge	6	F	Washington	Washington
						(Replaced Gallatin)				
						William Hoge	7	F	Washington	Washington

	COUNTIES					REPRESENTATIVES				
County	Aggregate	Slave	%S	sq.mi.	P/sq.mi.	Representative	Cong.	Pty.	Address	County

AT LARGE

County	Aggregate	Slave	%S	sq.mi.	P/sq.mi.	Representative	Cong.	Pty.	Address	County
Bristol	3,211	98	3.0	25	128.4	Benjamin Bourn	3	Ad	Bristol	Bristol
Kent	8,848	63	0.7	173	51.1	Francis Malbone	3	Ad	Newport	Newport
Newport	14,300	366	2.5	115	124.3					
Providence	24,391	82	3.3	416	58.6	Benjamin Bourn[r]	4	Ad	Bristol	Bristol
Washington	18,075	339	1.8	321	56.3	(Retired in 1796)				
TOTALS	68,825	948	1.3	1,050	65.5	Elisha R. Potter	4	Ad	Kingston	Washington
						(Replaced Bourn)				
						Francis Malbone	4	Ad	Newport	Newport
						Christopher G. Champlin	5	F	Newport	Newport
						Elisha R. Potter[r]	5	F	Kingston	Washington
						(Retired in 1797)				
						Thomas Tillinghast	5	R	East Greenwich	Kent
						(Replaced Potter)				
						John Brown	6	F	Providence	Providence
						Christopher G. Champlin	6	F	Newport	Newport
						Joseph Stanton	7	R	Charlestown	Washington
						Thomas Tillinghast	7	R	East Greenwich	Kent

	COUNTIES					REPRESENTATIVES				
County	Aggregate	Slave	%S	sq.mi.	P/sq.mi.	Representative	Cong.	Pty.	Address	County

DISTRICT 1 (CHARLESTOWN)

County	Aggregate	Slave	%S	sq.mi.	P/sq.mi.	Representative	Cong.	Pty.	Address	County
Charlestown	66,990	50,633	75.5	3,246	20.6	Alexander Gillon[†]	3	A-Ad	Charleston	Charlestown
						(Died October 6, 1794)				
						William L. Smith	3	Ad	Charleston	Charlestown
						(Replaced Gillon)				
						William L. Smith	4	Ad	Charleston	Charlestown
						William L. Smith[r]	5	F	Charleston	Charlestown
						Thomas Pinckney	5	F	Charleston	Charlestown
						(Replaced Smith)				
						Thomas Pinckney	6	F	Charleston	Charlestown
						Thomas Lowndes	7	F	Charleston	Charlestown

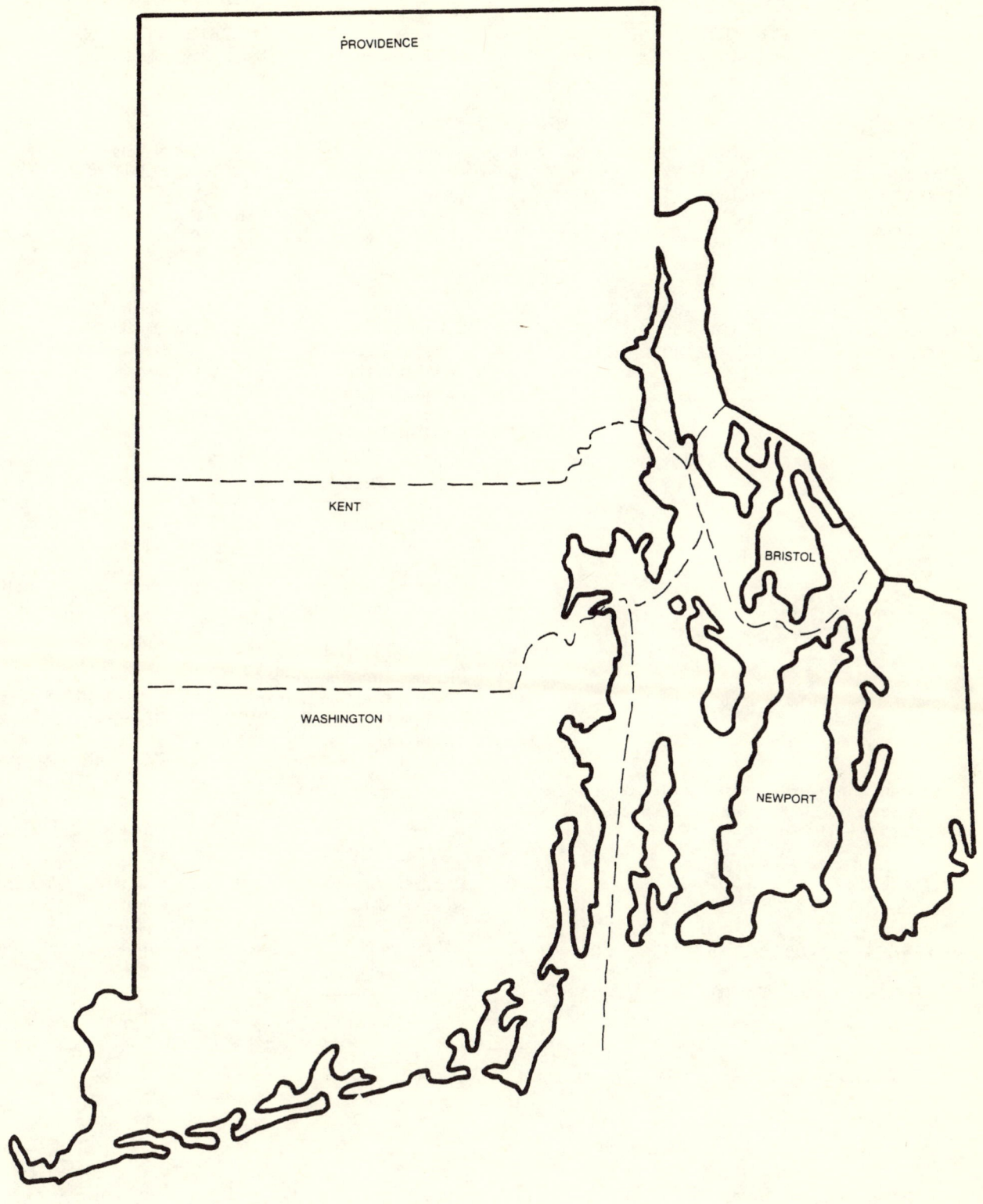

COUNTIES						REPRESENTATIVES				
County	Aggregate	Slave	%S	sq.mi.	P/sq.mi.	Representative	Cong.	Pty.	Address	County

DISTRICT 2 (BEAUFORT)

County	Aggregate	Slave	%S	sq.mi.	P/sq.mi.	Representative	Cong.	Pty.	Address	County
Beaufort	18,753	14,236	75.9	1,793	10.5	John Hunter	3	A-Ad	Newberry	Orangeburg
Orangeburg	18,513	5,931	32.0	4,345	4.3	Wade Hampton	4	A-Ad	Columbia	Orangeburg
TOTALS	37,266	20,167	54.1	6,138	6.1	John Rutledge, Jr.	5	F	----	Orangeburg
						John Rutledge, Jr.	6	F	----	Orangeburg
						John Rutledge, Jr.	7	F	----	Orangeburg

DISTRICT 3 (CHERAW)

County	Aggregate	Slave	%S	sq.mi.	P/sq.mi.	Representative	Cong.	Pty.	Address	County
Cheraw	10,706	3,229	30.1	2,122	5.4	Lemuel Benton	3	A-Ad	Darlington	Cheraw
Georgetown	22,122	13,131	59.3	4,715	4.7	Lemuel Benton	4	A-Ad	Darlington	Cheraw
TOTALS	32,828	16,360	49.8	6,837	4.8	Lemuel Benton	5	R	Darlington	Cheraw
						Benjamin Huger	6	F	Georgetown	Georgetown
						Benjamin Huger	7	F	Georgetown	Georgetown

DISTRICT 4 (CAMDEN)

County	Aggregate	Slave	%S	sq.mi.	P/sq.mi.	Representative	Cong.	Pty.	Address	County
Camden	38,265	8,865	23.4	5,675	6.7	Richard Winn	3	A-Ad	Winnesboro	Camden
						Richard Winn	4	A-Ad	Winnesboro	Camden
						Thomas Sumter	5	F	Statesburg	Camden
						Thomas Sumter	6	F	Statesburg	Camden
						Thomas Sumter[r]	7	F	Statesburg	Camden
						(Resigned December 15, 1801)				
						Richard Winn	7	R	Winnesboro	Camden
						(Replaced Sumter)				

DISTRICT 5 (NINETY-SIX)

County	Aggregate	Slave	%S	sq.mi.	P/sq.mi.	Representative	Cong.	Pty.	Address	County
						Robert Goodloe Harper	3	A-Ad	----	Ninety-Six
Ninety-Six[a]	38,701	7,074	18.3	3,924	9.9	Robert Goodloe Harper	4	Ad	----	Ninety-Six
						Robert Goodloe Harper	5	F	----	Ninety-Six
						Robert Goodloe Harper	6	F	----	Ninety-Six
						William Butler	7	R	Edgefield	Ninety-Six

[a]Population figures are estimated; returns are included with
those of Washington and Pinckney Counties in 1790 census.

DISTRICT 6 (WASHINGTON)

County	Aggregate	Slave	%S	sq.mi.	P/sq.mi.	Representative	Cong.	Pty.	Address	County
Pinckney						Andrew Pickens	3	A-Ad	Pendleton	Washington
Washington[a]	19,781	2,143	10.8	2,687	7.4	Samuel Earle	4	A-Ad	Pendleton	Washington
Pinckney	15,247	1,851	12.1	1,345	11.3	William Smith	5	R	Spartanburg	Washington
TOTALS	35,028	3,994	11.4	4,032	8.7	Abraham Nott	6	F	Union	Washington
						Thomas Moore	7	R	Spartanburg	Washington

[a]Total figures are estimated; there were no census returns for this district.

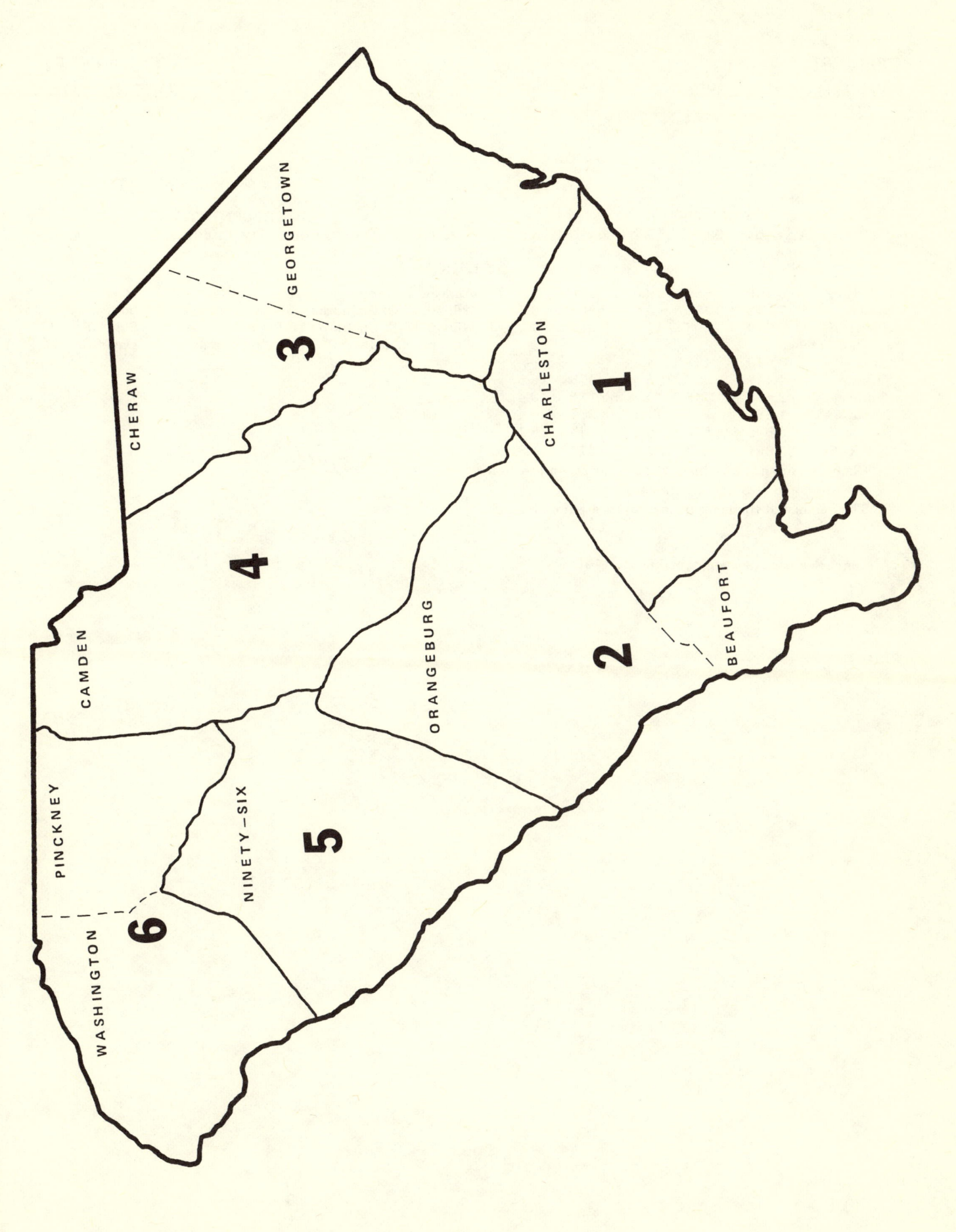

	COUNTIES						REPRESENTATIVES				
County	Aggregate	Slave	%S	sq.mi.	P/sq.mi.	Representative	Cong.	Pty.	Address	County	

						AT LARGE					
Davidson	3,459	659	19.0	4,196	0.8	Andrew Jackson	4	A-Ad	Nashville	Davidson
Greene	7,741	454	5.8	2,209	3.5	William C. C. Claiborne[a]	5	R	----	Sullivan
Hawkins	6,970	807	11.5	3,983	1.7	William C. C. Claiborne	6	R	----	Sullivan
South of French						William Dickson	7	R	Nashville	Davidson
Broad[b]	3,619	163	4.5	----	----					
Sullivan	4,447	297	6.6	413	10.8					
Sumner	2,196	348	15.8	5,116	0.4					
Tennessee	1,387	154	11.1	3,311	0.4					
Washington	5,872	535	9.1	1,149	5.1					
TOTALS	35,691	3,417	9.5	20,377[c]	1.8					

[a]Claiborne did not take his seat until the second session.

[b]Location and area undetermined.

[c]The balance of the lands in the state were Indian lands.

[1] Tennessee became a state on June 1, 1796.

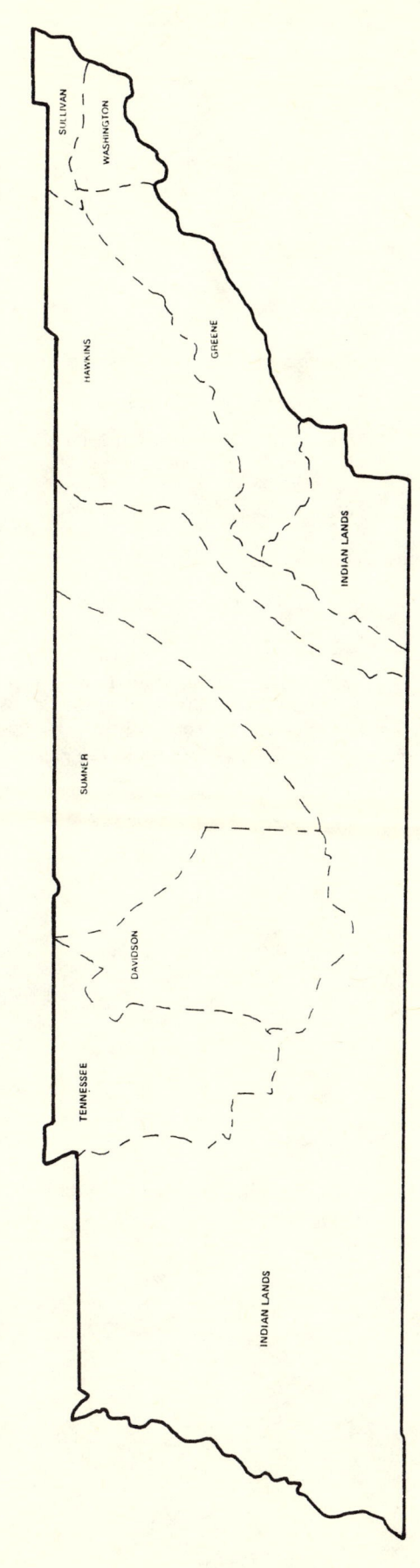

		COUNTIES						REPRESENTATIVES			
County	Aggregate	Slave	%S	sq.mi.	P/sq.mi.	Representative	Cong.	Pty.	Address	County

DISTRICT 1 (EASTERN)

County	Aggregate	Slave	%S	sq.mi.	P/sq.mi.	Representative	Cong.	Pty.	Address	County
Orange[a]	10,529	----	----	3,159	3.3	Nathaniel Niles	3	A-Ad	West Fairlee	Windsor
Windham	17,693	----	----	784	22.5	Daniel Buck	4	F	Norwich	Windsor
Windsor	15,748	----	----	962	16.3	Lewis R. Morris	5	F	Springfield	Windsor
TOTALS	43,970	----	----	4,905	9.0	Lewis R. Morris	6	F	Springfield	Windsor
						Lewis R. Morris	7	F	Springfield	Windsor

[a]That part of the state heretofore included in Orange and Caldeonia Counties.

DISTRICT 2 (WESTERN)

County	Aggregate	Slave	%S	sq.mi.	P/sq.mi.	Representative	Cong.	Pty.	Address	County
Addison	6,449	----	----	784	8.2	Israel Smith	3	A-Ad	Rutland	Rutland
Bennington	12,254	16	0.1	672	18.2	Israel Smith	4	A-Ad	Rutland	Rutland
Chittendon[a]	7,301	----	----	1,983	3.7	Matthew Lyon	5	R	Fair Haven	Rutland
Rutland	15,565	----	----	927	16.7	Matthew Lyon	6	R	Fair Haven	Rutland
TOTALS	41,569	16	0.03	4,366	9.5	Israel Smith	7	R	Rutland	Rutland

[a]That tract of land heretofore included in Chittenden and Franklin Counties.

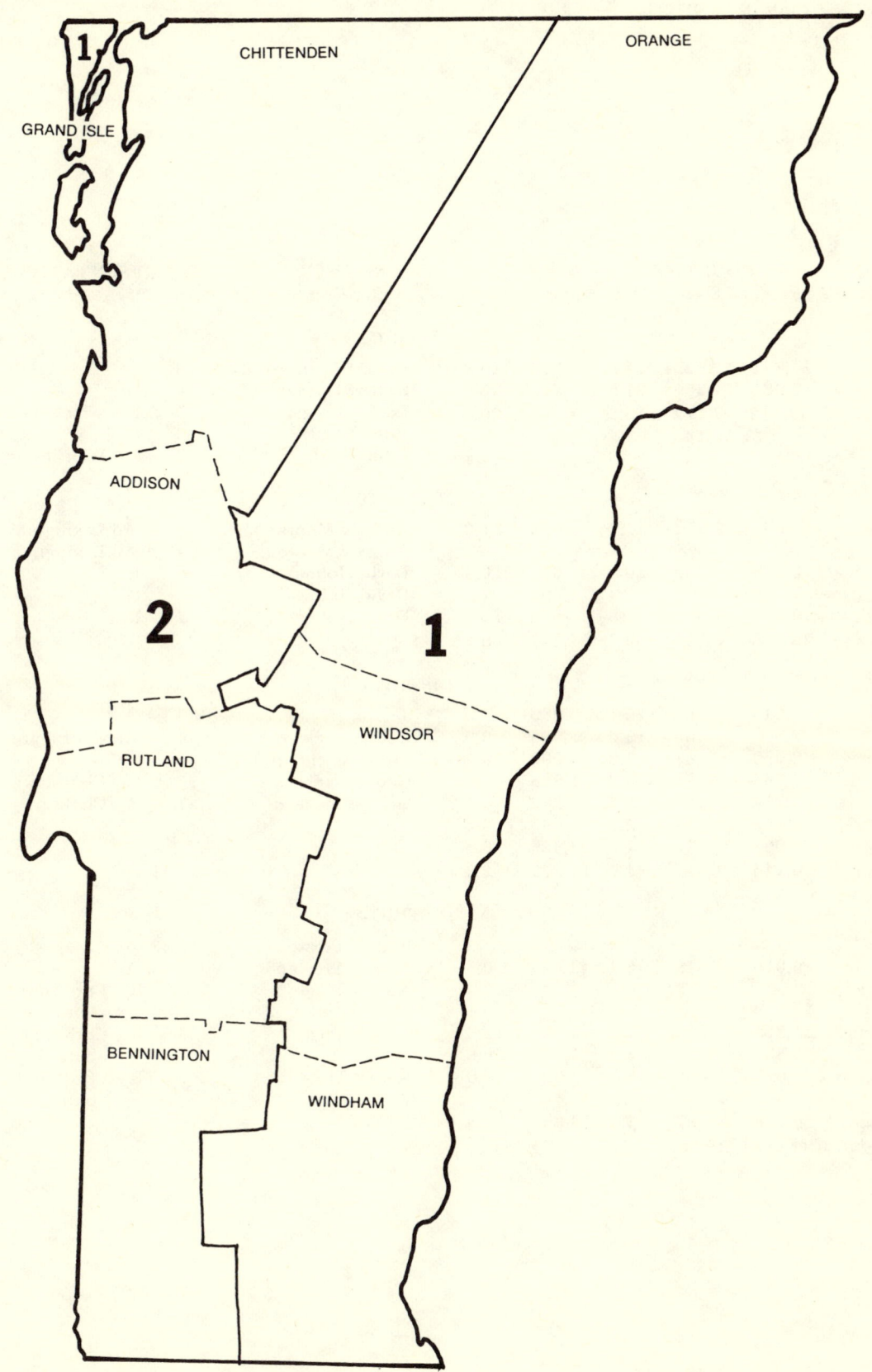

COUNTIES						REPRESENTATIVES				
County	Aggregate	Slave	%S	sq.mi.	P/sq.mi.	Representative	Cong.	Pty.	Address	County
DISTRICT 1										
Berkeley	19,731	2,922	14.8	760	25.9	Robert Rutherford	3	Ad	----	Frederick
Frederick	19,681	4,250	21.5	729	26.9	Robert Rutherford	4	Ad	----	Frederick
TOTALS	39,412	7,172	18.2	1,489	26.4	Daniel Morgan	5	F	Winchester	Frederick
						Robert Page	6	R	----	Frederick
						John Smith	7	R	Winchester	Frederick
DISTRICT 2										
Augusta	10,866	1,222	11.2	986	11.0	Andrew Moore	3	A-Ad	Lexington	Augusta
Bath[a]	----	----	----	956	----	Andrew Moore	4	A-Ad	Lexington	Augusta
Rockbridge	6,548	682	10.4	601	10.8	David Holmes	5	R	----	----
Rockingham	7,449	772	10.3	965	7.7	David Holmes	6	R	----	----
Shenandoah	10,510	512	48	823	12.7	David Holmes	7	R	----	----
TOTALS	35,373	3,188	9.0	4,331	8.2					

[a]Created after 1790 census.

COUNTIES						REPRESENTATIVES				
DISTRICT 3										
Hampshire	7,346	454	6.1	969	7.5	Joseph Neville	3	A-Ad	----	Hampshire
Hardy	7,336	369	5.0	1,063	6.9	George Jackson	4	A-Ad	Clarksburg	Harrison
Harrison	2,080	67	3.2	3,099	0.7	James Machir	5	F	----	----
Monongalia	4,768	154	3.2	1,348	3.1	George Jackson	6	R	Clarksburg	Harrison
Ohio	5,212	281	5.3	1,269	4.1	George Jackson	7	R	Clarksburg	Harrison
Pendleton	2,452	73	2.9	695	3.5					
Randolph	951	19	1.9	2,429	0.4					
TOTALS	30,145	1,417	4.7	10,872	2.8					

COUNTIES						REPRESENTATIVES				
DISTRICT 4										
Grayson[a]						Francis Preston	3	A-Ad	----	Montgomery
Greenbrier	6,015	319	5.3	12,425	0.5	Francis Preston	4	A-Ad	----	Montgomery
Kanawha[a]						Abram Trigg	5	R	Christiansburg	Montgomery
Lee[a]										
Montgomery	13,228	828	6.2	3,624	2.6	Abram Trigg	6	R	Christiansburg	Montgomery
Russell	3,338	190	5.6	4,024	0.6					
Washington	5,625	450	8.0	624	9.0	Abram Trigg	7	R	Christiansburg	Montgomery
Wyeth[a]										
TOTALS	28,206	1,787	6.3	20,697	1.4					

[a]Created after the 1790 census.

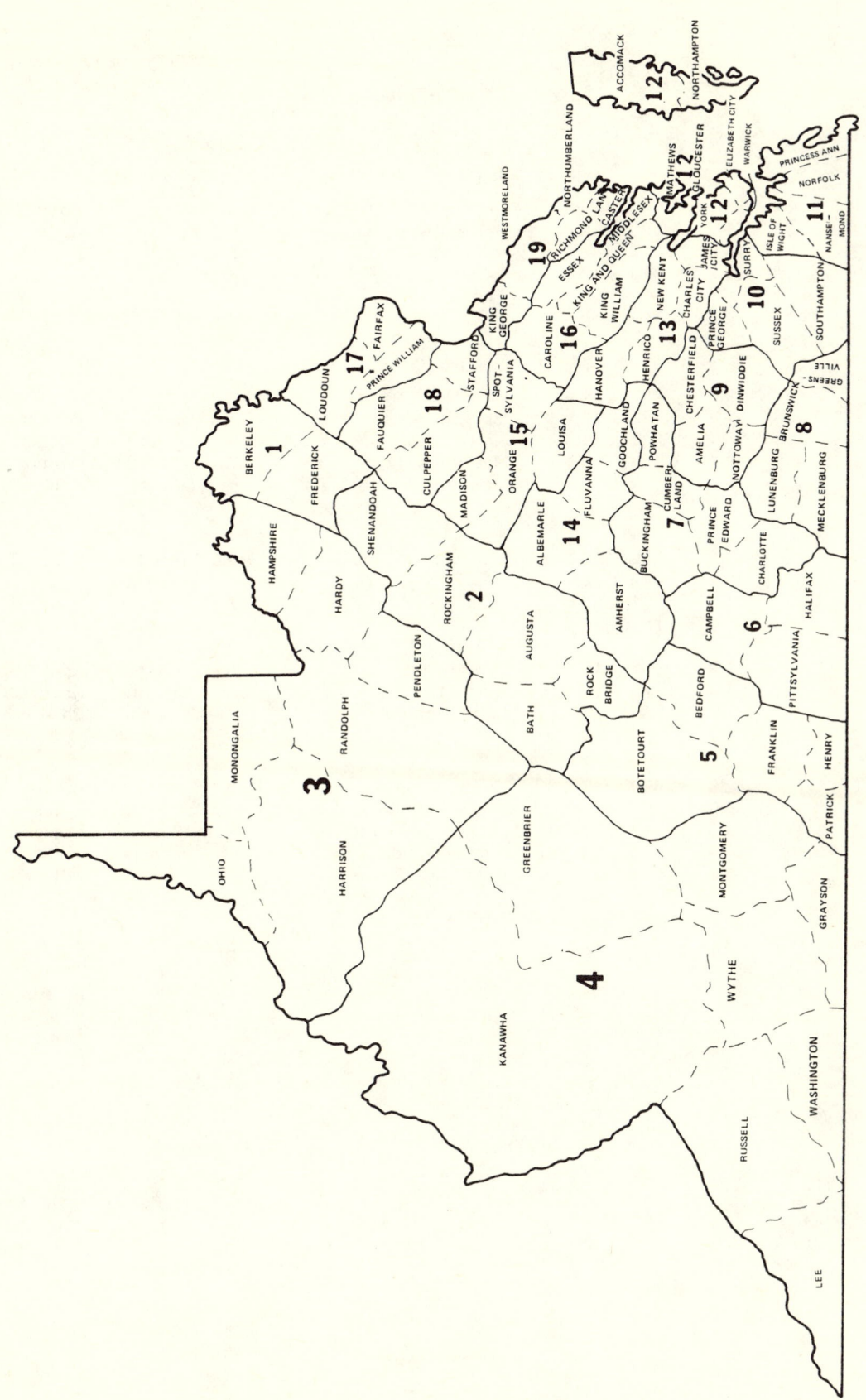

| COUNTIES | | | | | | REPRESENTATIVES | | | | |
County	Aggregate	Slave	%S	sq.mi.	P/sq.mi.	Representative	Cong.	Pty.	Address	County

DISTRICT 5

County	Aggregate	Slave	%S	sq.mi.	P/sq.mi.	Representative	Cong.	Pty.	Address	County
Bedford	10,531	2,754	26.1	727	14.4	George Hancock	3	Ad	----	Botetourt
Botetourt	10,524	1,259	11.9	1,590	6.6	George Hancock	4	Ad	----	Botetourt
Franklin	6,842	1,073	15.6	716	9.5	John Trigg	5	R	----	Bedford
Henry	8,479	1,551	18.2	845	10.0	John Trigg	6	R	----	Bedford
Patrick[a]	----	----	----	----	----	John Trigg	7	R	----	Bedford
TOTALS	36,376	6,637	18.2	3,878	9.5					

DISTRICT 6

County	Aggregate	Slave	%S	sq.mi.	P/sq.mi.	Representative	Cong.	Pty.	Address	County
Campbell	7,685	2,488	32.3	669	11.4	Isaac Coles	3	A-Ad	Chatham	Pittsylvania
Halifax	14,722	5,565	37.8	796	18.4	Isaac Coles	4	A-Ad	Chatham	Pittsylvania
Pittsylvania	11,579	2,979	25.7	1,001	11.5	Matthew Clay	5	R	Halifax	Halifax
TOTALS	33,986	11,032	32.4	2,466	13.7	Matthew Clay	6	R	Halifax	Halifax
						Matthew Clay	7	R	Halifax	Halifax

[a]Created after 1790 census.

DISTRICT 7

County	Aggregate	Slave	%S	sq.mi.	P/sq.mi.	Representative	Cong.	Pty.	Address	County
Buckingham	9,779	4,168	42.6	737	13.2	Abraham B. Venable	3	A-Ad	Prince Edward Court House	Prince Edward
Charlotte	10,078	4,816	47.7	470	21.4					
Cumberland	8,153	4,434	54.3	291	28.0	Abraham B. Venable	4	A-Ad	Prince Edward Court House	Prince Edward
Powhatan	6,822	4,325	63.3	261	26.1					
Prince Edward	8,100	3,986	49.2	407	19.9	Abraham B. Venable	5	R	Prince Edward Court House	Prince Edward
TOTALS	42,932	21,729	50.6	2,166	19.8	John Randolph	6	R	Charlotte	Charlotte
						John Randolph	7	R	Charlotte	Charlotte

DISTRICT 8

County	Aggregate	Slave	%S	sq.mi.	P/sq.mi.	Representative	Cong.	Pty.	Address	County
Brunswick	12,827	6,776	52.8	579	22.2	Thomas Claiborne	3	A-Ad	----	Brunswick
Greensville	6,362	3,620	56.9	299	21.3	Thomas Claiborne	4	A-Ad	----	Brunswick
Lunenburg	8,959	4,332	48.3	442	20.3	Thomas Claiborne	5	R	----	Brunswick
Mecklenburg	14,733	6,762	45.9	612	24.0	Samuel Goode	6	F	Invermay	Mecklenburg
TOTALS	42,881	21,490	50.1	1,932	22.2	Thomas Claiborne	7	R	----	Brunswick

DISTRICT 9

County	Aggregate	Slave	%S	sq.mi.	P/sq.mi.	Representative	Cong.	Pty.	Address	County
Amelia	18,097	11,307	62.4	624	26.7	William B. Giles	3	A-Ad	Amelia	Amelia
Chesterfield	14,214	7,487	52.6	442	32.2	William B. Giles	4	A-Ad	Amelia	Amelia
Dinwiddie	13,934	7,334	52.6	507	27.5	William B. Giles[r]	5	R	Amelia	Amelia
Nottoway[a]	----	----	----	----	----	(Resigned October, 1798)				
TOTALS	46,245	26,128	56.4	1,573	28.5	Joseph Eggleston	5	R	Amelia	Amelia
						(Replaced Giles December, 1798)				
						Joseph Eggleston	6	R	Amelia	Amelia
						William B. Giles	7	R	Amelia	Amelia

[a]Included in Amelia county statistics.

DISTRICT 10

County	Aggregate	Slave	%S	sq.mi.	P/sq.mi.	Representative	Cong.	Pty.	Address	County
Prince George	8,173	4,519	55.2	276	29.6	Carter B. Harrison	3	A-Ad	----	Prince George
Southampton	12,864	559	4.3	602	21.4	Carter B. Harrison	4	A-Ad	----	Prince George
Surrey	6,227	368	5.9	277	22.5	Carter B. Harrison	5	R	----	Prince George
Sussex	10,554	5,387	51.0	494	21.4	Edwin Gray	6	F	----	Southampton
TOTALS	37,818	10,833	28.6	1,649	22.9	Edwin Gray	7	F	----	Southampton

COUNTIES						REPRESENTATIVES				
County	Aggregate	Slave	%S	sq.mi.	P/sq.mi.	Representative	Cong.	Pty.	Address	County

DISTRICT 11

COUNTIES						REPRESENTATIVES				
Isle of Wight	9,028	1,551	17.1	317	28.5	Josiah Parker	3	Ad	Macclesfield	Isle of Wight
Nansemond	9,010	3,817	42.3	408	22.0	Josiah Parker	4	Ad	Macclesfield	Isle of Wight
Norfolk	14,524	5,345	36.8	394	36.4	Josiah Parker	5	F	Macclesfield	Isle of Wight
Princess Anne	7,793	3,202	41.0	259	30.0	Josiah Parker	6	F	Macclesfield	Isle of Wight
TOTALS	40,355	13,915	34.4	1,378	29.3	Thomas Newton, Jr.	7	R	Norfolk	Norfolk

DISTRICT 12

COUNTIES						REPRESENTATIVES				
Accomack	13,959	4,262	30.5	476	29.3	John Page	3	Ad	"Rosewell"	Gloucester
Elizabeth						John Page	4	Ad	"Rosewell"	Gloucester
City	3,450	1,876	54.3	69	50.0	Thomas Evans	5	F	----	Accomack
Gloucester	13,498	7,063	52.3	228	59.2	Thomas Evans	6	F	----	Accomack
Mathews[a]	----	----	----	89	----	John Stratton	7	F	Eastville	Northampton
Northampton	6,889	3,244	47.0	220	31.3					
Warwick	1,690	996	58.9	75	22.5					
York	5,233	2,760	52.7	129	40.6					
TOTALS	44,719	20,201	45.1	1,286	34.8					

[a]Created after 1790 census.

DISTRICT 13

COUNTIES						REPRESENTATIVES				
Charles City	5,588	3,141	56.2	181	30.9	Samuel Griffin	3	A-Ad	----	James City
Hanover	14,754	8,223	55.7	465	31.7	John Clopton	4	A-Ad	Tunstall	New Kent
Henrico	12,000	5,819	48.4	229	52.4	John Clopton	5	R	Tunstall	New Kent
James City	4,070	2,405	59.0	152	26.8	John Marshall[r]	6	F	Richmond	Henrico
New Kent	6,239	3,700	59.3	210	29.7	(Resigned June, 1800)				
TOTALS	42,651	23,288	54.6	1,237	34.5	Littleton W. Tazewell	6	R	Williamsburg	James City
						(Replaced Marshall)				
						John Clopton	7	R	Tunstall	New Kent

DISTRICT 14

COUNTIES						REPRESENTATIVES				
Albemarle	12,585	5,579	44.3	740	17.0	Francis Walker	3	A-Ad	Cobham	Albemarle
Amherst	13,703	5,296	38.6	941	14.6	Samuel J. Cabell	4	A-Ad	New Market	Albemarle
Fluvanna	3,921	1,466	37.3	288	13.6	Samuel J. Cabell	5	R	New Market	Albemarle
Goochland	9,053	4,656	51.4	289	31.3	Samuel J. Cabell	6	R	New Market	Albemarle
TOTALS	39,262	16,997	43.2	2,258	17.4	Samuel J. Cabell	7	R	New Market	Albemarle

DISTRICT 15

COUNTIES						REPRESENTATIVES				
Louisa	8,467	4,573	54.0	517	16.4	James Madison	3	A-Ad	"Mont-	Orange
Madison[a]	6,963	2,751	37.2	327	21.3				pelier"	
Orange	9,921	4,421	44.5	508	19.5	James Madison	4	A-Ad	"Mont-	Orange
Spott-									pelier"	
sylvania	11,252	5,933	52.7	409	27.5	John Dawson	5	R	----	----
TOTALS	36,603	17,678	48.2	1,761	20.8	John Dawson	6	R	----	----
						John Dawson	7	R	----	----

[a]Became a part of the 15th District with its creation in 1793.

DISTRICT 16

COUNTIES						REPRESENTATIVES				
Caroline	10,292	1,148	11.1	545	18.9	Anthony New	3	A-Ad	----	----
Essex	9,122	5,440	59.6	250	36.4	Anthony New	4	A-Ad	----	----
King						Anthony New	5	R	----	----
and Queen	9,377	5,143	54.8	318	29.5	Anthony New	6	R	----	----
King William	8,128	5,151	63.3	278	29.2	Anthony New	7	R	----	----
Middlesex	4,140	2,558	61.7	130	31.8					
TOTALS	41,059	19,440	47.3	1,521	26.9					

COUNTIES						REPRESENTATIVES				
County	Aggregate	Slave	%S	sq.mi.	P/sq.mi.	Representative	Cong.	Pty	Address	County

DISTRICT 17

County	Aggregate	Slave	%S	sq.mi.	P/sq.mi.	Representative	Cong.	Pty	Address	County
Fairfax	12,320	4,574	37.1	425	28.9	Richard Bland Lee	3	Ad	Leesylvania	Prince William
Loudoun	18,962	4,030	21.2	517	36.7	Richard Brent	4	A-Ad	----	Prince William
Prince						Richard Brent	5	R	----	Prince William
William	11,615	4,704	40.4	347	33.5	Levin Powell	6	F	----	----
TOTALS	42,897	13,308	31.0	1,289	33.3	Richard Brent	7	R	----	Prince William

DISTRICT 18

County	Aggregate	Slave	%S	sq.mi.	P/sq.mi.	Representative	Cong.	Pty	Address	County
Culpepper	15,142	5,750	37.2	656	23.0	John Nicholas	3	A-Ad	----	----
Fauquier	17,892	6,642	37.1	660	27.1	John Nicholas	4	A-Ad	----	----
Stafford	9,588	4,036	42.0	270	35.5	John Nicholas	5	R	----	----
TOTALS	42,622	16,428	38.5	1,586	26.9	John Nicholas	6	R	----	----
						Philip R. Thompson	7	R	----	----

DISTRICT 19

County	Aggregate	Slave	%S	sq.mi.	P/sq.mi.	Representative	Cong.	Pty	Address	County
King George	7,366	4,157	56.4	176	41.8	John Heath	3	A-Ad	Heathsville	Northumberland
Lancaster	5,638	3,236	57.3	137	41.1					
Northumberland	9,163	4,460	48.6	190	48.2	John Health	4	A-Ad	Heathsville	Northumberland
Richmond	6,985	3,984	57.0	190	36.4	Walter Jones	5	R	----	Northumberland
Westmoreland	7,722	4,425	57.3	229	33.7	Henry Lee	6	F	----	----
TOTALS	36,874	20,262	54.9	922	39.9	John Taliaferro	7	R	Fredericksburg	King George

3

Off–Year Districting

1794, 1798

COUNTIES						REPRESENTATIVES				
County	Aggregate	Slave	%S	sq.mi.	P/sq.mi.	Representative	Cong.	Pty.	Address	County

FIRST WESTERN DISTRICT

Berkshire	33,885	----	----	941	36.0	Theodore Sedgewick[r]	4	Ad	Sheffield	Berkshire
Towns in Hampshire County:						Thomson J. Skinner	4	R	----	Berkshire
Rowe, Cummington, Plainfield, Worthington, Hawley,						(Replaced Sedgewick)				
Charlemont						Thomson J. Skinner	5	R	----	Berkshire
Total, towns	5,229	----	----	150	34.9	Theodore Sedgewick	6	F	Sheffield	Berkshire
TOTALS	39,114	----	----	1,091	35.9	John Bacon	7	R	Stockbridge	Berkshire

SECOND WESTERN DISTRICT

Towns in Hampshire County:						William Lyman	4	A-Ad	North-ampton	Hampshire
Westfield, Russell, Hatfield, Deerfield, Northampton,										
Blandford, Southampton, Greenfield, Gill, Granville,						William Shepard	5	F	Westfield	Hampshire
Chesterfield, Conway, Ashfield, Southwick, Williams-						William Shepard	6	F	Westfield	Hampshire
burgh Whately, Norwich, West Springfield, West						William Shepard	7	F	Westfield	Hampshire
Hampton, Montgomery, Colerain, Barnardston,										
Shelburne, Goshen, Leyden, Northfield, Montague,										
Sunderland, Hadley, Chester, Buckland, Health,										
Middlefield, East Hampton.										
Total, towns	42,664	----	----	800	53.3					

THIRD WESTERN DISTRICT

Towns in Hampshire County:						Samuel Lyman	4	F	Springfield	Hampshire
Brimfield, Pelham, Palmer, New Salem, Greenfield,						Samuel Lyman	5	F	Springfield	Hampshire
Amherst, Monson, Belchertown, Shutesbury, Ware,						Samuel Lyman[r]	6	F	Springfield	Hampshire
Springfield, South Brimfield, Holland, Warwick,						Ebeneazer Mattoon	6	F	North Amherst	Hampshire
Orange, Wilbraham, Granby, Leverett, Wendell,						(Replaced Lyman)				
Longmeadow, South Hadley, Ludlow.						Ebeneazer Mattoon	7	F	North Amherst	Hampshire
Total, towns	25,549	----	----	906	28.2					
Towns in Worcester County:										
Western, Petersham, New Braintree, Barre, Sturbridge,										
Athol, Templeton, Toyalston, Gerry, Winchendon,										
Gardner, Hardwick.										
Total, towns	13,780	----	----	650	21.2					
TOTALS	39,329	----	----	1,556	25.3					

FOURTH WESTERN DISTRICT

Towns in Worcester County:						Dwight Foster	4	F	Brookfield	Worcester
Mendon, Brookfield, Oxford, Worcester, Leicester,						Dwight Foster	5	F	Brookfield	Worcester
Rutland, Sutton, Uxbridge, Shrewsbury, Dudley,						Dwight Foster[r]	6	F	Brookfield	Worcester
Grafton, Upton, Holden, Leominster, Lancaster,						Levi Lincoln[r]	7	R	Worcester	Worcester
Douglass, Spencer, Charlton, Oakham, Paxton, Hub-						Seth Hastings	7	F	Mendon	Worcester
bardton, Westminster, Princeton, Northbridge, Ward,						(Replaced Lincoln)				
Milford, Sterling, Boylston.										
Total, towns	38,091	----	----	650	73.0					

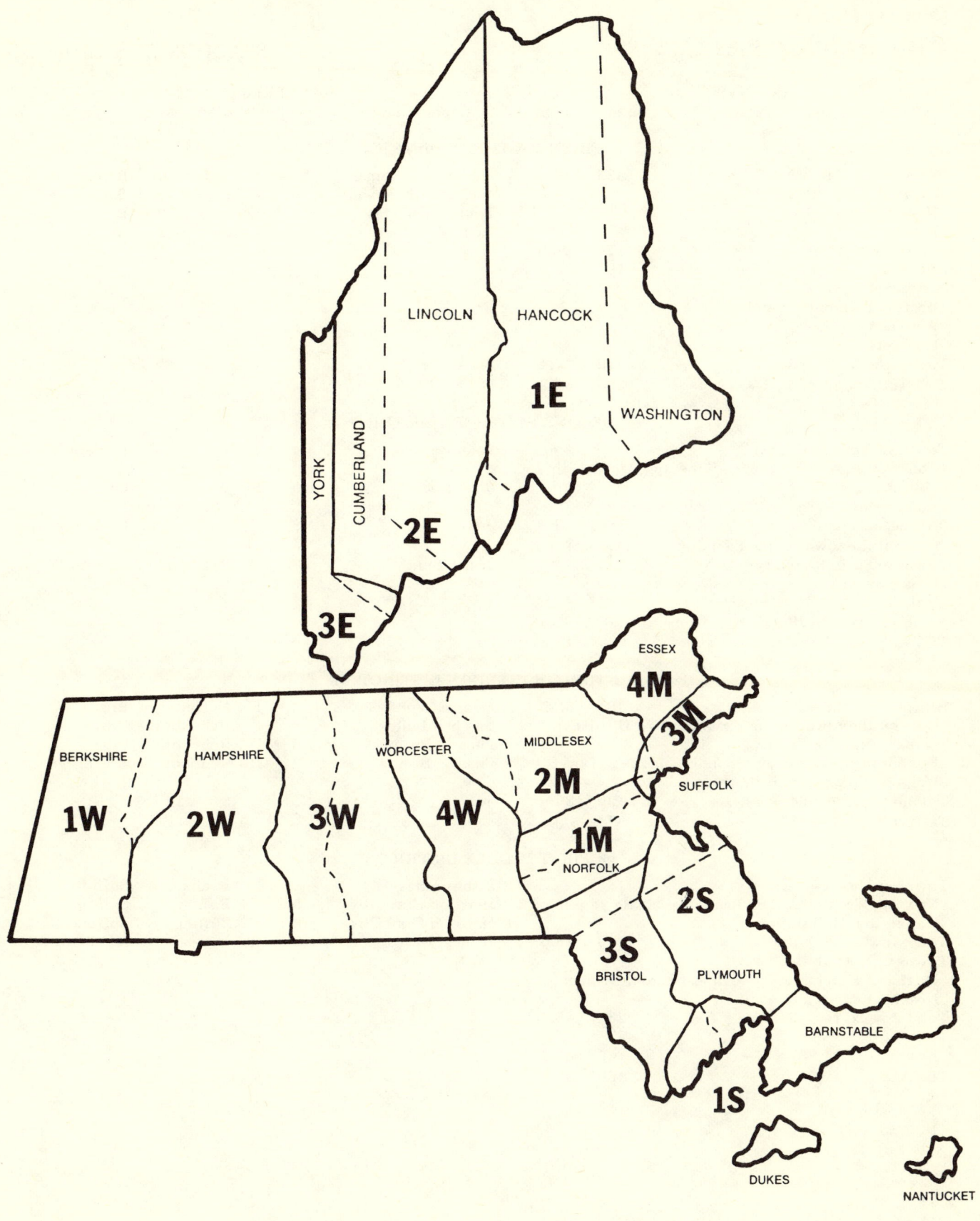

LINCOLN

HANCOCK

1E

WASHINGTON

YORK

CUMBERLAND

2E

3E

ESSEX

4M

3M

SUFFOLK

BERKSHIRE

HAMPSHIRE

WORCESTER

MIDDLESEX

2M

1M

1W

2W

3W

4W

NORFOLK

2S

3S

BRISTOL

PLYMOUTH

BARNSTABLE

1S

DUKES

NANTUCKET

COUNTIES						REPRESENTATIVES				
County	Aggregate	Slave	%S	sq.mi.	P/sq.mi.	Representative	Cong.	Pty.	Address	County

FIRST SOUTHERN DISTRICT

Barnstable	19,293	----	----	393	49.1	Nathaniel Freeman	4	F	Sandwich	Barnstable
Towns in Bristol County:						Nathaniel Freeman	5	F	Sandwich	Barnstable
New Bedford						Lemuel Williams	6	F	New Bedford	Bristol
Dartmouth						Lemuel Williams	7	F	New Bedford	Bristol
Total, towns	7,021	----	----	70	100.3					
Dukes	3,118	----	----	104	30.0					
Nantucket	5,617	----	----	46	122.1					
Towns in Plymouth County:										
Wareham										
Rochester										
Total, towns	3,316	----	----	70	47.4					
TOTALS	38,365	----	----	683	56.2					

SECOND SOUTHERN DISTRICT

Towns in Norfolk County						John Reed	4	F	West Bridgewater	Plymouth
Cohasset, Braintree, Quincy, Randolph, Weymouth,										
Milton.						John Reed	5	F	West Bridgewater	Plymouth
Total, towns	7,182	----	----	90	79.8					
Plymouth	26,757	----	----	584	45.8	John Reed	6	F	West Bridgewater	Plymouth
(Except the towns in the First Southern District)										
Towns in Suffolk County:						Josiah Smith	7	R	Pembroke	Plymouth
Hingham										
Hull										
Total, towns	2,229	----	----	70	31.8					
TOTALS	36,168	----	----	744	48.6					

THIRD SOUTHERN DISTRICT

Bristol	26,859	----	----	484	55.5	George Leonard	4	F	Norton	Bristol
(Except the towns in the First Southern District)						Stephen Bullock	5	F	Rehoboth	Bristol
Towns in Norfolk County:						Phanvel Bishop	6	R	Rehoboth	Bristol
Foxborough, Wrentham, Franklin, Medfield, Dover,						Phanvel Bishop	7	R	Rehoboth	Bristol
Walpole, Stoughton, Bellingham.										
Total, towns	8,094	----	----	90	89.9					
TOTALS	34,953	----	----	574	60.9					

FIRST MIDDLE DISTRICT

Towns in Middlesex County:						Fisher Ames	4	F	Dedham	Suffolk
Newton, Weston, East Sudbury, Natick, Sherburne,						Harrison Gray Otis	5	F	Boston	Suffolk
Hopkinton, Holliston.						Harrison Gray Otis	6	F	Boston	Suffolk
Total, towns	6,978	----	----	200	35.0	William Eustis	7	R	----	Middlesex
Towns in Norfolk County:										
Roxbury, Dorchester, Brookline, Sharon, Dedham,										
Needham, Medway.										
Total, towns	10,830	----	----	234	46.3					
Town of										
Boston	24,937	----	----	46	542.1					
TOTALS	42,745	----	----	480	89.0					

| COUNTIES | | | | | | REPRESENTATIVES | | | |
County	Aggregate	Slave	%S	sq.mi.	P/sq.mi.	Representative	Cong.	Pty.	Address	County

SECOND MIDDLE DISTRICT

Towns in Middlesex County:
 Charlestown, Cambridge, Watertown, Concord, Sudbury, Groton, Marlboro', Framingham, Dunstable, Stow, Lexington, Littleton, Westford, Townsend, Acton, Dracut, Chelmsford, Waltham, Shirley, Pepperel, Lincoln, Ashby, Carlisle, Boxboro', Tinsboro'.

						Joseph B. Varnum	4	R	Dracut	Middlesex
						Joseph B. Varnum	5	R	Dracut	Middlesex
						Joseph B. Varnum	6	R	Dracut	Middlesex
						Joseph B. Varnum	7	R	Dracut	Middlesex

Total, towns 30,479 ---- ---- 625 48.8
Towns in Worcester County:
 Ashburnham, Fitchburgh, Lunenburgh, Harvard, Westboro', Bolton, Berlin, Northboro', Southboro'.
Total, towns 9,321 ---- ---- 209 44.6
TOTALS 39,800 ---- ---- 834 47.8

THIRD MIDDLE DISTRICT

Towns in Essex County:
 Salem, Marblehead, Lynn, Lynnfield, Danvers, Middleton, Beverly, Manchester.

						Benjamin Goodhue[r]	4	F	Salem	Essex
						Samuel Sewall	4	F	Marblehead	Essex
						(Replaced Goodhue December, 1796)				

Total, towns 26,117 ---- ---- 100 261.2
Towns in Middlesex County:
 Reading, Stoneham, Medford, Malden, Tewksbury, Wilmington, Woburn, Bedford, Billerica.

						Samuel Sewall	5	F	Marblehead	Essex
						Samuel Sewall[r]	6	F	Marblehead	Essex
						Nathan Read	6	F	Salem	Essex
						(Replaced Sewall November, 1800)				

Total, towns 9,471 ---- ---- 40 236.8
Towns in Suffolk County:

| | | | | | | Nathan Read | 7 | F | Salem | Essex |

Chelsea 849 ---- ---- 10 84.9
TOTALS 36,437 ---- ---- 150 242.9

FOURTH MIDDLE DISTRICT

Towns in Essex County:
 Salisbury, Almesbury, Methuen, Haverhill, Andover, Bradford, Boxford, Newbury, Newbury Port, Rowley, Ipswich, Hamilton, Wenham, Gloucester, Topsfield.

| | | | | | | Theophilis Bradbury | 4 | F | Newbury Port | Essex |
| | | | | | | Theophilis Bradbury | 5 | F | Newbury Port | Essex |

Total, towns 35,079 ---- ---- 394 89.0

| | | | | | | Bailey Bartlett | 6 | F | Haverhill | Essex |
| | | | | | | Manasseh Cutler | 7 | F | Hamilton | Essex |

FIRST EASTERN DISTRICT

| Hancock | 9,549 | ---- | ---- | 12,030 | 0.8 | Henry Dearborn | 4 | R | Monmouth | Lincoln |
| Lincoln | 18,250e | ---- | ---- | 16,034 | 1.9 | Isaac Parker | 5 | F | ---- | ---- |

 (Except towns and plantations in Lincoln County that are part of the Second Eastern District)

| | | | | | | Silas Lee | 6 | F | Wiscasset | Lincoln |
| | | | | | | Silas Lee | 7 | F | Wiscasset | Lincoln |

| Washington | 2,758 | ---- | ---- | 3,504 | 0.8 | | | | | |
| TOTALS | 30,557 | ---- | ---- | 31,568 | 0.9 | | | | | |

SECOND EASTERN DISTRICT

Cumberland	25,450	----	----	3,269	6.9	Peleg Wadsworth	4	F	Port Land	Cumberland
						Peleg Wadsworth	5	F	Port Land	Cumberland
						Peleg Wadsworth	6	F	Port Land	Cumberland
						Peleg Wadsworth	7	F	Port Land	Cumberland

 (Except the towns of Bridgeton, Standish and Flintstown)
Towns in Lincoln County:
 Topsham, Winthrop, Readfield, Bath, Bowdoin, Green, Monmouth, Mount Vernon, Sandwich, Livermore, Recomecko, mouth of Sandy River, Sandy River No. 1, Sandy River No. 2.
Total, towns 11,712 ---- ---- 8,698 1.4
TOTALS 37,162 ---- ---- 11,965 3.1   79

COUNTIES / REPRESENTATIVES

County	Aggregate	Slave	%S	sq.mi.	P/sq.mi.	Representative	Cong.	Pty.	Address	County
						THIRD EASTERN DISTRICT				
Towns in Cumberland County:						Samuel Thatcher	4	F	Warren	Lincoln
Bridgetown, Standish, Flintstown.						Samuel Thatcher	5	F	Warren	Lincoln
Total, towns	2,242	----	----	400	5.6	Samuel Thatcher	6	F	Warren	Lincoln
York	37,729	----	----	3,937	9.6	Richard Cutts	7	R	Pepperell	York
TOTALS	39,971	----	----	4,036	9.9					

COUNTIES / REPRESENTATIVES

County	Aggregate	Slave	%S	sq.mi.	P/sq.mi.	Representative	Cong.	Pty	Address	County
						DISTRICT 1				
Kings	27,428	1,259	4.5	70	391.8	Jonathan Havens[†]	6	R	Shelter	Suffolk
Queens	16,893	1,528	9.0	108	156.4	(Died October 24, 1799)			Island	
Richmond	4,563	675	14.7	58	7817.0	John Smith	6	R	Mastic	Suffolk
Suffolk	19,464	886	4.5	1,218	16.0	(Replaced Havens)				
TOTALS	68,348	4,348	6.3	1,454	47.0	John Smith	7	R	Mastic	Suffolk
						DISTRICT 2				
City of						Edward Livingston	6	R	City of New York	
New York	45,048	2,133	5.2	20	2252.0	Samuel L. Mitchell	7	R	City of New York	
(Except Ward No. 7)										
						DISTRICT 3				
City of						Philip Van Cortlandt	6	R	Croton	Westchester
New York,						Philip Van Cortlandt	7	R	Croton	Westchester
Ward No. 7	15,394	133[a]	0.9	3	5131.3					
Towns in Orange County:										
Clarkes Town										
Haverstraw										
Hempstead										
Orange Town										
Total, towns	6,353	551	8.6	176	36.0					
Westchester	27,428	1,259	4.5	443	61.9					
TOTALS	49,175	1,943	3.9	622	79.1					

[a]There are no ward statistics for slave population in New York City. This figure represents one-tenth of the slave population of the city.

County	Aggregate	Slave	%S	sq.mi.	P/sq.mi.	Representative	Cong.	Pty	Address	County
						DISTRICT 4				
Delaware	10,228	16	0.1	1,443	14.9	Lucas C. Elmendorf	6	R	Kingston	Ulster
Orange						Lucas C. Elmendorf	7	R	Kingston	Ulster
(remainder)	29,355	1,145	11.6	833	35.2					
Ulster	24,855	2,257	9.0	2,121	11.7					
TOTALS	64,438	3,418	5.3	4,397	14.6					

80

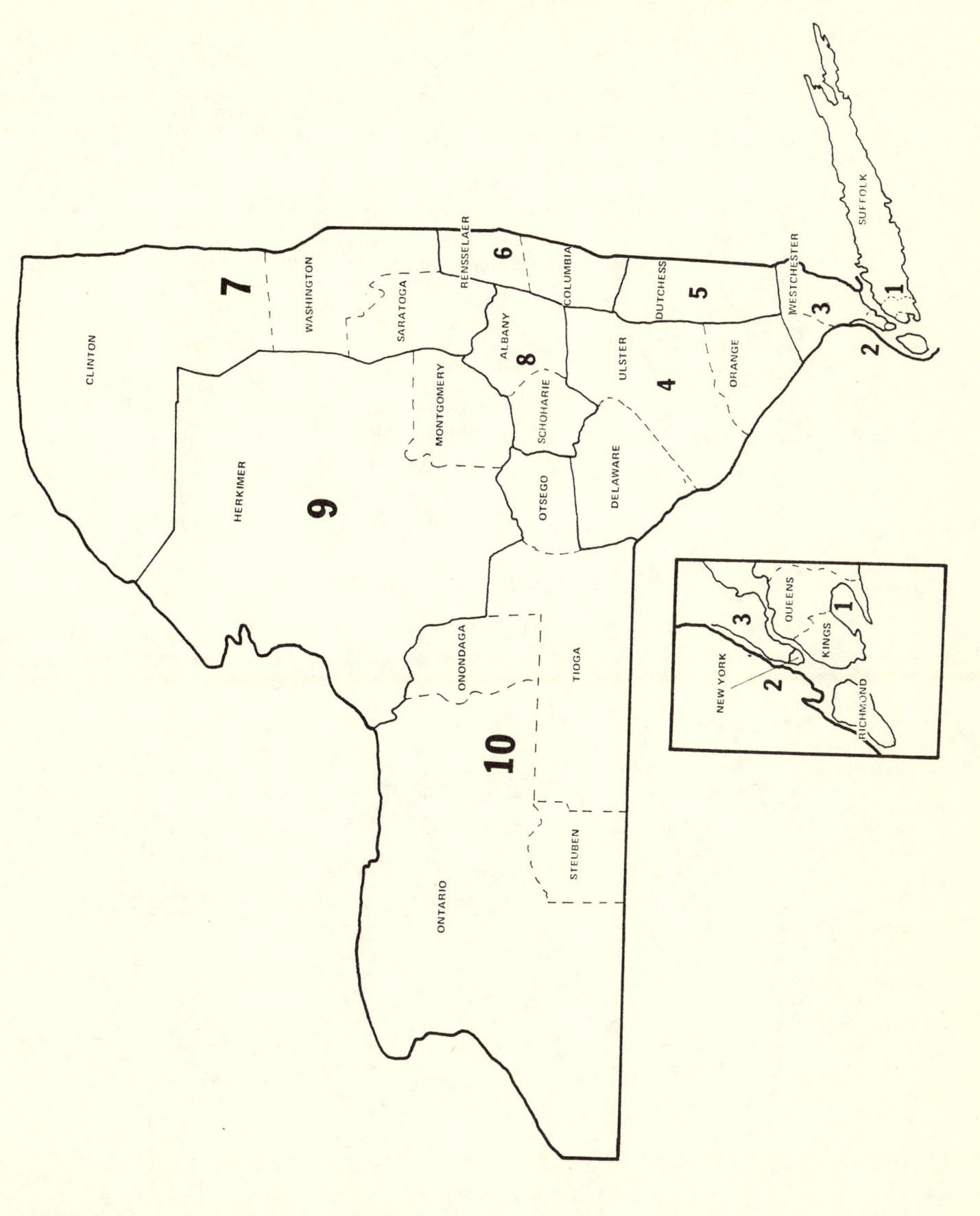

County	COUNTIES Aggregate	Slave	%S	sq.mi.	P/sq.mi.	Representative	REPRESENTATIVES Cong.	Pty	Address	County
						DISTRICT 5				
Dutchess	47,775	1,609	3.3	1,044	45.7	Theodorus Bailey	6	R	Pough-keepsie	Dutchess
						Thomas Tillotson[r]	7	R	Red Hook	Dutchess
						Theodorus Bailey (Replaced Tillotson)	7	R	Pough-keepsie	Dutchess
						DISTRICT 6				
Columbia	35,322	1,471	4.1	645	54.7	John Bird	6	F	Troy	Rensselaer
Rensselaer	30,442	890	2.9	665	45.7	John Bird[r]	7	F	Troy	Rensselaer
TOTALS	65,764	2,361	3.5	1,310	50.2	(Resigned July 25, 1801)				
						John P. Van Ness (Replaced Bird)	7	R	----	----
						DISTRICT 7				
Clinton	8,514	416	1.2	4,556	11.8	John Thompson	6	R	Stillwater	Saratoga
Saratoga	24,483	358	1.4	818	29.9	David Thomas	7	R	Salem	Washington
Washington	35,574	80	0.2	1,723	20.6					
TOTALS	68,571	854	1.2	7,097	9.6					
						DISTRICT 8				
Albany City of Albany[a]	34,043	1,808	5.3	1,386	24.6	Henry Glen	6	F	Schenectady	Albany
						Killian Van Rensselaer	7	F	Albany	Albany
Schoharie	9,808	354	3.6	624	15.7					
TOTALS	43,851	2,162	4.9	2,010	21.8					

[a]Included in Albany County statistics.

County	COUNTIES Aggregate	Slave	%S	sq.mi.	P/sq.mi.	Representative	REPRESENTATIVES Cong.	Pty	Address	County
						DISTRICT 9				
Herkimer	14,479	61	0.4	11,771	3.5	Jonas Platt	6	F	----	----
Montgomery	21,700	466	2.1	2,641	8.2	Benjamin Walker	7	F	----	----
TOTALS	36,179	527	1.4	14,412	3.1					
						DISTRICT 10				
Onondaga	7,406	11	0.1	2,954	2.5	William Cooper	6	F	Cooperstown	Otsego
Ontario	15,218	57	0.4	9,244	1.6	Thomas Morris	7	F	Canandaigua	Ontario
Otsego	21,636	48	0.2	1,013	21.3					
Steuben	1,788	22	1.2	1,510	2.8					
Tioga	6,889	17	0.2	2,443	4.1					
TOTALS	52,937	155	0.2	17,164	3.5					

4

Congressional Districts

1802–1811
8th–12th Congresses

COUNTIES						REPRESENTATIVES				
County	Aggregate	Slave	%S	sq.mi.	P/sq.mi.	Representative	Cong.	Pty	Address	County

AT LARGE

COUNTIES						REPRESENTATIVES				
Fairfield	38,208	276	0.72	626	61.0	Simeon Baldwin	8	F	New Haven	New Haven
Hartford	42,147	67	0.15	739	57.0	Samuel Dana	8	F	Middletown	Middlesex
Litchfield	42,214	47	0.11	925	45.6	John Davenport	8	F	Stamford	Fairfield
Middlesex	19,874	72	0.36	372	53.4	Calvin Goddard	8	F	Plainville	Windham
New Haven	32,162	236	0.73	604	53.2	Roger Griswold	8	F	Lyme	Middlesex
New London	34,614	209	0.6	667	51.9	John Smith	8	F	Sharon	Litchfield
Tolland	14,319	9	0.06	416	34.4	Benjamin Talmadge	8	F	Litchfield	Litchfield
Windham	28,222	35	0.1	514	54.9					
TOTALS	251,760	951	0.37	4,863	51.8	Samuel Dana	9	F	Middletown	Middlesex
						John Davenport	9	F	Stamford	Fairfield
						Calvin Goddard[r] (Resigned in 1805)	9	F	Plainville	Windham
						Roger Griswold[r] (Resigned in 1805)	9	F	Lyme	Middlesex
						Timothy Pitkin (Replaced Goddard and Griswold)	9	F	Farmington	Hartford
						Lewis Sturges (Replaced Goddard and Griswold)	9	F	Fairfield	Fairfield
						Jonathan O. Moseley	9	F	East Haddam	Middlesex
						John Cotton Smith[r] (Resigned in 1806)	9	F	Sharon	Litchfield
						Theodore Dwight	9	F	Hartford	Hartford
						Benjamin Tallmadge	9	F	Litchfield	Litchfield
						Epaphroditus Champion	10	F	East Haddam	Middlesex
						Samuel Dana	10	F	Middletown	Middlesex
						John Davenport	10	F	Stamford	Fairfield
						Jonathan O. Moseley	10	F	East Haddam	Middlesex
						Timothy Pitkin	10	F	Farmington	Hartford
						Lewis Sturges	10	F	Fairfield	Fairfield
						Benjamin Tallmadge	10	F	Litchfield	Litchfield
						Epaphroditus Champion	11	F	East Haddam	Middlesex
						Samuel Dana[r] (Resigned May, 1810)	11	F	Middletown	Middlesex
						Ebenezer Huntington (Replaced Dana December, 1810)	11	W	Norwich	New London
						John Davenport	11	F	Stamford	Fairfield
						Jonathan O. Moseley	11	F	East Haddam	Middlesex
						Timothy Pitkin	11	F	Farmington	Hartford
						Lewis Sturges	11	F	Fairfield	Fairfield
						Benjamin Tallmadge	11	F	Litchfield	Litchfield

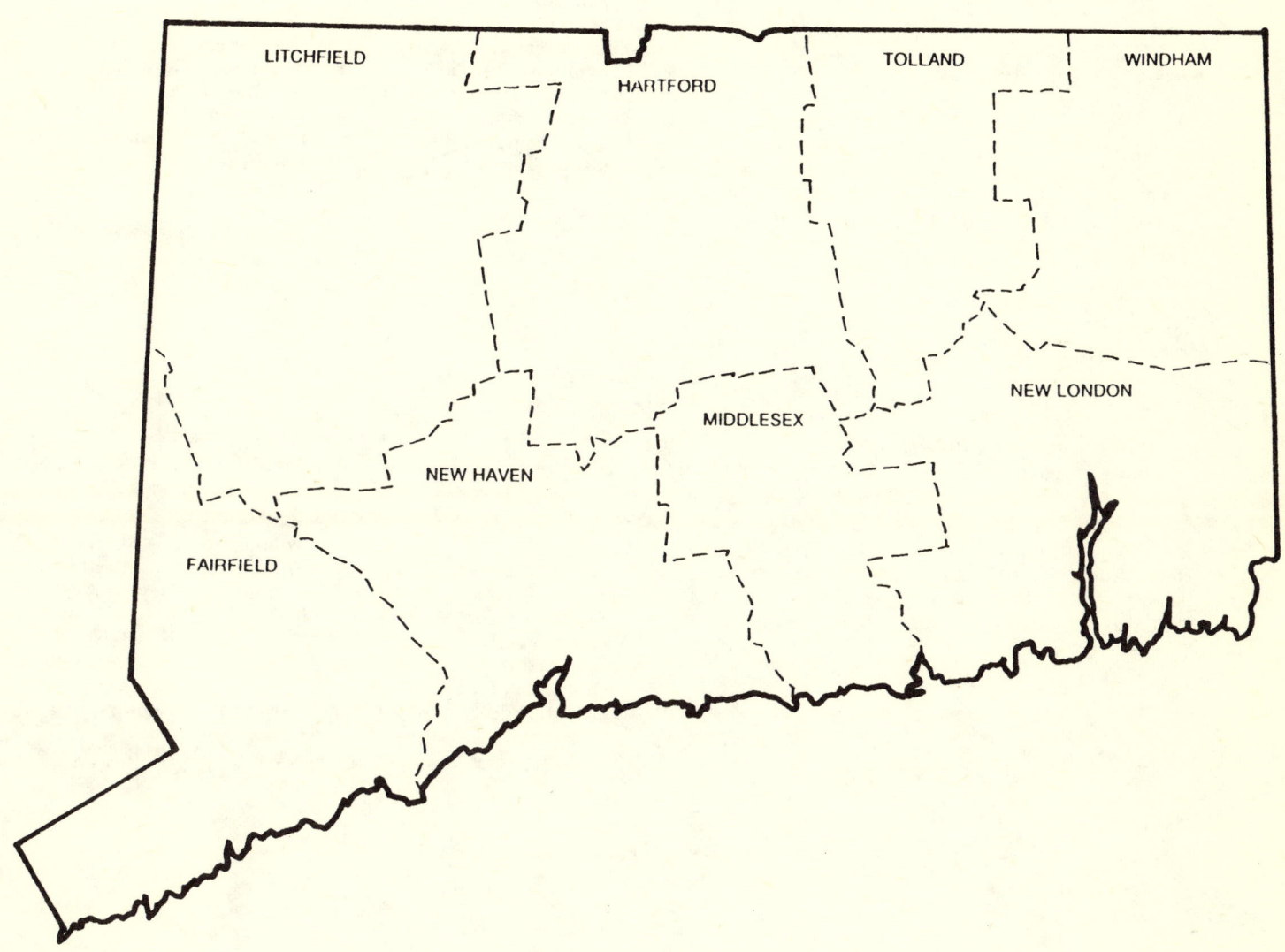

| COUNTIES | | | | | | REPRESENTATIVES | | | | |
County	Aggregate	Slave	%S	sq.mi.	P/sq.mi.	Representative	Cong.	Pty	Address	County
						Epaphroditus Champion	12	F	East Haddam	Middlesex
						John Davenport	12	F	Stamford	Fairfield
						Lyman Law	12	F	New London	New London
						Jonathan O. Moseley	12	F	East Haddam	Middlesex
						Timothy Pitkin	12	F	Farmington	Hartford
						Lewis B. Sturges	12	F	Fairfield	Fairfield
						Benjamin Tallmadge	12	F	Litchfield	Litchfield

DELAWARE
1 CONGRESSMAN

| COUNTIES | | | | | | REPRESENTATIVES | | | | |
County	Aggregate	Slave	%S	sq.mi.	P/sq.mi.	Representative	Cong.	Pty	Address	County
						AT LARGE				
Kent	19,554	1,485	7.5	594	32.9	Caesar A. Rodney	8	R	Wilmington	New Castle
New Castle	25,361	1,838	7.2	438	57.9	James M. Broom	9	F	Wilmington	New Castle
Sussex	19,358	2,830	14.6	950	20.4	James M. Broom[r]	10	F	Wilmington	New Castle
TOTALS	64,273	6,153	9.5	1,982	32.4	(Resigned before Congress assembled)				
						Nicholas Van Dyke (Replaced Broom)	10	F	----	New Castle
						Nicholas Van Dyke	11	F	----	New Castle
						Henry M. Ridgely	12	F	Dover	Kent

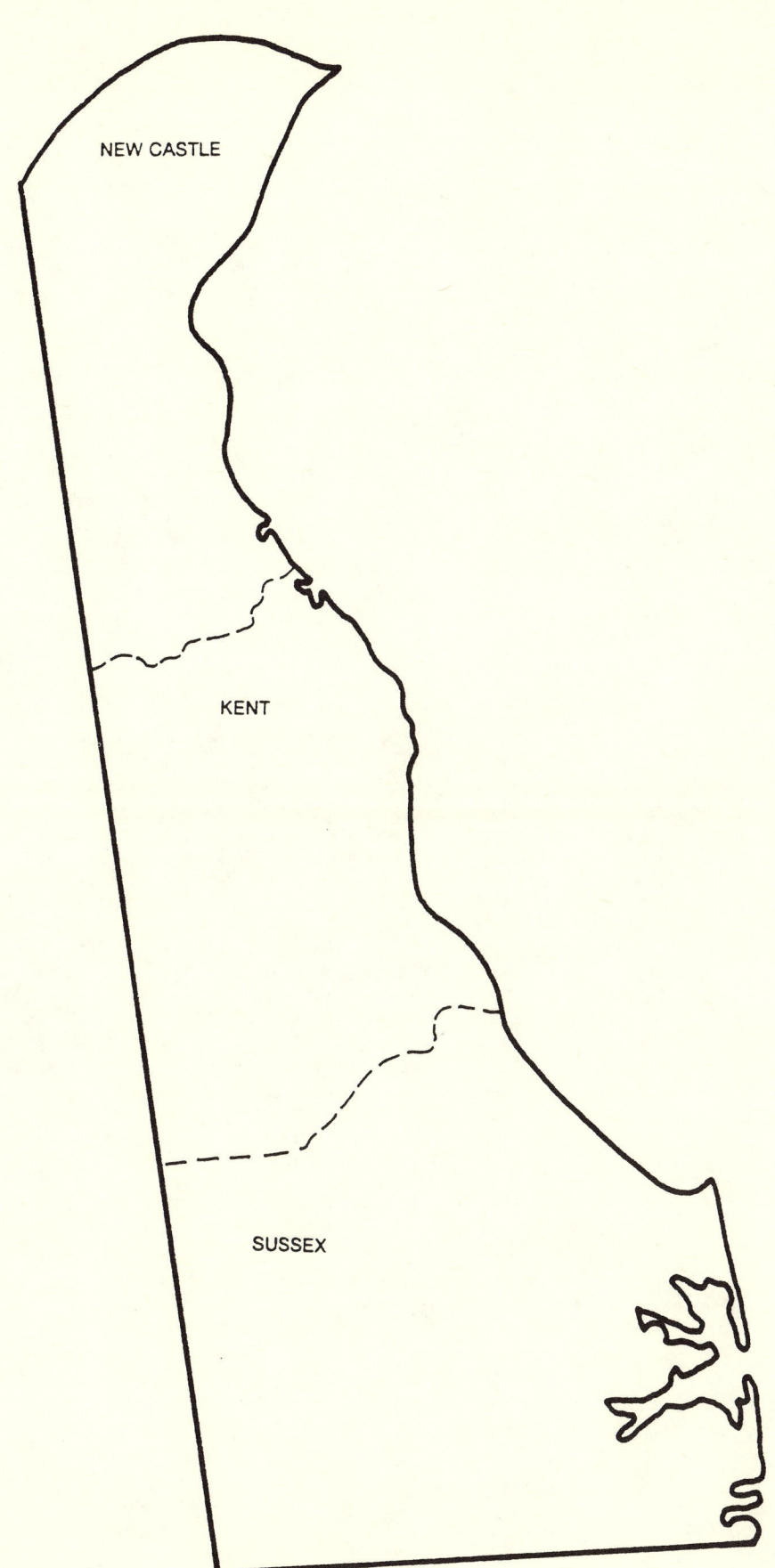

COUNTIES						REPRESENTATIVES				
County	Aggregate	Slave	%S	sq.mi.	P/sq.mi.	Representative	Cong.	Pty	Address	County
						AT LARGE				
Bryan	2,836	2,306	81.3	443	6.4	Joseph Bryan	8	R	Savannah	Chatham
Bulloch	1,913	269	14.0	935	2.0	Peter Early	8	R	Scull Shoals	Greene
Burke	9,506	2,967	31.2	831	11.4	Samuel Hammond	8	R	Augusta	Richmond
Camden	1,681	735	43.7	1,187	1.4	David Meriwether	8	R	----	Wilkes
Chatham	12,946	9,049	69.8	445	29.1					
Columbia	8,345	3,008	36.0	543	15.4	Joseph Bryan[r]	9	R	Savannah	Chatham
Effingham	2,072	762	36.7	480	4.3	(Resigned in 1806)				
Elbert	10,094	2,816	27.8	459	22.0	Dennis Smelt	9	R	Savannah	Chatham
Franklin	6,859	959	13.9	928	7.4	(Replaced Bryan)				
Glynn	1,874	1,092	58.3	412	4.5	Peter Early	9	R	Scull Shoals	Greene
Green	10,761	3,657	33.9	453	23.7	David Meriwether	9	R	----	Wilkes
Hancock	14,456	4,835	33.4	528	27.4	Cowles Mead[ce]	9	R	----	----
Jackson	7,736	1,400	18.0	919	8.4	(Contested by Thomas Spalding)				
Jefferson	5,684	1,642	28.8	530	10.7	Thomas Spalding	9	(----)	----	MacIntosh
Liberty	5,313	3,940	74.1	916	5.8	(Replaced Mead)				
Lincoln	4,766	1,433	30.1	193	24.7	(Resigned in 1806)				
McIntosh	2,660	1,819	68.3	426	6.2	William W. Bibb	9	R	Petersburg	Elbert
Montgomery	3,180	435	13.6	2,925	1.2	(Replaced Spalding)				
Oglethorpe	9,780	3,089	31.5	455	21.5					
Richmond	5,473	2,691	49.1	323	16.9	William W. Bibb	10	R	Petersburg	Elbert
Screven	3,019	766	25.3	651	4.6	Howell Cobb	10	R	Louisville	Jefferson
Warren	8,329	2,058	24.7	427	19.5	Dennis Smelt	10	R	Savannah	Chatham
Washington	10,300	2,668	25.9	674	15.3	George M. Troup	10	R	Dublin	Washington
Wilkes	13,103	5,008	38.2	518	25.3					
TOTALS	162,685	59,404	36.5	16,601[a]	9.8	William W. Bibb	11	R	Petersburg	Elbert
						Howell Cobb	11	R	Louisville	Jefferson
						Dennis Smelt	11	R	Savannah	Chatham
						George M. Troup	11	R	Dublin	Washington
						William W. Bibb	12	R	Petersburg	Elbert
						Howell Cobb[r]	12	R	Louisville	Jefferson
						(Resigned in 1812)				
						William Barnett	12	R	Washington	Wilkes
						(Replaced Cobb)				
						Bolling Hall	12	R	Milledgeville	Greene
						George M. Troup	12	R	Dublin	Washington

[a]Indian lands comprised the balance of the territory within the present boundaries of the state.

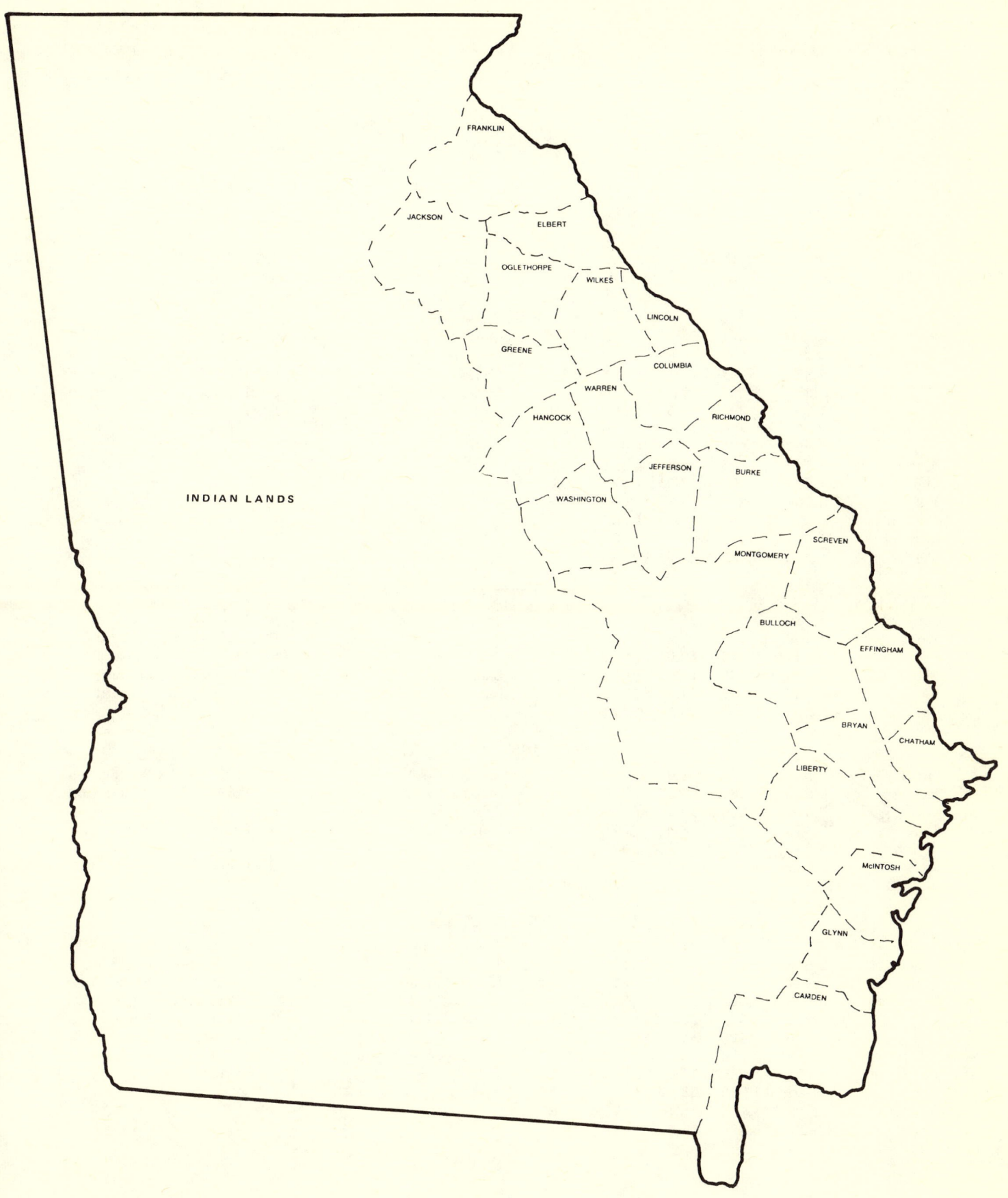

	COUNTIES						REPRESENTATIVES			
County	Aggregate	Slave	%S	sq.mi.	P/sq.mi.	Representative	Cong.	Pty	Address	County

DISTRICT 1

County	Aggregate	Slave	%S	sq.mi.	P/sq.mi.	Representative	Cong.	Pty	Address	County
Adair[a]	----	----	----	804	----	Matthew Lyon	8	R	Eddysville	Caldwell
Barren	4,784	505	10.5	32	5.1	Matthew Lyon	9	R	Eddysville	Caldwell
Christian	2,318	297	12.8	1,133	2.0	Matthew Lyon	10	R	Eddysville	Caldwell
Cumberland	3,284	236	7.1	410	8.0	Matthew Lyon	11	R	Eddysville	Caldwell
Henderson	1,468	390	26.5	1,326	1.1	Anthony New	12	R	Lexington	Fayette
Livingston	2,856	456	15.9	3,749	0.76					
Logan	5,807	775	13.3	1,089	5.3					
Muhlenberg	1,443	125	8.6	681	2.1					
Ohio	1,228	151	12.2	1,938	0.6					
Pulaski	3,161	232	7.3	653	4.8					
Warren[a]	----	----	----	1,135	----					
Wayne[a]	----	----	----	530	----					
TOTALS	26,349	3,167	12.0	14,380	1.3					

[a]Created after 1800 census.

DISTRICT 2

County	Aggregate	Slave	%S	sq.mi.	P/sq.mi.	Representative	Cong.	Pty	Address	County
Garrard	6,186	1,259	20.3	236	26.2	John Boyle	8	R	Lancaster	Garrard
Knox	1,109	62	5.5	3,307	0.3	John Boyle	9	R	Lancaster	Garrard
Lincoln	8621	1,776	20.6	775	11.1	John Boye	10	R	Lancaster	Garrard
Madison	10,490	1,726	16.4	1,664	6.3	Samuel McKee	11	R	Lancaster	Garrard
Mercer	9,646	2,316	24.0	439	21.9	Samuel McKee	12	R	Lancaster	Garrard
TOTALS	36,034	7,139	19.8	6,421	5.6					

DISTRICT 3

County	Aggregate	Slave	%S	sq.mi.	P/sq.mi.	Representative	Cong.	Pty	Address	County
Breckinridge	809	41	5.0	741	1.0	Matthew Walton	8	R	Springfield	Washington
Bullitt	3,542	969	27.3	300	11.8	Matthew Walton	9	R	Springfield	Washington
Green	6,096	836	13.7	559	10.9	John Rowan	10	R	Louisville	Jefferson
Hardin	3,643	325	8.9	1,377	2.6	Henry Crist	11	(----)	Shepherds-ville	Bullitt
Jefferson	8,744	2,406	27.5	375	23.3					
Nelson	9,866	1,902	19.2	437	22.5	Stephen Ormsby	12	R	Louisville	Jefferson
TOTALS	41,750	7,901	18.9	4,514	9.2					

DISTRICT 4

County	Aggregate	Slave	%S	sq.mi.	P/sq.mi.	Representative	Cong.	Pty	Address	County
Boone	1,534	325	21.1	249	6.1	Thomas Sandford	8	R	Covington	Campbell
Bracken	2,603	243	9.3	204	12.7	Thomas Sandford	9	R	Covington	Campbell
Campbell	1,943	279	14.3	314	6.1	Richard M. Johnson	10	R	Great Crossings	Scott
Franklin	5,078	1,369	26.9	218	23.2					
Gallatin	1,291	329	25.4	430	3.0	Richard M. Johnson	11	R	Great Crossings	Scott
Harrison	4,056	406	10.0	308	13.1					
Henry	3,258	406	12.4	519	6.2	Richard M. Johnson	12	R	Great Crossings	Scott
Pendleton	1,613	240	14.8	654	2.4					
Scott	8,007	1,910	23.8	409	19.5					
Shelby	8,191	1,487	18.1	574	14.2					
TOTALS	37,574	6,994	18.6	3,879	9.7					

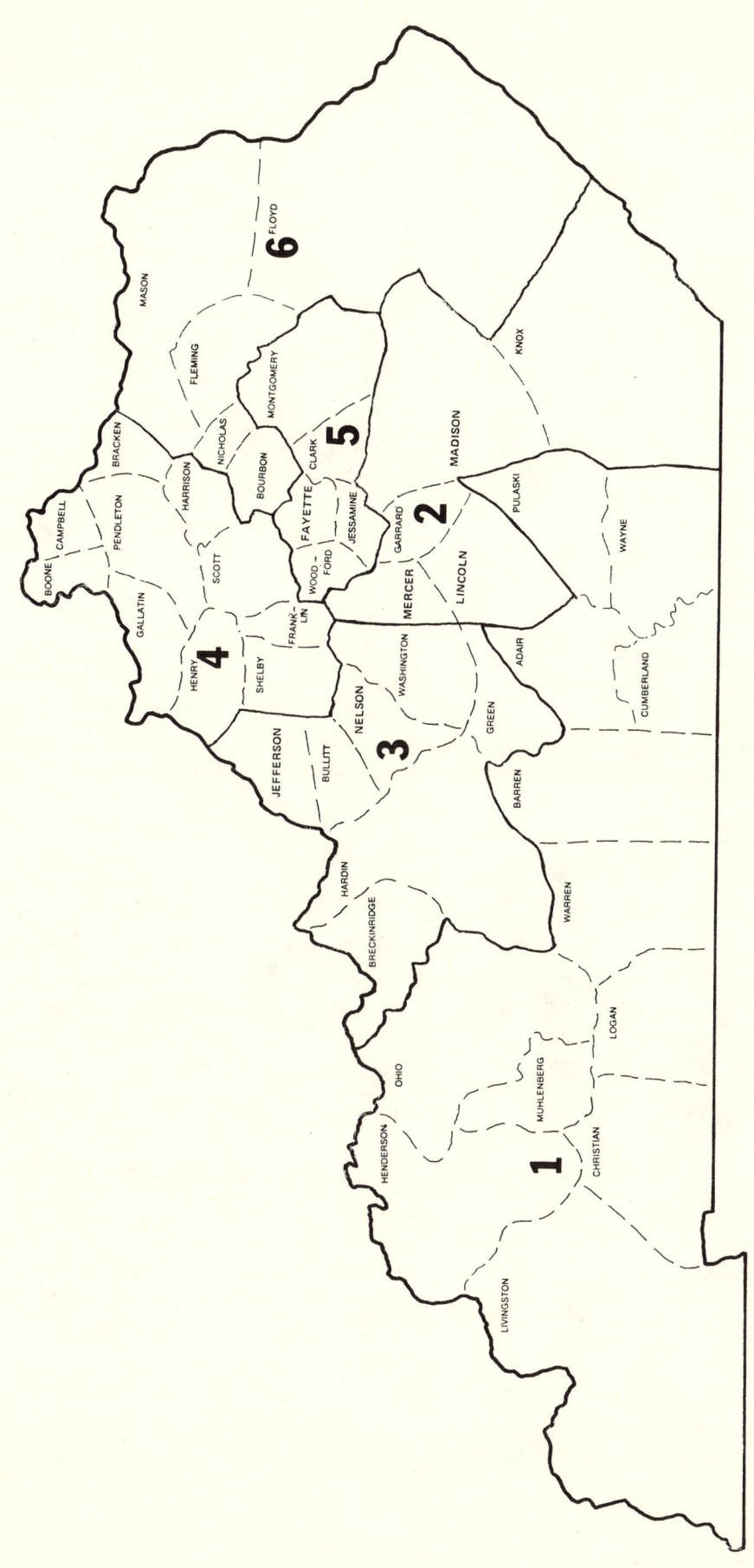

| COUNTIES | | | | | | REPRESENTATIVES | | | | |
County	Aggregate	Slave	%S	sq.mi.	P/sq.mi.	Representative	Cong.	Pty	Address	County
						DISTRICT 5				
Clark	7,653	1,561	20.3	309	24.8	John Fowler	8	R	Lexington	Fayette
Fayette	14,028	4,225	30.1	280	50.1	John Fowler	9	R	Lexington	Fayette
Jessamine	5,461	1,561	28.5	177	30.9	Benjamin Howard	10	R	Lexington	Fayette
Montgomery	6,988	767	10.9	1,051	6.6	Benjamin Howard[r]	11	R	Lexington	Fayette
Woodford	6,624	2,058	31.0	193	34.3	William T. Barry	11	R	Lexington	Fayette
TOTALS	40,754	10,172	24.9	2,010	20.3	(Replaced Howard)				
						Henry Clay	12	R	Lexington	Fayette
						DISTRICT 6				
Bourbon	6,782	2,136	31.4	300	22.6	George M. Bedinger	8	(----)	Blue Licks Springs	Nicholas
Fleming	5,016	254	5.0	990	5.1					
Floyd	478	----	----	4,343	0.1	George M. Bedinger	9	(----)	Blue Licks Springs	Nicholas
Mason	12,182	1,747	14.3	1,691	7.2					
Nicholas	2,925	322	11.0	204	14.4	Joseph Desha	10	R	Mays Lick	Mason
TOTALS	27,383	4,459	16.2	7,528	3.6	Joseph Desha	11	R	Mays Lick	Mason
						Joseph Desha	12	R	Mays Lick	Mason

MARYLAND
8 DISTRICTS
9 CONGRESSMEN

| COUNTIES | | | | | | REPRESENTATIVES | | | | |
County	Aggregate	Slave	%S	sq.mi.	P/sq.mi.	Representative	Cong.	Pty.	Address	County
						DISTRICT 1				
Calvert	8,297	4,101	49.4	217	38.2	John Campbell	8	F	Port Tobacco	Charles
Charles	19,172	9,558	49.8	459	41.8	John Campbell	9	F	Port Tobacco	Charles
St. Marys	13,699	6,399	46.7	373	36.6	John Campbell	10	F	Port Tobacco	Charles
TOTALS	41,168	20,058	48.7	1,049	39.2	John Campbell	11	F	Port Tobacco	Charles
						Philip Stuart	12	F	Port Tobacco	Charles
						DISTRICT 2				
Anne- Arundel	20,411	9,114	44.6	674	30.3	Walter Bowie	8	R	Nottingham	Prince Georges
						Leonard Covington	9	R	Aquasco	Prince Georges
Prince						Archibald Van Horne	10	R	----	Prince Georges
Georges	21,185	12,191	57.5	485	43.7	Archibald Van Horne	11	R	----	Prince Georges
TOTALS	41,596	21,305	51.2	1,159	35.9	Joseph Kent	12	R	Bladensburg	Prince Georges

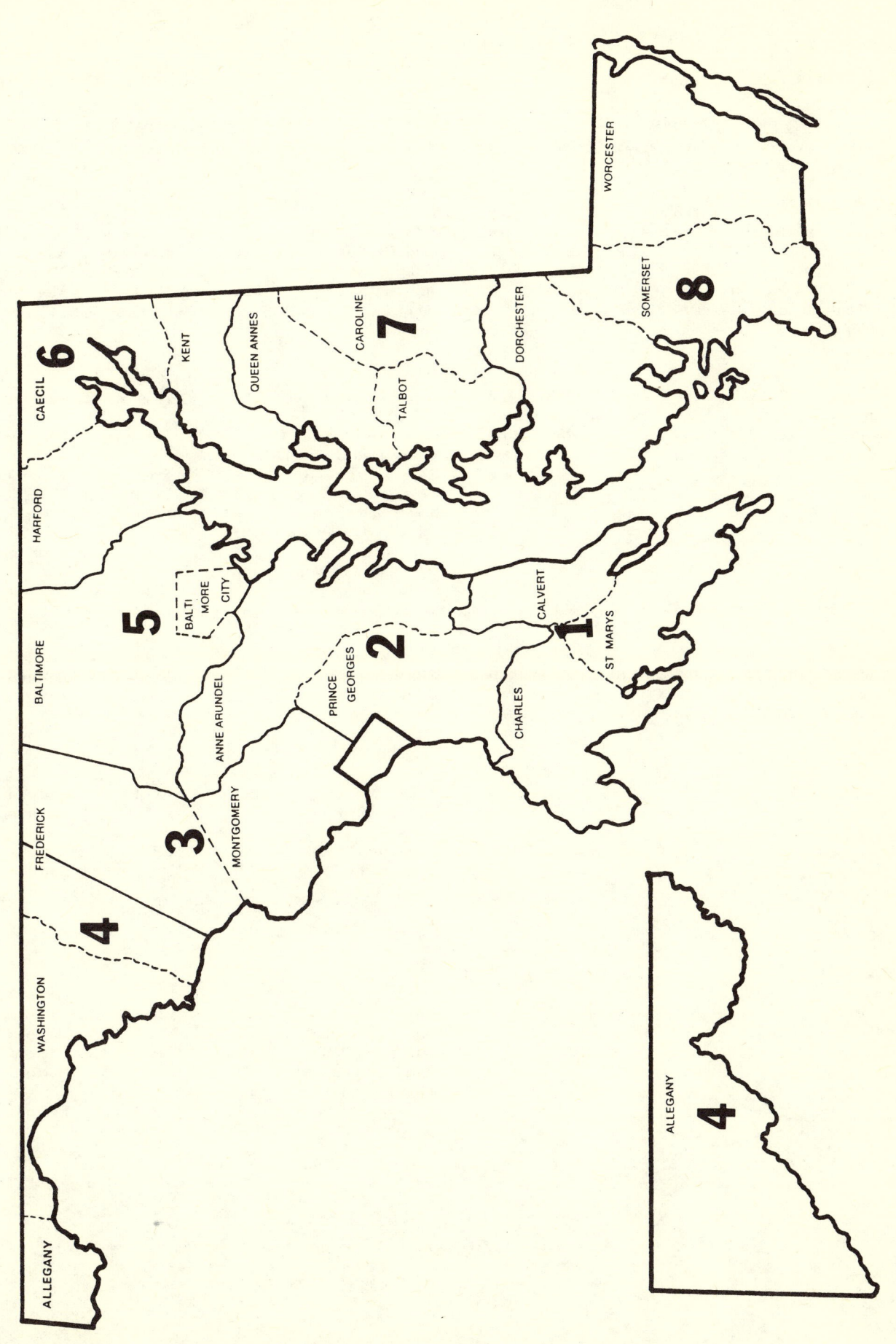

ALLEGANY 4

WASHINGTON FREDERICK 4

ALLEGANY

BALTIMORE 5

MONTGOMERY 3

BALTI MORE CITY

ANNE ARUNDEL

PRINCE GEORGES 2

CHARLES

CALVERT 1

ST MARYS

HARFORD

CAECIL 6

KENT

QUEEN ANNES

CAROLINE 7

TALBOT

DORCHESTER

WORCESTER

SOMERSET 8

County	Aggregate	Slave	%S	sq.mi.	P/sq.mi.	Representative	Cong.	Pty.	Address	County
		COUNTIES					REPRESENTATIVES			

DISTRICT 3

County	Aggregate	Slave	%S	sq.mi.	P/sq.mi.	Representative	Cong.	Pty.	Address	County
Frederick[a]	15,761	2,286	14.5	395	39.9	Thomas Plater	8	F	Georgetown	Montgomery
Montgomery	15,058	6,288	41.7	495	30.4	Patrick Magruder	9	R	Rockville	Montgomery
TOTALS	30,819	8,574	27.8	890	34.6	Philip B. Key	10	F	Rockville	Montgomery
						Philip B. Key	11	F	Rockville	Montgomery
						Philip B. Key	12	F	Rockville	Montgomery

[a]"That part of Frederick County adjacent as far as Monocacy from the mouth thereof to the Pennsylvania line," One-half of census figures were assigned to this portion of the county.

DISTRICT 4

County	Aggregate	Slave	%S	sq.mi.	P/sq.mi.	Representative	Cong.	Pty.	Address	County
Allegheny	5,804	499	8.5	928	6.3	Daniel Hiester[†]	8	R	Hagerstown	Washington
Frederick[a]	15,761	2,286	14.5	395	39.9	(Died March 7, 1804)				
Washington	16,450	2,200	13.3	459	35.9	Roger Nelson	8	R	Frederick	Frederick
TOTALS	38,015	4,985	13.1	1,782	21.3	(Replaced Hiester)				
						Roger Nelson	9	R	Frederick	Frederick
						Roger Nelson	10	R	Frederick	Frederick
						Roger Nelson[r]	11	R	Frederick	Frederick
						(Resigned May 14, 1810)				
						Samuel Ringgold	11	R	Hagerstown	Washington
						(Replaced Nelson)				
						Samuel Ringgold	12	R	Hagerstown	Washington

[a]"Remainder of Frederick County." One-half of census figures were assigned to this portion of the county.

DISTRICT 5

County	Aggregate	Slave	%S	sq.mi.	P/sq.mi.	Representative	Cong.	Pty.	Address	County
Baltimore	32,516	6,830	21.0	929	35.0	William MacCreery	8	R	Reistertown	Baltimore
City of						Nicholas R. Moore	8	R	Ruxton	Baltimore
Baltimore	26,514	2,843	10.7	78	339.9					
TOTALS	59,030	9,673	16.4	1,007	58.6	William McCreery	9	R	Reistertown	Baltimore
						Nicholas R. Moore	9	R	Ruxton	Baltimore
						William McCreery	10	R	Reistertown	Baltimore
						Nicholas R. Moore	10	R	Ruxton	Baltimore
						Alexander McKim	11	R	City of Baltimore	
						Nicholas R. Moore	11	R	Buxton	Baltimore
						Peter Little	12	R	City of Baltimore	
						Alexander McKim	12	R	City of Baltimore	

DISTRICT 6

County	Aggregate	Slave	%S	sq.mi.	P/sq.mi.	Representative	Cong.	Pty.	Address	County
Caecil	9,018	2,103	23.3	362	42.0	John Archer	8	R	Churchville	Harford
Harford	17,626	4,264	24.2	453	38.9	John Archer	9	R	Churchville	Harford
Kent	11,771	4,474	38.0	281	41.9	John Montgomery	10	R	Bel Air	Harford
TOTALS	38,415	10,841	28.2	1,096	35.1	John Montgomery	11	R	Bel Air	Harford
						John Montgomery[r]	12	R	Bel Air	Harford
						(Resigned April 29, 1811)				
						Stevenson Archer	12	R	Bel Air	Harford
						(Replaced Montgomery)				

| | COUNTIES | | | | | REPRESENTATIVES | | | | |
| County | Aggregate | Slave | %S | sq.mi. | P/sq.mi. | Representative | Cong. | Pty. | Address | County |

DISTRICT 7

County	Aggregate	Slave	%S	sq.mi.	P/sq.mi.	Representative	Cong.	Pty.	Address	County
Caroline	9,226	1,865	20.2	321	28.7	Joseph H. Nicholson	8	R	Easton	Talbot
Queen						Joseph H. Nicholson[r]	9	R	Easton	Talbot
Annes	14,857	6,517	43.8	375	39.6	(Resigned March, 1806)				
Talbot	13,436	4,775	35.5	261	51.5	Edward Lloyd	9	R	Wye Mills	Talbot
TOTALS	37,619	13,157	35.0	957	39.3	(Replaced Nicholson)				
						Edward Lloyd	10	R	Wye Mills	Talbot
						John Brown	11	R	Centerville	Queen Annes
						John Brown[r]	12	R	Centerville	Queen Annes
						(Resigned in 1810)				
						Robert Wright	12	R	Queenstown	Queen Annes
						(Replaced Brown)				

DISTRICT 8

County	Aggregate	Slave	%S	sq.mi.	P/sq.mi.	Representative	Cong.	Pty.	Address	County
Dorchester	16,346	4,566	27.9	594	27.5	John Dennis	8	F	----	Somerset
Somerset	17,358	7,432	42.8	560	31.0	Charles Goldsborough	9	F	Cambridge	Dorchester
Worcester	16,370	4,398	25.6	639	25.6	Charles Goldsborough	10	F	Cambridge	Dorchester
TOTALS	50,074	16,396	32.7	1,793	27.9	Charles Goldsborough	11	F	Cambridge	Dorchester
						Charles Goldsborough	12	F	Cambridge	Dorchester

COUNTIES						REPRESENTATIVES				
County	Aggregate	Slave	%S	sq.mi.	P/sq.mi.	Representative	Cong.	Pty.	Address	County

DISTRICT 1 (HAMPSHIRE SOUTH)[a]

All towns lying south of a line created by the towns of:						Thomas Dwight	8	F	Springfield	Hampshire
Belchertown	1,878	----	----	----[b]	----	William Ely	9	F	Springfield	Hampshire
Granby	786	----	----	----	----	William Ely	10	F	Springfield	Hampshire
Hadley	1,073	----	----	----	----	William Ely	11	F	Springfield	Hampshire
North-						William Ely	12	F	Springfield	Hampshire
ampton	2,190	----		----	----					
Norwich	959	----	----	----	----					
Middlefield	877	----	----	----	----					
South Hadley	801	----	----	----	----					
Ware	997	----	----	----	----					
Westhampton	756	----	----	----	----					
Worthington	1,223	----	----	----	----					
The towns south of the line which are included in this district are as follows:										
Amherst	1,358	----	----	----	----					
Chesterfield	1,323	----	----	----	----					
Goshen	724	----	----	----	----					
Hatfield	809	----	----	----	----					
Pelham	1,144	----	----	----	----					
Plainfield	797	----	----	----	----					
TOTALS[c]	36,216	----	----	619	58.5					

[a]Hampshire South District is roughly similar to the present county of Hampden.

[b]No data are available for the size of these towns.

[c]This figure represents one-half of the population of Hampshire County.

DISTRICT 2 (HAMPSHIRE NORTH)

All towns in Hampshire not included in Hampshire South (District 1),						Samuel Taggart	8	F	Colrain	Hampshire
						Samuel Taggart	9	F	Colrain	Hampshire
totals:	36,216	----	----	1,237	29.3	Samuel Taggart	10	F	Colrain	Hampshire
						Samuel Taggart	11	F	Colrain	Hampshire
						Samuel Taggart	12	F	Colrain	Hampshire

DISTRICT 3 (SUFFOLK)

Towns in Suffolk County:						William Eustis	8	R	Boston	Suffolk
Boston and						Josiah Quincy	9	F	Boston	Suffolk
Islands	----	----	----	----	----	Josiah Quincy	10	F	Boston	Suffolk
Chelsea and						Josiah Quincy	11	F	Boston	Suffolk
Islands	----	----	----	----	----	Josiah Quincy	12	F	Boston	Suffolk
Hingham	----	----	----	----	----					
Hull	----	----	----	----	----					
Total, towns	28,015	----	----	56	500.3					

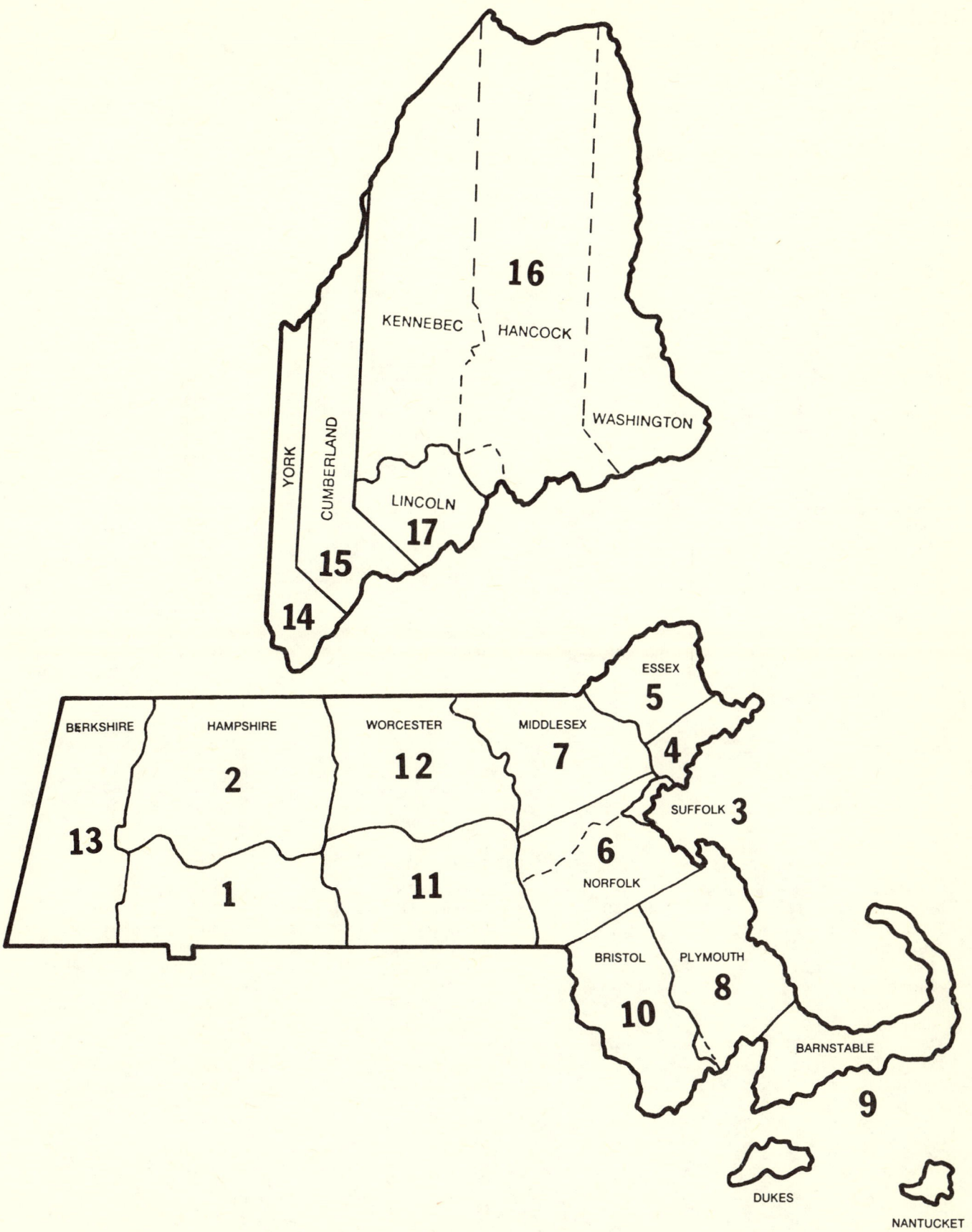

KENNEBEC

HANCOCK

16

WASHINGTON

YORK

CUMBERLAND

LINCOLN

17

15

14

BERKSHIRE

HAMPSHIRE

WORCESTER

MIDDLESEX

ESSEX

5

2

12

7

4

13

SUFFOLK 3

6

1

11

NORFOLK

BRISTOL

PLYMOUTH

8

10

BARNSTABLE

9

DUKES

NANTUCKET

| COUNTIES | | | | | | REPRESENTATIVES | | | | |
| County | Aggregate | Slave | %S | sq.mi. | P/sq.mi. | Representative | Cong. | Pty. | Address | County |

DISTRICT 3 (CONTINUED)

Towns in Middlesex County:

Charleston	2,751	----	----	20[a]	137.6					
Maiden	1,059	----	----	20	53.0					
Medford	1,114	----	----	20	55.7					
Total, towns	4,924			60	82.1					
TOTALS	37,862	----	----	116	326.4					

[a]The square mile figure for each town was unavailable. This figure represents the square miles per county divided by the number of towns in the county.

DISTRICT 4 (ESSEX SOUTH)[a]

Towns in Essex County:

Beverly	3,881	----	----	----	----	Jacob Crowninshield	8	R	Salem	Essex
Danvers	2,643	----	----	----	----	Jacob Crowninshield	9	R	Salem	Essex
Gloucester	5,313	----	----	----	----	Jacob Crowninshield[†]	10	R	Salem	Essex
Lynn	2,837	----	----	----	----	(Died April, 1808)				
Lynnfield	468	----	----	----	----	Joseph Story	10	R	Salem	Essex
Manchester	1,082	----	----	----	----	(Replaced Crowninshield December, 1808)				
Marblehead	5,211	----	----	----	----	Benjamin Pickman, Jr.	11	(----)	Salem	Essex
Salem	9,457	----	----	----	----	William Reed	12	F	Marblehead	Essex
Wenham	476	----	----	----	----					
TOTALS	31,368	----	----	194	161.6					

[a]This district covered the southern quarter of Essex County.

DISTRICT 5 (ESSEX NORTH)

All other towns in Essex County not included in Essex South (District 4).						Manasseh Cutler	8	F	Hamilton	Essex
Total, towns	29,827	----	----	300	99.4	Jeremiah Nelson	9	F	Newburyport	Essex
Towns in Middlesex County:						Edward St. Loe Livermore	10	F	Newburyport	Essex
Readingtown	2,025	----	----	20	101.3					
TOTALS	31,852	----	----	320	99.5	Edward St. Loe Livermore	11	F	Newburyport	Essex
						Leonard White	12	R	Haverhill	Essex

DISTRICT 6 (NORFOLK)

All towns and districts in Norfolk County, total:	27,216	----	----	394	69.1	Ebeneazer Seaver	8	R	Roxbury	Norfolk
Towns in Middlesex County:						Ebeneazer Seaver	9	R	Roxbury	Norfolk
Holliston	783	----	----	----	----	Ebeneazer Seaver	10	R	Roxbury	Norfolk
Hopkinton	1,372	----	----	----	----	Ebeneazer Seaver	11	R	Roxbury	Norfolk
Nantick	694	----	----	----	----	Ebeneazer Seaver	12	R	Roxbury	Norfolk
Newton	1,491	----	----	----	----					
Sherburne	776	----	----	----	----					
Total, towns:	5,116	----	----	100	51.2					
TOTALS	36,665	----	----	494	65.5					

COUNTIES						REPRESENTATIVES				
County	Aggregate	Slave	%S	sq.mi.	P/sq.mi.	Representative	Cong.	Pty.	Address	County

DISTRICT 7 (MIDDLESEX)

All towns in Middlesex, except Readingtown, and those						Joseph B. Varnum	8	R	Dracut	Middlesex
in Suffolk and Norfolk Counties,						Joseph B. Varnum	9	R	Dracut	Middlesex
total:	34,053	----	----	645	52.8	Joseph B. Varnum	10	R	Dracut	Middlesex
						Joseph B. Varnum	11	R	Dracut	Middlesex
						Joseph B. Varnum[r]	12	R	Dracut	Middlesex
						(Resigned June, 1811)				
						William M. Richardson	12	F	Groton	Middlesex
						(Replaced Varnum January 1812)				

DISTRICT 8 (PLYMOUTH)

Plymouth	30,073	----	----	654	46.0	Nahum Mitchell	8	F	East Bridgewater	Plymouth
						Joseph Barker	9	R	Middleboro	Plymouth
						Joseph Barker	10	R	Middleboro	Plymouth
						William Baylies[ce]	11	WR	Bridgewater	Plymouth
						(Served until election successfully contested in 1809)				
						Charles Turner, Jr.	11	WR	Scituate	Plymouth
						(Successfully contested election of Baylies and took seat June 1809)				
						Charles Turner, Jr.	12	WR	Scituate	Plymouth

DISTRICT 9 (BARNSTABLE)

Barnstable	19,293	----	----	393	49.1	Lemuel Williams	8	F	New Bedford	Bristol
Town in Bristol County:						Isiah Green	9	R	Barnstable	Barnstable
New Bedford	4,361	----	----	37	117.9	Isiah Green	10	R	Barnstable	Barnstable
Dukes	3,118	----	----	104	30.0	Gideon Gardner	11	R	Nantucket	Nantucket
Nantucket	5,617	----	----	46	122.1	Isiah Green	12	R	Barnstable	Barnstable
TOTALS	32,389	----	----	580	55.8					

DISTRICT 10 (BRISTOL)

All towns in Bristol County, except New Bedford,						Phanuel Bishop	8	R	Rehoboth	Bristol
total:	29,519	----	----	517	57.1	Phanuel Bishop	9	R	Rehoboth	Bristol
						Josiah Dean	10	R	Raynham	Bristol
						Laban Wheaton	11	F	Easton	Bristol
						Laban Wheaton	12	F	Easton	Bristol

DISTRICT 11 (WORCESTER SOUTH)

Towns in Worcester County:						Seth Hastings	8	F	Mendon	Worcester
Brookfield	3,284	----	----	----	----	Seth Hastings	9	F	Mendon	Worcester
Charlton	2,120	----	----	----	----	Jabez Upham	10	(----)	Brookfield	Worcester
Douglass	1,083	----	----	----	----	Jabez Upham[r]	11	(----)	Brookfield	Worcester
Grafton	985	----	----	----	----	(Resigned in 1810)				
Leicester	1,103	----	----	----	----	Joseph Allen	11	(----)	Worcester	Worcester
Mendon	1,628	----	----	----	----	(Replaced Upham December, 1810)				
Milford	907	----	----	----	----	Elijah Bringham	12	F	Westboro	Worcester
New Raintree	875	----	----	----	----					
Northborough	698	----	----	----	----					
Northbridge	544	----	----	----	----					
Shrewsbury	1,048	----	----	----	----					
Southborough	871	----	----	----	----					
Spencer	1,433	----	----	----	----					

COUNTIES						REPRESENTATIVES				
County	Aggregate	Slave	%S	sq.mi.	P/sq.mi.	Representative	Cong.	Pty.	Address	County

DISTRICT 11 (CONTINUED)

County	Aggregate	Slave	%S	sq.mi.	P/sq.mi.	Representative	Cong.	Pty.	Address	County
Starbridge	1,846	----	----	----	----					
Sutton	2,513	----	----	----	----					
Upton	854	----	----	----	----					
Uxbridge	1,404	----	----	----	----					
Westboro	922	----	----	----	----					
Western	979	----	----	----	----					
Worcester	2,411	----	----	----	----					
TOTALS	27,508	----	----	755	36.4					

DISTRICT 12 (WORCESTER NORTH)

All towns in Worcester County not included in
Worcester South (District 11),

County	Aggregate	Slave	%S	sq.mi.	P/sq.mi.	Representative	Cong.	Pty.	Address	County
totals:	32,210	----	----	754	42.8	William Stedman	8	F	Lancaster	Worcester
						William Stedman	9	F	Lancaster	Worcester
						William Stedman	10	F	Lancaster	Worcester
						William Stedman[r]	11	F	Lancaster	Worcester
						(Resigned July, 1810)				
						Abijah Bigelow	11	F	Leominster	Worcester
						(Replaced Stedman December, 1810)				
						Abijah Bigelow	12	F	Leominster	Worcester

DISTRICT 13 (BERKSHIRE)

County	Aggregate	Slave	%S	sq.mi.	P/sq.mi.	Representative	Cong.	Pty.	Address	County
Berkshire	33,885	----	----	941	36.0	Thompson J. Skinner[r]	8	(----)	----	----
						(Resigned August, 1804)				
						Simon Larned	8	(----)	Pittsfield	Berkshire
						(Replaced Skinner November, 1804)				
						Barnabas Bidwell	9	(----)	Stockbridge	Berkshire
						Barnabas Bidwell[r]	10	(----)	Stockbridge	Berkshire
						(Resigned July, 1807)				
						Ezekiel Bacon	10	R	Pittsfield	Berkshire
						(Replaced Bidwell November, 1807)				
						Ezekiel Bacon	11	R	Pittsfield	Berkshire
						Ezekiel Bacon	12	R	Pittsfield	Berkshire

DISTRICT 14 (YORK)

County	Aggregate	Slave	%S	sq.mi.	P/sq.mi.	Representative	Cong.	Pty.	Address	County
York	37,729	----	----	2,937	12.8	Richard Cutts	8	R	Saco or Pepperelboro	York
						Richard Cutts	9	R	Saco or Pepperelboro	York
						Richard Cutts	10	R	Pepperelboro	York
						Richard Cutts	11	R	Pepperelboro	York
						Richard Cutts	12	R	Pepperelboro	York

DISTRICT 15 (CUMBERLAND)

County	Aggregate	Slave	%S	sq.mi.	P/sq.mi.	Representative	Cong.	Pty.	Address	County
Cumberland	37,918	----	----	3,669	10.3	Peleg Wadsworth	8	(----)	Portland	Cumberland
						Peleg Wadsworth	9	(----)	Portland	Cumberland
						Daniel Ilsley	10	R	Falmouth	Cumberland
						Ezekiel Whitman	11	F	Portland	Cumberland
						William Widgery	12	R	Portland	Cumberland

| COUNTIES | | | | | | REPRESENTATIVES | | | | |
| County | Aggregate | Slave | %S | sq.mi. | P/sq.mi. | Representative | Cong. | Pty. | Address | County |

DISTRICT 16 (KENNEBEC)

County	Aggregate	Slave	%S	sq.mi.	P/sq.mi.	Representative	Cong.	Pty.	Address	County
Hancock	11,269	----	----	12,743	0.9	Phineas Bruce	8	(----)	Machias	Washington
(Except those towns included in District 17)						(Never served due to illness)				
Kennebec	24,402	----	----	7,925	3.1	John Chandler	9	(----)	Monmouth	Kennebec
Washington	4,436	----	----	3,504	1.3	John Chandler	10	(----)	Monmouth	Kennebec
TOTALS	40,107	----	----	24,172	1.7	Barzillai Gannett	11	R	Gardener	Kennebec
						Barzillai Gannett[r]	12	R	Gardener	Kennebec
						(Resigned in 1812--never qualified for seat)				
						Francis Carr	12	R	Orrington	Hancock
						(Replaced Gannett June, 1812)				

DISTRICT 17 (LINCOLN)

County	Aggregate	Slave	%S	sq.mi.	P/sq.mi.	Representative	Cong.	Pty.	Address	County
Lincoln	30,100	----	----	1,617	18.6	Samuel Thatcher	8	R	Warren	Lincoln
Towns in Hancock County:						Orchard Cook	9	(----)	Wiscasset	Lincoln
Bedfast	674	----	----	----	----	Orchard Cook	10	(----)	Wiscasset	Lincoln
Deer Isle	1,094	----	----	----	----	Orchard Cook	11	(----)	Wiscasset	Lincoln
Ducktrap	686	----	----	----	----	Peleg Tallman	12	R	Bath	Lincoln
Isleborough	483	----	----	----	----					
Northport	482	----	----	----	----					
Prospect	770	----	----	----	----					
Venalhaven	858	----	----	----	----					
Total, towns	5,049	----	----	300	16.8					
TOTALS	35,147	----	----	1,917	18.3					

COUNTIES						REPRESENTATIVES				
County	Aggregate	Slave	%S	sq.mi.	P/sq.mi.	Representative	Cong.	Pty.	Address	County
						AT LARGE				
Cheshire	38,825	----	----	1,174	33.1	Silas Betton	8	F	Salem	Rockingham
Coos[a]	----	----	----	----	----	Clifton Claggett	8	F	Litchfield	Hillsborough
Grafton	23,093	8	----	3,852	6.0	David Hough	8	F	Lebanon	Grafton
Hillsborough	43,899	----	----	1,477	29.7	Samuel Hunt	8	F	Charleston	Cheshire
Rockingham	45,427	----	----	1,041	43.6	Samuel Tenney	8	F	Exeter	Rockingham
Strafford	32,614	----	----	1,414	23.1					
TOTALS	183,658	8	----	8,958	20.5	Silas Betton	9	F	Salem	Rockingham
						Caleb Ellis	9	(----)	Claremont	Cheshire
						David Hough	9	F	Lebanon	Grafton
						Thomas W. Thompson	9	(----)	Concord	Rockingham
						Samuel Tenney	9	F	Exeter	Rockingham
						Peter Carleton	10	R	Landaff	Grafton
						Daniel M. Durell	10	(----)	Dover	Strafford
						Francis Gardner	10	(----)	Keene	Cheshire
						Jedediah K. Smith	10	(----)	Amherst	Hillsborough
						Clement Storer	10	(----)	Portsmouth	Rockingham
						Daniel Blaisdell	11	F	Canaan	Strafford
						John C. Chamberlain	11	F	Charlestown	Cheshire
						William Hale	11	F	Dover	Strafford
						Nathaniel A. Haven	11	F	Portsmouth	Rockingham
						James Wilson	11	F	Peterboro	Hillsborough
						Josiah Bartlett, Jr.	12	(----)	Stratham	Rockingham
						Samuel Dinsmore	12	R	Keene	Cheshire
						Obed Hall	12	R	Bartlett	Strafford
						John A. Harper	12	R	Meredith Bridge	Strafford
						George Sullivan	12	F	Exeter	Rockingham

[a]Created in 1803 - not in the 1800 census.

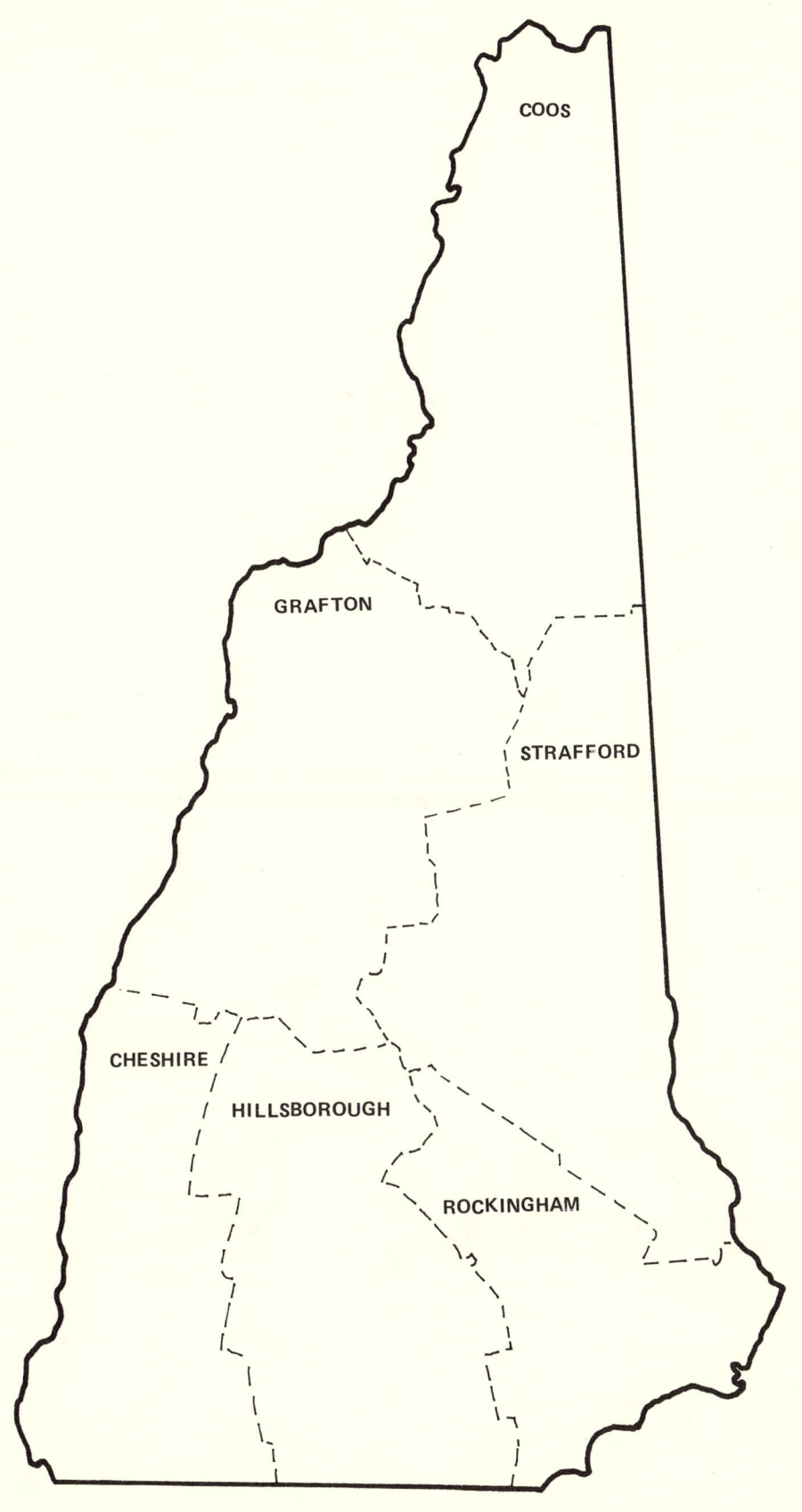

COUNTIES						REPRESENTATIVES				
County	Aggregate	Slave	%S	sq.mi.	P/sq.mi.	Representative	Cong.	Pty.	Address	County
						AT LARGE				
Bergen	15,156	2,825	18.6	426	35.6	Adam Boyd	8	R	Hackensack	Bergen
Burlington	21,521	188	0.9	819	26.3	Ebenezer Elmer	8	R	Bridgetown	Cumberland
Cape May	3,066	98	3.2	267	11.5	William Helmes	8	R	Hacketts-town	Sussex
Cumberland	9,529	75	0.8	500	19.1					
Essex	22,269	1,521	6.8	233	95.6	James Mott	8	R	Middletown	Monmouth
Gloucester	16,115	61	0.4	1,119	14.4	James Sloan	8	R	Newtontown	Gloucester
Hunterdon	21,261	1,220	5.7	651	32.7	Henry Southard	8	R	Basking Ridge	Somerset
Middlesex	17,890	1,564	8.7	312	57.3					
Monmouth	19,872	1,633	8.2	1,118	17.8					
Morris	17,750	775	4.4	468	37.9	Ezra Darby	9	R	Scotch Plains	Essex
Salem	11,371	85	0.8	365	31.2	Ebenezer Elmer	9	R	Bridgetown	Cumberland
Somerset	12,815	1,863	14.5	307	41.7	William Helmes	9	R	Hacketts-town	Sussex
Sussex	22,534	514	2.3	889	25.3					
TOTALS	211,149	12,422	6.0	7,474	28.3	John Lambert	9	R	Lamberts-ville	Hunterdon
						James Sloan	9	R	Newtontown	Gloucester
						Henry Southard	9	R	Basking Ridge	Somerset
						Ezra Darby[†]	10	R	Scotch Plains	Essex
						Adam Boyd (Replaced Darby)	10	R	Hackensack	Bergen
						William Helmes	10	R	Hacketts-town	Sussex
						John Lambert	10	R	Lamberts-ville	Hunterdon
						Thomas Newbold	10	R	Springfield	Burlington
						James Sloan	10	R	Newtontown	Gloucester
						Henry Southard	10	R	Basking Ridge	Somerset
						Adam Boyd	11	R	Hackensack	Bergen
						James Cox[†]	11	R	Monmouth	Monmouth
						John A. Scudder (Replaced Cox)	11	R	Monmouth	Monmouth
						William Helmes	11	R	Hacketts-town	Sussex
						Jacob Hufty	11	R	Salem	Salem
						Thomas Newbold	11	R	Springfield	Burlington
						Henry Southard	11	R	Basking Ridge	Somerset

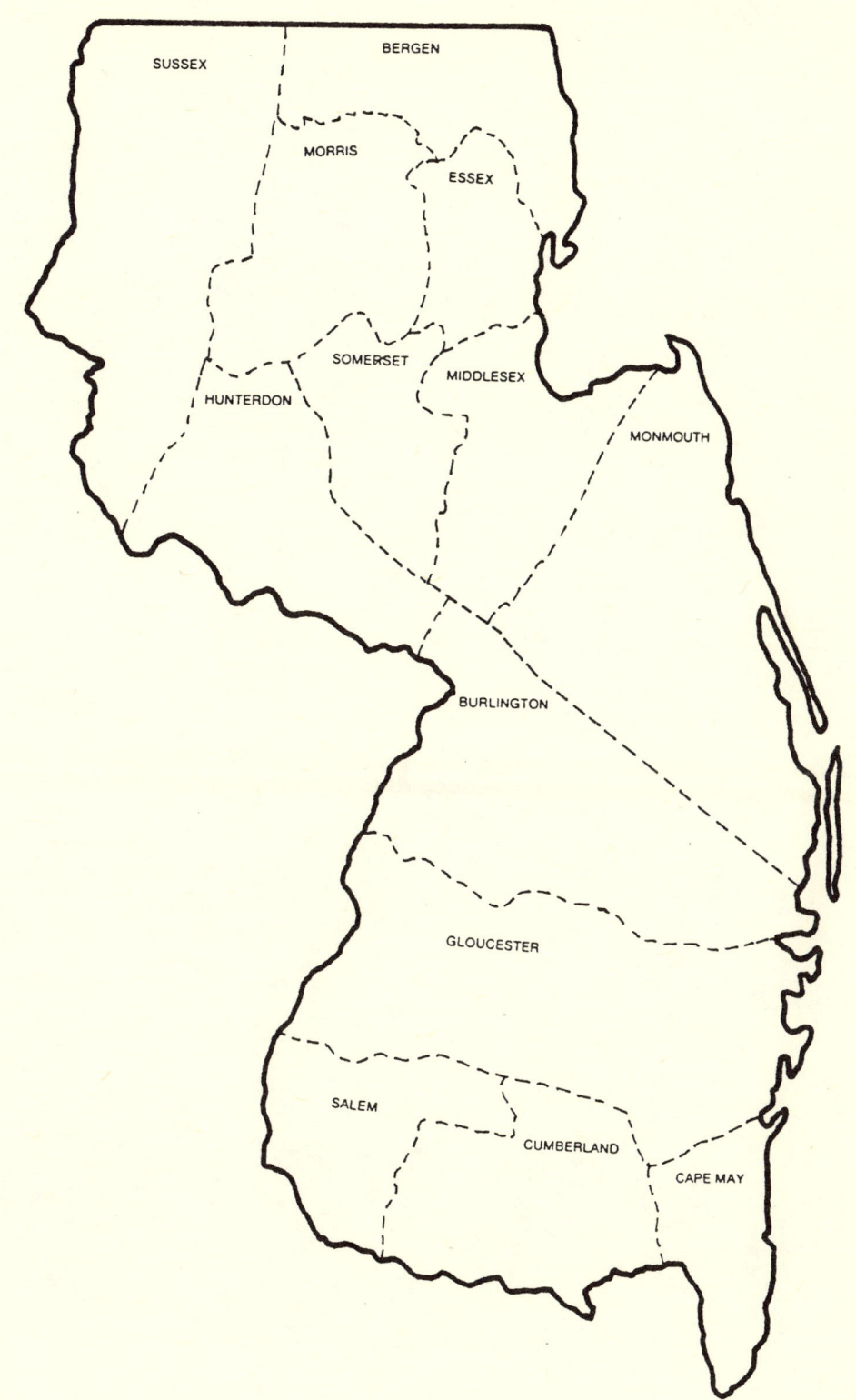

COUNTIES						REPRESENTATIVES				
County	Aggregate	Slave	%S	sq.mi.	P/sq.mi.	Representative	Cong.	Pty.	Address	County
						Adam Boyd	12	R	Hackensack	Bergen
						Lewis Condict	12	R	Morristown	Morris
						Jacob Hufty	12	R	Salem	Salem
						George C. Maxwell	12	R	Raritan	Middlesex
						James Morgan	12	F	South Amboy	Middlesex
						Thomas Newbold	12	R	Springfield	Burlington

COUNTIES						REPRESENTATIVES				
County	Aggregate	Slave	%S	sq.mi.	P/sq.mi.	Representative	Cong.	Pty.	Address	County
DISTRICT 1										
Queens	16,893	1,528	9.0	108	156.4	John Smith[r]	8[1]	R	Mastigo	Suffolk
Suffolk	19,464	886	4.5	929	20.9	(Resigned February 23, 1804)				
TOTALS	36,357	2,414	6.6	1,037	35.0	Samuel Riker	8	(----)	Newtown	Suffolk
						(Replaced Smith)				
DISTRICT 2										
Kings	27,428	1,259	4.5	70	391.8	Joshua Sands	8	(----)	Brooklyn	Kings
First, Second, Third, and Fifth Wards of New York City,										
totals:	23,005	1,613	7.0	828	2875.6					
Richmond	4,563	675	14.7	58	78.7					
TOTALS	54,996	3,547	6.4	136	404.4					
DISTRICT 3										
Fourth, Sixth, and Seventh Wards of New York City,						Samuel L. Mitchell[r]	8	R	City of New York	
totals:	37,484	1,255	3.3	48	780.9	(Resigned November 22, 1804)				
						George Clinton, Jr.	8	R	City of New York	
						(Replaced Mitchell)				
DISTRICT 4										
Rockland	6,353	551	8.6	176	36.0	Philip Van Cortland	8	F	Croton	Westchester
Westchester	27,428	1,259	4.5	443	61.9					
TOTALS	33,781	1,810	5.3	619	54.6					
DISTRICT 5										
Orange	29,355	1,145	3.9	833	35.2	Andrew McCord	8	(----)	Stoney Ford	Orange
DISTRICT 6										
Dutchess	47,775	1,609	3.3	1,044	45.7	Isaac Bloom[†]	8	(----)	Clinton	Dutchess
						(Died April 26, 1803)				
						Daniel C. Verplanck	8	F	Fishkill	Dutchess
						(Replaced Bloom)				

COUNTIES						REPRESENTATIVES				
County	Aggregate	Slave	%S	sq.mi.	P/sq.mi.	Representative	Cong.	Pty.	Address	County
DISTRICT 7										
Greene	12,584	520	4.1	653	19.2	Josiah Hasbrouck	8	(----)	New Paltz	Ulster
Ulster	24,855	2,257	9.0	1,141	21.7					
TOTALS	37,439	2,777	7.4	1,793	20.8					

County	Aggregate	Slave	%S	sq.mi.	P/sq.mi.	Representative	Cong.	Pty.	Address	County
COUNTIES						REPRESENTATIVES				
DISTRICT 8										
Columbia	35,322	1,471	4.1	645	54.7	Henry Livingston	8	(----)	Linlithgo	Columbia
DISTRICT 9										
Albany	34,043	1,808	5.3	733	46.4	Killian K.				
City of Albany[a]						Van Rensselaer	8	F	Albany	Albany

[a]Included in Albany County statistics.

County	Aggregate	Slave	%S	sq.mi.	P/sq.mi.	Representative	Cong.	Pty.	Address	County
DISTRICT 10										
Rensselaer	30,442	890	2.9	665	45.7	George Tibbits	8	F	Troy	Rensselaer
DISTRICT 11										
Clinton	8,514	58	0.7	1,823	4.6	Beriah Palmer	8	(----)	Ballston Spa	Saratoga
Essex[a]										
Saratoga	24,483	358	1.4	818	29.9					
TOTALS	32,997	416	1.2	2,641	12.5					

[a]Included in Clinton County statistics.

County	Aggregate	Slave	%S	sq.mi.	P/sq.mi.	Representative	Cong.	Pty.	Address	County
DISTRICT 12										
Washington	35,574	80	0.2	1,723	20.6	David Thomas	8	R	Salem	Washington
DISTRICT 13										
Montgomery	21,700	466	2.1	2,641	8.2	Thomas Sammons	8	R	Johnstown	Montgomery
Schoharie	9,808	354	3.6	624	15.7					
TOTALS	31,508	820	2.6	3,265	9.6					
DISTRICT 14										
Delaware	10,228	16	0.15	1,443	14.9	Erastus Root	8	R	Delhi	Delaware
Otsego	21,636	48	0.2	1,013	21.3					
TOTALS	31,864	64	0.2	2,456	12.9					
DISTRICT 15										
Herkimer	14,479	61	0.4	4,020	3.5	Gaylord Griswold	8	F	----	Herkimer
Oneida	22,047	50	0.2	2,187	4.6					
St. Lawrence[a]	----	----	----	2,768	----					
TOTALS	36,526	111	0.3	8,975	4.0					

[a]Created after 1800 census.

County	Aggregate	Slave	%S	sq.mi.	P/sq.mi.	Representative	Cong.	Pty.	Address	County
DISTRICT 16										
Chenango	15,666	16	0.1	1,564	10.0	John Patterson	8	(----)	Lisle	Tioga
Onondaga	7,406	11	0.1	1,295	5.7					
Tioga	6,889	17	0.2	1,653	4.1					
TOTALS	29,961	44	0.1	4,512	6.6					

County	Aggregate	Slave	%S	sq.mi.	P/sq.mi.	Representative	Cong.	Pty.	Address	County
COUNTIES						REPRESENTATIVES				
DISTRICT 17										
Cayuga	15,871	53	0.3	1,940	8.1	Oliver Phelps	8	R	Canandaigua	Ontario
Ontario	15,218	57	0.5	9,244	1.6					
Steuben	1,788	22	1.2	1,510	1.1					
TOTALS	32,877	132	0.4	12,694	2.5					

[1]Congressmen for the Ninth through Twelfth Congresses are given in the apportionments of 1804 and 1808.

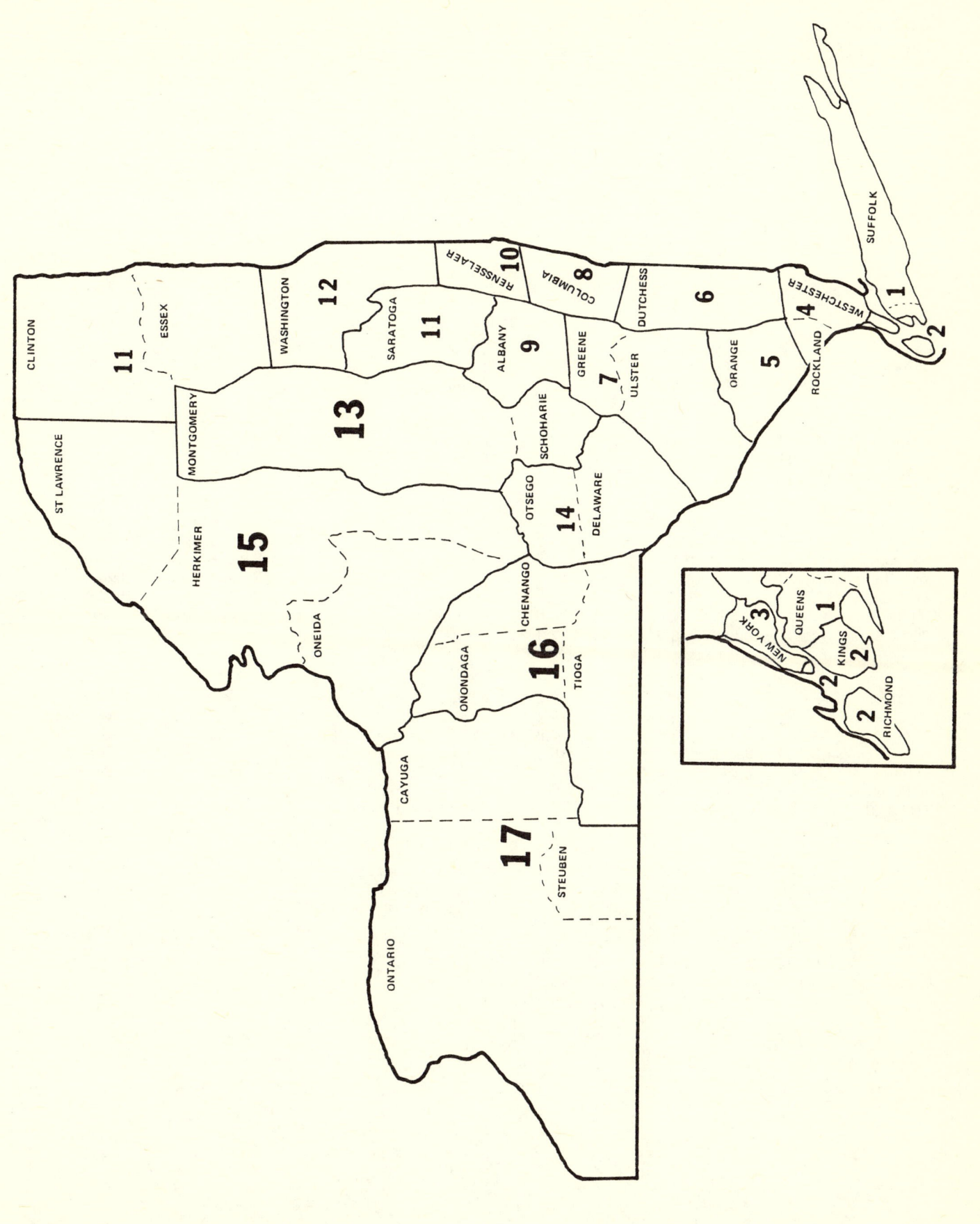

COUNTIES						REPRESENTATIVES				
County	Aggregate	Slave	%S	sq.mi.	P/sq.mi.	Representative	Cong.	Pty.	Address	County
DISTRICT 1										
Camden	4,191	1,170	27.9	239	12.5	Thomas Wynns	8	F	Winton	Hertford
Chowan	3,830	1,760	45.9	173	22.1	Thomas Wynns	9	F	Winton	Hertford
Currituck	6,928	1,530	22.0	246	28.2	Lemuel Sawyer	10	R	Elizabeth City	Pasquotank
Gates	5,881	2,688	45.7	337	17.5					
Hertford	6,701	2,864	4.0	353	19.0	Lemuel Sawyer	11	R	Elizabeth City	Pasquotank
Pasquotank	5,037	1,593	31.6	228	22.1					
Perquimans	5,609	1,980	35.3	246	22.8	Lemuel Sawyer	12	R	Elizabeth City	Pasquotank
TOTALS	38,177	13,585	35.6	1,822	21.0					
DISTRICT 2										
Bertie	10,998	5,387	48.9	698	15.8	Willis Alston	8	R	Littleton	Halifax
Halifax	13,563	7,020	51.7	734	18.5	Willis Alston	9	R	Littleton	Halifax
Martin	5,312	1,646	30.9	455	11.7	Willis Alston	10	R	Littleton	Halifax
North-						Willis Alston	11	R	Littleton	Halifax
ampton	12,331	6,206	50.3	536	23.0	Willis Alston	12	R	Littleton	Halifax
TOTALS	42,204	20,259	48.0	2,423	17.4					
DISTRICT 3										
Beaufort	5,441	1,674	30.7	826	6.6	William Kennedy	8	F	Washington	Beaufort
Edgecombe	9,898	3,580	36.1	510	19.4	Thomas Blount	9	R	Tarboro	Edgecombe
Hyde	4,783	1,386	28.9	613	7.8	Thomas Blount	10	R	Tarboro	Edgecombe
Pitt	8,910	2,792	31.3	655	13.6	William Kennedy	11	F	Washington	Beaufort
Tyrell	3,363	849	25.2	781	4.3	Thomas Blount†	12	R	Tarboro	Edgecombe
Washington	2,165	305	14.0	343	6.3	William Kennedy	12	F	Washington	Beaufort
TOTALS	34,560	10,586	30.6	3,728	9.3	(Replaced Blount)				
DISTRICT 4										
Cataret	3,962	796	20.0	536	7.4	William Blackledge	8	R	Spring Hill	Craven
Craven	7,778	2,863	36.8	1,037	7.5	William Blackledge	9	R	Spring Hill	Craven
Green	4,218	1,496	35.4	267	15.8	William Blackledge	10	R	Spring Hill	Craven
Lenoir	3,898	1,457	37.3	400	9.7	John Stanley	11	R	New Bern	Craven
Jones	4,241	1,899	44.7	467	9.1	William Blackledge	12	R	Spring Hill	Craven
Johnston	6,301	1,763	27.9	797	7.9					
Wayne	6,772	1,988	29.3	557	12.2					
TOTALS	37,170	12,262	32.9	4,061	9.2					

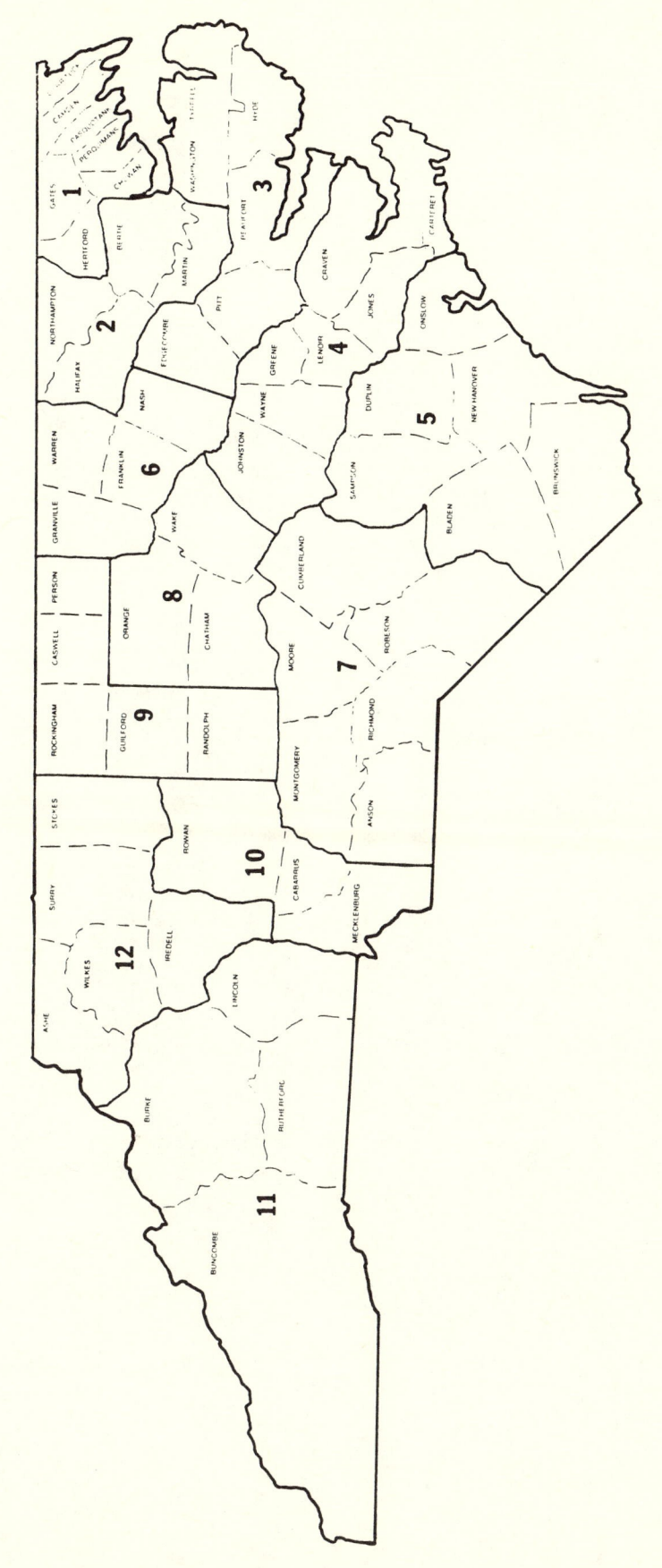

COUNTIES						REPRESENTATIVES				
County	Aggregate	Slave	%S	sq.mi.	P/sq.mi.	Representative	Cong.	Pty.	Address	County

DISTRICT 5

County	Aggregate	Slave	%S	sq.mi.	P/sq.mi.	Representative	Cong.	Pty.	Address	County
Bladen	6,963	2,278	32.7	1,828	3.8	James Gillespie	8	R	Kenansville	Duplin
Brunswick	4,110	1,614	39.2	856	4.8	James Gillespie†	9	R	Kenansville	Duplin
Duplin	6,796	1,864	27.4	815	8.3	(Died January, 1805)				
New Hanover	5,371	2,933	54.6	1,056	5.1	Thomas Kenan	9	R	Kenansville	Duplin
Onslow	5,474	1,757	32.0	765	7.2	(Replaced Gillespie)				
Sampson	6,719	1.712	25.4	945.	7.1	Thomas Kenan	10	R	Kenansville	Duplin
TOTALS	35,433	12,157	34.3	6,256	5.7	Thomas Kenan	11	R	Kenansville	Duplin
						William R. King	12	R	Wilmington	New Hanover

DISTRICT 6

County	Aggregate	Slave	%S	sq.mi.	P/sq.mi.	Representative	Cong.	Pty.	Address	County
Franklin	8,473	3,667	43.2	491	17.3	Nathaniel Macon	8	R	Warrenton	Warren
Granville	14,015	6,106	43.5	686	20.4	Nathaniel Macon	9	R	Warrenton	Warren
Nash	6,975	2,596	37.2	544	12.8	Nathaniel Macon	10	R	Warrenton	Warren
Warren	11,046	5,905	53.4	524	21.1	Nathaniel Macon	11	R	Warrenton	Warren
TOTALS	40,509	18,274	45.1	2,245	18.0	Nathaniel Macon	12	R	Warrenton	Warren

DISTRICT 7

County	Aggregate	Slave	%S	sq.mi.	P/sq.mi.	Representative	Cong.	Pty.	Address	County
Anson	8,146	1,290	15.0	633e	12.9	Samuel Purviance	8	F	Fayetteville	Cumberland
Cumberland	7,608	2,097	27.5	1,093e	6.9	Duncan McFarland	9	R	Laurel Hill	Richmond
Montgomery	7,677	1,373	17.8	761	10.1	John Culpepper	10	F	Allenton	----
Moore	4,767	608	12.7	704	6.8	Archibald McBride	11	R	Carthage	Moore
Richmond	5,623	875	15.5	794	7.1	Archibald McBride	12	R	Carthage	Moore
Robeson	6,666	960	14.4	900e	7.4					
TOTALS	40,487	7,203	17.7	4,885e	8.2					

DISTRICT 8

County	Aggregate	Slave	%S	sq.mi.	P/sq.mi.	Representative	Cong.	Pty.	Address	County
Chatham	11,645	2,708	23.2	709	16.4	Richard Stanford	8	R	Hawsfield	Chatham
Orange	15,657	3,327	21.2	1,123	13.9	Richard Stanford	9	R	Hawsfield	Chatham
Wake	12,768	3,906	30.5	858	14.9	Richard Stanford	10	R	Hawsfield	Chatham
TOTALS	40,070	9,941	24.8	2,690	14.9	Richard Stanford	11	R	Hawsfield	Chatham
						Richard Stanford	12	R	Hawsfield	Chatham

DISTRICT 9

County	Aggregate	Slave	%S	sq.mi.	P/sq.mi.	Representative	Cong.	Pty.	Address	County
Caswell	8,701	2,788	32.0	428e	20.3	Marmaduke Williams	8	R	----	Caswell
Guilford	9,442	905	9.5	655	14.4	Marmaduke Williams	9	R	----	Caswell
Person	6,402	2,082	32.5	401	15.9	Marmaduke Williams	10	R	----	Caswell
Randolph	9,234	607	6.5	798	11.6	James Cochran	11	R	Roxboro	Person
Rockingham	8,277	1,633	19.7	569	14.5	James Cochran	12	R	Roxboro	Person
TOTALS	42,056	8,015	19.1	2,851	14.8					

DISTRICT 10

County	Aggregate	Slave	%S	sq.mi.	P/sq.mi.	Representative	Cong.	Pty.	Address	County
Cabarus	5,061	695	13.7	363	14.0	Nathaniel Alexander	8	R	Charlotte	Mecklenburg
Mecklenburg	10,317	1,931	18.7	530	19.5	Nathaniel Alexander	9	R	Charlotte	Mecklenburg
Rowan	19,415	2,532	13.0	1,337	14.5	Evans S. Alexander	9	R	Salisbury	Rowan
TOTALS	34,793	5,158	14.8	2,230	15.6	Evans S. Alexander	10	R	Salisbury	Rowan
						Joseph Person	11	F	Salisbury	Rowan
						Joseph Person	12	F	Salisbury	Rowan

County	Aggregate	Slave	%S	sq.mi.	P/sq.mi.	Representative	Cong.	Pty.	Address	County
COUNTIES						REPRESENTATIVES				

DISTRICT 11

County	Aggregate	Slave	%S	sq.mi.	P/sq.mi.	Representative	Cong.	Pty.	Address	County
Buncomb	5,774	334	6.4	489	11.8	James Holland	8	R	Rutherford	Rutherford
Burke	9,799	776	7.9	511	19.2	James Holland	9	R	Rutherford	Rutherford
Lincoln	12,568	1,479	11.7	297	42.3	James Holland	10	R	Rutherford	Rutherford
Rutherford	10,696	1,047	9.7	563	18.99	James Holland	11	R	Rutherford	Rutherford
TOTALS	38,837	3,636	9.3	1,860	20.9	Israel Pickens	12	R	Morgantown	Burke

DISTRICT 12

County	Aggregate	Slave	%S	sq.mi.	P/sq.mi.	Representative	Cong.	Pty.	Address	County
Ashe	2,783	85	3.0	651	4.3	Joseph Winston	8	R	Germantown	Stokes
Iredell	8,761	1,481	16.9	572	15.3	Joseph Winston	9	R	Germantown	Stokes
Stokes	10,516	1,359	12.9	876e	12.0	Meshack Franklin	10	R	----	Surrey
Surrey	9,405	962	10.2	872e	10.8	Meshack Franklin	11	R	----	Surrey
Wilkes	7,247	790	10.9	757	9.6	Meshack Franklin	12	R	----	Surrey
TOTALS	38,712	4,677	12.0	3,728e	10.4					

COUNTIES						REPRESENTATIVES				
County	Aggregate	Slave	%S	sq.mi.	P/sq.mi.	Representative	Cong.	Pty.	Address	County

OHIO

There is no mention of Ohio in the census of 1800, except for an overall population figure, given below:

State of Ohio, total: 6,407 ---- ---- ---- ----

Representative	Cong.	Pty.	Address	County
Jeremiah Morrow	8	R	Twenty-Mile Stand	Warren
Jeremiah Morrow	9	R	Twenty-Mile Stand	Warren
Jeremiah Morrow	10	R	Twenty-Mile Stand	Warren
Jeremiah Morrow	11	R	Twenty-Mile Stand	Warren
Jeremiah Morrow	12	R	Twenty-Mile Stand	Warren

[1] Ohio became a state on March 1, 1803.

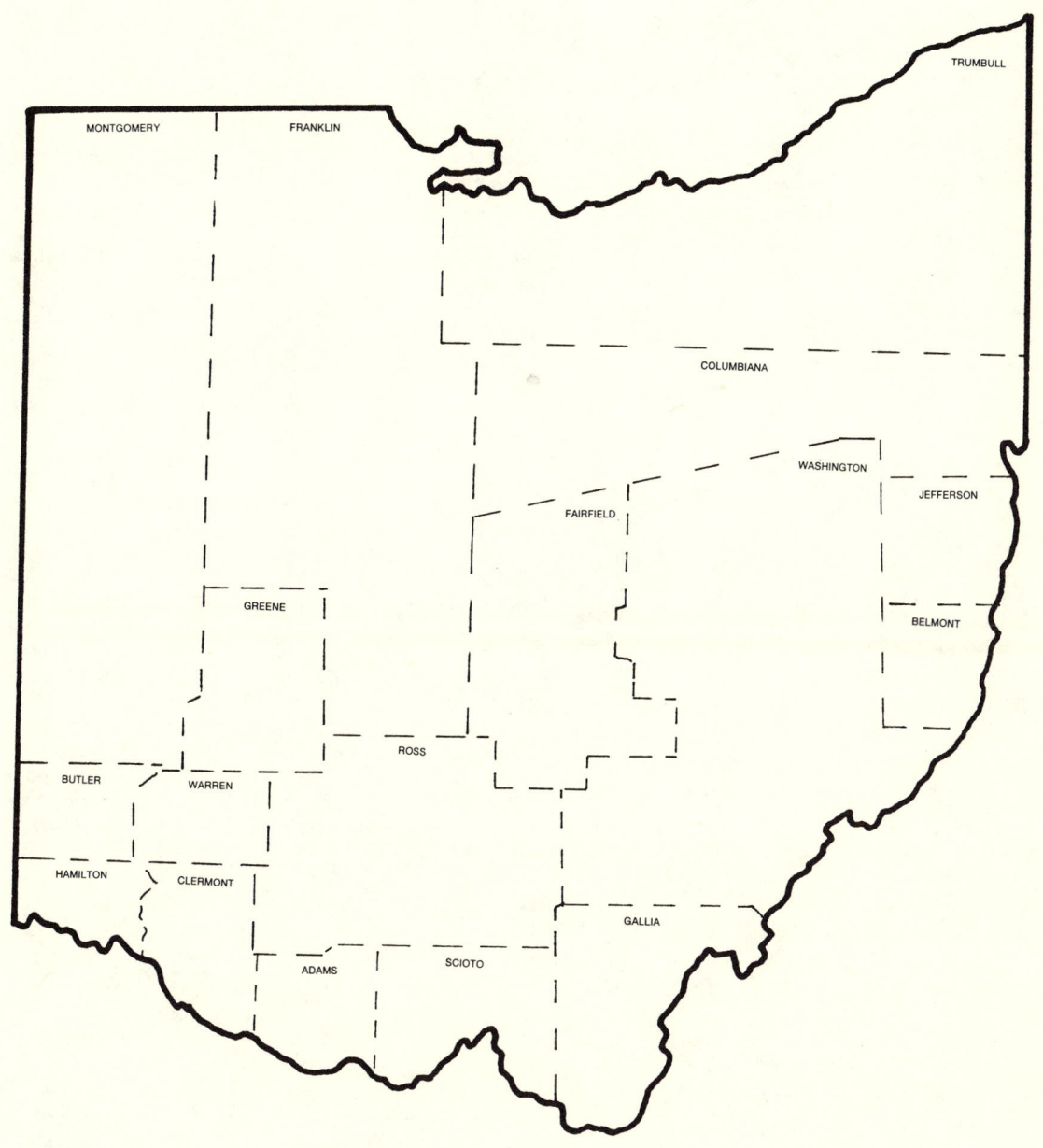

	COUNTIES					REPRESENTATIVES				
County	Aggregate	Slave	%S	sq.mi.	P/sq.mi.	Representative	Cong.	Pty.	Address	County

DISTRICT 1 [a]

County	Aggregate	Slave	%S	sq.mi.	P/sq.mi.	Representative	Cong.	Pty.	Address	County
Delaware	12,809	7	0.05	184	69.6	Joseph Clay	8	F	City of Philadelphia	
Philadelphia	89,789	30	0.03	100	897.0	Michael Leib	8	R	City of Philadelphia	
City of						Jacob Richards	8	R	Chester	Delaware
Philadelphia	41,220	55	0.1	29	1421.0					
TOTALS	143,818	92	0.06	313	459.4	Joseph Clay	9	F	City of Philadelphia	
						Michael Leib[r]	9	R	City of Philadelphia	
						John Porter	9	(----)	City of Philadelphia	
						(Replaced Leib)				
						Jacob Richards	9	R	Chester	Delaware
						Joseph Clay[r]	10	F	City of Philadelphia	
						Benjamin Say	10	(----)	City of Philadelphia	
						(Replaced Clay)				
						William Milnor	10	F	City of Philadelphia	
						John Porter	10	(----)	City of Philadelphia	
						Jacob Richards	10	R	Chester	Delaware
						William Anderson	11	R	Chester	Delaware
						William Milnor	11	F	City of Philadelphia	
						John Porter	11	(----)	City of Philadelphia	
						Benjamin Say[r]	11	(----)	City of Philadelphia	
						Adam Seybert	11	R	City of Philadelphia	
						(Replaced Say)				
						William Anderson	12	R	Chester	Delaware
						William Milnor	12	F	City of Philadelphia	
						Adam Seybert	12	R	City of Philadelphia	

[a]District 1 has one too many representatives for the 10th and 11th Congresses, while District 3 lacks one representative for each of those Congresses. We were unable to account for this situation, although J. Richards and W. Anderson may have represented District 3.

DISTRICT 2

County	Aggregate	Slave	%S	sq.mi.	P/sq.mi.	Representative	Cong.	Pty.	Address	County
Bucks	27,496	59	0.2	614	44.7	Robert Brown	8	R	Weaversville	Northampton
Luzerne	12,839	18	0.1	2,571	4.9	Frederick Conrad	8	F	Worcester	Montgomery
Montgomery	24,150	33	0.1	496	48.6				Township	
North-						Isaac Van Horne	8	R	Tollbury	Bucks
ampton	30,062	8	0.02	1,478	20.3				Township	
Wayne	2,562	1	0.03	1,544	1.6	Robert Brown	9	R	Weaversville	Northampton
TOTALS	97,109	119	0.1	6,703	14.4	Frederick Conrad	9	F	Worcester	Montgomery
									Township	
						John Pugh	9	R	Doylestown	Bucks
						Robert Brown	10	R	Weaversville	Northampton
						John Pugh	10	R	Doylestown	Bucks
						Matthias Richards	10	(----)	Pottstown	Montgomery

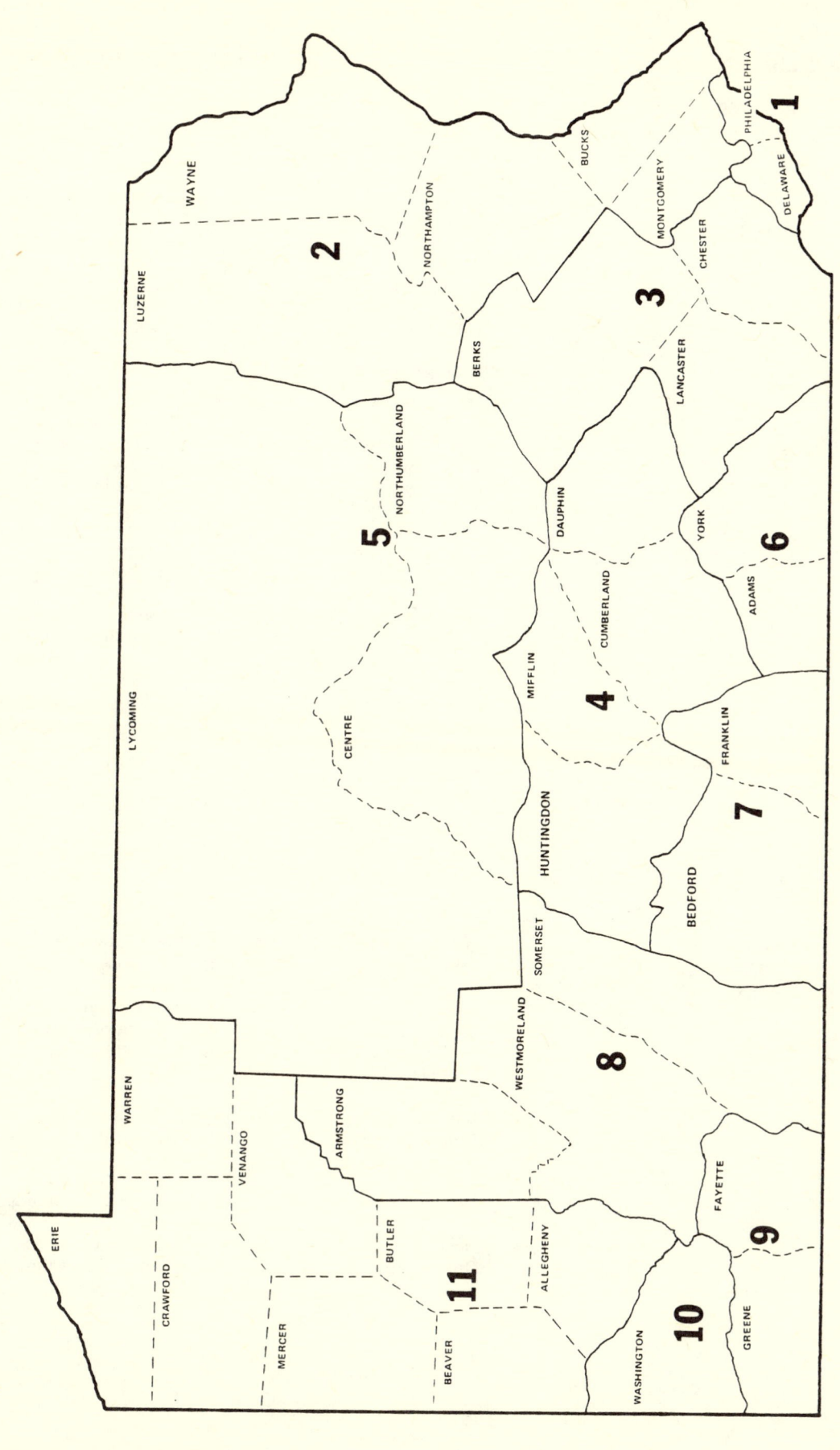

COUNTIES						REPRESENTATIVES				
County	Aggregate	Slave	%S	sq.mi.	P/sq.mi.	Representative	Cong.	Pty.	Address	County

DISTRICT 2 (CONTINUED)

						Robert Brown	11	R	Weaversville	Northampton
						Matthias Richards	11	(----)	Franklin	Montgomery
						John Ross	11	(----)	Easton	Northampton
						Robert Brown	12	R	Weaversville	Northampton
						Jonathan Roberts	12	R	Norristown	Montgomery
						William Rodman	12	R	Bristol	Bucks

DISTRICT 3[a]

County	Aggregate	Slave	%S	sq.mi.	P/sq.mi.	Representative	Cong.	Pty.	Address	County
Berks	32,407	19	0.05	1,646	19.6	Isaac Anderson	8	R	Charlestown Township	Chester
Chester	32,093	46	0.1	761	42.1					
Lancaster	43,403	178	0.4	946	45.8	Joseph Hiester	8	F	Reading	Berks
TOTALS	107,903	243	0.2	3,353	32.1	John Whitehill	8	(----)	Salisbury Township	Lancaster
						Isaac Anderson	9	R	Charlestown Township	Chester
						Christian Lower[†] (Died; not replaced)	9	(----)	Tulpehocken Township	Berks
						John Whitehill	9	(----)	Salisbury Township	Lancaster
						John Hiester	10	(----)	Parker Ford	Berks
						Robert Jenkins	10	(----)	Churchtown	Lancaster
						Daniel Hiester	11	(----)	Westchester	Chester
						Robert Jenkins	11	(----)	Churchtown	Lancaster
						Rober Davis	12	D	Charlestown	Chester
						John M. Hyneman	12	D	Reading	Berks
						Joseph Lefever	12	D	Paradise	Lancaster

[a]See note to District 1.

DISTRICT 4

County	Aggregate	Slave	%S	sq.mi.	P/sq.mi.	Representative	Cong.	Pty.	Address	County
Blair (Created from Huntingdon)						David Bard	8	R	Frankstown	Blair
Cumberland	25,386	228	0.9	1,106	22.9	John A. Hanna	8	R	Harrisburg	Dauphin
Dauphin	22,270	93	0.4	881	25.2					
Huntingdon	13,008	32	0.2	1,425	9.1	David Bard	9	R	Frankstown	Blair
Mifflin[a]	13,609	23	0.2	817	16.6	John A. Hanna[†]	9	R	Harrisburg	Dauphin
TOTALS	74,273	376	0.5	4,229	17.5	Robert Whitehill (Replaced Hanna)	9	R	Camp Hill	Cumberland
						David Bard	10	R	Frankstown	Blair
						Robert Whitehill	10	R	Camp Hill	Cumberland
						David Bard	11	R	Frankstown	Blair
						Robert Whitehill	11	R	Camp Hill	Cumberland
						David Bard	12	R	Frankstown	Blair
						Robert Whitehill	12	R	Camp Hill	Cumberland

[a]Entered as one with Centre County in District 5.

118

| COUNTIES | | | | | | REPRESENTATIVES | | | | |
County	Aggregate	Slave	%S	sq.mi.	P/sq.mi.	Representative	Cong.	Pty.	Address	County

DISTRICT 5

County	Aggregate	Slave	%S	sq.mi.	P/sq.mi.	Representative	Cong.	Pty.	Address	County
Centre[a]	13,609	23	0.2	1,914	7.1	Andrew Gregg	8	R	Bellefonte	Centre
Lycoming	5,414	39	0.7	9,327	0.58	Andrew Gregg	9	R	Bellefonte	Centre
Montour (Created from Northumberland)						Daniel Montgomery	10	R	Danville	Montour
Northum-						George Smith	11	R	----	----
berland	21,098	19	0.09	1,067	19.7	George Smith	12	R	----	----
TOTALS	40,121	81	0.2	12,308	3.2					

[a]Entered as one with Mifflin County in District 4.

DISTRICT 6

County	Aggregate	Slave	%S	sq.mi.	P/sq.mi.	Representative	Cong.	Pty.	Address	County
Adams	13,172	114	0.9	526	25.0	John Stewart	8	D	York	York
York	25,643	77	0.3	909	28.2	James Kelly	9	(----)	----	York
TOTALS	38,815	191	0.5	1,435	27.0	James Kelly	10	(----)	----	York
						William Crawford	11	R	Gettysburg	Adams
						William Crawford	12	R	Gettysburg	Adams

DISTRICT 7

County	Aggregate	Slave	%S	sq.mi.	P/sq.mi.	Representative	Cong.	Pty.	Address	County
Bedford	12,039	5	0.04	1,453	8.2	John Rea	8	R	Chambers-burg	Franklin
Franklin	19,638	181	0.9	754	26.0					
TOTALS	31,677	186	0.6	2,207	14.3	John Rea	9	R	Chambers-burg	Franklin
						John Rea	10	R	Chambers-burg	Franklin
						John Rea	11	R	Chambers-burg	Franklin
						William Piper	12	R	Bloody Run	Bedford

DISTRICT 8

County	Aggregate	Slave	%S	sq.mi.	P/sq.mi.	Representative	Cong.	Pty.	Address	County
Armstrong	2,399	1	0.04	1,249	1.9	William Findley	8	R	Youngstown	Westmoreland
Somerset	10,188	0	0.0	1,770	5.7	William Findley	9	R	Youngstown	Westmoreland
West-						William Findley	10	R	Youngstown	Westmoreland
moreland	22,726	136	0.6	1,849	12.1	William Findley	11	R	Youngstown	Westmoreland
TOTALS	35,313	137	0.4	4,868	7.2	William Findley	12	R	Youngstown	Westmoreland

DISTRICT 9

County	Aggregate	Slave	%S	sq.mi.	P/sq.mi.	Representative	Cong.	Pty.	Address	County
Fayette	20,159	92	0.5	802	25.1	John Smilie	8	R	Fayette	Fayette
Greene	8,605	22	0.3	578	14.8	John Smilie	9	R	Fayette	Fayette
TOTALS	28,764	114	0.4	1,380	20.8	John Smilie	10	R	Fayette	Fayette
						John Smilie	11	R	Fayette	Fayette
						John Smilie	12	R	Fayette	Fayette

DISTRICT 10

County	Aggregate	Slave	%S	sq.mi.	P/sq.mi.	Representative	Cong.	Pty.	Address	County
Washington	28,298	84	0.3	857	33.0	William Hoge[r]	8	F	Washington	Washington
						John Hoge	8	R	----	Washington
						(Replaced William Hoge)				
						John Hamilton	9	F	Washington	Washington
						William Hoge	10	F	Washington	Washington
						Aaron Lyle	11	R	West Middletown	Washington
						Aaron Lyle	12	R	West Middletown	Washington

	COUNTIES					REPRESENTATIVES				
County	Aggregate	Slave	%S	sq.mi.	P/sq.mi.	Representative	Cong.	Pty.	Address	County

DISTRICT 11

	COUNTIES					REPRESENTATIVES				
Allegheny	15,087	79	0.5	728	2.0	John B. C. Lucas	8	R	Pittsburgh	Allegheny
Beaver	5,776	4	0.06	807	7.1	John B. C. Lucas[r]	9	R	Pittsburgh	Allegheny
Butler	3,916	1	0.02	794	4.9	Samuel Smith	9	F	Erie	Erie
Crawford	2,346	5	0.2	1,012	2.3	(Replaced Lucas)				
Erie	1,468	2	0.1	813	1.8	Samuel Smith	10	F	Erie	Erie
Mercer	3,228	5	0.2	670	4.8	Samuel Smith	11	F	Erie	Erie
Venango	1,130	0	0.0	878	1.2	Abner Lacock	12	R	Beavertown	Allegheny or
Warren	233	0	0.0	905	0.25					Beaver
TOTALS	33,184	96	0.3	6,607	5.0					

RHODE ISLAND
2 CONGRESSMEN AT LARGE

	COUNTIES					REPRESENTATIVES				
County	Aggregate	Slave	%S	sq.mi.	P/sq.mi.	Representative	Cong.	Pty.	Address	County

AT LARGE

	COUNTIES					REPRESENTATIVES				
Bristol	3,801	46	1.2	25	152.0	Nehemiah Knight	8	R	Cranston	Providence
Kent	8,487	20	0.2	173	49.1	Joseph Stanton, Jr.	8	R	Charlestown	Washington
Newport	14,845	185	1.2	115	129.1					
Providence	25,854	5	0.02	416	62.1	Nehemiah Knight	9	R	Cranston	Providence
Washington	16,135	124	0.8	321	50.3	Joseph Stanton, Jr.	9	R	Charlestown	Washington
TOTALS	69,122	380	0.5	1,050	65.8					
						Nehemiah Knight[†] (Died June, 1808)	10	R	Cranston	Providence
						Richard Jackson, Jr. (Replaced Knight December, 1808)	10	F	Providence	Providence
						Isaac Wilbour	10	F	Little Compton	Newport
						Richard Jackson, Jr.	11	F	Providence	Providence
						Elisha R. Potter	11	F	Kingston	Washington
						Richard Jackson, Jr.	12	F	Providence	Providence
						Elisha R. Potter	12	F	Kingston	Washington

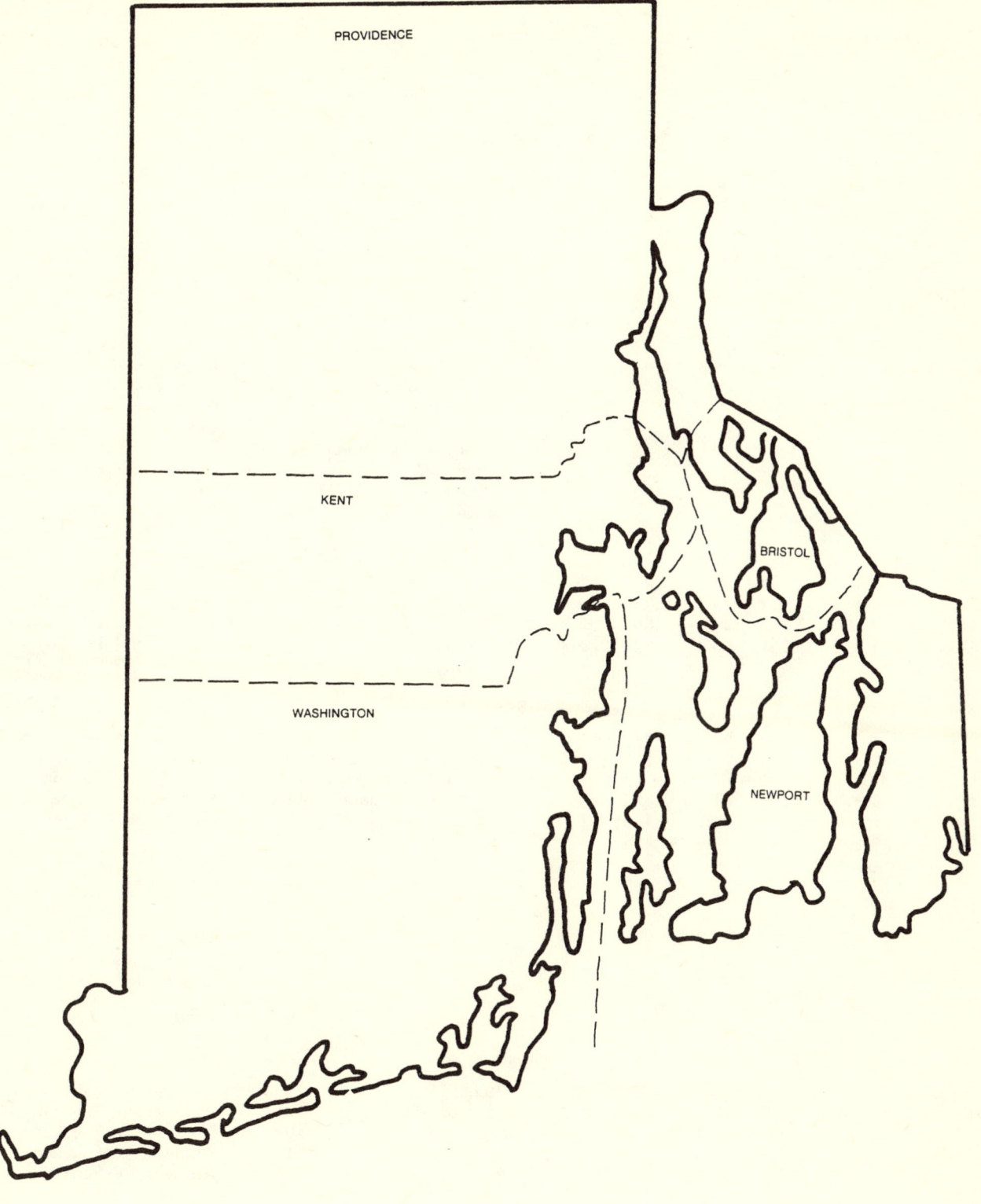

PROVIDENCE

KENT

WASHINGTON

BRISTOL

NEWPORT

	COUNTIES						REPRESENTATIVES				
County	Aggregate	Slave	%S	sq.mi.	P/sq.mi.	Representative	Cong.	Pty.	Address	County

DISTRICT 1

County	Aggregate	Slave	%S	sq.mi.	P/sq.mi.	Representative	Cong.	Pty.	Address	County
Charleston	57,480	41,945	72.9	2,049	28.0	Thomas Lowrdes	8	F	Charleston	Charleston
						Robert Marion	9	(----)	Charleston	Charleston
						Robert Marion	10	(----)	Charleston	Charleston
						Robert Marion[r]	11	(----)	Charleston	Charleston
						(Resigned December 4, 1810)				
						Langdon Cheves	11	R	Charleston	Charleston
						(Replaced Marion January, 1811)				
						Langdon Cheves	12	R	Charleston	Charleston

DISTRICT 2

County	Aggregate	Slave	%S	sq.mi.	P/sq.mi.	Representative	Cong.	Pty.	Address	County
Barnwell	6,406	1,690	26.3	1,927	3.3	William Butler	8	R	Saluda	Edgefield
Beaufort	20,428	16,031	78.5	1,793	11.3	William Butler	9	R	Saluda	Edgefield
Edgefield	18,130	5,006	27.6	1,602	11.3	William Butler	10	R	Saluda	Edgefield
TOTALS	44,964	22,727	50.5	5,322	8.4	William Butler	11	R	Saluda	Edgefield
						William Butler	12	R	Saluda	Edgefield

DISTRICT 3

County	Aggregate	Slave	%S	sq.mi.	P/sq.mi.	Representative	Cong.	Pty.	Address	County
Darlington[a]	5,295	2,336	44.1	849	6.2	Benjamin Huger	8	F	Georgetown	Georgetown
Georgetown	22,938	16,568	72.2	2,246	10.2	David Williams	9	R	Society Hill	Darlington
Horry (created from Georgetown County)						David Williams	10	R	Society Hill	Darlington
Marion	6,914	2,155	31.1	894	7.7	Robert Witherspoon	11	R	Mayesville	Sumter
Marlborough[a]	4,059	1,393	34.3	483	8.4	David Williams	12	R	Society Hill	Darlington
TOTALS	39,206	22,452	57.2	4,472	8.7					

[a]Part of Cheraw County in the 1800 census.

DISTRICT 4

County	Aggregate	Slave	%S	sq.mi.	P/sq.mi.	Representative	Cong.	Pty.	Address	County
Colleton	24,903	20,471	82.2	1,618	15.3	Wade Hampton	8	R	Columbia	Richland
Orangburg	15,766	5,356	33.9	2,418	6.5	O'Brien Smith	9	(----)	----	Colleton
Richland	6,097	3,033	49.7	748	8.1	John Taylor	10	R	Columbia	Richland
TOTALS	46,766	28,860	61.7	4,784	9.7	John Taylor	11	R	Columbia	Richland
						William Lowrdes	12	R	Jacksonboro	Colleton

DISTRICT 5

County	Aggregate	Slave	%S	sq.mi.	P/sq.mi.	Representative	Cong.	Pty.	Address	County
Chesterfield	5,216	1,148	22.0	790	6.6	Richard Winn	8	R	Winnesboro	Fairfield
Fairfield	10,087	1,968	19.5	696	14.4	Richard Winn	9	R	Winnesboro	Fairfield
Kershaw	7,340	2,530	34.4	781	9.3	Richard Winn	10	R	Winnesboro	Fairfield
Lancaster	6,012	1,076	17.8	502	11.9	Richard Winn	11	R	Winnesboro	Fairfield
Sumter	13,103	6,563	50.0	1,680	7.7	Richard Winn	12	R	Winnesboro	Fairfield
TOTALS	41,758	13,285	31.8	4,449	9.3					

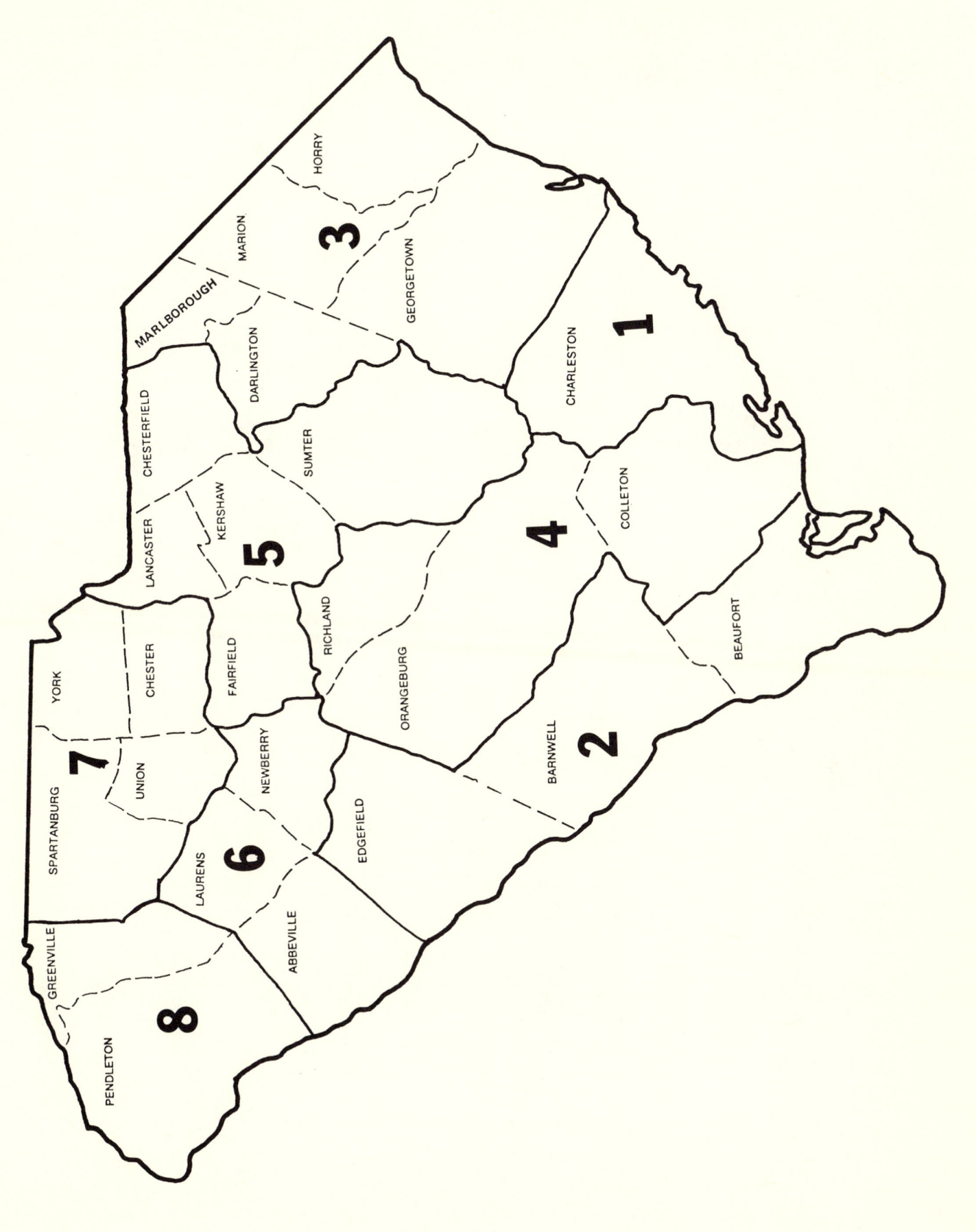

County	COUNTIES Aggregate	Slave	%S	sq.mi.	P/sq.mi.	Representative	REPRESENTATIVES Cong.	Pty.	Address	County
						DISTRICT 6				
Abbeville	13,553	2,964	21.8	976	13.8	Levi Casey	8	(----)	----	Newberry
Laurens	12,809	1,919	14.98	711	18.0	Levi Casey	9	(----)	----	Newberry
Newberry	12,006	2,204	18.3	635	18.9	Levi Casey†	10	(----)	----	Newberry
TOTALS	38,368	7.087	18.4	2,322	16.5	(Died November 3, 1807)				
						John Calhoun (Replaced Casey)	10	R	Calhoun Mills	Abbeville
						John Calhoun	11	R	Calhoun Mills	Abbeville
						John Calhoun	12	R	Calhoun Mills	Abbeville
						DISTRICT 7				
Chester	8,185	1,164	14.2	584	14.0	Thomas Moore	8	R	Prices Store	Spartanburgh
Spartan-						Thomas Moore	9	R	Prices Store	Spartanburgh
burgh	12,122	1,467	12.1	831	14.5	Thomas Moore	10	R	Prices Store	Spartanburgh
Union	10,137	1,697	16.7	514	19.7	Thomas Moore	11	R	Prices Store	Spartanburgh
York	10,248	1,804	17.6	684	14.9	Thomas Moore	12	R	Prices Store	Spartanburgh
TOTALS	40,692	6,132	15.0	2,613	15.5					
						DISTRICT 8				
Greenville	9,504	1,439	15.1	792	12.0	John B. Earle	8	(----)	----	Pendleton
Pendleton	19,374	2,224	11.4	1,895	10.2	Elias Earle	9	R	Centerville	Greenville
TOTALS	28,878	3,663	12.6	2,687	10.7	Lemuel J. Alston	10	(----)	Greenville	Greenville
						Lemuel J. Alston	11	(----)	Greenville	Greenville
						Elias Earle	12	R	Centerville	Pendleton

TENNESSEE
3 DISTRICTS
3 CONGRESSMEN

County	COUNTIES Aggregate	Slave	%S	sq.mi.	P/sq.mi.	Representative	REPRESENTATIVES Cong.	Pty.	Address	County
						DISTRICT 1 (WASHINGTON)				
Carter	4,813	208	4.3	641	7.5	John Rhea	8	R	Sullivan or Blountville	Sullivan
Greene	7,610	471	6.1	613	12.4					
Hawkins	6,563	811	12.4	710	9.2	John Rhea	9	R	Sullivan or Blountville	Sullivan
Sullivan	10,218	491	4.8	413	24.7					
Washington	6,379	533	8.3	508	12.6	John Rhea	10	R	Sullivan or Blountville	Sullivan
TOTALS	35,583	2,514	7.0	2,885	12.3					
						John Rhea	11	R	Sullivan or Blountville	Sullivan
						John Rhea	12	R	Sullivan or Blountville	Sullivan

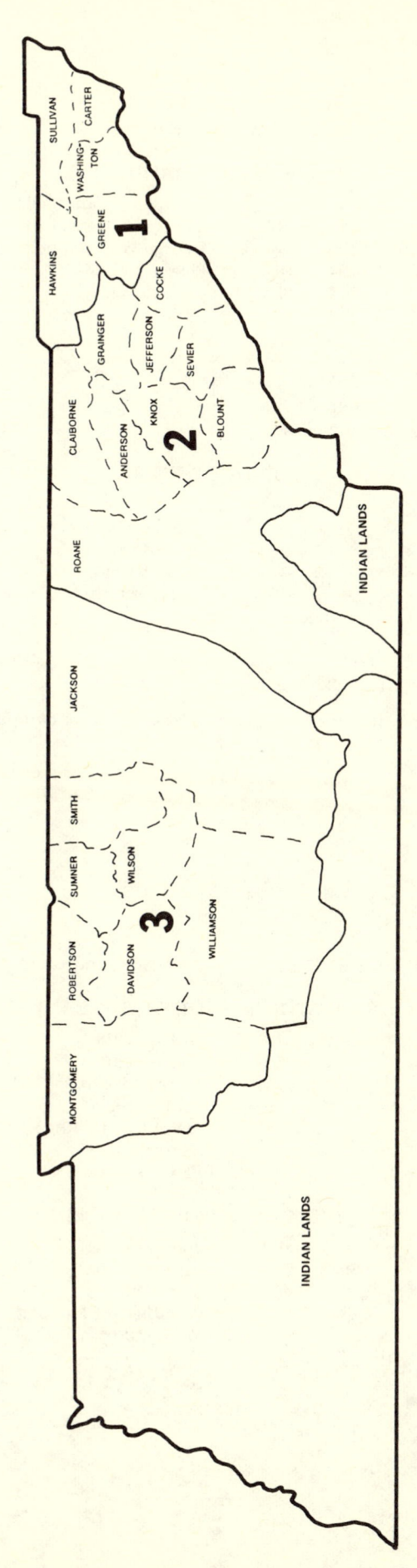

| COUNTIES | | | | | | REPRESENTATIVES | | | | |
| County | Aggregate | Slave | %S | sq.mi. | P/sq.mi. | Representative | Cong. | Pty. | Address | County |

DISTRICT 2 (HAMILTON)

County	Aggregate	Slave	%S	sq.mi.	P/sq.mi.	Representative	Cong.	Pty.	Address	County
Anderson[b]	----	----	----	335	----	George W. Campbell	8	R	Knoxville	Knox
Blount	5,585	345	6.1	575	9.7	George W. Campbell	9	R	Knoxville	Knox
Claiborne[b]	----	----	----	895	----	George W. Campbell	10	R	Knoxville	Knox
Cocke	9,017	695	7.7	424	21.3	Pleasant M. Miller	11	R	Knoxville	Knox
Grainger	7,367	496	6.7	282	26.1	John Sevier	12	R	Knoxville	Knox
Jefferson[a]	9,017	695	7.7	274	32.9					
Knox	12,446	1,298	10.4	508	24.5					
Roane[b]	----	----	----	4,515	----					
Sevier	3,419	162	4.7	597	5.7					
TOTALS	46,851	3,691	7.9	8,405	5.6					

[a]Combined with Cocke County in the 1800 census.

[b]Created after 1800 census.

DISTRICT 3 (MERO)

County	Aggregate	Slave	%S	sq.mi.	P/sq.mi.	Representative	Cong.	Pty.	Address	County
Davidson	9,965	3,087	20.97	----[a]	----[a]	William Dickson	8	R	Nashville	Davidson
Jackson[b]	----	----	----	----	----	William Dickson	9	R	Nashville	Davidson
Montgomery	2,899	821	28.3	----	----	Jesse Wharton	10	R	Nashville	Davidson
Robertson	----	----	----	----	----	Robert Weakley	11	R	Nashville	Davidson
Smith[b]	----	----	----	----	----	Felix Grundy	12	R	Nashville	Davidson
Sumner	4,616	1,284	2,781	----	----					
Williamson	2,868	693	24.1	----	----					
Robertson	4,280	863	20.2	----	----					
TOTALS	27,889	7,477	26.8	12,623	2.2					

[a]Because of rapidly changing county boundaries, only district totals were computed for square mile and population per square mile data.

[b]Created after 1800 census.

VERMONT
4 DISTRICTS
4 CONGRESSMEN

| COUNTIES | | | | | | REPRESENTATIVES | | | | |
| County | Aggregate | Slave | %S | sq.mi. | P/sq.mi. | Representative | Cong. | Pty. | Address | County |

DISTRICT 1 (SOUTHWESTERN)

County	Aggregate	Slave	%S	sq.mi.	P/sq.mi.	Representative	Cong.	Pty.	Address	County
Bennington	14,616	----	----	672	21.6	Gideon Olin	8	R	Shaftsbury	Bennington
Rutland	23,813	----	----	927	25.6	Gideon Olin	9	R	Shaftsbury	Bennington
TOTALS	38,429	----	----	1,599	24.0	James Witherell[r]	10	R	Fairhaven	Rutland
						Samuel Shaw	10	R	Castleton	Rutland
						(Replaced Witherell)				
						Samuel Shaw	11	R	Castleton	Rutland
						Samuel Shaw	12	R	Castleton	Rutland

DISTRICT 2 (SOUTHEASTERN)

County	Aggregate	Slave	%S	sq.mi.	P/sq.mi.	Representative	Cong.	Pty.	Address	County
Windham	23,581	----	----	784	30.0	James Elliott	8	F	Brattleboro	Windham
Windsor	26,944	----	----	962	28.0	James Elliott	9	F	Brattleboro	Windham
TOTALS	50,525	----	----	1,746	28.9	James Elliott	10	F	Brattleboro	Windham
						Jonathan H. Hubbard	11	F	Windsor	Windsor
						William Strong	12	R	Hartford	Windsor

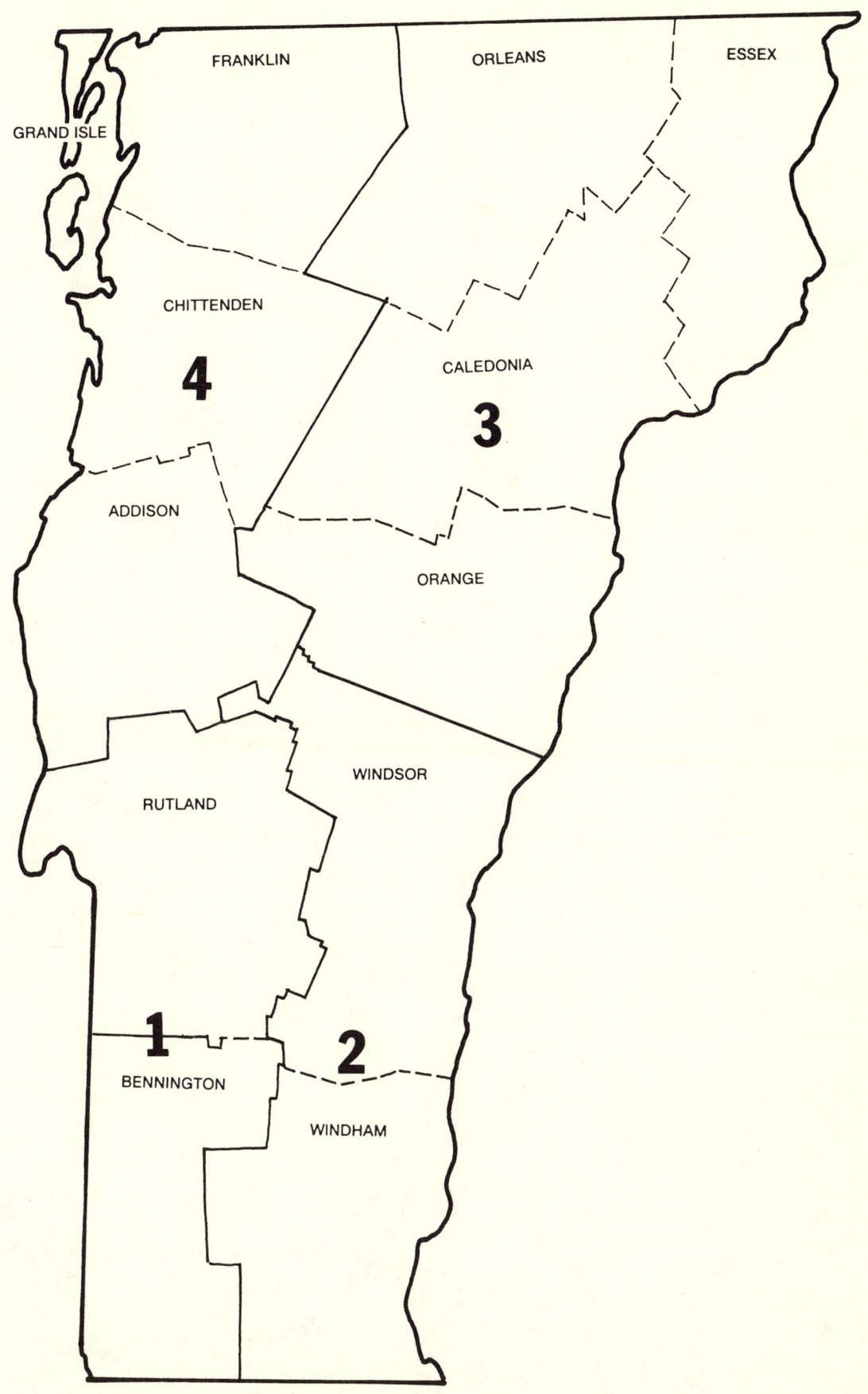

GRAND ISLE

FRANKLIN

ORLEANS

ESSEX

CHITTENDEN

4

CALEDONIA

3

ADDISON

ORANGE

RUTLAND

WINDSOR

1

2

BENNINGTON

WINDHAM

COUNTIES						REPRESENTATIVES				
County	Aggregate	Slave	%S	sq.mi.	P/sq.mi.	Representative	Cong.	Pty.	Address	County

DISTRICT 3 (NORTHEASTERN)

County	Aggregate	Slave	%S	sq.mi.	P/sq.mi.	Representative	Cong.	Pty.	Address	County
Caledonia	9,377	----	----	845	11.0	William Chamberlain	8	F	Peacham	Caledonia
Essex	1,479	----	----	663	2.2	James Fisk	9	R	Barre	Orange
Orange	18,238	----	----	832	21.9	James Fisk	10	R	Barre	Orange
Orleans	1,439	----	----	905	1.5	William Chamberlain	11	F	Peacham	Caledonia
TOTALS	30,533	----	----	3,245	9.4	James Fisk	12	R	Barre	Orange

DISTRICT 4 (NORTHWESTERN)

County	Aggregate	Slave	%S	sq.mi.	P/sq.mi.	Representative	Cong.	Pty.	Address	County
Addison	13,417	----	----	784	17.1	Martin Chittenden	8	F	Williston	Chittendon
Chittendon	12,778	----	----	1,048	12.1	Martin Chittenden	9	F	Williston	Chittendon
Franklin	8,782	----	----	838	10.4	Martin Chittenden	10	F	Williston	Chittendon
TOTALS	34,977	----	----	2,670	13.1	Martin Chittenden	11	F	Williston	Chittendon
						Martin Chittenden	12	F	Williston	Chittendon

VIRGINIA
22 DISTRICTS
22 CONGRESSMEN

COUNTIES						REPRESENTATIVES				
County	Aggregate	Slave	%S	sq.mi.	P/sq.mi.	Representative	Cong.	Pty.	Address	County

DISTRICT 1

County	Aggregate	Slave	%S	sq.mi.	P/sq.mi.	Representative	Cong.	Pty.	Address	County
Brooke	4,706	288	6.1	171	27.5	John G. Jackson	8	R	Clarksburg	Harrison
Harrison	4,848	245	5.0	2,939	1.6	John G. Jackson	9	R	Clarksburg	Harrison
Monongolia	8,540	163	1.9	1,348	6.3	John G. Jackson	10	R	Clarksburg	Harrison
Ohio	4,740	257	5.4	1,160	4.0	John G. Jackson[r]	11	R	Clarksburg	Harrison
Randolph	1,826	85	4.6	2,429	0.8	William McKinley	11	R	----	Ohio
Wood	1,218	61	5.0	803	1.5	(Replaced Jackson)				
TOTALS	25,878	1,099	4.2	8,850	2.9	Thomas Wilson	12	F	Morgantown	Monongolia

DISTRICT 2

County	Aggregate	Slave	%S	sq.mi.	P/sq.mi.	Representative	Cong.	Pty.	Address	County
Berkeley	21,506	3,679	17.1	760	28.3	James Stephenson	8	F	Martinsburg	Berkeley
Hampshire	8,348	587	7.0	970	8.6	John Morrow*	9	(----)	----	----
Jefferson[a]						John Morrow*	10	(----)	----	----
TOTALS	29,854	4,266	14.2	1,730	17.2	James Stephenson	11	F	Martinsburg	Berkeley
						John Baker	12	F	Shepherds-town	Jefferson

[a]Created after the 1800 census.

DISTRICT 3

County	Aggregate	Slave	%S	sq.mi.	P/sq.mi.	Representative	Cong.	Pty.	Address	County
Frederick	24,944	5,118	20.5	679	36.7	John Smith	8	R	Winchester	Frederick
Shenandoah	13,823	738	5.3	942	14.7	John Smith	9	R	Winchester	Frederick
TOTALS	38,767	5,856	15.1	1,621	23.9	John Smith	10	R	Winchester	Frederick
						John Smith	11	R	Winchester	Frederick
						John Smith	12	R	Winchester	Frederick

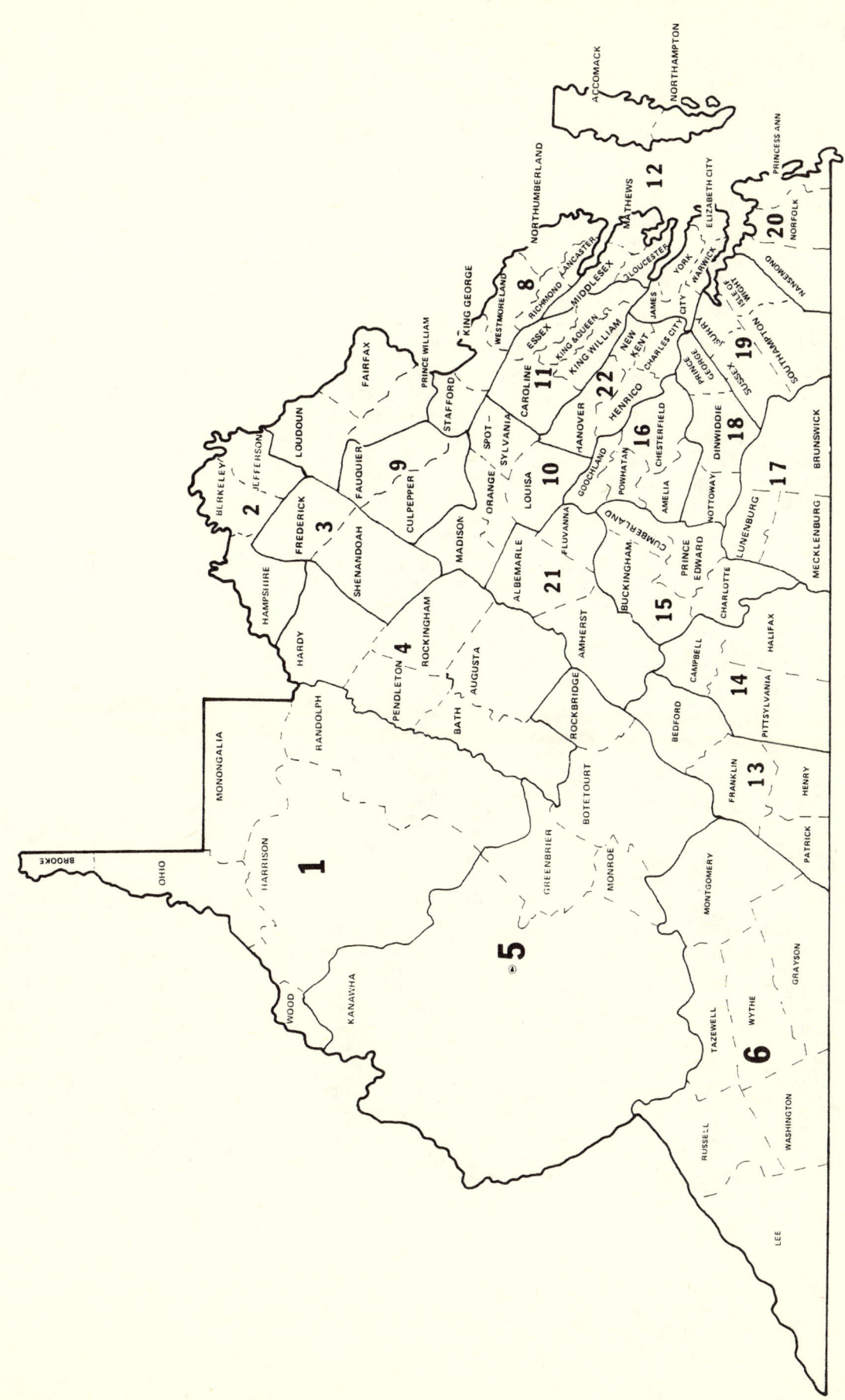

	COUNTIES					REPRESENTATIVES				
County	Aggregate	Slave	%S	sq.mi.	P/sq.mi.	Representative	Cong.	Pty.	Address	County

DISTRICT 4

County	Aggregate	Slave	%S	sq.mi.	P/sq.mi.	Representative	Cong.	Pty.	Address	County
Augusta	11,342	1,946	17.1	986	11.5	David Holmes	8	R	----	----
Bath	5,505	11	0.2	956	5.8	David Holmes	9	R	----	----
Hardy	6,627	623	9.4	1,685	3.9	David Holmes	10	R	----	----
Pendleton	3,962	124	3.1	695	5.7	Jacob Swoope	11	F	Staunton	Augusta
Rockingham	10,374	1,052	10.1	865	11.9	William McCoy	12	R	Franklin	Pendleton
TOTALS	37,810	3,745	9.9	5,187	7.3					

DISTRICT 5

County	Aggregate	Slave	%S	sq.mi.	P/sq.mi.	Representative	Cong.	Pty.	Address	County
Botetourt	10,427	1,343	12.8	1,590	6.5	Thomas Lewis[ce]	8	(----)	----	Rockbridge
Greenbrier	4,319	271	6.2	2,639	1.6	Andrew Moore[r]	8	(----)	Fairfield	Rockbridge
Kanawha	3,239	231	7.1	6,540	0.5	Alexander Wilson	8	(----)	----	----
Monroe	4,178	189	4.5	473	8.8	Alexander Wilson	9	(----)	----	----
Rockbridge	8,936	1,070	11.9	601	14.8	Alexander Wilson	10	(----)	----	----
TOTALS	31,099	3,104	9.9	11,843	2.6	James Breckinridge	11	F	Fincastle	Botetourt
						James Breckinridge	12	F	Fincastle	Botetourt

DISTRICT 6

County	Aggregate	Slave	%S	sq.mi.	P/sq.mi.	Representative	Cong.	Pty.	Address	County
Grayson	3,912	170	4.3	946	4.1	Abram Trigg	8	(----)	"Buchanan's Bottom"	Montgomery
Lee	3,538	243	6.8	1,350	2.6					
Montgomery	9,044	968	10.7	1,468	6.2	Abram Trigg	9	(----)	"Buchanan's Bottom"	Montgomery
Russell	4,808	352	7.3	1,323	3.6					
Tazewell	2,127	219	10.2	3,375	0.6	Abram Trigg	10	(----)	"Buchanan's Bottom"	Montgomery
Washington	9,536	817	8.5	613	15.5					
Wythe	6,380	831	13.0	895	7.1	Daniel Sheffey	11	F	Wythe	Wythe
TOTALS	39,345	3,600	9.1	9.970	3.9	Daniel Sheffey	12	F	Wythe	Wythe

DISTRICT 7

County	Aggregate	Slave	%S	sq.mi.	P/sq.mi.	Representative	Cong.	Pty.	Address	County
Fairfax	13,317	6,078	45.6	399	33.4	Philip R. Thompson	8	R	Fairfax	Fairfax
Loudoun	20,523	4,990	24.3	517	39.7	Philip R. Thompson	9	R	Fairfax	Fairfax
Prince						John Love	10	R	Alexandria	Fairfax
William	12,733	5,416	42.5	347	36.7	John Love	11	R	Alexandria	Fairfax
TOTALS	46,573	16,484	35.3	1,263	36.9	Joseph Lewis, Jr.	12	F	Upperville	----

DISTRICT 8

County	Aggregate	Slave	%S	sq.mi.	P/sq.mi.	Representative	Cong.	Pty.	Address	County
King George	6,749	3,987	59.0	176	38.3	Walter Jones	8	R	----	Northumberland
Lancaster	5,375	3,126	58.1	137	39.2	Walter Jones	9	R	----	Northumberland
Northumberland	7,803	3,903	50.0	190	41.0	Walter Jones	10	R	----	Northumberland
Richmond[a]										
Stafford	9,971	4,343	43.5	270	36.9	Walter Jones	11	R	----	Northumberland
Westmoreland	13,744	7,826	56.9	419	32.8					
TOTALS	43,642	23,185	53.1	1,192	36.6	John P. Hungerford[ce]	12	R	Leedstown	Westmoreland
						John Taliaferro	12	R	Fredericksburg	King George

(Successfully contested the election of Hungerford)

[a]Combined with Westmoreland County in the 1800 census.

130

COUNTIES						REPRESENTATIVES				
County	Aggregate	Slave	%S	sq.mi.	P/sq.mi.	Representative	Cong.	Pty.	Address	County

DISTRICT 9

County	Aggregate	Slave	%S	sq.mi.	P/sq.mi.	Representative	Cong.	Pty.	Address	County
Culpepper	18,100	7,348	40.5	656	27.6	Joseph Lewis, Jr.	8	F	Upperville	Fauquier
Fauquier	21,329	8,754	41.0	660	32.3	Joseph Lewis, Jr.	9	F	Upperville	Fauquier
TOTALS	39,429	16,102	40.8	1,316	29.9	Joseph Lewis, Jr.	10	F	Upperville	Fauquier
						Joseph Lewis, Jr.	11	F	Upperville	Fauquier
						Aylett Hawes	12	R	Woodville	Culpepper

DISTRICT 10

County	Aggregate	Slave	%S	sq.mi.	P/sq.mi.	Representative	Cong.	Pty.	Address	County
Louisa	11,892	5,992	50.3	517	23.0	John Dawson	8	R	----	----
Madison	8,322	3,436	41.2	327	25.4	John Dawson	9	R	----	----
Orange	11,449	5,242	45.7	508	22.5	John Dawson	10	R	----	----
Spott-						John Dawson	11	R	----	----
sylvania	13,007	6,830	52.5	409	31.8	John Dawson	12	R	----	----
TOTALS	44,670	21,500	48.1	1,761	25.4					

DISTRICT 11

County	Aggregate	Slave	%S	sq.mi.	P/sq.mi.	Representative	Cong.	Pty.	Address	County
Caroline	17,238	10,581	61.3	545	31.6	Anthony New	8	R	----	----
Essex	9,508	5,767	60.6	250	38.0	James M. Garnett	9	R	Loretto	Essex
King						James M. Garnett	10	R	Loretto	Essex
and Queen	9,779	5,380	55.0	318	30.8	John Roane	11	R	Uppowac	King William
King William	9,055	5,744	63.4	278	32.6	John Roane	12	R	Uppowac	King William
TOTALS	45,580	27,472	60.2	1,391	32.8					

DISTRICT 12

County	Aggregate	Slave	%S	sq.mi.	P/sq.mi.	Representative	Cong.	Pty.	Address	County
Accomack	15,693	4,429	28.2	476	32.9	Thomas Griffin	8	F	Yorktown	York
Elizabeth						Burwell Bassett	9	R	Williamsburg	James City
City	2,779	1,522	66.7	69	40.3	Burwell Bassett	10	R	Williamsburg	James City
Gloucester	7,981	4,909	61.5	228	35.0	Burwell Bassett	11	R	Williamsburg	James City
James City	3,931	2,389	60.7	152	25.8	Burwell Bassett	12	R	Williamsburg	James City
Mathews	5,806	2,804	48.2	89	65.2					
Middlesex	4,203	2,516	59.8	130	32.3					
Northampton	6,302	3,178	50.4	220	28.6					
Warwick	1,659	1,024	61.7	90	18.4					
City of										
Williamsburg[a]	----	----	----	----	----					
York	2,231	2,020	90.5	129	17.3					
TOTALS	50,585	24,791	49.0	1,583	31.9					

[a]Included in James City County statistics.

DISTRICT 13

County	Aggregate	Slave	%S	sq.mi.	P/sq.mi.	Representative	Cong.	Pty.	Address	County
Bedford	14,115	4,097	29.0	727	19.4	John Trigg[†]	8	R	----	Bedford
Franklin	9,302	1,574	16.9	716	12.9	Christopher Clark (Replaced Trigg)	8	R	New London	Bedford
Henry	5,249	1,415	269	381	13.8	Christopher Clark[r]	9	R	New London	Bedford
Patrick	4,331	649	14.9	464	9.3	William Burrill (Replaced Clark)	9	R	Rocky Mount	Franklin
TOTALS	32,997	7,735	23.4	2,288	14.4	William Burwell	10	R	Rocky Mount	Franklin
						William Burwell	11	R	Rocky Mount	Franklin
						William Burwell	12	R	Rocky Mount	Franklin

COUNTIES						REPRESENTATIVES				
County	Aggregate	Slave	%S	sq.mi.	P/sq.mi.	Representative	Cong.	Pty.	Address	County

DISTRICT 14

County	Aggregate	Slave	%S	sq.mi.	P/sq.mi.	Representative	Cong.	Pty.	Address	County
Campbell	10,066	3,671	36.4	669	17.0	Matthew Clay	8	R	Halifax	Halifax
Halifax	19,377	7,911	40.8	796	24.3	Matthew Clay	9	R	Halifax	Halifax
Pittsylvania	12,697	4,133	32.5	1,001	12.7	Matthew Clay	10	R	Halifax	Halifax
TOTALS	42,140	15,715	37.2	2,466	17.0	Matthew Clay	11	R	Halifax	Halifax
						Matthew Clay	12	R	Halifax	Halifax

DISTRICT 15

County	Aggregate	Slave	%S	sq.mi.	P/sq.mi.	Representative	Cong.	Pty.	Address	County
Buckingham	13,409	6,336	47.2	737	18.2	John Randolph	8	R	Charlotte	Charlotte
Charlotte	7,912	6,283	79.4	470	16.8	John Randolph	9	R	Charlotte	Charlotte
Cumberland	9,857	5,711	57.9	291	33.9	John Randolph	10	R	Charlotte	Charlotte
Prince						John Randolph	11	R	Charlotte	Charlotte
Edward	10,962	5,921	54.0	407	26.9	John Randolph	12	R	Charlotte	Charlotte
TOTALS	42,140	24,251	57.5	1,905	22.1					

DISTRICT 16

County	Aggregate	Slave	%S	sq.mi.	P/sq.mi.	Representative	Cong.	Pty.	Address	County
Amelia	9,432	6,585	69.8	366	25.8	John W. Eppes	8	R	----	----
Chesterfield	14,188	7,852	55.3	442	32.0	John W. Eppes	9	R	----	----
Goochland	9,696	4,803	49.5	289	33.6	John W. Eppes	10	R	----	----
Powhatan	7,669	5,031	65.6	269	28.5	John W. Eppes	11	R	----	----
TOTALS	40,985	24,271	59.2	1,366	30.0	James Pleasants	12	R	Goochland	Goochland

DISTRICT 17

County	Aggregate	Slave	%S	sq.mi.	P/sq.mi.	Representative	Cong.	Pty.	Address	County
Brunswick	16,309	9,422	57.7	579	28.2	Thomas Claiborne	8	(----)	----	Brunswick
Greenville	6,362	4,620	72.6	299	21.3					
Lunenberg	10,581	5,876	55.5	442	23.9	John Claiborne	9	(----)	----	Brunswick
Mecklenberg	17,008	8,676	51.0	612	27.8	John Claiborne[r]	10	(----)	----	Brunswick
TOTALS	43,898	23,974	54.6	1,633	26.9	Thomas Gholson, Jr.	10	R	Brunswick	Brunswick
						(Replaced Claiborne)				
						Thomas Gholson, Jr.	11	R	Brunswick	Brunswick
						Thomas Gholson, Jr.	12	R	Brunswick	Brunswick

DISTRICT 18

County	Aggregate	Slave	%S	sq.mi.	P/sq.mi.	Representative	Cong.	Pty.	Address	County
Dinwiddie	11,853	6,866	57.9	507	23.4	Peterson Goodwyn	8	R	Petersburg	Dinwiddie
Nottoway	9,403	5,983	63.6	308	30.5	Peterson Goodwyn	9	R	Petersburg	Dinwiddie
Prince George	7,425	4,388	58.9	276	26.9	Peterson Goodwyn	10	R	Petersburg	Dinwiddie
Town of						Peterson Goodwyn	11	R	Petersburg	Dinwiddie
Petersburg	3,521	1,487	42.2	8	440.1	Peterson Goodwyn	12	R	Petersburg	Dinwiddie
TOTALS	32,204	18,716	58.1	1,099	29.3					

DISTRICT 19

County	Aggregate	Slave	%S	sq.mi.	P/sq.mi.	Representative	Cong.	Pty.	Address	County
Isle of						Edwin Gray	8	R	----	Southampton
Wight	8,342	4,029	48.2	317	26.3	Edwin Gray	9	R	----	Southampton
South-						Edwin Gray	10	R	----	Southampton
ampton	13,923	6,625	47.5	602	23.1	Edwin Gray	11	R	----	Southampton
Surrey	6,535	3,258	49.8	277	23.6	Edwin Gray	12	R	----	Southampton
Sussex	11,062	5,988	54.1	494	22.4					
TOTALS	39,862	19,900	49.9	1,690	23.6					

COUNTIES						REPRESENTATIVES				
County	Aggregate	Slave	%S	sq.mi.	P/sq.mi.	Representative	Cong.	Pty.	Address	County

DISTRICT 20

County	Aggregate	Slave	%S	sq.mi.	P/sq.mi.	Representative	Cong.	Pty.	Address	County
Nansemond	11,127	4,408	39.6	408	27.3	Thomas Newton, Jr.	8	R	Norfolk	Norfolk
Norfolk	18,920	4,735	25.0	394	48.0	Thomas Newton, Jr.	9	R	Norfolk	Norfolk
Borough of						Thomas Newton, Jr.	10	R	Norfolk	Norfolk
Norfolk	18,920	4,735	25.0	53	356.9	Thomas Newton, Jr.	11	R	Norfolk	Norfolk
Princess Anne	8,859	3,574	40.3	259	34.2	Thomas Newton, Jr.	12	R	Norfolk	Norfolk
TOTALS	57,826	17,452	30.1	1,114	51.9					

DISTRICT 21

County	Aggregate	Slave	%S	sq.mi.	P/sq.mi.	Representative	Cong.	Pty.	Address	County
Albemarle	16,439	7,436	45.2	740	22.2	Thomas M. Randolph	8	R	"Monti-cello"	Albemarle
Amherst	16,807	7,462	44.3	941	17.8					
Fluvanna	5,122	1,920	37.4	288	17.8	Thomas M. Randolph	9	R	"Monti-cello"	Albemarle
TOTALS	38,368	16,818	43.8	1,969	19.5					
						Wilson C. Nicholas	10	R	Charlottes-ville	Albemarle
						Wilson C. Nicholas[r]	11	R	Charlottes-ville	Albemarle
						David S. Garland (Replaced Nicholas)	11	R	Clifford	Amherst
						Hugh Nelson	12	R	Milton	Albemarle

DISTRICT 22

County	Aggregate	Slave	%S	sq.mi.	P/sq.mi.	Representative	Cong.	Pty.	Address	County
Charles City	5,365	3,013	56.1	181	29.6	John Clopton	8	R	Tunstall	New Kent
Hanover	14,403	8,192	56.8	465	30.9	John Clopton	9	R	Tunstall	New Kent
Henrico	9,149	4,608	50.3	229	39.9	John Clopton	10	R	Tunstall	New Kent
New Kent	6,363	3,622	56.9	210	30.3	John Clopton	11	R	Tunstall	New Kent
City of						John Clopton	12	R	Tunstall	New Kent
Richmond	5,737	2,293	39.9	60	95.6					
TOTALS	41,017	21,728	52.9	1,145	35.8					

5

Off–Year Districting

1804, 1808

	COUNTIES					REPRESENTATIVES				
County	Aggregate	Slave	%S	sq.mi.	P/sq.mi.	Representative	Cong.	Pty.	Address	County

DISTRICT 1

Queens	16,893	1,528	9.0	108	156.4	Eliphalet Wickes	9	(----)	Jamica	Queens
Suffolk	19,464	886	4.5	929	20.9	Samuel Riker	10	(----)	Newtown	Queens
TOTALS	36,357	2,414	6.6	1,037	35.0					

DISTRICT 2

Kings	27,428	1,259	4.5	70	391.8	Gurden S. Mumford	9	F	----	Kings
Richmond	4,563	675	14.7	58	78.7	Gurden S. Mumford	10	F	----	Kings
TOTALS	31,991	1,934	6.0	128	250.0					

DISTRICT 3

City and County of New York	60,489	2,868	4.7	53	1141.3	George Clinton, Jr.	9	R	New York City	
						George Clinton, Jr.	10	R	New York City	

DISTRICT 4

Rockland	6,353	551	8.5	176	36.0	Philip Van Cortland	9	F	Croton	Westchester
Westchester	27,428	1,259	4.5	443	61.9	Philip Van Cortland	10	R	Croton	Westchester
TOTALS	33,781	1,810	5.3	619	54.6					

DISTRICT 5

Orange	29,355	1,145	3.9	833	35.2	John Blake, Jr.	9	(----)	Montgomery	Orange
						John Blake, Jr.	10	(----)	Montgomery	Orange

DISTRICT 6

Dutchess	47,775	1,609	3.3	1,044	45.7	Daniel C. Verplanck	9	F	Fishkill	Dutchess
						Daniel C. Verplanck	10	F	Fishkill	Dutchess

DISTRICT 7

Green	12,584	520	4.1	653	19.2	Martin G. Schneman	9	R	Catskill	Green
Ulster	24,855	2,257	9.0	1,141	21.7	Barent Gardiner	10	F	Kingston	Ulster
TOTALS	37,439	2,777	7.4	1,793	20.8					

DISTRICT 8

Columbia	35,322	1,471	4.1	645	54.7	Henry W. Livingston	9	(----)	Lithlingo	Columbia
						James L. Van Alen	10	F	Kinderhook	Columbia

DISTRICT 9

City and County of Albany	34,043	1,808	5.3	733	46.4	Killian Van Rensselaer	9	F	Albany	Albany
						Killian Van Rensselaer	10	F	Albany	Albany

| | COUNTY | | | | | | REPRESENTATIVES | | | | |
County	Aggregate	Slave	%S	sq.mi.	P/sq.mi.	Representative	Cong.	Pty.	Address	County

DISTRICT 10

County	Aggregate	Slave	%S	sq.mi.	P/sq.mi.	Representative	Cong.	Pty.	Address	County
Rensselaer	30,442	890	2.9	665	45.7	Josiah Masters	9	R	Schaghticoke	Rensselaer
						Josiah Masters	10	R	Schaghticoke	Rensselaer

DISTRICT 11

County	Aggregate	Slave	%S	sq.mi.	P/sq.mi.	Representative	Cong.	Pty.	Address	County
Clinton	8,514	58	0.7	1,823	4.6	Peter Sailly	9	R	Plattsbury	Clinton
Saratoga	24,483	358	1.4	818	29.9	John Thompson	10	R	Stillwater	Saratoga
TOTALS	32,997	416	1.2	2,641	25.0					

DISTRICT 12

County	Aggregate	Slave	%S	sq.mi.	P/sq.mi.	Representative	Cong.	Pty.	Address	County
Washington	35,574	80	0.2	1,723	20.6	David Thomas	9	R	Salem	Washington
						David Thomas[r]	10	R	Salem	Washington
						(Resigned May 1, 1808)				
						Nathan Wilson	10	R	Salem	Washington
						(Replaced Thomas)				

DISTRICT 13

County	Aggregate	Slave	%S	sq.mi.	P/sq.mi.	Representative	Cong.	Pty.	Address	County
Montgomery	21,700	466	2.1	2,641	8.2	Thomas Sammons	9	R	Johnstown	Montgomery
Schoharie	9,808	354	3.6	624	15.7	Peter Swart	10	(----)	Schoharie	Schoharie
TOTALS	31,508	820	2.6	3,265	9.6					

DISTRICT 14

County	Aggregate	Slave	%S	sq.mi.	P/sq.mi.	Representative	Cong.	Pty.	Address	County
Delaware	10,228	16	0.2	1,443	14.9	John Russell	9	(----)	Cooperstown	Otsego
Otsego	21,636	48	0.2	1,013	21.3	John Russell	10	(----)	Cooperstown	Otsego
TOTALS	31,864	64	0.2	2,456	12.9					

DISTRICT 15

County	Aggregate	Slave	%S	sq.mi.	P/sq.mi.	Representative	Cong.	Pty.	Address	County
Herkimer	14,479	61	0.4	1,443	3.5	Nathan Williams	9	R	Utica	Oneida
Oneida	22,047	50	0.2	2,187	4.6	William Kirkpatrick	10	R	Salina	Oneida
St. Lawrence[a]	----	----	----	2,768	----					
TOTALS	36,526	111	0.3	6,398	5.7					

[a]Created after 1800 census.

DISTRICT 16

County	Aggregate	Slave	%S	sq.mi.	P/sq.mi.	Representative	Cong.	Pty.	Address	County
Chenango	15,666	16	0.1	1,564	10.0	Uri Tracy	9	R	Oxford	Chanango
Onondaga	7,406	11	0.1	1,295	5.7	Uri Tracy	10	R	Oxford	Chenango
Tioga	6,889	17	0.2	1,653	4.1					
TOTALS	29,961	44	0.1	4,512	6.6					

DISTRICT 17

County	Aggregate	Slave	%S	sq.mi.	P/sq.mi.	Representative	Cong.	Pty.	Address	County
Cayuga	15,871	53	0.3	1,940	8.1	Silas Halsey	9	R	Lodi	Cayuga
Genessee[a]	----	----	----	----	----	John Harris	10	(----)	Aurelias	----
Ontario	15,218	57	0.4	9,244	1.6					
Steuben	1,788	22	1.2	1,510	1.1					
TOTALS	32,877	132	0.4	12,694	2.5					

[a]Created after 1800 census.

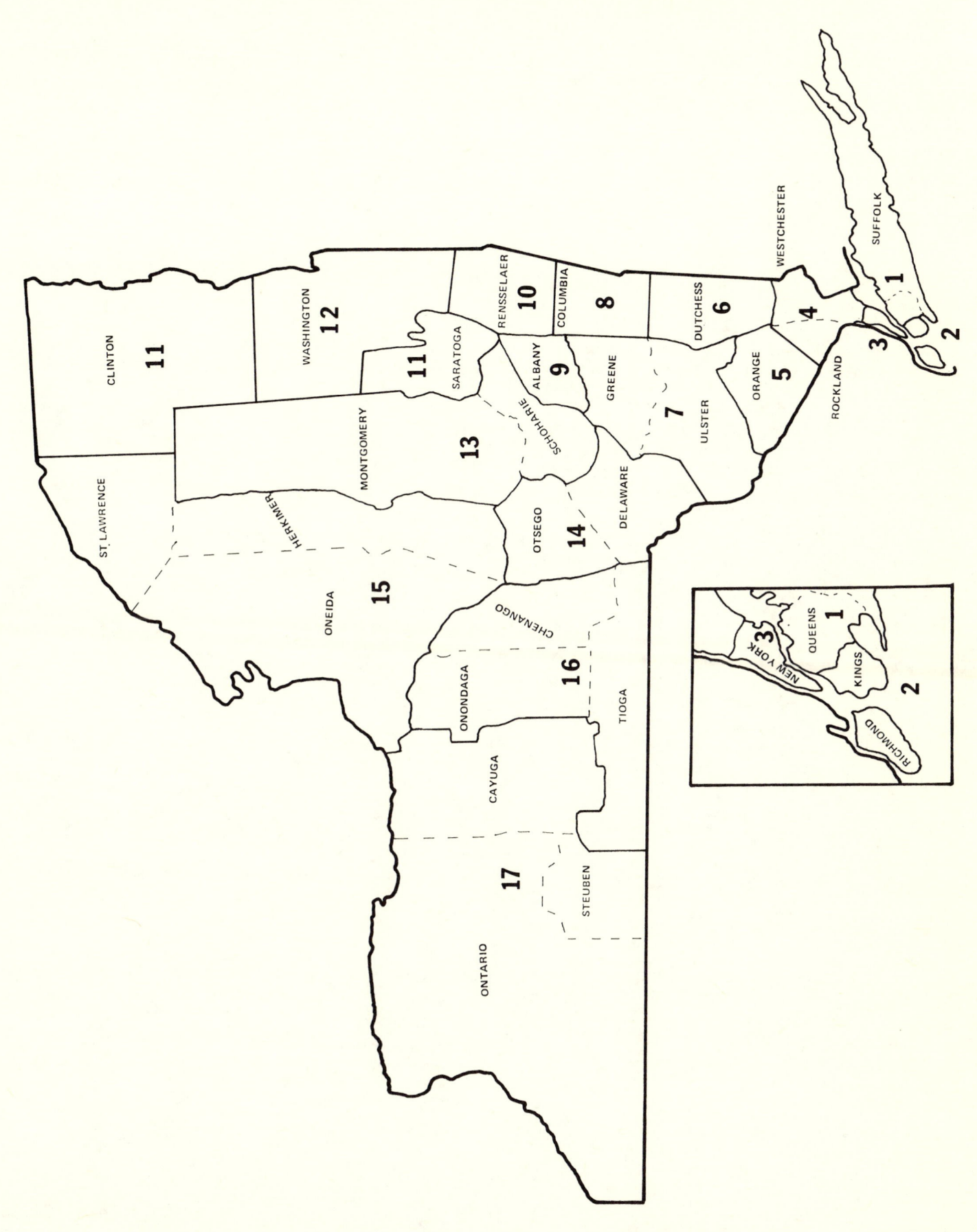

| County | COUNTIES | | | | | Representative | REPRESENTATIVES | | | County |
	Aggregate	Slave	%S	sq.mi.	P/sq.mi.		Cong.	Pty.	Address	
DISTRICT 1										
Kings	8,303	1,118	13.4	70	118.6	Ebenezer Sage	11	R	Sag Harbor	Suffolk
Queens	19,336	809	4.1	108	17.3	Ebenezer Sage	12	R	Sag Harbor	Suffolk
Suffolk	21,113	413	2.0	1,218	17.3					
TOTALS	48,752	2,340	4.8	1,396	34.9					
DISTRICT 2										
City and						William Denning[r]	11	(----)	New York City	
County of						(Resigned before qualifying)				
New York	96,373	1,686	1.8	64	1505.0	Samuel L. Mitchell	11	R	New York City	
Richmond	5,347	427	8.0	58	92.1	(Replaced Denning December 4, 1810)				
Rockland	7,758	316	18.7	176	44.0	Gurden S. Mumford	11	F	New York City	
TOTALS	109,478	2,429	2.2	298	367.4					
						Samuel L. Mitchell	12	R	New York City	
						William Paulding, Jr.	12	R	New York City	
DISTRICT 3										
Orange	34,347	966	2.8	833	41.2	Jonathan Fisk	11	R	Newburgh	Orange
Westchester	30,272	982	3.2	443	68.3	Pierre Van Cortland, Jr.	12	R	Peekskill	Westchester
TOTALS	64,619	1,858	2.9	1,276	50.6					
DISTRICT 4										
Dutchess	51,363	1,262	2.5	813	63.2	James Emott	11	F	Pough-keepsie	Dutchess
						James Emott	12	F	Pough-keepsie	Dutchess
DISTRICT 5										
Green	19,536	367	1.8	653	29.9	Barent Gardiner	11	F	Kingston	Ulster
Ulster	26,576	1,437	5.4	1,141	23.2	Thomas B. Cooke	12	R	Catskill	Green
TOTALS	46,112	1,804	3.9	1,794	25.7					
DISTRICT 6										
Columbia	32,390	879	2.7	645	50.2	Herman Knickerbocker	11	F	Schaghticoke	Rensselaer
Rensselaer	36,309	750	2.0	665	54.6	Robert L. Livingston	11	F	Hudson	Columbia
Washington	44,289	315	0.7	836	52.9					
TOTALS	112,988	1,944	1.7	2,146	52.6	Asa Fitch	12	F	Salem	Washington
						Robert L. Livingston[r]	12	F	Hudson	Columbia
						(Resigned May 6, 1812)				
						Thomas P. Grosvenor	12	F	Hudson	Columbia
						(Replaced Livingston January 20, 1813)				

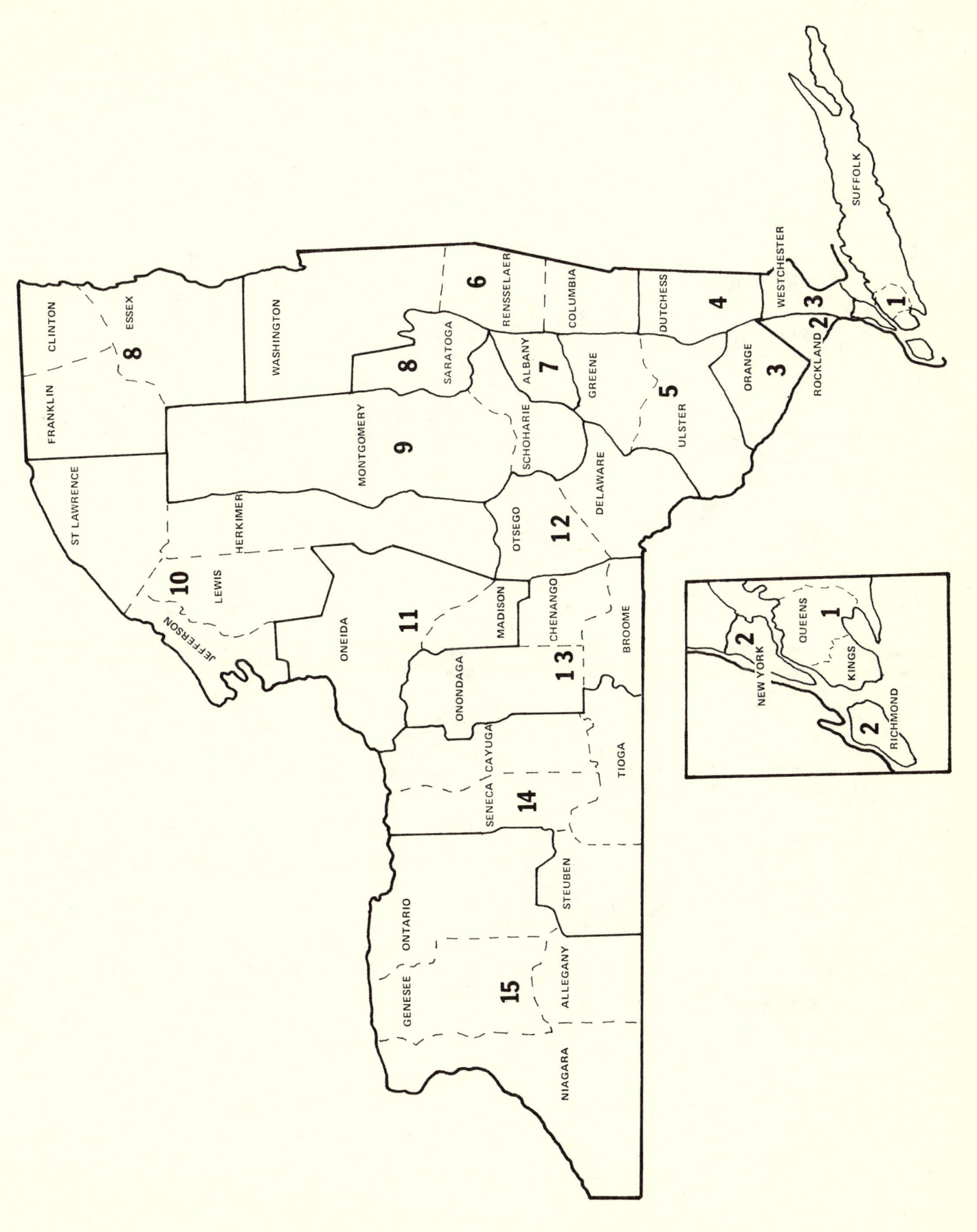

| | COUNTIES | | | | | REPRESENTATIVES | | | | |
County	Aggregate	Slave	%S	sq.mi.	P/sq.mi.	Representative	Cong.	Pty.	Address	County
DISTRICT 7										
City and						Killian Van Rensselaer	11	F	City of Albany	
County of						Harmanus Bleecker	12	F	City of Albany	
Albany	34,661	772	2.1	1,179	29.4					
DISTRICT 8										
Clinton	8,002	29	0.4	1,059	7.5	John Thompson	11	R	Stillwater	Saratoga
Essex	9,477	----	----	1,826	5.1	Benjamin Pond	12	R	Schroon	Clinton
Franklin	2,617	3	0.1	1,674	1.5					
Saratoga	33,147	107	0.3	818	40.5					
TOTALS	53,243	139	0.3	5,377	9.9					
DISTRICT 9										
Montgomery	41,214	712	1.7	906	45.5	Thomas Scammons	11	R	Johnstown	Montgomery
Schoharie	18,945	316	1.6	624	30.3	Thomas Scammons	12	R	Johnstown	Montgomery
TOTALS	60,159	1,028	1.7	1,530	39.3					
DISTRICT 10										
Herkimer	22,046	64	----	1,435	15.4	John Nicholson	11	R	Herkimer	Herkimer
Jefferson	15,104	----	----	1,294	11.7	Silas Stow	12	F	Lowville	Herkimer
Lewis	6,433	4	----	1,291	4.9					
St. Lawrence	7,885	5	----	2,168	6.0					
TOTALS	51,468	73	----	6,188	8.3					
DISTRICT 11										
Madison	25,144	35	----	661	37.9	Thomas P. Gold	11	F	Whitestown	Oneida
Oneida	33,792	81	0.3	1,223	27.6	Thomas P. Gold	12	F	Whitestown	Oneida
TOTALS	58,936	116	----	1,884	31.3					
DISTRICT 12										
Delaware	20,303	55	0.2	1,443	14.0	Erastus Root	11	R	Delhi	Delaware
Otsego	38,802	74	0.4	1,013	76.6	Arunah Metcalf	12	R	Otsego	Otsego
TOTALS	59,105	129	0.2	2,456	24.1					
DISTRICT 13										
Broome	8,130	23	0.3	714	11.3	Uri Tracy	11	R	Oxford	Chenango
Chenango	21,704	13	0.1	903	24.0	Uri Tracy	12	R	Oxford	Chenango
Onondaga	25,987	50	0.2	794	32.7					
TOTALS	55,821	86	0.1	2,411	23.2					
DISTRICT 14										
Cayuga	29,843	75	0.3	1,180	25.2	Vincent Mathews	11	F	Elmira	Tioga
Seneca	16,609	101	0.6	890	18.6	Daniel Avery	12	R	Aurora	Cayuga
Steuben	7,246	87	1.2	2,457	2.9					
Tioga	7,899	61	0.8	939	8.4					
TOTALS	61,597	324	0.5	5,466	11.3					

| COUNTIES | | | | | | REPRESENTATIVES | | | | |
| County | Aggregate | Slave | %S | sq.mi. | P/sq.mi. | Representative | Cong. | Pty. | Address | County |

DISTRICT 15

County	Aggregate	Slave	%S	sq.mi.	P/sq.mi.	Representative	Cong.	Pty.	Address	County
Allegany[a]						Peter B. Porter	11	R	Buffalo	Ontario
Genesee	12,588	11	----	1,894	6.6	Peter B. Porter	12	R	Buffalo	Ontario
Niagara	8,971	8	----	1,590	5.6					
Ontario	42,032	212	0.5	2,244	18.7					
TOTALS	63,591	231	0.4	5,728	11.1					

[a]Created in 1806 from Genesee County.

6
Congressional Districts

1812–1821
13th–17th Congresses

COUNTIES						REPRESENTATIVES				
County	Aggregate	Slave	%S	sq.mi.	P/sq.mi.	Representative	Cong.	Pty.	Address	County

AT LARGE

County	Aggregate	Slave	%S	sq.mi.	P/sq.mi.	Representative	Cong.	Pty.	Address	County
Fairfield	40,950	83	0.2	626	65.4	Epaphroditus				
Hartford	44,733	17	---	739	60.5	Champion	13	F	East Haddam	Middlesex
Litchfield	41,375	4	----	925	44.8	John Davenport	13	F	Stamford	Fairfield
Middlesex	20,723	57	0.3	372	55.7	Lyman Law	13	F	New London	New London
New Haven	37,064	51	0.1	604	61.4	Jonathan O. Moseley	13	F	East Haddam	Middlesex
New London	34,707	77	0.2	667	52.0	Timothy Pitkin	13	F	Farmington	Hartford
Tolland	13,779	----	----	416	33.1	Lewis B. Sturges	13	F	Fairfield	Fairfield
Windham	28,611	21	0.1	514	55.7	Benjamin Tallmadge	13	F	Litchfield	Litchfield
TOTALS	261,942	310	0.1	4,863	53.9					
						Epaphroditus				
						Champion	14	F	East Haddam	Middlesex
						John Davenport	14	F	Stamford	Fairfield
						Lyman Law	14	F	New London	New London
						Jonathan O. Moseley	14	F	East Haddam	Middlesex
						Timothy Pitkin	14	F	Farmington	Hartford
						Lewis B. Sturges	14	F	Fairfield	Fairfield
						Benjamin Tallmadge	14	F	Litchfield	Litchfield
						Uriel Holmes[r]	15	F	Litchfield	Litchfield
						(Resigned in 1818)				
						Sylvester Gilbert	15	(----)	Hebron	Tolland
						(Replaced Holmes October, 1818)				
						Ebenezer Huntington	15	F	Norwich	New London
						Jonathan O. Moseley	15	F	East Haddam	Middlesex
						Timothy Pitkin	15	F	Farmington	Hartford
						Samuel B. Sherwood	15	F	Saugatuck	Fairfield
						Nathaniel Terry	15	(----)	Hartford	Hartford
						Thomas S. Williams	15	D	Hartford	Hartford
						Henry W. Edwards	16	R	New Haven	New Haven
						Samuel A. Foote	16	F	Cheshire	New Haven
						Jonathan O. Moseley	16	F	East Haddam	Middlesex
						Elisha Phelps	16	R	Simsbury	Hartford
						John Russ	16	R	Hartford	Hartford
						James Stevens	16	R	Stamford	Fairfield
						Gideon Tomlinson	16	R	Fairfield	Fairfield
						Noyes Barber	17	R	Groton	New London
						Daniel Burrows	17	R	Hebron	Tolland
						Henry W. Edwards	17	R	New Haven	New Haven
						John Russ	17	R	Hartford	Hartford
						Ansel Sterling	17	(----)	Sharon	Litchfield
						Ebenezer Stoddard	17	R	West Wood-stock	Windham
						Gideon Tomlinson	17	R	Fairfield	Fairfield

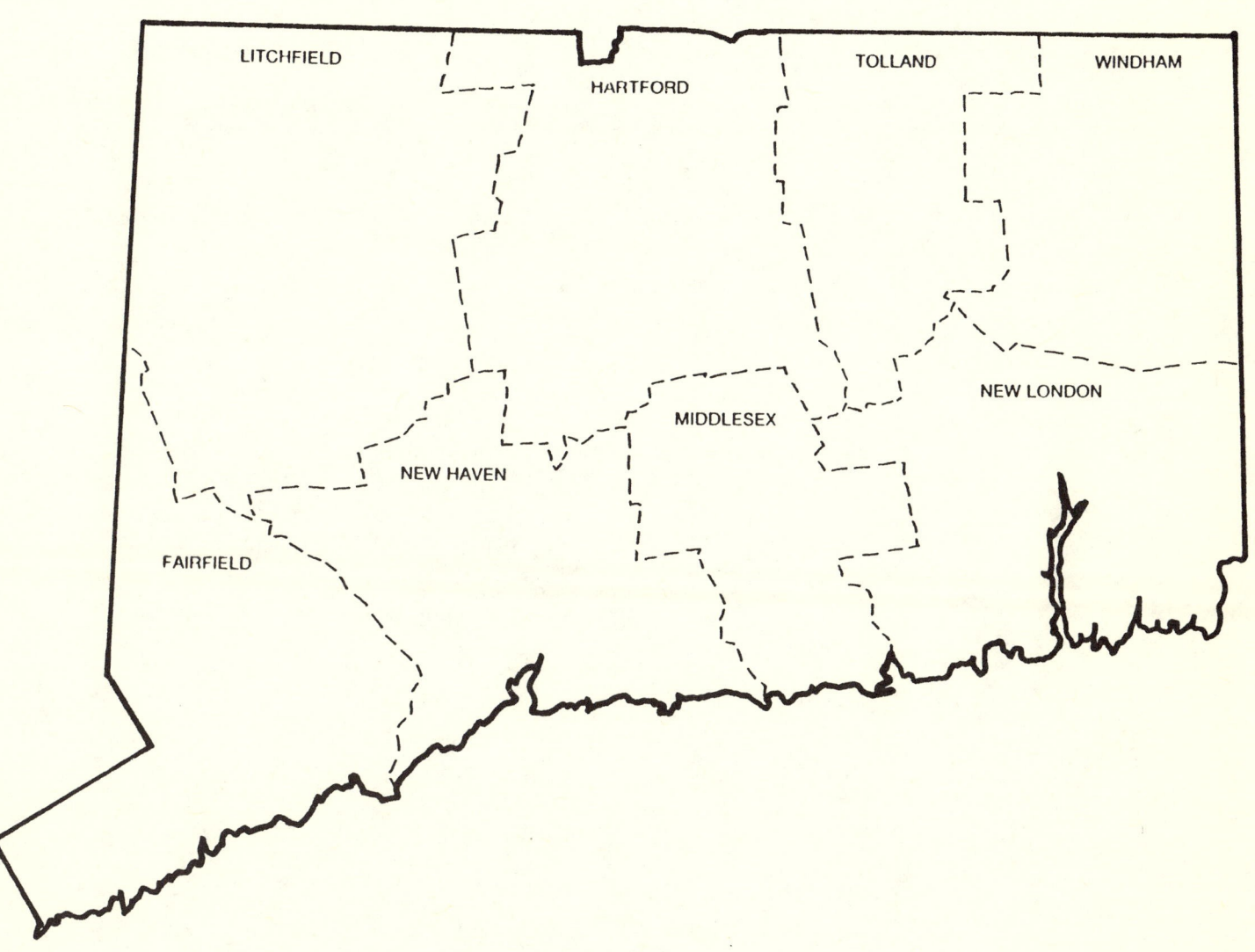

COUNTIES						REPRESENTATIVES				
County	Aggregate	Slave	%S	sq.mi.	P/sq.mi.	Representative	Cong.	Pty.	Address	County
						AT LARGE				
Kent	20,495	728	3.6	594	34.5	Thomas Cooper	13	F	Georgetown	Sussex
New Castle	24,429	1,027	4.2	438	55.8	Henry M. Ridgely	13	F	Dover	Kent
Sussex	27,750	2,402	8.7	950	29.2					
TOTALS	72,674	4,157	5.7	1,982	36.7	Thomas Clayton	14	F	Dover	Kent
						Thomas Cooper	14	F	Georgetown	Sussex
						Willard Hall	15	R	Dover	Kent
						Louis McLane	15	F	Wilmington	New Castle
						Willard Hall[r]	16	R	Dover	Kent
						(Resigned January, 1821)				
						Louis McLane	16	F	Wilmington	New Castle
						Louis McLane	17	F	Wilmington	New Castle
						Caesar A. Rodney[r]	17	R	Wilmington	New Castle
						(Resigned January, 1822)				
						Daniel Rodney	17	F	Leures	Sussex
						(Replaced C. A. Rodney December, 1822)				

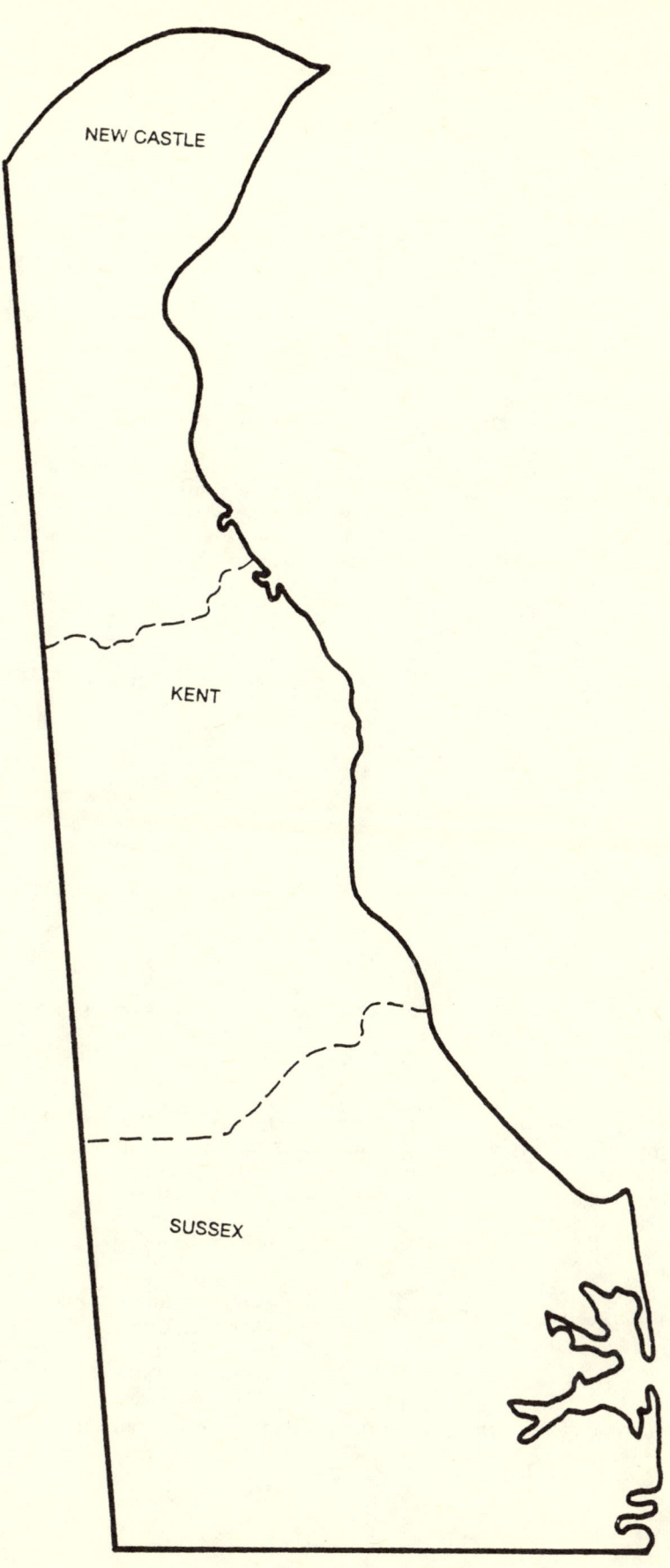

COUNTIES						REPRESENTATIVES				
County	Aggregate	Slave	%S	sq.mi.	P/sq.mi.	Representative	Cong.	Pty.	Address	County

AT LARGE

County	Aggregate	Slave	%S	sq.mi.	P/sq.mi.	Representative	Cong.	Pty.	Address	County
Baldwin	6,356	2,550	40.1	255	24.9	William Barnett	13	R	Washington	Wilkes
Bryan	2,827	2,264	80.1	443	6.4	William W. Bibb[r]	13	R	Petersburg	Elbert
Bulloch	2,306	426	18.5	935	2.5	(Resigned November, 1813)				
Burke	10,858	4,691	43.2	831	13.1	Alfred Cuthbert	13	R	Eatonton	Putnam
Camden	3,941	2,687	68.2	1,187	3.3	(Replaced Bibb October, 1814)				
Chatham	13,540	9,748	72.0	445	30.4	John Forsyth	13	R	Augusta	Richmond
Clarke	7,628	2,594	34.0	302	25.3	Bolling Hall	13	R	Milledgeville	Baldwin
Columbia	11,242	5,980	53.2	543	20.7	Thomas Telfair	13	R	Savannah	Chatham
Effingham	2,586	1,010	39.1	480	5.4	George M. Troup	13	R	Dublin	Laurens
Elbert	12,156	4,574	37.6	459	26.5					
Franklin	10,815	1,656	15.3	898	12.0	Alfred Cuthbert[r]	14	R	Eatonton	Putnam
Glynn	3,417	2,845	83.3	412	8.3	(Resigned November, 1816)				
Greene	11,679	5,236	44.8	415	28.1	Zadock Cook	14	(----)	Watkinsville	Clark
Hancock	13,330	6,456	48.4	498	26.8	(Replaced Cuthbert January, 1817)				
Jackson	10,569	1,816	17.2	517	20.4	John Forsyth	14	R	Augusta	Richmond
Jefferson	6,111	2,336	38.2	530	11.5	Bolling Hall	14	R	Milledgeville	Baldwin
Jones	8,597	2,587	30.1	402	21.4	Wilson Lumpkin	14	R	Lexington	Wilkes
Laurens	2,210	485	21.9	1,123	2.0	Thomas Telfair	14	R	Savannah	Chatham
Liberty	6,228	4,808	77.2	916	6.8	Richard Henry Wilde	14	R	Augusta	Richmond
Lincoln	4,555	2,212	48.6	193	23.6					
McIntosh	3,739	2,957	79.1	426	8.8	Joel Abbot	15	R	Washington	Wilkes
Montgomery	2,954	747	25.3	1,774	1.7	Thomas W. Cobb	15	(----)	Lexington	Wilkes
Morgan	8,369	2,418	28.9	356	23.5	Zadock Cook	15	(----)	Watkinsville	Clark
Oglethorpe	12,297	5,435	44.2	415	29.6	Joel Crawford	15	R	Milledgeville	Baldwin
Pulaski	2,093	528	25.2	970	2.2	John Forsyth[r]	15	R	Augusta	Richmond
Putnam	10,029	3,220	32.1	339	29.6	(Resigned November, 1818)				
Randolph	7,573	1,821	24.0	373	20.3	Robert R. Reid	15	R	Augusta	Richmond
Richmond	6,189	3,436	55.5	323	19.2	(Replaced Forsyth February, 1819)				
Scriven	4,477	1,816	40.6	651	6.9	William Terrell	15	R	Sparta	Hancock
Tattnall	2,206	542	24.6	1,044	2.1					
Telfair	744	218	29.3	440	1.7	Joel Abbot	16	R	Washington	Wilkes
Twiggs	3,405	642	18.9	364	9.4	Thomas W. Cobb	16	(----)	Lexington	Wilkes
Walton	1,026	60	5.8	330	3.1	Joel Crawford	16	R	Milledgeville	Baldwin
Warren	8,725	3,048	34.9	314	27.8	John A. Cuthbert	16	R	Eatonton	Putnam
Wayne	676	254	37.6	1,202	0.6	Robert R. Reid	16	R	Augusta	Richmond
Washington	9,940	3,513	35.3	674	14.7	William Terrell	16	R	Sparta	Hancock
Wilkenson	2,154	318	14.8	458	4.7					
Wilkes	14,887	7,284	48.9	498	29.9	Joel Abbot	17	R	Washington	Wilkes
TOTALS	252,433	105,218	41.7	22,735[a]	11.1	Alfred Cuthbert	17	R	Eatonton	Putnam
						George R. Gilmer	17	R	Lexington	Wilkes
						Robert R. Reid	17	R	Augusta	Richmond
						Edward F. Tattnall	17	(----)	Savannah	Chatham
						Wiley Thompson	17	R	Elberton	Elbert

[a]Indian lands comprised the balance of the territory within the present boundaries of the state.

INDIAN LANDS

FRANKLIN

JACKSON
ELBERT

CLARKE OGLETHORPE
WALTON WILKES
LINCOLN
MORGAN GREENE
COLUMBIA
WARREN
JASPER PUTNAM
HANCOCK RICHMOND
JEFFERSON
BURKE
JONES BALDWIN
WASHINGTON
WILKINSON
MONTGOMERY SCRIVEN
TWIGGS
LAURENS
BULLOCH
EFFINGHAM
PULASKI
TATTNALL
BRYAN
CHATHAM
LIBERTY
TELFAIR
WAYNE
McINTOSH
GLYNN
CAMDEN

COUNTIES					REPRESENTATIVES				
County	Aggregate	Slave	%S	sq.mi.	P/sq.mi.	Representative	Cong.	Pty.	Address	County

DISTRICT 1

County	Aggregate	Slave	%S	sq.mi.	P/sq.mi.	Representative	Cong.	Pty.	Address	County
Bath[a]	----	----	----	367	----	James Clark	13	R	Winchester	Clark
Clark	11,519	2,934	25.4	259	44.5	James Clark[r]	14	R	Winchester	Clark
Estill	2,082	133	6.4	697	3.0	Thomas Fletcher	14	R	Winchester	Clark
Greenup	2,369	484	20.4	901	2.6	(Replaced Clark December, 1816)				
Fleming	8,947	549	6.1	640	14.0	David Trimble	15	R	Sterling	Montgomery
Floyd	3,485	115	3.3	3,013	1.2	David Trimble	16	R	Sterling	Montgomery
Montgomery	12,975	1,767	13.6	507	25.6	David Trimble	17	R	Sterling	Montgomery
TOTALS	41,377	5,982	14.5	6,384	6.5					

[a]Created after 1810 census.

DISTRICT 2

County	Aggregate	Slave	%S	sq.mi.	P/sq.mi.	Representative	Cong.	Pty.	Address	County
Fayette	21,370	6,764	31.6	280	76.3	Henry Clay[r]	13	R	Lexington	Fayette
Jessamine	8,377	2,483	29.6	177	47.3	(Resigned January, 1814)				
Woodford	9,659	3,414	35.3	193	50.0	Joseph H. Hawkins	13	R	Lexington	Fayette
TOTALS	39,406	12,661	32.1	650	60.6	(Replaced Clay March, 1814)				
						Henry Clay	14	R	Lexington	Fayette
						Henry Clay	15	R	Lexington	Fayette
						Henry Clay	16	R	Lexington	Fayette
						Samuel H. Woodson	17	F	Lexington	Fayette

DISTRICT 3

County	Aggregate	Slave	%S	sq.mi.	P/sq.mi.	Representative	Cong.	Pty.	Address	County
Boone	3,608	656	18.2	249	14.5	Richard M. Johnson	13	R	Great Crossing	Scott
Campbell	3,473	472	13.6	314	11.1					
Franklin	8,013	2,201	27.5	218	36.8	Richard M. Johnson	14	R	Great Crossing	Scott
Gallatin	3,307	688	20.8	430	7.7					
Harrison	7,752	1,105	14.2	308	25.2	Richard M. Johnson	15	R	Great Crossing	Scott
Pendleton	3,061	386	12.6	654	4.7					
Scott	12,419	3,732	30.0	409	30.4	William Brown	16	(----)	Cynthiana	Harrison
TOTALS	41,633	9,240	22.2	2,582	16.1	John T. Johnson	17	JD	Georgetown	Scott

DISTRICT 4

County	Aggregate	Slave	%S	sq.mi.	P/sq.mi.	Representative	Cong.	Pty.	Address	County
Bourbon	18,009	4,169	23.1	300	60.0	Joseph Desha	13	R	Mays Lick	Mason
Bracken	3,706	358	9.6	204	18.2	Joseph Desha	14	R	Mays Lick	Mason
Lewis	2,357	284	12.0	486	4.9	Joseph Desha	15	R	Mays Lick	Mason
Nicholas	4,898	509	10.4	229	21.4	Thomas Metcalfe	16	R	Carlisle	Nicholas
Mason	11,071	2,065	18.6	304	36.4	Thomas Metcalfe	17	R	Carlisle	Nicholas
TOTALS	40,041	7,385	18.4	1,523	26.3					

DISTRICT 5

County	Aggregate	Slave	%S	sq.mi.	P/sq.mi.	Representative	Cong.	Pty.	Address	County
Breckenridge	3,430	----	----	741	4.6	Samuel Hopkins	13	R	Henderson	Henderson
Caldwell	4,268	579	13.5	1,924	2.2	Alney McLean	14	(----)	Greenville	Muhlenberg
Christian	11,020	1,766	16.0	933	11.8	Anthony New	15	R	Elkton	Todd
Grayson	2,301	103	4.5	496	4.6	Alney McLean	16	(----)	Greenville	Muhlenberg
Henderson	4,703	1,514	32.2	775	6.0	Anthony New	17	R	Elkton	Todd
Hopkins	2,964	412	13.9	892	3.3					

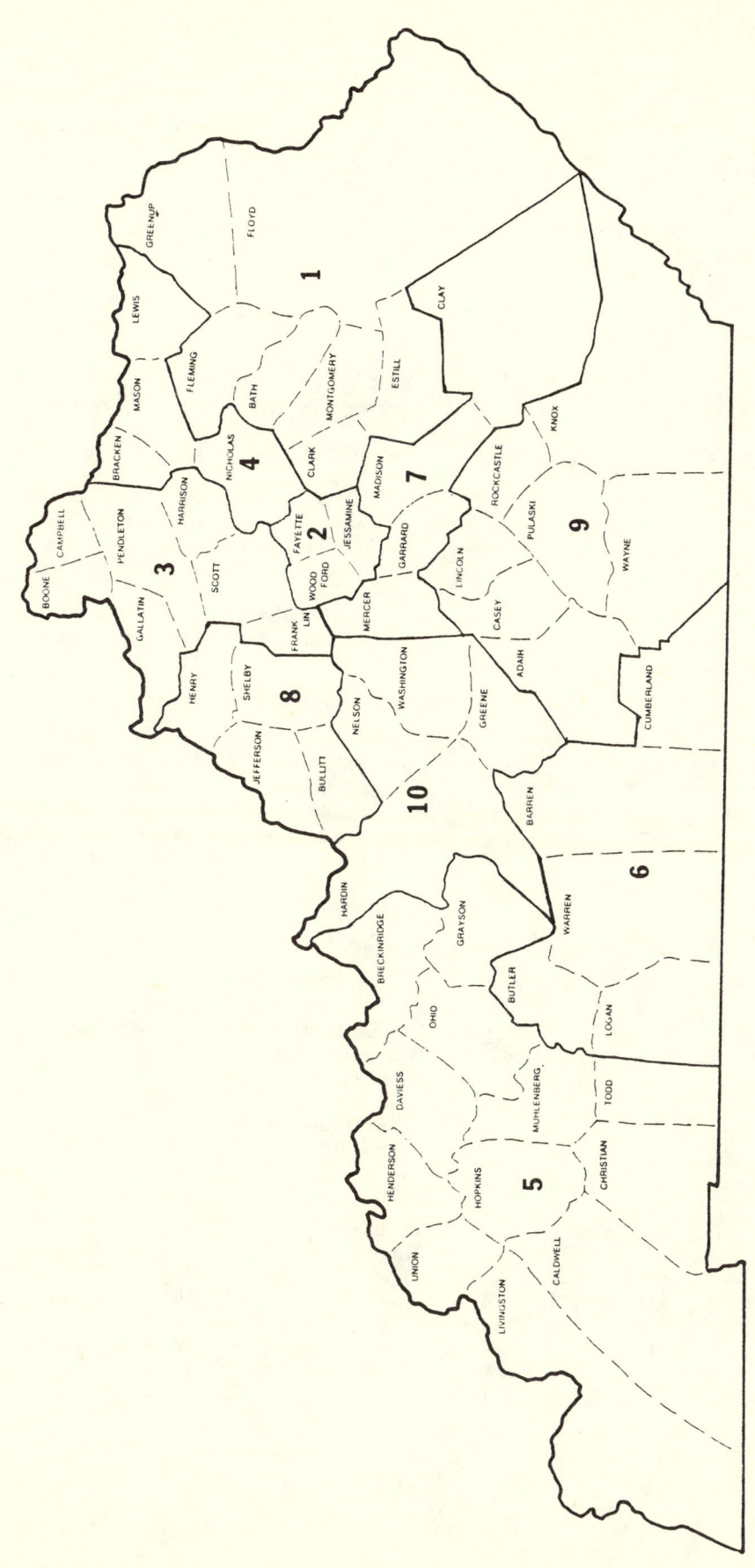

| County | COUNTIES | | | | | REPRESENTATIVES | | | | |
	Aggregate	Slave	%S	sq.mi.	P/sq.mi.	Representative	Cong.	Pty.	Address	County
DISTRICT 5 (CONTINUED)										
Livingston	3,674	718	19.5	1,824	2.0					
Muhlenberg	4,181	480	11.5	481	8.7					
Ohio	3,719	533	14.3	596	6.2					
Union[a]	----	----	-----	----	----					
TOTALS	40,260	6,105	15.2	8,662	4.6					

[a]Created after 1800 census.

County	Aggregate	Slave	%S	sq.mi.	P/sq.mi.	Representative	Cong.	Pty.	Address	County
DISTRICT 6										
Barren	11,286	1,724	15.3	1,498	7.5	Solomon P. Sharp	13	R	Bowling Green	Warren
Butler	2,181	274	12.6	443	4.9					
Cumberland	6,191	922	14.9	500	12.4	Solomon P. Sharp	14	R	Bowling Green	Warren
Logan	12,123	2,486	20.5	702	17.3					
Warren	11,937	1,498	12.5	1,147	10.4	David Walker	15	AR	Russellville	Logan
TOTALS	43,718	6,904	15.8	4,290	10.2	David Walker†	16	AR	Russellville	Logan
						(Died March, 1820)				
						Francis Johnson	16	AR	Bowling Green	Warren
						(Replaced Walker November, 1820)				
						Francis Johnson	17	AR	Bowling Green	Warren

County	Aggregate	Slave	%S	sq.mi.	P/sq.mi.	Representative	Cong.	Pty.	Address	County
DISTRICT 7										
Clay	2,398	141	5.9	2,610	0.9	Samuel McKee	13	R	Lancaster	Garrard
Garrard	9,186	2,083	22.7	236	38.9	Samuel McKee	14	R	Lancaster	Garrard
Madison	15,540	3,037	19.5	783	19.8	George Robertson	15	JD	Lancaster	Garrard
Mercer	12,630	3,284	26.0	439	28.8	George Robertson	16	JD	Lancaster	Garrard
TOTALS	39,754	8,545	21.5	4,068	9.8	George Robertson[r]	17	JD	Lancaster	Garrard
						(Resigned before Congress assembled)				
						John S. Smith	17	R	Richmond	Madison
						(Replaced Robertson December, 1821)				

County	Aggregate	Slave	%S	sq.mi.	P/sq.mi.	Representative	Cong.	Pty.	Address	County
DISTRICT 8										
Bullitt	4,311	976	22.6	300	14.4	Stephen Ormsby	13	R	Louisville	Jefferson
Jefferson	13,399	4,347	32.4	375	35.7	Stephen Ormsby	14	R	Louisville	Jefferson
Henry	6,777	1,137	16.8	519	13.1	Richard D. Anderson	15	JD	Louisville	Jefferson
Shelby	14,877	3,144	20.9	574	26.0	Richard D. Anderson	16	JD	Louisville	Jefferson
TOTALS	39,364	9,574	24.3	1,768	22.3	Wingfield Bullock†	17	(----)	Shelbyville	Shelby
						(Died October, 1821)				
						James D. Breckinridge	17	(----)	Louisville	Jefferson
						(Replaced Bullock January, 1822)				

County	Aggregate	Slave	%S	sq.mi.	P/sq.mi.	Representative	Cong.	Pty.	Address	County
DISTRICT 9										
Adair	6,011	956	15.9	608	9.9	Thomas Montgomery	13	R	Stanford	Lincoln
Casey	3,285	242	7.4	435	7.6	Micah Taul	14	R	Monticello	Wayne
Knox	5,875	307	5.2	2,117	2.8	Tunstall Quarles	15	R	Somerset	Pulaski
Lincoln	8,676	2,341	26.9	340	25.5	Tunstall Quarles[r]	16	R	Somerset	Pulaski
Pulaski	6,897	468	6.8	653	10.6	(Resigned June, 1820)				
Rockcastle	1,731	163	9.4	311	5.6	Thomas Montgomery	16	R	Stanford	Lincoln
Wayne	5,320	230	4.3	858	6.2	(Replaced Quarles November, 1820)				
TOTALS	37,795	4,707	12.4	5,322	7.1	Thomas Montgomery	17	R	Stanford	Lincoln

	COUNTIES					REPRESENTATIVES				
County	Aggregate	Slave	%S	sq.mi.	P/sq.mi.	Representative	Cong.	Pty.	Address	County
					DISTRICT 10					
Green	6,735	1,401	20.8	559	12.0	William P. Duval	13	R	Bardstown	Nelson
Hardin	7,531	840	11.1	1,301	5.8	Benjamin Hardin	14	R	Bardstown	Nelson
Nelson	14,078	3,110	22.1	437	32.2	Thomas Speed	15	(----)	Bardstown	Nelson
Washington	13,248	2,245	16.9	750	17.7	Benjamin Hardin	16	AR	Bardstown	Nelson
TOTALS	41,592	7,596	18.2	3,047	13.6	Benjamin Hardin	17	AR	Bardstown	Nelson

COUNTIES						REPRESENTATIVES				
County	Aggregate	Slave	%S	sq.mi.	P/sq.mi.	Representative	Cong.	Pty.	Address	County

AT LARGE

County	Aggregate	Slave	%S	sq.mi.	P/sq.mi.	Representative	Cong.	Pty.	Address	County
Ascension	2,219	1,031	46.4	240	9.2	Thomas B. Robertson	13	R	New Orleans	
Assumption	2,472	547	22.7	238	10.4	Thomas B. Robertson	14	R	New Orleans	
Attakapas	7,369	3,132	42.5	4,389	1.7	Thomas B. Robertson[r]	15	R	New Orleans	
Avoyelles	1,209	404	33.4	1,267	1.0	(Resigned April, 1818)				
Baton Rouge	1,463	675	46.1	881	1.7	Thomas Butler	15	R	St. Francis-ville	West Feliciana
Catahoula	1,164	348	29.8	950	1.2					
Concordia	2,895	1,581	54.6	1,344	2.2	(Replaced Robertson November, 1818)				
Iberville	2,679	1,205	44.9	224	12.0	Thomas Butler	16	R	St. Francis-ville	West Feliciana
LaFourche	1,995	289	14.4	2,509	0.5					
Natchitoches	2,870	1,476	51.4	8,819	0.3	Josiah S. Johnston	17	R	Alexandria	Rapides
Opelousas	5,048	1,670	33.0	6,348	0.8					
Ouachita	1,077	284	26.3	5,569	0.2					
Plaquemines	1,549	753	48.6	1,544	1.0					
Pointe Coupee	4,539	3,187	70.2	563	8.1					
Rapides	2,200	1,081	49.1	3,523	0.6					
St. Bernard	1,020	382	3.1	566	1.8					
St. Charles	3,291	2,321	70.5	294	11.2					
St. James	3,955	1,952	49.3	167	23.7					
St. John the Baptist	2,990	1,518	50.7	227	13.2					
TOTALS	52,004	23,836	45.8	40,637	1.3					

	COUNTIES					REPRESENTATIVES				
County	Aggregate	Slave	%S	sq.mi.	P/sq.mi.	Representative	Cong.	Pty.	Address	County
DISTRICT 1										
Calvert	8,805	3,937	49.1	217	40.6	Philip Stuart	13	F	Port Tobacco	Charles
Charles	20,245	12,435	61.0	459	44.1					
St. Marys	12,794	6,000	46.8	373	34.3	Philip Stuart	14	F	Port Tobacco	Charles
TOTALS	41,844	22,372	53.5	1,049	39.9					
						Philip Stuart	15	F	Port Tobacco	Charles
						Raphael Neale	16	R	Leonardtown	St. Marys
						Raphael Neale	17	R	Leonardtown	St. Marys
DISTRICT 2										
Ann Arundel	26,668	11,693	43.8	674	39.6	Joseph Kent	13	R	Bladensburg	Prince Georges
						John C. Herbert	14	F	Vannsville	Prince Georges
Prince Georges	20,589	9,189	44.6	485	42.5	John C. Herbert	15	F	Vannsville	Prince Georges
						Joseph Kent	16	R	Bladensburg	Prince Georges
TOTALS	47,257	20,882	44.2	1,159	40.8	Joseph Kent	17	R	Bladensburg	Prince Georges
DISTRICT 3										
Frederick[a]	17,218	2,835	16.4	395	43.6	Alexander C. Hanson	13	F	Rockville	Montgomery
Montgomery	17,980	7,572	42.1	495	36.3	Alexander C. Hanson	14	F	Rockville	Montgomery
TOTALS	35,198	10,407	29.6	890	39.5	George Peters	15	R	Darmestown	Montgomery
						Henry R. Warfield	16	F	Middleburg	----
						George Peters	17	R	Darmestown	Montgomery

[a]"That part of Frederick County adjacent as far as Monocracy from mouth of thereof to the Pennsylvania line." One-half of census figures were assigned to this portion of the county.

	COUNTIES					REPRESENTATIVES				
DISTRICT 4										
Allegheny	6,909	620	8.9	928	7.4	Samuel Ringgold	13	R	Hagerstown	Washington
Frederick[a]	17,218	2,835	16.4	395	43.6	George Baer	14	F	Frederick	Frederick
Washington	18,730	2,656	14.1	459	40.8	Samuel Ringgold	15	R	Hagerstown	Washington
TOTALS	42,857	6,111	14.2	1,782	33.7	Samuel Ringgold	16	R	Hagerstown	Washington
						John Nelson	17	R	Frederick	Frederick

[a]"Remainder of Frederick County." One-half census figures were assigned to this portion of the county.

	COUNTIES					REPRESENTATIVES				
DISTRICT 5										
Baltimore	29,255	6,697	22.8	929	31.5	Alex McKim	13	R	City of Baltimore	
City of Baltimore	35,583	3,713	10.4	78	456.2	Nicholas R. Moore	13	R	Ruxton	Baltimore
TOTALS	64,838	10,410	16.0	1,007	64.4	Nicholas R. Moore	14	R	Ruxton	Baltimore
						Samuel Smith	14	R	City of Baltimore	
						Peter Little	15	R	Freedom	Baltimore
						Samuel Smith	15	R	City of Baltimore	

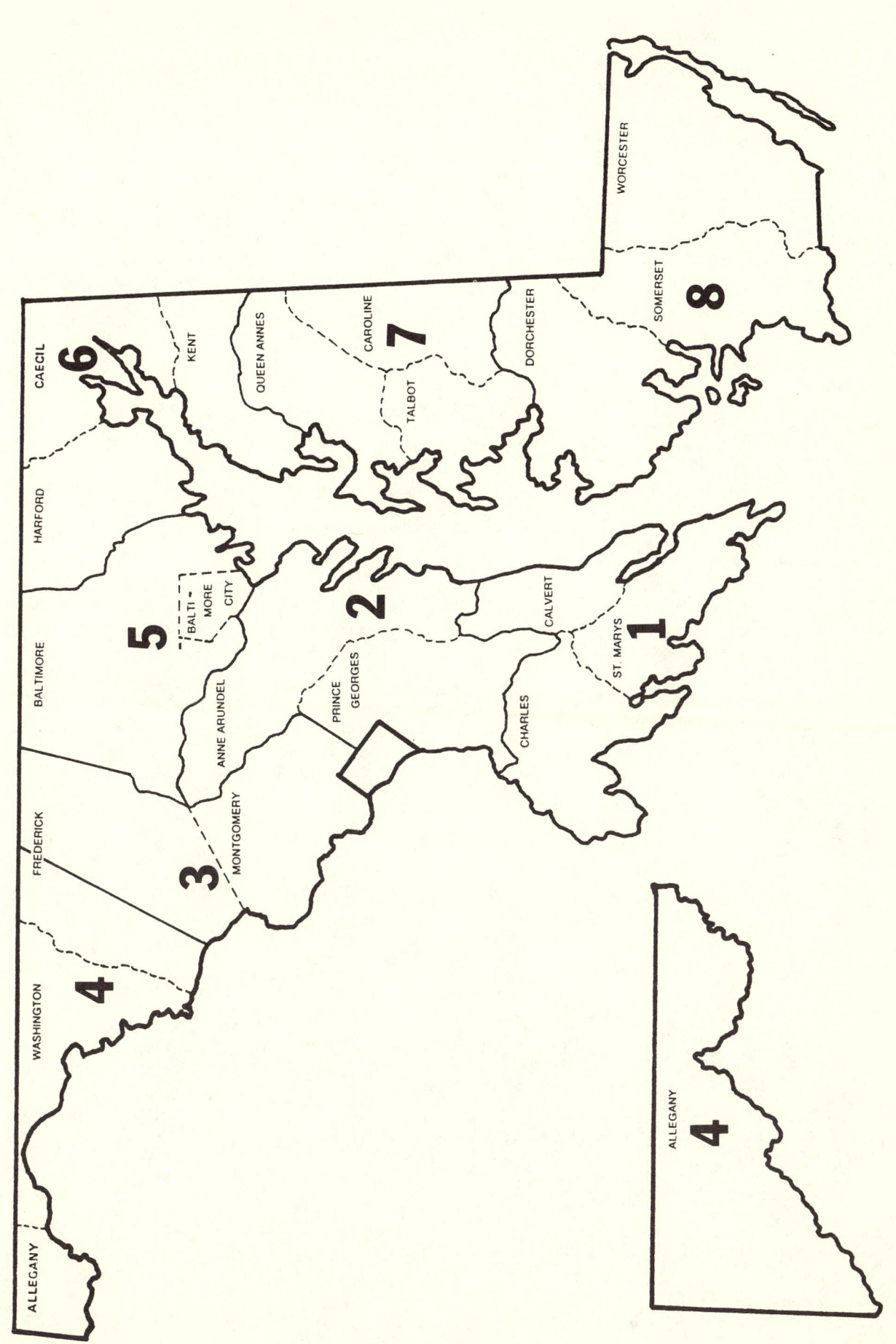

| | COUNTIES | | | | | | REPRESENTATIVES | | | |
County	Aggregate	Slave	%S	sq.mi.	P/sq.mi.	Representative	Cong.	Pty.	Address	County

DISTRICT 5 (CONTINUED)

						Peter Little	16	R	Freedom	Baltimore
						Samuel Smith	16	R	City of Baltimore	
						Peter Little	17	R	Freedom	Baltimore
						Samuel Smith[r]	17	R	City of Baltimore	
						(Resigned December 17, 1822)				
						Isaac McKim	17	R	City of Baltimore	
						(Replaced Smith)				

DISTRICT 6

Cecil	13,066	2,467	18.8	362	36.0	Stevenson Archer	13	R	Bel Air	Harford
Harford	21,258	4,431	20.8	453	46.9	Stevenson Archer	14	R	Bel Air	Harford
Kent	11,450	4,249	37.1	281	40.7	Philip Reed	15	R	Chestertown	Kent
TOTALS	45,774	11,147	24.4	1,096	41.8	Stevenson Archer	16	R	Bel Air	Harford
						Jeremiah Cosden[ce]	17	R	Elkton	Cecil
						Philip Reed	17	R	Chestertown	Kent
						(Successfully contested the election of Cosden)				

DISTRICT 7

Caroline	9,453	1,520	16.0	321	29.4	Robert Wright	13	R	Queenstown	Queen Annes
Queen Annes	16,648	6,381	38.3	375	44.4	Robert Wright	14	R	Queenstown	Queen Annes
Talbot	14,230	4,078	34.2	261	54.5	Thomas Culbreth	15	R	Denton	Caroline
TOTALS	40,331	11,979	29.7	957	42.1	Thomas Culbreth	16	R	Denton	Caroline
						Robert Wright	17	R	Queenstown	Queen Annes

DISTRICT 8

Dorchester	18,108	5,032	27.7	594	30.5	Charles Goldsborough	13	F	Cambridge	Dorchester
Somerset	17,195	6,975	40.5	560	30.7	Charles Goldsborough	14	F	Cambridge	Dorchester
Worcester	16,971	4,427	26.0	639	26.5	Thomas Bayly	15	R	Princess Ann	Somerset
TOTALS	52,274	16,434	31.4	1,793	29.2	Thomas Bayly	16	R	Princess Ann	Somerset
						Thomas Bayly	17	R	Princess Ann	Somerset

MASSACHUSETTS
20 DISTRICTS
20 CONGRESSMEN

| | COUNTIES | | | | | | REPRESENTATIVES | | | |
County	Aggregate	Slave	%S	sq.mi.	P/sq.mi.	Representative	Cong.	Pty.	Address	County

DISTRICT 1

Town in Middlesex County:						Artemis Ward	13	F	Boston	Suffolk
Cambridge	2,323	----	----	10	232.0	Artemis Ward	14	F	Boston	Suffolk
Suffolk	34,381	----	----	56	613.9	Timothy Fuller	15	R	Boston	Suffolk
TOTALS	36,704	----	----	66	556.1	Timothy Fuller	16	R	Boston	Suffolk
						Timothy Fuller	17	R	Boston	Suffolk

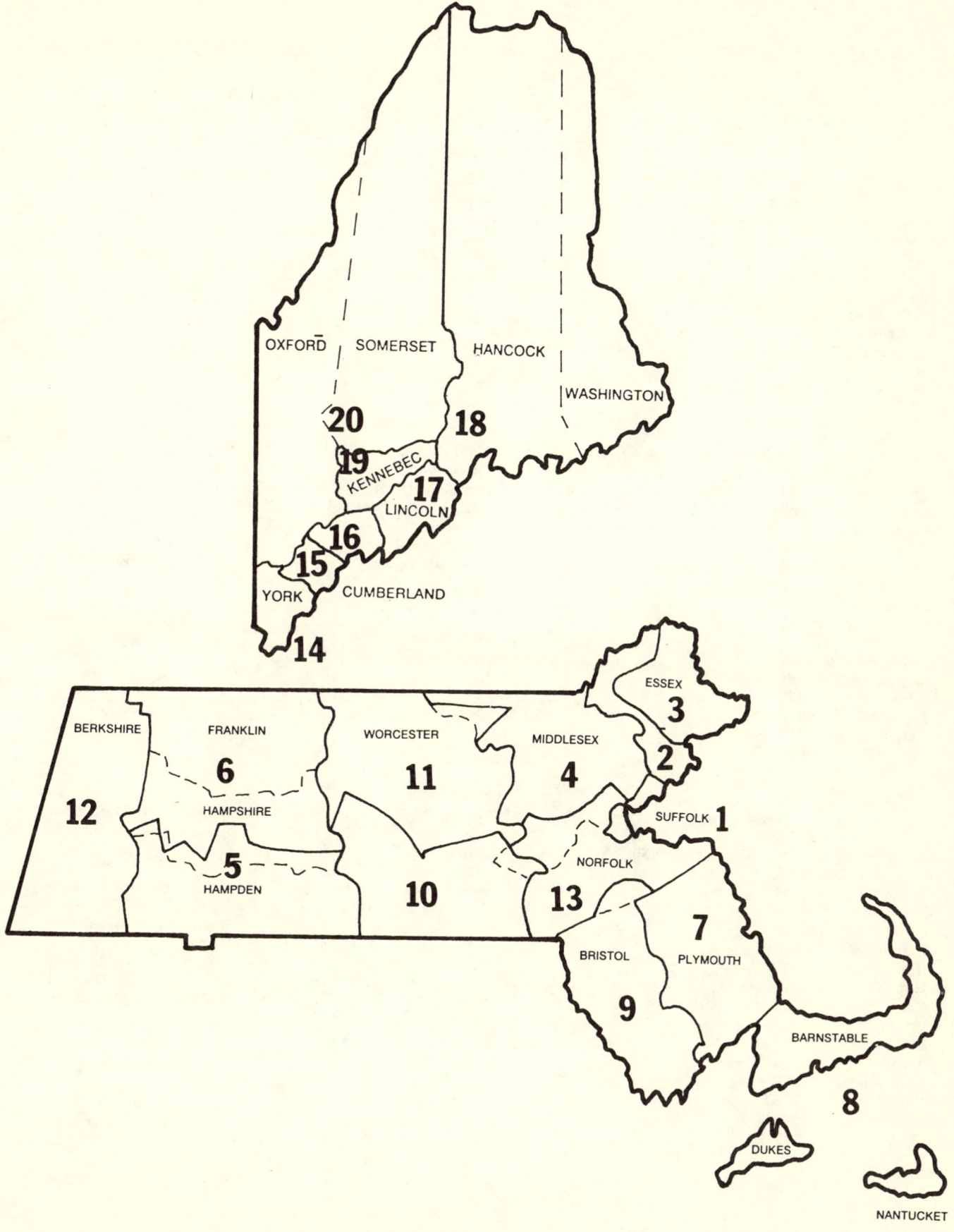

OXFORD SOMERSET HANCOCK

WASHINGTON

20

19 KENNEBEC

18

17 LINCOLN

16

15

YORK CUMBERLAND

14

BERKSHIRE FRANKLIN WORCESTER MIDDLESEX

ESSEX

3

2

6

HAMPSHIRE

11

4

SUFFOLK **1**

12

5

HAMPDEN

10

NORFOLK

13

BRISTOL PLYMOUTH

7

9

BARNSTABLE

8

DUKES

NANTUCKET

| COUNTIES | | | | | | REPRESENTATIVES | | | | |
| County | Aggregate | Slave | %S | sq.mi. | P/sq.mi. | Representative | Cong. | Pty. | Address | County |

DISTRICT 2 (ESSEX SOUTH)

County	Aggregate	Slave	%S	sq.mi.	P/sq.mi.	Representative	Cong.	Pty.	Address	County
Towns in Essex County:						William Reed	13	F	Marblehead	Essex
Amesbury	1,890	----	----	----	----	Jeremiah Nelson*	14	(----)	Newburyport	
Andover	3,164	----	----	----	----	Nathaniel Silsbee	15	R	Salem	Essex
Danvers	3,127	----	----	----	----	Nathaniel Silsbee	16	R	Salem	Essex
Haverhill	2,682	----	----	----	----	Gideon Barstow	17	R	Salem	Essex
Lynn	4,087	----	----	----	----					
Lynnfield	509	----	----	----	----					
Marblehead	5,900	----	----	----	----					
Methuen	1,181	----	----	----	----					
Middleton	541	----	----	----	----					
Salem	12,613	----	----	----	----					
TOTALS	35,694	----	----	194	184.0					

DISTRICT 3 (ESSEX NORTH)

County	Aggregate	Slave	%S	sq.mi.	P/sq.mi.	Representative	Cong.	Pty.	Address	County
Towns and districts of Essex not included in Essex South:						Timothy Pickering	13	F	Wenham	Essex
Beverly	4,608	----	----	----	----	Timothy Pickering[r]	14	F	Wenham	Essex
Boxford	880	----	----	----	----	Jeremiah Nelson	14	F	Newburyport	Essex
Bradford	1,369	----	----	----	----	(Replaced Pickering)				
Gloucester &						Jeremiah Nelson	15	F	Newburyport	Essex
Thatcher's						Jeremiah Nelson	16	F	Newburyport	Essex
Isle	5,943	----	----	----	----	Jeremiah Nelson	17	F	Newburyport	Essex
Hamilton	780	----	----	----	----					
Ipswich	3,569	----	----	----	----					
Manchester	1,137	----	----	----	----					
Newbury	5,006	----	----	----	----					
Newburyport	7,634	----	----	----	----					
Rowley	1,682	----	----	----	----					
Salisbury	2,047	----	----	----	----					
Topsfield	815	----	----	----	----					
Wenham	554	----	----	----	----					
TOTALS	36,094	----	----	300	120.3					

DISTRICT 4 (MIDDLESEX)

County	Aggregate	Slave	%S	sq.mi.	P/sq.mi.	Representative	Cong.	Pty.	Address	County
Towns and districts of Middlesex, total:	52,789	----	----	----	----	William M. Richardson[r] (Resigned April, 1814)	13	F	Groton	Middlesex
The following towns in Middlesex County are NOT included in this district:						Samuel Dana (Replaced Richardson September, 1814)	13	R	Groton	Middlesex
Ashby	(1,103)	----	----	----	----	Asahel Stearns	14	F	Charlestown	Middlesex
Brighton	(608)	----	----	----	----	Jonathan Mason	15	F	Boston	Middlesex
Cambridge	(2,323)	----	----	----	----	Jonathan Mason[r] (Resigned May, 1820)	16	F	Boston	Middlesex
Framingham	(1,670)	----	----	----	----					
Holliston	(989)	----	----	----	----	Benjamin Gorham (Replaced Mason November, 1820)	16	(----)	Boston	Middlesex
Hopkinton	(1,345)	----	----	----	----					
Newton	(1,709)	----	----	----	----	Benjamin Gorham	17	(----)	Boston	Middlesex
Peperell	(1,333)	----	----	----	----					
Sherburne	(770)	----	----	----	----					
Shirley	(814)	----	----	----	----					
Townsend	(1,246)	----	----	----	----					
Natick	(766)	----	----	----	----					
Watertown	(1,531)	----	----	----	----					
TOTALS	36,582	----	----	244	150.0					

COUNTIES						REPRESENTATIVES				
County	Aggregate	Slave	%S	sq.mi.	P/sq.mi.	Representative	Cong.	Pty.	Address	County

DISTRICT 5 (HAMPSHIRE SOUTH)

County	Aggregate	Slave	%S	sq.mi.	P/sq.mi.	Representative	Cong.	Pty.	Address	County
Towns and districts of Hampden County,						William Ely	13	F	Springfield	Hampden
total:	25,525	----	----	----	----	Elijah H. Mills	14	F	Northampton	Hampshire
Towns in Hampshire County:						Elijah H. Mills	15	F	Northampton	Hampshire
Belchertown	2,220	----	----	----	----	Samuel Lathrop	16	R	West Springfield	Hampden
Easthampton	660	----	----	----	----					
Granby	850	----	----	----	----	Samuel Lathrop	17	R	West Springfield	Hampden
Hadley	1,247	----	----	----	----					
Middlefield	822	----	----	----	----					
Northampton	2,631	----	----	----	----					
Norwich	968	----	----	----	----					
South Hadley	902	----	----	----	----					
Southampton	1,171	----	----	----	----					
Ware	996	----	----	----	----					
Westhampton	793	----	----	----	----					
Worthington	1,391	----	----	----	----					
TOTALS	40,226	----	----	872	46.1					

DISTRICT 6 (HAMPSHIRE NORTH)

County	Aggregate	Slave	%S	sq.mi.	P/sq.mi.	Representative	Cong.	Pty.	Address	County
Towns and districts in Hampshire County not included in Hampshire South,						Samuel Taggert	13	F	Colrain	Franklin
						Samuel Taggert	14	F	Colrain	Franklin
total:	10,824	----	----	----	----	Samuel C. Allen	15	(----)	Greenfield	Franklin
Towns and districts in Franklin County,						Samuel C. Allen	16	(----)	Northfield	Franklin
total:	25,525	----	----	----	----	Samuel C. Allen	17	(----)	Greenfield	Franklin
TOTALS	36,349	----	----	984	36.9					

DISTRICT 7 (PLYMOUTH)

County	Aggregate	Slave	%S	sq.mi.	P/sq.mi.	Representative	Cong.	Pty.	Address	County
Towns and districts in Plymouth County,						William Baylies	13	R	Bridgewater	Plymouth
total:	35,169	----	----	654	53.8	William Baylies	14	R	Bridgewater	Plymouth
						Zabdrel Sampson	15	R	Plymouth	Plymouth
						Zabdrel Sampson[r] (Resigned April, 1820)	16	R	Plymouth	Plymouth
						Aaron Hobart (Replaced Sampson December, 1820)	16	R	Hanover	Plymouth
						Aaron Hobart	17	R	Hanover	Plymouth

DISTRICT 8 (BARNSTABLE)

County	Aggregate	Slave	%S	sq.mi.	P/sq.mi.	Representative	Cong.	Pty.	Address	County
Towns and districts in Barnstable County,						John Reed	13	F	Yarmouth	Barnstable
total:	22,211	----	----	393	56.5	John Reed	14	F	Yarmouth	Barnstable
Dukes	3,290	----	----	104	31.6	Walter Folger, Jr.	15	R	Nantucket	Nantucket
Nantucket	6,807	----	----	46	82.8	Walter Folger, Jr.	16	R	Nantucket	Nantucket
Town in Bristol County:						John Reed	17	F	Yarmouth	Barnstable
New Bedford	5,651	----	----	37	152.7					
TOTALS	37,959	----	----	580	65.4					

DISTRICT 9 (BRISTOL)

County	Aggregate	Slave	%S	sq.mi.	P/sq.mi.	Representative	Cong.	Pty.	Address	County
Towns and districts in Bristol County, except New Bedford (see District 8),						Laban Wheaton	13	F	Easton	Bristol
						Laban Wheaton	14	F	Easton	Bristol
total:	31,517	----	----	524	71.0	Marcus Morton	15	R	Taunton	Bristol
						Marcus Morton	16	R	Taunton	Bristol
						Francis Baylies	17	(----)	Taunton	Bristol

163

COUNTIES						REPRESENTATIVES				
County	Aggregate	Slave	%S	sq.mi.	P/sq.mi.	Representative	Cong.	Pty.	Address	County

DISTRICT 10 (WORCESTER SOUTH)

Towns in Worcester County:						Elijah Brigham	13	F	Westboro	Worcester
Barre	1,971	----	----	----	----	Elijah Brigham†	14	F	Westboro	Worcester
Brookfield	3,170	----	----	----	----	(Died February, 1816)				
Charlton	2,180	----	----	----	----	Benjamin Adams	14	F	Uxbridge	Worcester
Dana	625	----	----	----	----	(Replaced Brigham December, 1816)				
Douglas	1,142	----	----	----	----	Benjamin Adams	15	F	Uxbridge	Worcester
Dudley	1,226	----	----	----	----	Benjamin Adams	16	F	Uxbridge	Worcester
Grafton	946	----	----	----	----	Jonathan Russell	17	R	Mendon	Worcester
Hardwick	1,657	----	----	----	----					
Mendon	1,819	----	----	----	----					
Milford	973	----	----	----	----					
New Braintree	912	----	----	----	----					
North Brookfield (not listed in census)										
Northbridge	713	----	----	----	----					
Oxford	1,277	----	----	----	----					
Petersham	1,490	----	----	----	----					
Spencer	1,453	----	----	----	----					
Sturbridge	1,927	----	----	----	----					
Sutton	2,660	----	----	----	----					
Upton	995	----	----	----	----					
Uxbridge	1,404	----	----	----	----					
Ward	540	----	----	----	----					
Westborough	1,045	----	----	----	----					
Western	1,014	----	----	----	----					
Worcester	2,577	----	----	----	----					
Total, towns	33,716	----	----	755	----					
Towns in Middlesex County:										
Holliston	989	----	----	----	----					
Hopkinton	1,345	----	----	----	----					
Total, towns	2,334	----	----	40	----					
TOTALS	36,050	----	----	795	45.3					

DISTRICT 11 (WORCESTER NORTH)

Towns and districts in Worcester County not included						Abijah Bigelow	13	F	Leominster	Worcester
in Worcester South,						Solomon Strong	14	F	Westminster	Worcester
total:	31,191	----	----	----	----	Solomon Strong	15	F	Westminster	Worcester
Towns in Middlesex County:						Jonas Kendall	16	F	Leominster	Worcester
Ashby	1,103	----	----	----	----	Lewis Bigelow	17	(----)	Petersham	Worcester
Pepperell	1,333	----	----	----	----					
Shirley	814	----	----	----	----					
Townsend	1,246	----	----	----	----					
Total, towns	4,496	----	----	----	----					
TOTALS	35,687	----	----	754	47.3					

DISTRICT 12 (BERKSHIRE)

Towns, districts, and plantations of Berkshire County,						Daniel Dewey[r]	13	F	Williamstown	Berkshire
total:	35,907	----	----	941	38.2	(Resigned February, 1814)				
						John W. Hulbert	13	F	Pittsfield	Berkshire
						(Replaced Dewey September, 1814)				
						John W. Hulbert	14	F	Pittsfield	Berkshire
						Henry Shaw	15	F	Lanesboro	Berkshire
						Henry Shaw	16	F	Lanesboro	Berkshire
						Henry W. Dwight	17	(----)	Stockbridge	Berkshire

COUNTIES						REPRESENTATIVES				
County	Aggregate	Slave	%S	sq.mi.	P/sq.mi.	Representative	Cong.	Pty.	Address	County

DISTRICT 13 (NORFOLK)

Towns and districts in Norfolk County,						Nathaniel Ruggles	13	F	Boston	Norfolk
total:	28,241	----	----	394	----	Nathaniel Ruggles	14	F	Boston	Norfolk
The following towns in Norfolk County are NOT						Nathaniel Ruggles	15	F	Boston	Norfolk
included in this district:						Edward Dowse[r]	16	R	Dedham	Norfolk
Foxborough	(870)	----	----	(54)	----	(Resigned May, 1820)				
Sharon	(1,000)	----	----	(18)	----	William Eustis	16	R	Boston	Norfolk
Stoughton	(1,134)	----	----	(18)	----	(Replaced Dowse November, 1820)				
Towns in Middlesex County:						William Eustis	17	R	Boston	Norfolk
Brighton	608	----	----	----	----					
Framingham	1,670	----	----	----	----					
Natick	766	----	----	----	----					
Newton	1,709	----	----	----	----					
Sherburne	770	----	----	----	----					
Watertown	1,531	----	----	----	----					
Total, towns	7,054	----	----	120	----					
TOTALS	32,291	----	----	460	70.2					

DISTRICT 14 (FIRST EASTERN)

Towns, districts, and plantations in York County,						Cyprus King	13	F	Saco	York
total:	35,045	----	----	1,001	----	Cyprus King	14	F	Saco	York
The following towns in York County are NOT							15[a]			
included in this district:						John Holmes	16	R	Alfred	York
Buxton	(2,324)	----	----	----	----	Joseph Dane[b]	17	(----)	Kennebunk	York
Cornish	(971)	----	----	----	----					
Limington	(1,774)	----	----	----	----					
Parsonfield	(1,763)	----	----	(100)	----					
TOTALS	28,213	----	----	901	31.3					

[a]No representative is listed in the BDAC for this district.

[b]This districts became the state of Maine on March 15, 1820. Representatives to the Seventeenth Congress were elected from the state.

DISTRICT 15 (SECOND EASTERN)

Towns in Cumberland County:						George Bradbury	13	F	Portland	Cumberland
Cape						George Bradbury	14	F	Portland	Cumberland
Elizabeth	1,415	----	----	----	----	Ezekiel Whitman	15	F	Portland	Cumberland
Falmouth	4,105	----	----	----	----	Ezekiel Whitman	16	F	Portland	Cumberland
Gorham	2,632	----	----	----	----	Ezekiel Whitman[r]	17	F	Portland	Cumberland
North						(Resigned June, 1822)				
Yarmouth	3,295	----	----	----	----	Mark Harris	17	(----)	Portland	Cumberland
Portland	7,169	----	----	----	----	(Replaced Whitman December, 1822)				
Scarborough	2,094	----	----	----	----					
Standish	1,378	----	----	----	----					
Windham	1,613	----	----	----	----					
Total, towns	23,701	----	----	----	----					
Towns in York County:										
Buxton	2,324	----	----	----	----					
Cornish	971	----	----	----	----					
Limington	1,774	----	----	----	----					
Parsonfield	1,763	----	----	----	----					
Total, towns	6,832	----	----	100	----					
TOTALS	30,533	----	----	390	78.3					

	COUNTIES					REPRESENTATIVES				
County	Aggregate	Slave	%S	sq.mi.	P/sq.mi.	Representative	Cong.	Pty.	Address	County

DISTRICT 16 (THIRD EASTERN)

Towns in Cumberland County:						Samuel Davis	13	F	Bath	Lincoln
Brunswick	2,682	----	----	----	----	Samuel S. Connor*	14	(----)	Waterville	Kennebec
Durham	1,772	----	----	----	----	Benjamin Orr	15	F	Brunswick	Cumberland
Freeport	2,184	----	----	----	----	James Parker*	16	(----)	Bardner	----
Gray	1,310	----	----	----	----	Ebenezer Herrick	17	(----)	Bowdoinham	Lincoln
Harpswell	1,190	----	----	----	----					
Minot	2,020	----	----	----	----					
New										
Gloucester	1,649	----	----	----	----					
Otisfield	912	----	----	----	----					
Pegypscot	805	----	----	----	----					
Poland	850	----	----	----	----					
Pownal	872	----	----	----	----					
Raymond	826	----	----	----	----					
Thompson's Pond & Shaker's Settlement Plantation	191	----	----	----	----					
Total, towns	17,263	----	----	----	----					
Towns in Lincoln County:										
Bath	2,491	----	----	----	----					
Bowdoin	1,649	----	----	----	----					
Bowdoinham	1,412	----	----	----	----					
Dresden	1,096	----	----	----	----					
Georgetown	1,998	----	----	----	----					
Lewistown	1,033	----	----	----	----					
Lisbon	1,614	----	----	----	----					
Litchfield	1,847	----	----	----	----					
Topsham	1,271	----	----	----	----					
Wales Plantation	471	----	----	----	----					
Total, towns	14,882	----	----	----	----					
TOTALS	32,145	----	----	720	44.6					

DISTRICT 17 (FOURTH EASTERN)

Towns, districts, and plantations in Lincoln County, except those included in the Third Eastern District, total:	18,163	----	----	----	----	Abiel Wood	13	F	Wiscasset	Lincoln
						Benjamin Brown	14	(----)	Waldoborough	Lincoln
Towns in Hancock County:						John Gage	15	(----)	Augusta	----
Deer Isle	1,507	----	----	----	----	Mark L. Hill	16	(----)	Phippsburg	Lincoln
Isleborough	583	----	----	----	----	Mark L. Hill	17	(----)	Phippsburg	Lincoln
Lincolnville	1,013	----	----	----	----					
Northport	780	----	----	----	----					
Vinalhaven	1,052	----	----	----	----					
Total, towns	4,935	----	----	----	----					
TOTALS	23,098	----	----	1,080	21.4					

COUNTIES						REPRESENTATIVES				
County	Aggregate	Slave	%S	sq.mi.	P/sq.mi.	Representative	Cong.	Pty.	Address	County

DISTRICT 18 (FIFTH EASTERN)

Towns, districts, and plantations in Hancock County, except those included in the Fourth Eastern District,						John Wilson	13	F	Belfast	Hancock
						James Carr	14	(----)	Bangor	Hancock
total:	20,161	----	----	13,030	----	John Wilson	15	F	Belfast	Hancock
All towns, districts, and plantations in Washington County,						Martin Kinsley	16	(----)	Hampden	Hancock
						William D. Williamson	17	(----)	Bangor	Hancock
total:	7,870	----	----	3,504	----					
TOTALS	28,031	----	----	16,684	1.7					

DISTRICT 19 (SIXTH EASTERN)

Towns, districts, and plantations in Kennebec County,						James Parker	13	R	Gardiner	Kennebec
total:	32,564	----	----	1,146	28.4	Thomas Rice	14	(----)	Augusta	Kennebec
						Thomas Rice	15	(----)	Augusta	Kennebec
						Joshua Cushman	16	R	Winslow	Kennebec
						Joshua Cushman	17	R	Winslow	Kennebec

DISTRICT 20 (SEVENTH EASTERN)

Towns in Cumberland County:						Levi Hubbard	13	R	Paris	Oxford
Baldwin	546	----	----	33.3	----	Albion K. Parris	14	R	Paris	Oxford
Bridgeton	882	----	----	33.3	----	Albion K. Parris[r]	15	R	Paris	Oxford
Harrison	439	----	----	33.3	----	(Resigned February, 1818)				
Oxford	17,630	----	----	4,845	----	Enoch Lincoln	15	R	Paris	Oxford
Somerset	12,910	----	----	5,294	----	(Replaced Parris December, 1818)				
TOTALS	32,407	----	----	10,239	3.2	Enoch Lincoln	16	R	Paris	Oxford
						Enoch Lincoln	17	R	Paris	Oxford

COUNTIES						REPRESENTATIVES				
County	Aggregate	Slave	%S	sq.mi.	P/sq.mi.	Representative	Cong.	Pty.	Address	County
DISTRICT 1										
Rockingham	50,175	----	----	1,041	48.2	Bradbury Cilley	13	F	Nottingham	Rockingham
						Daniel Webster	13	F	Portsmouth	Rockingham
						Bradbury Cilley	14	F	Nottingham	Rockingham
						Daniel Webster	14	F	Portsmouth	Rockingham
						Josiah Butler	15	R	South Deerfield	Rockingham
						John F. Parrott	15	R	Portsmouth	Rockingham
						Josiah Butler	16	R	South Deerfield	Rockingham
						William Plumer, Jr.	16	R	Epping	Rockingham
						Josiah Butler	17	R	South Deerfield	Rockingham
						William Plumer, Jr.	17	R	Epping	Rockingham
DISTRICT 2										
Strafford	41,595	----	----	1,414	29.4	William Hale	13	F	Dover	Strafford
						William Hale	14	F	Dover	Strafford
						Nathaniel Upham	15	R	Rochester	Strafford
						Nathaniel Upham	16	R	Rochester	Strafford
						Nathaniel Upham	17	R	Rochester	Strafford
DISTRICT 3										
Hillsboro	49,595	----	----	1,474	34.6	Samuel Smith	13	F	Peterboro	Hillsboro
						Charles H. Atherton	14	F	Amherst	Hillsboro
						Clifton Clagett	15	(----)	Amherst	Hillsboro
						Clifton Clagett	16	(----)	Amherst	Hillsboro
						Matthew Harvey	17	R	Hopkinton	Hillsboro
DISTRICT 4										
Grafton	28,462	----	----	1,732	16.4	Jeduthum Wilcox	13	F	Orford	Grafton
Coos	3,991	----	----	2,120	1.9	Jeduthum Wilcox	14	F	Orford	Grafton
TOTALS	32,453	----	----	3,852	8.4	Arthur Livermore	15	R	Plymouth	Grafton
						Arthur Livermore	16	R	Plymouth	Grafton
						Thomas Whipple, Jr.	17	R	Wentworth	Grafton

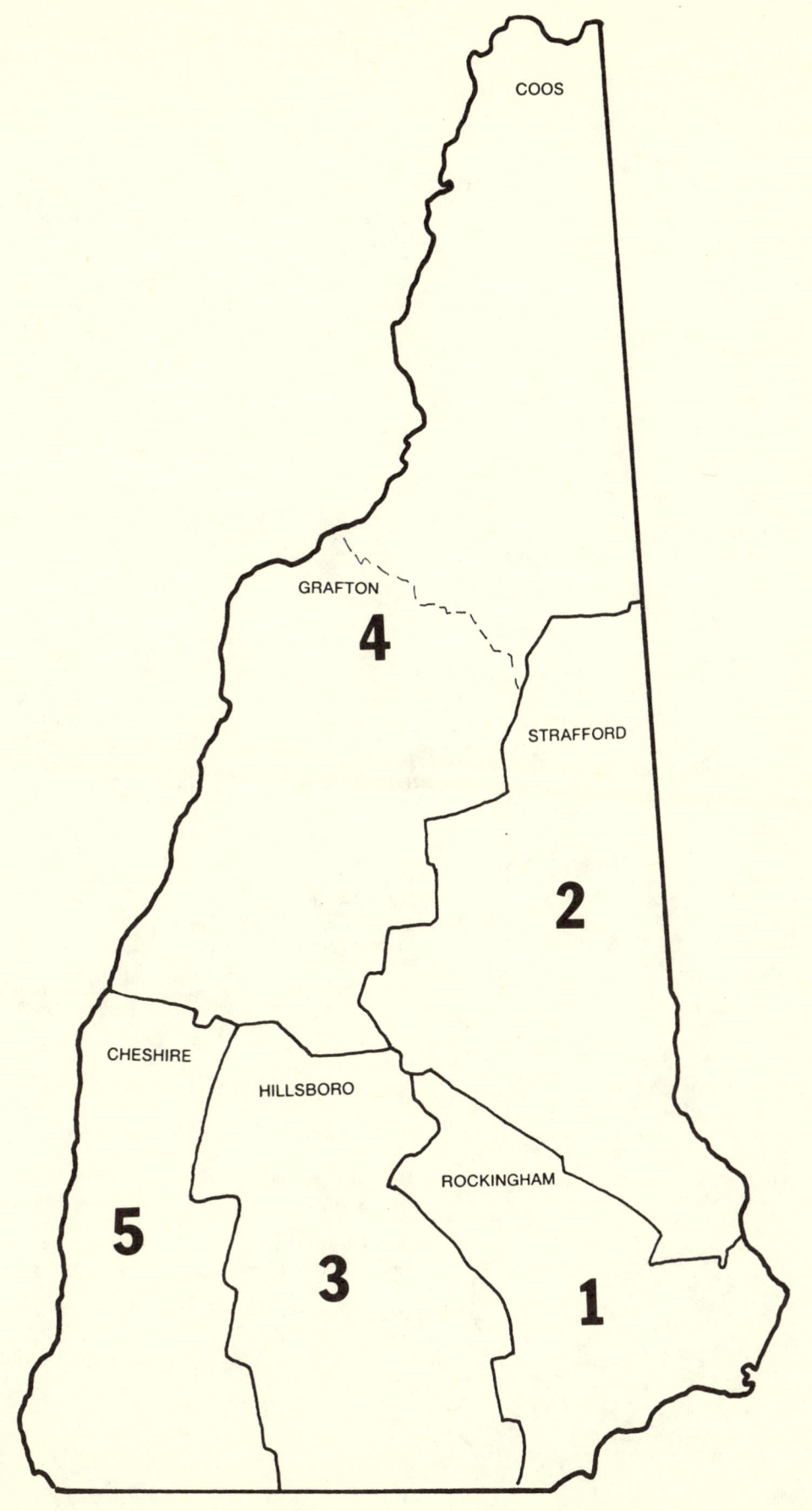

COUNTIES						REPRESENTATIVES				
County	Aggregate	Slave	%S	sq.mi.	P/sq.mi.	Representative	Cong.	Pty.	Address	County

DISTRICT 5

County	Aggregate	Slave	%S	sq.mi.	P/sq.mi.	Representative	Cong.	Pty.	Address	County
Cheshire	40,988	----	----	1,174	34.9	Roger Vose	13	F	Walpole	Cheshire
						Roger Vose	14	F	Walpole	Cheshire
						Salma Hale	15	R	Keene	Cheshire
						Juseph Buffum, Jr.	16	R	West-moreland	Cheshire
						Aaron Matson	17	(----)	Stoddard	Cheshire

NEW JERSEY[1]

3 DISTRICTS
6 CONGRESSMEN

COUNTIES						REPRESENTATIVES				
County	Aggregate	Slave	%S	sq.mi.	P/sq.mi.	Representative	Cong.	Pty.	Address	County

DISTRICT 1

County	Aggregate	Slave	%S	sq.mi.	P/sq.mi.	Representative	Cong.	Pty.	Address	County
Bergen	16,603	2,180	13.1	426	39.0	Lewis Condict	13	R	Morristown	Morris
Essex	25,984	1,129	4.3	233	111.5	Thomas Ward	13	R	Newark	Essex
Morris	21,828	856	3.9	468	46.6					
Sussex	25,539	478	1.9	889	28.7	Lewis Condict	14	R	Morristown	Morris
TOTALS	89,954	4,643	5.2	2,016	44.6	Thomas Ward	14	R	Newark	Essex
						Charles Kinsey	15	(----)	Paterson	Bergen
						John Linn	15	(----)	Monroe	Sussex
						John Condit[r] (Retired November, 1819)	16	R	Orange	Essex
						Charles Kinsey (Replaced Condit February 2, 1820)	16	(----)	Paterson	Bergen
						John Linn† (Died January 25, 1821; not replaced)	16	(----)	Monroe	Sussex
						George Cassedy	17	R	Hackensack	Bergen
						Lewis Condict	17	R	Morristown	Morris

DISTRICT 2

County	Aggregate	Slave	%S	sq.mi.	P/sq.mi.	Representative	Cong.	Pty.	Address	County
Hunterdon	24,553	1,119	4.6	651	37.7	James Schureman	13	F	New Brunswick	Middlesex
Middlesex	20,381	1,298	6.3	312	65.3					
Monmouth	22,150	1,504	6.8	1,118	19.8	Richard Stockton	13	F	Princeton	Somerset
Somerset	13,728	1,968	13.4	307	48.0					
TOTALS	81,812	5,889	7.2	2,388	34.3	Benjamin Bennet	14	(----)	Middletown	Monmouth
						Henry Southard	14	R	Baskingridge	Somerset
						Benjamin Bennet	15	(----)	Middletown	Monmouth
						Henry Southard	15	R	Baskingridge	Somerset
						Henry Southard	16	R	Baskingridge	Somerset
						Bernard Smith	16	(----)	New Brunswick	Middlesex

[1] Thirteenth Congress by districts, all others at large.

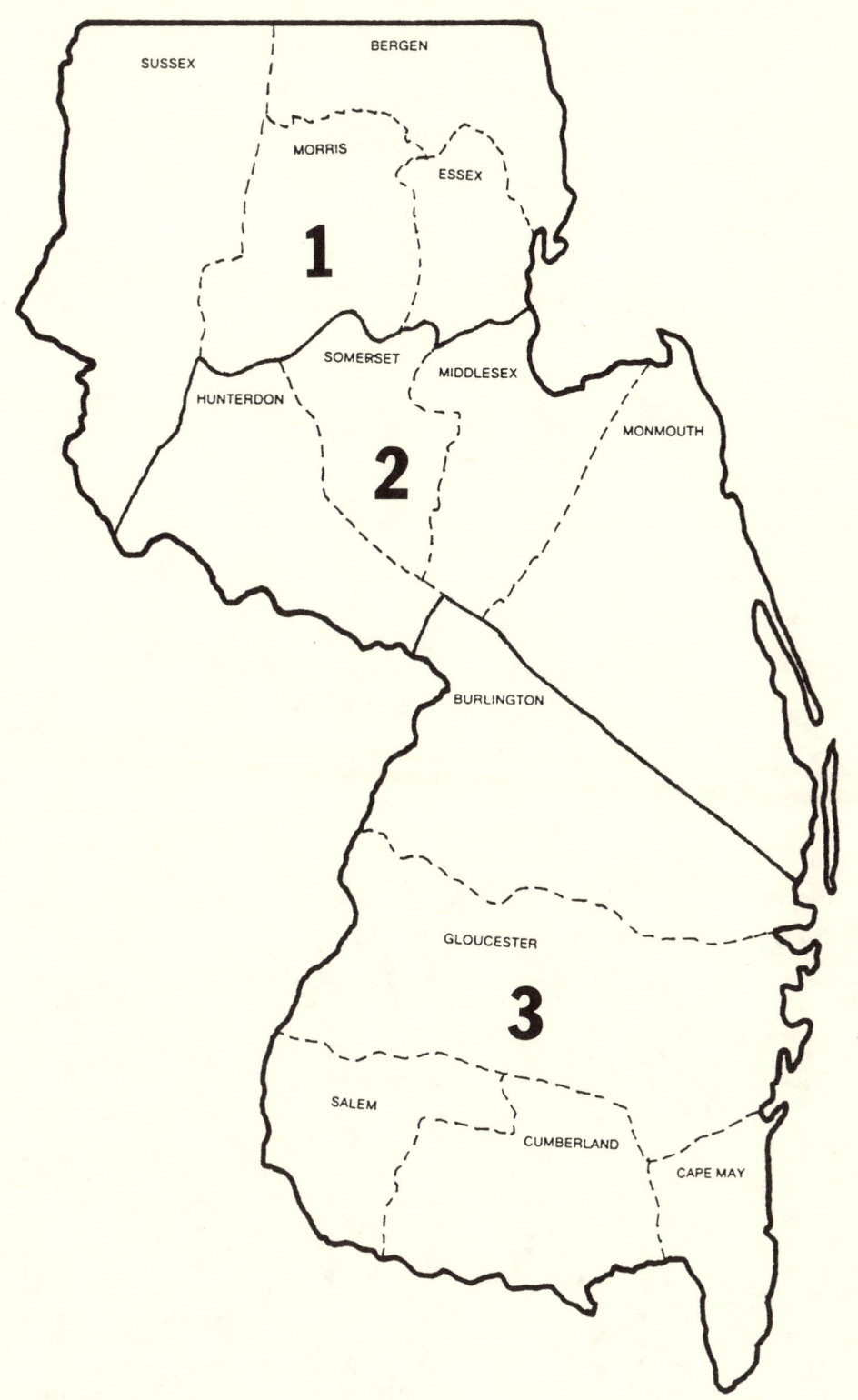

SUSSEX

BERGEN

MORRIS

ESSEX

1

SOMERSET

MIDDLESEX

HUNTERDON

2

MONMOUTH

BURLINGTON

GLOUCESTER

3

SALEM

CUMBERLAND

CAPE MAY

DISTRICT 2 (CONTINUED)

County	Aggregate	Slave	%S	sq.mi.	P/sq.mi.	Representative	Cong.	Pty.	Address	County
						George Holcombe	17	R	Allentown	Monmouth
						Samuel Swan	17	NR	Somerville	Somerset

DISTRICT 3

County	Aggregate	Slave	%S	sq.mi.	P/sq.mi.	Representative	Cong.	Pty.	Address	County
Burlington	24,979	93	0.4	819	30.5	William Coxe	13	F	Burlington	Burlington
Cape May	3,632	81	2.2	267	13.6	Jacob Hufty†	13	R	Salem	Salem
Cumberland	12,670	42	0.3	500	25.3	(Died May, 1814)				
Gloucester	19,744	74	0.4	1,119	17.6	Thomas Bines	13	R	Pennsville	Salem
Salem	13,761	29	2.2	365	35.0	(Replaced Hufty November, 1814)				
TOTALS	73,786	319	0.4	3,070	24.0					
						Ezra Baker	14	(----)	Tuckerton	Burlington
						Ephraim Bateman	14	R	Cedarville	Cumberland
						Ephraim Bateman	15	R	Cedarville	Cumberland
						Joseph Bloomfield	15	R	Burlington	Burlington
						Ephraim Bateman	16	R	Cedarville	Cumberland
						Joseph Bloomfield	16	R	Burlington	Burlington
						Ephraim Bateman	17	R	Cedarville	Cumberland
						James Matlock	17	NR	Woodbury	Gloucester

NEW YORK
21 DISTRICTS
27 CONGRESSMEN

County	Aggregate	Slave	%S	sq.mi.	P/sq.mi.	Representative	Cong.	Pty.	Address	County

DISTRICT 1

County	Aggregate	Slave	%S	sq.mi.	P/sq.mi.	Representative	Cong.	Pty.	Address	County
Kings	8,303	1,118	13.4	70	118.6	John Lefferts	13	R	Brooklyn	Kings
New York City,						Ebeneazer Sage	13	R	Sag Harbor	Suffolk
First Ward	9,637	169	1.8		24818.5					
New York City,						Henry Crocheron	14	R	Castletown	Richmond
Second Ward	9,637	169	1.8		24818.5	George Townsend	14	R	Oyster Bay	Queens
Queens	19,336	809	4.1	108	17.3					
Richmond	5,347	427	8.0	58	92.1	Tredwell Scudder	15	(----)	Islip	Suffolk
TOTALS	73,373	3,105	4.2	1,458	50.5	George Townsend	15	R	Oysters Bay	Queens
						Ebeneazer Sage ce	16	R	Sag Harbor	Suffolk
						(Never appeared to claim the seat. Election contested by James Guyon, Jr.)				
						James Guyon, Jr.	16	F	Richmond	Richmond
						(Contested election of Sage. Took seat January, 1820)				
						Silas Wood	16	R	Huntington	Suffolk
						Churchill Cambreleng	17	R	New York City	
						Silas Wood	17	R	Huntington	Suffolk

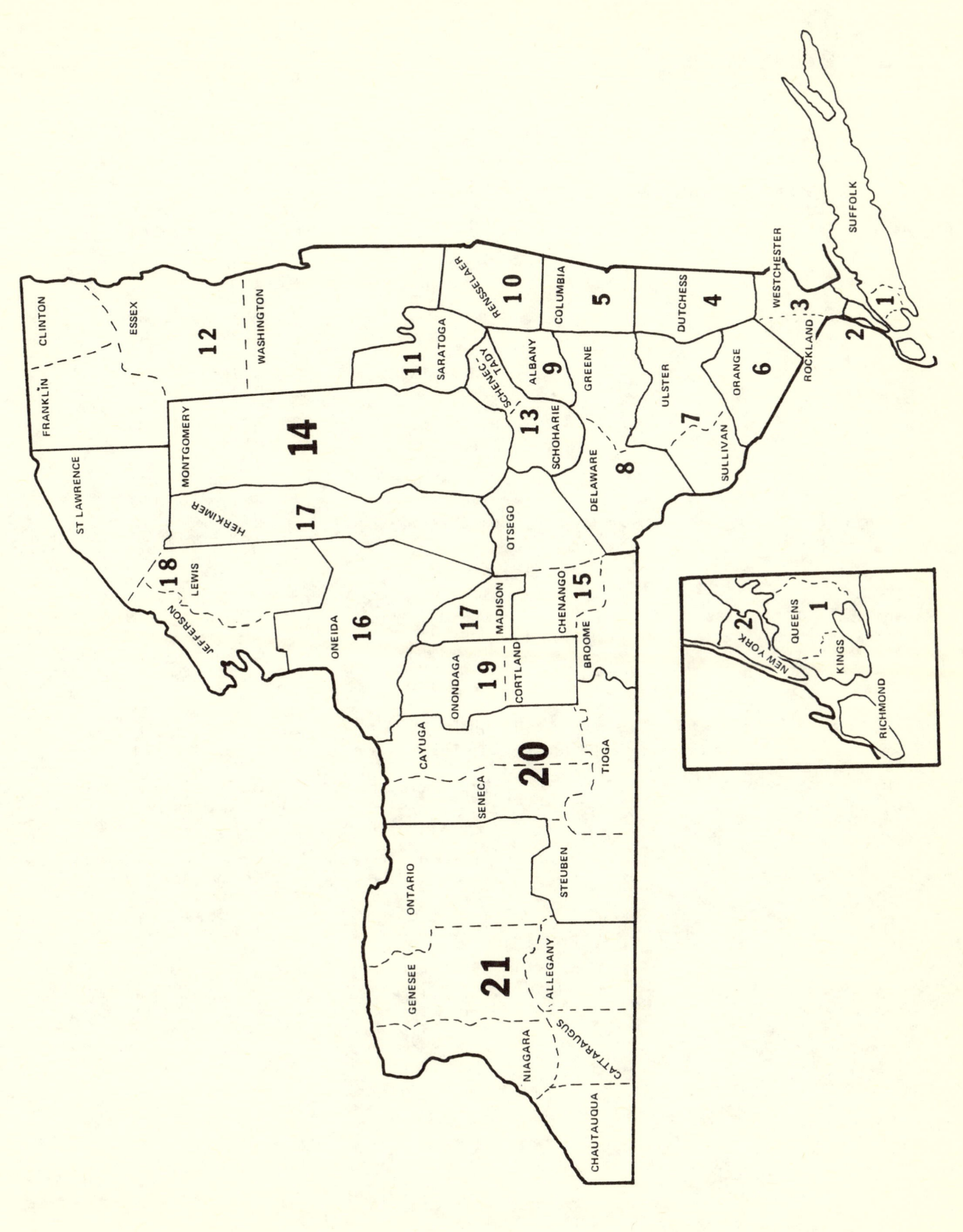

COUNTIES						REPRESENTATIVES				
County	Aggregate	Slave	%S	sq.mi.	P/sq.mi.	Representative	Cong.	Pty.	Address	County

DISTRICT 2

Third, Fourth, Fifth, Sixth, Seventh, Eighth, Ninth, and Tenth Wards of New York City,						Egbert Benson[r] (Resigned August, 1813)	13[a]	(----)	New York City	
total:	77,096	1,352	1.8	16	4818.5	William Irving (Replaced Benson January, 1814)	13	R	New York City	
						Samuel Hopkins	13	R	New York City	
						Jonathan Post, Jr.	13	F	New York City	
						William Irving	14	R	New York City	
						Peter H. Wendover	14	R	New York City	
						William Irving	15	R	New York City	
						Peter H. Wendover	15	R	New York City	
						Henry Meigs	16	R	New York City	
						Peter H. Wendover	16	R	New York City	
						Cadwallader D. Colden	17	F	New York City	
						John J. Morgan	17	R	New York City	

[a]Extra representative in this Congress for unknown reason. The Twenty-first District, a 2-member district, has only one representative for this Congress.

DISTRICT 3

Rockland	7,758	316	18.7	176	44.0	Peter Denoyelles	13	(----)	Haverstraw	Rockland
Westchester	30,272	982	3.2	443	68.3	Johnathan Ward	14	R	New Rochelle	Westchester
TOTALS	38,030	1,298	3.4	619	61.4					
						Caleb Tompkins	15	(----)	White Plains	Westchester
						Caleb Tompkins	16	(----)	White Plains	Westchester
						Jeremiah H. Pierson	17	F	Ramapo	Rockland

DISTRICT 4

All of Dutchess County except the towns of Clinton and Rhinebeck,						Thomas J. Oakley	13	F	Pough-keepsie	Dutchess
total:	51,363	1,262	2.5	813	63.2	Abraham H. Schenck	14	R	Fishkill Landing	Dutchess
						James Tallmadge, Jr.	15	R	Pough-keepsie	Dutchess

(Elected to fill vacancy upon the death of Representative-elect H. B. Lee. Took seat December, 1817).

						Randall S. Street	16	R	Pough-keepsie	Dutchess
						William W. Van Wyck	17	R	Fishkill	Dutchess

DISTRICT 5

Columbia	32,390	879	2.7	645	50.2	Thomas P. Grosvenor	13	F	Hudson	Columbia
Towns in Dutchess County:[a]						Thomas P. Grosvenor	14	F	Hudson	Columbia
Clinton						Philip J. Schuyler	15	F	Rhinebeck	Dutchess
Rhinebeck						James Strong	16	F	Hudson	Columbia
						Walter Patterson	17	(----)	Livingston	Columbia

[a]The printed census contains no population data for towns in New York.

	COUNTIES					REPRESENTATIVES				
County	Aggregate	Slave	%S	sq.mi.	P/sq.mi.	Representative	Cong.	Pty.	Address	County

DISTRICT 6

Orange	34,347	966	2.8	833	41.2	Jonathan Fisk	13	R	Newburgh	Orange
						Jonathan Fisk[r]	14	R	Newburgh	Orange
						(Resigned March, 1815)				
						James W. Wilken	14	R	Goshen	Orange
						(Replaced Fisk December, 1815)				
						James W. Wilken	15	R	Goshen	Orange
						Walter Case	16	R	Newberry	Orange
						Selah Tuthill[†]	17	(----)	Goshen	Orange
						(Died September, 1821)				
						Charles Borland, Jr.	17	(----)	Wardsbridge	Orange
						(Replaced Tuthill, December, 1821)				

DISTRICT 7

Sullivan	6,108	43	0.7	980	6.2	Abraham J. Hasbrouck	13	R	Kingston	Ulster
Ulster	26,576	1,437	5.4	1,141	23.2	Samuel R. Betts[a]	14	R	Newburgh	Orange
TOTALS	32,684	1,480	4.5	2,121	15.4	Josiah Hasbrouck	15	(----)	New Paltz	Ulster
						Jacob H. DeWitt	16	R	Kingston	Ulster
						Charles H. Ruggles	17	(----)	Kingston	Ulster

[a]Listed in District 7 by ICPR despite his address.

DISTRICT 8

Delaware	20,303	55	0.2	1,443	14.0	Samuel Sherwood	13	F	Delhi	Delaware
Greene	19,536	367	1.8	653	29.9	John Adams[ce]	14	R	Catskill	Greene
TOTALS	39,839	422	1.1	2,096	19.0	(Resigned December, 1815 after election successfully contested by Erastus Root)				
						Erastus Root	14	R	Delhi	Delaware
						(Successfully contested election of Adams. Took seat December, 1815)				
						Dorrance Kirtland	15	R	Coxsackie	Greene
						Robert Clark	16	R	Roseville	Delaware
						Richard McCarty	17	R	Coxsackie	Greene

DISTRICT 9

Albany	34,661	772	2.1	1,179	29.4	John Lovett	13	F	Albany	Albany
						John Lovett	14	F	Albany	Albany
						Rensselaer Westerlo	15	F	Albany	Albany
						Solomon Van Rensselaer	16	F	Albany	Albany
						Solomon Van Rensselaer[r]	17	F	Albany	Albany
						(Resigned January, 1822)				
						Stephen Van Rensselaer	17	NR	Albany	Albany
						(Replaced Solomon Van Rensselaer March, 1822)				

DISTRICT 10

Rensselaer	36,309	750	2.0	665	54.6	Hosea Moffitt	13	F	Nassau	Rensselaer
						Hosea Moffitt	14	F	Nassau	Rensselaer
						John P. Cushman	15	(----)	Troy	Rensselaer
						John D. Dickinson	16	F	Troy	Rensselaer
						John D. Dickinson	17	F	Troy	Rensselaer

| | | COUNTIES | | | | | REPRESENTATIVES | | | |
County	Aggregate	Slave	%S	sq.mi.	P/sq.mi.	Representative	Cong.	Pty.	Address	County
						DISTRICT 11				
Saratoga	33,147	107	0.3	818	40.5	John W. Taylor	13	R	Ballston Spa	Saratoga
						John W. Taylor	14	R	Ballston Spa	Saratoga
						John W. Taylor	15	R	Ballston Spa	Saratoga
						John W. Taylor	16	R	Ballston Spa	Saratoga
						John W. Taylor	17	R	Ballston Spa	Saratoga
						DISTRICT 12				
Clinton	8,002	29	0.4	1,059	7.5	Elisha I. Winter	13	F	Peru	Clinton
Essex	9,477	----	----	1,826	5.1	Zebulon R. Shipherd	13	F	Granville	Washington
Franklin	2,617	3	0.1	1,674	1.5					
Washington	44,289	315	0.7	836	52.9	Asa Adgate	14	R	Chesterfield	Essex
TOTALS	64,385	347	0.5	5,395	11.9	John Savage	14	R	Salem	Washington
						John Palmer	15	R	Plattsburg	Clinton
						John Savage	15	R	Salem	Washington
						Ezra C. Gross	16	R	Elizabeth	Essex
						Nathaniel Pitcher	16	R	Sandy Hill	Washington
						Nathaniel Pitcher	17	R	Sandy Hill	Washington
						Reuban H. Walworth	17	R	Plattsburg	Clinton
						DISTRICT 13				
Schenectady	10,201	318	3.1	207	49.2	Alexander Boyd	13	F	Middlebury	Schoharie
Schoharie	18,945	316	1.6	624	30.3		14ᵃ			
TOTALS	29,146	634	2.1	831	35.0	Thomas Lawyer	15	(----)	Cobleskill	Schoharie
						Harmanus Peek	16	(----)	Schenectady	Schenectady
						John Gebhard	17	(----)	Schoharie	Schoharie

ᵃSee District 16.

						DISTRICT 14				
Montgomery	41,214	712	1.7	906	45.5	Jacob Markell	13	F	Manheim	Montgomery
						Daniel Cady	14	F	Johnston	Montgomery
							15ᵃ			
						John Fay	16	R	Northampton	Montgomery
						Alfred Conkling	17	NR	Canajoharie	Montgomery

ᵃSee District 17.

						DISTRICT 15				
Broome	8,130	23	0.3	714	11.3	John M. Bowersᶜᵉ	13	(----)	Cooperstown	Otsego
Chenango	21,704	13	0.1	903	24.0	(Resigned December, 1813 after election successfully				
Otsego	38,802	74	0.4	1,013	76.6	contested by Isaac Williams, Jr.)				
TOTALS	68,636	110	0.2	2,630	26.1	Isaac Williams, Jr.	13	R	Cooperstown	Otsego
						Joel Thompson	13	F	Smyrna	Chenango
						James Birdsall	14	R	Norwhich	Chenango
						Jabez D. Hammond	14	R	Cherry Valley	Otsego
						John R. Drake	15	(----)	Oswego	Tioga
						Isaac Williams, Jr.	15	R	Cooperstown	Otsego

COUNTIES						REPRESENTATIVES				
County	Aggregate	Slave	%S	sq.mi.	P/sq.mi.	Representative	Cong.	Pty.	Address	County

DISTRICT 15 (CONTINUED)

County	Aggregate	Slave	%S	sq.mi.	P/sq.mi.	Representative	Cong.	Pty.	Address	County
						Joseph S. Lyman	16	(----)	Cooperstown	Otsego
						Robert Monell	16	R	Greene	Chenango
						Samuel Campbell	17	NR	Columbus	Chenango
						James Hawkes	17	(----)	Richfield	Otsego

DISTRICT 16

County	Aggregate	Slave	%S	sq.mi.	P/sq.mi.	Representative	Cong.	Pty.	Address	County
Oneida	33,792	81	0.3	1,223	27.6	Morris S. Miller	13	F	Utica	Oneida
						Thomas R. Gold[a]	14	F	Whitestown	Oneida
						John B. Yates[a]	14	R	Utica	Oneida
						Henry R. Storrs	15	F	Whitestown	Oneida
						Henry R. Storrs	16	F	Whitestown	Oneida
						Joseph Kirkland	17	(----)	Utica	Oneida

[a]Both men are listed by ICPR as from this district. One probably represents District 13.

DISTRICT 17

County	Aggregate	Slave	%S	sq.mi.	P/sq.mi.	Representative	Cong.	Pty.	Address	County
Herkimer	22,046	64	----	1,435	54.7	William S. Smith	13	F	Lebanon	Madison
Madison	25,144	35	----	661	37.9	Westel Willoughby, Jr.	14	R	Herkimer	Herkimer
TOTALS	47,190	99	----	2,096	22.5	Thomas H. Hubbard[a]	15	R	Hamilton	Madison
						John Herkimer[a]	15	R	Danube	Herkimer
						Aaron Hackley, Jr.	16	(----)	Herkimer	Herkimer
						Thomas H. Hubbard	17	R	Hamilton	Madison

[a]Both men are listed by ICPR as from this district. One probably represents District 14.

DISTRICT 18

County	Aggregate	Slave	%S	sq.mi.	P/sq.mi.	Representative	Cong.	Pty.	Address	County
Jefferson	15,140	---	----	1,294	11.7	Moss Kent	13	F	Leraysville	Jefferson
Lewis	6,433	4	----	1,291	4.9	Moss Kent	14	F	Leraysville	Jefferson
St. Lawrence	7,885	5	----	2,168	6.0	David A. Ogden	15	F	Madrid	St. Lawrence
TOTALS	29,458	9	----	5,353	5.5	William D. Ford	16	R	Watertown	Jefferson
						Micah Sterling	17	F	Watertown	Jefferson

DISTRICT 19

County	Aggregate	Slave	%S	sq.mi.	P/sq.mi.	Representative	Cong.	Pty.	Address	County
Cortland	8,869	----	----	502	17.6	James Geddes	13	F	Onondaga	Onondaga
Onondaga	25,987	50	0.2	794	32.7	Victory Birdseye	14	F	Pompey	Onondaga
TOTALS	34,856	50	0.1	1,296	26.9	James Porter	15	R	Skaneatles	Onondaga
						George Hall	16	R	Onondaga	Onondaga
						Elisha Litchfield	17	R	Delphi	Onondaga

DISTRICT 20

County	Aggregate	Slave	%S	sq.mi.	P/sq.mi.	Representative	Cong.	Pty.	Address	County
Cayuga	29,843	75	0.3	1,180	25.2	Daniel Avery	13	R	Aurora	Cayuga
Seneca	16,609	101	0.6	890	18.6	Oliver C. Comstock	13	R	Trumansburg	Seneca
Steuban	7,246	87	1.2	2,457	2.9					
Tioga	7,899	61	0.8	939	8.4	Oliver C. Comstock	14	R	Trumansburg	Seneca
TOTALS	61,597	324	0.5	5,466	11.3	Enos T. Throop[r]	14	R	Auburn	Cayuga
						(Resigned June, 1816)				
						Daniel Avery	14	R	Aurora	Cayuga
						(Replaced Throop December, 1816)				
						Oliver C. Comstock	15	R	Trumansburg	Seneca
						Daniel Cruger	15	R	Bath	Steuban

	COUNTIES					REPRESENTATIVES				
County	Aggregate	Slave	%S	sq.mi.	P/sq.mi.	Representative	Cong.	Pty.	Address	County

DISTRICT 20 (CONTINUED)

						Representative	Cong.	Pty.	Address	County
						Caleb Baker	16	(----)	Elmira	Tioga
						Jonathan Richmond	16	(----)	Aurora	Cayuga
						William B. Rochester	17	R	Bath	Steuban
						David Woodcock	17	R	Ithaca	Seneca

DISTRICT 21[a]

County	Aggregate	Slave	%S	sq.mi.	P/sq.mi.	Representative	Cong.	Pty.	Address	County
Allegheny	1,942	21	----	1,047	1.8	Nathaniel W. Howell	13	(----)	Canandaigua	Ontario
Cattaraugus (not listed in 1810 census)				1,318						
Chatauqua (not listed in 1810 census)				1,081		Micah Brooks	14	(----)	East Broomfield	Ontario
Genesee	12,588	11	----	1,894	6.6					
Niagara	8,971	8	----	1,590	5.6	Peter B. Porter	14	R	Buffalo	Niagara
Ontario	42,032	212	0.5	2,244	18.7	(Resigned January, 1816)				
TOTALS	65,533	252	0.4	6,775	9.6	Archibald S. Clark	14	(----)	Clark	Niagara
						(Replaced Porter December, 1816)				
						Benjamin Ellicott	15	R	Batavia	Genesee
						John C. Spencer	15	R	Canandaigua	Ontario
						Nathaniel Allen	16	(----)	Richmond	Ontario
						Albert H. Tracy	16	R	Buffalo	Niagara
						Elijah Spencer	17	R	Benton	Ontario
						Albert H. Tracy	17	R	Buffalo	Niagara

[a]District 21 was split in 1821. The northeast portion remained as District 21, while the remainder became District 22.

NORTH CAROLINA
13 DISTRICTS
13 CONGRESSMEN

	COUNTIES					REPRESENTATIVES				
County	Aggregate	Slave	%S	sq.mi.	P/sq.mi.	Representative	Cong.	Pty.	Address	County

DISTRICT 1

County	Aggregate	Slave	%S	sq.mi.	P/sq.mi.	Representative	Cong.	Pty.	Address	County
Camden	5,347	1,411	26.3	239	22.7	William H. Murfree	13	R	Murfreesboro	Hertford
Chowan	5,297	2,789	52.6	173	30.6	William H. Murfree	14	R	Murfreesboro	Hertford
Currituck	6,985	1,631	23.3	246	28.4	Lemuel Sawyer	15	R	Elizabeth City	Pasquotank
Gates	10,366	1,469	14.1	337	30.8					
Hertford	6,052	2,805	46.3	353	17.1	Lemuel Sawyer	16	R	Elizabeth City	Pasquotank
Pasquotank	7,674	2,295	29.9	228	33.7					
Perquimans	6,052	2,017	33.3	246	24.6	Lemuel Sawyer	17	R	Elizabeth City	Pasquotank
TOTALS	47,773	14,417	30.2	1,822	26.2					

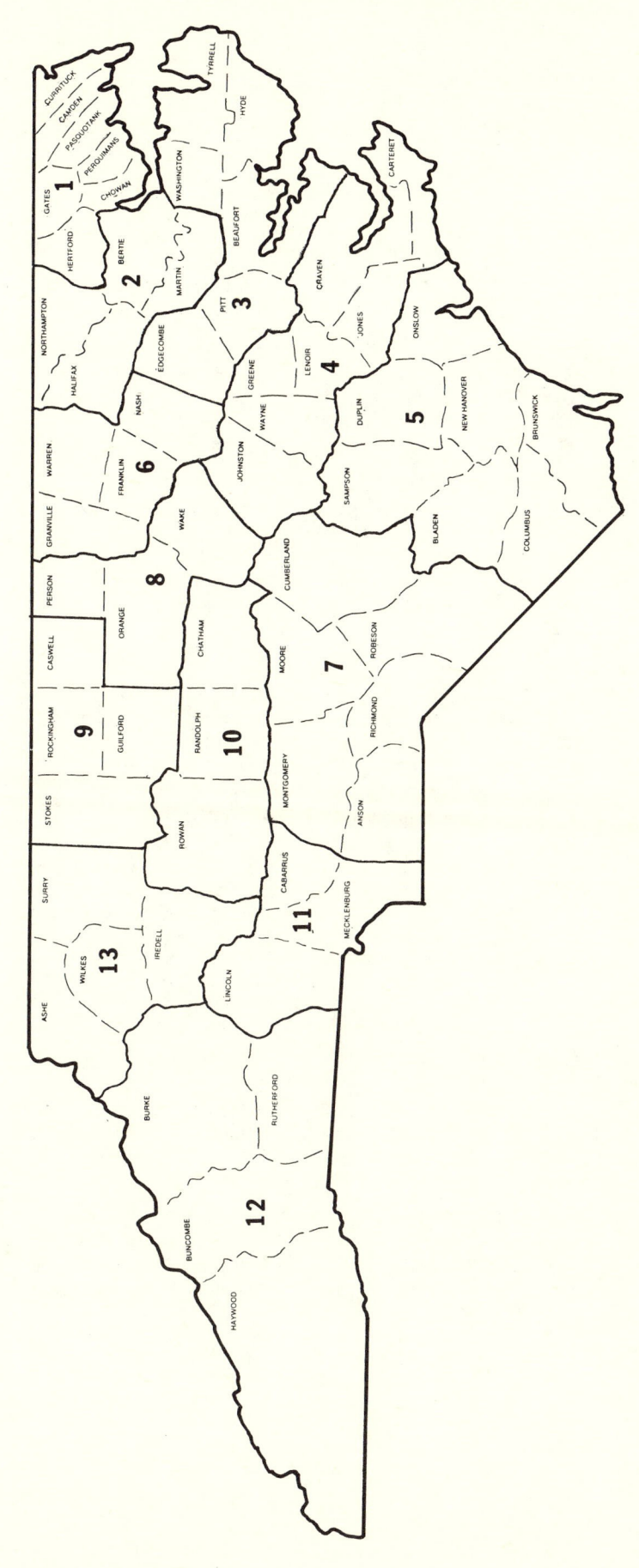

COUNTIES						REPRESENTATIVES				
County	Aggregate	Slave	%S	sq.mi.	P/sq.mi.	Representative	Cong.	Pty.	Address	County

DISTRICT 2

County	Aggregate	Slave	%S	sq.mi.	P/sq.mi.	Representative	Cong.	Pty.	Address	County
Bertie	11,218	6,059	54.0	698	16.0	Willis Alston	13	R	Littleton	Halifax
Halifax	15,620	6,624	42.4	734	21.3	Joseph H. Bryan	14	(----)	Windsor	Bertie
Martin	5,987	2,357	39.4	455	13.2	Joseph H. Bryan	15	(----)	Windsor	Bertie
Northampton	13,082	7,258	55.5	536	24.4	Hutchins G. Burton	16	R	Halifax	Halifax
TOTALS	45,907	22,298	48.6	2,423	18.9	Hutchins G. Burton	17	R	Halifax	Halifax

DISTRICT 3

County	Aggregate	Slave	%S	sq.mi.	P/sq.mi.	Representative	Cong.	Pty.	Address	County
Beaufort	7,203	2,568	35.6	826	8.7	William Kennedy	13	F	Washington	Beaufort
Edgecombe	12,423	5,707	45.9	560	24.4	James W. Clark	14	R	Tarboro	Edgecombe
Hyde	6,029	1,852	30.7	613	9.8	Thomas H. Hall	15	R	Tarboro	Edgecombe
Pitt	9,169	3,589	39.1	655	14.0	Thomas H. Hall	16	R	Tarboro	Edgecombe
Tyrrel	3,364	910	27.0	781	4.3	Thomas H. Hall	17	R	Tarboro	Edgecombe
Washington	10,166	5,330	52.4	343	29.6					
TOTALS	48,354	19,956	41.3	3,778	12.8					

DISTRICT 4

County	Aggregate	Slave	%S	sq.mi.	P/sq.mi.	Representative	Cong.	Pty.	Address	County
Cateret	4,823	1,172	24.3	536	9.0	William Gaston	13	F	New Bern	Craven
Craven	12,676	5,650	44.5	1,037	12.2	William Gaston	14	F	New Bern	Craven
Greene	4,865	1,842	37.9	307	15.8	Jesse Slocumb	15	F	Waynesborough	Wayne
Johnston	6,867	2,330	33.9	972	7.9					
Jones	4,968	2,375	47.8	467	10.6	Jesse Slocumb†	16	F	Waynesborough	Wayne
Lenoir	5,572	2,440	43.8	400	13.9	(Died December, 1820)				
Wayne	8,687	2,756	31.7	607	14.3	William S. Blackledge	16	R	New Bern	Wayne
TOTALS	48,458	18,565	38.3	4,226	11.5	(Replaced Slocumb February, 1821)				
						William S. Blackledge	17	R	New Bern	Wayne

DISTRICT 5

County	Aggregate	Slave	%S	sq.mi.	P/sq.mi.	Representative	Cong.	Pty.	Address	County
Bladen	5,671	1,985	35.0	883	6.4	William R. King	13	R	Wilmington	New Hanover
Brunswick	4,778	2,254	47.2	856	5.6	William R. Kingͫ	14	R	Wilmington	New Hanover
Columbus	3,022	703	23.3	945	4.1	(Resigned November, 1816)				
Duplin	7,863	2,416	30.7	815	9.6	Charles Hooks	14	R	Duplin	Bladen
New Hanover	11,465	6,442	56.1	185	62.0	(Replaced King December, 1816)				
Onslow	6,609	2,299	34.5	765	8.7	James Owen	15	R	Elizabethtown	Bladen
Sampson	6,620	2,049	30.9	945	7.0					
TOTALS	46,088	18,148	39.4	5,397	8.5	Charles Hooks	16	R	Duplin	Bladen
						Charles Hooks	17	R	Duplin	Bladen

DISTRICT 6

County	Aggregate	Slave	%S	sq.mi.	P/sq.mi.	Representative	Cong.	Pty.	Address	County
Franklin	10,366	1,469	14.2	540	19.2	Nathaniel Macon	13	R	Warrenton	Warren
Granville	15,576	7,746	49.7	686	22.7	Nathaniel Macon	14	R	Warrenton	Warren
Nash	7,268	2,897	39.9	644	11.3	Weldon N. Edwards	15	R	Warrenton	Warren
Warren	11,004	6,282	57.1	474	23.2	Weldon N. Edwards	16	R	Warrenton	Warren
TOTALS	44,214	18,394	41.6	2,355	18.8	Weldon N. Edwards	17	R	Warrenton	Warren

DISTRICT 7

County	Aggregate	Slave	%S	sq.mi.	P/sq.mi.	Representative	Cong.	Pty.	Address	County
Anson	8,831	2,325	26.3	633	13.9	John Culpepper	13	F	Allenton	Robeson
Cumberland	9,382	2,796	29.5	1,257	7.5	John Culpepper	14	F	Allenton	Robeson
Montgomery	8,430	1,699	20.1	886	9.5	Alexander McMillian†	15	(----)	----	----
Moore	6,307	944	14.8	959	6.6	(Died in 1817)				
Richmond	6,695	1,301	19.4	794	8.4	James Stewart	15	(----)	Laurinburg	Richmond
Robeson	7,528	1,340	17.8	1,338	5.6	(Replaced McMillian January, 1818)				
TOTALS	47,233	10,405	22.0	5,867	8.0	John Culpepper	16	F	Wadesboro	Anson

COUNTIES					REPRESENTATIVES				
County	Aggregate	Slave	%S	sq.mi.	P/sq.mi.	Representative	Cong.	Pty.	Address	County

DISTRICT 7 (CONTINUED)

| | | | | | | Archibald McNeil | 17 | (----) | McNeil's Store | Moore |

DISTRICT 8

County	Aggregate	Slave	%S	sq.mi.	P/sq.mi.	Representative	Cong.	Pty.	Address	County
Orange	20,135	4,701	23.3	1,123	17.9	Israel Pickens	13	R	Morgantown	Orange
Person	6,642	2,573	38.7	401	16.6	Israel Pickens	14	R	Morgantown	Orange
Wake	17,086	5,878	34.4	858	19.9	James S. Smith	15	R	Hillsboro	Orange
TOTALS	43,863	13,152	30.0	2,382	18.4	James S. Smith	16	R	Hillsboro	Orange
						Josiah Crudup	17	NR	Raleigh	Wake

DISTRICT 9

County	Aggregate	Slave	%S	sq.mi.	P/sq.mi.	Representative	Cong.	Pty.	Address	County
Caswell	11,757	4,299	36.5	428	27.5	Bartlett Yancy	13	F	Caswell	Caswell
Guilford	11,420	1,467	12.8	655	17.4	Bartlett Yancy	14	F	Caswell	Caswell
Rockingham	10,316	2,114	20.4	569	18.1	Thomas Settle	15	R	Lenox Castle	Rockingham
Stokes	11,645	1,746	14.9	876	13.3	Thomas Settle	16	R	Lenox Castle	Rockingham
TOTALS	45,138	9,626	21.3	2,528	17.9	Romnus M. Saunders	17	R	Milton	Caswell

DISTRICT 10

County	Aggregate	Slave	%S	sq.mi.	P/sq.mi.	Representative	Cong.	Pty.	Address	County
Chatham	12,977	3,635	28.0	709	18.3	Joseph Pearson	13	F	Salisbury	Rowan
Randolph	10,112	798	7.8	798	12.7	William C. Love	14	R	Salisbury	Rowan
Rowan	21,543	3,257	15.1	1,337	16.1	George Mumford	15	R	Salisbury	Rowan
TOTALS	44,632	7,690	17.2	2,844	15.7	Charles Fisher	15	R	Salisbury	Rowan
						Charles Fisher	16	R	Salisbury	Rowan
						John Long	17	NR	Long Mills	Randolph

DISTRICT 11

County	Aggregate	Slave	%S	sq.mi.	P/sq.mi.	Representative	Cong.	Pty.	Address	County
Cabarus	6,158	1,234	20.0	363	17.0	Peter Forney	13	R	Lincolnton	Lincoln
Lincoln	16,359	2,489	15.2	1,047	15.6	Daniel M. Forney	14	R	Lincolnton	Lincoln
Mecklenburg	14,272	3,494	24.4	1,069	13.4	Daniel M. Forney^r	15	R	Lincolnton	Lincoln
TOTALS	36,789	7,217	19.6	2,479	14.8	(Resigned in 1818)				
						William Davidson	15	F	Charlotte	Mecklenburg
						(Replaced Forney December, 1818)				
						William Davidson	16	F	Charlotte	Mecklenburg
						Henry W. Connor	17	R	Sherills Ford	Lincoln

DISTRICT 12

County	Aggregate	Slave	%S	sq.mi.	P/sq.mi.	Representative	Cong.	Pty.	Address	County
Buncombe	9,277	695	7.4	1,575	5.9	Richard Sanford	13	R	Hawfield	----
Burke	11,007	1,433	13.0	2,188	5.0	Richard Sanford†	14	R	Hawfield	----
Haywood	2,780	171	6.1	3,414	0.8	(Died April, 1816)				
Rutherford	13,202	979	7.4	1,180	11.2	Samuel Dickens	14	(----)	Mt. Tirzah	----
TOTALS	36,266	3,278	9.0	8,357	4.3	(Replaced Sanford December, 1816)				
						Felix Walker	15	R	Waynesville	Haywood
						Felix Walker	16	R	Waynesville	Haywood
						Felix Walker	17	R	Waynesville	Haywood

		COUNTIES				REPRESENTATIVES				
County	Aggregate	Slave	%S	sq.mi.	P/sq.mi.	Representative	Cong.	Pty.	Address	County

DISTRICT 13

Ash	3,964	147	3.7	968	4.1	Meshack Franklin	13	R	----	Surry
Iredell	10,972	2,432	22.1	831	13.2	Lewis Williams	14	F	Panther Creek	Surry
Surry	5,965	2,790	46.7	862	6.9					
Wilkes	9,054	1,194	13.1	757	12.0	Lewis Williams	15	F	Panther Creek	Surry
TOTALS	29,955	6,563	21.9	3,418	8.7	Lewis Williams	16	F	Panther Creek	Surry
						Lewis Williams	17	F	Panther Creek	Surry

OHIO
6 DISTRICTS
6 CONGRESSMEN

		COUNTIES				REPRESENTATIVES				
County	Aggregate	Slave	%S	sq.mi.	P/sq.mi.	Representative	Cong.	Pty.	Address	County

DISTRICT 1

Butler	11,150	----	----	484	23.0	John McLean	13	R	Lebanon	Warren
Hamilton	15,258	----	----	487	31.3	John McLean[r]	14	R	Lebanon	Warren
Preble	3,304	----	----	414	8.0	(Resigned in 1816)				
Warren	9,925	----	----	400	24.8	William Henry Harrison	14	R	Cincinnati	Hamilton
TOTALS	39,637	----	----	1,785	22.2	(Replaced McLean December, 1816)				
						William Henry Harrison	15	R	Cincinnati	Hamilton
						Thomas R. Ross	16	R	Lebanon	Warren
						Thomas R. Ross	17	R	Lebanon	Warren

DISTRICT 2

Adams	9,434	----	----	383	24.6	John Alexander	13	R	Xenia	Greene
Clermont	9,965	----	----	905	11.0	John Alexander	14	R	Xenia	Greene
Clinton	2,674	----	----	332	8.1	John W. Campbell	15	R	West Union	Adams
Fayette	1,854	----	----	390	4.8	John W. Campbell	16	R	West Union	Adams
Greene	5,870	----	----	365	16.1	John W. Campbell	17	R	West Union	Adams
Highland	5,766	----	----	468	12.3					
TOTALS	35,563	----	----	2,843	12.5					

DISTRICT 3

Athens	2,791	----	----	1,090	2.6	Duncan McArthur†	13	R	Chillicothe	Ross
Gallia	4,181	----	----	1,266	3.3	(Died April, 1813)				
Pickaway	7,124	----	----	376	18.9	William Creighton	13	R	Chillicothe	Ross
Ross	15,514	----	----	1,122	13.8	(Replaced McArthur June, 1813)				
Scioto	3,399	----	----	835	4.1	William Creighton	14	R	Chillicothe	Ross
Washington	5,991	----	----	1,342	4.5	Levi Barber	15	(----)	Point Harmer	Washington
TOTALS	39,000	----	----	6,031	6.5	Henry Brush	16	(----)	Chillicothe	Ross
						Levi Barber	17	(----)	Point Harmer	Washington

COUNTIES						REPRESENTATIVES				
County	Aggregate	Slave	%S	sq.mi.	P/sq.mi.	Representative	Cong.	Pty.	Address	County

DISTRICT 4

County	Aggregate	Slave	%S	sq.mi.	P/sq.mi.	Representative	Cong.	Pty.	Address	County
Belmont	11,087	----	----	744	14.9	James Caldwell	13	R	St. Clairsville	Belmont
Guernsey	3,051	----	----	716	4.3	James Caldwell	14	R	St. Clairsville	Belmont
Jefferson	17,260	----	----	690	25.0	Samuel Herrick	15	R	Zanesville	Muskingum
Muskingum &						Samuel Herrick	16	R	Zanesville	Muskingum
Coshocton						David Chambers	17	NR	Zanesville	Muskingum
of 1811	10,036	----	----	1,373	7.3					
TOTALS	41,444	----	----	3,523	11.8					

DISTRICT 5

County	Aggregate	Slave	%S	sq.mi.	P/sq.mi.	Representative	Cong.	Pty.	Address	County
Champaign	6,303	----	----	3,203	2.0	James Kilbourne	13	R	Worthington	Franklin
Darke & Miami	3,941	----	----	5,010	0.8	James Kilbourne	14	R	Worthington	Franklin
Delaware	2,000	----	----	2,412	0.8	Philemon Beecher	15	F	Lancaster	Fairfield
Fairfield	11,361	----	----	860	13.2	Philemon Beecher	16	F	Lancaster	Fairfield
Franklin	3,486	----	----	506	6.9	Joseph Vance	17	R	Urbana	Champaign
Licking	3,852	----	----	564	6.8					
Madison	1,603	----	----	394	4.1					
Montgomery	7,722	----	----	443	17.4					
TOTALS	40,268	----	----	13,392	3.0					

DISTRICT 6

County	Aggregate	Slave	%S	sq.mi.	P/sq.mi.	Representative	Cong.	Pty.	Address	County
Ashtabula (organized in 1811)[a]						Reasin Beale[r]	13	R	Wooster	Wayne
Columbiana	10,878	----	----	1,582	6.9	(Resigned June, 1814)				
Cuyahoga &						David Clendenin	13	(----)	Youngstown	Trumbull
Huron of						(Replaced Beale December, 1814)				
1812	2,995	----	----	1,513	2.0	David Clendenin	14	(----)	Youngstown	Trumbull
Geauga[b]						Peter Hitchcock	15	(----)	Burton	Geauga
Knox	2,149	----	----	1,452	1.5	John Sloane	16	R	Wooster	Wayne
Portage &						John Sloane	17	R	Wooster	Wayne
Medina of										
1812	2,995	----	----	1,513	2.0					
Richland[c]										
Stark	2,734	----	----	609	4.5					
Trumbull	8,671	----	----	1,234	7.0					
Tuscarawas	3,045	----	----	753	4.0					
Wayne[d]										
TOTALS	31,931	----	----	9,539	3.3					

[a]Half of Astabula given to Trumbull and half to Geauga.
[b]Not mentioned in the 1810 census.
[c]Land area of Richland attributed to Knox.
[d]Land area of Wayne attributed to Columbiana.

COUNTIES						REPRESENTATIVES				
County	Aggregate	Slave	%S	sq.mi.	P/sq.mi.	Representative	Cong.	Pty.	Address	County

DISTRICT 1

County	Aggregate	Slave	%S	sq.mi.	P/sq.mi.	Representative	Cong.	Pty.	Address	County
Delaware	14,734	----	----	184	80.0	William Anderson	13	R	Chester	Delaware
Philadelphia	57,488	6	----	100	574.8	John Conrad	13	R	Germantown	Philadelphia
City of						Charles J. Ingersoll	13	R	City of Philadelphia	
Philadelphia	53,722	2	----	29	1852.5	Adam Seybert	13	R	City of Philadelphia	
TOTALS	125,944	8	----	313	402.4					
						Joseph Hopkinson	14	F	City of Philadelphia	
						William Milnor	14	F	City of Philadelphia	
						Thomas Smith	14	F	Darby	Delaware
						Jonathan Williams† (Died May, 1815)	14	(----)	City of Philadelphia	
						John Sergeant (Replaced Williams December, 1815)	14	F	City of Philadelphia	
						William Anderson	15	R	Chester	Delaware
						Joseph Hopkinson	15	F	City of Philadelphia	
						John Sergeant	15	F	City of Philadelphia	
						Adam Seybert	15	R	City of Philadelphia	
						Samuel Edwards	16	F	Chester	Delaware
						Thomas Forrest	16	(----)	City of Philadelphia	
						Joseph Hemphill	16	F	City of Philadelphia	
						John Sergeant	16	F	City of Philadelphia	
						Samuel Edwards	17	F	Chester	Delaware
						Joseph Hemphill	17	F	City of Philadelphia	
						William Milnor[r] (Resigned May, 1822)	17	F	City of Philadelphia	
						Thomas Forrest (Replaced Milnor December, 1822)	17	(----)	City of Philadelphia	
						John Sergeant	17	F	City of Philadelphia	

DISTRICT 2

County	Aggregate	Slave	%S	sq.mi.	P/sq.mi.	Representative	Cong.	Pty.	Address	County
Chester	39,596	7	----	761	52.0	Roger Davis	13	R	Charlestown	Chester
Montgomery	29,703	3	----	496	59.8	Jonathan Roberts[r] (Resigned February, 1814)	13	R	Norristown	Montgomery
TOTALS	69,299	10	----	1,257	55.1	Samuel Henderson (Replaced Roberts November, 1814)	13	R	Norristown	Montgomery
						William Darlington	14	R	West Chester	Chester
						John Hahn	14	R	Pottsgrove	Union
						Isaac Darlington	15	F	West Chester	Chester
						Levi Pawling	15	R	Norristown	Montgomery

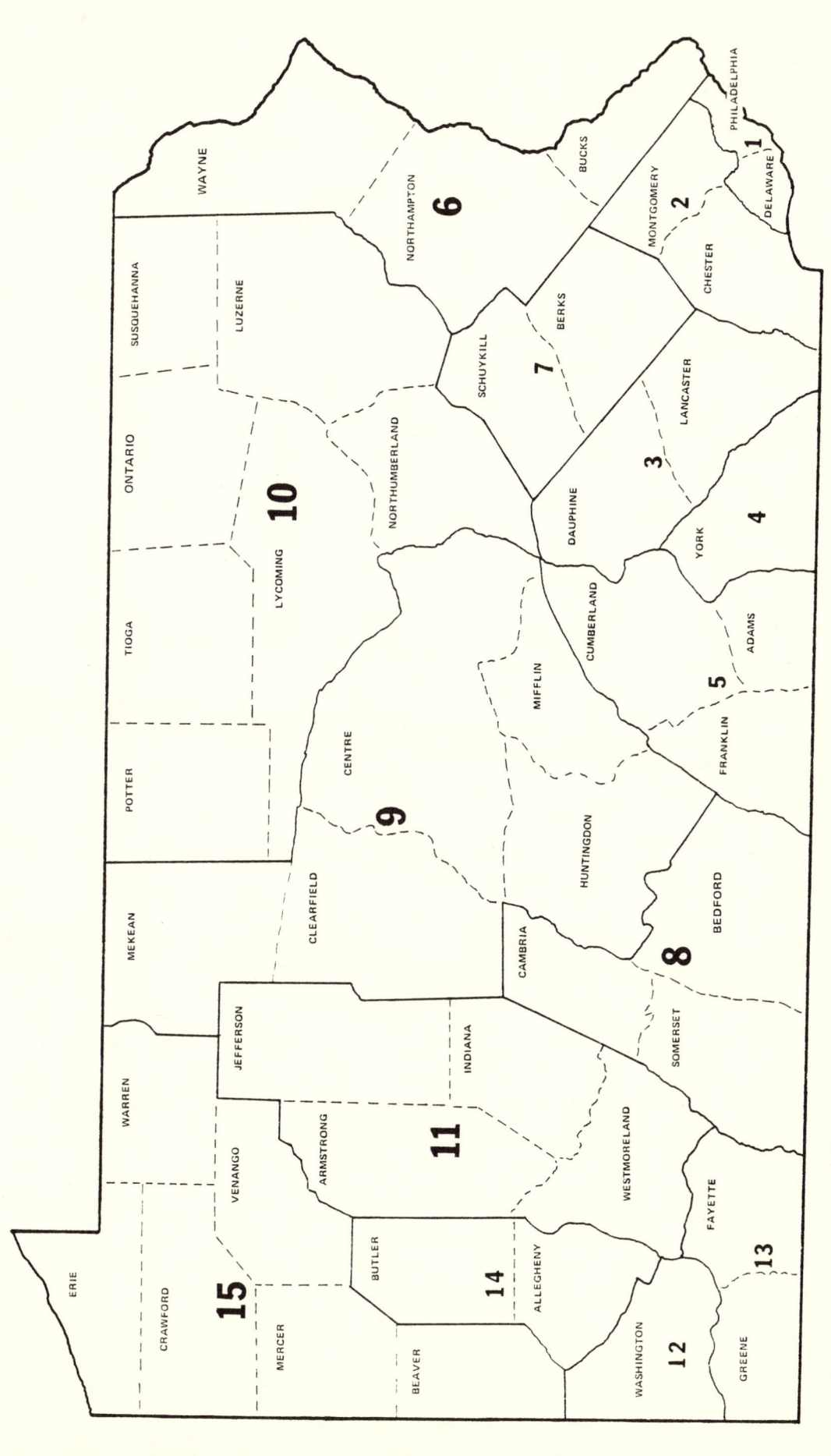

COUNTIES						REPRESENTATIVES				
County	Aggregate	Slave	%S	sq.mi.	P/sq.mi.	Representative	Cong.	Pty.	Address	County

DISTRICT 2 (CONTINUED)

						William Darlington	16	R	Westchester	Chester
						Samuel Gross	16	R	Trappe	Montgomery
						William Darlington	17	R	Westchester	Chester
						Samuel Gross	17	R	Trappe	Montgomery

DISTRICT 3

County	Aggregate	Slave	%S	sq.mi.	P/sq.mi.	Representative	Cong.	Pty.	Address	County
Dauphin	31,883	26	----	881	36.1	John Gloninger[r]	13	R	Lebanon	Lancaster
Lancaster	53,927	44	----	946	57.0	(Resigned August, 1813)				
TOTALS	85,810	70	----	1,827	47.0	Edward Crouch	13	R	Paxtang	----
						(Replaced Gloninger December, 1813)				
						James Whitehill[r]	13	(----)	Strasburg	Lancaster
						(Resigned September, 1814)				
						Amos Slaymaker	13	(----)	Lancaster	Lancaster
						(Replaced Whitehill December, 1814)				
						Amos Ellmaker	14	(----)	Harrisburg	Dauphin
						(Never qualified for the seat)				
						James M. Wallace	14	(----)	Hummels-town	Dauphin
						(Took seat December, 1815)				
						John Whiteside	14	R	Lancaster	Lancaster
						James M. Wallace	15	(----)	Hummels-town	Dauphin
						John Whiteside	15	R	Lancaster	Lancaster
						Jacob Hibshman	16	R	Ephrata	Lancaster
						James M. Wallace	16	(----)	Hummels-town	Dauphin
						James Buchanan	17	R	Lancaster	Lancaster
						John Phillips	17	F	Hummels-town	Dauphin

DISTRICT 4

County	Aggregate	Slave	%S	sq.mi.	P/sq.mi.	Representative	Cong.	Pty.	Address	County
York	31,958	22	----	909	35.2	Hugh Glasgow	13	(----)	York	York
						Hugh Glasgow	14	(----)	York	York
						Jacob Spangler[r]	15	F	York	York
						(Resigned April, 1818)				
						Jacob Hostetter	15	R	Hanover	York
						(Replaced Spangler November, 1818)				
						Jacob Hostetter	16	R	Hanover	York
						James S. Mitchell	17	R	Rossville	York

COUNTIES						REPRESENTATIVES				
County	Aggregate	Slave	%S	sq.mi.	P/sq.mi.	Representative	Cong.	Pty.	Address	County

DISTRICT 5

County	Aggregate	Slave	%S	sq.mi.	P/sq.mi.	Representative	Cong.	Pty.	Address	County
Adams	15,152	71	0.5	526	28.8	William Crawford	13	R	Gettysburg	Adams
Cumberland	26,757	307	1.1	1,106	24.1	Robert Whitehill†	13	(----)	Camp Hill	Cumberland
Franklin	23,083	87	0.4	754	30.6	(Died April, 1813)				
TOTALS	64,992	465	0.7	2,386	28.2	John Rea	13	R	Chambersburg	Franklin
						(Replaced Whitehill May, 1813)				
						William Crawford	14	R	Gettysburg	Adams
						William Maclay	14	R	Fannetsburg	Franklin
						Andrew Boden	15	(----)	Carlisle	Cumberland
						William Maclay	15	R	Fannetsburg	Franklin
						Andrew Boden	16	(----)	Carlisle	Cumberland
						David Fullerton[r]	16	(----)	Greencastle	Franklin
						(Resigned May, 1820)				
						Thomas E. McCullough	16	(----)	Chambersburg	Franklin
						(Replaced Fullerton November, 1820)				
						James Duncan[r]	17	(----)	Carlisle	Cumberland
						(Resigned before Congress assembled)				
						John Findlay	17	R	Chambersburg	Franklin
						(Replaced Duncan December, 1821)				
						James McSherry	17	(----)	Petersburg	Adams

DISTRICT 6

County	Aggregate	Slave	%S	sq.mi.	P/sq.mi.	Representative	Cong.	Pty.	Address	County
Bucks	32,371	11	----	614	52.7	Robert Brown	13	R	Weaversville	Northampton
Northampton	38,145	----	----	1,478	25.8	Samuel D. Ingham	13	R	New Hope	Bucks
Wayne	4,125	3	----	1,544	2.6					
TOTALS	74,641	14	----	3,636	20.5	Samuel D. Ingham	14	R	New Hope	Bucks
						John Ross	14	F	Easton	Northampton
						Samuel D. Ingham[r]	15	R	New Hope	Bucks
						(Resigned July, 1818)				
						Samuel Moore	15	R	Doylestown	Bucks
						(Replaced Ingham November, 1818)				
						John Ross[r]	15	F	Easton	Northampton
						(Resigned February, 1818)				
						Thomas J. Rogers	15	R	Easton	Northampton
						Replaced Ross March, 1818)				
						Samuel Moore	16	R	Doylestown	Bucks
						Thomas J. Rogers	16	R	Easton	Northampton
						Samuel Moore[r]	17	R	Doylestown	Bucks
						(Resigned May, 1822)				
						Samuel D. Ingham	17	R	New Hope	Bucks
						(Replaced Moore December, 1822)				
						Thomas J. Rogers	17	R	Easton	Northampton

	COUNTIES					REPRESENTATIVES				
County	Aggregate	Slave	%S	sq.mi.	P/sq.mi.	Representative	Cong.	Pty.	Address	County

DISTRICT 7

Berks	43,146	4	----	1,646	26.2	John Hyneman[r] (Resigned August, 1813)	13	R	Reading	Berks
Schuylkill (created in 1811)						Daniel Udree (Replaced Hyneman December, 1813)	13	R	Reading	Berks
TOTALS	43,146	4	----	1,646	26.2	Joseph Hiester	14	F	Reading	Berks
						Joseph Hiester	15	F	Reading	Berks
						Joseph Hiester[r] (Resigned December, 1820)	16	F	Reading	Berks
						Daniel Udree (Replaced Hiester January, 1821)	16	R	Reading	Berks
						Ludwig Worman† (Died October, 1822)	17	F	Pottstown	Berks
						Daniel Udree (Replaced Worman December, 1822)	17	R	Reading	Berks

DISTRICT 8

Bedford	15,746	1	----	1,453	10.8	William Piper	13	(----)	Bloodyrun	Bedford
Cambria	2,117	6	----	692	3.0	William Piper	14	(----)	Bloodyrun	Bedford
Somerset	11,284	----	----	1,078	10.4	Alexander Ogle	15	R	Somerset	Somerset
TOTALS	29,147	7	----	3,223	9.0	Robert Philson	16	(----)	Somerset	Somerset
						John Tod	17	R	Bedford	Bedford

DISTRICT 9

Blair (created after the 1810 census)						David Bard	13	(----)	Frangstown	Blair
Centre &						David Bard† (Died March, 1815)	14	(----)	Frangstown	Blair
Clearfield	10,681	1	----	2,510	4.2	Thomas Burnside[r] (Replaced Bard December 1815; resigned December, 1816)	14	(----)	Bellefonte	Centre
Huntingdon	14,778	----	----	1,425	10.3					
McKean	142	1	----	1,192	0.12					
Mifflin	12,132	9	----	817	14.8	William P. Maclay (Replaced Burnside December, 1816)	14	R	Lewistown	Mifflin
TOTALS	37,733	11	----	5,944	6.3	William P. Maclay	15	R	Lewistown	Mifflin
						William P. Maclay	16	R	Lewistown	Mifflin
						John Brown	17	(----)	Lewistown	Mifflin

DISTRICT 10

Luzerne & Susquehanna	18,109	----	----	2,571	7.0	Jared Irwin	13	R	Sunbury	Northumberland
Lycoming & Ontario	11,006	2	----	1,944	5.6	Isaac Smith	13	R	Jersey Shore	Lycoming
Northumberland	36,327	3	----	1,067	34.0	Jared Irwin	14	R	Sunbury	Northumberland
Potter	29	----	----	1,092	0.02	William Wilson	14	(----)	Williamsport	Lycoming
Tioga	1,687	----	----	1,146	0.8	David Scott[r]	15	(----)	----	----
TOTALS	67,158	5	----	7,820	8.58	John Murray (Replaced Scott)	15	(----)	Milton	Northumberland
						William Wilson	15	(----)	Williamsport	Lycoming
						George Denison	16	R	Wilkes-Barre	Luzerne
						John Murray	16	(----)	Milton	Northumberland

| COUNTIES | | | | | | REPRESENTATIVES | | | | |
County	Aggregate	Slave	%S	sq.mi.	P/sq.mi.	Representative	Cong.	Pty.	Address	County

DISTRICT 10 (CONTINUED)

						George Denison	17	R	Wilkes-Barre	Luzerne
						William Cox Ellis[r]	17	F	Muncy	Lycoming
						Thomas Murray, Jr.	17	R	Milton	Northum- berland
						(Replaced Ellis)				

DISTRICT 11

Armstrong	6,143	----	----	1,249	4.9	William Findley	13	R	Youngstown	Westmoreland
Indiana	6,214	----	----	825	7.5	William Findley	14	R	Youngstown	Westmoreland
Jefferson	161	----	----	1,278	0.12	David Marchand	15	(----)	Greenburg	Westmoreland
West-						David Marchand	16	(----)	Greenburg	Westmoreland
moreland	26,392	20	----	1,024	25.7	George Plumer	17	R	Robbstown	Westmoreland
TOTALS	38,910	20	----	4,376	8.9					

DISTRICT 12

Washington	36,289	36	----	857	42.3	Aaron Lyle	13	R	West Middleton	Washington
						Aaron Lyle	14	R	West Middleton	Washington
						Thomas Patterson	15	R	West Middleton	Washington
						Thomas Patterson	16	R	West Middleton	Washington
						Thomas Patterson	17	R	West Middleton	Washington

DISTRICT 13

Fayette	24,714	58	----	802	30.8	Isaac Griffin	13	R	New Geneva	Fayette
Greene	12,544	10	----	578	21.7	Isaac Griffin	14	R	New Geneva	Fayette
TOTALS	37,258	68	----	1,380	27.0	Christian Tarr	15	(----)	Brownsville	Fayette
						Christian Tarr	16	(----)	Brownsville	Fayette
						Andrew Stewart	17	R	Uniontown	Fayette

DISTRICT 14

Allegheny	25,317	24	----	728	34.7	Adamson Tannehill	13	R	Pittsburgh	Allegheny
Butler	7,346	----	----	794	9.2	John Woods[a]	14	F	Pittsburgh	Allegheny
TOTALS	32,663	24	----	1,522	21.5	Henry Baldwin	15	F	Pittsburgh	Allegheny
						Henry Baldwin	16	F	Pittsburgh	Allegheny
						Henry Baldwin[r]	17	F	Pittsburgh	Allegheny
						Walter Forward	17	R	Pittsburgh	Allegheny
						(Replaced Baldwin)				

[a]Never qualified because of illness.

DISTRICT 15

Beaver	12,168	8	----	807	15.0	Abner Lacock[r]	13	R	Beavertown	Beaver
Crawford	6,178	2	----	1,012	6.1	Thomas Wilson	13	R	Erie	Erie
Erie	3,758	18	----	813	4.6	(Replaced Lacock)				
Mercer	8,277	3	----	670	12.3	Thomas Wilson	14	R	Erie	Erie
Venango	3,060	----	----	878	3.4	Robert Moore	15	(----)	Beavertown	Beaver
Warren	827	----	----	905	0.9	Robert Moore	16	(----)	Beavertown	Beaver
TOTALS	34,268	31	----	5,085	6.7	Patrick Farrelly	17	R	Meadville	Crawford

COUNTIES						REPRESENTATIVES				
County	Aggregate	Slave	%S	sq.mi.	P/sq.mi.	Representative	Cong.	Pty.	Address	County
						AT LARGE				
Bristol	5,072	37	----	25	3197.2	Richard Jackson	13	F	Providence	Providence
Kent	9,834	4	----	202	48.7	Elisha R. Potter	13	F	Kingston	Washington
Newport	16,294	44	0.3	103	158.2					
Providence	30,709	13	----	413	74.4	John L. Boss	14	F	Newport	Newport
Washington	14,962	10	0.1	340	44.0	James B. Mason	14	F	Providence	Providence
TOTALS	76,871	108	0.1	1,083	70.1					
						John L. Boss	15	F	Newport	Newport
						James B. Mason	15	F	Providence	Providence
						Samuel Eddy	16	R	Providence	Providence
						Nathaniel Hazard†	16	R	Newport	Newport
						(Died December, 1820)				
						Job Durfee	17	R	Tiverton	Newport
						Samuel Eddy	17	R	Providence	Providence

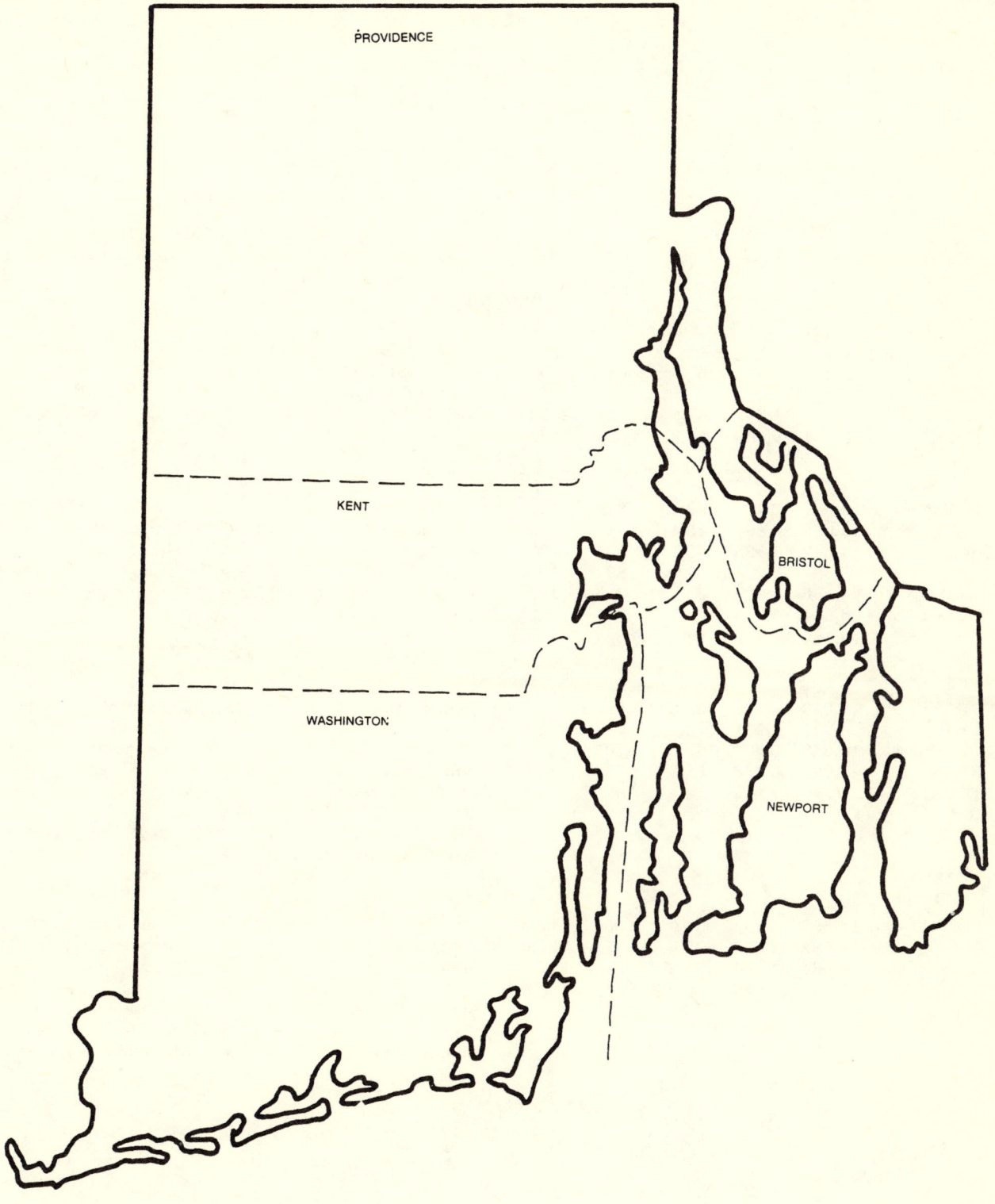

	COUNTIES						REPRESENTATIVES			
County	Aggregate	Slave	%S	sq.mi.	P/sq.mi.	Representative	Cong.	Pty.	Address	County

DISTRICT 1

All of Charleston County except those parishes included						Langdon Cheves	13	R	City of Charleston	
in District 9,						Henry Middleton	14	R	City of Charleston	
total:	31,256	27,393	87.6	1,644	19.1	Henry Middleton	15	R	City of Charleston	
City of						Charles Pinckney	16	R	City of Charleston	
Charleston	24,711	11,671	47.2	17	1453.6	Joel R. Poinsett	17	R	City of Charleston	
TOTALS	55,967	39,064	69.8	1,661	33.7					

DISTRICT 2

Darlington	9,047	2,731	30.1	849	10.6	Theodore Gourdin	13	R	Pineville	Williamsburg
Georgetown	15,679	13,867	88.4	812	19.3	Benjamin Huger	14	(----)	Georgetown	Georgetown
Horry	4,349	1,398	32.1	1,154	3.1	James Ervin	15	PT	Darlington	Darlington
Marion	8,884	2,771	31.1	894	9.9	James Ervin	16	PT	Darlington	Darlington
Marlboro	4,966	1,709	34.4	483	10.2	Thomas R. Mitchell	17	(----)	Georgetown	Georgetown
Williamsburg	6,871	4,518	65.7	1,434	4.7					
TOTALS	49,796	26,994	54.2	5,626	8.9					

DISTRICT 3

Barnwell	12,280	4,153	33.8	1,927	6.3	John J. Chappell	13	SWR	Columbia	Richland
Lexington	6,641	1,911	28.7	717	9.2	John J. Chappell	14	SWR	Columbia	Richland
Orangeburg	13,229	6,564	49.6	1,701	7.7	Joseph Bellinger	15	R	Duncansville	Barnwell
Richland	9,027	5,238	58.0	748	12.0	James Overstreet	16	(----)	Kings Creek	Barnwell
TOTALS	41,177	17,866	43.4	5,093	8.1	James Overstreet†	17	(----)	Kings Creek	Barnwell
						(Died May, 1822)				
						Andrew Govan	17	(----)	Orangeburg	Orangeburg
						(Replaced Overstreet)				

DISTRICT 4

Fairfield	11,857	4,034	34.0	696	17.0	David R. Evans	13	R	Winnsboro	Fairfield
Laurens	14,982	3,308	22.0	711	21.0	William Woodward	14	(----)	Monticello	Fairfield
Newberry	13,964	4,006	28.6	635	21.9	Starling Tucker	15	(----)	Mountain Shoals	Laurens
TOTALS	40,803	11,348	27.8	2,042	20.0	Starling Tucker	16	(----)	Mountain Shoals	Laurens
						Starling Tucker	17	(----)	Mountain Shoals	Laurens

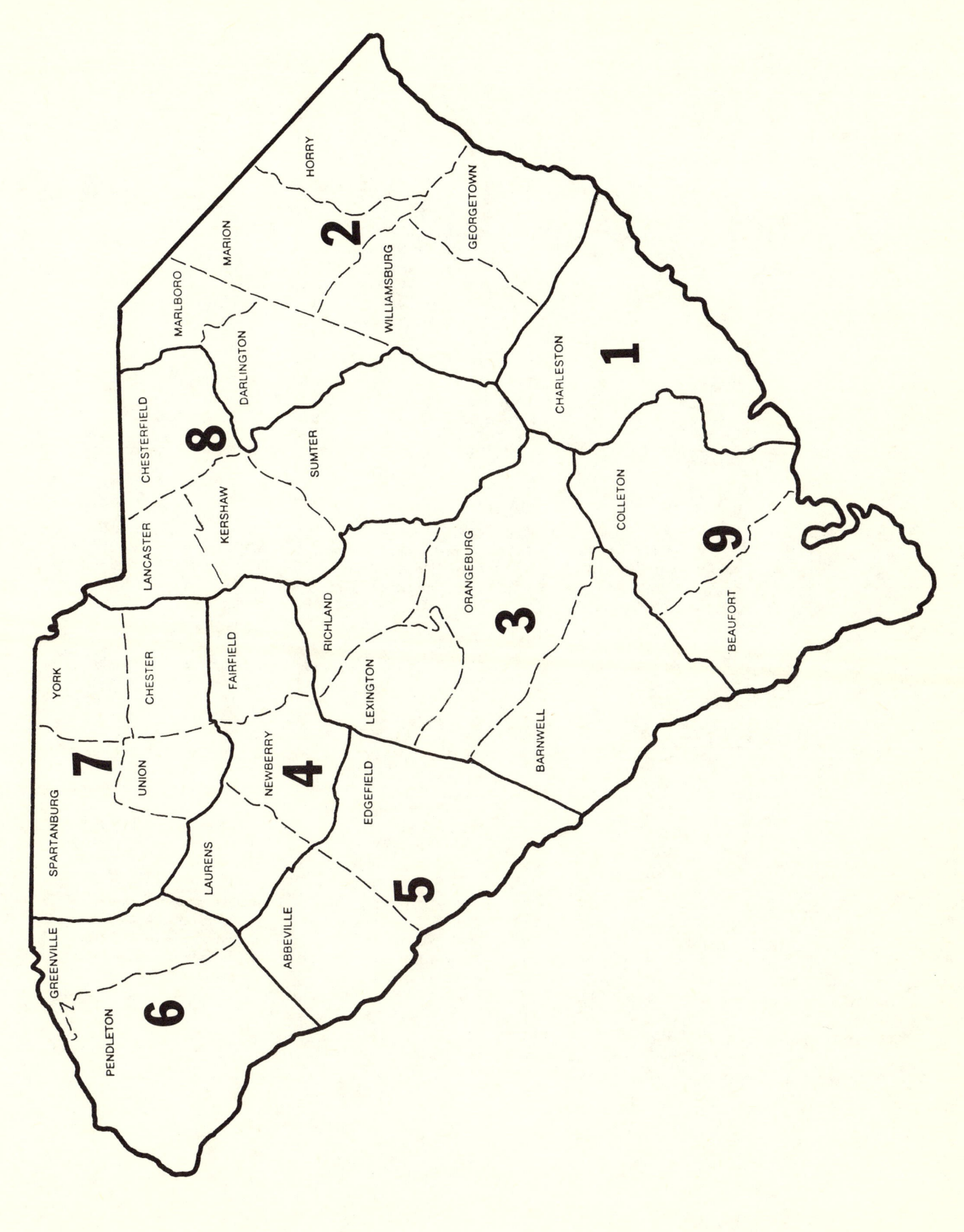

	COUNTIES					REPRESENTATIVES				
County	Aggregate	Slave	%S	sq.mi.	P/sq.mi.	Representative	Cong.	Pty.	Address	County

DISTRICT 5

Abbeville	21,156	6,672	31.5	976	21.6	John C. Calhoun	13	WR	Willington	Abbeville
Edgefield	23,610	8,576	36.3	1,602	14.7	John C. Calhoun	14	WR	Willington	Abbeville
TOTALS	44,766	15,248	34.1	2,578	17.4	John C. Calhoun^r	15	WR	Willington	Abbeville
						(Resigned November, 1817)				
						Eldrid Simkins	15	R	Edgefield	Edgefield
						(Replaced Calhoun February, 1818)				
						Eldrid Simkins	16	R	Edgefield	Edgefield
						George McDuffie	17	R	Edgefield	Edgefield

DISTRICT 6

Greenville	13,133	2,353	17.9	792	16.5	Elias Earle	13	R	Centerville	Greenville
Pendleton	22,897	3,485	15.2	1,895	12.0	John Taylor	14	(----)	Pendleton	Pendleton
TOTALS	36,030	5,838	16.2	2,687	13.4	Elias Earle	15	R	Centerville	Greenville
						Elias Earle	16	R	Centerville	Greenville
						John Wilson	17	(----)	Golden Grove	Pendleton

DISTRICT 7

Chester	11,479	2,743	23.8	584	19.6	Samuel Farrow	13	WR	Spartanburg	Spartanburg
Spartanburg	14,254	2,391	16.7	1,225	11.6	Thomas Moore	14	(----)	Prices Store	Spartanburg
Union	10,995	2,846	25.8	514	21.3	Wilson Nesbitt	15	R	New Hope	Spartanburg
York	10,332	3,164	30.6	684	15.1	John McCreary	16	(----)	Cedarshoals	Chester
TOTALS	47,060	11,144	23.7	3,007	15.7	Joseph Gist	17	R	Pinckneyville	Union

DISTRICT 8

Chesterfield	5,564	1,639	29.4	790	7.0	John Kershaw	13	R	Camden	Kershaw
Kershaw	9,867	4,847	49.1	781	12.6	William Mayrant^r	14	(----)	Stateburg	Sumter
Lancaster	6,318	1,646	26.0	502	12.5	(Resigned October, 1816)				
Sumter	19,054	11,638	61.0	1,680	11.3	Stephen Miller	14	R	Stateburg	Sumter
TOTALS	40,803	19,770	48.5	3,753	10.9	(Replaced Mayrant January, 1817)				
						Stephen Miller	15	R	Stateburg	Sumter
						Joseph Brevard	16	NR	Camden	Kershaw
						James Blair^r	17	R	Camden	Kershaw
						(Resigned August, 1822)				
						John Carter	17	(----)	Camden	Kershaw
						(Replaced Blair)				

DISTRICT 9

Parishes in Charleston County:^a						William Lowndes	13	R	Jacksonboro	Colleton
Colleton	2,404	2,107	87.6	126	19.1	William Lowndes	14	R	Jacksonboro	Colleton
St. Andrews	2,404	2,107	87.6	126	19.1	William Lowndes	15	R	Jacksonboro	Colleton
St. John	2,404	2,107	87.6	126	19.1	William Lowndes	16	R	Jacksonboro	Colleton
Total, parishes	7,212	6,321	87.6	378	19.1	William Lowndes^r	17	R	Jacksonboro	Colleton
Beaufort	25,887	20,914	80.7	1,793	14.4	James Hamilton, Jr.	17	SRR	Colleton	Charleston
Colleton	26,359	21,558	82.9	1,618	16.2	(Replaced Lowndes)				
TOTALS	59,458	48,793	82.1	3,789	15.7					

^aThe third census contains no parish data. The number used in this table represent the mean parish population multiplied by the number of parishes in the district.

		COUNTIES				REPRESENTATIVES				
County	Aggregate	Slave	%S	sq.mi.	P/sq.mi.	Representative	Cong.	Pty.	Address	County
DISTRICT 1										
Carter	4,190	262	6.3	641	6.5	John Rhea	13	R	Sullivan	Sullivan
Green	9,713	655	6.7	613	15.8	Samuel Powell	14	(----)	Rogersville	Hawkins
Hawkins	7,643	930	12.1	710	10.8	John Rhea	15	R	Sullivan	Sullivan
Sullivan	6,847	773	11.3	413	16.6	John Rhea	16	R	Sullivan	Sullivan
Washington	7,740	850	11.0	508	15.2	John Rhea	17	R	Sullivan	Sullivan
TOTALS	36,133	3,470	9.6	2,885	12.5					
DISTRICT 2										
Blount	8,839	805	9.1	575	15.3	John Sevier	13	R	Knoxville	Knox
Claiborne	4,798	327	6.8	556	8.6	John Sevier[r]	14	R	Knoxville	Knox
Cocke	5,154	436	8.5	424	12.1	William G. Blount	14	R	Knoxville	Knox
Grainger	6,397	537	8.4	444	14.4	(Replaced Sevier)				
Jefferson	7,309	783	10.7	324	22.5	William G. Blount	15	R	Knoxville	Knox
Knox	10,171	1,271	12.5	508	20.0	John Cocke	16	R	Rutledge	Grainger
Sevrer	4,595	294	6.4	597	7.7	John Cocke	17	R	Rutledge	Grainger
TOTALS	47,263	4,453	9.4	3,428	13.8					
DISTRICT 3										
Anderson	3,959	260	6.6	335	11.8	Thomas K. Harris	13	R	Sparta	White
Bledsoe[a]						Isaac Thomas	14	R	Sparta	White
Campbell	2,668	103	3.9	451	5.9	Franklin Jones	15	(----)	Winchester	Franklin
Franklin	5,730	709	12.3	627	9.1	Franklin Jones	16	(----)	Winchester	Franklin
Overton	5,643	355	6.3	1,273	4.4	Franklin Jones	17	(----)	Winchester	Franklin
Rhea	2,504	214	8.5	1,180	2.1					
Roane	5,581	670	12.0	2,902	1.9					
Warren	5,725	476	8.3	1,151	5.0					
White	4,028	283	7.0	660	6.1					
TOTALS	35,838	3,070	8.6	8,579	4.2					

[a]Created in 1807 from Roane County; not included in the 1810 census.

		COUNTIES				REPRESENTATIVES				
DISTRICT 4										
Jackson	5,401	481	8.9	628	8.6	John H. Bowen	13	R	Gallatin	Sumner
Smith	11,649	2,201	18.9	741	15.7	Bennett H. Henderson	14	(----)	Henderson-ville	----
Sumner	13,792	3,734	27.0	534	25.8					
Wilson	11,952	2,297	19.2	567	21.0	Samuel Hogg	15	R	Lebanon	Wilson
TOTALS	42,794	8,713	20.4	2,470	17.3	Robert Allen	16	R	Carthage	Smith
						Robert Allen	16	R	Carthage	Smith

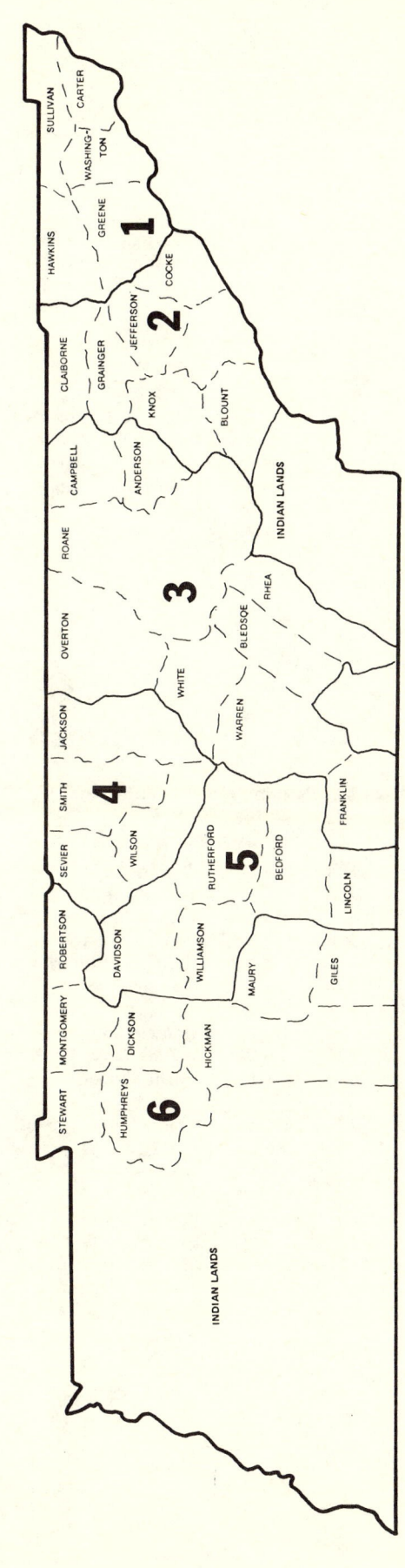

COUNTIES						REPRESENTATIVES				
County	Aggregate	Slave	%S	sq.mi.	P/sq.mi.	Representative	Cong.	Pty.	Address	County

DISTRICT 5

County	Aggregate	Slave	%S	sq.mi.	P/sq.mi.	Representative	Cong.	Pty.	Address	County
Bedford	18,242	1,180	6.5	859	21.2	Felix Grundy[r]	13	WR	Nashville	Davidson
Davidson	15,608	6,305	40.3	813	19.2	Newton Cannon	13	R	Harpeth	Williamson
Lincoln	6,104	720	11.8	640	9.5	(Replaced Grundy)				
Rutnerford	10,265	2,701	26.3	883	11.6	Newton Cannon	14	R	Harpeth	Williamson
Williamson	13,153	3,985	30.3	593	22.2	Thomas Claiborne	15	R	Nashville	Davidson
TOTALS	63,372	14,891	23.5	3,788	16.7	Newton Cannon	16	R	Harpeth	Williamson
						Newton Cannon	17	R	Harpeth	Williamson

DISTRICT 6

County	Aggregate	Slave	%S	sq.mi.	P/sq.mi.	Representative	Cong.	Pty.	Address	County
Dickson	4,516	980	21.7	485	9.3	Parry W. Humphreys	13	R	----	----
Giles	4,546	733	16.1	619	7.3	James B. Reynolds	14	R	Clarksville	Montgomery
Hickman	2,583	245	9.5	8,283	0.3	George W. L. Marr	15	(----)	Clarksville	Montgomery
Humphreys	1,511	132	8.7	4,793	0.3	Henry H. Bryan	16	(----)	Palmyra	Montgomery
Maury	10,359	2,626	25.3	614	16.9	Henry H. Bryan	17	(----)	Palmyra	Montgomery
Montgomery	8,021	2,629	32.8	539	14.9					
Robertson	7,270	1,608	22.1	476	15.3					
Stewart	4,262	779	18.3	470	9.1					
TOTALS	43,068	9,732	22.6	16,279	2.6					

VERMONT[1]

6 CONGRESSMEN AT LARGE

COUNTIES						REPRESENTATIVES				
County	Aggregate	Slave	%S	sq.mi.	P/sq.mi.	Representative	Cong.	Pty.	Address	County

AT LARGE

County	Aggregate	Slave	%S	sq.mi.	P/sq.mi.	Representative	Cong.	Pty.	Address	County
Addison	19,993	----	----	784	25.5	William C. Bradley	13	R	Westminster	Windham
Bennington	15,893	----	----	672	23.6	Ezra Butler	13	R	Waterbury	Washington
Caledonia	18,740	----	----	612	30.6	James Fisk	13	R	Barre	Orange
Chittenden	18,120	----	----	590	30.7	Charles Rich	13	R	Shorham	Addison
Essex	2,887	----	----	663	4.4	Richard Skinner	13	R	Manchester	Bennington
Franklin	16,615	----	----	755	22.0	William Strong	13	R	Hartford	Windsor
Grand Isle	3,445	----	----	83	41.5					
Orange	25,247	----	----	690	36.6	Daniel Chipman[†]	14	F	Middlebury	Addison
Orleans	5,650	----	----	905	6.2	(Died May, 1815; not replaced)				
Rutland	29,486	----	----	927	31.8	Luther Jewett	14	F	St. Johns-bury	Caledonia
Washington[a]	----	----	----	840	----					
Windham	26,760	----	----	784	34.1	Chauncey Langdon	14	F	Castleton	Rutland
Windsor	34,877	----	----	962	36.3	Asa Lyon	14	F	Grand Isle	Grand Isle
TOTALS	217,713	----	----	9,267	23.5	Charles Marsh	14	F	Woodstock	Windsor
						John Noyes	14	F	Brattleboro	Windham
						Herman Allen[r]	15	R	Burlington	Chittenden
						(Resigned April 20, 1818; not replaced)				
						Samuel C. Crafts	15	R	Craftsbury	Orleans
						William Hunter	15	R	Windsor	Windsor
						Orsamus C. Merrill	15	R	Bennington	Bennington
						Charles Rich	15	R	Shoreham	Addison

[1] Elections for the Seventeenth Congress were by district.

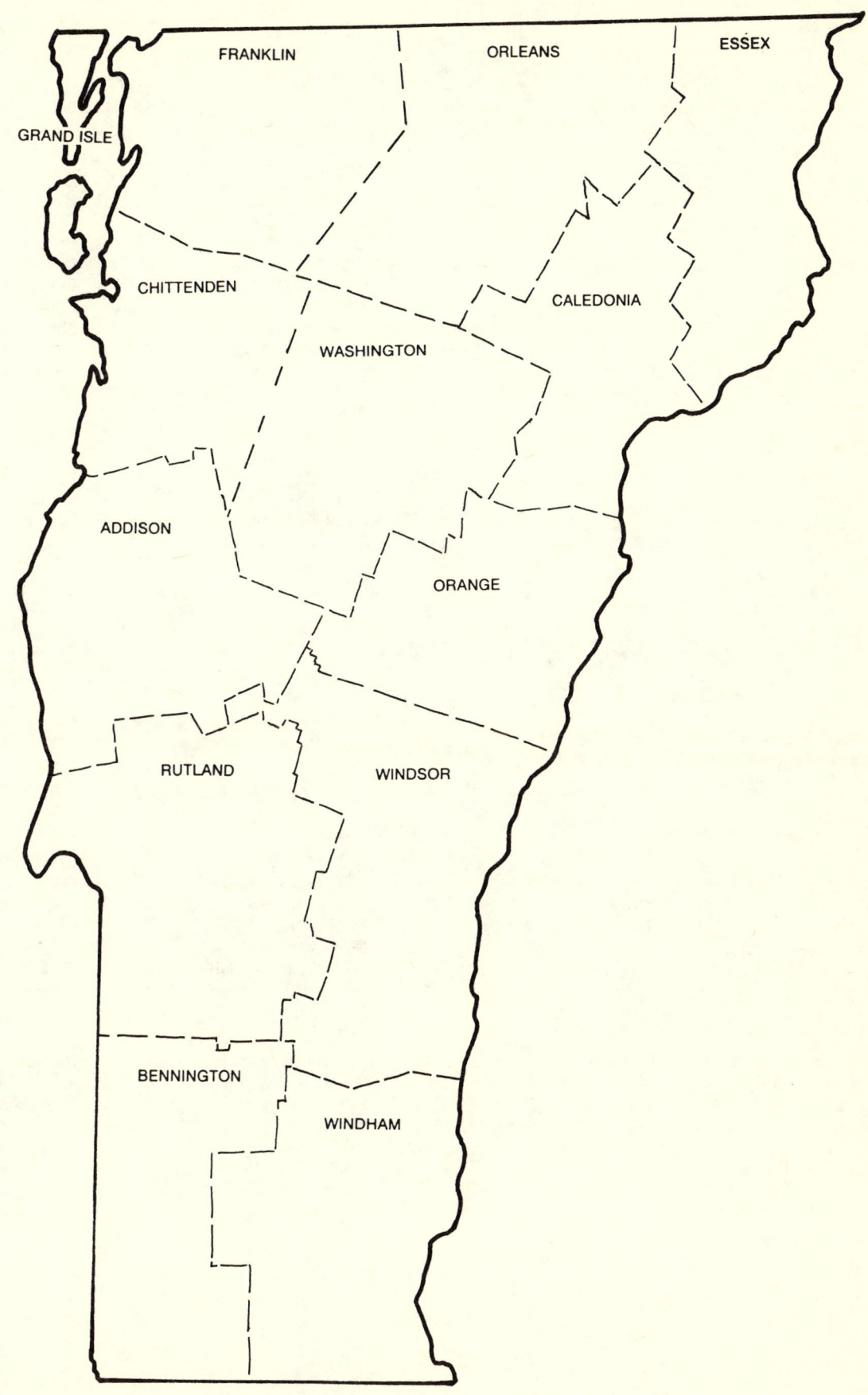

	COUNTIES					REPRESENTATIVES				
County	Aggregate	Slave	%S	sq.mi.	P/sq.mi.	Representative	Cong.	Pty.	Address	County

AT LARGE (CONTINUED)

						Mark Richards	15	R	Westminster	Windham
						Samuel C. Crafts	16	R	Craftsbury	Orleans
						Ezra Meech	16	R	Charlotte	Chittenden
						Orsamus C. Merrill[ce]	16	R	Bennington	Bennington
						Rollin C. Mallary	16	(----)	Poultney	Rutland
						Charles Rich	16	R	Shoreham	Addison
						Mark Richards	16	R	Westminster	Windham
						William Strong	16	R	Hartford	Windsor
						Samuel C. Crafts	17	R	Craftsbury	Orleans
						Elias Keyes	17	R	Stockbridge	Windsor
						Rollin C. Mallary	17	(----)	Poultney	Rutland
						John Mattocks	17	W	Peacham	Caledonia
						Charles Rich	17	R	Shoreham	Addison
						Phineas White	17	R	Putney	Windham

[a]Created from Addison, Chittenden, Orange, and Caledonia Counties after the 1810 census.

VIRGINIA
23 DISTRICTS
23 CONGRESSMEN

	COUNTIES					REPRESENTATIVES				
County	Aggregate	Slave	%S	sq.mi.	P/sq.mi.	Representative	Cong.	Pty.	Address	County

DISTRICT 1

County	Aggregate	Slave	%S	sq.mi.	P/sq.mi.	Representative	Cong.	Pty.	Address	County
Brooke	5,843	332	5.6	171	34.2	John G. Jackson	13	R	Clarksburg	Harrison
Harrison	9,958	459	4.6	2,939	3.4	John G. Jackson	14	R	Clarksburg	Harrison
Monongalia	12,793	351	2.7	1,348	9.5	James Pindall	15	F	Clarksburg	Harrison
Ohio	8,175	440	5.3	1,160	7.0	James Pindall[r]	16	F	Clarksburg	Harrison
TOTALS	36,769	1,582	4.2	5,618	6.5	Edward B. Jackson (Replaced Pindall)	16	R	Clarksburg	Harrison
						Edward B. Jackson	17	R	Clarksburg	Harrison

DISTRICT 2

County	Aggregate	Slave	%S	sq.mi.	P/sq.mi.	Representative	Cong.	Pty.	Address	County
Berkeley	11,479	1,529	13.4	549	20.9	Francis White	13	(----)	Romney	Hampshire
Hampshire	9,784	929	9.4	969	10.0	Magnus Tate	14	F	Martinsburg	Berkeley
Hardy	5,525	749	13.5	1,063	5.2	Edward Colston	15	F	Martinsburg	Berkeley
Jefferson	11,851	3,532	29.8	211	56.2	Thomas Van Swearingen	16	(----)	Shepherds-town	Jefferson
TOTALS	38,639	6,739	17.4	2,792	13.8					
						Thomas Van Swearingen[r]	17	(----)	Shepherds-town	Jefferson
						James Stephenson (Replaced Van Swearingen)	17	F	Martinsburg	Berkeley

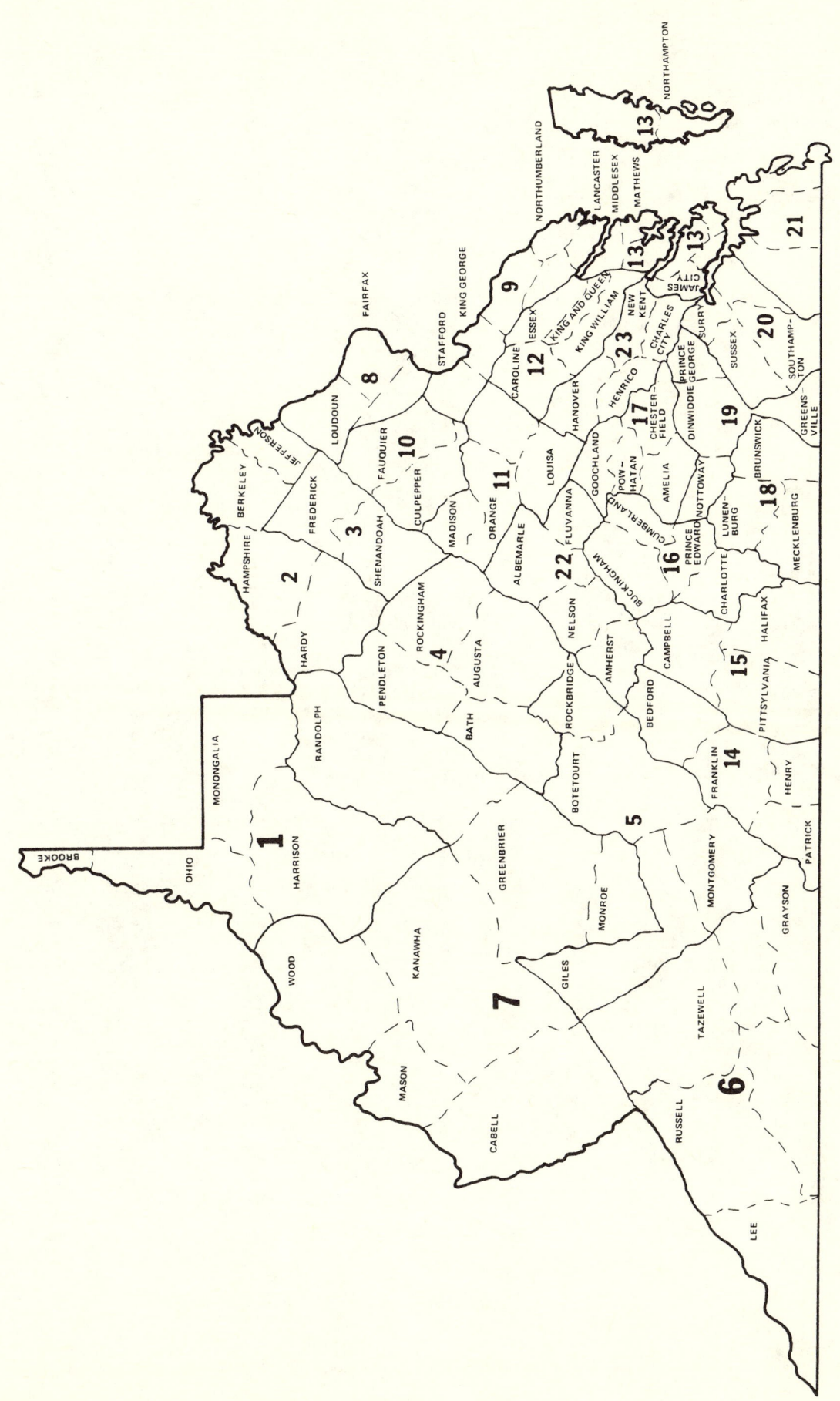

COUNTIES						REPRESENTATIVES				
County	Aggregate	Slave	%S	sq.mi.	P/sq.mi.	Representative	Cong.	Pty.	Address	County

DISTRICT 3

County	Aggregate	Slave	%S	sq.mi.	P/sq.mi.	Representative	Cong.	Pty.	Address	County
Frederick	22,574	6,417	28.4	679	33.2	John Smith	13	R	----	Frederick
Shenandoah	13,646	1,038	7.6	942	14.5	Henry				
TOTALS	36,220	7,455	20.6	1,621	22.3	St. George Tucker	14	F	Winchester	Frederick
							15	F	Winchester	Frederick
						Jared Williams	16	JR	Newton	Frederick
						Jared Williams	17	JR	Newton	Frederick

DISTRICT 4

County	Aggregate	Slave	%S	sq.mi.	P/sq.mi.	Representative	Cong.	Pty.	Address	County
Augusta	14,308	2,880	20.1	986	14.5	William McCoy	13	R	Franklin	Pendleton
Bath	4,837	882	18.2	956	5.0	William McCoy	14	R	Franklin	Pendleton
Pendleton	4,239	262	6.1	695	6.0	William McCoy	15	R	Franklin	Pendleton
Rockingham	12,758	1,491	11.6	865	14.7	William McCoy	16	R	Franklin	Pendleton
TOTALS	36,142	5,515	15.2	3,502	10.3	William McCoy	17	R	Franklin	Pendleton

DISTRICT 5

County	Aggregate	Slave	%S	sq.mi.	P/sq.mi.	Representative	Cong.	Pty.	Address	County
Botetourt	13,301	2,275	17.1	1,590	8.4	James Breckinridge	13	F	Fincastle	Botetourt
Giles	3,745	242	6.4	1,017	3.7	James Breckinridge	14	F	Fincastle	Botetourt
Montgomery	8,409	1,099	13.0	1,105	7.6	John Floyd	15	R	New Bern	Montgomery
Rockbridge	10,318	1,724	16.7	601	17.2	John Floyd	16	R	New Bern	Montgomery
TOTALS	35,773	5,340	14.9	4,313	8.3	John Floyd	17	R	New Bern	Montgomery

DISTRICT 6

County	Aggregate	Slave	%S	sq.mi.	P/sq.mi.	Representative	Cong.	Pty.	Address	County
Grayson	4,941	270	5.4	946	5.2	Daniel Sheffey	13	F	Wythe	Wythe
Lee	4,694	336	7.1	1,350	3.5	Daniel Sheffey	14	F	Wythe	Wythe
Russell	6,136	386	6.2	1,323	4.6	Alexander Smyth	15	(----)	Wythe	Wythe
Tazewell	3,007	328	10.9	2,228	1.3	Alexander Smyth	16	(----)	Wythe	Wythe
Washington	12,136	1,448	11.9	988	12.3	Alexander Smyth	17	(----)	Wythe	Wythe
Wythe	8,356	1,157	13.8	895	9.3					
TOTALS	39,270	3,925	9.9	7,730	5.1					

DISTRICT 7

County	Aggregate	Slave	%S	sq.mi.	P/sq.mi.	Representative	Cong.	Pty.	Address	County
Cabell	2,717	221	8.1	2,385	1.1	Hugh Caperton	13	F	Union	Monroe
Greenbrier	5,914	494	8.3	1,592	3.7	Ballard Smith	14	(----)	Lewisburg	Greenbrier
Kenawha	3,866	352	9.1	6,573	0.58	Ballard Smith	15	(----)	Lewisburg	Greenbrier
Mason	1,991	249	12.5	694	2.8	Ballard Smith	16	(----)	Lewisburg	Greenbrier
Monroe	5,444	376	6.9	473	11.5	William Smith	17	(----)	Lewisburg	Greenbrier
Randolph	2,854	111	3.8	1,834	1.5					
Wood	3,036	450	14.8	1,184	2.5					
TOTALS	25,822	2,253	8.7	14,735	1.7					

DISTRICT 8

County	Aggregate	Slave	%S	sq.mi.	P/sq.mi.	Representative	Cong.	Pty.	Address	County
Fairfax	13,111	5,942	45.3	399	32.9	Joseph Lewis, Jr.*	13	F	Upperville	----
Loudoun	21,338	5,157	24.1	517	41.3	Joseph Lewis, Jr.*	14	F	Upperville	----
Prince						Charles F. Mercer	15	R	Aldie	Loudoun
William	11,311	5,220	46.1	347	32.6	Charles F. Mercer	16	R	Aldie	Loudoun
TOTALS	45,760	16,319	35.7	1,263	36.2	Charles F. Mercer	17	R	Aldie	Loudoun

COUNTIES						REPRESENTATIVES				
County	Aggregate	Slave	%S	sq.mi.	P/sq.mi.	Representative	Cong.	Pty.	Address	County

DISTRICT 9

County	Aggregate	Slave	%S	sq.mi.	P/sq.mi.	Representative	Cong.	Pty.	Address	County
King						John P. Hungerford	13	R	Leedstown	Westmoreland
George	6,754	3,876	57.3	176	38.4	John P. Hungerford	14	R	Leedstown	Westmoreland
Lancaster	5,592	3,112	55.6	137	40.8	William L. Ball	15	R	Lancaster	Lancaster
Northum-						William L. Ball	16	R	Lancaster	Lancaster
berland	8,308	3,847	46 3	190	43.7	William L. Ball	17	R	Lancaster	Lancaster
Richmond	6 214	3,178	51.1	190	32.7					
Stafford	9 830	4,195	42.6	270	36.4					
West-										
moreland	8,102	4,080	50.3	229	35.4					
TOTALS	44,800	22,288	49.7	1,192	37.6					

DISTRICT 10

County	Aggregate	Slave	%S	sq.mi.	P/sq.mi.	Representative	Cong.	Pty.	Address	County
Culpepper	18,967	8,312	43.8	656	28.9	Aylett Hawes	13	R	Woodville	Culpepper
Fauquier	22,689	10,361	45.6	660	34.4	Aylett Hawes	14	R	Woodville	Culpepper
TOTALS	41,656	18,673	44.8	1,316	31.6	George F. Strother	15	R	Culpepper	Culpepper
						George F. Strother	16	R	Culpepper	Culpepper
						Thomas L. Moore	16	(----)	Warrenton	Fauquier
						(Replaced Strother)				
						Thomas L. Moore	17	(----)	Warrenton	Fauquier

DISTRICT 11

County	Aggregate	Slave	%S	sq.mi.	P/sq.mi.	Representative	Cong.	Pty.	Address	County
Louisa	11,900	6,430	54.0	517	23.0	John Dawson†	13	R	----	----
Madison	8,381	3,970	47.3	327	25.6	Philip P. Barbour	13	R	Orange	Orange
Orange	12,323	6,516	52.8	508	24.3	(Replaced Dawson)				
Spott-						Philip P. Barbour	14	R	Orange	Orange
sylvania	13,296	7,135	53.6	409	32.5	Philip P. Barbour	15	R	Orange	Orange
TOTALS	45,900	24,051	52.3	1,761	26.1	Philip P. Barbour	16	R	Orange	Orange
						Philip P. Barbour	17	R	Orange	Orange

DISTRICT 12

County	Aggregate	Slave	%S	sq.mi.	P/sq.mi.	Representative	Cong.	Pty.	Address	County
King						John Roane	13	R	Rumford	King
and Queen	10,988	6,003	54.6	318	34.6				Academy	William
King William	9,285	5,188	55.8	278	33.4	William H. Roane	14	R	Dunkirk	King and
Essex &										Queen
Caroline	26,920	16,423	61.0	795	33.9	Robert S. Garnett	15	R	Lloyds	Essex
TOTALS	47,193	27,614	58.5	1,391	33.9	Robert S. Farnett	16	R	Lloyds	Essex
						Robert S. Garnett	17	R	Lloyds	Essex

DISTRICT 13

County	Aggregate	Slave	%S	sq.mi.	P/sq.mi.	Representative	Cong.	Pty.	Address	County
Accomack	15,743	4,542	28.8	476	33.0	Thomas M. Bayly	13	R	Drummond	Accomack
Elizabeth						Burwell Bassett	14	R	Williamsburg	James City
City	3,608	1,734	48.1	69	52.3	Burwell Bassett	15	R	Williamsburg	James City
Gloucester	10,427	5,798	55.6	228	45.7	Severn E. Parker	16	(----)	Eastville	Northampton
James City	4,094	2,320	56.6	152	26.9	Burwell Bassett	17	R	Williamsburg	James City
Matthews	4,227	2,068	48.9	89	47.5					
Middlesex	4,414	2,476	56.0	130	33.9					
Northampton	7,474	3,350	44.8	220	33.9					
Warwick	1,835	1,120	61.0	75	24.5					
York	5,187	2,931	56.5	129	40.2					
TOTALS	57,009	26,339	42.6	1,568	36.4					

		COUNTIES						REPRESENTATIVES			
County	Aggregate	Slave	%S	sq.mi.	P/sq.mi.	Representative	Cong.	Pty.	Address	County

DISTRICT 14

County	Aggregate	Slave	%S	sq.mi.	P/sq.mi.	Representative	Cong.	Pty.	Address	County
Bedford	16,148	6,147	38.1	727	22.2	William A. Burwell	13	R	Rocky Mount	Franklin
Franklin	10,724	2,672	24.9	716	14.9					
Henry	5,611	1,755	31.2	381	14.7	William A. Burwell	14	R	Rocky Mount	Franklin
Patrick	4,695	724	15.4	464	10.1					
TOTALS	37,178	11,298	30.4	2,288	16.2	William A. Burwell	15	R	Rocky Mount	Franklin
						William A. Burwell	16	R	Rocky Mount	Franklin
						Jabez Leftwich	17	(----)	Liberty	Bedford

DISTRICT 15

County	Aggregate	Slave	%S	sq.mi.	P/sq.mi.	Representative	Cong.	Pty.	Address	County
Campbell	11,001	5,368	48.7	669	16.4	John Kerr	13	R	Mt. Pleasant	----
Halifax	22,133	9,663	43.6	796	27.8	Matthew Clay†	14	R	Halifax	Halifax
Pittsylvania	17,172	6,312	36.7	1,001	17.2	John Kerr	14	R	Mt. Pleasant	----
TOTALS	50,306	21,343	42.4	2,466	20.4	(Replaced Clay)				
						William J. Lewis	15	R	Lynchburg	Campbell
						George Tucker	16	R	Lynchburg	Campbell
						George Tucker	17	R	Lynchburg	Campbell

DISTRICT 16

County	Aggregate	Slave	%S	sq.mi.	P/sq.mi.	Representative	Cong.	Pty.	Address	County
Buckingham	20,059	11,675	58.2	737	27.2	John W. Eppes	13	R	Charles City	Buckingham
Charlotte	13,161	7,597	57.7	470	28.0	John Randolph	14	R	Charlotte	Charlotte
Cumberland	9,992	6,012	60.1	291	34.3	Archibald Austin	15	R	Buckingham	Buckingham
Prince						John Randolph	16	R	Charlotte	Charlotte
Edward	12,409	6,996	56.3	407	30.5	John Randolph	17	R	Charlotte	Charlotte
TOTALS	55,621	32,280	58.0	1,905	29.2					

DISTRICT 17

County	Aggregate	Slave	%S	sq.mi.	P/sq.mi.	Representative	Cong.	Pty.	Address	County
Amelia	10,594	7,186	67.8	366	28.9	James Pleasants	13	R	Goochland	Goochland
Chesterfield	9,979	6,015	60.2	442	22.6	James Pleasants	14	R	Goochland	Goochland
Goochland	10,203	5,464	53.5	289	35.3	James Pleasants	15	R	Goochland	Goochland
Powhatan	8,073	5,091	63.1	269	30.0	James Pleasants[r]	16	R	Goochland	Goochland
TOTALS	38,849	23,756	61.1	1,366	28.4	William S. Archer	16	R	Amelia	Amelia
						(Replaced Pleasants)				
						William S. Archer	17	R	Amelia	Amelia

DISTRICT 18

County	Aggregate	Slave	%S	sq.mi.	P/sq.mi.	Representative	Cong.	Pty.	Address	County
Brunswick	15,411	9,368	60.7	579	26.6	Thomas Gholson, Jr.	13	R	Brunswick	Brunswick
Lunenburg	12,265	7,155	58.3	442	27.7	Thomas Gholson, Jr.†	14	R	Brunswick	Brunswick
Mecklenburg	18,453	10,264	55.6	612	30.2	Thomas M. Nelson	14	R	Mecklenburg	Mecklenburg
TOTALS	46,129	26,787	58.1	1,633	28.2	(Replaced Gholson)				
						Thomas M. Nelson	15	R	Mecklenburg	Mecklenburg
						Mark Alexander	16	SRR	"Lombardy Grove"	----
						Mark Alexander	17	SRR	"Lombardy Grove"	----

	COUNTIES					REPRESENTATIVES				
County	Aggregate	Slave	%S	sq.mi.	P/sq.mi.	Representative	Cong.	Pty.	Address	County

DISTRICT 19

County	Aggregate	Slave	%S	sq.mi.	P/sq.mi.	Representative	Cong.	Pty.	Address	County
Dinwiddie	12,524	7,442	59.4	507	24.7	Peterson Goodwyn	13	R	Petersburg	Dinwiddie
Greensville	6,853	4,599	67.1	299	22.9	Peterson Goodwyn	14	R	Petersburg	Dinwiddie
Nottoway	9,278	6,368	68.6	308	30.1	Peterson Goodwyn†	15	R	Petersburg	Dinwiddie
Prince George						John Pegram	15	(----)	Dinwiddie	Dinwiddie
George	8,050	4,486	55.7	276	29.2	(Replaced Goodwyn)				
TOTALS	36,705	22,895	62.4	1,390	28.0	James Jones	16	R	Hendersonville	Nottoway
						James Jones	17	R	Hendersonville	Nottoway

DISTRICT 20

County	Aggregate	Slave	%S	sq.mi.	P/sq.mi.	Representative	Cong.	Pty.	Address	County
Isle						James Johnson[a]	13	R	Suffolk	Nansemond
of Wight	9,186	4,041	43.9	317	28.9	James Johnson	14	R	Suffolk	Nansemond
Southampton	13,497	6,406	47.4	602	22.4	James Johnson	15	R	Suffolk	Nansemond
Surry	6,855	3,440	51.0	317	28.9	James Johnson[r]	16	R	Lawrenceville	Brunswick
Sussex	11,362	6,344	55.8	494	23.0					
TOTALS	40,900	20,231	49.5	1,690	24.2	John C. Grey	16	(----)	Courtland	Southampton
						(Replaced Johnson November, 1820)				
						Arthur Smith	17	(----)	Smithfield	Isle of Wight

[a]Johnson's address never in the Twentieth District.

DISTRICT 21

County	Aggregate	Slave	%S	sq.mi.	P/sq.mi.	Representative	Cong.	Pty.	Address	County
Nansemond	10,324	4,462	43.2	408	25.3	Thomas Newton, Jr.	13	R	Norfolk	Norfolk
Norfolk	13,679	5,647	41.2	394	34.7	Thomas Newton, Jr.	14	R	Norfolk	Norfolk
Borough of						Thomas Newton, Jr.	15	R	Norfolk	Norfolk
Norfolk[a]	----	----	----	53	----	Thomas Newton, Jr.	16	R	Norfolk	Norfolk
Princess						Thomas Newton, Jr.	17	R	Norfolk	Norfolk
Anne	9,498	3,926	41.3	259	36.7					
TOTALS	33,501	14,035	41.9	1,114	30.1					

[a]Included in Norfolk County statistics.

DISTRICT 22

County	Aggregate	Slave	%S	sq.mi.	P/sq.mi.	Representative	Cong.	Pty.	Address	County
Albemarle	18,268	9,226	50.5	740	24.7	Hugh Nelson	13	R	Milton	Albemarle
Amherst	10,548	5,207	49.3	470	22.4	Hugh Nelson	14	R	Milton	Albemarle
Fluvanna	4,775	2,142	44.8	288	16.6	Hugh Nelson	15	R	Milton	Albemarle
Nelson	9,684	4,679	48.3	471	20.6	Hugh Nelson	16	R	Milton	Albemarle
TOTALS	43,275	21,254	49.1	1,969	22.0	Hugh Nelson	17	R	Milton	Albemarle

DISTRICT 23

County	Aggregate	Slave	%S	sq.mi.	P/sq.mi.	Representative	Cong.	Pty.	Address	County
Charles City	5,786	3,023	58.2	181	31.9	John Clopton	13	R	Tunstall	New Kent
Hanover	15,082	8,454	56.1	465	32.4	John Clopton†	14	R	Tunstall	New Kent
Henrico	9,945	4,846	48.7	229	43.4	John Tyler	14	R	Charles City	Charles City
New Kent	6,478	3,725	57.5	210	30.8	(Replaced Clopton)				
City of						John Tyler	15	R	Charles City	Charles City
Richmond	9,736	3,748	38.4	60	162.3	John Tyler	16	R	Charles City	Charles City
TOTALS	47,027	23,796	50.6	1,145	41.1	Andrew Stevenson	17	R	Richmond	Henrico

7

Congressional Districts

1822–1831
18th–22nd Congresses

	COUNTIES					REPRESENTATIVES				
County	Aggregate	Slave	%S	sq.mi.	P/sq.mi.	Representative	Cong.	Pty.	Address	County

DISTRICT 1 (NORTHERN)

County	Aggregate	Slave	%S	sq.mi.	P/sq.mi.	Representative	Cong.	Pty.	Address	County
Decatur[a]	----	----	----	403	----	Gabriel Moore	18	D	Huntsville	Madison
Jackson	8,751	539	6.2	1,079	8.1	Gabriel Moore	19	JD	Huntsville	Madison
Lauderdale	4,963	1,378	27.8	662	7.5	Gabriel Moore	20	JD	Huntsville	Madison
Lawrence	8,652	2,941	34.0	685	12.6	Clement C. Clay	21	JD	Huntsville	Madison
Limestone	9,871	2,919	29.6	546	18.1	Clement C. Clay	22	D	Huntsville	Madison
Madison	17,481	8,622	49.3	400	43.7					
TOTALS	49,723	16,399	33.0	3,775	13.2					

[a]Created after 1820 census.

DISTRICT 2 (MIDDLE)

County	Aggregate	Slave	%S	sq.mi.	P/sq.mi.	Representative	Cong.	Pty.	Address	County
Bibb	3,676	746	20.3	930	2.9	John McKee	18	(----)	Tuscaloosa	Tuscaloosa
Blount	2,415	175	7.2	1,319	1.8	John McKee	19	(----)	Tuscaloosa	Tuscaloosa
Franklin	4,988	1,667	33.4	670	7.4	John McKee	20	(----)	Tuscaloosa	Tuscaloosa
Greene	4,554	1,691	37.1	1,289	3.5	Robert E. B. Baylor	21	JD	Tuscaloosa	Tuscaloosa
Jefferson[a]	----	----	----	1,115	----	Samuel W. Mardis	22	D	Montevallo	Shelby
Marengo	2,933	866	29.5	978	3.0					
Marion[b]	----	----	----	403	----					
Morgan	5,263	858	16.3	690	7.6					
Perry	3,646	988	27.1	954	3.8					
Pickens[b]	----	----	----	400	----					
St. Clair	4,166	539	12.9	640	6.5					
Shelby	2,416	405	16.8	798	3.1					
Tuscaloosa	8,229	2,335	28.4	1,033	8.0					
TOTALS	42,286	10,270	24.3	11,219	3.8					

[a]Created in 1819, although not included in 1820 census.
[b]Created after 1820 census.

DISTRICT 3 (SOUTHERN)

County	Aggregate	Slave	%S	sq.mi.	P/sq.mi.	Representative	Cong.	Pty.	Address	County
Autauga	3,853	1,647	42.7	773	5.0	George W. Owen	18	JD	Claiborne	Mobile
Baldwin	1,713	1,001	58.4	1,677	1.0	George W. Owen	19	JD	Claiborne	Mobile
Butler	1,405	569	40.5	1,334	1.1	George W. Owen	20	JD	Claiborne	Mobile
Clarke	5,839	1,835	31.4	1,232	4.7	Dixon Hall Lewis	21	SRD	Montgomery	Montgomery
Conecuh	5,713	1,931	33.8	1,714	3.3	Dixon Hall Lewis	22	SRD	Montgomery	Montgomery
Covington[a]	----	----	----	984	----					
Dallas	6,003	2,677	44.6	976	6.2					
Henry	2,638	626	23.7	946	2.8					
Mobile	2,672	836	31.3	1,240	2.1					
Montgomery	6,604	2,655	40.2	840	7.9					
Monroe	8,838	3,794	42.9	1,032	8.6					
Pike[a]	----	----	----	1,500	----					
Washington	8,652	1,631	18.9	986	8.8					
Wilcox	2,917	1,354	46.4	899	3.2					
TOTALS	56,847	20,556	36.2	16,133	3.5					

[a]Created after 1820 census.

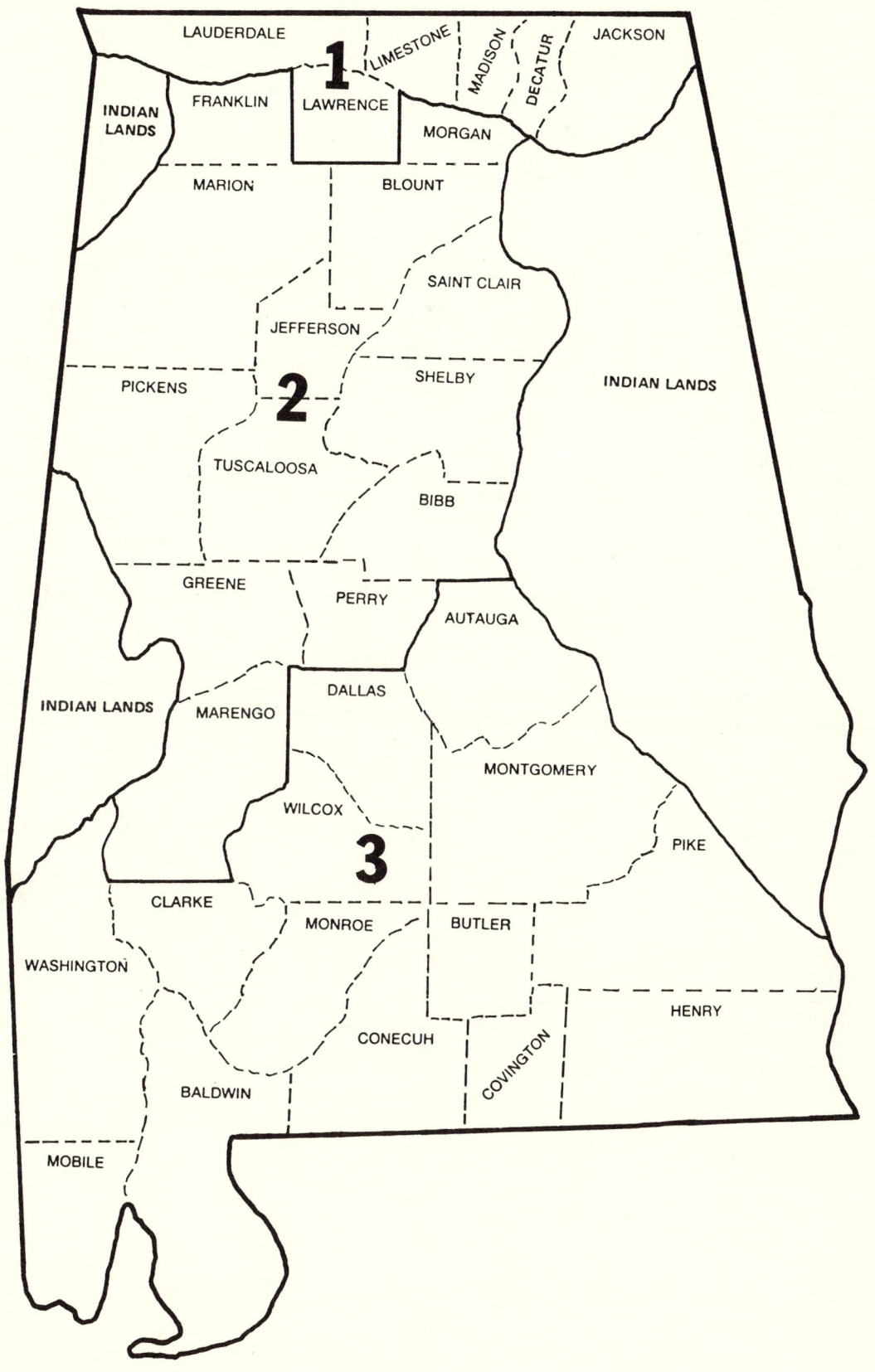

	COUNTIES					REPRESENTATIVES				
County	Aggregate	Slave	%S	sq.mi.	P/sq.mi.	Representative	Cong.	Pty.	Address	County
						AT LARGE				
Fairfield	42,739	27	----	626	68.3	Noyes Barber	18	D	Groton	New London
Hartford	47,264	15	----	739	64.0	Samuel A. Foote	18	NR	Cheshire	New Haven
Litchfield	41,267	3	----	925	44.6	Ansel Sterling	18	(----)	Sharon	Litchfield
Middlesex	22,405	9	----	372	60.3	Ebenezer Stoddard	18	(----)	Woodstock	Windham
New Haven	39,616	16	----	604	65.6	Gideon Tomlinson	18	D	Fairfield	Fairfield
New London	35,943	11	----	667	53.9	Lemuel Whitman	18	D	Farmington	Hartford
Windham	31,684	12	----	514	61.6					
TOTALS	275,248	95	----	4,863	56.6	John Baldwin	19	(----)	Windham	Windham
						Noyes Barber	19	D	Groton	New London
						Ralph Ingersoll	19	D	New Haven	New Haven
						Elisha Phelps	19	D	Simsbury	Hartford
						Orange Merwin	19	D	New Milford	Litchfield
						Gideon Tomlinson	19	D	Fairfield	Fairfield
						John Baldwin	20	(----)	Windham	Windham
						Noyes Barber	20	D	Groton	New London
						Ralph Ingersoll	20	D	New Haven	New Haven
						Orange Merwin	20	D	New Milford	Litchfield
						Elisha Phelps	20	D	Simsbury	Hartford
						David Plant	20	NR	Stratford	Fairfield
						Noyes Barber	21	D	Groton	New London
						William Ellsworth	21	NR	Hartford	Hartford
						Jabez Huntington	21	NR	Litchfield	Litchfield
						Ralph Ingersoll	21	D	New Haven	New Haven
						William L. Storrs	21	NR	Middletown	Middlesex
						Ebenezer Young	21	NR	Killingly Center	Windham
						Noyes Barber	22	NR	Groton	New London
						William Ellsworth	22	NR	Hartford	Hartford
						Jabez Huntington	22	NR	Litchfield	Litchfield
						Ralph Ingersoll	22	NR	New Haven	New Haven
						William L. Storrs	22	NR	Middletown	Middlesex
						Ebenezer Young	22	NR	Killingly Center	Windham

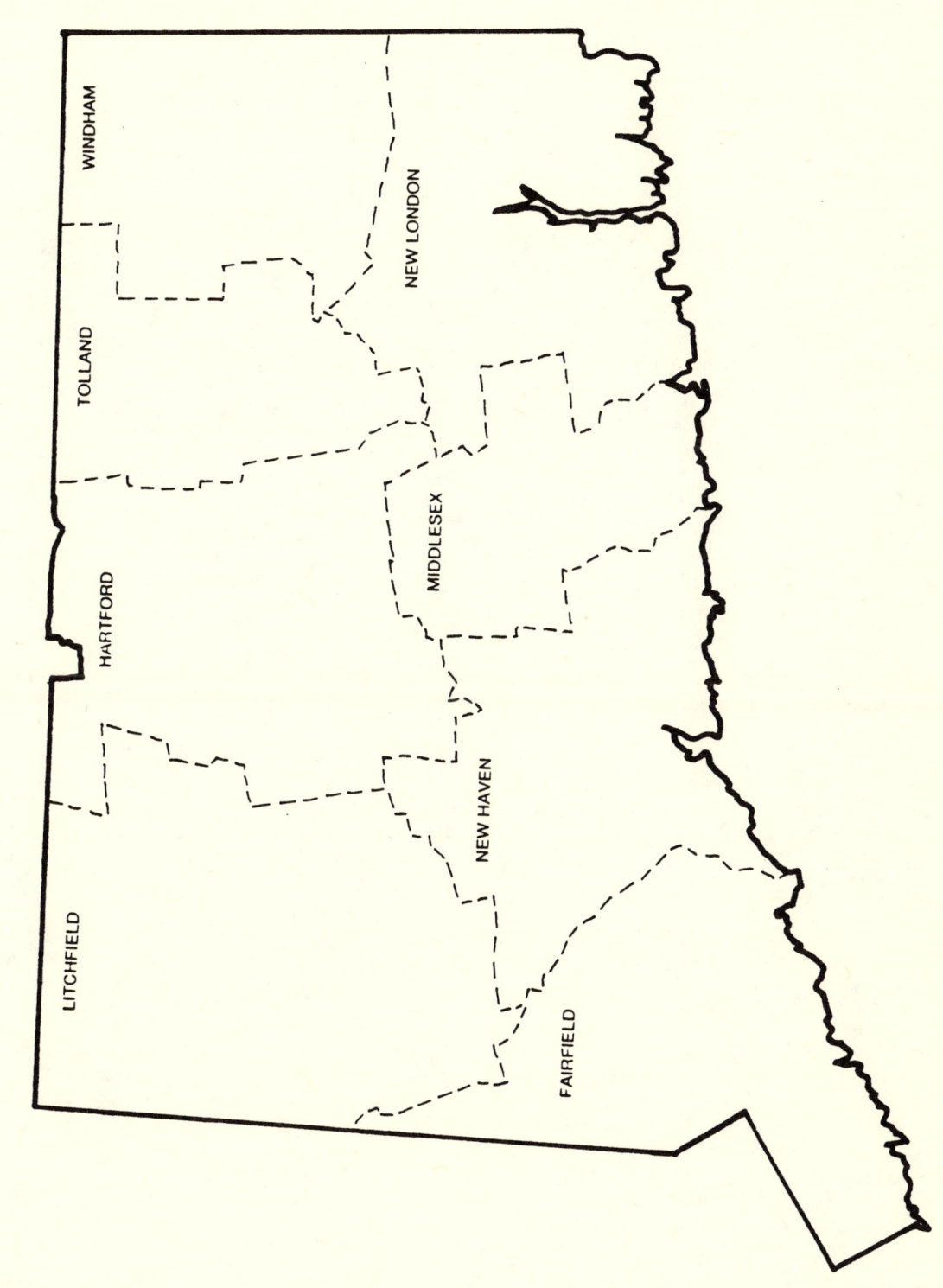

County	COUNTIES Aggregate	Slave	%S	sq.mi.	P/sq.mi.	Representative	REPRESENTATIVES Cong.	Pty.	Address	County
						AT LARGE				
Kent	20,793	1,070	5.1	594	35.0	Louis McLane	18	F	Wilmington	Newcastle
Newcastle	27,899	1,178	4.2	438	63.7	Louis McLane[r]	19	F	Wilmington	Newcastle
Sussex	24,057	2,246	9.3	950	25.3	(Resigned March, 1827)				
TOTALS	72,749	4,494	6.2	1,982	36.7	Kensey Johns, Jr.	19	F	Newcastle	Newcastle
						(Replaced McLane December, 1827)				
						Kensey Johns, Jr.	20	F	Newcastle	Newcastle
						Kensey Johns, Jr.	21	F	Newcastle	Newcastle
						John J. Milligan	22	NR	Wilmington	Newcastle

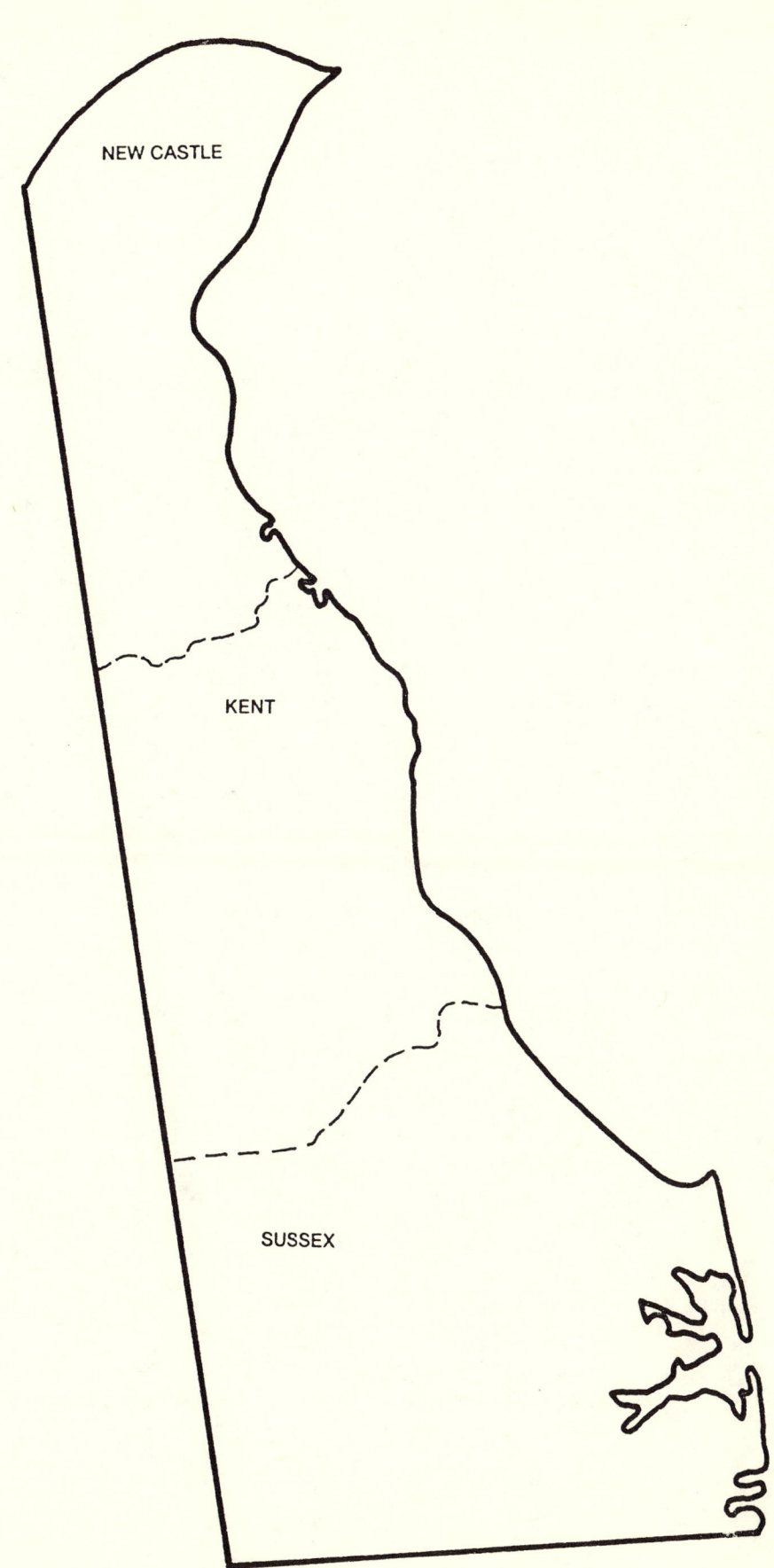

COUNTIES						REPRESENTATIVES				
County	Aggregate	Slave	%S	sq.mi.	P/sq.mi.	Representative	Cong.	Pty.	Address	County

AT LARGE: EIGHTEENTH AND NINETEENTH CONGRESSES

County	Aggregate	Slave	%S	sq.mi.	P/sq.mi.	Representative	Cong.	Pty.	Address	County
						Joel Abbott	18	D	Washington	Wilkes
						George Cary	18	(----)	Appling	Columbia
						Thomas W. Cobb[r]	18	(----)	Greensboro	Greene
						(Resigned December, 1824)				
						Richard H. Wilde	18	D	Augusta	Richmond
						(Replaced Cobb February, 1825)				
						Alfred Cuthbert	18	D	Eatonton	Putnam
						John Forsyth	18	D	Augusta	Richmond
						Edward F. Tattnall	18	(----)	Savannah	Chatham
						Wiley Thompson	18	D	Elberton	Elbert
						George Cary	19	(----)	Appling	Columbia
						Alfred Cuthbert	19	D	Eatonton	Putnam
						John Forsyth	19	D	Augusta	Richmond
						Charles E. Haynes	19	D	Sparta	Hancock
						James E. Meriwether	19	(----)	Athens	Clarke
						Edward F. Tattnall	19	(----)	Savannah	Chatham
						Wiley Thompson	19	D	Elberton	Elbert

DISTRICT 1

County	Aggregate	Slave	%S	sq.mi.	P/sq.mi.	Representative	Cong.	Pty.	Address	County
Bryan	3,021	2,238	74.0	443	6.8	Edward F. Tattnall[r]	20	(----)	Savannah	Chatham
Bulloch	2,578	697	27.0	935	2.7	(Resigned before Congress assembled)				
Chatham	7,214	6,467	89.6	445	16.2	George R. Gilmer	20	D	Lexington	Oglethorpe
Effingham	3,018	1,347	44.6	480	6.3	(Replaced Tattnall)				
Emanuel	2,928	367	12.5	1,037	2.8					
Laurens	5,436	1,975	36.3	1,123	4.8					
Liberty	6,695	5,037	75.2	916	7.3					
McIntosh	5,129	3,715	72.4	426	12.0					
Montgomery	1,869	703	37.6	737	2.5					
Scriven	3,941	1,833	46.5	651	6.1					
Tattnall	2,644	568	21.4	1,044	2.5					
TOTALS	44,473	24,947	56.1	8,237	5.4					

DISTRICT 2

County	Aggregate	Slave	%S	sq.mi.	P/sq.mi.	Representative	Cong.	Pty.	Address	County
Burke	11,577	5,820	50.2	831	13.9	John Forsyth[r]	20	D	Augusta	Richmond
Columbia	12,695	7,420	58.4	543	23.4	(Resigned November, 1827, having been elected Governor)				
Jefferson	6,362	2,680	42.1	530	12.0	Richard H. Wilde	20	D	Augusta	Richmond
Lincoln	6,458	3,063	47.4	193	33.5	(Replaced Forsyth)				
Richmond	8,608	4,831	56.1	323	26.6					
Wilkes	16,912	9,356	55.3	498	33.9					
TOTALS	62,612	33,170	53.0	2,918	21.5					

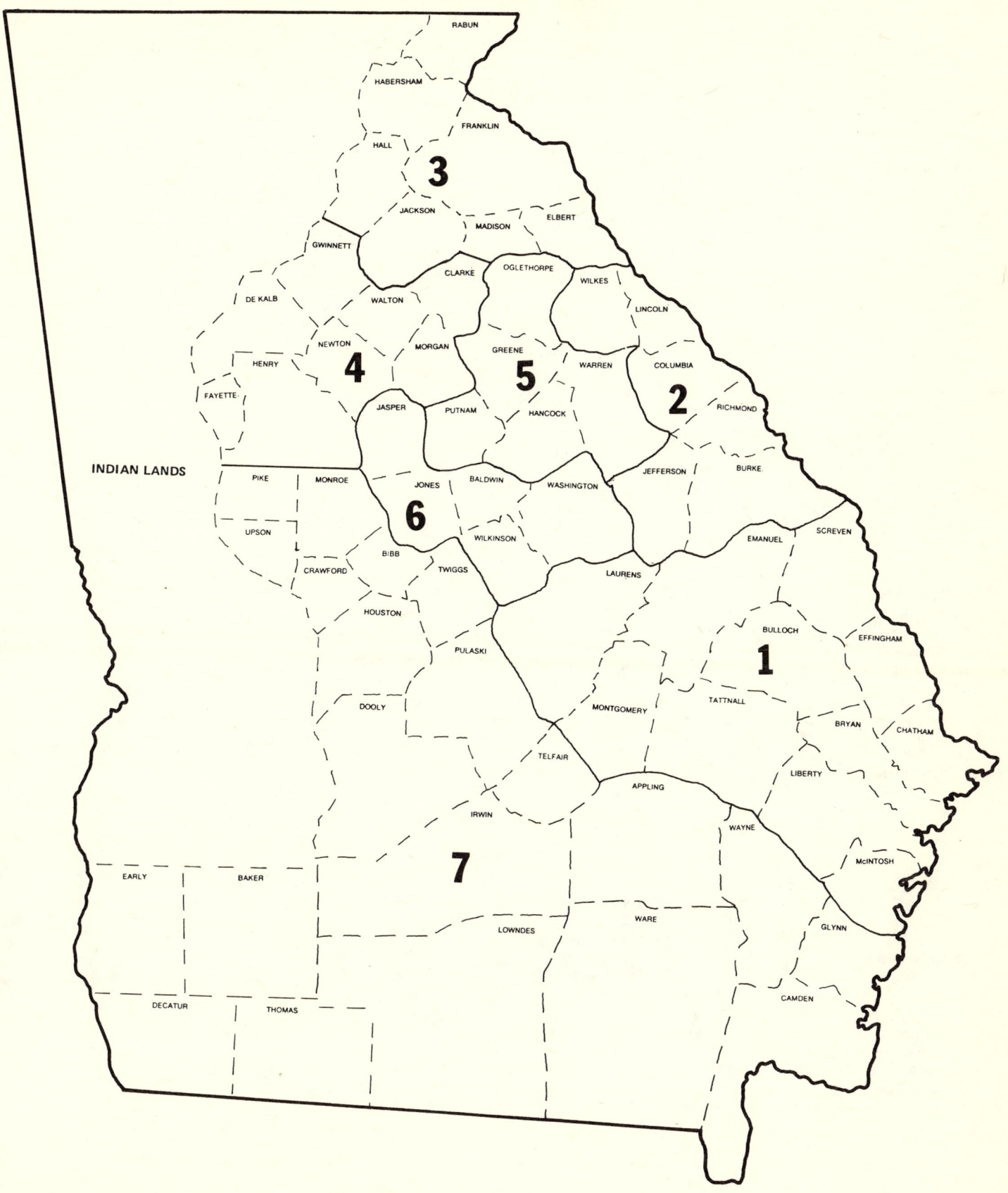

INDIAN LANDS

RABUN

HABERSHAM

FRANKLIN

HALL

3

JACKSON

MADISON

ELBERT

GWINNETT

DE KALB

WALTON

CLARKE

OGLETHORPE

WILKES

LINCOLN

NEWTON

MORGAN

GREENE

WARREN

COLUMBIA

HENRY

4

5

RICHMOND

FAYETTE

JASPER

PUTNAM

HANCOCK

2

PIKE

MONROE

JONES

BALDWIN

WASHINGTON

JEFFERSON

BURKE

UPSON

6

WILKINSON

SCREVEN

CRAWFORD

BIBB

EMANUEL

TWIGGS

LAURENS

HOUSTON

BULLOCH

EFFINGHAM

PULASKI

1

DOOLY

MONTGOMERY

TATTNALL

BRYAN

CHATHAM

TELFAIR

LIBERTY

APPLING

WAYNE

McINTOSH

EARLY

BAKER

IRWIN

7

WARE

GLYNN

DECATUR

THOMAS

LOWNDES

CAMDEN

| | COUNTIES | | | | | REPRESENTATIVES | | | | |
| County | Aggregate | Slave | %S | sq.mi. | P/sq.mi. | Representative | Cong. | Pty. | Address | County |

DISTRICT 3

County	Aggregate	Slave	%S	sq.mi.	P/sq.mi.	Representative	Cong.	Pty.	Address	County
Elbert[a]	----	----	----	----	----	Wiley Thompson	20	D	Elberton	Elbert
Franklin	9,040	1,774	19.6	898	10.1					
Habersham	3,145	277	8.8	525	6.0					
Hall	5,086	399	7.8	200	25.4					
Jackson	8,355	1,997	23.9	517	16.2					
Madison	3,735	904	24.2	281	13.3					
Rabon[a]	----	----	----	----	----					
TOTALS	29,361	5,351	18.2	3,149	9.3					

[a]Created after 1820 census.

DISTRICT 4

County	Aggregate	Slave	%S	sq.mi.	P/sq.mi.	Representative	Cong.	Pty.	Address	County
Clarke	8,767	3,461	39.4	302	29.0	Wilson Lumpkin	20	D	Madison	Morgan
De Kalb[a]	----	----	----	519	----					
Fayette[a]	----	----	----	199	----					
Gwinnett	4,589	538	11.7	250	18.4					
Henry[a]	----	----	----	717	----					
Morgan	13,520	6,045	44.7	356	37.9					
Newton[a]	----	- ----	----	399	----					
Walton	4,192	631	15.0	330	12.7					
TOTALS	31,068	10,675	34.4	3,072	10.1					

[a]Created after 1820 census.

DISTRICT 5

County	Aggregate	Slave	%S	sq.mi.	P/sq.mi.	Representative	Cong.	Pty.	Address	County
Greene	13,589	6,931	51.0	415	30.7	Charles E. Haynes	20	D	Sparta	Hancock
Hancock	12,734	6,863	53.9	498	25.6					
Oglethorpe	14,046	7,338	52.2	415	33.8					
Putnam	15,475	7,241	46.7	339	45.6					
Warren	10,630	4,041	38.0	314	33.9					
TOTALS	66,474	32,414	48.8	2,009	33.1					

DISTRICT 6

County	Aggregate	Slave	%S	sq.mi.	P/sq.mi.	Representative	Cong.	Pty.	Address	County
Baldwin	5,665	3,042	53.6	255	22.2	Tomlinson Fort	20	D	Milledgeville	Baldwin
Jasper	14,614	5,494	37.5	373	39.2					
Jones[a]	16,570	6,886	41.5	402	41.2					
Washington	10,627	3,898	36.6	674	15.7					
Wilkinson	6,992	1,463	20.9	458	15.3					
TOTALS	54,468	20,783	38.7	2,162	25.2					

[a]Town of Clinton used for population statistics.

DISTRICT 7

County	Aggregate	Slave	%S	sq.mi.	P/sq.mi.	Representative	Cong.	Pty.	Address	County
Appling	1,264	78	6.1	1,327	0.9	John Floyd	20	D	Jefferson	Jackson
Baker[a]	----	----	----	1,435	----					
Bibb[a]	----	----	----	254	----					
Camden[a]	3,402	2,095	61.6	1,187	30.4					
Crawford[a]	----	----	----	315	----					
Decatur[a]	----	----	----	821	----					
Dooley[a]	----	----	----	1,229	----					
Early	768	216	28.1	954	0.8	[a]Created after 1820 census.				
Glynn	3,418	2,760	80.7	412	8.3					
Houston[a]	----	----	----	711	----					
Irwin	411	39	9.4	2,036	0.2					
Loundes[a]	----	----	----	2,671	----					
Monroe	10,477	3,462	33.0	489	21.4					
Pike[a]	----	----	----	320	----					

COUNTIES						REPRESENTATIVES				
County	Aggregate	Slave	%S	sq.mi.	P/sq.mi.	Representative	Cong.	Pty.	Address	County

DISTRICT 7 (CONTINUED)

County	Aggregate	Slave	%S	sq.mi.	P/sq.mi.
Pulaski	5,283	2,021	38.2	970	5.4
Telfair	2,104	646	30.7	440	4.8
Thomas[a]	----	----	----	1,007	----
Twiggs	----	----	----	364	----
Upson[a]	----	----	----	334	----
Ware[a]	----	----	----	3,035	----
Wayne	1,010	333	32.9	914	1.1
Twiggs	10,447	3,462	33.1	364	28.7
TOTALS	38,620	18,112	49.5	21,225	1.8

[a]Created after 1820 census.

AT LARGE: TWENTY-FIRST AND TWENTY-SECOND CONGRESSES

Representative	Cong.	Pty.	Address	County
Thomas F. Foster	21	D	Greensboro	Greene
Charles E. Haynes	21	D	Sparta	Hancock
Henry G. Lamar	21	D	Macon	Bibb
(Elected to fill vacancy caused when Representative-Elect George Gilmer failed to signify his acceptance)				
Wilson Lumpkin	21	D	Monroe	Walton
Wiley Thompson	21	D	Elberton	Elbert
James M. Wayne	21	JD	Savannah	Chatham
Richard H. Wilde	21	D	Augusta	Richmond
Thomas F. Foster	22	D	Greensboro	Greene
Henry G. Lamar	22	D	Macon	Bibb
Wilson Lumpkin[r]	22	D	Monroe	Walton
(Resigned before Congress assembled)				
Augustin S. Clayton	22	SRD	Athens	Clarke
(Replaced Lumpkin)				
Daniel Newman	22	SRD	McDonough	Henry
Wiley Thompson	22	D	Elberton	Elbert
James M. Wayne	22	JD	Savannah	Chatham
Richard H. Wilde	22	D	Augusta	Richmond

[1]Elections were held at large for the Eighteenth, Nineteenth, Twenty-first and Twenty-second Congresses, and by districts for the Twentieth Congress.

	COUNTIES						REPRESENTATIVES			
County	Aggregate	Slave	%S	sq.mi.	P/sq.mi.	Representative	Cong.	Pty.	Address	County
AT LARGE										
Alexander	626	----	----	373	1.6	John McLean	15	D	Shawnee-	Gallatin
Bond	2,931	27	0.9	448	6.5				town	
Clark	931	1	0.1	1,140	0.8	Daniel P. Cook	16	NR	Edwardsville	Madison
Crawford	3,022	----	----	1,183	2.5	Daniel P. Cook	17	NR	Edwardsville	Madison
Edwards	3,444	7	2.0	447	7.7	Daniel P. Cook	18	NR	Edwardsville	Madison
Franklin	1,763	8	0.5	863	2.0	Daniel P. Cook	19	NR	Edwardsville	Madison
Gallatin	3,155	267	8.4	794	3.9	Joseph Duncan	20	JD	Brownsville	----
Jackson	1,542	37	2.3	605	2.5	Joseph Duncan	21	JD	Brownsville	----
Jefferson	691	----	----	573	1.2	Joseph Duncan	22	JD	Brownsville	----
Johnson	843	14	1.6	449	1.8					
Madison	13,550	122	0.9	733	18.4					
Monroe	1,537	12	0.8	382	4.0					
Pope	2,610	----	----	625	4.1					
Randolph	3,492	233	6.6	1,033	3.3					
St. Clair	5,253	98	1.8	673	7.8					
Washington	1,517	26	1.1	998	1.5					
Wayne	1,114	3	0.3	865	1.2					
White	4,828	50	1.0	502	9.6					
Union	2,362	24	1.0	416	5.6					
TOTALS	55,211	929	1.6	13,102	4.2					

[1]Illinois became a state in December, 1818. Counties listed are those included in the 1810 census.

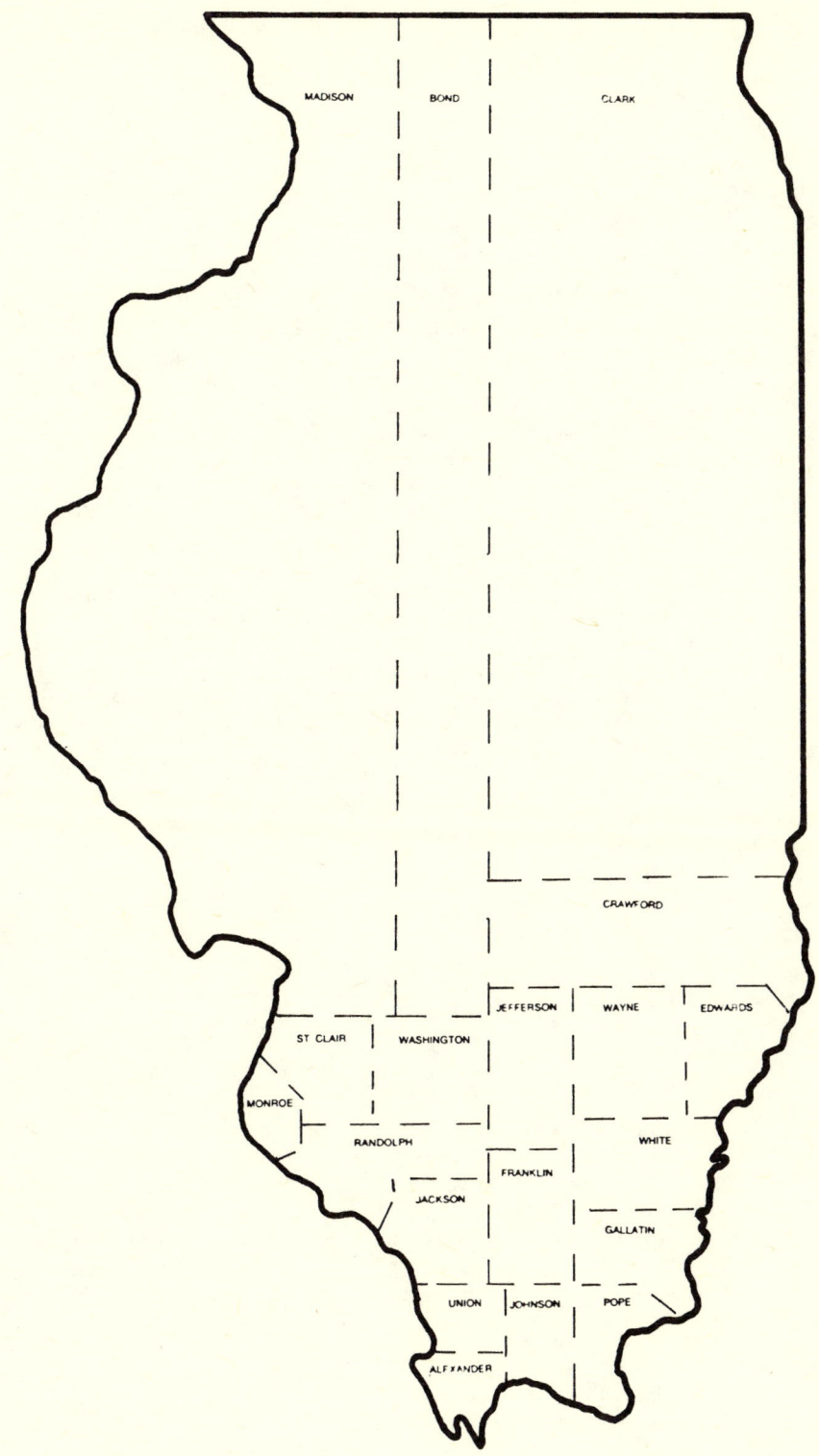

| County | COUNTIES | | | | | Representative | REPRESENTATIVES | | | |
	Aggregate	Slave	%S	sq.mi.	P/sq.mi.		Cong.	Pty.	Address	County

PROVISIONAL CONGRESSMEN FROM INDIANA
FOURTEENTH THROUGH SEVENTEENTH CONGRESSES

						Representative	Cong.	Pty.	Address	County
						William Hendricks	14	R	Madison	Jefferson
						(Took Seat December, 1816)				
						William Hendricks	15	R	Madison	Jefferson
						William Hendricks	16	R	Madison	Jefferson
						William Hendricks[r]	17	R	Madison	Jefferson
						(Resigned July, 1822)				
						Jonathan Jennings	17	R	Charlestown	Clark
						(Replaced Hendricks December, 1822)				

DISTRICT 1

County	Aggregate	Slave	%S	sq.mi.	P/sq.mi.	Representative	Cong.	Pty.	Address	County
Davies	3,432	----	----	430	8.0	William Prince†	18	(----)	Princeton	Gibson
Dubois	1,168	----	----	433	2.7	(Died September, 1824)				
Gibson	10,763	----	----	560	19.2	Jacob Call	18	(----)	Princeton	Gibson
Greene[a]	----	----	----	549	----	(Replaced Prince)				
Knox	5,437	----	----	516	10.5	Ratliff Boon	19	JD	Boonville	Warwick
Lawrence	4,116	----	----	459	9.0	Thomas H. Blake	20	NR	Terre Haute	Vigo
Martin	1,032	----	----	300	3.4	Ratliff Boon	21	JD	Boonville	Warwick
Monroe	2,679	----	----	386	6.9	Ratliff Boon	22	JD	Boonville	Warwick
Morgan	3,498	----	----	350	----					
Orange	5,368	----	----	405	13.3					
Owen	838	1	----	390	2.1					
Park[a]	----	----	----	600	----					
Pike	1,472	----	----	273	5.4					
Posey	4,061	11	----	350	11.6					
Putnam[a]	----	----	----	364	----					
Spencer	1,882	3	----	396	4.8					
Sullivan	3,498	8	----	507	6.9					
Vanderburgh	1,798	8	----	303	5.9					
Vigo	3,390	----	----	415	8.2					
Wabash	147	----	----	2,692	0.05					
Warwick	1,749	1	----	391	4.5					
TOTALS	52,830	32	----	11,069	4.8					

[a]Created after 1820 census.

DISTRICT 2

County	Aggregate	Slave	%S	sq.mi.	P/sq.mi.	Representative	Cong.	Pty.	Address	County
Bartholomew[a]	----	-----	----	721	----	Jonathan Jennings	18	R	Charleston	Clark
Clark	8,709	----	----	384	22.7	Jonathan Jennings	19	NR	Charleston	Clark
Crawford	2,683	----	----	312	8.3	Jonathan Jennings	20	NR	Charleston	Clark
Delaware	2,356	----	----	1,699	2.2	Jonathan Jennings	21	NR	Charleston	Clark
Floyd	2,776	----	----	149	18.6	John Carr	22	JD	Charleston	Clark
Harrison	7,875	----	----	479	16.4					
Jackson	4,010	----	----	520	7.7					
Jefferson	8,038	----	----	366	22.0					
Jennings	2,000	118	5.9	377	5.3					
Marion[a]	----	----	----	392	----					

[a]Created after 1820 census.

	COUNTIES					REPRESENTATIVES				
County	Aggregate	Slave	%S	sq.mi.	P/sq.mi.	Representative	Cong.	Pty.	Address	County

DISTRICT 2 (CONTINUED)

	COUNTIES					REPRESENTATIVES				
Scott	2,334	6	----	193	12.1					
Washington	9,039	----	----	516	17.5					
TOTALS	49,720	124	0.2	6,108	8.1					

DISTRICT 3

County	Aggregate	Slave	%S	sq.mi.	P/sq.mi.	Representative	Cong.	Pty.	Address	County
Dearborn	11,468	----	----	393	29.2	John Test	18	R	Brookville	Franklin
Delaware	1,321	----	----	1,013	1.3	John Test	19	NR	Brookville	Franklin
Fayette	5,950	----	----	215	27.7	Oliver H. Smith	20	JD	Connersville	Fayette
Randolph	1,808	----	----	2,431	0.7	John Test	21	NR	Lawrence- burg	Dearborn
Ripley	1,822	----	----	442	4.1					
Switzerland	3,934	----	----	221	17.8	Jonathan McCarty	22	JD	Connersville	Fayette
Union[a]	----	----	----	168	----					
Wayne	12,119	----	----	405	29.9					
TOTALS	41,198	----	----	5,682[2]	7.3					

[1]Indiana became a state on December 11, 1816.

[2]Indian lands in Indiana totaled 13,328 square miles.

[a]Created after 1820 census.

KENTUCKY
12 DISTRICTS
12 CONGRESSMEN

	COUNTIES					REPRESENTATIVES				
County	Aggregate	Slave	%S	sq.mi.	P/sq.mi.	Representative	Cong.	Pty.	Address	County

DISTRICT 1

County	Aggregate	Slave	%S	sq.mi.	P/sq.mi.	Representative	Cong.	Pty.	Address	County
Bath	7,961	1,224	15.3	287	27.8	David Trimble	18	D	Mount Sterling	Montgomery
Fleming	12,186	1,144	9.3	640	19.0					
Floyd	8,207	197	2.4	1,120	7.3	David Trimble	19	D	Mount Sterling	Montgomery
Greenup	4,311	566	13.1	907	4.8					
Lawrence	----	----	----	665	----	Henry Daniel	20	JD	Mount Sterling	Montgomery
Lewis	3,976	464	11.6	486	8.2					
Montgomery	9,587	2,054	21.4	414	23.2	Henry Daniel	21	JD	Mount Sterling	Montgomery
Pike	----	----	----	1,267	----					
TOTALS	46,228	5,649	12.2	5,785	8.0	Henry Daniel	22	JD	Mount Sterling	Montgomery

DISTRICT 2

County	Aggregate	Slave	%S	sq.mi.	P/sq.mi.	Representative	Cong.	Pty.	Address	County
Bourbon	17,664	5,165	29.2	300	58.9	Thomas Metcalfe	18	D	Carlisle	Nicholas
Bracken	5,280	676	12.8	254	20.8	Thomas Metcalfe	19	D	Carlisle	Nicholas
Mason	13,588	3,366	24.7	289	47.0	Thomas Metcalfe[r]	20	JD	Carlisle	Nicholas
Nicholas	7,973	924	11.5	204	39.1	John Chambers (Replaced Metcalfe)	20	NR	Washington	Mason
TOTALS	44,505	10,131	22.7	1,047	42.5	Nicholas D. Coleman	21	JD	Washington	Mason
						Thomas A. Marshall	22	NR	Paris	Bourbon

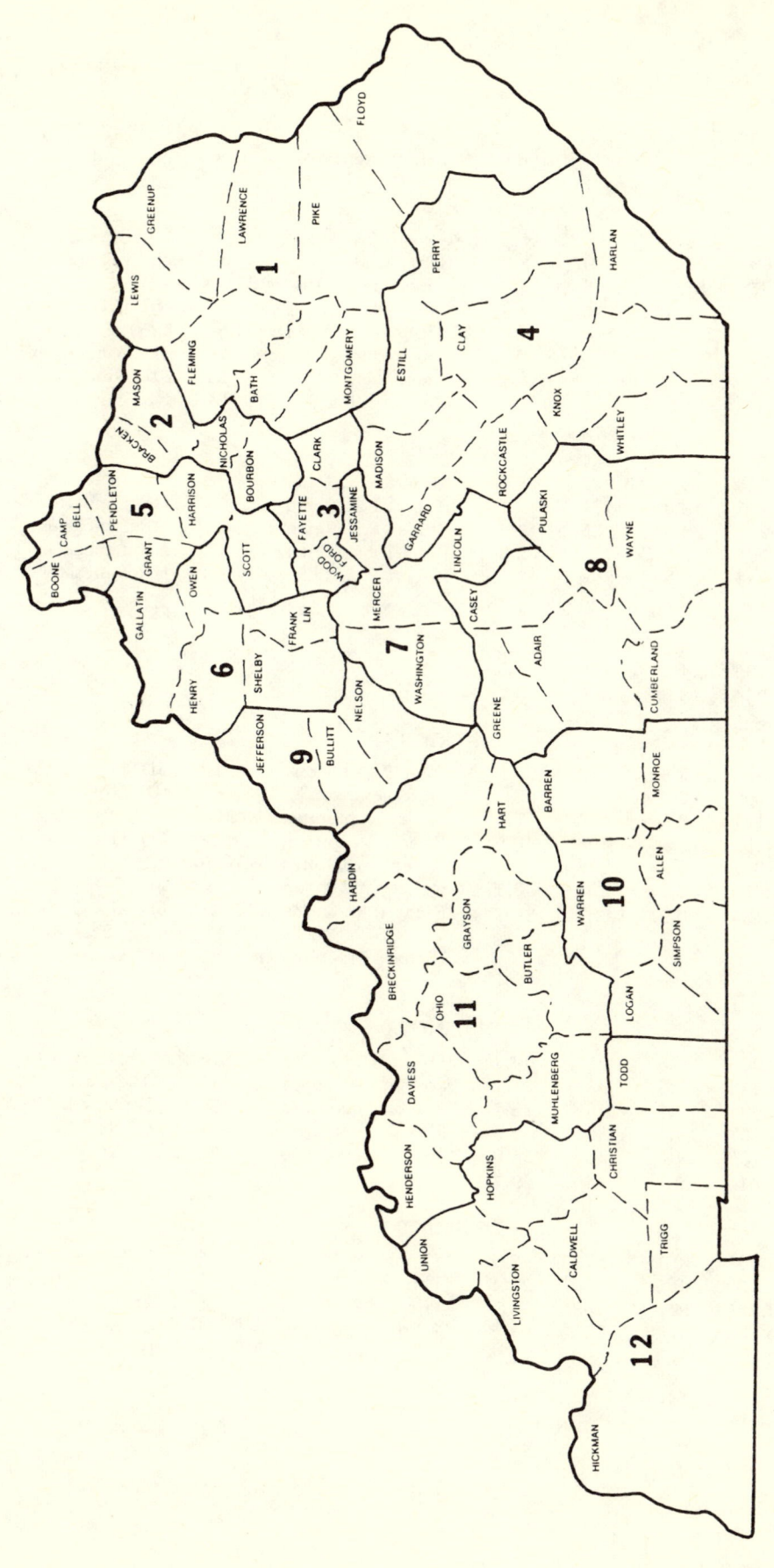

COUNTIES						REPRESENTATIVES				
County	Aggregate	Slave	%S	sq.mi.	P/sq.mi.	Representative	Cong.	Pty.	Address	County

DISTRICT 3

County	Aggregate	Slave	%S	sq.mi.	P/sq.mi.	Representative	Cong.	Pty.	Address	County
Clark	11,449	3,463	30.2	259	44.2	Henry Clay	18	NR	Lexington	Fayette
Fayette	23,250	7,633	32.8	280	83.0	Henry Clay[r]	19	NR	Lexington	Fayette
Woodford	12,207	4,678	38.3	193	63.2	(Resigned April, 1825)				
TOTALS	49,609	15,774	33.6	732	67.8	James Clark	19	NR	Winchester	Clark
						(Replaced Clay December, 1825)				
						James Clark	20	SD	Winchester	Clark
						James Clark	21	SD	Winchester	Clark
						Chilton Allan	22	NR	Winchester	Clark

DISTRICT 4

County	Aggregate	Slave	%S	sq.mi.	P/sq.mi.	Representative	Cong.	Pty.	Address	County
Clay	4,393	285	6.4	1,208	3.6	Robert P. Letcher	18	R	Lancaster	Garrard
Estill	3,507	281	8.0	471	7.4	Robert P. Letcher	19	NR	Lancaster	Garrard
Garrard	10,851	2,918	26.8	236	46.0	Robert P. Letcher	20	NR	Lancaster	Garrard
Harlan	1,961	108	5.5	779	2.5	Robert P. Letcher	21	NR	Lancaster	Garrard
Knox	3,661	337	9.2	809	4.5	Robert P. Letcher	22	NR	Lancaster	Garrard
Madison	15,954	4,154	26.0	696	22.9					
Perry[a]	----	----	----	1,491	----					
Rockcastle	2,249	155	6.8	431	5.2					
Whitley	2,340	96	4.1	539	4.3					
TOTALS	44,916	8,334	18.5	6,660	6.7					

[a]Created after 1820 census.

DISTRICT 5

County	Aggregate	Slave	%S	sq.mi.	P/sq.mi.	Representative	Cong.	Pty.	Address	County
Boone	6,542	1,296	19.8	249	26.3	John T. Johnson	18	JD	Georgetown	Scott
Campbell	7,022	897	12.7	314	22.4	James Johnson[†]	19	D	Great Crossings	Scott
Grant	1,805	137	12.6	249	7.3	(Died September, 1826)				
Harrison	12,278	2,137	17.4	308	39.8	Robert McHatton	19	JD	Georgetown	Scott
Pendleton	3,086	318	10.3	279	11.0	(Replaced Johnson December, 1926)				
Scott	14,219	4,620	32.4	284	50.1	Robert McHatton	20	JD	Georgetown	Scott
TOTALS	44,952	9,405	20.9	1,683	26.7	Richard M. Johnson	21	JD	Great Crossings	Scott
						Richard M. Johnson	22	JD	Great Crossings	Scott

DISTRICT 6

County	Aggregate	Slave	%S	sq.mi.	P/sq.mi.	Representative	Cong.	Pty.	Address	County
Franklin	11,024	2,907	26.3	211	99.7	David White	18	(----)	New Castle	Henry
Gallatin	7,075	1,242	17.5	335	21.1	Joseph Lecompte	19	D	New Castle	Henry
Henry	10,816	2,004	18.5	469	23.1	Joseph Lecompte	20	JD	New Castle	Henry
Owen	2,031	207	10.1	351	5.8	Joseph Lecompte	21	JD	New Castle	Henry
Shelby	21,047	5,158	24.5	383	55.0	Joseph Lecompte	22	JD	New Castle	Henry
TOTALS	51,993	11,518	22.1	1,749	29.7					

DISTRICT 7

County	Aggregate	Slave	%S	sq.mi.	P/sq.mi.	Representative	Cong.	Pty.	Address	County
Jessamine	9,297	2,802	30.1	177	52.5	Thomas P. Moore	18	D	Harrodsburg	Mercer
Lincoln	9,979	3,053	30.5	340	29.4	Thomas P. Moore	19	D	Harrodsburg	Mercer
Mercer	15,587	3,825	24.5	439	35.5	Thomas P. Moore	20	JD	Harrodsburg	Mercer
Washington	15,947	3,734	23.4	650	24.5	John Kincaid	21	D	Stanford	Lincoln
TOTALS	50,810	13,414	26.4	1,606	31.6	John Adair	22	D	Harrodsburg	Mercer

	COUNTIES					REPRESENTATIVES				
County	Aggregate	Slave	%S	sq.mi.	P/sq.mi.	Representative	Cong.	Pty.	Address	County
						DISTRICT 8				
Adair	8,765	1,509	17.2	810	10.8	Richard A. Buckner	18	NR	Greenburg	Green
Casey	4,349	456	10.4	435	10.0	Richard A. Buckner	19	NR	Greenburg	Green
Cumberland	8,058	1,332	16.5	410	19.7	Richard A. Buckner	20	NR	Greenburg	Green
Green	11,943	3,241	27.1	559	21.4	Nathan Gaither	21	D	Columbia	Adair
Pulaski	7,597	637	8.3	653	11.6	Nathan Gaither	22	D	Columbia	Adair
Wayne	7,951	553	6.9	440	18.0					
TOTALS	48,663	7,728	15.8	3,307	14.7					
						DISTRICT 9				
Bullitt	5,831	1,245	21.3	300	19.4	Charles A. Wickliffe	18	D	Bardstown	Nelson
Jefferson	20,768	5,855	28.1	425	48.9	Charles A. Wickliffe	19	D	Bardstown	Nelson
Nelson	16,273	3,866	23.7	630	25.8	Charles A. Wickliffe	20	JD	Bardstown	Nelson
TOTALS	42,872	10,966	25.6	1,355	31.6	Charles A. Wickliffe	21	D	Bardstown	Nelson
						Charles A. Wickliffe	22	D	Bardstown	Nelson
						DISTRICT 10				
Allen	5,327	723	13.5	351	15.2	Francis Johnson	18	NR	Bowling Green	Warren
Barren	10,328	2,446	23.6	668	15.5					
Logan	14,423	4,019	27.8	563	25.6	Francis Johnson	19	NR	Bowling Green	Warren
Monroe	4,956	498	10.0	334	14.8					
Simpson	4,852	803	16.5	239	6.0	Joel Yancey	20	JD	Glasgow	Barren
Warren	3,470	2,554	72.6	696	5.0	Joel Yancey	21	JD	Glasgow	Barren
TOTALS	43,356	11,043	25.5	2,851	13.8	Christopher Tompkins	22	NR	Glasgow	Barren
						DISTRICT 11				
Breckinridge	7,485	1,269	16.9	741	10.1	Philip Thompson	18	(----)	Yellow Banks	Daviess
Butler	3,083	867	28.1	443	7.0					
Daviess	3,876	852	21.9	652	5.9	William S. Young	19	D	Elizabeth-town	Hardin
Grayson	4,055	184	4.5	596	6.8					
Hancock	----	----	----	----	----	William S. Young†	20	JD	Elizabeth-town	Hardin
Hardin	10,498	1,466	13.9	1,081	9.7	(Died September, 1827)				
Hart	4,181	596	14.2	520	8.0	John Calhounce	20	NR	Hardinsburg	Breckinridge
Henderson	5,714	2,265	39.6	433	13.2	(Elected to replace Young; election contested by Thomas				
Muhlenberg	4,979	575	12.2	521	9.6	Chilton)				
Ohio	3,879	468	12.0	696	5.6	Thomas Chilton	20	NR	Elizabeth-town	Hardin
TOTALS	47,750	8,542	17.8	5,683	8.4					
						(Successfully contested the election of Calhoun; took seat January, 1828)				
						Thomas Chilton	21	NR	Elizabeth-town	Hardin
						Albert E. Hawes	22	JD	Hawesville	Hancock
						DISTRICT 12				
Caldwell	9,022	1,444	16.0	1,900	4.7	Robert P. Henry	18	NR	Hopkinsville	Christian
Christian	10,459	3,491	33.3	725	14.4	Robert P. Henry†	19	NR	Hopkinsville	Christian
Hickmana	----	----	----	----	----	(Died November, 1826)				
Hopkins	5,322	782	14.6	692	7.7	John F. Henry	19	NR	Hopkinsville	Christian
Livingston	5,824	1,020	17.5	1,799	3.2	(Replaced Robert Henry December, 1826)				
Todd	5,089	1,729	33.9	376	13.5	Chittenden Lyon	20	JD	Eddysville	Caldwell
Trigg	3,871	816	21.0	408	9.5	Chittenden Lyon	21	JD	Eddysville	Caldwell
Union	3,470	1,035	29.8	490	7.1	Chittenden Lyon	22	D	Eddysville	Caldwell
TOTALS	43,057	10,317	24.0	6,390	6.7					

aCreated after 1820 census.

COUNTIES						REPRESENTATIVES				
County	Aggregate	Slave	%S	sq.mi.	P/sq.mi.	Representative	Cong.	Pty.	Address	County

DISTRICT 1

County	Aggregate	Slave	%S	sq.mi.	P/sq.mi.	Representative	Cong.	Pty.	Address	County
'Orleans'*[1]						Edward Livingston	18	D	New Orleans	----
New Orleans	14,175	7,591	53.6		73.1	Edward Livingston	19	D	New Orleans	----
City of New				566		Edward Livingston	20	D	New Orleans	----
Orleans	27,176	7,355	27.1		73.1	Edward D. White	21	W	Donaldsville	Ascension
Plaquemines	2,354	1,566	66.5	1,544	1.5	Edward D. White	22	W	Donaldsville	Ascension
St. Bernard	2,635	1,923	72.8	294	9.0					
Subtotal	46,340	18,435	39.8	2,404	19.3					
'German Coast'*										
St. Charles	3,862	2,987	77.3	227	17.0					
St. John	3,854	2,209	57.3	253	15.2					
Subtotal	7,716	5,196	67.4	480	16.1					
'Acadia'*										
Ascension	3,728	2,129	57.1	250	14.9					
St. James	5,660	3,086	54.5	306	18.5					
Subtotal	9,388	5,215	55.5	556	16.9					
'La Fourche'	3,755	968	25.8	2,509	1.5					
TOTALS[2]	67,199	29,814	44.4	5,949	11.3					

DISTRICT 2

County	Aggregate	Slave	%S	sq.mi.	P/sq.mi.	Representative	Cong.	Pty.	Address	County
'Feliciana'	12,732	7,167	56.3	859	14.8	Henry H. Gurley	18	W	Baton Rouge	West Baton Rouge
'Iberville'	4,414	2,279	51.6	407	10.8					
'Pointe						Henry H. Gurley	19	W	Baton Rouge	West Baton Rouge
Coupee	4,912	3,630	73.9	563	8.7					
Subtotal	22,058	13,076	59.3	1,829	12.1	Henry H. Gurley	20	W	Baton Rouge	West Baton Rouge
East Baton										
Rouge	5,220	2,076	39.8	459	11.4	Henry H. Gurley	21	W	Baton Rouge	West Baton Rouge
West Baton										
Rouge	2,335	1,303	55.8	450	5.2	Philemon Thomas	22	D	Baton Rouge	West Baton Rouge
Subtotal	7,555	3,379	44.7	909	8.3					
Florida Parishes:[3]										
St. Helena	3,026	830	27.4	1,882	1.6					
St. Tammany	1,723	631	36.6	887	1.9					
Washington	2,517	559	22.2	665	3.8					
Subtotal	7,266	2,020	27.8	3,434	2.1					
TOTAL	36,879	18,475	50.0	6,172	6.0					

NATCHITOCHES

OUACHITA

CONCORDIA

CATAHOULA

RAPIDES

3

AVOYELLES

OPELOUSAS

ST. LANDRY

FELICIANA

ST. HELENA

WASHINGTON

POINTE
COUPEE

EAST
BATON
ROUGE

2

ST. TAMMANY

WEST
BATON ROUGE

IBERVILLE

ATTAKAPAS

ST. MARTIN

ASCENSION

ST. JAMES

ST. JOHN

ST. CHARLES

ST. BERNARD

ORLEANS

ASSUMPTION

LAFOURCHE

PLAQUEMINES

1

COUNTIES						REPRESENTATIVES				
County	Aggregate	Slave	%S	sq.mi.	P/sq.mi.	Representative	Cong.	Pty.	Address	County

DISTRICT 3

County	Aggregate	Slave	%S	sq.mi.	P/sq.mi.	Representative	Cong.	Pty.	Address	County
'Attakapas'*	12,063	5,707	47.3	3,543	3.4	William L. Brent	18	W	St. Martins-ville	Attakapas
'Concordia'	2,626	1,787	68.0	1,830	1.4					
'Natchi-toches'*	7,486	2,326	31.1	9,530	0.8	William L. Brent	19	W	St. Martins-ville	Attakapas
'Opelousas'4	10,085	3,951	39.2	7,274	1.4	William L. Brent	20	W	St. Martins-ville	Attakapas
'Ouachita'	2,896	836	3.5	4,765	0.6					
'Rapides'	6,065	3,489	57.2	3,269	1.9	Walter H. Overton	21	D	Alexandria	Rapides
Subtotal	41,221	18,096	43.9	30,211	1.4	Henry A. Bullard	22	W	Alexandria	Rapides
Avoyelles	2,245	782	34.8	941	2.4					
Assumption	3,576	1,149	32.1	356	10.0					
Catahoula	2,287	751	32.8	1,250	1.8					
Subtotal	8,108	2,682	33.1	2,547	3.4					
TOTALS	49,329	20,778	42.1	32,758	1.5					

[1] The names in quotations are those used in the 1822 act which divided the state into three districts. Some of the names are parishes, while those marked with quotes and an asterisk (*) apparently refer to sections of the state. Parishes were assigned to these sections after consulting with persons familiar with early Louisiana politics. Other parishes, not mentioned in the act, were assigned to districts in the same manner. Internal evidence, mainly the residence of Congressmen through 1842, indicates that our assignment of unnamed counties is correct.

[2] The totals for District 1 seem much too large. If the totals indicated by the act are correct, District 1 had 43.8 per cent of Louisiana's total population. This would make Louisiana the most mal-apportioned state in the U.S. from 1789 to 1842.

[3] It is assumed that the "Florida Parishes" belong in District 2. They were not mentioned in the districting act.

[4] Data for Opelousas is omitted in the 1820 census; it can be found in the retrospective section of the 1830 census. Catahoula, Aroyelles, and Assumption were not mentioned in the districting act and were assigned to District 3.

MAINE
7 DISTRICTS
7 CONGRESSMEN

COUNTIES						REPRESENTATIVES				
County	Aggregate	Slave	%S	sq.mi.	P/sq.mi.	Representative	Cong.	Pty.	Address	County

DISTRICT 1 (YORK)

County	Aggregate	Slave	%S	sq.mi.	P/sq.mi.	Representative	Cong.	Pty.	Address	County
York	46,283	----	----	1,001	46.2	William Burleigh	18	NR	South Ber-Berwick	York
						William Burleigh	19	NR	South Berwick	York
						William Burleigh† (Died July, 1827)	20	NR	South Berwick	York
						Rufus McIntire (Replaced Burleigh December, 1827)	20	JD	Parsonsfield	York
						Rufus McIntire	21	JD	Parsonsfield	York
						Rufus McIntire	22	JD	Parsonsfield	York

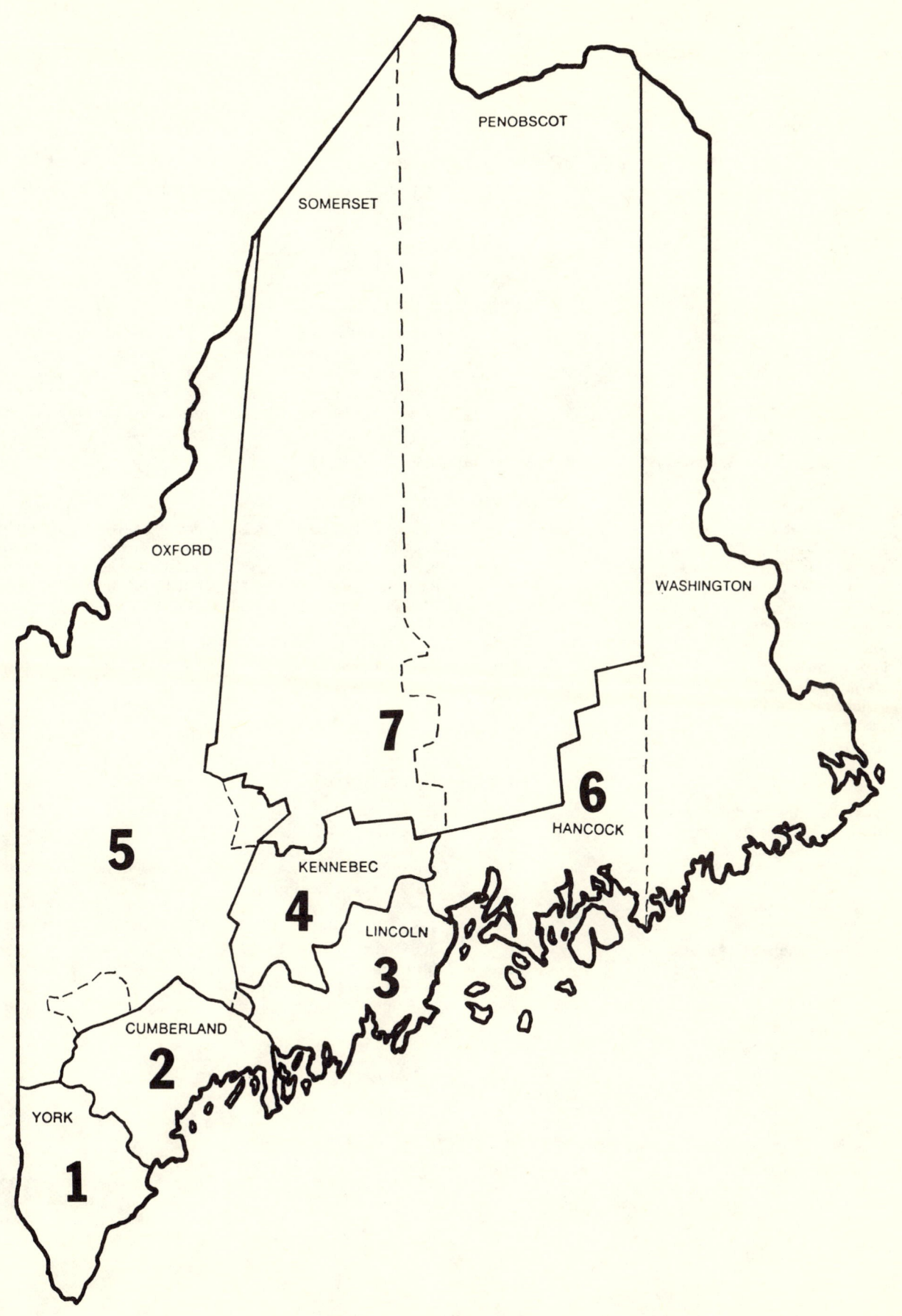

PENOBSCOT

SOMERSET

OXFORD

WASHINGTON

7

5

6

HANCOCK

KENNEBEC

4

LINCOLN

3

CUMBERLAND

2

YORK

1

COUNTIES						REPRESENTATIVES				
County	Aggregate	Slave	%S	sq.mi.	P/sq.mi.	Representative	Cong.	Pty.	Address	County

DISTRICT 2 (CUMBERLAND)

All of Cumberland County, except those towns included						Stephen Longfellow	18	F	Portland	Cumberland
in District 5,						John Anderson	19	JR	Portland	Cumberland
total:	36,045	----	----	972	37.1	John Anderson	20	JR	Portland	Cumberland
						John Anderson	21	JR	Portland	Cumberland
						John Anderson	22	JR	Portland	Cumberland

DISTRICT 3 (LINCOLN)

All of Lincoln County, except those towns included in						Ebeneazer Herrick	18	(----)	Bowdoinham	Lincoln
Districts 4 and 5,						Ebeneazer Herrick	19	(----)	Bowdoinham	Lincoln
total:[a]	36,987	----	----	661	55.9	Joseph F. Wingate	20	D	Bath	Lincoln
						Joseph F. Wingate	21	D	Bath	Lincoln
						Edward Kavanagh	22	D	Damariscotta Mills	Lincoln

[a]No census data is available on the town of Washington in Lincoln County.

DISTRICT 4 (KENNEBEC)

All of Kennebec County, except those towns included						Joshua Cushman	18	D	Winslow	Kennebec
in District 5,						Peleg Sprague	19	NR	Hallowell	Kennebec
total:	33,611	----	----	997	26.9	Peleg Sprague	20	NR	Hallowell	Kennebec
Towns in Lincoln County:						Peleg Sprague[r]	21	NR	Hallowell	Kennebec
Appleton	511	----	----	----	----	(Resigned, having been elected to the Senate)				
Montville	1,266	----	----	----	----	George Evans	21	NR	Gardiner	Kennebec
Montville						(Replaced Sprague December, 1829)				
Plantation	409	----	----	----	----	George Evans	22	NR	Gardiner	Kennebec
Palermo	1,056	----	----	----	----					
Patricktown	292	----	----	----	----					
Total, towns	3,534	----	----	----	----					
TOTALS	37,145	----	----	997	37.3					

DISTRICT 5 (OXFORD)

Towns in Cumberland County:						Enoch Lincoln	18	(----)	Paris	Oxford
Baldwin	1,120	----	----	----	----	Enoch Lincoln[r]	19	(----)	Paris	Oxford
Bridgeton	1,160	----	----	----	----	(Resigned January, 1826)				
Harrison	789	----	----	----	----	James W. Ripley	19	D	Fryeburg	Oxford
Minot	2,524	----	----	----	----	(Replaced Lincoln December, 1826)				
Otisfield	1,107	----	----	----	----	James W. Ripley	20	D	Fryeburg	Oxford
Total, towns	6,700	----	----	170	39.4	James W. Ripley[r]	21	JR	Fryeburg	Oxford
Towns in Kennebec County:						(Resigned March, 1830)				
Greene	1,309	----	----	----	----	Cornelius Holland	21	D	Canton	Oxford
Temple	615	----	----	----	----	(Replaced Ripley December, 1830)				
Wilton	1,115	----	----	----	----	Cornelius Holland	22	D	Canton	Oxford
Total, towns	3,039	----	----	103	39.5					
Towns in Lincoln County:										
Lewiston	1,312	----	----	----	----					
Lisbon	2,240	----	----	----	----					
Wales	515	----	----	----	----					
Total, towns	4,067	----	----	103	39.5					
Oxford	27,104	----	----	3,080	8.8					
TOTALS	40,910	----	----	3,456	11.8					

	COUNTIES					REPRESENTATIVES				
County	Aggregate	Slave	%S	sq.mi.	P/sq.mi.	Representative	Cong.	Pty.	Address	County
DISTRICT 6 (HANCOCK & WASHINGTON)										
Hancock	42,623	----	----	1,736	24.6	Jeremiah O'Brien	18	D	Machias	Washington
Washington	12,744	----	----	3,504	3.6	Jeremiah O'Brien	19	D	Machias	Washington
TOTALS	55,367	----	----	5,240	10.6	Jeremiah O'Brien	20	D	Machias	Washington
						Leonard Jarvis	21	D	Ellsworth	Hancock
						Leonard Jarvis	22	D	Ellsworth	Hancock
DISTRICT 7 (SOMERSET & PENOBSCOT)										
Penobscot	13,870	----	----	11,294	1.2	David Kidder	18	NR	Norridge-wock	Somerset
Somerset	21,787	----	----	6,794	3.2					
TOTALS	35,657	----	----	18,088	2.0	David Kidder	19	NR	Norridge-wock	Somerset
						Samuel Butman	20	(----)	Dixmont	Penobscot
						Samuel Butman	21	(----)	Dixmont	Penobscot
						James Bates	22	D	Norridge-wock	Somerset

COUNTIES						REPRESENTATIVES				
County	Aggregate	Slave	%S	sq.mi.	P/sq.mi.	Representative	Cong.	Pty.	Address	County
DISTRICT 1										
Calvert	8,073	3,985	49.3	217	37.2	Raphael Neale	18	D	Leonardtown	St. Marys
Charles	16,500	9,419	57.0	459	35.9	Clement Dorsey	19	(----)	Chaptico	St. Marys
St. Marys	12,974	6,619	51.0	373	34.8	Clement Dorsey	20	(----)	Chaptico	St. Marys
TOTALS	37,547	20,023	53.3	1,049	35.8	Clement Dorsey	21	(----)	Chaptico	St. Marys
						Daniel Jenifer	22	NR	Allens Fresh	Charles
DISTRICT 2										
Ann Arundel	27,165	10,301	37.9	674	40.3	Joseph Kent	18	D	Bladensburg	Prince Georges
Prince						Joseph Kent[r]	19	D	Bladensburg	Prince Georges
Georges	20,216	9,031	44.6	485	41.7	John C. Weems	19	D	Waterloo*	Calvert*
TOTALS	47,381	19,332	40.8	1,159	40.9	(Replaced Kent)				
						John C. Weems	20	D	Waterloo*	Calvert*
						Benedict J. Semmes	21	D	Piscataway	Prince Georges
						Benedict J. Semmes	22	D	Piscataway	Prince Georges
DISTRICT 3										
Frederick[a]	20,229	3,842	18.9	395	51.2	Henry R. Warfield	18	F	Middleburg	Frederick
Montgomery	16,400	6,396	39.0	495	33.1	George Peter	19	D	Darnestown	Frederick
TOTALS	36,629	10,238	27.9	890	41.2	George C. Washington	20	NR	Rockville	Montgomery
						George C. Washington	21	NR	Rockville	Montgomery
						George C. Washington	22	NR	Rockville	Montgomery

[a]The part of Frederick east of the Monocracy River.

COUNTIES						REPRESENTATIVES				
DISTRICT 4										
Allegheny	8,654	798	9.2	928	9.3	John Lee	18	D	Petersville	Frederick
Frederick[a]	20,229	3,842	18.9	395	51.2	Thomas C.				
Washington	23,072	3,201	13.8	459	50.3	Worthington	19	D	Frederick	Frederick
TOTALS	51,955	7,841	15.1	1,782	29.2	Michael C. Sprigg	20	D	Frostburg	Allegheny
						Michael C. Sprigg	21	D	Frostburg	Allegheny
						Francis Thomas	22	D	Frederick	Frederick

[a]The part of Frederick west of the Monocracy River.

COUNTIES						REPRESENTATIVES				
DISTRICT 5										
Baltimore	33,463	6,720	20.0	929	36.0	Samuel Smith[r]	18	(----)	City of Baltimore	
City of						(Resigned December, 1822)				
Baltimore	62,738	4,357	6.9	78	804.0	Isaac McKim	18	D	City of Baltimore	
TOTALS	96,201	11,077	11.5	1,007	95.5	(Replaced Smith January, 1823)				
						Peter Little	18	D	Freedom	Baltimore
						John Barney	19	F	City of Baltimore	
						Peter Little	19	D	Freedom	Baltimore

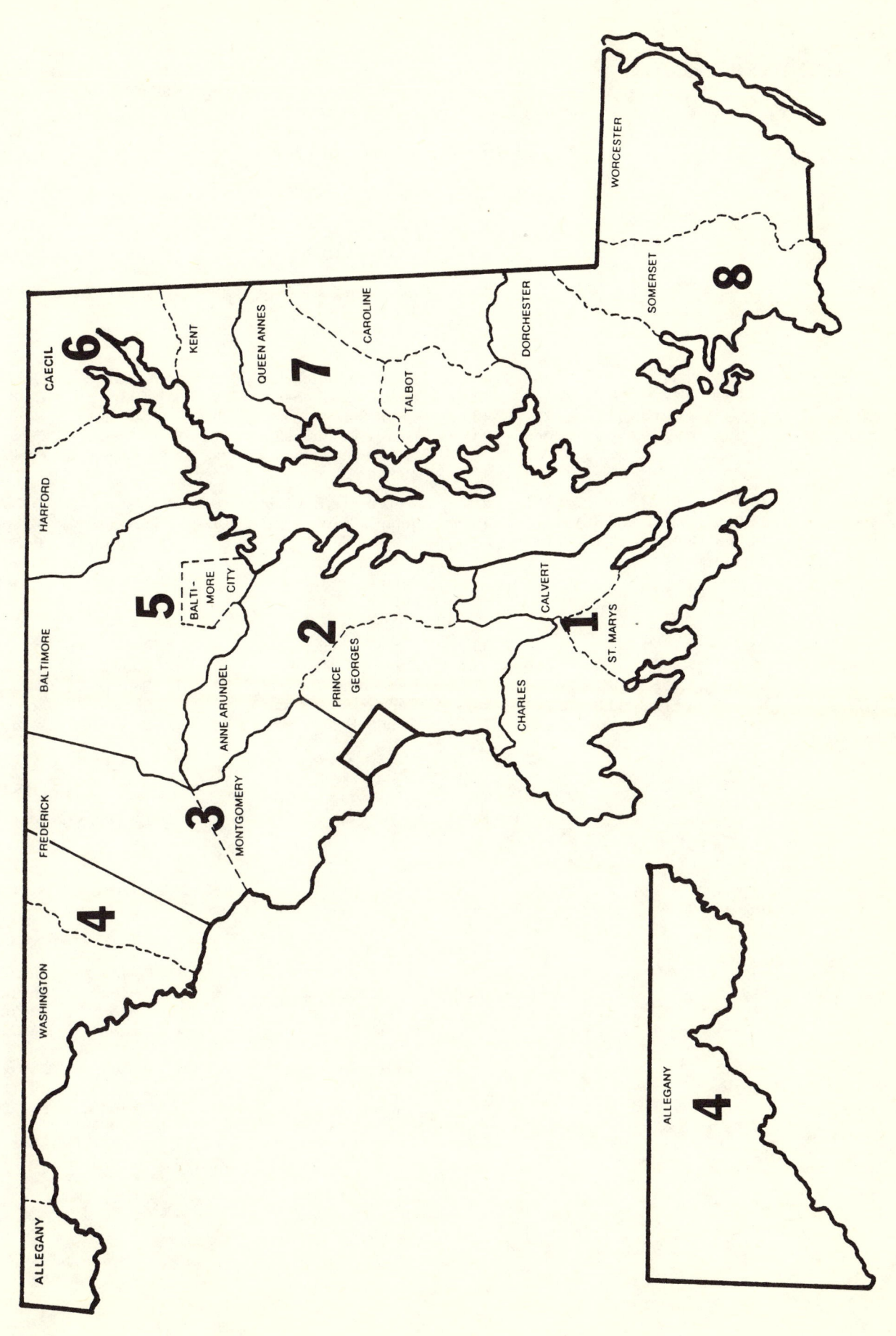

COUNTIES						REPRESENTATIVES				
County	Aggregate	Slave	%S	sq.mi.	P/sq.mi.	Representative	Cong.	Pty.	Address	County

DISTRICT 5 (CONTINUED)

						John Barney	20	F	City of Baltimore	
						Peter Little	20	D	Freedom	Baltimore
						Elias Brown	21	NR	Freedom	Baltimore
						Benjamin C. Howard	21	D	City of Baltimore	
						Benjamin C. Howard	22	D	City of Baltimore	
						John T. H. Worthington	22	D	Golden	Baltimore

DISTRICT 6

County	Aggregate	Slave	%S	sq.mi.	P/sq.mi.	Representative	Cong.	Pty.	Address	County
A Caecil	16,048	2,343	14.5	362	44.2	George E. Mitchell	18	D	Elkton	Cecil
Harford	15,924	3,320	20.8	453	35.2	George E. Mitchell	19	D	Elkton	Cecil
Kent	11,453	4,071	35.5	281	40.8	Levin Gale	20	(----)	Elkton	Cecil
TOTALS	43,425	9,734	22.4	1,096	39.6	George E. Mitchell	21	D	Elkton	Cecil
						George E. Mitchell	22	D	Elkton	Cecil

DISTRICT 7

County	Aggregate	Slave	%S	sq.mi.	P/sq.mi.	Representative	Cong.	Pty.	Address	County
Caroline	10,108	1,574	15.5	321	31.5	William Heyward, Jr.	18	D	Easton	Talbot
Queen Anns	14,952	5,588	37.3	375	39.9	John L. Kerr	19	NR	Easton	Talbot
Talbot	14,389	4,768	33.1	261	55.1	John L. Kerr	20	NR	Easton	Talbot
TOTALS	39,449	11,930	30.2	957	41.2	Richard Spencer	21	D	Easton	Talbot
						John L. Kerr	22	NR	Easton	Talbot

DISTRICT 8

County	Aggregate	Slave	%S	sq.mi.	P/sq.mi.	Representative	Cong.	Pty.	Address	County
Dorchester	17,759	5,168	29.1	594	29.9	John S. Spence	18	D	Poplartown	Worcester*
Somerset	19,579	7,258	37.0	560	35.0	Robert N. Martin	19	D	Princess Ann	Somerset
Worcester	17,421	4,145	23.7	639	27.3	Ephraim K. Wilson	20	D	Snow Hill	Somerset
TOTALS	54,759	16,571	30.3	1,793	30.5	Ephraim K. Wilson	21	D	Snow Hill	Somerset
						John S. Spence	22	D	Berlin	Worcester

MASSACHUSETTS
13 DISTRICTS
13 CONGRESSMEN

COUNTIES						REPRESENTATIVES				
County	Aggregate	Slave	%S	sq.mi.	P/sq.mi.	Representative	Cong.	Pty.	Address	County

DISTRICT 1 (SUFFOLK)

County	Aggregate	Slave	%S	sq.mi.	P/sq.mi.	Representative	Cong.	Pty.	Address	County
City of Boston[b]	42,656	----	----	8	5412.0	Daniel Webster	18[a]	F	Boston	Suffolk
						Timothy Fuller	18[a]	D	Boston	Suffolk
						Daniel Webster	19	AR	Boston	Suffolk
						Daniel Webster[r] (Resigned May, 1827)	20	AR	Boston	Suffolk
						Benjamin Gorham (Replaced Webster)	20	AR	Boston	Suffolk
						Benjamin Gorham	21	AR	Boston	Suffolk

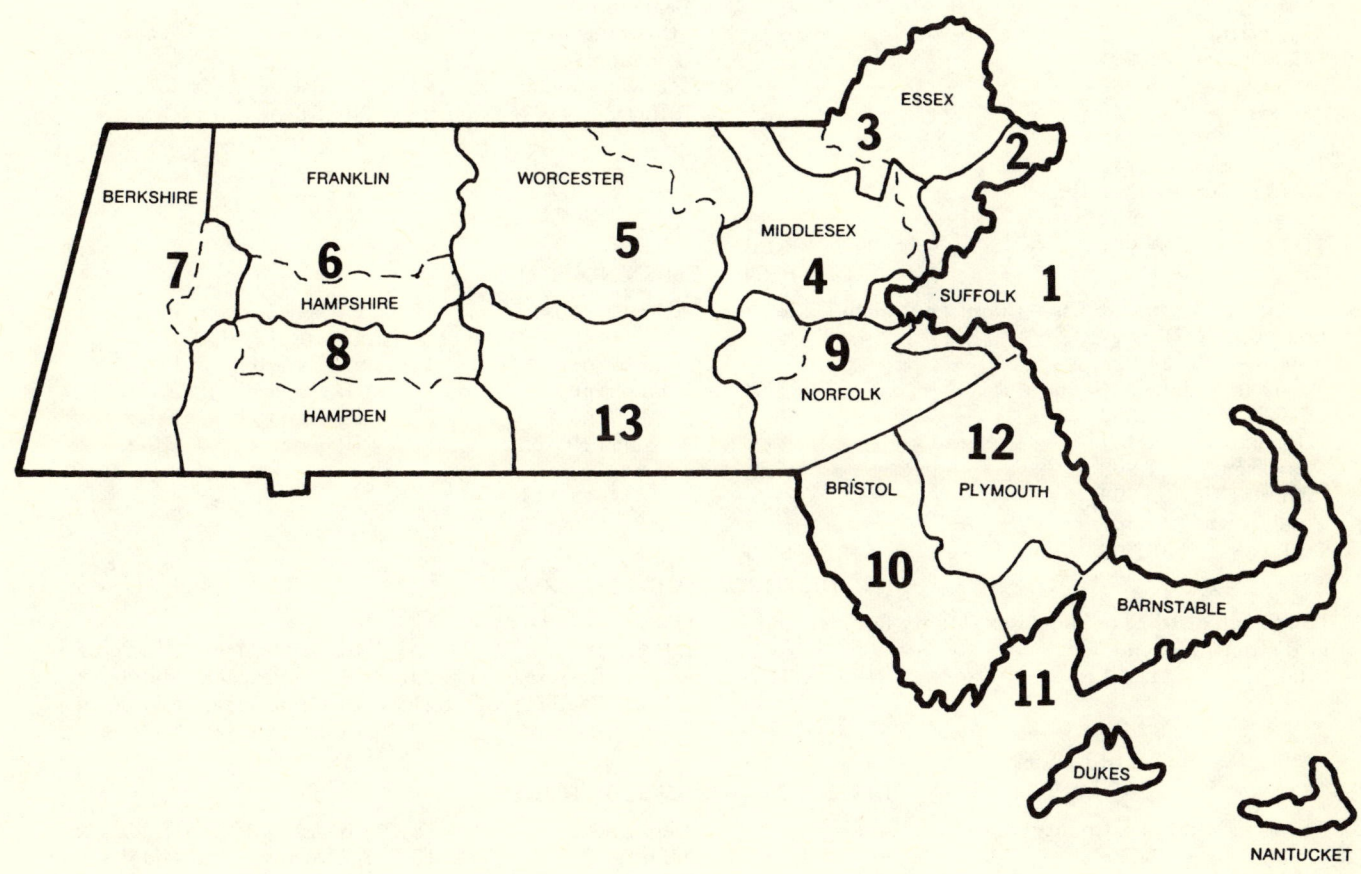

| | COUNTIES | | | | | REPRESENTATIVES | | | | |
| County | Aggregate | Slave | %S | sq.mi. | P/sq.mi. | Representative | Cong. | Pty. | Address | County |

DISTRICT 1 (CONTINUED)

| | | | | | | Nathan Appleton | 22 | NR | Boston | Suffolk |

[a]The addresses of two representatives are in this district. See District 4; Fuller probably represented that district.
[b]Excluding the town of Chelsea (see District 2).

DISTRICT 2 (ESSEX SOUTH)

Towns in Essex County:						Benjamin W.				
Beverly	4,283	----	----	----	----	Crowninshield	18	D	Salem	Essex
Danvers	3,646	----	----	----	----	Benjamin W.				
Gloucester	6,384	----	----	----	----	Crowninshield	19	AR	Salem	Essex
Lynn	4,515	----	----	----	----	Benjamin W.				
Lynnfield	596	----	----	----	----	Crowninshield	20	AR	Salem	Essex
Manchester	1,201	----	----	----	----	Benjamin W.				
Marblehead	5,630	----	----	----	----	Crowninshield	21	AR	Salem	Essex
Salem	11,346	----	----	----	----	Rufus Choate	22	NR	Salem	Essex
Saugus	748	----	----	----	----					
Total, towns	38,349	----	----	----	----					
Town in Suffolk County:										
Chelsea	642	----	----	----	----					
TOTALS	38,991	----	----	155	251.6					

DISTRICT 3 (ESSEX NORTH)

Towns and districts in Essex County not included in						Jeremiah Nelson	18	F	Newbury-port	Essex
Essex South (District 2),										
total:	34,921	----	----	----	----	John Varnum	19	NR	Haverhill	Essex
Towns in Middlesex County:						John Varnum	20	NR	Haverhill	Essex
Bellerica	1,380	----	----	----	----	John Varnum	21	NR	Haverhill	Essex
Dracut	1,407	----	----	----	----	Jeremiah Nelson	22	NR	Essex	Essex
Tewksbury	1,008	----	----	----	----					
Wilmington	790	----	----	----	----					
Total, towns	4,585	----	----	----	----					
TOTALS	39,506	----	----	442	89.0					

DISTRICT 4 (MIDDLESEX)

Towns and districts in Middlesex County not included						(Timothy Fuller)[a]	18	D		
in Districts 3, 5, and 9,						Edward Everett	19	NR	Cambridge	Middlesex
total:	41,011	----	----	450	91.0	Edward Everett	20	NR	Cambridge	Middlesex
						Edward Everett	21	NR	Cambridge	Middlesex
						Edward Everett	22	NR	Cambridge	Middlesex

[a]See Footnote a of District 1.

DISTRICT 5 (WORCESTER NORTH)

Towns in Middlesex County:						John Locke	18	AR	Ashby	Middlesex
Ashby	1,188	----	----	----	----	John Locke	19	AR	Ashby	Middlesex
Groton	1,897	----	----	----	----	John Locke	20	AR	Ashby	Middlesex
Pepperell	1,439	----	----	----	----	Joseph G. Kendall	21	NR	Leominster	Middlesex
Shirley	922	----	----	----	----	Joseph G. Kendall	22	NR	Leominster	Middlesex
Townsend	1,482	----	----	----	----					
Total, towns	6,928	----	----	----	----					
Towns and districts in Worcester County not included										
in Worcester South (District 13),										
total:	32,422	----	----	----	----					
TOTALS	39,350	----	----	930	42.0					

County	Aggregate	Slave	%S	sq.mi.	P/sq.mi.	Representative	Cong.	Pty.	Address	County

COUNTIES / REPRESENTATIVES

DISTRICT 6 (FRANKLIN)

County	Aggregate	Slave	%S	sq.mi.	P/sq.mi.	Representative	Cong.	Pty.	Address	County
Franklin	29,268	----	----	----	----	Samuel C. Allen	18	R	Greenfield	Franklin
Towns in Hampshire County:						Samuel C. Allen	19	AR	Greenfield	Franklin
Amherst	1,917	----	----	----	----	Samuel C. Allen	20	AR	Greenfield	Franklin
Chesterfield	1,447	----	----	----	----	George Grennell, Jr.	21	NR	Greenfield	Franklin
Enfield	873	----	----	----	----	George Grennell, Jr.	22	NR	Greenfield	Franklin
Goshen	632	----	----	----	----					
Greenwich	778	----	----	----	----					
Hadley	1,461	----	----	----	----					
Hatfield	823	----	----	----	----					
Pelham	1,278	----	----	----	----					
Prescott (not included in the 1820 census)										
Williamsburg	1,087	----	----	----	----					
Total, towns	10,296	----	----	----	----					
TOTALS	39,564	----	----	938	42.0					

DISTRICT 7 (BERKSHIRE)

County	Aggregate	Slave	%S	sq.mi.	P/sq.mi.	Representative	Cong.	Pty.	Address	County
Berkshire	35,720	----	----	----	----	Henry W. Dwight	18	R	Stockbridge	Berkshire
Towns in Hampshire County:						Henry W. Dwight	19	AR	Stockbridge	Berkshire
Cummington	1,060	----	----	----	----	Henry W. Dwight	20	AR	Stockbridge	Berkshire
Middlefield	755	----	----	----	----	Henry W. Dwight	21	AR	Stockbridge	Berkshire
Plainfield	936	----	----	----	----	George N. Briggs	22	NR	Lanesboro	Berkshire
Worthington	1,276	----	----	----	----					
Total, towns	4,027	----	----	----	----					
TOTALS	39,747	----	----	1,064	37.0					

DISTRICT 8 (HAMPDEN)

County	Aggregate	Slave	%S	sq.mi.	P/sq.mi.	Representative	Cong.	Pty.	Address	County
Hampden	28,021	----	----	----	----	Samuel Lathrop	18	R	West Springfield	Hampden
Towns in Hampshire County:										
Belchertown	2,426	----	----	----	----	Samuel Lathrop	19	R	West Springfield	Hampden
East Hampton	712	----	----	----	----	Isaac C. Bates	20	AR	Northampton	Hampshire
Granby	1,066	----	----	----	----					
Northampton	2,854	----	----	----	----	Isaac C. Bates	21	AR	Northampton	Hampshire
Norwich	849	----	----	----	----					
South Hampton	1,160	----	----	----	----	Isaac C. Bates	22	AR	Northampton	Hampshire
South Hadley	1,047	----	----	----	----					
Ware	1,154	----	----	----	----					
Westhampton	896	----	----	----	----					
Total, towns	12,164	----	----	----	----					
TOTALS	40,185	----	----	828	49.0					

| COUNTIES | | | | | | REPRESENTATIVES | | | | |
County	Aggregate	Slave	%S	sq.mi.	P/sq.mi.	Representative	Cong.	Pty.	Address	County

DISTRICT 9 (NORFOLK)

County	Aggregate	Slave	%S	sq.mi.	P/sq.mi.	Representative	Cong.	Pty.	Address	County
Towns in Middlesex County:						John Bailey	18	AR	Canton	Norfolk
Brighton	702	----	----	----	----	John Bailey	19	AR	Canton	Norfolk
Framingham	2,037	----	----	----	----	John Bailey	20	AR	Canton	Norfolk
Holliston	1,655	----	----	----	----	John Bailey	21	AR	Canton	Norfolk
Hopkinton	1,655	----	----	----	----	Henry A. S. Dearborn	22	NR	Brookline	Norfolk
Natick	849	----	----	----	----					
Newton	1,850	----	----	----	----					
Sherburne	811	----	----	----	----					
Total, towns	8,946	----	----	----	----					
Towns and districts in Norfolk County, except those included in Barnstable (District 11),										
total:	26,213	----	----	----	----					
TOTALS	35,159	----	----	496	81.0					

DISTRICT 10 (BRISTOL)

County	Aggregate	Slave	%S	sq.mi.	P/sq.mi.	Representative	Cong.	Pty.	Address	County
Towns and districts in Bristol County, except the town of Raynham (see District 12),						Francis Baylies	18	R	Taunton	Bristol
						Francis Baylies	19	JD	Taunton	Bristol
total:	38,766	----	----	484	80.1	James L. Hodges	20	NR	Taunton	Bristol
						James L. Hodges	21	NR	Taunton	Bristol
						James L. Hodges	22	NR	Taunton	Bristol

DISTRICT 11 (BARNSTABLE)

County	Aggregate	Slave	%S	sq.mi.	P/sq.mi.	Representative	Cong.	Pty.	Address	County
Barnstable	24,026	----	----	400	60.1	John Reed	18	AR	Yarmouth	Barnstable
Dukes	3,292	----	----	51	64.5	John Reed	19	AR	Yarmouth	Barnstable
Nantucket	7,266	----	----	107	67.9	John Reed	20	AR	Yarmouth	Barnstable
Towns in Plymouth County:						John Reed	21	AR	Yarmouth	Barnstable
Carver	839	----	----	----	----	John Reed	22	NR	Yarmouth	Barnstable
Rochester	3,034	----	----	----	----					
Wareham	952	----	----	----	----					
Total, towns	4,825	----	----	132	36.5					
TOTALS	39,409	----	----	690	57.1					

DISTRICT 12 (PLYMOUTH)

County	Aggregate	Slave	%S	sq.mi.	P/sq.mi.	Representative	Cong.	Pty.	Address	County
Town in Bristol County:						Aaron Hobart	18	AR	Hanover	Plymouth
Raynham	1,071	----	----	----	----	Aaron Hobart	19	AR	East Bridgewater	Plymouth
Towns in Norfolk County:										
Cohasset	1,099	----	----	----	----	Joseph Richardson	20	AR	Hingham	Plymouth
Quincy	1,623	----	----	----	----	Joseph Richardson	21	AR	Hingham	Plymouth
Weymouth	2,407	----	----	----	----	John Quincy Adams	22	NR	Quincy	Norfolk
Total, towns	5,129	----	----	----	----					
Towns and districts of Plymouth County, except those included in Barnstable (District 11),										
total:	28,486	----	----	----	----					
TOTALS	34,686	----	----	625	55.5					

COUNTIES						REPRESENTATIVES				
County	Aggregate	Slave	%S	sq.mi.	P/sq.mi.	Representative	Cong.	Pty.	Address	County

DISTRICT 13 (WORCESTER SOUTH)

Towns in Worcester County:						Jonas Sibley	18	D	Worcester	Worcester
Brookfield, Charlton, Dudley, Dugless, Grafton, Hardwick, Leicester, Mendon, Milbury, Milford, Northborough, New Braintree, Northbridge, North Brookfield, Oakham, Oxford, Paxton, Shrewsbury, Southborough, Southbridge, Spencer, Sturbridge, Sutton, Upton, Ward, Westborough, Western, Worcester.						John Davis	19	NR	Worcester	Worcester
						John Davis	20	NR	Worcester	Worcester
						John Davis	21	NR	Worcester	Worcester
						John Davis	22	NR	Worcester	Worcester
total, towns	40,503	----	----	765	53.0					

COUNTIES						REPRESENTATIVES				
County	Aggregate	Slave	%S	sq.mi.	P/sq.mi.	Representative	Cong.	Pty.	Address	County
						AT LARGE				
Adams	9,892	2,593	26.2	367	26.9	George Poindexter	15	(----)	Woodville	Wilkinson
Amite	6,853	2,833	41.3	616	11.1	(Took seat December 15, 1817 when Mississippi became a				
Claiborne	5,963	3,087	51.8	498	12.0	state)				
Covington	2,230	406	18.2	574	3.9	Christopher Rankin	16	D	Natchez	Adams
Franklin	3,821	1,535	40.2	681	5.6	Christopher Rankin	17	D	Natchez	Adams
Greene	1,445	380	26.3	774	1.9	Christopher Rankin	18	JD	Natchez	Adams
Hancock	1,594	321	20.1	1,963	0.8	Christopher Rankin[†]	19	JD	Natchez	Adams
Jackson	1,682	321	19.1	1,132	1.5	(Died March, 1826)				
Jefferson	6,822	3,635	53.3	508	13.4	William Haile	19	JD	Woodville	Wilkinson
Lawrence	4,916	991	20.0	969	5.1	(Replaced Rankin December, 1826)				
Marion	3,116	1,232	39.5	988	3.1	William Haile[r]	20	JD	Woodville	Wilkinson
Monroe	2,721	522	19.2	875	3.1	(Resigned September, 1828)				
Perry	2,037	491	24.1	1,134	1.8	Thomas Hinds	20	JD	Greenville	Jefferson
Pike	4,430	531	12.0	687	6.5	(Replaced Haile December, 1828)				
Warren	2,693	1,166	43.3	685	3.9	Thomas Hinds	21	JD	Greenville	Jefferson
Wayne	3,323	1,065	32.0	896	3.7	Franklin E. Plummer	22	JD	Westville	Simpson
Wilkinson	9,718	5,761	59.3	571	17.0					
TOTALS	73,264	26,870	36.7	13,918	5.3					

----

[1] Mississippi became a state on December 10, 1817.

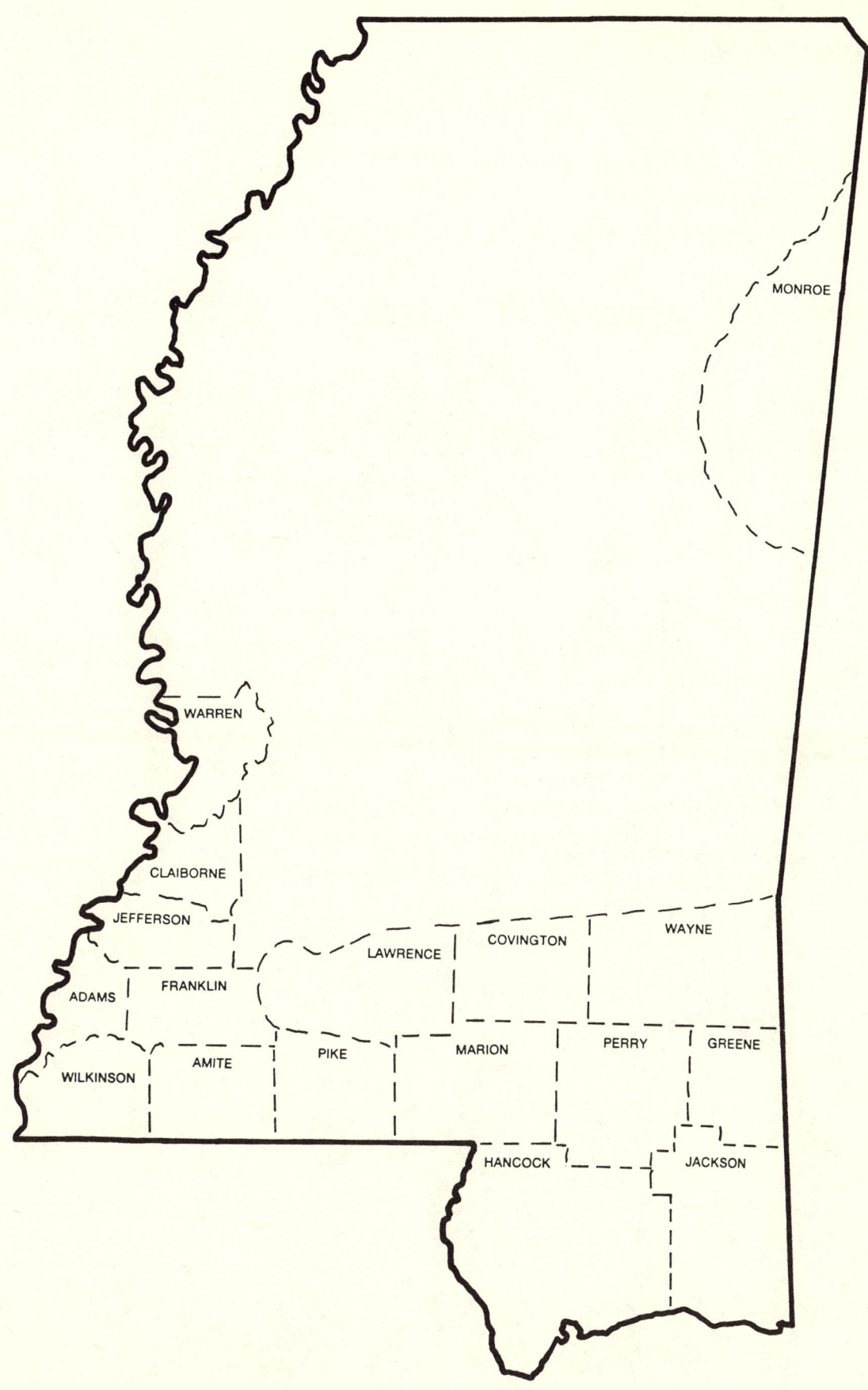

COUNTIES						REPRESENTATIVES				
County	Aggregate	Slave	%S	sq.mi.	P/sq.mi.	Representative	Cong.	Pty.	Address	County
						AT LARGE				
Cape						John Scott	17	CR	St. Genevieve	St. Genevieve
Girardeau	5,968	865	14.4	1,195	5.0	John Scott	18	CR	St. Genevieve	St. Genevieve
Cooper	6,959	637	9.1	566	12.3	John Scott	19	CR	St. Genevieve	St. Genevieve
Franklin	2,379	209	8.7	934	2.5	Edward Bates	20	JD	St. Louis	St. Louis
Howard[a]	7,960	1,342	16.8	----	----	Spencer D. Pettis	21	JD	Fayette	Howard
Howard[b]	5,466	753	13.7	----	----	Spencer D. Pettis†	22	JD	Fayette	Howard
Jefferson	1,835	207	11.2	668	2.8	(Died August, 1831)				
Lincoln	1,662	242	14.5	625	2.7	William H. Ashley	22	W	St. Louis	St. Louis
Madison	2,047	364	17.7	927	2.2	(Replaced Pettis)				
Montgomery	3,074	526	17.1	534	5.8					
New Madrid	2,296	291	12.6	2,538	0.9					
Pike	3,747	676	18.0	681	5.5					
St. Charles	3,970	682	17.1	551	7.2					
St. Genevieve	4,962	983	19.8	499	9.9					
St. Louis	10,049	1,810	18.0	100	100.5					
Wayne	1,443	197	13.6	6,907	0.2					
TOTALS	63,817	9,784	15.3	16,725	3.8					

[a]The part of Howard west of the Bonne Femme Creek.

[b]The part of Howard east of the Bonne Femme Creek.

[1]Missouri became a state August 10, 1821.

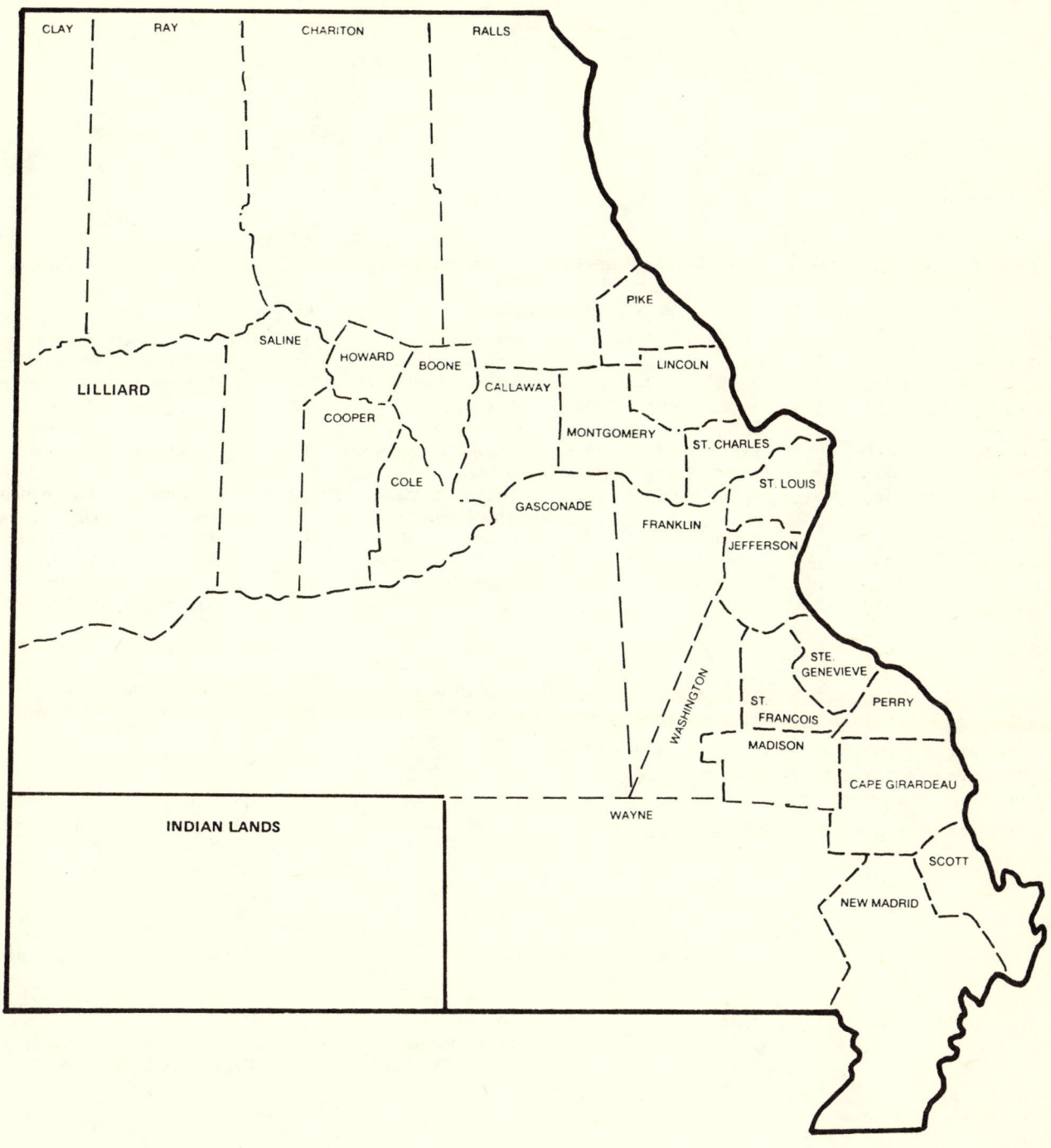

CLAY RAY CHARITON RALLS

LILLIARD

SALINE

HOWARD BOONE

COOPER

COLE

CALLAWAY

PIKE

LINCOLN

MONTGOMERY

ST. CHARLES

ST. LOUIS

FRANKLIN

JEFFERSON

GASCONADE

WASHINGTON

STE.
GENEVIEVE

ST.
FRANCOIS

PERRY

MADISON

CAPE GIRARDEAU

WAYNE

SCOTT

NEW MADRID

INDIAN LANDS

COUNTIES						REPRESENTATIVES				
County	Aggregate	Slave	%S	sq.mi.	P/sq.mi.	Representative	Cong.	Pty.	Address	County
						AT LARGE				
Cheshire	45,376	----	----	1,254	36.1	Ichabod Bartlett	18	OR	Portsmouth	Rockingham
Coos	5,549	----	----	1,820	3.0	Matthew Harvey	18	R	Hopkinton	Hillsborough
Grafton	32,989	----	----	1,732	19.0	Arthur Livermore	18	R	Plymouth	Grafton
Hillsborough	35,524	----	----	887	40.0	Aaron Matson	18	(----)	Stoddard	Cheshire
Merrimack[a]	32,281	----	----	930	34.7	William Plumer, Jr.	18	R	Epping	Rockingham
Rockingham	41,325	----	----	691	59.8	Thomas Whipple, Jr.	18	R	Wentworth	Grafton
Strafford	51,117	----	----	1,414	29.8					
TOTALS	244,161	----	----	8,728	28.0	Ichabod Bartlett	19	OR	Portsmouth	Rockingham
						Titus Brown	19	OR	Francestown	Hillsborough
						Nehemiah Eastman	19	R	Farmington	Strafford
						Jonathan Harvey	19	OR	Sutton	Merrimack
						Joseph Healy	19	OR	Washington	Cheshire
						Thomas Whipple, Jr.	19	OR	Wentworth	Grafton
						David Barker, Jr.	20	OR	Rochester	Strafford
						Ichabod Bartlett	20	OR	Portsmouth	Rockingham
						Titus Brown	20	OR	Francestown	Hillsborough
						Jonathan Harvey	20	OR	Sutton	Merrimack
						Joseph Healy	20	OR	Washington	Cheshire
						Thomas Whipple, Jr.	20	OR	Wentworth	Grafton
						John Brodhead	21	JD	Newmarket	Rockingham
						Thomas Chandler	21	JD	Hillsborough	Hillsborough
						Joseph Hammons	21	JD	Farmington	Strafford
						Jonathan Harvey	21	JD	Sutton	Merrimack
						Henry Hubbard	21	JD	Charlestown	Cheshire
						John W. Weeks	21	JD	Lancaster	Coos
						John Brodhead	22	JD	Newmarket	Rockingham
						Thomas Chandler	22	JD	Hillsborough	Hillsborough
						Joseph Hammons	22	JD	Farmington	Strafford
						Jonathan Harvey	22	JD	Sutton	Merrimack
						Henry Hubbard	22	JD	Charleston	Cheshire
						John W. Weeks	22	JD	Lancaster	Coos

[a]Created from Rockingham and Hillsborough in 1824.

[1]New Hampshire congressmen were elected at large throughout this apportionment. An act of December 16, 1824, divided the state into six districts, but it was rescinded before the following election. Even though elections were held at large, the state followed an informal districting arrangement, with each major county supplying one representative. The single exception to this rule is the Eighteenth Congress, in which Rockingham County elected two congressmen.

COUNTIES						REPRESENTATIVES				
County	Aggregate	Slave	%S	sq.mi.	P/sq.mi.	Representative	Cong.	Pty.	Address	County

AT LARGE

County	Aggregate	Slave	%S	sq.mi.	P/sq.mi.	Representative	Cong.	Pty.	Address	County
Bergen	18,178	1,683	9.2	420	43.3	George Cassedy	18	D	Hackensack	Bergen
Burlington	28,822	82	0.2	819	35.2	Lewis Condict	18	D	Morristown	Morris
Cape May	4,265	28	0.7	267	16.0	Daniel Garrison	18	D	Salem	Salem
Cumberland	12,668	18	0.1	500	25.3	George Holcombe	18	D	Allentown	Monmouth
Essex	30,793	659	2.1	233	132.2	James Matlack	18	NR	Woodbury	Gloucester
Gloucester	23,089	39	0.2	1,119	20.6	Samuel Swan	18	NR	Somerville	Somerset
Hunterdon	28,604	616	2.1	651	43.9					
Middlesex	21,470	1,012	4.7	312	68.8	George Cassedy	19	D	Hackensack	Bergen
Monmouth	25,038	1,248	4.9	1,118	22.4	Lewis Condict	19	D	Morristown	Morris
Morris	20,368	657	3.0	468	44.4	Daniel Garrison	19	D	Salem	Salem
Salem	14,022	15	0.1	365	38.4	George Holcombe	19	D	Allentown	Monmouth
Somerset	16,506	1,122	6.7	307	53.8	Samuel Swan	19	D	Somerville	Somerset
Sussex	32,752	378	1.1	889	36.8	Ebenezer Tucker	19	D	Tuckerton	Burlington
TOTALS	262,907	7,557	2.8	7,468	35.2					

Representative	Cong.	Pty.	Address	County
Lewis Condict	20	AR	Morristown	Morris
George Holcombe† (Died January 14, 1828)	20	JD	Allentown	Monmouth
James F. Randolph (Replaced Holcombe)	20	NR	New Brunswick	Middlesex
Isaac Pierson	20	AR	Orange	Essex
Hedge Thompson† (Died July 23, 1828)	20	AR	Salem	Salem
Thomas Sinnickson (Replaced Thompson)	20	NR	Salem	Salem
Samuel Swan	20	AR	Somerville	Somerset
Ebenezer Tucker	20	AR	Tuckerton	Burlington
Lewis Condict	21	NR	Morristown	Morris
Richard M. Cooper	21	NR	Camden	Gloucester
Thomas H. Hughes	21	NR	Cold Spring	Cape May
Isaac Pierson	21	NR	Orange	Essex
James F. Randolph	21	NR	New Brunswick	Middlesex
Samuel Swan	21	NR	Somerville	Somerset
Lewis Condict	22	NR	Morristown	Morris
Silas Condict	22	NR	Newark	Essex
Richard M. Cooper	22	NR	Camden	Gloucester
Thomas H. Hughes	22	NR	Cold Spring	Cape May
James F. Randolph	22	NR	New Brunswick	Middlesex
Isaac Southard	22	NR	Somerville	Somerset

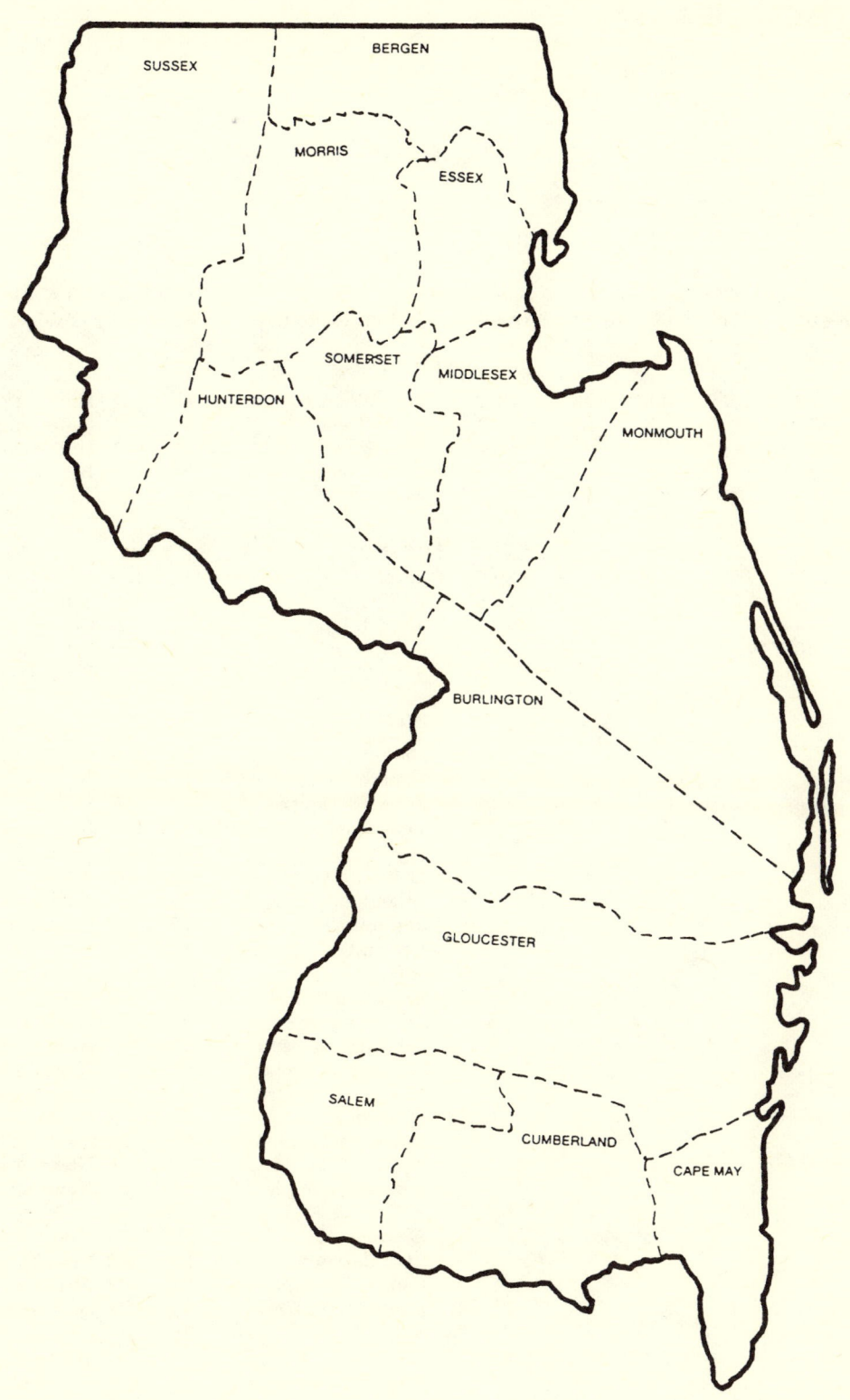

County	COUNTIES Aggregate	Slave	%S	sq.mi.	P/sq.mi.	Representative	REPRESENTATIVES Cong.	Pty.	Address	County
						DISTRICT 1				
Queens	21,519	559	2.5	397	54.2	Silas Wood	18	D	Huntington	Suffolk
Suffolk	24,272	323	1.3	929	26.1	Silas Wood	19	D	Huntington	Suffolk
TOTALS	45,791	882	1.9	1,326	34.5	Silas Wood	20	D	Huntington	Suffolk
						James Lent	21	JD	Newtown	Queens
						James Lent	22	JD	Newtown	Queens
						DISTRICT 2				
Kings	11,187	879	7.8	70	159.7	Jacob Tyson	18	(----)	Castletown	Richmond
Richmond	6,135	532	9.0	58	11.5	Joshua Sands	19	(----)	Brooklyn	Kings
Rockland	8,837	715	8.0	176	50.2	John J. Wood	20	JD	Clarkstown	Rockland
TOTALS	26,159	2,126	8.1	304	172.0	Jacob Crocheron	21	JD	Smithfield	Richmond
						John T. Borgen	22	JD	Brooklyn	Kings
						DISTRICT 3				
City and County of New York	123,706	516	0.4	64	1932.9	Churchill C. Cambreleng	18	D	New York City	
						John J. Morgan	18	D	New York City	
						Peter Sharpe	18	(----)	New York City	
						Churchill C. Cambreleng	19	D	New York City	
						Jeromus Johnson	19	D	New York City	
						Gulian C. Verplank	19	D	New York City	
						Churchill C. Cambreleng	20	D	New York City	
						Jeromus Johnson	20	D	New York City	
						Gulian C. Verplank	20	D	New York City	
						Churchill C. Cambreleng	21	D	New York City	
						Jeromus Johnson	21	D	New York City	
						Gulian C. Verplank	21	D	New York City	
						Churchill C. Cambreleng	22	JD	New York City	
						Gulian C. Verplank	22	JD	New York City	
						Campbell P. White	22	JD	New York City	

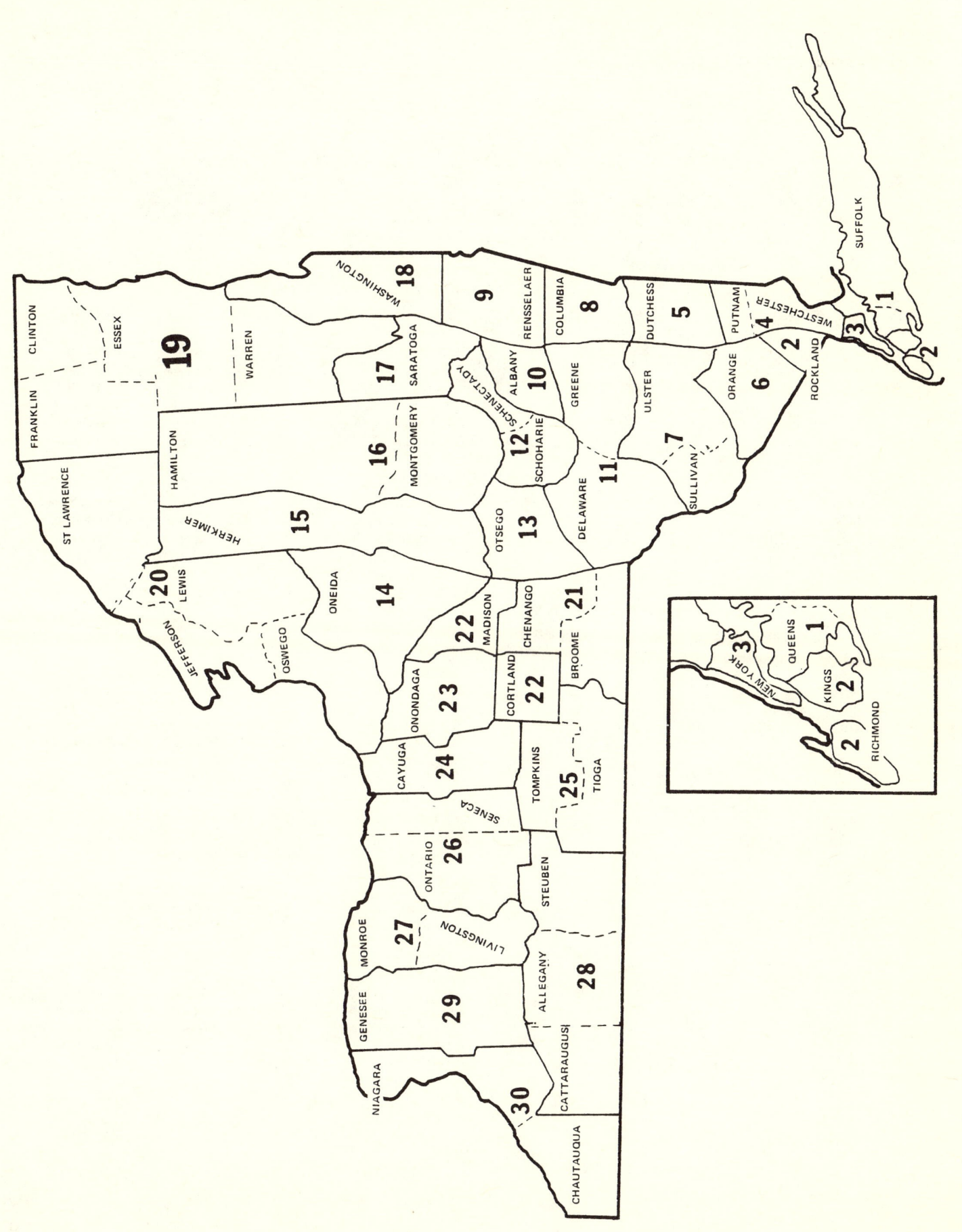

County	COUNTIES Aggregate	Slave	%S	sq.mi.	P/sq.mi.	REPRESENTATIVES Representative	Cong.	Pty.	Address	County
						DISTRICT 4				
Putnam	11,268	49	0.4	231	48.7	Joel Frost	18	NR	Carmel	Putnam
Westchester	32,638	205	0.6	443	73.6	Aaron Ward	19	D	Mt. Pleasant	Westchester
TOTALS	43,906	254	0.5	674	65.1	Aaron Ward	20	D	Mt. Pleasant	Westchester
						Henry B. Cowles	21	(----)	Carmel	Putnam
						Aaron Ward	22	JD	Mt. Pleasant	Westchester
						DISTRICT 5				
Dutchess	46,615	772	1.6	813	57.3	William W. Van Wyck	18	D	Fishkill	Dutchess
						Bartow White	19	(----)	Fishkill	Dutchess
						Thomas J. Oakley[r] (Resigned May, 1828)	20	D	Pough- keepsie	Dutchess
						Thomas Taber II (Replaced Oakley December, 1828)	20	D	Dover	Dutchess
						Abraham Bockee	21	JD	Federal Store	Dutchess
						Edmund H. Pendleton	22	NR	Hyde Park	Dutchess
						DISTRICT 6				
Orange	41,218	1,134	2.7	833	49.4	Hector Craig	18	JD	Chester	Orange
						John Hallock, Jr.	19	D	Ridgebury	Orange
						John Hallock, Jr.	20	D	Ridgebury	Orange
						Hector Craig[r] (Resigned May, 1830)	21	JD	Craigville	Orange
						Samuel W. Eager (Replaced Craig December, 1830)	21	R	Montgomery	Orange
						Samuel J. Wilkin	22	NR	Goshen	Orange
						DISTRICT 7				
Sullivan	8,900	77	0.8	980	9.0	Lemuel Jenkins	18	D	Blooming- burg	Sullivan
Ulster	30,934	2,423	7.8	1,141	27.1					
TOTALS	39,834	2,500	6.2	2,121	18.7	Abraham B. Hasbrouck	19	NR	Kingston	Ulster
						George O. Beldon	20	D	Monticello	Sullivan
						Charles G. DeWitt	21	JD	Kingston	Ulster
						John C. Brodhead	22	JD	Modena	Ulster
						DISTRICT 8				
Columbia	38,330	761	2.0	645	59.4	James Strong	18	F	Hudson	Columbia
						James Strong	19	F	Hudson	Columbia
						James Strong	20	F	Hudson	Columbia
						James Strong	21	F	Hudson	Columbia
						John King	22	JD	North Lebanon	Columbia
						DISTRICT 9				
Rensselaer	40,153	433	1.0	665	60.3	James L. Hogeboom	18	NR	Castleton	Rensselaer
						William McManus	19	(----)	Troy	Rensselaer
						John D. Dickinson	20	NR	Troy	Rensselaer
						John D. Dickinson	21	NR	Troy	Rensselaer
						Job Pierson	22	JD	Schaghticoke	Rensselaer

COUNTIES						REPRESENTATIVES				
County	Aggregate	Slave	%S	sq.mi.	P/sq.mi.	Representative	Cong.	Pty.	Address	County

DISTRICT 10

City and County of Albany	38,114	413	1.0	526	72.4	Stephen Van Rensselaer	18	NR	City of Albany	
						Stephen Van Rensselaer	19	NR	City of Albany	
						Stephen Van Rensselaer	20	NR	City of Albany	
						Ambrose Spencer	21	D	City of Albany	
						Gerrit Y. Lansing	22	JD	City of Albany	

DISTRICT 11

Delaware	26,587	73	0.3	1,443	18.4	Charles A. Foote	18	D	Delhi	Delaware
Green	22,996	134	0.6	653	35.2	Henry Ashley	19	(----)	Catskill	Greene
TOTALS	49,583	207	0.4	2,096	23.9	Selah R. Hobbie	20	JD	Delhi	Delaware
						Perkins King	21	D	Freehold	Green
						Erastus Root	22	JD	Delhi	Delaware

DISTRICT 12

Schenectady	23,154	302	1.3	207	111.8	Lewis Eaton	18	(----)	Schoharie Bridge	Schoharie
Schoharie	23,619	84	0.4	624	37.8					
TOTALS	46,773	386	0.8	831	56.2	William Dietz	19	D	Schoharie	Schoharie
						John I DeGraff	20	D	Schenectady	Schenectady
						Peter I. Borst	21	JD	Middleburg	Schoharie
						Joseph Boock	22	JD	Middleburg	Schoharie

DISTRICT 13

Otsego	44,856	17	----	1,013	44.3	Isaac Williams, Jr.	18	D	Cooperstown	Otsego
						William G. Angel	19	NR	Burlington	Otsego
						Samuel Chase	20	NR	Cooperstown	Otsego
						William G. Angel	21	JD	Burlington	Otsego
						William G. Angel	22	JD	Burlington	Otsego

DISTRICT 14

Oneida	50,997	9	----	1,223	41.7	Henry R. Storrs	18	F	Whitestown	Oneida
						Henry R. Storrs	19	F	Whitestown	Oneida
						Henry R. Storrs	20	F	Whitestown	Oneida
						Henry R. Storrs	21	F	Whitestown	Oneida
						Samuel Beardsley	22	JD	Utica	Oneida

DISTRICT 15

Herkimer	31,017	72	----	1,435	21.6	John Herkimer	18	D	Danube	Herkimer
						Michael Hoffman	19	D	Herkimer	Herkimer
						Michael Hoffman	20	D	Herkimer	Herkimer
						Michael Hoffman	21	D	Herkimer	Herkimer
						Michael Hoffman	22	JD	Herkimer	Herkimer

DISTRICT 16

Hamilton	1,251	1	----	1,735	0.7	John W. Cady	18	NR	Johnstown	Montgomery
Montgomery	37,569	349	0.9	907	41.4	Henry Markell	19	D	Palentine	Montgomery
TOTALS	38,820	350	0.9	2,642	14.7	Henry Markell	20	D	Palentine	Montgomery
						Benedict Arnold	21	(----)	Amsterdam	Montgomery
						Nathan Soule	22	JD	Fort Plain	Montgomery

County	COUNTIES Aggregate	Slave	%S	sq.mi.	P/sq.mi.	Representative	REPRESENTATIVES Cong.	Pty.	Address	County
						DISTRICT 17				
Saratoga	36,052	123	0.3	818	44.1	John W. Taylor	18	D	Ballston Spa	Saratoga
						John W. Taylor	19	D	Ballston Spa	Saratoga
						John W. Taylor	20	D	Ballston Spa	Saratoga
						John W. Taylor	21	D	Ballston Spa	Saratoga
						John W. Taylor	22	JD	Ballston Spa	Saratoga
						DISTRICT 18				
Washington	38,831	150	0.4	836	46.4	Henry C. Martindale	18	NR	Sandy Hill	Washington
						Henry C. Martindale	19	NR	Sandy Hill	Washington
						Henry C. Martindale	20	NR	Sandy Hill	Washington
						Henry C. Martindale	21	NR	Sandy Hill	Washington
						Nathan Pitcher	22	D	Sandy Hill	Washington
						DISTRICT 19				
Clinton	12,070	2	----	1,059	11.3	John Richards	18	(----)	Johnsburg	Warren
Essex	12,811	3	----	1,823	7.0	Henry H. Ross	19	NR	Essex	Essex
Franklin	4,439	----	----	1,674	2.6	Richard Keese	20	D	Keeseville	Clinton
Warren	9,453	7	----	887	10.6	Isaac Finch	21	D	Jay	Essex
TOTALS	38,773	12	----	5,443	7.1	William Hogan	22	JD	Hogansburg	Lincoln
						DISTRICT 20				
Jefferson	32,952	5	----	1,294	25.4	Ela Collins	18	D	Lowville	Lewis
Lewis	9,227	----	----	1,291	7.1	Egbert Ten Eyck	18	(----)	Watertown	Jefferson
Oswego	12,374	----	----	964	12.8					
St. Lawrence	16,037	8	----	2,768	5.8	Nicoll Fosdick	19	NR	Morristown	St. Lawrence
TOTALS	70,590	13	----	6,317	11.7	Egbert Ten Eyck[ce]	19	(----)	Watertown	Jefferson
						(Served until December, 1825)				
						Daniel Hugunin, Jr.	19	(----)	Oswego	Oswego
						(Replaced Ten Eyck December, 1825)				
						Rudolph Bunner	20	NR	Oswego	Oswego
						Silas Wright, Jr.	20	D	Canton	St. Lawrence
						George Fisher[ce]	21	(----)	Oswego	Oswego
						(Served until February, 1830; election successfully contested by Silas Wright, Jr.)				
						Silas Wright, Jr.[r]	21	D	Canton	St. Lawrence
						(Replaced Fisher February, 1830; resigned March, 1830)				
						Jonah Sanford	21	JD	Oswego	Oswego
						(Replaced Wright December, 1830)				
						Joseph Hawkins	21	NR	Henderson	Jefferson
						Charles Dayan	22	JD	Lowville	Lewis
						Daniel Wardwell	22	JD	Mannsville	Jefferson
						DISTRICT 21				
Broome	14,343	46	0.3	714	20.0	Lot Clark	18	NR	Norwhich	Chenango
Chenango	31,215	7	----	903	34.5	Elias Whitmore	19	D	Windsor	Broome
TOTALS	45,558	53	0.1	1,617	28.2	John C. Clark	20	D	Bainbridge	Chenango
						Robert Monell	21	D	Greene	Chenango
						John A. Collier	22	NR	Binghampton	Broome

254

County	COUNTIES					REPRESENTATIVES				
County	Aggregate	Slave	%S	sq.mi.	P/sq.mi.	Representative	Cong.	Pty.	Address	County
						DISTRICT 22				
Courtland	16,507	3	----	502	30.8	Justin Dwinnell	18	(----)	Cazenovia	Madison
Madison	32,208	10	----	661	48.7	John Miller	19	(----)	Troxton	Cortland
TOTALS	48,715	13	----	1,163	41.9	John G. Stower	20	JD	Hamilton	Madison
						Thomas Beekman	21	(----)	Peterboro	Madison
						Edward C. Reed	22	JD	Homer	Cortland
						DISTRICT 23				
Onondaga	47,467	59	0.1	794	59.8	Elisha Litchfield	18	D	Delphi	Onondaga
						Luther Badger	19	(----)	Jamesville	Onondaga
						Jonas Earll, Jr.	20	D	Onondaga	Onondaga
						Jonas Earll, Jr.	21	D	Onondaga	Onondaga
						Freeborn G. Jewett	22	JD	Skaneatles	Onondaga
						DISTRICT 24				
Cayuga	38,897	48	----	698	55.7	Rowland Day	18	D	Simpronius	Cayuga
						Charles Kellogg	19	(----)	Kelloggsville	Cayuga
						Nathaniel Garrow	20	D	Auburn	Cayuga
						Gershom Powers	21	JD	Auburn	Cayuga
						Ulysses F. Doubleday	22	JD	Auburn	Cayuga
						DISTRICT 25				
Tioga	16,971	104	0.6	939	18.0	Samuel Lawrence	18	D	Johnson Settlement	Tioga
Tompkins	20,681	6	----	813	25.4					
TOTALS	37,652	110	0.9	1,752	21.5	Charles Humphrey	19	D	Ithaca	Tompkins
						David Woodcock	20	D	Ithaca	Tompkins
						Thomas Maxwell	21	D	Elmira	Tompkins
						Gamaliel H. Barstow	22	NR	Nichols	Tioga
						DISTRICT 26				
Ontario	73,392	----	----	1,400	52.4	Dudley Marvin	18	NR	Canandaigua	Ontario
Seneca	23,619	84	0.4	530	44.5	Robert S. Rose	18	NR	Geneva	Ontario
TOTALS	97,011	84	----	1.930	50.3					
						Dudley Marvin	19	NR	Canandaigua	Ontario
						Robert S. Rose	19	NR	Geneva	Ontario
						Dudley Marvin	20	NR	Canandaigua	Ontario
						John Maynard	20	NR	Ovid Village	Seneca
						Jehiel H. Halsey	21	JD	Lodi	Seneca
						Robert S. Rose	21	NR	Geneva	Ontario
						William Babcock	22	NR	Pen Yan	Ontario
						John Dickson	22	NR	West Bloomfield	Ontario
						DISTRICT 27				
Livingston[a]	22,745	----	----	638	35.6	Moses Hayden	18	(----)	York	Livingston
Monroe[a]	4,898	----	----	675	7.3	Moses Hayden	19	(----)	York	Livingston
TOTALS	27,643	----	----	1,313	21.0	Daniel D. Barnard	20	(----)	Rochester	Monroe
						Timothy Childs	21	(----)	Rochester	Monroe
						Frederick Whittlesey	22	NR	Rochester	Monroe

[a]These counties were created from Genesee and Ontario after the 1820 census. Their population was computed by multiplying the population per square mile figure of their parent counties by the square miles in each new county.

COUNTIES						REPRESENTATIVES				
County	Aggregate	Slave	%S	sq.mi.	P/sq.mi.	Representative	Cong.	Pty.	Address	County

DISTRICT 28

Allegheny	1,942	21	1.0	1,047	1.8	William B. Rochester	18	D	Bath	Steuben
Cattaraugus	4,090	2	----	1,318	3.1	Timothy H. Porter	19	(----)	Olean	Cattaraugus
Steuben	7,246	87	1.2	1,410	5.1	John McGee	20	D	Bath	Steuben
TOTALS	13,278	128	0.8	3,775	3.5	John McGee	21	D	Bath	Steuben
						Grattan Wheeler	22	NR	Wheeler	Steuben

DISTRICT 29

Genesee	45,325	35	----	1,494	30.3	Isaac Wilson[ce]	18	(----)	Middlebury	Genesee
						(Election successfully contested by Parmenio Adams)				
						Parmenio Adams	18	NR	Batavia	Genesee
						(Took seat January, 1824)				
						Parmenio Adams	19	NR	Batavia	Genesee
						David E. Evans[r]	20	D	Batavia	Genesee
						(Resigned May, 1827)				
						Phineas L. Tracy	20	NR	Batavia	Genesee
						(Replaced Evans December, 1827)				
						Phineas L. Tracy	21	NR	Batavia	Genesee
						Phineas L. Tracy	22	NR	Batavia	Genesee

DISTRICT 30

Chautauque	12,568	3	----	1,081	14.9	Albert H. Tracy	18	D	Buffalo	Erie
Erie[a]	----	----	----	----	----	Daniel G. Garnsey	19	JD	Fredonia	Chautauque
Niagara	22,990	15	----	1,590	43.2	Daniel G. Garnsey	20	JD	Fredonia	Chautauque
TOTALS	35,558	18	----	2,671	13.3	Ebeneazer F. Norton[r]	21	D	Buffalo	Erie
						(Resigned February, 1831; apparently not replaced)				
						Bates Cooke	22	NR	Lewiston	Niagara

[a]Created in 1821; included in Niagara County figures.

NORTH CAROLINA
13 DISTRICTS
13 CONGRESSMEN

COUNTIES						REPRESENTATIVES				
County	Aggregate	Slave	%S	sq.mi.	P/sq.mi.	Representative	Cong.	Pty.	Address	County

DISTRICT 1

Camden	6,347	1,329	20.9	239	26.5	Alfred M. Gatlin	18	(----)	Edenton	Chowan
Chowan	6,464	3,469	53.6	173	37.3	Lemuel Sawyer	19	D	Elizabeth City	Pasquotank
Currituck	8,098	1,854	22.8	246	32.9					
Gates	6,837	2,685	39.2	337	20.2	Lemuel Sawyer	20	D	Elizabeth City	Pasquotank
Hertford	7,712	3,244	42.0	353	21.8					
Pasquotank	8,008	2,616	32.6	228	35.1	William B. Shepard	21	NR	Elizabeth City	Pasquotank
Perquimans	6,857	2,465	35.9	246	27.8					
TOTALS	50,323	17,662	35.0	1,822	27.6	William B. Shepard	22	NR	Elizabeth City	Pasquotank

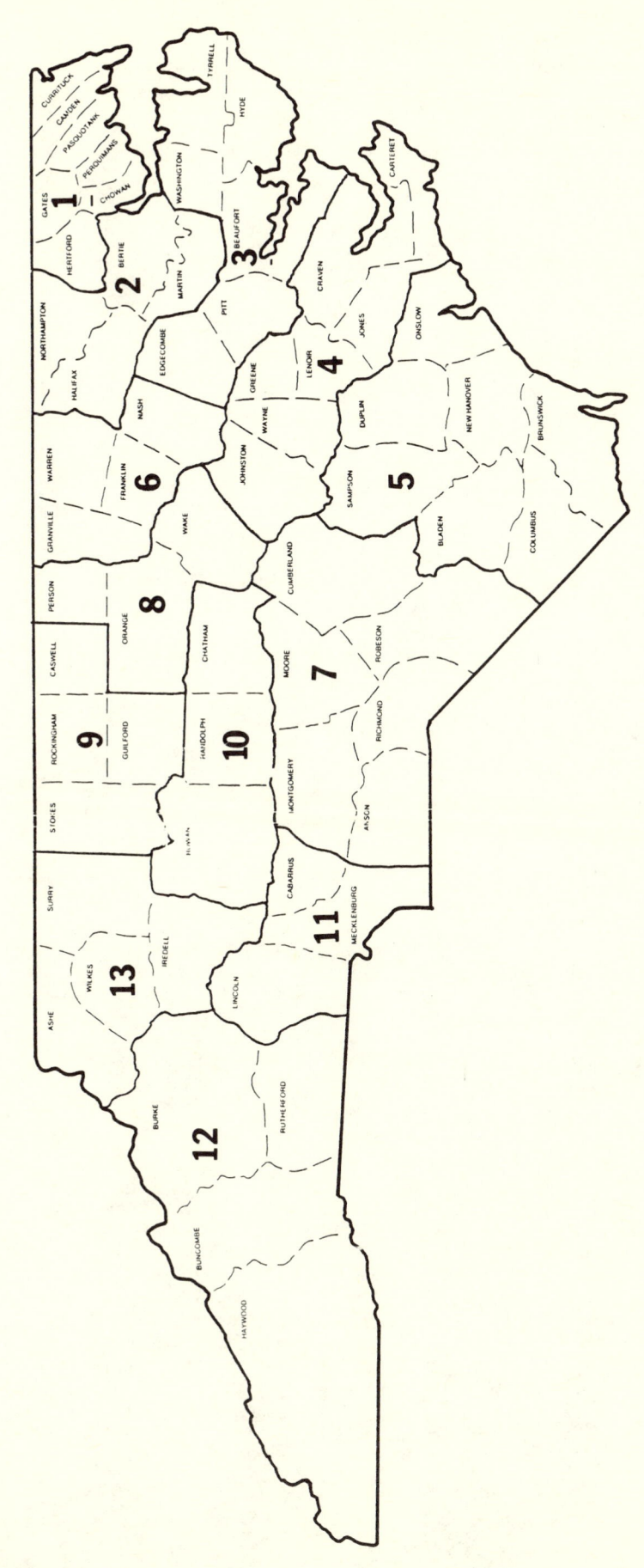

COUNTIES						REPRESENTATIVES				
County	Aggregate	Slave	%S	sq.mi.	P/sq.mi.	Representative	Cong.	Pty.	Address	County

DISTRICT 2

County	Aggregate	Slave	%S	sq.mi.	P/sq.mi.	Representative	Cong.	Pty.	Address	County
Bertie	10,805	5,725	52.9	698	15.4	Hutchins G. Burton[r]	18	NR	Halifax	Halifax
Halifax	17,237	7,181	41.6	734	23.4	(Resigned March, 1824)				
Martin	6,320	2,850	45.0	455	13.8	George Outlaw	18	JR	Windsor	Bertie
North-						(Replaced Burton January, 1825)				
ampton	13,242	7,263	54.8	536	24.7	Willis Alston	19	D	Hyde Park	Halifax
TOTALS	47,604	23,019	48.3	2,423	19.6	Willis Alston	20	D	Hyde Park	Halifax
						Willis Alston	21	D	Hyde Park	Halifax
						John Branch	22	D	Enfield	Halifax
						(Served as Secretary of the Navy until May 21, 1831)				

DISTRICT 3

County	Aggregate	Slave	%S	sq.mi.	P/sq.mi.	Representative	Cong.	Pty.	Address	County
Beaufort	9,850	3,655	37.1	826	11.9	Thomas H. Hall	18	D	Tarboro	Edgecombe
Edgecombe	13,276	5,745	43.2	560	26.0	Richard Hines	19	D	Edgecombe	Edgecombe
Hyde	4,967	1,580	31.8	613	8.1	Thomas H. Hall	20	D	Tarboro	Edgecombe
Pitt	10,001	4,241	42.4	655	15.2	Thomas H. Hall	21	D	Tarboro	Edgecombe
Tyrrel	4,319	1,261	29.1	781	5.5	Thomas H. Hall	22	D	Tarboro	Edgecombe
Washington	3,986	1,667	41.8	343	11.6					
TOTALS	46,399	18,149	39.1	3,778	12.3					

DISTRICT 4

County	Aggregate	Slave	%S	sq.mi.	P/sq.mi.	Representative	Cong.	Pty.	Address	County
Cateret	5,609	1,329	23.6	536	10.4	Richard D. Spaight	18	D	New Bern	Craven
Craven	13,394	5,087	37.9	1,037	12.9	John H. Bryan	19	NR	New Bern	Craven
Green	4,523	2,174	47.9	307	14.7	John H. Bryan	20	NR	New Bern	Craven
Johnston	9,607	3,086	32.1	872	11.0	Jesse Speight	21	D	Stantonsburg	----
Jones	5,216	2,764	52.9	467	11.1	Jesse Speight	22	D	Stantonsburg	----
Lenoir	6,799	3,354	49.3	400	16.9					
Wayne	9,040	3,162	34.9	607	14.9					
TOTALS	54,188	20,956	38.6	4,226	12.8					

DISTRICT 5

County	Aggregate	Slave	%S	sq.mi.	P/sq.mi.	Representative	Cong.	Pty.	Address	County
Bladen	7,276	2,788	38.3	883	8.2	Charles Hooks	18	D	Dublin	Bladen
Brunswick	5,480	2,334	42.5	856	6.4	Gabriel Holmes	19	NR	Clinton	Sampson
Columbus	3,912	913	23.3	945	4.1	Gabriel Holmes	20	NR	Clinton	Sampson
Duplin	9,744	3,599	36.9	815	12.0	Gabriel Holmes†	21	NR	Clinton	Sampson
New Hanover	10,866	5,561	51.0	185	58.7	(Died September, 1829)				
Onslow	7,016	2,777	39.5	765	9.2	Edward B. Dudley	21	NR	Wilmington	New Hanover
Sampson	8,908	2,857	32.0	945	9.4	Replaced Holmes December, 1829)				
TOTALS	53,202	20,829	39.2	5,394	9.9	James I. McKay	22	D	Elizabeth-town	Bladen

DISTRICT 6

County	Aggregate	Slave	%S	sq.mi.	P/sq.mi.	Representative	Cong.	Pty.	Address	County
Franklin	9,741	3,985	40.9	540	18.0	Weldon N. Edwards	18	D	Warrenton	Warren
Granville	18,222	8,976	49.2	686	26.6	Weldon N. Edwards	19	D	Warrenton	Warren
Nash	8,185	3,445	42.0	644	12.7	Daniel Turner	20	D	Warrenton	Warren
Warren	11,158	6,754	60.5	474	23.5	Robert Potter	21	JD	Oxford	Granville
TOTALS	47,306	23,160	48.9	2,355	20.1	Robert Potter[r]	22	JD	Oxford	Granville
						(Resigned November, 1831)				
						Micajah T. Howkins	22	D	Warrenton	Warren
						(Replaced Potter January, 1832)				

COUNTIES						REPRESENTATIVES				
County	Aggregate	Slave	%S	sq.mi.	P/sq.mi.	Representative	Cong.	Pty.	Address	County

DISTRICT 7

County	Aggregate	Slave	%S	sq.mi.	P/sq.mi.	Representative	Cong.	Pty.	Address	County
Anson	12,534	3,476	27.7	633	19.8	John Culpepper	18	F	Lawrence-ville	Montgomery
Cumberland	14,446	4,751	32.8	1,257	11.5					
Moore	7,128	1,296	18.1	959	7.4	Archibald McNeill	19	R	McNeil's Store	Moore*
Montgomery	8,693	1,816	20.8	886	9.8					
Richmond	7,537	2,021	26.8	794	9.5	John Culpepper	20	F	Beard's Store	Montgomery
Robeson	8,204	2,099	25.5	1,338	6.1	Edmund Deberry	21	NR	Lawrence-ville	Montgomery
TOTALS	58,542	15,459	26.4	5,867	10.0					
						Lauchlin Bethune	22	JD	Fayetteville	Cumberland

DISTRICT 8

County	Aggregate	Slave	%S	sq.mi.	P/sq.mi.	Representative	Cong.	Pty.	Address	County
Orange	23,492	6,153	26.1	1,123	20.9	Willie P. Mangum	18	(----)	Red Mountain	Orange
Person	9,029	3,674	40.6	401	22.5					
Wake	20,102	7,417	36.8	858	23.4	Willie P. Mangum[r]	19	NR	Red Mountain	Orange
TOTALS	52,623	17,244	32.7	2,382	22.0	(Resigned March, 1826)				
						Daniel L. Barringer	19	D	Raleigh	Wake
						(Replaced Mangum December, 1826)				
						Daniel L. Barringer	20	D	Raleigh	Wake
						Daniel L. Barringer	21	D	Raleigh	Wake
						Daniel L. Barringer	22	D	Raleigh	Wake

DISTRICT 9

County	Aggregate	Slave	%S	sq.mi.	P/sq.mi.	Representative	Cong.	Pty.	Address	County
Caswell	13,253	5,707	43.0	428	31.0	Romulus M. Saunders	18	D	Milton	Caswell
Guilford	14,511	1,611	11.1	655	22.1	Romulus M. Saunders	19	D	Milton	Caswell
Rockingham	11,474	2,974	25.9	569	20.1	Augustine H.				
Stokes	14,033	2,204	15.7	876	16.0	Shepperd	20	D	Germantown	----
TOTALS	53,271	12,496	23.4	2,528	21.1	Augustine H.				
						Shepperd	21	D	Germantown	----
						Augustine H.				
						Shepperd	22	D	Germantown	----

DISTRICT 10

County	Aggregate	Slave	%S	sq.mi.	P/sq.mi.	Representative	Cong.	Pty.	Address	County
Chatham	12,667	3,808	30.0	709	17.9	John Long, Jr.	18	NR	Long's Mill	Randolph
Randolph	11,331	1,080	9.5	798	14.2	John Long, Jr.	19	NR	Long's Mill	Randolph
Rowan	26,009	5,381	20.6	1,337	19.4	John Long, Jr.	20	NR	Long's Mill	Randolph
TOTALS	50,007	10,269	20.5	2,844	17.5	Abraham Rencher	21	D	Pittsboro	Chatham
						Abraham Rencher	22	D	Pittsboro	Chatham

DISTRICT 11

County	Aggregate	Slave	%S	sq.mi.	P/sq.mi.	Representative	Cong.	Pty.	Address	County
Cabarrus	7,248	1,599	22.0	363	20.0	Henry W. Connor	18	D	Sherrill's Ford	Lincoln
Lincoln	18,147	3,329	18.3	1,047	17.3					
Mecklenburg	16,895	5,181	30.6	1,069	15.8	Henry W. Connor	19	D	Sherrill's Ford	Lincoln
TOTALS	42,290	10,109	23.9	2,479	17.1	Henry W. Connor	20	D	Sherrill's Ford	Lincoln
						Henry W. Connor	21	D	Sherrill's Ford	Lincoln
						Henry W. Connor	22	D	Sherrill's Ford	Lincoln

NORTH CAROLINA (continued)

COUNTIES / REPRESENTATIVES

County	Aggregate	Slave	%S	sq.mi.	P/sq.mi.	Representative	Cong.	Pty.	Address	County

DISTRICT 12

County	Aggregate	Slave	%S	sq.mi.	P/sq.mi.	Representative	Cong.	Pty.	Address	County
Buncombe	10,542	1,042	9.8	1,575	6.7	Robert B. Vance	18	D	Ashville	Buncombe
Burke	13,411	1,917	14.2	2,188	6.1	Samuel P. Carson	19	D	Pleasant Garden	----
Haywood	4,073	274	6.7	3,414	1.2					
Macon (created from Buncombe County in 1828)						Samuel P. Carson	20	D	Pleasant Garden	----
Rutherford	15,351	3,321	21.6	1,180	13.0					
TOTALS	43,377	6,554	15.1	8,357	5.2	Samuel P. Carson	21	D	Pleasant Garden	----
						Samuel P. Carson	22	D	Pleasant Garden	----

DISTRICT 13

County	Aggregate	Slave	%S	sq.mi.	P/sq.mi.	Representative	Cong.	Pty.	Address	County
Ashe	4,335	250	5.7	968	4.5	Lewis Williams	18	F	Panther Creek	Surry
Iredell	13,071	2,988	22.8	831	15.7					
Surry	12,320	1,365	11.0	862	14.3	Lewis Williams	19	NR	Panther Creek	Surry
Wilkes	9,967	1,191	11.9	757	13.2	Lewis Williams	20	NR	Panther Creek	Surry
TOTALS	39,693	5,794	14.5	3,418	11.6	Lewis Williams	21	NR	Panther Creek	Surry
						Lewis Williams	22	NR	Panther Creek	Surry

OHIO
14 DISTRICTS
14 CONGRESSMEN

COUNTIES / REPRESENTATIVES

County	Aggregate	Slave	%S	sq.mi.	P/sq.mi.	Representative	Cong.	Pty.	Address	County

DISTRICT 1

County	Aggregate	Slave	%S	sq.mi.	P/sq.mi.	Representative	Cong.	Pty.	Address	County
Clermont	15,820	----	----	506	31.3	James W. Gazley	18	JD	Cincinatti	Hamilton
Hamilton	31,764	----	----	487	65.2	James Findlay	19	JD	Cincinatti	Hamilton
TOTALS	47,584	----	----	993	47.9	James Findlay	20	JD	Cincinatti	Hamilton
						James Findlay	21	JD	Cincinatti	Hamilton
						James Findlay	22	JD	Cincinatti	Hamilton

DISTRICT 2

County	Aggregate	Slave	%S	sq.mi.	P/sq.mi.	Representative	Cong.	Pty.	Address	County
Butler	21,746	----	----	484	44.9	Thomas R. Ross	18	D	Lebanon	Warren
Warren	17,837	----	----	400	44.6	John Woods	19	W	Hamilton	Butler
TOTALS	39,583	----	----	884	44.8	John Woods	20	AR	Hamilton	Butler
						James Shields	21	JD	Dick's Mills	Butler
						Thomas Corwin	22	NR	Lebanon	Warren

COUNTIES						REPRESENTATIVES				
County	Aggregate	Slave	%S	sq.mi.	P/sq.mi.	Representative	Cong.	Pty.	Address	County

DISTRICT 3

County	Aggregate	Slave	%S	sq.mi.	P/sq.mi.	Representative	Cong.	Pty.	Address	County
Allen[a]	----	----	----	471	----	William McLean	18	AR	Piqua	Miami
Darke	3,717	----	----	630	5.9	William McLean	19	AR	Piqua	Miami
Mercer[a]	----	----	----	439	----	William McLean	20	AR	Piqua	Miami
Miami	8,851	----	----	426	20.8	Joseph H. Crane	21	AR	Dayton	Montgomery
Montgomery	15,999	----	----	443	36.1	Joseph H. Crane	22	NR	Dayton	Montgomery
Paulding[a]	----	----	----	396	----					
Preble	10,237	----	----	414	24.7					
Putnam[a]	----	----	----	462	----					
Shelby	2,106	----	----	342	6.2					
Van Wert[a]	----	----	----	396	----					
Williams[a]	----	----	----	440	----					
TOTALS	40,910	----	----	4,859	8.4					

[a]Created after 1820 census.

DISTRICT 4

County	Aggregate	Slave	%S	sq.mi.	P/sq.mi.	Representative	Cong.	Pty.	Address	County
Champaign	8,479	----	----	352	24.1	Joseph Vance	18	D	Urbana	Champaign
Clark	9,533	----	----	311	30.7	Joseph Vance	19	D	Urbana	Champaign
Green	10,529	8	----	346	30.4	Joseph Vance	20	NR	Urbana	Champaign
Hancock[a]	----	----	----	483	----	Joseph Vance	21	NR	Urbana	Champaign
Hardin[a]	----	----	----	462	----	Joseph Vance	22	NR	Urbana	Champaign
Henry[a]	----	----	----	567	----					
Logan	3,181	----	----	374	8.5					
Madison	4,799	----	----	470	10.2					
Union	1,996	----	----	353	3.7					
Wood	733	----	----	621	1.2					
TOTALS	39,250	8	----	4,339	9.0					

[a]Created after 1820 census.

DISTRICT 5

County	Aggregate	Slave	%S	sq.mi.	P/sq.mi.	Representative	Cong.	Pty.	Address	County
Adams	10,406	----	----	383	27.2	John W. Campbell	18	D	West Union	Adams
Brown	13,356	----	----	399	28.5	John W. Campbell	19	D	West Union	Adams
Clinton	8,085	----	----	332	24.4	William Russell	20	JD	West Union	Adams
Highland	12,308	----	----	468	26.3	William Russell	21	JD	West Union	Adams
TOTALS	44,155	----	----	1,582	27.9	William Russell	22	JD	West Union	Adams

DISTRICT 6

County	Aggregate	Slave	%S	sq.mi.	P/sq.mi.	Representative	Cong.	Pty.	Address	County
Fayette	6,316	----	----	390	16.2	Duncan McArthur	18	(a)	Chillicothe	Ross
Hocking	2,130	----	----	383	5.6	John Thomson	19	D	Chillicothe	Ross
Pickaway	13,149	----	----	376	35.0	William Creighton, Jr.r	20	AR	Chillicothe	Ross
Ross	20,619	----	----	673	45.8	(Resigned May 20, 1828)				
TOTALS	44,214	----	----	1,822	24.3	Francis S. Muhlenberg	20	NR	Circleville	Pickaway
						(Replaced Creighton December 19, 1828)				
						William Creighton, Jr.	21	AR	Chillicothe	Ross
						William Creighton, Jr.	22	NR	Chillicothe	Ross

[a]Elected as an advocate of the U.S. Bank.

County	Aggregate	Slave	%S	sq.mi.	P/sq.mi.	Representative	Cong.	Pty.	Address	County
						COUNTIES / REPRESENTATIVES				

DISTRICT 7

County	Aggregate	Slave	%S	sq.mi.	P/sq.mi.	Representative	Cong.	Pty.	Address	County
Athens	6,312	----	----	606	10.4	Samuel F. Vinton	18	NR	Gallipolis	Gallia
Gallia	7,098	----	----	465	15.3	Samuel F. Vinton	19	W	Gallipolis	Gallia
Jackson	3,746	----	----	549	6.8	Samuel F. Vinton	20	AR	Gallipolis	Gallia
Lawrence	3,499	----	----	387	9.0	Samuel F. Vinton	21	AR	Gallipolis	Gallia
Meigs	4,480	----	----	390	11.5	Samuel F. Vinton	22	NR	Gallipolis	Gallia
Pike	4,253	----	----	450	9.5					
Scioto	5,750	----	----	558	10.3					
Washington	10,425	----	----	485	21.5					
TOTALS	45,563	----	----	3,890	11.7					

DISTRICT 8

County	Aggregate	Slave	%S	sq.mi.	P/sq.mi.	Representative	Cong.	Pty.	Address	County
Coshocton	7,086	----	----	778	9.1	William Wilson	18	AR	Newark	Licking
Crawford[a]	----	----	----	432	----	William Wilson	19	AR	Newark	Licking
Delaware	7,639	----	----	588	13.0	William Wilson†	20	AR	Newark	Licking
Franklin	10,292	----	----	506	20.3	(Died June 6, 1827)				
Knox	8,326	----	----	584	14.3	William Stanbury	20	JD	Newark	Licking
Licking	11,861	----	----	564	21.0	(Replaced Wilson December 3, 1827)				
Marion[a]	----	----	----	486	----	William Stanbury	21	JD	Newark	Licking
TOTALS	45,204	----	----	3,938	11.5	William Stanbury	22	NR	Newark	Licking

[a]Created after 1820 census.

DISTRICT 9

County	Aggregate	Slave	%S	sq.mi.	P/sq.mi.	Representative	Cong.	Pty.	Address	County
Fairfield	16,633	----	----	485	34.3	Philemon Beecher	18	F	Lancaster	Fairfield
Muskingum	17,824	----	----	625	28.5	Philemon Beecher	19	F	Lancaster	Fairfield
Perry	8,429	----	----	424	19.9	Philemon Beecher	20	AR	Lancaster	Fairfield
TOTALS	42,886	----	----	1,534	28.0	William W. Irvin	21	JD	Lancaster	Fairfield
						William W. Irvin	22	JD	Lancaster	Fairfield

DISTRICT 10

County	Aggregate	Slave	%S	sq.mi.	P/sq.mi.	Representative	Cong.	Pty.	Address	County
Belmont	20,329	----	----	448	45.4	John Patterson	18	D	St. Clairsville	Belmont
Guernsey	9,292	----	----	610	15.2	David Jennings[r]	19	(----)	St. Clairsville	Belmont
Monroe	4,645	----	----	468	9.9	(Resigned May 25, 1826)				
Morgan	5,297	----	----	498	10.6	Thomas Shannon	19	D	Barnesville	Belmont
TOTALS	39,563	----	----	2,024	19.5	(Replaced Jennings December 4, 1826)				
						John Davenport	20	AR	Barnesville	Belmont
						William Kennon, Sr.	21	JD	St. Clairsville	Belmont
						William Kennon, Sr.	22	NR	St. Clairsville	Belmont

DISTRICT 11

County	Aggregate	Slave	%S	sq.mi.	P/sq.mi.	Representative	Cong.	Pty.	Address	County
Jefferson	18,531	----	----	395	46.9	John C. Wright	18	AR	Steubanville	Jefferson
Harrison	14,345	----	----	378	37.9	John C. Wright	19	AR	Steubanville	Jefferson
Tuscarawas	8,328	----	----	564	14.8	John C. Wright	20	AR	Steubanville	Jefferson
TOTALS	41,204	----	----	1,337	30.8	John M. Goodenow[r]	21	JD	Steubanville	Jefferson
						(Resigned April 9, 1830)				
						Humphrey H. Leawitt	21	JD	Steubanville	Jefferson
						(Replaced Goodenow December 6, 1830)				
						Humphrey H. Leawitt	22	JD	Steubanville	Jefferson

DISTRICT 12

County	Aggregate	Slave	%S	sq.mi.	P/sq.mi.	Representative	Cong.	Pty.	Address	County
Columbiana	22,023	----	----	798	27.6	John Sloane	18	W	Wooster	Wayne
Stark	12,406	----	----	609	20.4	John Sloane	19	W	Wooster	Wayne
Wayne	11,933	----	----	784	15.2	John Sloane	20	AR	Wooster	Wayne
TOTALS	46,362	----	----	2,191	21.2	John Thomson	21	JD	New Lisbon	Columbiana
						John Thomson	22	JD	New Lisbon	Columbiana

COUNTIES						REPRESENTATIVES				
County	Aggregate	Slave	%S	sq.mi.	P/sq.mi.	Representative	Cong.	Pty.	Address	County
DISTRICT 13										
Ashtabula	7,382	7	----	767	9.6	Elisha Whittlesey	18	AR	Canfield	Trumbell
Geauga	7,791	----	----	560	13.9	Elisha Whittlesey	19	AR	Canfield	Trumbell
Portage	10,095	----	----	667	15.1	Elisha Whittlesey	20	AR	Canfield	Trumbell
Trumbull	15,556	4	----	850	18.3	Elisha Whittlesey	21	AR	Canfield	Trumbell
TOTALS	40,824	11	----	2,844	14.4	Elisha Whittlesey	22	NR	Canfield	Trumbell
DISTRICT 14										
Cuyahoga	6,328	----	----	572	11.1	Mordecai Bartley	18	AR	Mansfield	Richland
Huron	6,675	----	----	1,176	5.7	Mordecai Bartley	19	AR	Mansfield	Richland
Medina	3,082	----	----	488	6.3	Mordecai Bartley	20	AR	Mansfield	Richland
Richland	9,169	----	----	868	10.6	Mordecai Bartley	21	AR	Mansfield	Richland
Sandusky	852	----	----	420	2.0	Eleutheros Cooke	22	NR	Sandusky	Sandusky
Seneca[a]	----	----	----	414	----					
TOTALS	26,106	----	----	3,938	6.6					

[a]Created after 1820 census.

PENNSYLVANIA
18 DISTRICTS
31 CONGRESSMEN

COUNTIES						REPRESENTATIVES				
County	Aggregate	Slave	%S	sq.mi.	P/sq.mi.	Representative	Cong.	Pty.	Address	County
DISTRICT 1										
Towns in Philadelphia County:						Samuel Breck	18	F	City of Philadelphia	
Blockley	2,655	----	----	----	----	John Wurts	19	NR	City of Philadelphia	
Moya-						Joel B. Sutherland	20	JD	City of Philadelphia	
mensing	3,963	----	----	----	----	Joel B. Sutherland	21	JD	City of Philadelphia	
Passyunk	1,638	----	----	----	----	Joel B. Sutherland	22	D	City of Philadelphia	
Total, towns	8,256	----	----	----	----					
Wards in the City of Philadelphia:										
Cedar	8,904	----	----	----	----					
Kingsessing	11,188	----	----	----	----					
New Market	5,889	----	----	----	----					
Total, wards	15,981	----	----	----	----					
Southwark	14,713	----	----	----	----					
TOTALS	38,950	----	----	15	2597.0					
DISTRICT 2										
All wards in the City of Philadelphia not included in						Joseph Hemphill	18	F	City of Philadelphia	
District 1,						Joseph Hemphill[r]	19	F	City of Philadelphia	
total:	49,009	2	----	14	3500.6	(Resigned in 1826)				
						Thomas Kittera	19	F	City of Philadelphia	
						(Replaced Hemphill December 4, 1826)				
						John Sergeant	20	F	City of Philadelphia	
						Joseph Hemphill	21	JD	City of Philadelphia	
						Henry Horn	22	JD	City of Philadelphia	

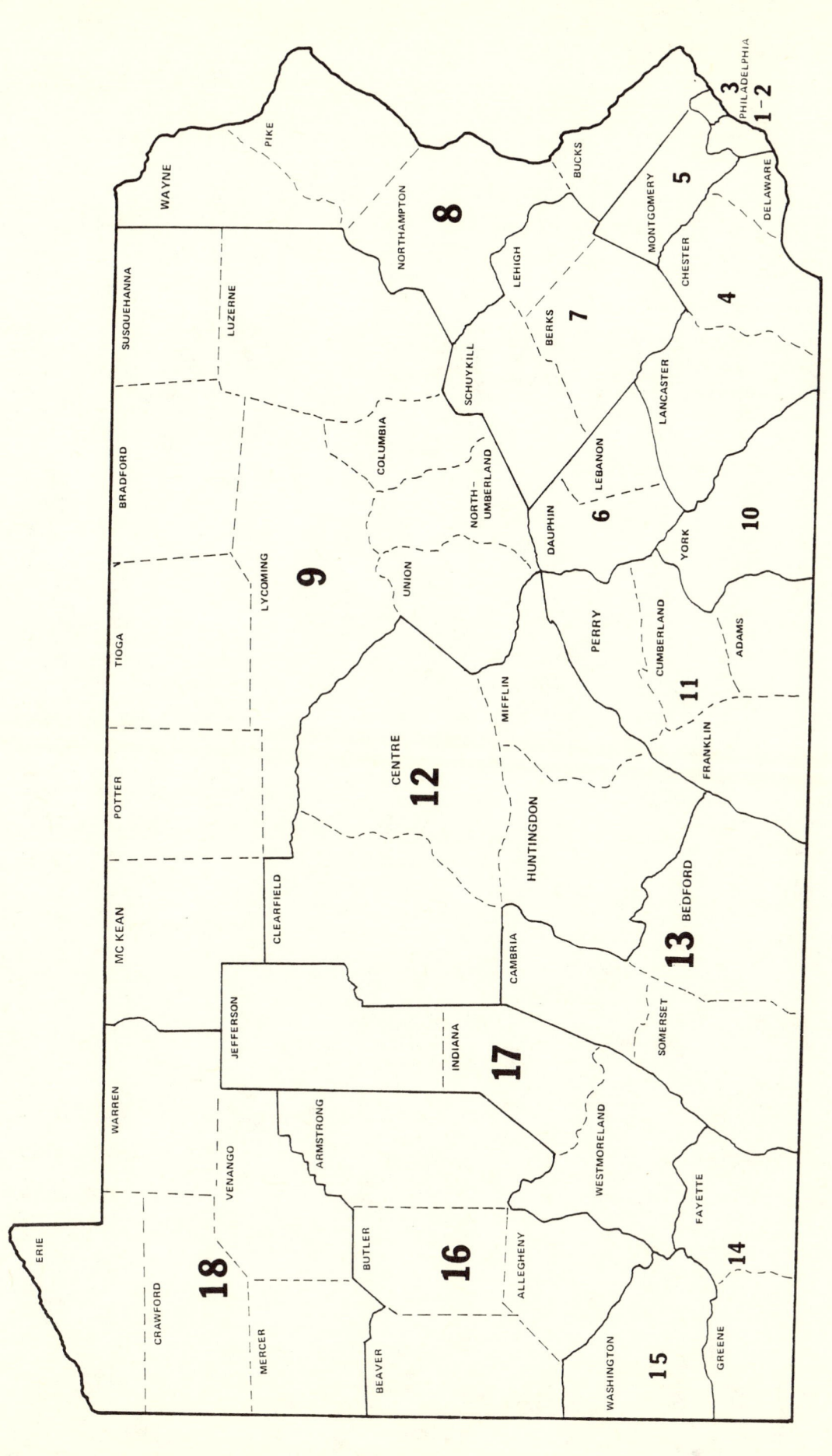

COUNTIES / REPRESENTATIVES

County	Aggregate	Slave	%S	sq.mi.	P/sq.mi.	Representative	Cong.	Pty.	Address	County
						DISTRICT 3				
All of Philadelphia County not included in District 1,						Daniel H. Miller	18	JD	City of Philadelphia	
total:	63,851	4	----	100	638.5	Daniel H. Miller	19	JD	City of Philadelphia	
						Daniel H. Miller	20	JD	City of Philadelphia	
						Daniel H. Miller	21	JD	City of Philadelphia	
						John G. Watmough	22	NR	City of Philadelphia	
						DISTRICT 4				
Chester	44,451	7	----	761	58.4	James Buchanan	18	D	Lancaster	Lancaster
Delaware	14,810	1	----	184	80.5	Samuel Edwards	18	F	Chester	Delaware
Lancaster	68,336	21	----	946	72.2	Isaac Wayne	18	F	Warren[a]	Chester
TOTALS	127,597	29	----	1,891	67.5					
						James Buchanan	19	D	Lancaster	Lancaster
						Samuel Edwards	19	F	Chester	Delaware
						Charles Miner	19	F	West Chester	Chester
						Samuel Anderson	20	F	Providence	----
						James Buchanan	20	D	Lancaster	Lancaster
						Charles Miner	20	F	West Chester	Chester
						James Buchanan	21	D	Lancaster	Lancaster
						Joshua Evans, Jr.	21	D	Paoli	Chester
						George G. Leiper	21	D	Leiperville	Delaware
						Joshua Evans, Jr.	22	D	Paoli	Chester
						William Hiester	22	NR	New Holland	Lancaster
						David Potts, Jr.	22	NR	Pottstown	Chester

[a]The Biographical Directory of the American Congress lists Wayne's address as Warren, a town in the Eighteenth District. All evidence points to Wayne having represented the Fourth District. Chester County seems to have been his only residence of any duration.

County	Aggregate	Slave	%S	sq.mi.	P/sq.mi.	Representative	Cong.	Pty.	Address	County
						DISTRICT 5				
Montgomery	35,793	3	----	496	72.2	Philip S. Markley	18	D	Norristown	Montgomery
						Philip S. Markley	19	D	Norristown	Montgomery
						John B. Sterigere	20	D	Upper Dublin	Montgomery
						John B. Sterigere	21	JD	Norristown	Montgomery
						Joel K. Mann	22	D	Jenkintown	Montgomery
						DISTRICT 6				
Dauphin	21,653	9	----	518	41.8	Robert Harris	18	(----)	Harrisburg	Dauphin
Lebanon	16,988	4	----	363	46.8	Robert Harris	19	(----)	Harrisburg	Dauphin
TOTALS	38,641	13	----	881	43.8	Innis Green	20	D	Dauphin	Dauphin
						Innis Green	21	JD	Dauphin	Dauphin
						John C. Bucher	22	(----)	Harrisburg	Dauphin

COUNTIES						REPRESENTATIVES				
County	Aggregate	Slave	%S	sq.mi.	P/sq.mi.	Representative	Cong.	Pty.	Address	County

DISTRICT 7

Berks	46,275	----	----	862	53.7	Daniel Udree	18	D	Reading	Berks
Lehigh	18,895	----	----	348	54.3	Henry Wilson	18	D	Allentown	Lehigh
Schuylkill	11,339	----	----	784	14.5					
TOTALS	76,509	----	----	1,994	38.4	William Addams	19	D	Reading	Berks
						Henry Wilson†	19	D	Allentown	Lehigh
						(Died August 14, 1826)				
						Jacob Krebs	19	D	Orwingsburg	Schuylkill
						(Replaced Wilson December, 1826)				
						William Addams	20	D	Reading	Berks
						Joseph Fry, Jr.	20	D	Fryburg	Lehigh
						Joseph Fry, Jr.	21	JD	Fryburg	Lehigh
						Henry A. P. Muhlenberg	21	JD	Reading	Berks
						Henry King	22	D	Allentown	Lehigh
						Henry A. P. Muhlenberg	22	D	Reading	Berks

DISTRICT 8

Bucks	37,842	2	----	614	61.6	Samuel D. Ingham	18	(----)	New Hope	Bucks
North-ampton	31,765	----	----	1,478	21.4	Thomas J. Rogers[r]	18	D	Easton	Northampton
						(Resigned April 20, 1824)				
Pike	2,894	1	----	803	3.6	George Wolf	18	D	Easton	Northampton
Wayne	4,127	----	----	741	5.5	(Replaced Rogers December 9, 1824)				
TOTALS	76,628	3	----	3,636	21.0					
						Samuel D. Ingham	19	(----)	New Hope	Bucks
						George Wolf	19	D	Easton	Northampton
						Samuel D. Ingham	20	(----)	New Hope	Bucks
						George Wolf	20	D	Easton	Northampton
						Samuel D. Ingham[r]	21	JD	New Hope	Bucks
						Samuel A. Smith	21	D	Doylestown	Bucks
						(Replaced Ingham December 7, 1829)				
						George Wolf[r]	21	D	Easton	Northampton
						Peter Ihrie, Jr.	21	JD	Easton	Northampton
						(Replaced Wolf December 7, 1829)				
						Peter Ihrie, Jr.	22	JD	Easton	Northampton
						Samuel A. Smith	22	D	Rockhill	----

DISTRICT 9

Bradford	11,554	----	----	1,148	10.1	William Cox Ellis	18	F	Muncy	Lycoming
Columbia	17,621	----	----	484	36.4	George Kremer	18	(----)	Lewisburg	Union
Luzerne	20,027	1	----	1,738	11.5	Samuel McKean	18	D	Burlington	Bradford
Lycoming	13,517	3	----	1,944	6.9					
McKean	728	----	----	992	0.7	George Kremer	19	(----)	Lewisburg	Union
North-umberland	15,424	1	----	583	26.5	Samuel McKean	19	D	Burlington	Bradford
						Espy Van Horne	19	D	Williamsport	Lycoming
Potter	186	----	----	1,092	0.2					
Susquehanna	9,960	----	----	833	12.0	George Kremer	20	(----)	Lewisburg	Union
Tioga	4,021	----	----	1,146	3.5	Samuel McKean	20	D	Burlington	Bradford

| COUNTIES | | | | | | REPRESENTATIVES | | | | |
County	Aggregate	Slave	%S	sq.mi.	P/sq.mi.	Representative	Cong.	Pty.	Address	County

DISTRICT 9 (CONTINUED)

County	Aggregate	Slave	%S	sq.mi.	P/sq.mi.	Representative	Cong.	Pty.	Address	County
Union	18,619	3	----	318	58.5	Espy Van Horne	20	D	Williamsport	Lycoming
TOTALS	111,657	8	----	10,278	10.9					
						James Ford	21	JD	Lawrence-ville	Tioga
						Alem Marr	21	JD	Montrose	Susquehanna
						Philander Stephens	21	JD	Montrose	Susquehanna
						Lewis Dewart	22	JD	Sunbury	North-umberland
						James Ford	22	JD	Lawrence-ville	Tioga
						Philander Stephens	22	JD	Montrose	Susquehanna

DISTRICT 10

County	Aggregate	Slave	%S	sq.mi.	P/sq.mi.	Representative	Cong.	Pty.	Address	County
York	38,759	6	----	909	42.6	James S. Mitchell	18	D	Rossville	York
						James S. Mitchell	19	D	Rossville	York
						Adam King	20	D	York	York
						Adam King	21	JD	York	York
						Adam King	22	JD	York	York

DISTRICT 11

County	Aggregate	Slave	%S	sq.mi.	P/sq.mi.	Representative	Cong.	Pty.	Address	County
Adams	19,370	23	----	526	36.8	John Findlay	18	D	Chambers-burg	Franklin
Cumberland	23,606	17	----	555	42.5					
Franklin	31,892	19	----	754	42.3	James Wilson	18	D	Fairfield	Adams
Perry	11,342	1	----	551	20.6					
TOTALS	86,210	60	----	2,386	36.1	John Findlay	19	D	Chambers-burg	Franklin
						James Wilson	19	D	Fairfield	Adams
						William Ramsey	20	D	Carlisle	Cumberland
						James Wilson	20	D	Fairfield	Adams
						Thomas H. Crawford	21	JD	Chambers-burg	Franklin
						William Ramsey	21	JD	Carlisle	Cumberland
						Thomas H. Crawford	22	JD	Chambers-burg	Franklin
						William Ramsey† (Died September 29, 1831)	22	D	Carlisle	Cumberland
						Robert McCoy (Replaced Ramsey December 5, 1831)	22	D	Carlisle	Cumberland

DISTRICT 12

County	Aggregate	Slave	%S	sq.mi.	P/sq.mi.	Representative	Cong.	Pty.	Address	County
Centre	13,796	----	----	1,865	7.4	John Brown	18	(----)	Lewistown	Mifflin
Clearfield	2,342	----	----	1,740	1.3	John Mitchell	19	D	Bellefonte	Centre
Huntingdon	20,142	5	----	1,425	14.1	John Mitchell	20	D	Bellefonte	Centre
Mifflin	16,618	2	----	817	20.3	John Scott	21	JD	Alexandria	Huntingdon
TOTALS	52,898	7	----	5,847	9.0	Robert Allison	22	W	Huntingdon Center	Huntingdon

| County | COUNTIES | | | | | REPRESENTATIVES | | | | |
	Aggregate	Slave	%S	sq.mi.	P/sq.mi.	Representative	Cong.	Pty.	Address	County
						DISTRICT 13				
Bedford	20,248	5	----	1,453	13.9	John Tod[r]	18	D	Bedford	Bedford
Cambria	3,287	----	----	692	4.8	(Resigned in 1824)				
Somerset	13,974	----	----	1,078	13.0	Alexander Thomson	18	(----)	Bedford	Bedford
TOTALS	37,509	5	----	3,223	11.6	(Replaced Tod December 6, 1824)				
						Alexander Thomson[r]	19	(----)	Bedford	Bedford
						(Resigned May 1, 1826)				
						Chauncey Forward	19	D	Somerset	Somerset
						(Replaced Thomson December, 1826)				
						Chauncey Forward	20	D	Somerset	Somerset
						Chauncey Forward	21	D	Somerset	Somerset
						George Burd	22	D	Bedford	Bedford
						DISTRICT 14				
Fayette	27,285	21	----	802	34.0	Andrew Stewart	18	D	Uniontown	Fayette
Greene	15,554	7	----	578	26.9	Andrew Stewart	19	D	Uniontown	Fayette
TOTALS	42,839	28	----	1,380	31.0	Andrew Stewart	20	D	Uniontown	Fayette
						Thomas Irwin	21	D	Uniontown	Fayette
						Andrew Stewart	22	D	Uniontown	Fayette
						DISTRICT 15				
Washington	40,038	5	----	857	46.7	Thomas Patterson	18	D	West Middletown	Washington
						Joseph Lawrence	19	W	Washington	Washington
						Joseph Lawrence	20	W	Washington	Washington
						William McCreery	21	D	Florence	Washington
						Thomas M. T. McKenna McKenna	22	W	Washington	Washington
						DISTRICT 16[a]				
Allegheny	34,291	1	----	728	47.1	James Allison, Jr.	18	W	Beaver	Beaver
Armstrong	10,324	----	----	1,249	8.3	Walter Forward	18	D	Pittsburg	Allegheny
Beaver	15,340	5	----	807	19.0					
Butler	10,193	----	----	670	15.2	James Allison, Jr.[r]	19	W	Beaver	Beaver
TOTALS	70,148	6	----	3,454	20.3	Robert Orr, Jr.	19	D	Kittanning	Armstrong
						(Replaced Allison December 5, 1825)				
						James S. Stevenson	19	(----)	Pittsburg	Allegheny
						Robert Orr, Jr.	20	D	Kittanning	Armstrong
						James S. Stevenson	20	(----)	Pittsburg	Allegheny
						John Gilmore	21	JD	Butler	Butler
						William Wilkins[r]	21	(----)	Pittsburg	Allegheny
						Harmar Denny	21	AM	Pittsburg	Allegheny
						(Replaced Wilkins December 30, 1829)				
						Harmar Denny	22	AM	Pittsburg	Allegheny
						John Gilmore	22	JD	Butler	Butler

[a]Congressional Quarterly, Guide to U.S. Elections, lists the representatives of our District 16 as representing the counties of the Seventeenth Districts and those of our District 17 as representing the Sixteenth. Based on the residencies of the members in question, we believe our listing is correct.

COUNTIES   REPRESENTATIVES

County	Aggregate	Slave	%S	sq.mi.	P/sq.mi.	Representative	Cong.	Pty.	Address	County

DISTRICT 17[a]

County	Aggregate	Slave	%S	sq.mi.	P/sq.mi.	Representative	Cong.	Pty.	Address	County
Indiana	8,882	----	----	825	10.8	George Plumer	18	D	Robbstown	Westmoreland
Jefferson	561	----	----	652	0.9	George Plumer	19	D	Robbstown	Westmoreland
West-						Richard Coulter	20	I	Greensburg	Westmoreland
moreland	30,540	5	----	1,024	29.8	Richard Coulter	21	I	Greensburg	Westmoreland
TOTALS	39,983	5	----	2,501	16.0	Richard Coulter	22	D	Greensburg	Westmoreland

[a]See note to District 16.

DISTRICT 18

County	Aggregate	Slave	%S	sq.mi.	P/sq.mi.	Representative	Cong.	Pty.	Address	County
Crawford	9,397	----	----	1,012	9.3	Patrick Farrelly	18	D	Meadville	Crawford
Erie	8,553	1	----	813	10.5	Patrick Farrelly†	19	D	Meadville	Crawford
Mercer	11,681	1	----	670	17.4	Thomas H. Sill	19	NR	Erie	Erie
Venango	4,915	----	----	878	5.6	(Replaced Farrelly)				
Warren	1,976	----	----	905	2.2	Stephen Bablow	20	D	Meadville	Crawford
TOTALS	36,522	2	----	4,278	8.5	Thomas H. Sill	21	NR	Erie	Erie
						John Banks	22	W	Mercer	Mercer

RHODE ISLAND
2 CONGRESSMEN AT LARGE

COUNTIES   REPRESENTATIVES

County	Aggregate	Slave	%S	sq.mi.	P/sq.mi.	Representative	Cong.	Pty.	Address	County

AT LARGE

County	Aggregate	Slave	%S	sq.mi.	P/sq.mi.	Representative	Cong.	Pty.	Address	County
Bristol	5,637	2	----	25	225.5	Job Durfee	18	D	Twerton	Newport
Kent	10,228	7	----	202	50.6	Samuel Eddy	18	D	Providence	Providence
Newport	15,771	28	----	103	153.1					
Providence	35,736	4	----	413	86.5	Tristram Burges	19	NR	Providence	Providence
Washington	15,687	7	----	340	46.1	Dutee J. Pearce	19	NR	Newport	Newport
TOTALS	83,059	48	----	1,083	76.7					
						Tristram Burges	20	NR	Providence	Providence
						Dutee J. Pearce	20	NR	Newport	Newport
						Tristram Burges	21	NR	Providence	Providence
						Dutee J. Pearce	21	NR	Newport	Newport
						Tristram Burges	22	NR	Providence	Providence
						Dutee J. Pearce	22	NR	Newport	Newport

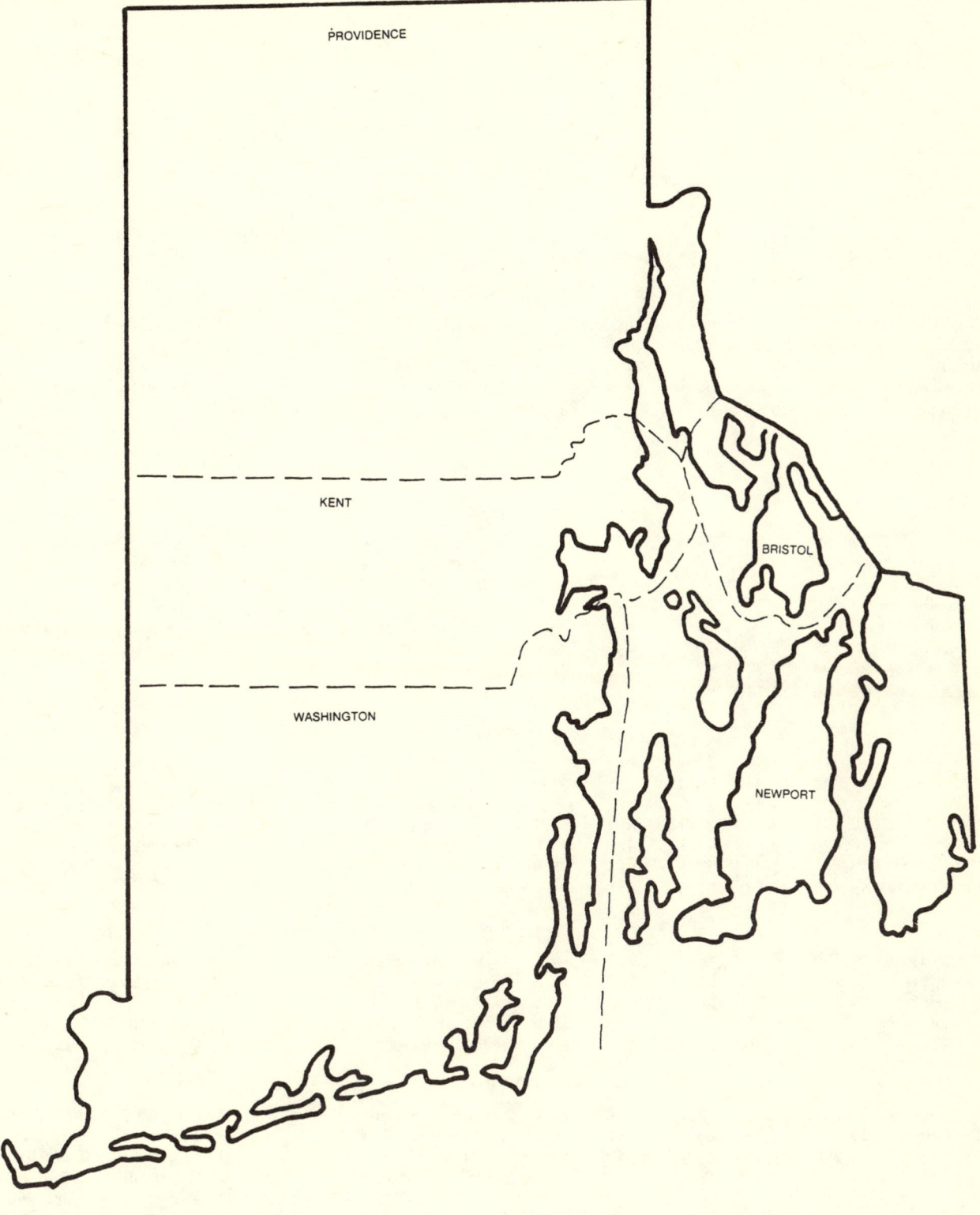

COUNTIES						REPRESENTATIVES				
County	Aggregate	Slave	%S	sq.mi.	P/sq.mi.	Representative	Cong.	Pty.	Address	County

DISTRICT 1

County	Aggregate	Slave	%S	sq.mi.	P/sq.mi.	Representative	Cong.	Pty.	Address	County
All of Charleston County not included in District 2,						Joel R. Poinsett	18	D	Charleston	Charleston
total:	34,113	24,041	70.5	1,626	21.0	Joel R. Poinsett[r]	19	D	Charleston	Charleston
City of						(Resigned March, 1825)				
Charleston	24,780	12,589	50.8	17	1457.6	William Drayton	19	UD	Charleston	Charleston
TOTALS	58,893	36,630	62.2	1,643	35.8	(Replaced Poinsett December, 1825)				
						William Drayton	20	UD	Charleston	Charleston
						William Drayton	21	UD	Charleston	Charleston
						William Drayton	22	UD	Charleston	Charleston

DISTRICT 2

County	Aggregate	Slave	%S	sq.mi.	P/sq.mi.	Representative	Cong.	Pty.	Address	County
Beaufort	32,199	27,339	84.9	1,793	18.0	James Hamilton, Jr.	18	SFT	Colleton	----
Parishes in Charleston County:						James Hamilton, Jr.	19	SFT	Colleton	----
Colleton	----	----	----	----	----	James Hamilton, Jr.	20	SFT	Colleton	----
St. Andrews	----	----	----	----	----	Robert W. Barnwell	21	D	Beaufort	Beaufort
St. Johns	----	----	----	----	----	Robert W. Barnwell	22	D	Beaufort	Beaufort
Total, parishes	8,527	6,010	70.5	406	21.0					
Colleton	26,404	21,770	82.4	1,618	16.3					
TOTALS	67,130	55,119	82.1	3,817	17.6					

DISTRICT 3

County	Aggregate	Slave	%S	sq.mi.	P/sq.mi.	Representative	Cong.	Pty.	Address	County
Darlington	10,949	4,473	40.8	849	12.9	Robert Campbell	18	(----)	Brownsville	Marlboro
Georgetown	17,603	15,846	90.0	812	21.6	Thomas R. Mitchell	19	(----)	Georgetown	Georgetown
Horry	5,025	1,434	28.5	1,154	4.9	Thomas R. Mitchell	20	(----)	Georgetown	Georgetown
Marion	10,201	3,463	33.9	894	11.4	John Campbell	21	SRW	Brownsville	Marlboro
Marlboro	6,425	3,033	47.2	483	13.3	Thomas R. Mitchell	22	(----)	Georgetown	Georgetown
Williamsburg	8,716	5,864	67.2	1,434	6.0					
TOTALS	58,919	34,113	57.8	5,626	10.4					

DISTRICT 4

County	Aggregate	Slave	%S	sq.mi.	P/sq.mi.	Representative	Cong.	Pty.	Address	County
Barnwell	14,750	6,336	43.0	1,927	7.7	Andrew Govan	18	(----)	Orangeburg	Orangeburg
Lexington	8,083	2,801	34.7	717	11.3	Andrew Govan	19	(----)	Orangeburg	Orangeburg
Orangeburg	15,653	8,829	56.4	1,701	9.2	William D. Martin	20	D	Barnwell	Barnwell
Richland	12,321	7,627	61.9	748	16.5	William D. Martin	21	D	Barnwell	Barnwell
TOTALS	50,807	25,593	50.3	5,093	10.0	John Felder	22	D	Orangeburg	Orangeburg

DISTRICT 5

County	Aggregate	Slave	%S	sq.mi.	P/sq.mi.	Representative	Cong.	Pty.	Address	County
Abbeville	23,167	9,615	41.5	976	23.7	George McDuffie	18	D	Edgefield	Edgefield
Edgefield	25,119	12,198	48.5	1,602	15.7	George McDuffie	19	D	Edgefield	Edgefield
TOTALS	48,286	21,813	45.3	2,578	18.7	George McDuffie	20	D	Edgefield	Edgefield
						George McDuffie	21	D	Edgefield	Edgefield
						George McDuffie	22	D	Edgefield	Edgefield

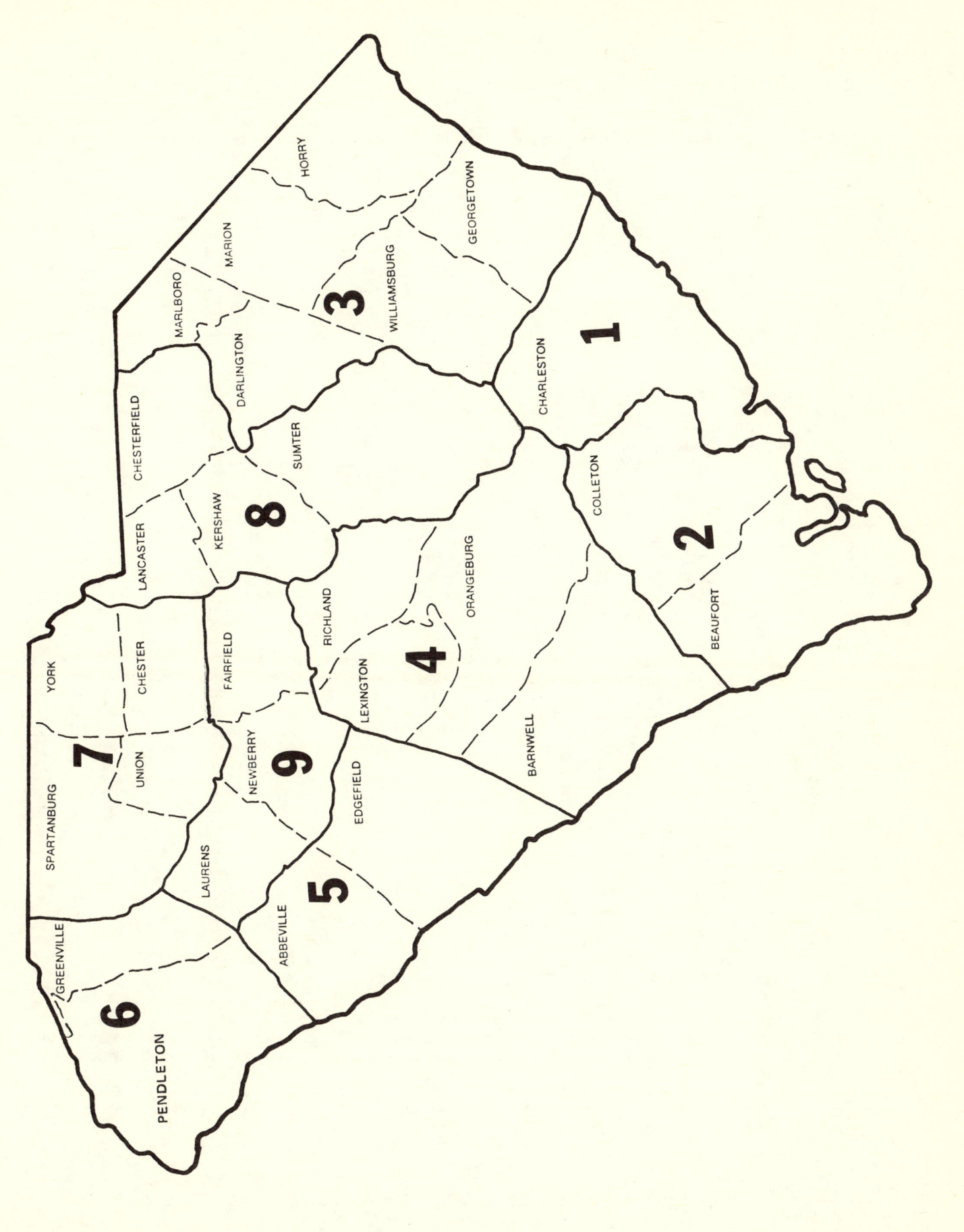

COUNTIES						REPRESENTATIVES				
County	Aggregate	Slave	%S	sq.mi.	P/sq.mi.	Representative	Cong.	Pty.	Address	County

DISTRICT 6

County	Aggregate	Slave	%S	sq.mi.	P/sq.mi.	Representative	Cong.	Pty.	Address	County
Greenville	14,530	3,423	23.6	792	18.3	John Wilson	18	(----)	Golden Grove	Pendleton
Pendleton	27,022	4,715	17.4	1,895	14.3					
TOTALS	41,552	8,138	19.5	2,687	15.4	John Wilson	19	(----)	Golden Grove	Pendleton
						Warren R. Davis	20	SRD	Pendleton	Anderson[a]
						Warren R. Davis	21	SRD	Pendleton	Anderson
						Warren R. Davis	22	SRD	Pendleton	Anderson

[a]Created from Pendleton in 1826.

DISTRICT 7

County	Aggregate	Slave	%S	sq.mi.	P/sq.mi.	Representative	Cong.	Pty.	Address	County
Chester	14,189	4,542	32.0	584	24.3	Joseph Gist	18	D	Pickneyville	Union
Spartanburg	16,989	3,308	19.5	1,225	13.9	Joseph Gist	19	D	Pickneyville	Union
Union	14,126	4,278	30.3	514	27.5	William T. Nuckolls	20	(----)	Spartanburg	Spartanburg
York	14,936	4,590	30.7	684	21.8	William T. Nuckolls	21	(----)	Hancockville	Union
TOTALS	60,240	16,718	27.7	3,007	20.0	William T. Nuckolls	22	(----)	Hancockville	Union

DISTRICT 8

County	Aggregate	Slave	%S	sq.mi.	P/sq.mi.	Representative	Cong.	Pty.	Address	County
Chesterfield	6,645	2,062	31.0	790	8.4	John Carter	18	(----)	Camden	Kershaw
Kershaw	11,706	6,590	56.3	781	15.0	John Carter	19	(----)	Camden	Kershaw
Lancaster	8,716	2,798	32.1	502	17.4	John Carter	20	(----)	Camden	Kershaw
Sumter[a]	25,369	16,143	63.6	1,680	15.1	James Blair	21	UD	Lynchwood	Lancaster
TOTALS	52,836	27,593	52.2	3,753	13.9	James Blair	22	D	Lynchwood	Lancaster

[a]Interpolated from data for 1810 and 1830.

DISTRICT 9

County	Aggregate	Slave	%S	sq.mi.	P/sq.mi.	Representative	Cong.	Pty.	Address	County
Fairfield	17,174	7,748	45.1	696	24.7	Starling Tucker	18	(----)	Mt. Shoals	Laurens
Laurens	17,682	4,893	27.6	711	24.9	Starling Tucker	19	(----)	Mt. Shoals	Laurens
Newberry	16,104	5,749	35.7	635	25.4	Starling Tucker	20	(----)	Mt. Shoals	Laurens
TOTALS	50,960	18,390	36.0	2,042	24.9	Starling Tucker	21	(----)	Mt. Shoals	Laurens
						John K. Griffin	22	SRW	Clinton	Laurens

TENNESSEE
9 DISTRICTS
9 CONGRESSMEN

COUNTIES						REPRESENTATIVES				
County	Aggregate	Slave	%S	sq.mi.	P/sq.mi.	Representative	Cong.	Pty.	Address	County

DISTRICT 1

County	Aggregate	Slave	%S	sq.mi.	P/sq.mi.	Representative	Cong.	Pty.	Address	County
Carter	4,835	345	7.1	641	7.5	John Blair	18	D	Jonesboro	Washington
Green	11,324	829	7.3	613	18.5	John Blair	19	D	Jonesboro	Washington
Hawkins	10,949	1,331	12.2	710	15.4	John Blair	20	D	Jonesboro	Washington
Sullivan	7,015	836	11.9	413	17.0	John Blair	21	D	Jonesboro	Washington
Washington	9,557	979	10.2	508	18.8	John Blair	22	D	Jonesboro	Washington
TOTALS	43,680	4,320	9.9	2,885	15.1					

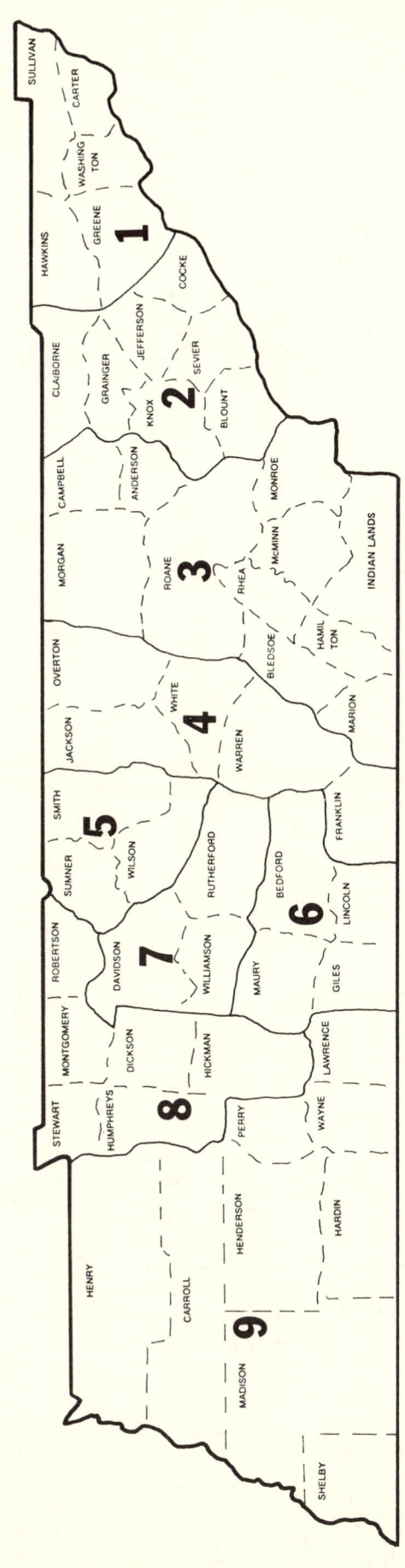

COUNTIES						REPRESENTATIVES				
County	Aggregate	Slave	%S	sq.mi.	P/sq.mi.	Representative	Cong.	Pty.	Address	County
DISTRICT 2										
Blount	11,258	1,050	9.3	575	19.6	John Cocke	18	(----)	Rutledge	Grainger
Claiborne	5,508	377	6.8	556	9.9	John Cocke	19	(----)	Rutledge	Grainger
Cocke	4,892	468	9.6	424	11.5	Pryor Lea	20	JD	Knoxville	Knox
Grainger	7,651	656	8.6	444	17.2	Pryor Lea	21	JD	Knoxville	Knox
Jefferson	8,953	892	10.0	324	27.6	Thomas D. Arnold	22	NR	Campbell	Greene
Knox	13,034	1,825	14.0	508	25.6				Station	
Sevier	4,772	290	6.1	597	8.0					
TOTALS	56,068	5,558	9.9	3,428	16.3					
DISTRICT 3										
Anderson	4,668	349	7.5	335	13.9	James Standifer	18	NR	Pikeville	Bledsoe
Bledsoe	4,005	361	9.0	677	5.9	James C. Mitchell	19	NR	Athens	McMinn
Campbell	4,244	116	2.7	451	9.4	James C. Mitchell	20	NR	Athens	McMinn
Hamilton	821	39	4.8	550	1.5	James Standifer	21	NR	Mountairy	----
McMinn	1,623	153	9.4	432	3.7	James Standifer	22	NR	Mountairy	----
Morgan	1,676	146	2.7	1,273	1.3					
Monroe	2,529	156	6.2	660	3.8					
Morgan	1,676	46	2.7	1,273	1.3					
Rhea	4,215	334	7.9	503	8.4					
Roane	7,895	814	10.3	1,629	4.8					
TOTALS	35,564	2,535	7.1	7,016	5.1					
DISTRICT 4										
Franklin	16,571	4,167	25.1	627	26.4	Jacob C. Isacks	18	(--)	Winchester	Franklin
Jackson	7,593	1,292	17.0	628	12.1	Jacob C. Isacks	19	(----)	Winchester	Franklin
Overton	7,128	665	9.3	914	7.8	Jacob C. Isacks	20	(----)	Winchester	Franklin
Warren	10,348	960	9.2	1,151	9.0	Jacob C. Isacks	21	(----)	Winchester	Franklin
White	8,701	593	6.8	660	13.2	Jacob C. Isacks	22	(----)	Winchester	Franklin
TOTALS	50,341	7,667	15.2	3,980	12.6					
DISTRICT 5										
Smith	17,580	3,554	20.2	741	23.7	Robert Allen	18	D	Carthage	Smith
Sumner	19,211	5,762	30.0	534	36.0	Robert Allen	19	D	Carthage	Smith
Wilson	18,730	3,844	20.5	567	33.0	Robert Desha	20	(----)	Gallatin	Sumner
TOTALS	55,521	13,160	23.7	1,842	30.1	Robert Desha	21	(----)	Gallatin	Sumner
						William Hall	22	D	Green	Sumner
									Garden	
DISTRICT 6										
Bedford	16,012	3,590	22.4	859	18.6	James T. Sandford	18	(----)	Columbia	Maury
Giles	12,558	3,267	26.0	619	20.3	James K. Polk	19	D	Columbia	Maury
Lincoln	14,761	2,250	15.2	640	23.0	James K. Polk	20	D	Columbia	Maury
Maury	22,141	6,420	29.0	614	36.0	James K. Polk	21	D	Columbia	Maury
TOTALS	65,472	15,527	23.7	2,732	24.0	James K. Polk	22	D	Columbia	Maury
DISTRICT 7										
Davidson	20,154	7,899	39.2	813	24.8	Samuel Houston	18	D	Nashville	Davidson
Rutherford	19,557	5,187	26.5	883	22.1	Samuel Houston	19	D	Nashville	Davidson
Williamson	20,640	6,972	33.8	593	34.8	John Bell	20	D	Nashville	Davidson
TOTALS	60,351	20,058	33.2	2,289	26.4	John Bell	21	D	Nashville	Davidson
						John Bell	22	D	Nashville	Davidson

| COUNTIES | | | | | | REPRESENTATIVES | | | | |
| County | Aggregate | Slave | %S | sq.mi. | P/sq.mi. | Representative | Cong. | Pty. | Address | County |

DISTRICT 8

County	Aggregate	Slave	%S	sq.mi.	P/sq.mi.	Representative	Cong.	Pty.	Address	County
Dickson	5,190	1,305	25.1	485	10.7	James B. Reynolds	18	D	Clarksville	Montgomery
Hickman	6,080	700	11.5	895	6.8	John H. Marable	19	NR	Yellow Creek	Montgomery
Humphreys	4,067	542	13.3	731	5.6	John H. Marable	20	NR	Yellow Creek	Montgomery
Montgomery	12,219	4,663	38.2	539	22.7	Cave Johnson	21	D	Clarksville	Montgomery
Robertson	9,938	2,520	25.3	476	20.9	Cave Johnson	22	D	Clarksville	Montgomery
Stewart	8,397	1,282	15.3	470	17.9					
TOTALS	45,891	11,012	23.9	3,596	12.8					

DISTRICT 9

County	Aggregate	Slave	%S	sq.mi.	P/sq.mi.	Representative	Cong.	Pty.	Address	County
Carroll[a]	----	----	----	2,096	----	Adam R. Alexander	18	F	Jackson	Madison
Hardin	1,462	136	9.3	1,256	1.2	Adam R. Alexander	19	F	Jackson	Madison
Henderson[a]	----	----	----	931	----	David Crockett	20	D	Trenton	Gibson
Henry[a]	----	----	----	1,966	----	David Crockett	21	D	Crockett	Gibson
Lawrence	3,271	204	6.2	634	5.2	William Fitzgerald[ce]	22	JD	Dresden	Weakly
Madison[a]	----	----	----	3,573	----	(Election unsuccessfully contested by David Crockett)				
Perry	2,384	223	9.4	411	5.8					
Shelby	354	103	29.1	755	0.5					
Wayne	2,459	72	2.9	739	3.3					
Weakley[a]	----	----	----	----	----					
TOTALS	9,930	738	7.4	12,363	0.8					

[a]Created after 1820 census.

County	Aggregate	Slave	%S	sq.mi.	P/sq.mi.	Representative	Cong.	Pty.	Address	County
		COUNTIES						REPRESENTATIVES		

DISTRICT 1

County	Aggregate	Slave	%S	sq.mi.	P/sq.mi.	Representative	Cong.	Pty.	Address	County
Bennington	16,125	----	----	672	23.9	William C. Bradley	18	D	Westminster	Windham
Towns in Rutland County:[a]						William C. Bradley	19	D	Westminster	Windham
Danby	1,305	----	----	----	----	Jonathan Hunt	20	NR	Brattleboro	Windham
Mt. Tabor	201	----	----	----	----	Jonathan Hunt	21	NR	Brattleboro	Windham
Pawlet	1,882	----	----	----	----	Jonathan Hunt†	22	NR	Brattleboro	Windham
Total, towns	3,388	----	----	111	30.5	(Died May, 1832)				
Windham	28,457	----	----	784	36.2	Hiland Hall	22	NR	Bennington	Bennington
TOTALS	47,970	----	----	1,567	30.6	(Replaced Hunt January, 1833)				

[a]The 1820 census does not list town data for Vermont. The town data used has been calculated on a ratio to the town data in the 1830 census.

DISTRICT 2

County	Aggregate	Slave	%S	sq.mi.	P/sq.mi.	Representative	Cong.	Pty.	Address	County
Addison	20,469	----	----	784	26.0	Rolland C. Mallary	18	(----)	Poultney	Rutland
All of Rutland County, except those towns included in						Rolland C. Mallary	19	(----)	Poultney	Rutland
District 1,						Rolland C. Mallary	20	(----)	Poultney	Rutland
total:	26,595	----	----	816	32.6	Rolland C. Mallary	21	(----)	Poultney	Rutland
TOTALS	47,064	----	----	1,600	29.4	Rolland C. Mallary†	22	(----)	Poultney	Rutland
						(Died April, 1831)				
						William Slade	22	NR	Middlebury	Addison
						(Replaced Mallary December, 1831)				

DISTRICT 3

County	Aggregate	Slave	%S	sq.mi.	P/sq.mi.	Representative	Cong.	Pty.	Address	County
Towns in Orange County:						Charles Rich†[a]	18	(----)	Shoreham	Addison
Braintree	1,093	----	----	----	----	(Died October, 1824)				
Randolph	2,481	----	----	----	----	Henry Olin[a]	18	(----)	Salisbury	Addison
Strafford	1,750	----	----	----	----	(Replaced Rich December, 1824)				
Thetford	1,911	----	----	----	----	George Wales	19	(----)	Hartford	Windsor
Turnbridge	1,736	----	----	----	----	George Wales	20	(----)	Hartford	Windsor
Total, towns	8,971	----	----	138	65.0	Horace Everett	21	NR	Windsor	Windsor
Windsor	38,233	----	----	962	39.7	Horace Everett	22	NR	Windsor	Windsor
TOTALS	56,175	----	----	1,100	51.1					

[a]Rich and Olin were placed in this district by process of elimination.

DISTRICT 4

County	Aggregate	Slave	%S	sq.mi.	P/sq.mi.	Representative	Cong.	Pty.	Address	County
Chittendon	16,055	----	----	520	30.8	Samuel C. Crafts	18	(----)	Craftsbury	Orleans
Franklin	17,192	----	----	755	22.7	Ezra Meech	19	D	Shelburn	Chittendon
Grand Isle	3,527	----	----	83	42.4	Benjamin Swift	20	F	St. Albans	Franklin
Orleans	6,976	----	----	890	7.8	Benjamin Swift	21	F	St. Albans	Franklin
TOTALS	43,750	----	----	2,248	19.5	Herman Allen	22	NR	Burlington	Chittendon

COUNTIES / REPRESENTATIVES — DISTRICT 5

County	Aggregate	Slave	%S	sq.mi.	P/sq.mi.	Representative	Cong.	Pty.	Address	County
Caledonia	16,669	----	----	612	27.2	Daniel A. A. Buck	18	D	Chelsea	Orange
Essex	3,284	----	----	663	4.9	John A. Mattocks	19	(----)	Peacham	Caledonia
All of Orange County, except those towns included in						Daniel A. A. Buck	20	D	Chelsea	Orange
District 3,						William Cahoon	21	AM	Lyndon	Caledonia
total:	15,710	----	----	552	28.5	William Cahoon	22	AM	Lyncon	Caledonia
Washington	14,113	----	----	840	16.8					
TOTALS	49,776	----	----	2,805	17.7					

VIRGINIA
22 DISTRICTS
22 CONGRESSMEN

COUNTIES / REPRESENTATIVES

County	Aggregate	Slave	%S	sq.mi.	P/sq.mi.	Representative	Cong.	Pty.	Address	County
DISTRICT 1										
Elizabeth City	3,789	1,643	43.3	69	54.9	Thomas Newton, Jr.	18	D	Norfolk	Norfolk
Nansemond	10,494	4,526	43.1	408	25.7	Thomas Newton, Jr.	19	NR	Norfolk	Norfolk
Norfolk	15,478	5,924	38.2	394	39.3	Thomas Newton, Jr.	20	NR	Norfolk	Norfolk
Borough of Norfolk	8,478	3,261	38.4	53	159.9	Thomas Newton, Jr.ce	21	NR	Norfolk	Norfolk
						(Election successfully contested by George Loyall)				
Princess Ann	8,768	2,905	33.1	259	33.8	George Loyall	21	JD	Norfolk	Norfolk
TOTALS	47,007	18,259	38.8	1,183	39.7	(Replaced Newton March, 1830)				
						Thomas Newton, Jr.	22	NR	Norfolk	Norfolk
DISTRICT 2										
Greensville	6,858	4,512	65.7	299	22.9	Arthur Smith	18	(----)	Smithfield	Isle of Wight
Isle of Wight	10,139	4,297	42.3	317	31.9	James Trezvant	19	(----)	Jerusalem	Southampton
Prince George	8,030	4,323	53.8	276	29.0	James Trezvant	20	(----)	Jerusalem	Southampton
						James Trezvant	21	(----)	Jerusalem	Southampton
Southampton	14,170	6,734	47.5	602	23.5	John Y. Mason	22	D	Hicksford	Greensville
Surry	6,594	3,340	50.6	277	23.8					
Sussex	11,884	7,045	59.2	494	24.0					
TOTALS	57,675	30,251	52.4	2,265	25.5					
DISTRICT 3										
Amelia	11,104	7,400	66.6	366	30.3	William S. Archer	18	R	Amelia	Amelia
Chesterfield	18,003	8,513	47.2	442	40.7	William S. Archer	19	R	Amelia	Amelia
Nottoway	9,658	6,670	69.1	308	31.4	William S. Archer	20	R	Elk Hill	Amelia
Town of Petersburg	6,690	2,891	43.2	8	836.2	William S. Archer	21	JD	Elk Hill	Amelia
Powhatan	8,292	5,476	66.0	269	30.8	William S. Archer	22	D	Elk Hill	Amelia
TOTALS	53,747	30,950	57.6	1,393	38.6					

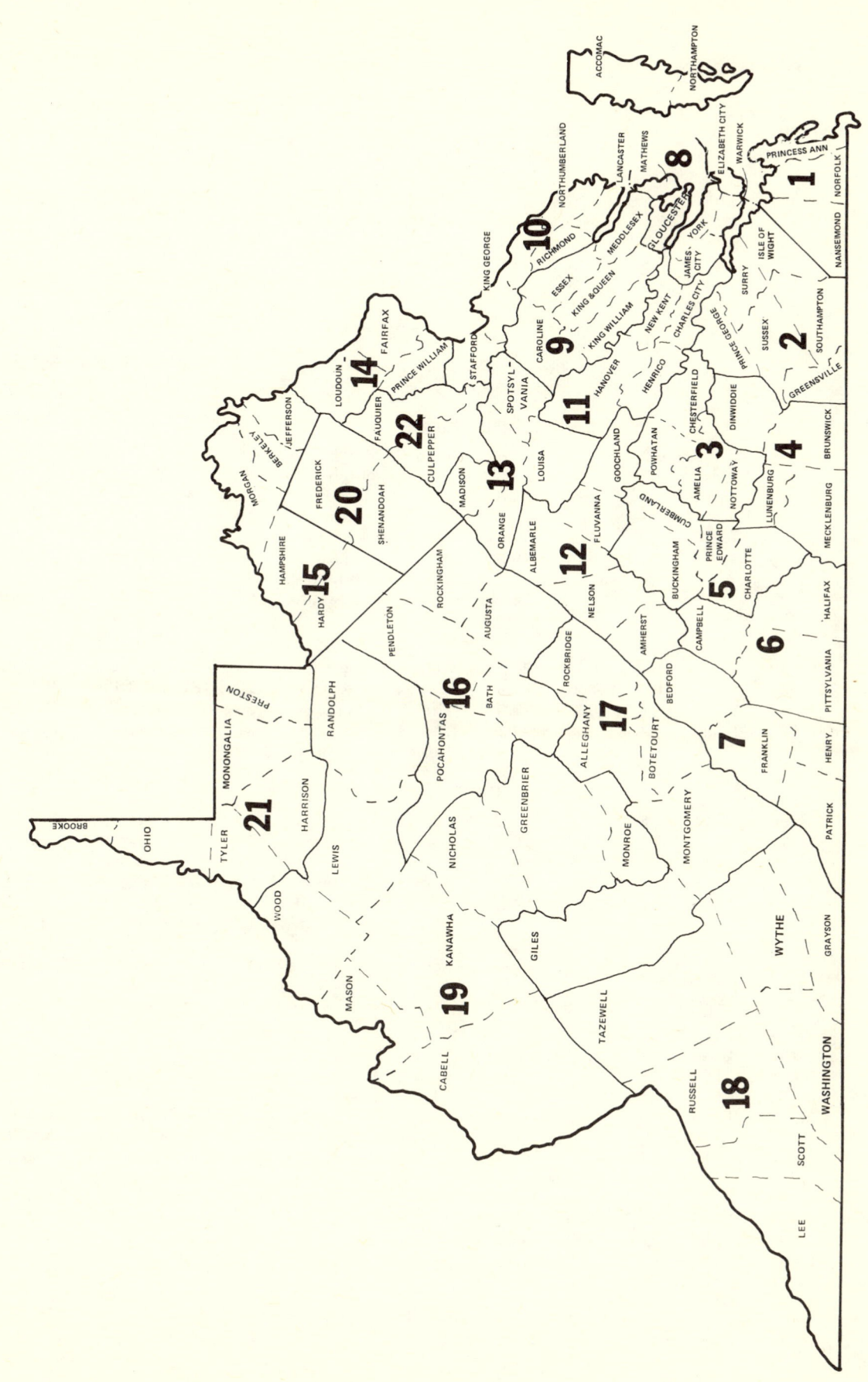

County	Aggregate	Slave	%S	sq.mi.	P/sq.mi.	Representative	Cong.	Pty.	Address	County

COUNTIES — **REPRESENTATIVES**

DISTRICT 4

County	Aggregate	Slave	%S	sq.mi.	P/sq.mi.	Representative	Cong.	Pty.	Address	County
Brunswick	16,687	10,081	60.4	579	28.8	Mark Alexander	18	SRD	"Lombardy Grove"	Mecklenburg
Dinwiddie	13,792	7,751	56.1	507	27.2					
Lunenburg	10,662	6,416	60.2	442	24.1	Mark Alexander	19	SRD	"Lombardy Grove"	Mecklenburg
Mecklenburg	19,786	10,853	54.8	612	32.3					
TOTALS	60,927	35,101	57.6	2,140	28.5	Mark Alexander	20	SRD	"Lombardy Grove"	Mecklenburg
						Mark Alexander	21	SRD	"Lombardy Grove"	Mecklenburg
						Mark Alexander	22	SRD	"Lombardy Grove"	Mecklenburg

DISTRICT 5

County	Aggregate	Slave	%S	sq.mi.	P/sq.mi.	Representative	Cong.	Pty.	Address	County
Buckingham	17,569	9,939	56.6	737	23.8	John Randolph	18	R	Charlotte	Charlotte
Charlotte	13,290	8,094	60.9	470	28.3	John Randolph[r]	19	R	Charlotte	Charlotte
Cumberland	11,023	6,813	61.8	291	37.8	(Resigned December, 1825)				
Prince						George W. Crump	19	JR	Cumberland	Cumberland
Edward	12,577	7,616	60.5	407	30.9	(Replaced Randolph February, 1826)				
TOTALS	54,459	32,462	59.6	1,905	28.6	John Randolph	20	R	Charlotte	Charlotte
						Thomas T. Bouldin	21	D	Charlotte	Charlotte
						Thomas T. Bouldin	22	D	Charlotte	Charlotte

DISTRICT 6

County	Aggregate	Slave	%S	sq.mi.	P/sq.mi.	Representative	Cong.	Pty.	Address	County
Campbell	16,569	7,445	44.9	669	24.8	George Tucker	18	D	Lynchburg	Campbell
Halifax	19,060	9,880	51.8	796	23.9	Thomas Davenport	19	F	Meadville	Halifax
Pittsylvania	21,323	8,484	59.7	1,001	21.3	Thomas Davenport	20	F	Meadville	Halifax
TOTALS	56,952	25,809	45.3	2,466	23.1	Thomas Davenport	21	F	Meadville	Halifax
						Thomas Davenport	22	F	Meadville	Halifax

DISTRICT 7

County	Aggregate	Slave	%S	sq.mi.	P/sq.mi.	Representative	Cong.	Pty.	Address	County
Bedford	19,305	8,041	41.6	727	26.5	Jabez Leftwich	18	(----)	Liberty	Bedford
Franklin	12,017	3,647	30.3	716	16.8	Nathaniel Claiborne	19	R	Rocky Mount	Franklin
Henry	5,624	2,178	38.7	381	14.8					
Patrick	5,089	1,163	22.8	464	10.9	Nathaniel Claiborne	20	R	Rocky Mount	Franklin
TOTALS	42,035	15,029	35.7	2,288	18.3	Nathaniel Claiborne	21	R	Rocky Mount	Franklin
						Nathaniel Claiborne	22	R	Rocky Mount	Franklin

DISTRICT 8

County	Aggregate	Slave	%S	sq.mi.	P/sq.mi.	Representative	Cong.	Pty.	Address	County
Accomack	15,966	4,480	28.1	476	33.5	Burwell Bassett	18	D	Williamsburg	James City
Gloucester	9,678	5,208	53.8	228	42.4	Burwell Bassett	19	D	Williamsburg	James City
James City	3,161	1,677	53.1	152	20.8	Burwell Bassett	20	D	Williamsburg	James City
Mathews	6,920	3,186	46.0	89	77.7	Richard Coke, Jr.	21	JD	Williamsburg	James City
Northampton	7,765	3,323	42.7	220	35.3	Richard Coke, Jr.	22	JD	Williamsburg	James City
Warwick	1,608	954	59.3	75	21.4					
City of Williamsburg	1,402	783	55.8	5	280.4					
York	4,384	2,165	49.3	129	33.9					
TOTALS	50,884	21,776	42.8	1,374	37.0					

| | COUNTIES | | | | | | REPRESENTATIVES | | | |
County	Aggregate	Slave	%S	sq.mi.	P/sq.mi.	Representative	Cong.	Pty.	Address	County

DISTRICT 9

Caroline	18,008	10,999	61.1	545	33.0	Robert S. Garnett	18	D	Lloyds	Essex
Essex	9,909	6,046	61.0	250	39.6	Robert S. Garnett	19	D	Lloyds	Essex
King						John J. Roane	20	D	Rumford	King William
and Queen	11,798	6,041	51.2	318	37.1	John J. Roane	21	D	Rumford	King William
King						John J. Roane	22	D	Rumford	King William
William	9,697	6,010	61.9	278	34.9					
Middlesex	4,057	2,166	53.3	130	31.3					
TOTALS	53,469	31,262	58.5	1,521	35.2					

DISTRICT 10

King George	6,110	3,504	57.3	176	74.7	William L. Ball†	18	D	Nuttsville	Lancaster
Lancaster	5,517	2,944	53.4	137	40.3	(Died February, 1824)				
North-						John Taliaferro	18	D	Fredericks-	King George
umberland	8,016	3,268	40.7	190	42.2	(Replaced Ball March, 1824)			burg	
Richmond	5,706	2,464	43.2	190	30.0	John Taliaferro	19	D	Fredericks-	King George
Stafford	9,517	4,368	45.8	270	35.2				burg	
West-						John Taliaferro	20	D	Fredericks-	King George
moreland	6,901	3,393	49.2	229	30.1				burg	
TOTALS	41,767	19,941	47.7	1,192	35.0	John Taliaferro	21	D	Fredericks-	King George
									burg	
						Joseph W. Chinn	22	D	Nuttsville	Lancaster

DISTRICT 11

Charles City	5,255	2,967	56.5	181	29.0	Andrew Stevenson	18	D	Richmond	Henrico
Hanover	12,267	8,756	57.3	465	32.8	Andrew Stevenson	19	D	Richmond	Henrico
Henrico	11,600	5,417	46.6	229	50.6	Andrew Stevenson	20	D	Richmond	Henrico
New Kent	6,630	3,759	56.6	210	31.6	Andrew Stevenson	21	D	Richmond	Henrico
City of						Andrew Stevenson	22	D	Richmond	Henrico
Richmond	5,706	4,387	76.8	60	95.1					
TOTALS	41,458	25,286	56.8	1,145	36.2					

DISTRICT 12

Albemarle	19,750	10,659	53.9	740	26.7	William C. Rives	18	D	Milton	Albemarle
Amherst	10,423	5,567	53.4	470	22.2	William C. Rives	19	D	Milton	Albemarle
Fluvanna	6,704	3,206	47.8	288	23.3	William C. Rives	20	D	Milton	Albemarle
Goochland	10,007	5,526	55.2	289	34.6	William C. Rivesʳ	21	JD	Milton	Albemarle
Nelson	10,187	5,660	55.6	471	21.6	(Resigned in 1829)				
TOTALS	57,071	30,618	53.6	2,258	25.3	William F. Gordon	21	D	Lindsey's	Albemarle
						(Replaced Rives January, 1830)			Store	
						William F. Gordon	22	D	Lindsey's	Albemarle
									Store	

DISTRICT 13

Louisa	13,746	7,848	57.1	517	26.6	Philip P. Barbour	18	D	Lucketsville	Orange
Madison	8,490	4,612	54.3	327	26.0	Robert Taylor	19	(----)	Orange	Orange
Orange	12,913	7,518	58.2	508	25.4	Philip P. Barbour	20	D	Gordonsville	Orange
Spott-						Philip P. Barbourʳ	21	JD	Gordonsville	Orange
sylvania	14,254	7,724	54.2	409	34.8	(Resigned October, 1830)				
TOTALS	49,403	27,702	56.1	1,761	28.1	John M. Patton	21	D	Fredericks-	Spottsylvania
									burg	
						(Replaced Barbour December, 1830)				
						John M. Patton	22	D	Fredericks-	Spottsylvania
									burg	

COUNTIES						REPRESENTATIVES				
County	Aggregate	Slave	%S	sq.mi.	P/sq.mi.	Representative	Cong.	Pty.	Address	County

DISTRICT 14

Fairfax	11,404	4,173	36.5	399	28.6	Charles F. Mercer	18	D	Aldie	Loudoun
Loudoun	22,702	5,729	25.2	517	43.9	Charles F. Mercer	19	D	Aldie	Loudoun
Prince						Charles F. Mercer	20	D	Aldie	Loudoun
William	9,419	4,380	46.5	347	27.1	Charles F. Mercer	21	D	Leesburg	Loudoun
TOTALS	43,525	14,282	32.8	1,263	34.5	Charles F. Mercer	22	NR	Leesburg	Loudoun

DISTRICT 15

Berkeley	11,211	1,898	16.9	316	35.5	Jesse Stephenson	18	F	Martinsburg	Berkeley
Hampshire	10,889	1,279	11.7	969	11.2	William Armstrong	19	D	Romney	Hampshire
Hardy	5,700	914	16.0	1,063	5.4	William Armstrong	20	D	Romney	Hampshire
Jefferson	13,087	4,136	31.6	211	62.0	William Armstrong	21	D	Romney	Hampshire
Morgan	2,500	98	3.9	233	10.7	William Armstrong	22	D	Romney	Hampshire
TOTALS	43,387	8,325	19.2	2,792	15.5					

DISTRICT 16

Augusta	16,742	3,512	20.9	986	17.0	William McCoy	18	D	Franklin	Pendleton
Bath	5,237	1,202	22.9	956	5.5	William McCoy	19	D	Franklin	Pendleton
Pendleton	4,846	381	7.8	695	7.0	William McCoy	20	D	Franklin	Pendleton
Pocahontas	3,239	46	1.4	943	3.4	William McCoy	21	D	Franklin	Pendleton
Rockingham	14,784	1,871	12.6	865	17.1	William McCoy	22	D	Franklin	Pendleton
TOTALS	44,848	7,012	15.6	4,445	10.1					

DISTRICT 17

Alleghany[a]	----	----	----	----	----	John Floyd	18	D	Newbern	Montgomery
Botetourt	13,589	2,806	20.6	1,590	8.5	John Floyd	19	D	Newbern	Montgomery
Giles	4,521	305	6.7	1,330	3.4	John Floyd	20	D	Newberg	Montgomery
Montgomery	8,733	1,255	14.3	1,105	7.9	Robert Craig	21	D	Montgomery	Montgomery
Rockbridge	11,945	2,612	21.9	601	19.9	Robert Craig	22	D	Montgomery	Montgomery
TOTALS	38,788	6,978	18.0	4,626	8.4					

[a]Created from Botetourt County in 1822.

DISTRICT 18

Grayson	5,598	345	6.1	946	5.9	Alexander Smyth	18	(----)	Wythe	Wythe
Lee	4,256	366	8.5	438	9.7	Benjamin Estil	19	NR	Abingdon	Washington
Russell	5,536	526	9.5	1,223	4.6	Alexander Smyth	20	(----)	Wythe	Wythe
Scott	4,263	258	6.1	950	4.5	Alexander Smyth†	21	(----)	Wythe	Wythe
Tazewell	3,916	463	11.8	2,228	1.8	(Died April, 1830)				
Washington	12,444	1,898	15.2	949	13.1	Joseph Draper	21	(----)	Wythe	Wythe
Wythe	9,692	1,533	15.8	460	21.1	(Replaced Smyth December, 1830)				
TOTALS	45,705	5,389	11.8	7,194	6.4	Charles C. Johnson†	22	(----)	Abingdon	Washington
						(Died June, 1832)				
						Joseph Draper	22	(----)	Wythe	Wythe
						(Replaced Johnson December, 1832)				

| COUNTIES | | | | | | REPRESENTATIVES | | | | |
County	Aggregate	Slave	%S	sq.mi.	P/sq.mi.	Representative	Cong.	Pty.	Address	County

DISTRICT 19

County	Aggregate	Slave	%S	sq.mi.	P/sq.mi.	Representative	Cong.	Pty.	Address	County
Cabell	4,789	392	8.1	2,685	1.8	William Smith	18	(----)	Lewisburg	Greenbrier
Greenbrier	4,507	736	16.3	1,026	4.4	William Smith	19	(----)	Lewisburg	Greenbrier
Kanawha	6,399	1,073	16.7	4,413	1.5	Lewis Maxwell	20	NR	Weston	Lewis
Lewis	4,247	556	13.1	835	5.1	Lewis Maxwell	21	NR	Weston	Lewis
Mason	4,868	593	12.2	1,878	2.6	Lewis Maxwell	22	NR	Weston	Lewis
Monroe	6,620	501	7.6	473	14.0					
Nicholas	1,853	48	2.5	1,193	1.6					
Randolph	2,652	115	4.3	1,457	1.8					
Wood	5,860	852	14.5	1,184	4.9					
TOTALS	41,795	4,866	11.6	15,144	2.8					

DISTRICT 20

County	Aggregate	Slave	%S	sq.mi.	P/sq.mi.	Representative	Cong.	Pty.	Address	County
Frederick	24,706	7,179	29.1	679	36.4	Jared Williams	18	JD	Newton	Frederick
Shenandoah	18,926	1,901	10.0	942	20.1	Alfred H. Powell	19	(----)	Winchester	Frederick
TOTALS	43,632	9,080	20.8	1,621	26.9	Robert Allen	20	D	Mount Jackson	Shenandoah
						Robert Allen	21	D	Mount Jackson	Shenandoah
						Robert Allen	22	D	Mount Jackson	Shenandoah

DISTRICT 21

County	Aggregate	Slave	%S	sq.mi.	P/sq.mi.	Representative	Cong.	Pty.	Address	County
Brooke	6,631	383	5.7	171	38.8	Joseph Johnson	18	D	Bridgeport	Harrison
Harrison	10,932	569	5.2	1,087	10.1	Joseph Johnson	19	D	Bridgeport	Harrison
Monongalia	11,060	375	3.4	755	14.6	Isaac Leffler	20	AR	Wheeling	Ohio
Ohio	9,184	419	4.6	106	86.6	Philip Doddridge	21	(----)	Wellsburg	Brooke
Preston	3,422	80	2.3	645	5.3	Philip Doddridge†	22	(----)	Wellsburg	Brooke
Tyler	2,314	100	4.3	619	3.7	(Died November, 1832)				
TOTALS	43,543	1,926	4.4	3,383	12.9	Joseph Johnson	22	D	Bridgeport	Harrison
						(Replaced Doddridge)				

DISTRICT 22

County	Aggregate	Slave	%S	sq.mi.	P/sq.mi.	Representative	Cong.	Pty.	Address	County
Culpepper	20,944	9,468	45.2	656	31.9	John S. Barbour	18	SRD	Culpepper	Culpepper
Fauquier	22,108	11,167	50.5	660	33.5	John S. Barbour	19	SRD	Culpepper	Culpepper
TOTALS	43,052	20,635	47.9	1,316	32.7	John S. Barbour	20	SRD	Culpepper	Culpepper
						John S. Barbour	21	SRD	Culpepper	Culpepper
						John S. Barbour	22	SRD	Culpepper	Culpepper

8
Congressional Districts

1832–1841
23rd–27th Congresses

	COUNTIES					REPRESENTATIVES				
County	Aggregate	Slave	%S	sq.mi.	P/sq.mi.	Representative	Cong.	Pty.	Address	County

DISTRICT 1

County	Aggregate	Slave	%S	sq.mi.	P/sq.mi.	Representative	Cong.	Pty.	Address	County
Benton[a]	----	----	----	----	----	Clement C. Clay	23	D	Huntsville	Madison
Blount	4,233	330	7.8	1,319	3.2	Reuben Chapman	24	D	Somerville	Morgan
Jackson	12,700	1,264	9.9	1,079	11.8	Reuben Chapman	25	D	Somerville	Morgan
Morgan	9,062	2,894	31.9	690	13.1	Reuben Chapman	26	D	Somerville	Morgan
Randolph[a]	----	----	----	----	----					
St. Clair	5,975	1,154	19.3	640	9.3					
TOTAL	59,960	19,269	32.1	4,531	13.2					

[a]Created after the census from Upper Creek lands

DISTRICT 2

County	Aggregate	Slave	%S	sq.mi.	P/sq.mi.	Representative	Cong.	Pty.	Address	County
Fayette	3,547	512	14.4	1,000	3.5	John McKinley	23	D	Florence	Lauderdale
Franklin	11,078	4,988	45.0	670	16.5	Joshua L. Martin	24	D	Athens	Limestone
Lauderdale	11,871	3,795	32.2	662	17.8	Joshua L. Martin	25	D	Athens	Limestone
Lawrence	14,984	6,556	43.7	685	21.9	David Hubbard	26	SRD	Courtland	Lawrence
Limestone	14,807	6,689	45.2	546	27.1					
Marion	4,058	600	14.8	740	5.5					
Walker	2,202	168	7.6	1,420	1.6					
TOTALS	62,457	23,308	37.3	5,723	10.9					

DISTRICT 3

County	Aggregate	Slave	%S	sq.mi.	P/sq.mi.	Representative	Cong.	Pty.	Address	County
Bibb	6,306	1,192	18.9	939	6.7	Samuel W. Mardis	23	D	Montevallo	Shelby
Greene	15,026	7,420	49.4	1.289	11.6	Joab Lawler	24	W	Mardisville	Talladega
Jefferson	6,855	1,715	25.0	1,115	6.2	Joab Lawler†	25	W	Mardisville	Talladega
Perry	11,490	4,318	37.6	954	12.0	(Died May, 1838)				
Pickens	6,622	1,631	24.6	887	7.5	George W. Crabb	25	W	Tuscaloosa	Tuscaloosa
Sumpter[a]	----	----	----	----	----	(Replaced Lawler December, 1838)				
Talladega[b]	----	----	----	----	----	George W. Crabb	26	W	Tuscaloosa	Tuscaloosa
Tuscaloosa	13,646	4,793	35.1	1,033	13.2					
TOTALS	59,945	21,069	35.1	6,217	9.6					

[a]Created after the census from Choctaw lands.

[b]Created after the census from central portion of Upper Creek lands.

DISTRICT 4

County	Aggregate	Slave	%S	sq.mi.	P/sq.mi.	Representative	Cong.	Pty.	Address	County
Antauga	11,874	5,990	50.4	773	15.4	Dixon H. Lewis	23	SRD	Lowndesboro	Lowndes
Barbour[a]	----	----	----	----	----	Dixon H. Lewis	24	SRD	Lowndesboro	Lowndes
Butler	5,650	1,739	30.8	1,334	5.0	Dixon H. Lewis	25	SRD	Lowndesboro	Lowndes
Chambers[a]	----	----	----	----	----	Dixon H. Lewis	26	SRD	Lowndesboro	Lowndes
Conecuh	7,108	1,878	26.4	1,714	4.1					
Covington	1,522	396	26.0	984	1.5					
Dale	2,031	269	13.2	2,024	1.0					
Henry	4,020	1,009	25.1	946	4.2					
Loundes	9,410	4,388	46.6	715	13.2					
Macon[a]	----	----	----	----	----					

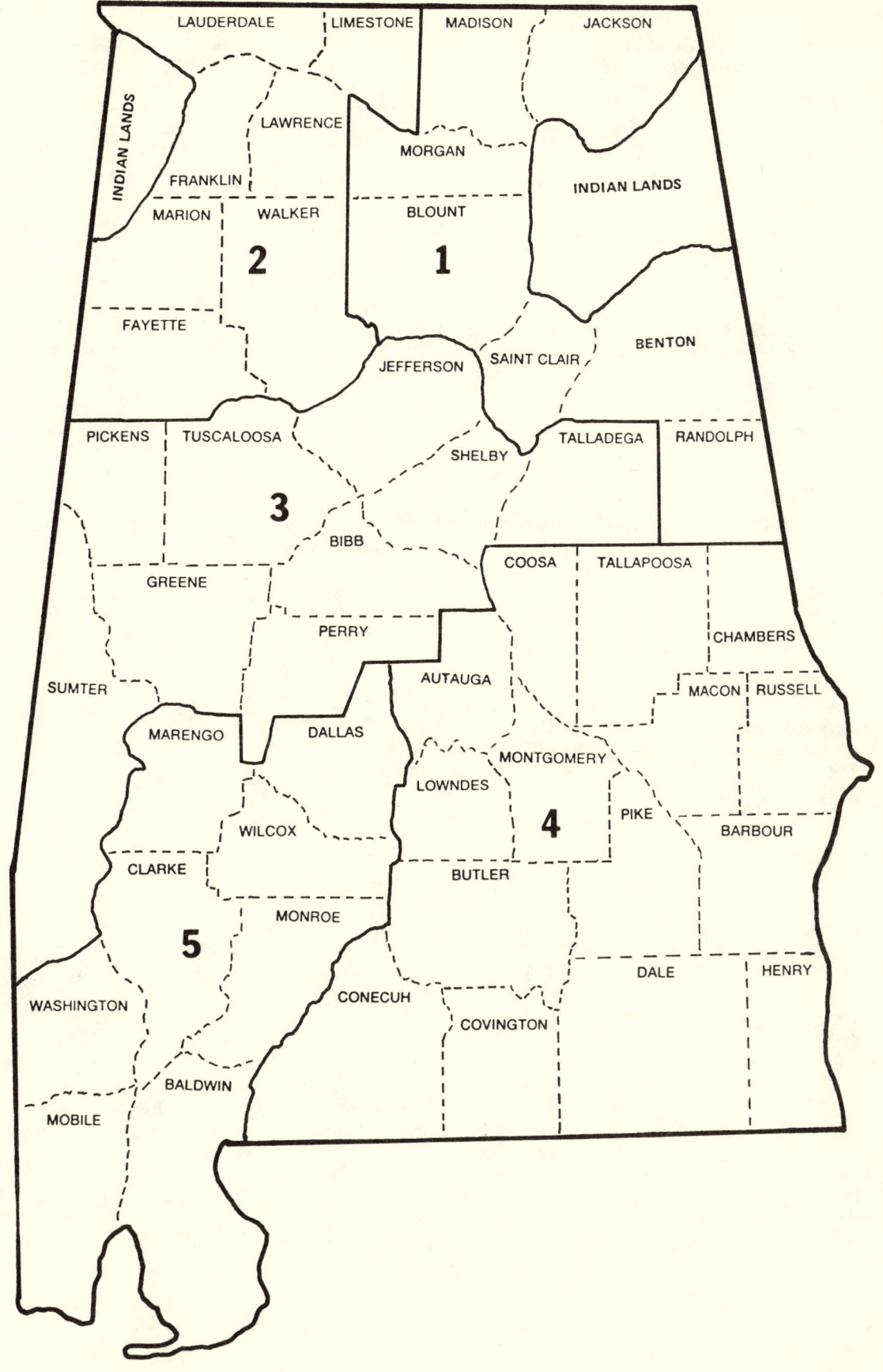

COUNTIES						REPRESENTATIVES				
County	Aggregate	Slave	%S	sq.mi.	P/sq.mi.	Representative	Cong.	Pty.	Address	County
						DISTRICT 4 (CONTINUED)				
Montgomery	12,695	6,450	50.8	840	15.1					
Pike	7,108	1,878	26.4	1,500	4.7					
Russell[a]	----	----	----	----	----					
Tallapoosa[a]	----	----	----	----	----					
TOTALS	61,418	23,997	39.1	10,830	5.7					

[a]Created after the census from southern half of Upper Creek lands.

				DISTRICT 5						
Baldwin	2,324	1,263	54.3	1,677	1.4	John Murphy	23	D	Claiborne	Mobile
Clarke	7,595	3,672	48.3	1,232	6.2	Francis S. Lynn	24	W	Demopolis	Marengo
Dallas	14,017	7,160	51.1	976	14.4	Francis S. Lynn	25	W	Demopolis	Marengo
Marengo	7,700	3,138	40.7	978	7.9	James Dellet	26	W	Claiborne	Mobile
Mobile	6,267	1,106	17.6	1,240	5.0					
Monroe	8,782	3,541	40.3	1,032	8.5					
Washington	3,474	1,532	44.1	986	3.5					
Wilcox	9,548	3,990	41.8	899	10.6					
TOTALS	59,707	24,402	42.5	9,020	6.6					

AT LARGE: TWENTY-SEVENTH CONGRESS

Representative	Cong.	Pty.	Address	County
Reuben Chapman	27	D	Somerville	Morgan
George Houston	27	D	Athens	Limestone
Dixon Lewis	27	D	Lowndesboro	Lowndes
William Winter Payne	27	D	Gainesville	Sumter
Benjamin Glover Shields	27	D	Demopolis	Marengo

[1]Elections were held by districts for the Twenty-third through Twenty-sixth Congresses, and at large for the Twenty-seventh Congress.

COUNTIES						REPRESENTATIVES				
County	Aggregate	Slave	%S	sq.mi.	P/sq.mi.	Representative	Cong.	Pty.	Address	County
						AT LARGE				
Arkansas	1,426	369	25.8	3,427	0.4		23[a]			
Chicot	1,165	270	23.1	1,753	0.7	Archibald Yell	24	VBD	Fayetteville	Washington
Clark	1,369	106	7.7	2,751	0.5	(Took seat December 5, 1836)				
Conway	982	87	8.8	2,525	0.4	Archibald Yell	25	VBD	Fayetteville	Washington
Crawford	2,440	622	25.4	2,166	1.1	Edward Cross	26	D	Washington	Hempstead
Crittenden	1,272	490	38.5	1,512	0.8	Edward Cross	27	D	Washington	Hempstead
Hempstead	2,512	522	20.7	1,542	1.6					
Hot Springs	458	52	11.3	2,813	0.2					
Independence	2,031	303	14.9	772	2.6					
Izard	1,266	57	4.5	4,491	0.3					

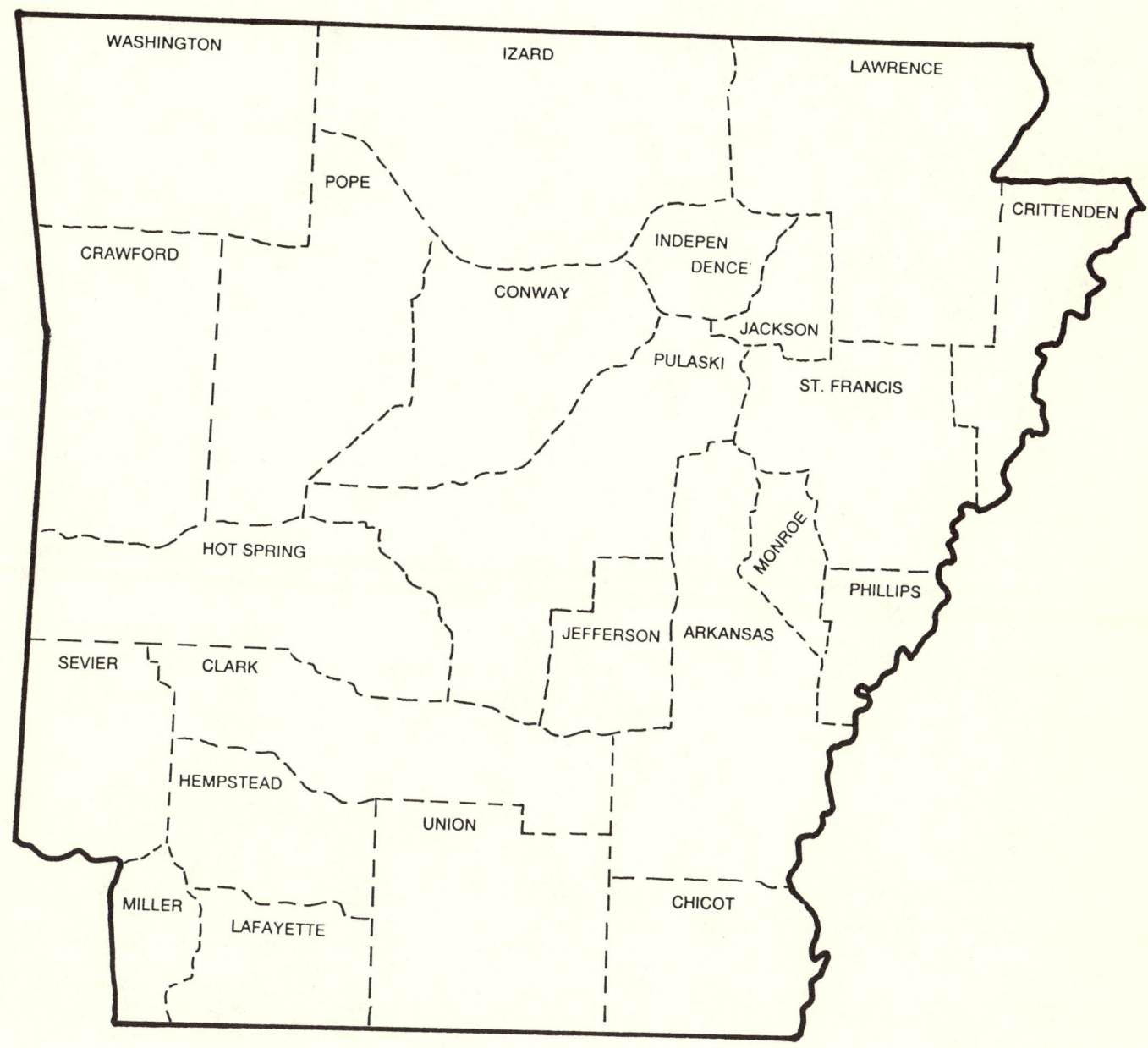

| COUNTIES | | | | | | REPRESENTATIVES | | | | |
County	Aggregate	Slave	%S	sq.mi.	P/sq.mi.	Representative	Cong.	Pty.	Address	County

AT LARGE (CONTINUED)

County	Aggregate	Slave	%S	sq.mi.	P/sq.mi.
Jackson	333	17	5.1	629	0.5
Jefferson	772	160	20.7	1,113	0.7
LaFayette	748	340	45.4	1,291	0.6
Lawrence	2,806	325	11.5	4,221	0.7
Miller	356	55	15.4	623	0.6
Monroe	461	75	16.2	627	0.7
Phillips	1,152	127	11.0	686	1.7
Pope	1,483	211	14.2	3,259	0.5
Pulaski	2,395	439	18.3	4,149	0.6
St. Frances	1,505	626	41.5	2,439	0.6
Sevier	634	66	10.4	1,677	0.4
Union	640	174	27.1	3,016	0.2
TOTALS	30,388	5,663	18.6	51,053	0.6

[a]Arkansas was not represented in the Twenty-third Congress.

[1]Arkansas became a state June 15, 1836.

CONNECTICUT
6 DISTRICTS/AT LARGE[1]
6 CONGRESSMEN

| COUNTIES | | | | | | REPRESENTATIVES | | | | |
County	Aggregate	Slave	%S	sq.mi.	P/sq.mi.	Representative	Cong.	Pty.	Address	County

AT LARGE: TWENTY-THIRD AND TWENTY-FOURTH CONGRESSES

Representative	Cong.	Pty.	Address	County
Noyes Barber	23	W	Groton	New London
William W. Ellsworth[r] (Resigned July, 1834)	23	W	Hartford	Hartford
Joseph Trumbull (Replaced Ellsworth December, 1834)	23	W	Hartford	Hartford
Samuel A. Foote[r] (Resigned May, 1834)	23	W	Cheshire	New Haven
Ebenezer Jackson, Jr. (Replaced Foote December, 1834)	23	W	Middletown	Middlesex
Jabez W. Huntington[r] (Resigned August, 1834)	23	W	Litchfield	Litchfield
Phineas Miner (Replaced Huntington December, 1834)	23	W	Litchfield	Litchfield
Samuel Tweedy	23	W	Danbury	Fairfield
Ebenezer Young	23	W	Killingly Center	Windham

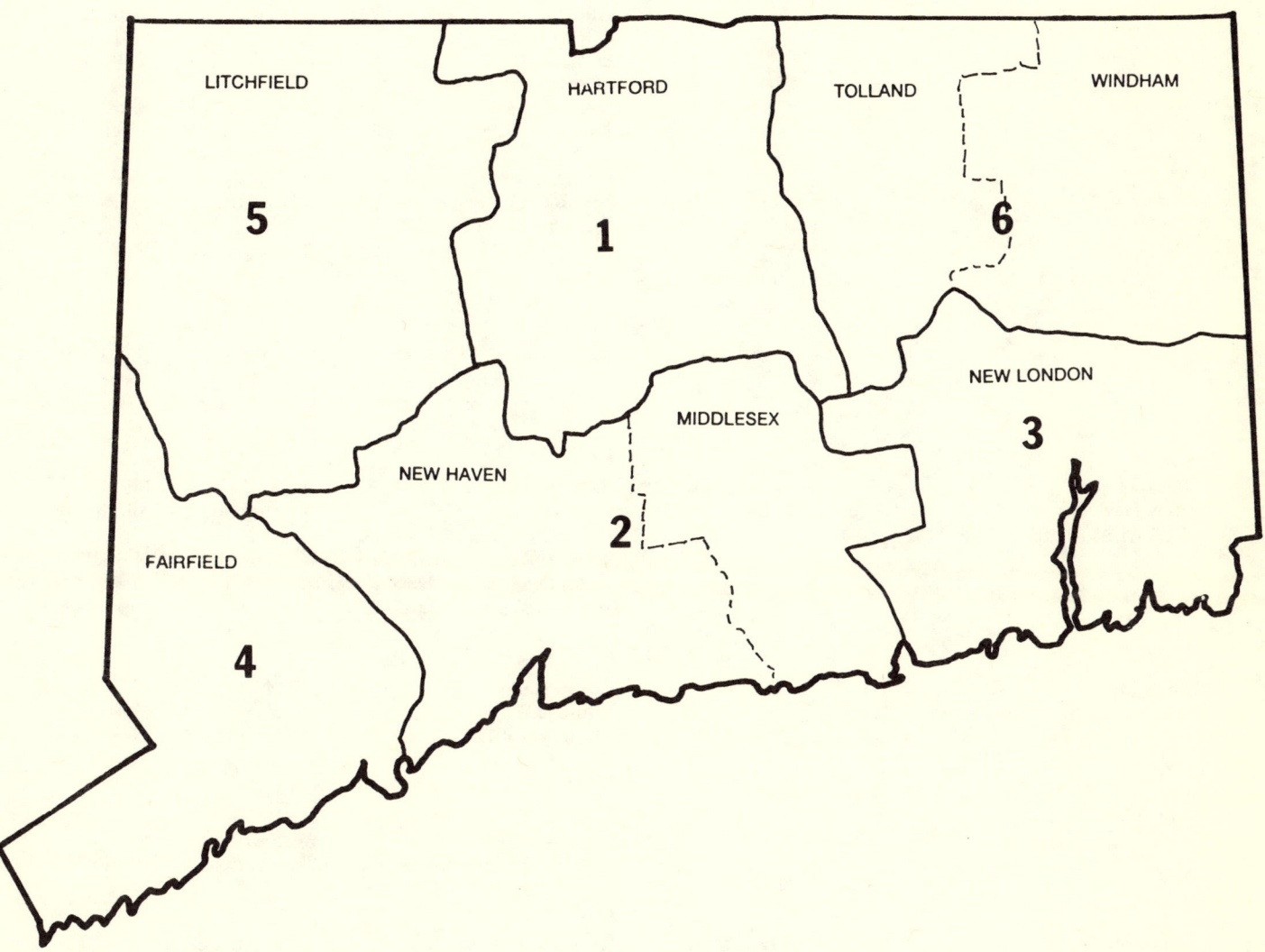

COUNTIES						REPRESENTATIVES				
County	Aggregate	Slave	%S	sq.mi.	P/sq.mi.	Representative	Cong.	Pty.	Address	County

AT LARGE: TWENTY-THIRD AND TWENTY-FOURTH CONGRESSES (CONTINUED)

County	Aggregate	Slave	%S	sq.mi.	P/sq.mi.	Representative	Cong.	Pty.	Address	County
						Elisha Haley	24	D	Mystic	New London
						Andrew T. Judson[r]	24	D	Canterbury	Windham
						(Resigned July, 1836)				
						Orrin Holt	24	D	Willington	Tolland
						(Replaced Judson December, 1836)				
						Samuel Ingham	24	D	Waybrook	Middlesex
						Lancelot Phelps	24	D	Hitchcock-ville	Litchfield
						Isaac Toucey	24	D	Hartford	Hartford
						Zalmon Wildman[†]	24	D	Danbury	Fairfield
						(Died December, 1835)				
						Thomas T. Whittlesey	24	D	Danbury	Fairfield
						(Replaced Wildman April, 1836)				

DISTRICT 1

County	Aggregate	Slave	%S	sq.mi.	P/sq.mi.	Representative	Cong.	Pty.	Address	County
Hartford	51,131	1	----	739	69.2	Isaac Toucey	25	D	Hartford	Hartford
						Joseph Trumbull	26	W	Hartford	Hartford
						Joseph Trumbull	27	W	Hartford	Hartford

DISTRICT 2

County	Aggregate	Slave	%S	sq.mi.	P/sq.mi.	Representative	Cong.	Pty.	Address	County
Middlesex	24,844	2	----	372	67.1	Samuel Ingham	25	D	Saybrook	Middlesex
New Haven	43,847	9	----	604	72.6	William Storrs[r]	26	W	Middletown	Middlesex
TOTALS	68,691	11	----	976	70.4	(Resigned July, 1840)				
						William W. Boardman	26	W	New Haven	New Haven
						(Replaced Storrs December, 1840)				
						William W. Boardman	27	W	New Haven	New Haven

DISTRICT 3

County	Aggregate	Slave	%S	sq.mi.	P/sq.mi.	Representative	Cong.	Pty.	Address	County
New London	42,201	2	----	667	63.3	Elisha Haley	25	D	Mystic	New London
						Thomas Williams	26	W	New London	New London
						Thomas Williams	27	W	New London	New London

DISTRICT 4

County	Aggregate	Slave	%S	sq.mi.	P/sq.mi.	Representative	Cong.	Pty.	Address	County
Fairfield	47,010	8	----	626	75.0	Thomas Whittlesey	25	D	Danbury	Fairfield
						Thomas B. Osborne	26	W	Fairfield	Fairfield
						Thomas B. Osborne	27	W	Fairfield	Fairfield

DISTRICT 5

County	Aggregate	Slave	%S	sq.mi.	P/sq.mi.	Representative	Cong.	Pty.	Address	County
Litchfield	42,858	2	----	925	46.3	Lancelot Phelps	25	D	Hitchcock-ville	Litchfield
						Truman Smith	26	W	Litchfield	Litchfield
						Truman Smith	27	W	Litchfield	Litchfield

DISTRICT 6

County	Aggregate	Slave	%S	sq.mi.	P/sq.mi.	Representative	Cong.	Pty.	Address	County
Tolland	18,702	1	----	416	44.9	Orrin Holt	25	D	Willington	Tolland
Windham	27,082	----	----	514	52.7	John H. Brockway	26	W	Ellington	Tolland
TOTALS	45,784	1	----	930	49.2	John H. Brockway	27	W	Ellington	Tolland

COUNTIES						REPRESENTATIVES				
County	Aggregate	Slave	%S	sq.mi.	P/sq.mi.	Representative	Cong.	Pty.	Address	County
					AT LARGE					
Kent	19,913	588	29.5	594	33.5	John J. Milligan	23	W	Wilmington	Newcastle
Newcastle	29,720	786	2.6	438	67.8	John J. Milligan	24	W	Wilmington	Newcastle
Sussex	27,115	1,918	7.0	950	28.5	John J. Milligan	25	W	Wilmington	Newcastle
TOTALS	76,748	3,292	4.3	1,982	39.7	Thomas Robinson, Jr.	26	D	Georgetown	Sussex
						George R. Rodney	27	W	New Castle	Newcastle

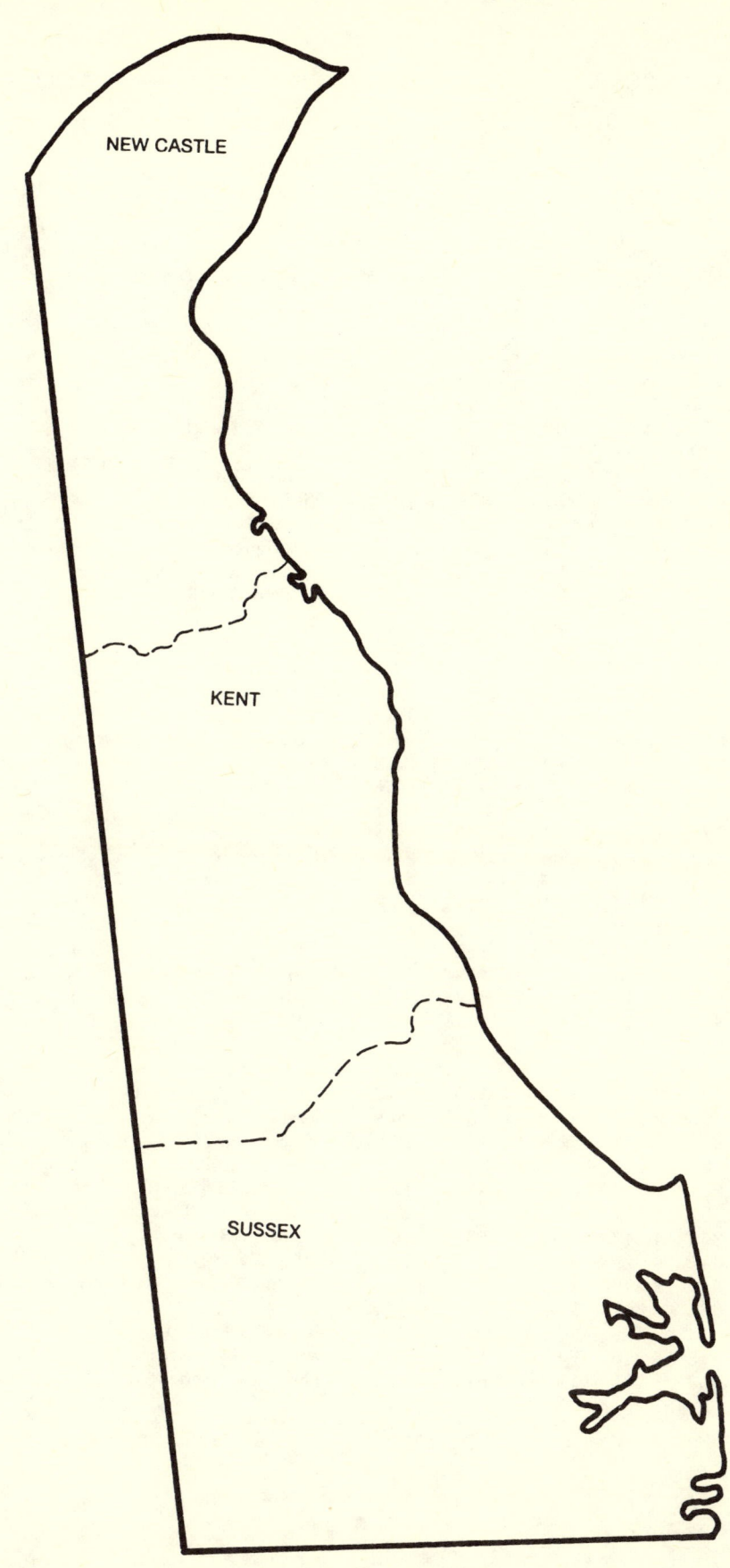

COUNTIES						REPRESENTATIVES				
County	Aggregate	Slave	%S	sq.mi.	P/sq.mi.	Representative	Cong.	Pty.	Address	County

AT LARGE

County	Aggregate	Slave	%S	sq.mi.	P/sq.mi.	Representative	Cong.	Pty.	Address	County
Appling	1,468	179	12.1	1,327	1.1	Augustin S. Clayton	23	SRD	Athens	Clark
Baker	1,253	454	36.2	1,435	0.9	John Coffee	23	D	Jacksonville	Telfair
Baldwin	7,295	4,542	62.2	255	28.6	Thomas F. Foster	23	D	Greenboro	Greene
Bibb	7,154	2,988	41.7	254	28.2	Roger L. Gamble	23	D	Louisville	Jefferson
Bryan	3,139	2,402	76.5	443	7.1	George R. Gilmer*	23	W	Lexington	Oglethorpe
Bulloch	2,587	650	25.1	935	2.8	Seaborn Jones	23	D	Columbus	Muscogee
Burke	11,833	6,641	56.1	831	14.2	William Schley	23	D	Augusta	Richmond
Butts	4,944	1,883	38.0	185	26.8	James M. Wayner	23	D	Savannah	Chatham
Camden	4,578	3,086	67.4	1,187	19.9	(Resigned January 13, 1835; not replaced until the Twenty-				
Campbell	3,323	613	18.4	230	14.4	fourth Congress)				
Carroll	3,419	487	14.2	770	4.4	Richard H. Wilde	23	D	Augusta	Richmond
Chatham	14,127	9,478	67.0	445	31.7					
Clarke	10,176	4,709	46.2	302	33.7	John Coffee†	24	D	Jacksonville	Telfair
Columbia	12,606	8,032	63.7	543	23.2	(Died September 25, 1835; news of his death did not reach				
Coweta	5,003	1,372	27.4	442	11.3	the voters before the election)				
Crawford	5,313	1,718	32.3	315	16.9	William C. Dawson	24	W	Greensboro	Greene
Decatur	3,854	1,308	33.9	821	4.7	(Replaced Coffee November 7, 1835)				
DeKalb	10,042	1,648	16.4	369	27.2	Seaton Grantland	24	D	Milledge-	Baldwin
Dooly	2,135	336	15.7	1,329	1.6				ville	
Early	2,051	490	23.8	954	2.1	Charles E. Haynes	24	D	Sparta	Hancock
Effingham	2,924	1,212	41.4	480	6.1	Jabez Y. Jackson	24	D	Clarkesville	Habersham
Elbert	12,354	5,765	46.6	358	34.5	(Elected to fill vacancy created by the resignation of J. Wayne				
Emanuel	2,673	465	17.3	1,037	2.6	in the Twenty-third Congress)				
Fayette	5,504	1,192	21.6	348	15.8	George W. Owens	24	D	Savannah	Chatham
Franklin	10,107	2,370	23.4	898	11.2	John W. A. Sanfordr	24	D	Milledge-	Baldwin
Glyn	4,567	3,968	86.8	412	11.1	(Resigned July 25, 1835)			ville	
Greene	12,549	7,475	59.5	403	31.1	Thomas Glascock	24	D	Augusta	Richmond
Gwinnett	13,289	2,334	17.5	437	30.4	(Replaced Sanford October 5, 1835)				
Habersham	10,671	909	8.5	525	20.3	William Schleyr	24	D	Augusta	Richmond
Hall	11,748	1,181	10.0	378	31.1	(Resigned July 1, 1835)				
Hancock	11,820	7,180	60.7	478	24.7	Jesse F. Cleveland	24	D	Decatur	DeKalb
Harris	5,105	2,269	44.4	465	10.9	(Replaced Schley October 5, 1835)				
Henry	10,566	2,571	24.3	532	19.9	James C. Terrellr	24	D	Carnesville	Franklin
Houston	7,369	2,193	29.7	711	10.4	(Resigned July 8, 1835)				
Irwin	1,180	110	9.3	2,036	0.6	Hopkins Holsey	24	D	Hamilton	Harris
Jackson	9,004	2,747	30.5	517	17.4	(Replaced Terrell October 5, 1835)				
Jasper	13,131	6,327	48.1	373	35.2	George W. B. Townsr	24	D	Talbotten	Talbot
Jefferson	7,309	4,147	56.7	530	13.8	(Resigned September 1, 1836)				
Jones	13,345	6,829	51.1	402	33.2	Julius C. Alford	24	W	Lagrange	Troup
Laurens	5,589	2,375	42.2	1,123	5.0	(Replaced Towns January 2, 1837)				
Lee	1,680	311	18.5	355	4.7					
Liberty	7,233	5,624	77.7	916	7.9	Jesse F. Cleveland	25	D	Decatur	DeKalb
Lincoln	6,145	3,276	53.3	193	31.8	William C. Dawson	25	W	Greensboro	Greene
Loundes	2,453	335	13.6	2,671	0.9	Thomas Glascock	25	D	Augusta	Richmond

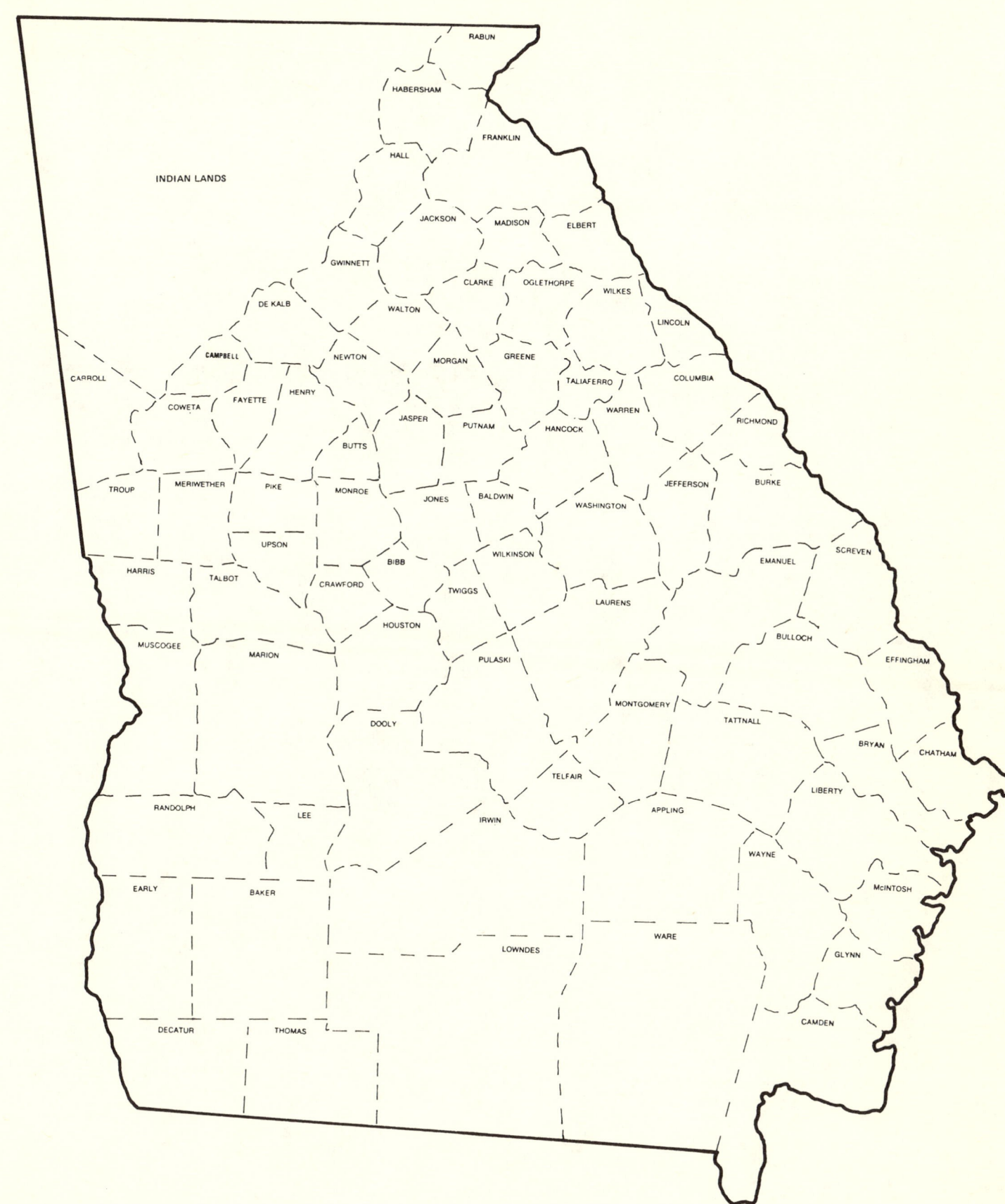

	COUNTIES					REPRESENTATIVES				
County	Aggregate	Slave	%S	sq.mi.	P/sq.mi.	Representative	Cong.	Pty.	Address	County

AT LARGE (CONTINUED)

County	Aggregate	Slave	%S	sq.mi.	P/sq.mi.	Representative	Cong.	Pty.	Address	County
Madison	4,646	1,259	27.0	281	16.5	Seaton Grantland	25	D	Milledge-ville	Baldwin
McIntosh	4,998	3,794	75.9	426	11.7					
Marion	1,436	109	7.5	1,610	0.9	Charles E. Haynes	25	D	Sparta	Hancock
Meriwether	4,422	1,349	31.5	499	8.9	Hopkins Holsey	25	D	Hamilton	Harris
Monroe	16,202	7,353	45.3	489	33.1	Jabez Jackson	25	D	Clarkesville	Habersham
Montgomery	1,269	335	26.3	737	1.7	George W. Owens	25	D	Savannah	Chatham
Morgan	12,046	7,155	59.3	356	33.8	George W. B. Towns	25	D	Talbotten	Talbot
Muscogee	3,508	1,240	35.3	925	3.8					
Newton	11,155	3,003	26.9	399	28.0	Julius C. Alford	26	W	Lagrange	Troup
Oglethorpe	13,618	7,940	58.3	435	31.1	Edward J. Black	26	W	Jacksonboro	Scriven
Pike	6,149	1,773	28.8	320	19.2	Walter T. Colquitt[r]	26	W	Columbus	Muscogee
Pulaski	4,906	1,765	35.9	970	5.1	(Resigned July 21, 1840)				
Putnam	13,261	7,707	58.1	339	39.1	Hines Holt	26	W	Columbus	Muscogee
Rabun	2,176	59	2.7	368	5.9	(Replaced Colquitt February 1, 1841)				
Randolph	2,191	682	31.1	1,071	2.0	Mark A. Cooper	26	W	Columbus	Muscogee
Richmond	11,644	6,246	53.6	323	36.0	William C. Dawson	26	W	Greensboro	Greene
Scriven	4,776	2,365	49.5	651	7.3	Richard W. Habersham	26	W	Clarkesville	Habersham
Talbot	5,940	1,799	30.2	593	7.3	Thomas Butler King	26	W	Waynesville	Wayne
Taliaferro	4,934	2,735	55.4	195	25.3	Eugenius A. Nisbet	26	W	Macon	Bibb
Tattnal	2,040	506	24.8	1,044	2.0	Lott Warren	26	W	Palmyra	----
Telfair	2,136	565	26.4	440	4.9					
Thomas	3,299	958	29.0	1,007	3.8	Julius C. Alford[r]	27	W	Lagrange	Troup
Troup	5,799	2,187	37.7	415	14.0	(Resigned October 1, 1841)				
Twiggs	8,031	3,561	44.3	364	22.1	Edward J. Black	27	D	Jacksonboro	Scriven
Upson	7,013	2,557	36.4	354	19.8	(Elected January 3, 1842 to fill in part vacancies created by				
Walton	10,929	3,163	28.9	330	33.1	the resignations of Alford, Dawson, and Nisbet)				
Ware	1,205	61	5.0	3,035	0.4	William C. Dawson[r]	27	W	Greensboro	Greene
Warren	10,946	4,693	42.8	427	25.6	(Resigned November 14, 1841)				
Washington	9,820	3,909	39.8	674	14.6	Walter T. Colquitt	27	D	Columbus	Muscogee
Wayne	963	276	28.6	914	1.1	(Elected January 3, 1842 to fill in part vacancies created by				
Wilkes	14,237	8,960	62.9	468	30.4	resignations of Alford, Dawson, and Nisbet)				
Wilkinson	6,513	1,922	29.5	458	14.2	Thomas F. Foster	27	W	Columbus	Muscogee
TOTALS	516,823	221,240	42.8	50,867	10.2	Roger L. Gamble	27	W	Louisville	Jefferson
						Richard W. Habersham[†]	27	W	Clarkesville	Habersham
						(Died December 2, 1842)				
						George W. Crawford	27	W	Augusta	Richmond
						(Replaced Habersham January 7, 1843)				
						Thomas Butler King	27	W	Waynesville	Wayne
						James A. Merriweather	27	W	Edenton	Putnam
						Eugenius A. Nisbet[r]	27	W	Macon	Bibb
						(Resigned October 12, 1841)				
						Mark A. Cooper	27	D	Columbus	Muscogee
						(Elected January 3, 1842 to fill in part vacancies created by				
						the resignations of Alford, Dawson, and Nisbet)				

| COUNTIES | | | | | | REPRESENTATIVES | | | | |
| County | Aggregate | Slave | %S | sq.mi. | P/sq.mi. | Representative | Cong. | Pty. | Address | County |

DISTRICT 1

County	Aggregate	Slave	%S	sq.mi.	P/sq.mi.	Representative	Cong.	Pty.	Address	County
Alexander	1,390	6	0.4	373	3.7	Charles Slade†	23	D	Carlyle	St. Clair
Bond	3,124	----	----	378	8.3	(Died July, 1834)				
Clinton	2,330	4	0.2	434	5.4	John Reynolds	23	D	Belleville	St. Clair
Franklin	4,083	9	----	863	4.7	(Replaced Slade December, 1834)				
Gallatin	7,405	184	2.4	794	9.3	John Reynolds	24	D	Belleville	St. Clair
Jackson	1,828	21	----	605	3.0	Adam Snyder	25	VBD	Belleville	St. Clair
Johnson	1,596	11	0.6	549	3.6	John Reynolds	26	D	Cadiz	St. Clair
Macoupin	1,990	----	----	872	2.3	John Reynolds	27	D	Belleville	St. Clair
Madison	6,221	24	0.4	733	8.5					
Monroe	2,000	38	1.9	382	5.2					
Perry	1,215	4	0.3	439	2.8					
Pope	3,316	25	0.8	624	5.3					
Randolph	4,429	211	4.7	594	7.5					
St. Clair	7,078	96	1.3	673	10.5					
Union	3,239	4	----	416	7.8					
Washington	1,675	13	0.8	564	2.9					
TOTALS	52,919	646	1.2	9,293	5.7					

DISTRICT 2

County	Aggregate	Slave	%S	sq.mi.	P/sq.mi.	Representative	Cong.	Pty.	Address	County
Clark	3,940	----	----	505	7.8	Zadoc Casey	23	D	Mt. Vernon	Jefferson
Clay	755	1	0.1	464	1.6	Zadoc Casey	24	D	Mt. Vernon	Jefferson
Coles[a]	----	----	----	1,273	----	Zadoc Casey	25	D	Mt. Vernon	Jefferson
Crawford	3,117	----	----	443	7.0	Zadoc Casey	26	D	Mt. Vernon	Jefferson
Edgar	4,071	----	----	628	6.5	Zadoc Casey	27	D	Mt. Vernon	Jefferson
Edwards	1,649	----	----	225	7.3					
Fayette	2,704	24	0.9	703	3.8					
Hamilton	2,616	2	0.1	435	6.0					
Jefferson	2,555	----	----	573	4.5					
Lawrence	3,668	----	----	738	5.0					
Marion	2,125	1	----	579	3.7					
Montgomery	2,953	4	----	981	3.0					
Shelby	2,972	1	----	1,120	2.6					
Vermilion	5,836	----	----	4,979	1.2					
Wabash	2,710	----	----	222	12.2					
Wayne	2,553	3	0.1	715	3.6					
White	6,091	----	----	502	12.1					
TOTALS	50,315	36	----	15,085	3.3					

[a]Created after 1830 census.

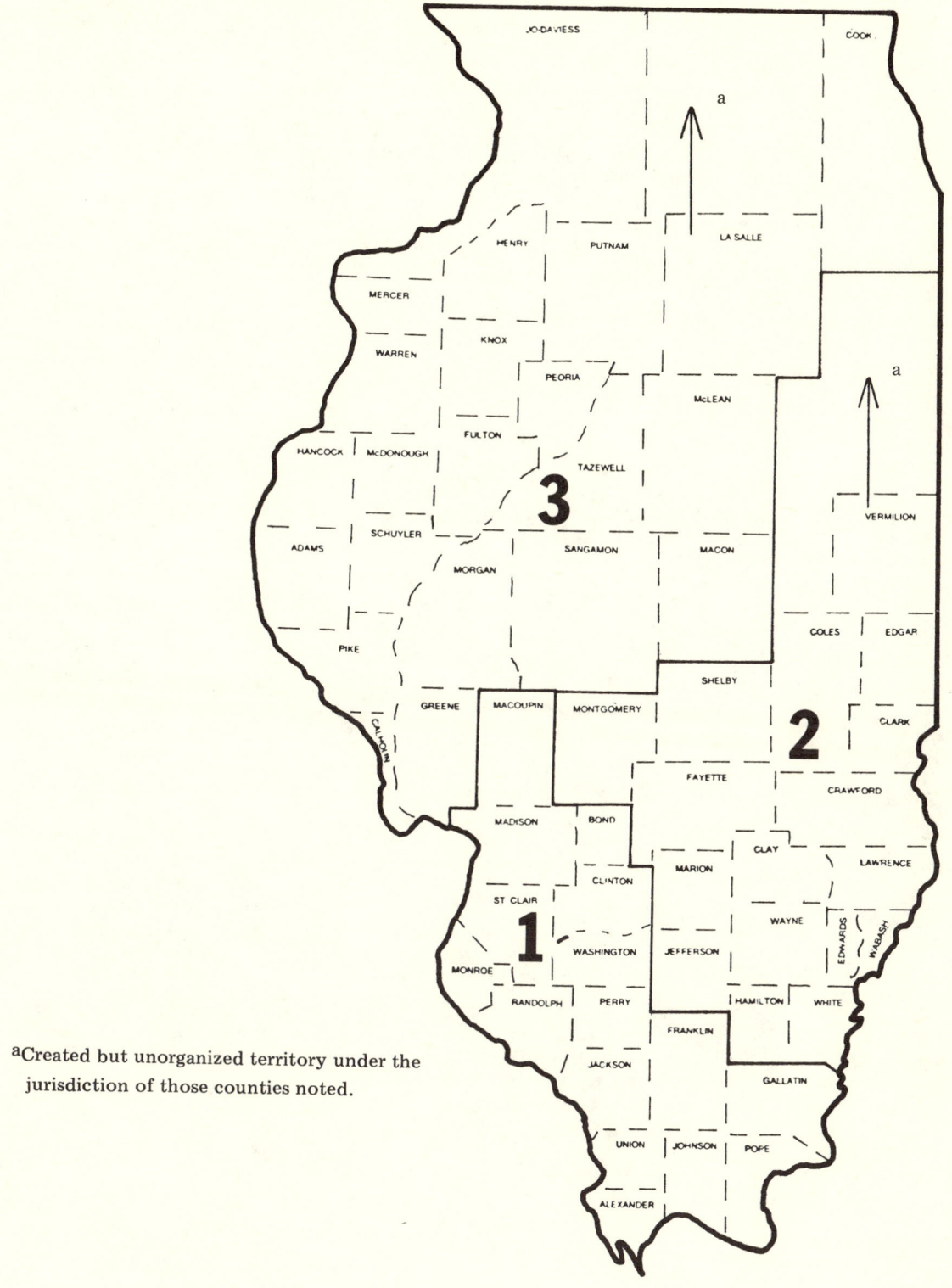

| | COUNTIES | | | | | REPRESENTATIVES | | | | |
| County | Aggregate | Slave | %S | sq.mi. | P/sq.mi. | Representative | Cong. | Pty. | Address | County |

DISTRICT 3

County	Aggregate	Slave	%S	sq.mi.	P/sq.mi.	Representative	Cong.	Pty.	Address	County
Adams	2,816	----	----	862	3.3	Joseph Duncan[r]	23	D	Jacksonville	Morgan
Calhoun	1,090	----	----	247	2.4	(Resigned September 21, 1834, having been elected Governor)				
Cook[a]	----	----	----	2,360	----	William L. May	23	D	Springfield	Sangamon
Fulton	1,841	----	----	877	2.1	(Replaced Duncan December, 1834)				
Greene	7,674	9	0.1	919	8.4	William L. May	24	D	Springfield	Sangamon
Hancock	483	----	----	797	0.6	William L. May	25	D	Springfield	Sangamon
Henry	41	----	----	856	0.1	John T. Stuart	26	W	Springfield	Sangamon
Jo Daviess	2,111	31	1.4	3,153	0.7	John T. Stuart	27	W	Springfield	Sangamon
Knox	274	----	----	778	0.4					
LaSalle[a]	----	----	----	5,940	----					
Macon	1,122	----	----	1,402	0.8					
McDonough[b]	----	----	----	----	----					
McLean[a]	----	----	----	2,045	----					
Mercer	26	----	----	556	0.1					
Morgan	12,714	----	----	1,183	10.7					
Peoria[c]	----	----	----	----	----					
Pike	2,396	----	----	828	2.9					
Putnam	1,310	----	----	2,281	0.5					
Sangamon	12,960	12	0.1	2,207	5.9					
Schuyler	2,959	----	----	1,322	2.2					
Tazewell	4,716	4	0.1	1,226	3.8					
Warren	308	----	----	917	0.4					
TOTALS	49,482	56	----	30,509	1.6					

[a]Created after 1830 census.

[b]Statistical information combined with Schuyler County in 1830 census.

[c]Statistical information combined with Putnam County in 1830 census.

INDIANA
7 DISTRICTS
7 CONGRESSMEN

| | COUNTIES | | | | | REPRESENTATIVES | | | | |
| County | Aggregate | Slave | %S | sq.mi. | P/sq.mi. | Representative | Cong. | Pty. | Address | County |

DISTRICT 1

County	Aggregate	Slave	%S	sq.mi.	P/sq.mi.	Representative	Cong.	Pty.	Address	County
Crawford	3,238	----	----	312	10.4	Ratliff Boon	23	JD	Boonville	Warrick
Dubois	1,778	----	----	433	4.1	Ratliff Boon	24	JD	Boonville	Warrick
Gibson	5,418	----	----	498	10.9	Ratliff Boon	25	JD	Boonville	Warrick
Harrison	10,273	----	----	479	21.4	George H. Proffit	26	W	Petersburg	Pike
Orange	7,901	----	----	405	19.5	George H. Proffit	27	W	Petersburg	Pike
Perry	3,369	----	----	384	8.8					
Pike	2,475	----	----	335	7.4					
Posey	6,549	----	----	412	15.9					
Spencer	3,196	----	----	396	8.1					
Vanderbourgh	2,611	----	----	214	12.2					
Warrick	2,877	1	----	391	7.4					
TOTALS	49,685	1	----	4,259	11.7					

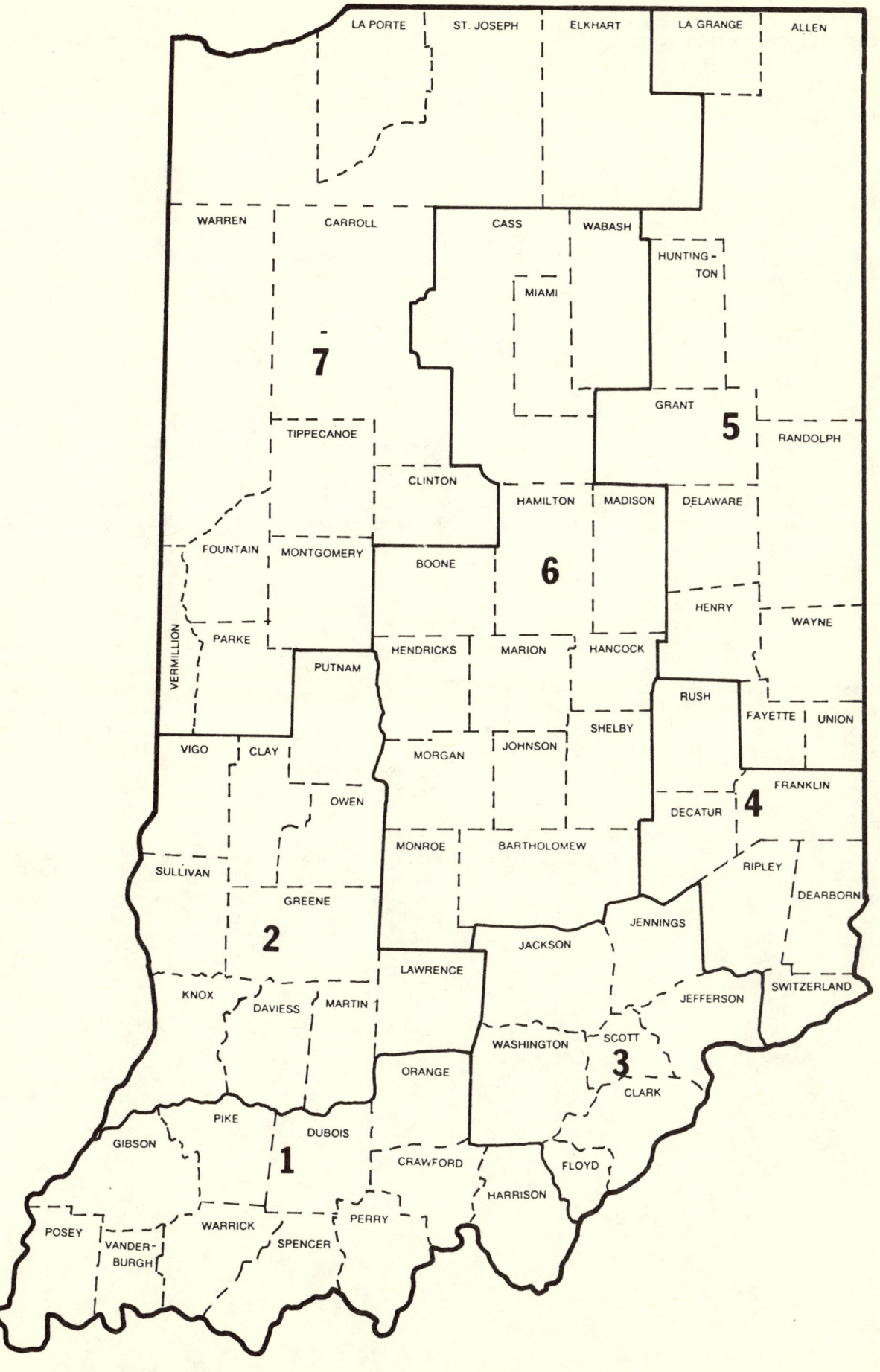

	COUNTIES					REPRESENTATIVES				
County	Aggregate	Slave	%S	sq.mi.	P/sq.mi.	Representative	Cong.	Pty.	Address	County

DISTRICT 2

County	Aggregate	Slave	%S	sq.mi.	P/sq.mi.	Representative	Cong.	Pty.	Address	County
Clay	1,616	----	----	364	4.4	John Ewing	23	W	Vincennes	Knox
Daviess	4,543	----	----	430	10.6	John W. Davis	24	D	Carlisle	Sullivan
Green	4,242	----	----	549	7.7	John Ewing	25	W	Vincennes	Knox
Knox	6,525	----	----	516	12.6	John W. Davis	26	D	Carlisle	Sullivan
Lawrence	9,234	----	----	459	20.1	Richard W. Thompson	27	W	Bedford	Lawrence
Martin	2,010	----	----	345	5.8					
Owen	4,017	----	----	390	10.3					
Putnam	8,262	----	----	390	21.2					
Sullivan	4,630	----	----	457	10.1					
Vigo	5,766	----	----	415	13.9					
TOTALS	50,845	----	----	4,315	11.8					

DISTRICT 3

County	Aggregate	Slave	%S	sq.mi.	P/sq.mi.	Representative	Cong.	Pty.	Address	County
Clark	10,686	----	----	384	27.8	John Carr	23	D	Charleston	Clark
Floyd	6,361	----	----	149	42.7	John Carr	24	D	Charleston	Clark
Jackson	4,870	----	----	520	9.4	William Graham	25	W	Vallonia	Jackson
Jefferson	11,465	----	----	366	31.3	John Carr	26	D	Charleston	Clark
Jennings	3,974	----	----	377	10.5	Joseph L. White	27	W	Madison	Jefferson
Scott	3,092	----	----	193	16.0					
Washington	13,064	----	----	516	25.3					
TOTALS	53,512	----	----	2,505	21.4					

DISTRICT 4

County	Aggregate	Slave	%S	sq.mi.	P/sq.mi.	Representative	Cong.	Pty.	Address	County
Dearborn	13,974	----	----	393	35.6	Amos Lane	23	D	Lawrence-burg	Dearborn
Decatur	5,887	1	----	370	15.9					
Franklin	10,190	----	----	394	25.9	Amos Lane	24	D	Lawrence-burg	Dearborn
Ripley	3,989	----	----	442	9.0					
Rush	9,707	----	----	409	23.7	George H. Dunn	25	W	Lawrence-burg	Dearborn
Switzerland	7,028	----	----	221	31.8					
TOTALS	50,775	1	----	2,229	22.8	Thomas Smith	26	D	Versailles	Ripley
						James H. Cravens	27	W	Marion	Ripley

DISTRICT 5

County	Aggregate	Slave	%S	sq.mi.	P/sq.mi.	Representative	Cong.	Pty.	Address	County
Allen	996	----	----	1,680	0.6	Jonathan McCarty	23	W	Fort Wayne	Allen
Delaware	2,374	----	----	396	6.0	Jonathan McCarty	24	W	Fort Wayne	Allen
Fayette	9,112	----	----	215	42.4	James Rariden	25	W	Centerville	Wayne
Grant[a]	----	----	----	688	----	James Rariden	26	W	Centerville	Wayne
Henry	6,497	----	----	400	16.2	Andrew Kennedy	27	D	Muncietown	Delaware
Huntington[a]	----	----	----	369	----					
La Grange[a]	----	----	----	381	----					
Randolph	3,912	----	----	843	4.6					
Union	7,944	----	----	168	47.3					
Wayne	18,571	----	----	405	45.8					
TOTALS	49,406	----	----	5,545	8.9					

[a]Created after 1830 census.

	COUNTIES					REPRESENTATIVES				
County	Aggregate	Slave	%S	sq.mi.	P/sq.mi.	Representative	Cong.	Pty.	Address	County

DISTRICT 6

County	Aggregate	Slave	%S	sq.mi.	P/sq.mi.	Representative	Cong.	Pty.	Address	County
Bartholomew	5,476	----	----	721	7.6	George L. Kennard	23	D	Indianapolis	Marion
Boon	621	----	----	427	1.4	George L. Kennard†	24	D	Indianapolis	Marion
Cass	1,162	----	----	1,076	1.1	(Died November, 1836)				
Hamilton	1,757	----	----	662	2.6	William Herod	24	W	Columbus	Bartholomew
Hancock	1,436	----	----	305	4.7	(Replaced Kennard December, 1836)				
Hendricks	3,975	----	----	417	9.5	William Herod	25	W	Columbus	Bartholomew
Johnson	4,019	----	----	315	12.7	William W. Wick	26	D	Indianapolis	Marion
Madison	2,238	----	----	453	4.9	David Wallace	27	W	Indianapolis	Marion
Marion	7,192	----	----	392	18.3					
Miami[a]	----	----	----	377	----					
Monroe	6,577	----	----	386	17.0					
Morgan	5,593	----	----	406	13.8					
Shelby	6,295	----	----	409	15.4					
Wabash[a]	----	----	----	398	----					
TOTALS	46,341	----	----	6,744	6.9					

[a]Created after 1830 census.

DISTRICT 7

County	Aggregate	Slave	%S	sq.mi.	P/sq.mi.	Representative	Cong.	Pty.	Address	County
Carroll	1,611	----	----	1,451	1.1	Edward A. Hannegan	23	D	Covington	Fountain
Clinton	1,423	----	----	407	3.5	Edward A. Hannegan	24	D	Covington	Fountain
Elkhart	935	----	----	1,415	0.7	Albert S. White	25	W	LaFayette	Tippecanoe
Fountain	7,619	----	----	397	19.2	Tilghman A. Howard[r]	26	D	Rockville	Parke
La Porte[a]	----	----	----	607	----	(Resigned August 1, 1840)				
Montgomery	7,317	----	----	507	14.4	Henry S. Lane	26	W	Crawfords-ville	Montgomery
Parke	7,535	----	----	445	16.9					
St. Joseph	287	----	----	2,257	0.1	(Replaced Howard December 7, 1840)				
Tippecanoe	7,187	----	----	500	14.4	Henry S. Lane	27	W	Crawfords-ville	Montgomery
Vermillion	5,692	----	----	263	21.6					
Warren	2,861	----	----	1,502	1.9					
TOTALS	42,467	----	----	9,751	4.4					

[a]Created after 1830 census.

| | COUNTIES | | | | | | REPRESENTATIVES | | | |
County	Aggregate	Slave	%S	sq.mi.	P/sq.mi.	Representative	Cong.	Pty.	Address	County
						DISTRICT 1				
Caldwell	8,324	1,774	21.3	573	14.5	Chittendon Lyon	23	D	Eddyville	Caldwell
Calloway	5,164	427	8.3	687	7.5	Linn Boyd	24	D	New Design	----
Graves	2,504	279	11.1	560	4.8	John L. Murray	25	D	Wadesboro	Callaway
Hickman	5,198	870	16.7	644	8.1	Linn Boyd	26	D	Cadiz	Trigg
Livingston	5,971	1,136	19.0	676	8.8	Linn Boyd	27	D	Cadiz	Trigg
McCracken	1,297	130	10.0	509	2.5					
Trigg	5,916	1,417	24.0	408	14.5					
Union	4,764	1,355	28.4	490	9.7					
TOTALS	39,138	7,388	18.9	4,547	8.6					
						DISTRICT 2				
Butler	3,058	453	14.8	440	7.0	Albert G. Hawes	23	D	Hawesville	Hancock
Christian	12,684	4,335	34.2	725	17.5	Albert G. Hawes	24	JD	Hawesville	Hancock
Daviess	5,209	1,324	25.4	612	8.5	Edward Rumsey	25	W	Greenville	Muhlenburg
Hancock	1,515	347	22.9	187	8.1	Phillip Triplett	26	W	Owensboro	Daviess
Henderson	6,659	2,559	38.4	433	15.4	Phillip Triplett	27	W	Owensboro	Daviess
Hopkins	6,763	1,325	19.6	692	9.8					
Muhlenburg	14,932	4,628	31.0	521	28.7					
Ohio	4,715	583	12.4	596	7.9					
TOTALS	55,535	15,554	28.0	4,206	13.2					
						DISTRICT 3				
Allen	6,485	956	14.7	351	18.5	Christopher Tompkins	23	W	Glasgow	Barren
Barren	15,079	3,735	24.8	598	25.2	Joseph R. Underwood	24	W	Bowling Green	Warren
Edmonson	2,642	278	10.5	220	12.0					
Logan	13,012	4,624	35.5	563	23.1	Joseph R. Underwood	25	W	Bowling Green	Warren
Monroe	5,340	645	12.1	334	16.0					
Simpson	5,815	1,232	21.2	239	24.3	Joseph R. Underwood	26	W	Bowling Green	Warren
Todd	8,680	3,168	36.5	376	23.1					
Warren	10,949	2,873	26.2	573	19.1	Joseph R. Underwood	27	W	Bowling Green	Warren
TOTALS	68,002	17,511	25.8	3,254	20.9					
						DISTRICT 4				
Adair	8,217	1,731	21.1	566	14.5	Martin Beaty	23	W	South Fork	Wayne
Casey	4,342	463	10.7	435	10.0	Sherrod Williams	24	W	Monticello	Wayne
Cumberland	8,624	1,692	19.6	410	21.0	Sherrod Williams	25	W	Monticello	Wayne
Pulaski	9,500	1,007	10.6	653	14.5	Sherrod Williams	26	W	Monticello	Wayne
Rockcastle	2,865	281	9.8	311	9.2	Bryan Y. Owsley	27	W	Jamestown	Russell
Russell	3,879	458	11.8	238	16.3					
Wayne	8,685	633	7.3	530	16.4					
Whitley	3,806	137	3.6	459	8.3					
TOTALS	49,918	6,402	12.8	3,602	13.9					

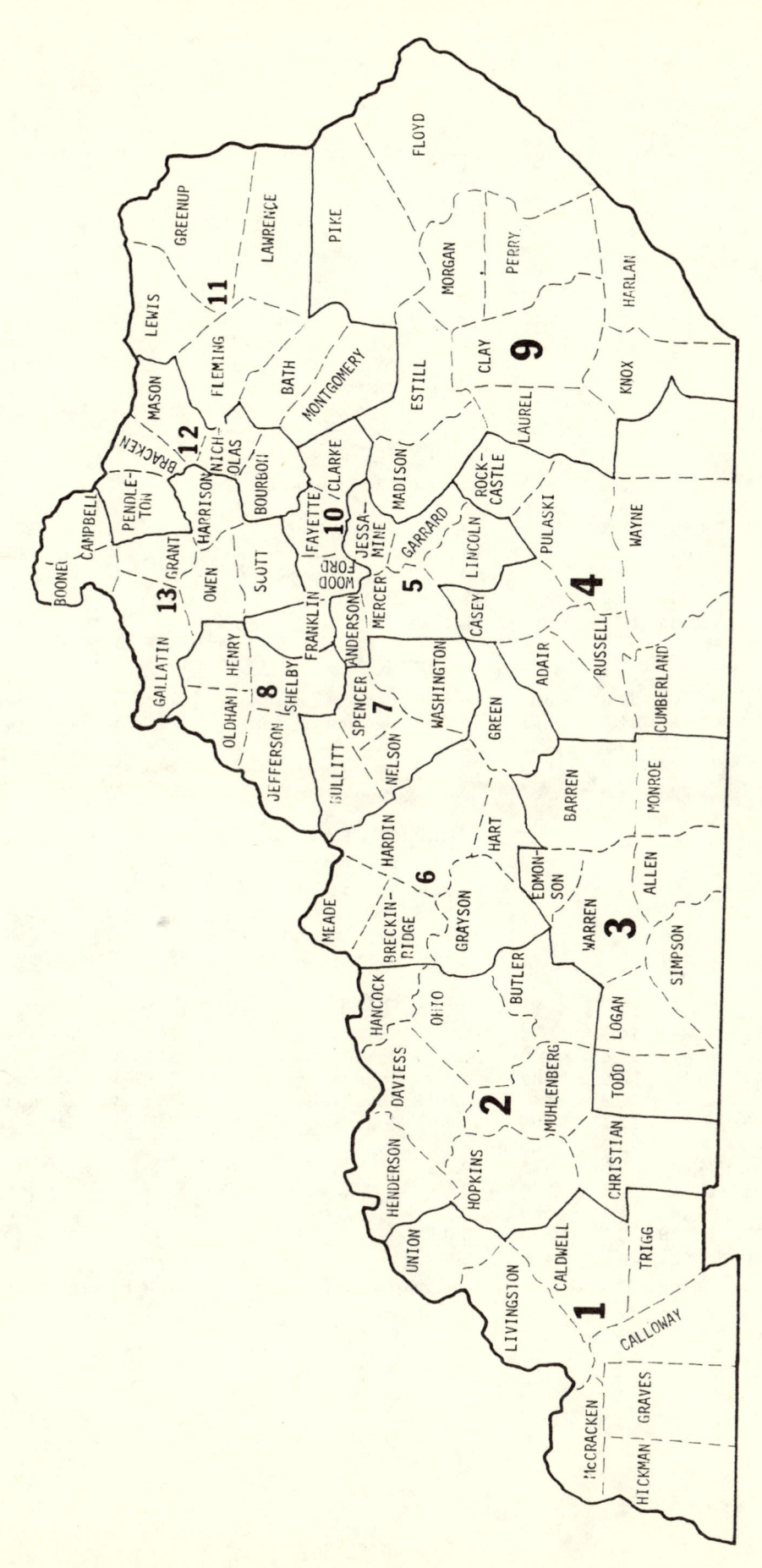

	COUNTIES					REPRESENTATIVES				
County	Aggregate	Slave	%S	sq.mi.	P/sq.mi.	Representative	Cong.	Pty.	Address	County

DISTRICT 5

Anderson	4,520	981	21.7	149	30.3	Robert P. Letcher[ce]	23	W	Lancaster	Garrard
Garrard	11,871	3,551	29.9	236	50.3	(Took seat December, 1834)				
Jassamine	9,960	3,379	33.9	177	56.3	James Harlan	24	W	Harrodsburg	Mercer
Lincoln	11,002	3,638	33.1	340	32.4	James Harlan	25	W	Harrodsburg	Mercer
Mercer	17,694	4,824	27.3	342	51.8	Simeon H. Anderson[†]	26	W	Lancaster	Garrard
TOTALS	55,047	16,373	29.7	1,244	44.3	(Died August, 1840)				
						John B. Thompson	26	W	Harrodsburg	Mercer
						(Replaced Anderson December, 1840)				
						John B. Thompson	27	W	Harrodsburg	Mercer

DISTRICT 6

Breckenridge	7,345	1,480	20.1	550	13.4	Thomas Chilton	23	W	Elizabeth-	Hardin
Grayson	3,880	238	6.1	596	6.5				town	
Green	13,138	3,461	26.3	559	23.5	John Calhoon	24	W	Hardinsburg	Breckenridge
Hardin	12,849	2,069	16.1	876	14.7	John Calhoon	25	W	Hardinsburg	Breckenridge
Hart	5,191	792	15.3	198	26.2	Willis Green	26	W	Green	Green
Meade	4,131	945	22.9	305	13.4	Willis Green	27	W	Green	Green
TOTALS	46,534	8,985	19.3	3,084	15.1					

DISTRICT 7

Bullitt	5,652	1,143	20.2	302	18.7	Benjamin Hardin	23	W	Bardstown	Nelson
Nelson	14,932	4,628	31.0	411	36.3	Benjamin Hardin	24	W	Bardstown	Nelson
Spencer	6,812	1,513	22.2	201	33.9	John Pope	25	I	Springfield	Washington
Washington	19,017	4,714	24.9	670	28.4	John Pope	26	D	Springfield	Washington
TOTALS	46,413	11,998	25.9	1,584	29.3	John Pope	27	W	Springfield	Washington

DISTRICT 8

Henry	11,387	2,463	21.6	289	39.4	Patrick H. Pope	23	D	Louisville	Jefferson
Jefferson	23,979	6,929	28.9	375	63.9	William J. Graves	24	W	New Castle	Henry
Oldham	9,588	2,405	25.1	284	33.8	William J. Graves	25	W	New Castle	Henry
Shelby	19,030	5,920	31.1	383	49.7	William J. Graves	26	W	New Castle	Henry
TOTALS	63,984	17,717	27.7	1,331	48.1	James C. Sprigg	27	W	Shelbyville	Shelby

DISTRICT 9

Clay	3,548	364	10.3	930	3.8	James Love	23	D	Barbourville	Knox
Estill	4,618	441	9.5	610	7.8	John White	24	W	Richmond	Madison
Floyd	4,347	139	3.2	1,532	2.8	John White	25	W	Richmond	Madison
Harlan	2,929	136	4.6	442	6.6	John White	26	W	Richmond	Madison
Knox	4,315	477	11.1	704	6.1	John White	27	W	Richmond	Madison
Laurel	2,206	126	5.7	533	4.1					
Madison	18,751	6,039	32.2	473	39.6					
Morgan[a]	2,857	46	1.6	796	3.6					
Perry	3,330	155	4.7	589	5.7					
Pike	2,677	78	2.9	880	3.0					
TOTALS	49,578	8,001	16.1	7,489	6.6					

[a]The legislature placed Morgan County in the eleventh district. We assume the statute is in error and place this county in the ninth district.

COUNTIES						REPRESENTATIVES				
County	Aggregate	Slave	%S	sq.mi.	P/sq.mi.	Representative	Cong.	Pty.	Address	County

DISTRICT 10

County	Aggregate	Slave	%S	sq.mi.	P/sq.mi.	Representative	Cong.	Pty.	Address	County
Clarke	13,051	4,486	34.4	259	50.4	Chilton Allan	23	D	Winchester	Clarke
Fayette	25,098	10,933	43.6	280	89.6	Chilton Allan	24	D	Winchester	Clarke
Franklin	9,254	3,092	33.4	211	43.9	Richard Hawes	25	W	Winchester	Clarke
Woodford	12,273	5,633	45.9	193	63.6	Richard Hawes	26	W	Winchester	Clarke
TOTALS	59,676	24,144	40.5	943	63.3	Thomas F. Marshall	27	W	Versailles	Woodford

DISTRICT 11

County	Aggregate	Slave	%S	sq.mi.	P/sq.mi.	Representative	Cong.	Pty.	Address	County
Bath	8,799	1,582	18.0	340	25.9	Amos Davis	23	W	Mount Sterling	Montgomery
Fleming	13,499	2,264	16.8	640	21.1					
Greenup	5,852	992	17.0	907	6.5	Richard French	24	D	Mount Sterling	Montgomery
Lawrence	3,900	81	2.1	665	5.9					
Lewis	5,229	464	8.9	486	10.8	Richard H. Menifee	25	W	Mount Sterling	Montgomery
Montgomery	10,240	2,580	25.2	467	21.9					
TOTALS	47,519	7,963	16.8	3,505	13.6	Landaff W. Andrews	26	W	Flemingsburg	Fleming
						Landaff W. Andrews	27	W	Flemingsburg	Fleming

DISTRICT 12

County	Aggregate	Slave	%S	sq.mi.	P/sq.mi.	Representative	Cong.	Pty.	Address	County
Bourbon	18,436	6,868	37.2	300	61.5	Thomas A. Marshall	23	W	Paris	Bourbon
Bracken	6,518	833	12.8	204	32.0	John Chambers	24	W	Washington	Mason
Mason	16,199	4,391	27.1	288	56.2	John Chambers	25	W	Washington	Mason
Nicholas	8,834	1,237	14.0	229	38.6	Garrett Davis	26	W	Paris	Bourbon
Pendleton	3,863	428	11.1	279	13.8	Garrett Davis	27	W	Paris	Bourbon
TOTALS	53,850	13,757	25.5	1,300	41.4					

DISTRICT 13

County	Aggregate	Slave	%S	sq.mi.	P/sq.mi.	Representative	Cong.	Pty.	Address	County
Boone	9,075	1,820	20.1	249	36.4	Richard M. Johnson	23	D	Great Crossings	Scott
Campbell	9,883	1,033	10.5	314	31.5					
Gallatin	6,674	1,184	17.7	330	20.2	Richard M. Johnson	24	JD	Great Crossings	Scott
Grant	2,986	266	8.9	249	12.0					
Harrison	13,234	2,788	21.1	330	40.1	William W. Southgate	25	W	Covington	Campbell
Owen	5,786	709	12.3	300	19.3	William O. Butler	26	D	Carrollton	Gallatin
Scott	14,677	5,452	37.1	284	51.7	William O. Butler	27	D	Carrollton	Gallatin
TOTALS	62,315	13,252	21.3	2,056	30.3					

COUNTIES						REPRESENTATIVES				
County	Aggregate	Slave	%S	sq.mi.	P/sq.mi.	Representative	Cong.	Pty.	Address	County

DISTRICT 1

COUNTIES						REPRESENTATIVES				
'Orleans'						Edward D. White[r]	23	W	Donaldsville	Ascension
Jefferson	6,846	4,907	71.6	369	18.6	(Resigned November, 1834)				
New						Henry Johnson	23	W	Donaldsville	Ascension
Orleans	49,826	16,453	33.0	197	252.9	(Replaced White December, 1834)				
Plaquemines	4,489	3,188	71.0	1,030	4.4	Henry Johnson	24	W	Donaldsville	Ascension
St. Bernard	3,356	2,519	75.0	514	6.5	Henry Johnson	25	W	Donaldsville	Ascension
Subtotal	64,517	27,067	41.9	2,110	30.6	Edward D. White	26	W	Thibodaux	La Fourche
'German Coast'						Edward D. White	27	W	Thibodaux	La Fourche
St. Charles	5,147	4,118	76.0	294	17.5					
St. John	5,677	3,493	60.5	227	25.0					
Subtotal	10,824	7,611	70.3	521	20.8					
'Acadia'										
Ascension	5,426	3,557	65.5	301	18.0					
St. James	7,616	5,029	66.0	253	30.1					
Subtotal	13,042	8,586	65.8	554	23.5					
'La Fourche'	5,503	2,153	39.1	1,141	4.8					
Terrebone[a]	2,121	1,033	48.7	1,368	1.6					
TOTALS	96,007	46,450	48.4	5,694	16.9					

[a]Created from 'La Fourche.'

DISTRICT 2

COUNTIES						REPRESENTATIVES				
East Baton						Philemon Thomas	23	D	Baton Rouge	West Baton
Rouge	6,698	3,348	49.9	459	14.6					Rouge
East						Eleazer W. Ripley	24	D	Jackson	Feliciana
Feliciana	8,247	4,652	56.4	454	18.2	Eleazer W. Ripley	25	D	Jackson	Feliciana
'Iberville'	7,049	4,507	63.9	427	16.5	(Never qualified due to prolonged illness, but apparently was				
'Pointe						never replaced)				
Coupee'	5,936	4,210	70.9	563	10.5	Thomas W. Chinn	26	W	Baton Rouge	West Baton
St. Helena	4,028	1,359	33.7	1,882	2.1	John B. Dawson	27	D	St. Francis-	West
St. Tammany	2,864	2,719	94.9	887	3.2				ville	Feliciana
Washington	2,286	587	25.6	665	3.4					
West Baton										
Rouge	3,084	1,932	62.6	403	7.6					
West										
Feliciana	8,629	6,345	73.5	405	21.3					
TOTALS	48,821	29,659	60.7	6,145	7.9					

	COUNTIES						REPRESENTATIVES			
County	Aggregate	Slave	%S	sq.mi.	P/sq.mi.	Representative	Cong.	Pty.	Address	County

DISTRICT 3

Assumption	5,669	1,886	33.2	356	15.9	Henry A. Bullard[r]	23	W	Alexandria	Rapides
'Attakapas'[a]						(Resigned January, 1834)				
Avoyelles	3,484	1,335	38.3	941	3.7	Rice Garland	23	W	Opelousas	Opelousas
Catahoula	2,581	920	35.6	1,250	2.1	(Replaced Bullard April, 1834)				
Claiborne	1,764	215	12.1	4,410	0.4	Rice Garland	24	W	Opelousas	Opelousas
'Concordia'	4,662	3,620	77.6	1,830	2.5	Rice Garland	25	W	Opelousas	Opelousas
Lafayette	5,653	6,669	17.9	283	20.0	Rice Garland[r]	26	W	Opelousas	Opelousas
'Natchi-						(Resigned July, 1840)				
toches'	7,905	3,571	45.1	5,120	1.5	John Moore	26	W	Franklin	Attakapas
'Opelousas'[a]						(Replaced Garland December, 1840)				
'Ouachita'	8,814	----	----	4,765	1.8	John Moore	27	W	Franklin	Attakapas
'Rapides'	7,575	5,328	70.3	3,269	2.3					
St. Landry	12,591	4,970	39.4	7,274	1.7					
St. Martins	7,205	3,987	55.3	736	9.8					
St. Marys	6,442	4,304	66.8	624	10.3					
TOTALS	74,345	36,805	49.5	30,858	2.4					

[a]Attakapas and Opelousas are not listed as political subdivisions in the 1830 census.

---

[1]Louisiana apparently continued to use the districts established by the Act of 1822. This act used both parish and regional names to locate the districts. Names used in the act are identified with quotes. Counties not mentioned in the original act and/or created after 1822 have been assigned to the districts within whose boundaries they lie. See discussion of Louisiana districts in the 1822 apportionment.

MAINE
8 DISTRICTS
8 CONGRESSMEN

	COUNTIES						REPRESENTATIVES			
County	Aggregate	Slave	%S	sq.mi.	P/sq.mi.	Representative	Cong.	Pty.	Address	County

DISTRICT 1 (YORK)

York	51,722	----	----	1,001	51.7	Rufus McIntire	23	JD	Parsonsfield	York
						John Fairfield	24	D	Saco	York
						John Fairfield[r]	25	D	Saco	York
						(Resigned December, 1838; not replaced)				
						Nathan Clifford	26	D	Newfield	York
						Nathan Clifford	27	D	Newfield	York

DISTRICT 2 (CUMBERLAND)

All of Cumberland County, except those towns included						Francis O. J. Smith	23	D	Portland	Cumberland
in District 5,						Francis O. J. Smith	24	D	Portland	Cumberland
total:	53,031	----	----	972	54.6	Francis O. J. Smith	25	D	Portland	Cumberland
						Albert Smith	26	D	Portland	Cumberland
						William Pitt				
						Fessenden	27	W	Portland	Cumberland

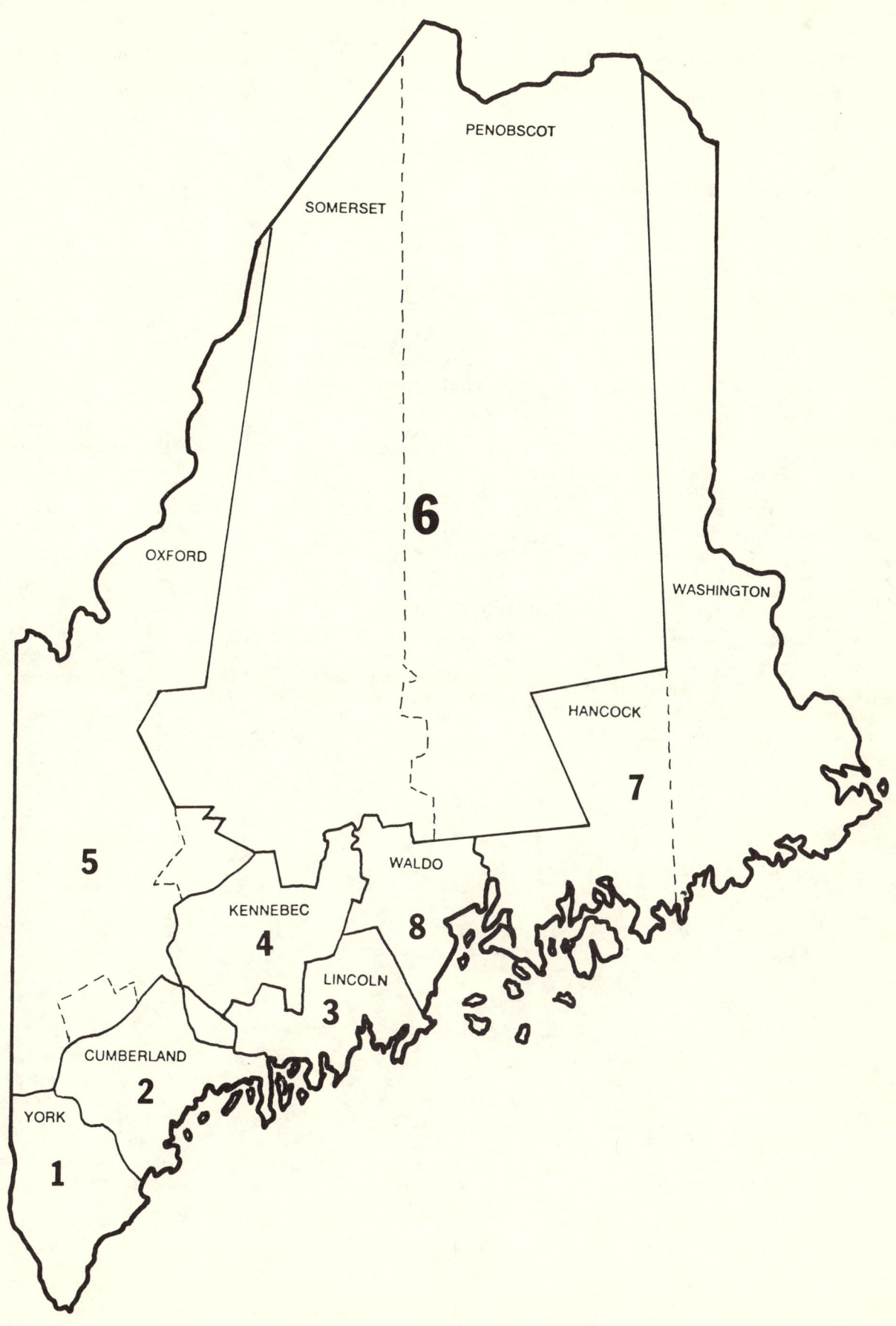

COUNTIES						REPRESENTATIVES				
County	Aggregate	Slave	%S	sq.mi.	P/sq.mi.	Representative	Cong.	Pty.	Address	County

DISTRICT 3 (LINCOLN)

All of Lincoln County, except those towns included in						Edward Kavanagh	23	D	Damariscotta Mills	Lincoln
Districts 4 and 5,										
total:	51,291	----	----	980	52.3	Jeremiah Bailey	24	W	Wiscasset	Lincoln
						Jonathan Cilley†	25	D	Thomaston	Lincoln
						(Killed in a duel February, 1838)				
						Edward Robinson	25	W	Thomaston	Lincoln
						(Replaced Cilley April, 1838)				
						Benjamin Randall	26	W	Bath	Lincoln
						Benjamin Randall	27	W	Bath	Lincoln

DISTRICT 4 (KENNEBEC AND SOMERSET)

All of Kennebec County, except those towns included						George Evans	23	NR	Gardiner	Kennebec
in Districts 5 and 8,						George Evans	24	W	Gardiner	Kennebec
total:	35,607	----	----	647	42.7	George Evans	25	W	Gardiner	Kennebec
The portion of Somerset County west of the Kennebec						George Evans	26	W	Gardiner	Kennebec
River, except the towns of Bloomfield and Norridgewock,						George Evans r	27	W	Gardiner	Kennebec
total:	18,690	----	----	4,026	4.6	(Reelected, but resigned, having been elected to the Senate)				
Town in Lincoln County:						David Bronson	27	W	Anson	Kennebec
Litchfield	1,308	----	----	40	32.7	(Replaced Evans May, 1841)				
TOTALS	55,605	----	----	4,713	11.8					

DISTRICT 5 (OXFORD)

Towns in Cumberland County:						Moses Mason, Jr.	23	D	Bethel	Oxford
Bridgeton	1,551	----	----	----	----	Moses Mason, Jr.	24	D	Bethel	Oxford
Harrison	1,068	----	----	----	----	Timothy J. Carter†	25	D	Paris	Oxford
Otisfield	1,274	----	----	----	----	(Died March 14, 1838)				
Minot	2,904	----	----	----	----	Virgil D. Parris	25	D	Buckfield	Oxford
Total, towns	6,797	----	----	140	44.6	(Replaced Carter May 29, 1838)				
Towns in Kennebec County:						Virgil D. Parris	26	D	Buckfield	Oxford
Greene	1,324	----	----	----	----	Nathaniel S. Littlefield	27	D	Bridgeton	Cumberland
Leeds	1,685	----	----	----	----					
Temple	795	----	----	----	----					
Wilton	1,640	----	----	----	----					
Total, towns	5,444	----	----	180	30.2					
Towns in Lincoln County:										
Lewiston	1,549	----	----	----	----					
Lisbon	2,423	----	----	----	----					
Wales	612	----	----	----	----					
Total, towns	4,584	----	----	60	76.4					
Oxford	35,211	----	----	3,080	11.4					
TOTALS	52,036	----	----	3,460	14.5					

DISTRICT 6 (PENOBSCOT AND SOMERSET)

Penobscot	31,530	----	----	11,294	2.8	Gorham Parks	23	D	Bangor	Penobscot
Somerset a	14,314	----	----	2,718	5.3	Gorham Parks	24	D	Bangor	Penobscot
TOTALS	45,844	----	----	14,012	3.3	Thomas Davee	25	D	Blanchard	Penobscot
						Thomas Davee	26	D	Blanchard	Penobscot
						Elisha H. Allen	27	D	Bangor	Penobscot

a "All that part of Somerset County on the east side of the Kennebec River, plus Norridgewock and Bloomfield on the west side of the Kennebec River." This area represents about forty percent of the land area of the county.

COUNTIES						REPRESENTATIVES				
County	Aggregate	Slave	%S	sq.mi.	P/sq.mi.	Representative	Cong.	Pty.	Address	County

DISTRICT 7 (HANCOCK AND WASHINGTON)

County	Aggregate	Slave	%S	sq.mi.	P/sq.mi.	Representative	Cong.	Pty.	Address	County
Hancock	24,336	----	----	1,736	14.0	Leonard Jarvis	23	D	Ellsworth	Hancock
Washington	21,294	----	----	3,504	6.0	Leonard Jarvis	24	D	Ellsworth	Hancock
TOTALS	45,630	----	----	5,240	8.7	Joseph C. Noyes	25	W	Eastport	Washington
						Joshua A. Lowell	26	D	East Machias	Washington
						Joshua A. Lowell	27	D	East Machias	Washington

DISTRICT 8 (WALDO)

County	Aggregate	Slave	%S	sq.mi.	P/sq.mi.	Representative	Cong.	Pty.	Address	County
Towns in Kennebec County:						Joseph Hall	23	D	Camden	Waldo
Albion	1,393	----	----	----	----	Joseph Hall	24	D	Camden	Waldo
Area between						Hugh J. Anderson	25	D	Belfast	Waldo
Pittfield &						Hugh J. Anderson	26	D	Belfast	Waldo
Clinton	99	----	----	50*	----	Alfred Marshall	27	D	China	Kennebec
China	2,233	----	----	----	----					
Clinton	2,124	----	----	----	----					
Unincorpo-rated place north of										
Albion	75	----	----	50*	----					
Vassal-borough	2,761	----	----	----	----					
Windsor	1,485	----	----	----	----					
Winslow	1,263	----	----	----	----					
Total, towns	11,433	----	----	350	32.7					
Waldo	29,788	----	----	737	40.4					
TOTALS	41,221	----	----	1,087	37.9					

	COUNTIES					REPRESENTATIVES				
County	Aggregate	Slave	%S	sq.mi.	P/sq.mi.	Representative	Cong.	Pty.	Address	County

DISTRICT 1

County	Aggregate	Slave	%S	sq.mi.	P/sq.mi.	Representative	Cong.	Pty.	Address	County
Dorchester	18,686	5,001	26.7	594	31.5	Littleton P. Dennis†	23	NR	Princess Ann	Somerset
Somerset	20,166	6,556	32.5	529	38.1	(Died April, 1834)				
Worcester	18,273	4,032	22.1	669	27.3	John N. Steele	23	W	Vienna	Dorchester
TOTALS	57,125	15,589	27.2	1,792	32.8	(Replaced Dennis June, 1834)				
						John N. Steele	24	W	Vienna	Dorchester
						John Dennis	25	W	Princess Ann	Somerset
						John Dennis	26	W	Princess Ann	Somerset
						Isaac D. Jones	27	W	Princess Ann	Somerset

DISTRICT 2

County	Aggregate	Slave	%S	sq.mi.	P/sq.mi.	Representative	Cong.	Pty.	Address	County
Caroline	9,070	1,177	12.9	321	28.3	Richard B. Carmichael	23	D	Centerville	Queen Anns
Cecil	15,432	1,705	11.0	362	42.6	James A. Pearce	24	W	Chestertown	Kent
Kent	10,501	2,991	28.5	281	37.4	James A. Pearce	25	W	Chestertown	Kent
Queen Anns	14,397	4,872	33.8	375	38.3	Philip F. Thomas	26	D	Easton	Talbot
Talbot	12,847	4,173	32.2	261	49.6	James A. Pearce	27	W	Chestertown	Kent
TOTALS	62,347	14,918	23.9	1,600	38.9					

DISTRICT 3

County	Aggregate	Slave	%S	sq.mi.	P/sq.mi.	Representative	Cong.	Pty.	Address	County
Baltimore	40,250	6,402	15.9	929	43.3	James Turner	23	NR	Wiseburg	Harford or Baltimore
Harford	13,372	2,947	22.0	453	29.5					
TOTALS	53,622	9,349	17.4	1.382	38.8	James Turner	24	W	Wiseburg	Harford or Baltimore
						John T. H. Worthington	25	D	Golden	Baltimore
						John T. H. Worthington	26	D	"Shewan"	Baltimore
						James W. Williams	27	D	Churchville	Harford

DISTRICT 4

County	Aggregate	Slave	%S	sq.mi.	P/sq.mi.	Representative	Cong.	Pty.	Address	County
Ann Arundel County and the City of Annapolis, total:	28,295	9,627	34.0	674	42.0	James P. Heath	23	D	City of Baltimore	
Wards of the City of Baltimore:						Isaac McKim	23	D	City of Baltimore	
One	5,430	219	4.0	----	----	Benjamin C. Howard	24	D	City of Baltimore	
Two	9,263	404	4.4	----	----	Isaac McKim	24	D	City of Baltimore	
Three	9,766	396	4.1	----	----					
Four	8,595	324	3.8	----	----	Benjamin C. Howard	25	D	City of Baltimore	
Five	4,024	229	5.7	----	----	Isaac McKim†	25	D	City of Baltimore	
Six	4,146	402	9.6	----	----	(Died April, 1838)				
Seven	3,936	395	10.0	----	----	John P. Kennedy	25	W	City of Baltimore	
Eight	4,942	173	3.5	----	----	(Replaced McKim April, 1838)				
Nine	4,636	357	7.7	----	----					
Ten	7,508	405	5.3	----	----	James Carroll	26	D	City of Baltimore	
Eleven	6,718	337	5.0	----	----	Solomon Hillen, Jr.	26	D	City of Baltimore	

[1] For the Twenty-third Congress, District 4 on the map was actually two separate districts; District 4 consisted of Baltimore Wards Six through Twelve, and District 5 consisted of Baltimore Wards One through Five and Ann Arundel County. Districts thereafter were numbered one higher than indicated on the map.

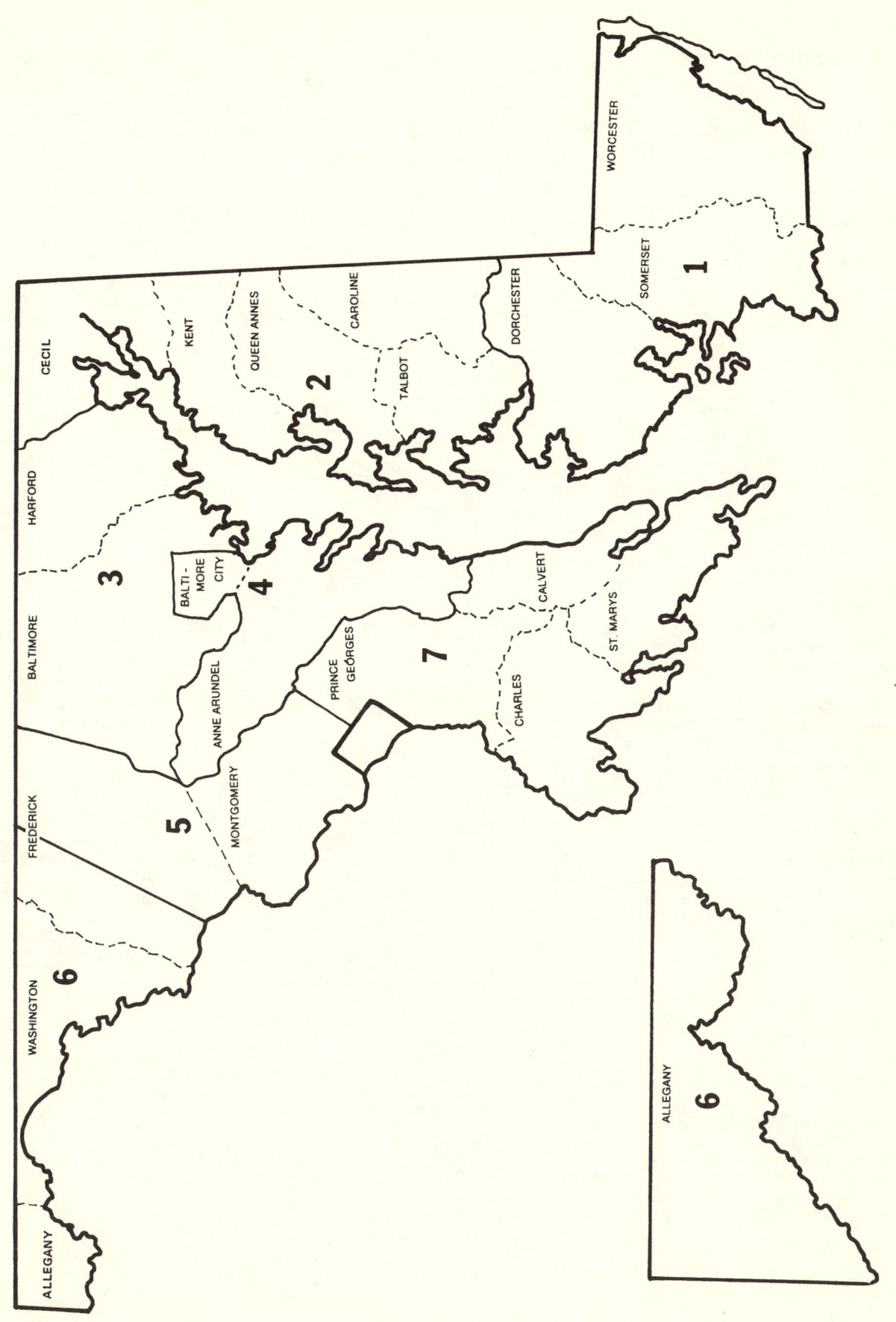

| | COUNTIES | | | | | REPRESENTATIVES | | | | |
| County | Aggregate | Slave | %S | sq.mi. | P/sq.mi. | Representative | Cong. | Pty. | Address | County |

DISTRICT 4 (CONTINUED)

County	Aggregate	Slave	%S	sq.mi.	P/sq.mi.	Representative	Cong.	Pty.	Address	County
Twelve	11,666	479	4.1	----	----	John P. Kennedy	27	W	City of Baltimore	
Total, wards	80,630	4,120	5.1	78	1033.7	Alexander Randall	27	W	Annapolis	Ann Arundel
TOTALS	108,925	13,747	12.6	752	144.8					

DISTRICT 5

County	Aggregate	Slave	%S	sq.mi.	P/sq.mi.	Representative	Cong.	Pty.	Address	County
Election Districts in Frederick County:						William Cost Johnson	23	W	Jefferson	Frederick
One	3,348	960	28.7	79	42.9	George C. Washington	24	W	Rockville	Montgomery
Three						William Cost Johnson	25	W	Jefferson	Frederick
(Fourteen)	7,666	1,447	18.9	79	97.0	William Cost Johnson	26	W	Jefferson	Frederick
Four	7,666	1,392	18.2	79	97.0	William Cost Johnson	27	W	Jefferson	Frederick
Five	2,779	187	6.7	79	35.2					
Six	3,314	195	17.0	79	41.9					
Seven	4,156	254	6.1	79	52.6					
Eight	5,415	661	12.2	79	68.5					
Nine	3,970	693	17.4	79	50.3					
Eleven	2,533	319	12.5	79	32.1					
Subtotal	40,847	6,108	14.9	711	57.5					
Montgomery	19,316	6,447	33.4	495	39.0					
TOTALS	60,163	12,555	20.9	1,206	49.9					

DISTRICT 6

County	Aggregate	Slave	%S	sq.mi.	P/sq.mi.	Representative	Cong.	Pty.	Address	County
Allegheny	10,609	818	7.7	428	24.8	Francis Thomas	23	D	Frederick	Frederick
Election Districts in Frederick County:						Francis Thomas	24	D	Frederick	Frederick
Two	2,828	486	17.2	79	35.8	Francis Thomas	25	D	Frederick	Frederick
Ten	1,281	22	1.7	79	16.2	Francis Thomas	26	D	Frederick	Frederick
Twelve[a]						John T. Mason	27	D	Hagerstown	Washington
Subtotal	4,109	508	12.4	158	26.0					
Washington	25,268	2,909	11.5	459	55.1					
TOTALS	39,986	4,235	10.6	1,045	38.3					

[a]The 1830 census contains no data on Election District 12.

DISTRICT 7

County	Aggregate	Slave	%S	sq.mi.	P/sq.mi.	Representative	Cong.	Pty.	Address	County
Calvert	8,900	3,899	43.8	217	41.0	John T. Stoddert	23	D	Harris Lot	Charles
Charles	17,769	10,129	57.0	459	38.7	Daniel Jenifer	24	W	Harris Lot	Charles
Prince						Daniel Jenifer	25	W	Harris Lot	Charles
Georges	20,474	8,889	43.4	485	42.2	Daniel Jenifer	26	W	Milton Hill	Charles
St. Marys	13,459	6,183	45.9	373	36.1	Augustus R. Sollers	27	W	Prince	Calvert
TOTALS	60,602	29,100	48.0	1,534	39.5				Frederick	

COUNTIES						REPRESENTATIVES				
County	Aggregate	Slave	%S	sq.mi.	P/sq.mi.	Representative	Cong.	Pty.	Address	County

DISTRICT 1

County	Aggregate	Slave	%S	sq.mi.	P/sq.mi.	Representative	Cong.	Pty.	Address	County
City of Boston	61,392	----	----	10	6139.2	Benjamin Gorham	23	NR	City of Boston	
						Abbott Lawrence	24	W	City of Boston	
						Richard Fletcher	25	W	City of Boston	
						Abbott Lawrence[r]	26	W	City of Boston	
						(Resigned September 18, 1840)				
						Robert C. Winthrop	26	W	City of Boston	
						(Replaced Lawrence December 7, 1840)				
						Robert C. Winthrop[r]	27	W	City of Boston	
						(Resigned May 25, 1842)				
						Nathan Appleton	27	W	City of Boston	
						(Replaced Winthrop June 9, 1842)				

DISTRICT 2

County	Aggregate	Slave	%S	sq.mi.	P/sq.mi.	Representative	Cong.	Pty.	Address	County
Towns in Essex County:						Rufus Choate[r]	23	NR	Salem	Essex
Beverly	4,073	----	----	----	----	(Resigned June 30, 1834)				
Chelsea	771	----	----	----	----	Stephen C. Phillips	23	W	Salem	Essex
Danvers	4,228	----	----	----	----	(Replaced Choate December 1, 1834)				
Gloucester	7,510	----	----	----	----	Stephen C. Phillips	24	W	Salem	Essex
Hamilton	748	----	----	----	----	Stephen C. Phillips[r]	25	W	Salem	Essex
Ipswich	2,949	----	----	----	----	(Resigned September 28, 1838)				
Lynn	6,138	----	----	----	----	Leverett Saltonstall	26	W	Salem	Essex
Lynnfield	617	----	----	----	----	Leverett Saltonstall	27	W	Salem	Essex
Manchester	1,236	----	----	----	----					
Marblehead	5,149	----	-----	----	----					
Salem	13,895	----	----	----	----					
Saugus	960	----	----	----	----					
South Essex	1,333	----	----	----	----					
Wenham	611	----	----	----	----					
TOTALS	50,218	----	----	158	317.8					

DISTRICT 3

County	Aggregate	Slave	%S	sq.mi.	P/sq.mi.	Representative	Cong.	Pty.	Address	County
All of Essex County not included in District 2, total:	33,412	----	----	336	99.4	Gayton P. Osgood	23	D	North Andover	Essex
Towns in Middlesex County:						Caleb Cushing	24	W	Newburyport	Essex
Bellerica	1,374	----	----	----	----	Caleb Cushing	25	W	Newburyport	Essex
Dracut	1,615	----	----	----	----	Caleb Cushing	26	W	Newburyport	Essex
Lowell	6,474	----	----	----	----	Caleb Cushing	27	W	Newburyport	Essex
Reading	1,806	----	----	----	----					
South Reading	1,311	----	----	----	----					
Tewksbury	1,527	----	----	----	----					
Wilmington	731	----	----	----	----					
Total, towns	14,838	----	----	50	296.8					
TOTALS	48,250	----	----	386	126.9					

322

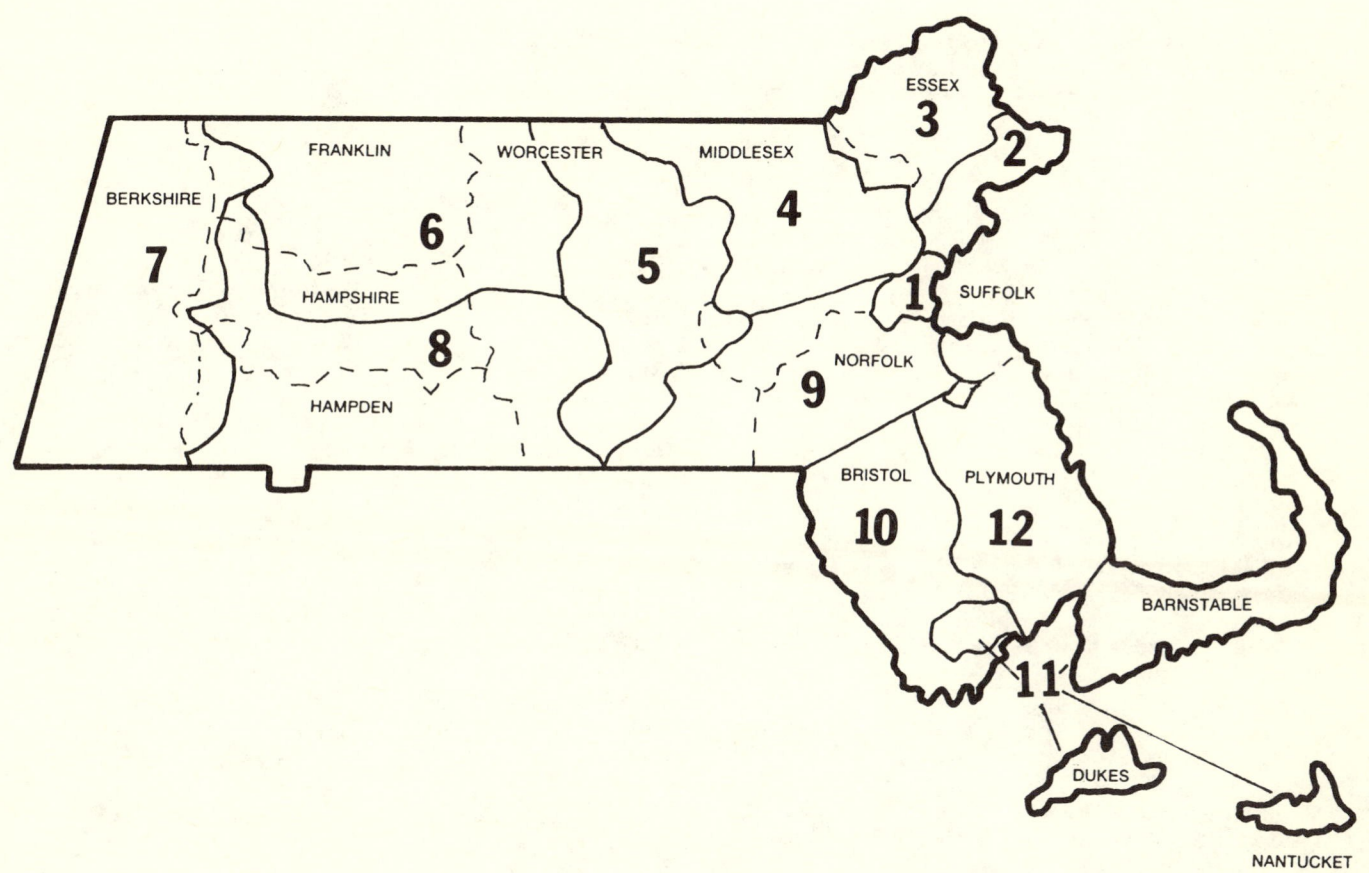

COUNTIES

County	Aggregate	Slave	%S	sq.mi.	P/sq.mi.

REPRESENTATIVES

Representative	Cong.	Pty.	Address	County

DISTRICT 4

Towns in Middlesex County:
Acton, Ashby, Bedford, Boxborough, Burlington, Cambridge, Carlisle, Charlestown, Chelmsford, Concord, Dunstable, Framingham, Groton, Lexington, Lincoln, Littleton, Malden, Marlboro, Medford, Peperell, Shirley, Stoneham, Stow, Sudbury, Townsend, Tynsboro, Waltham, Watertown, Wayland, West Cambridge, Westford, Westow, Woburn.
Total, towns 53,097 ---- ---- 675 78.7

Representative	Cong.	Pty.	Address	County
Edward Everett	23	NR	Charlestown	Middlesex
Samuel Hoar	24	W	Concord	Middlesex
William Parmenter	25	D	East Cambridge	Middlesex
William Parmenter	26	D	East Cambridge	Middlesex
William Parmenter	27	D	East Cambridge	Middlesex

DISTRICT 5

Towns in Worcester County:
Ashburnham, Belton, Berlin, Boylston, Charlton, Dudley, Fitchbury, Gardner, Grafton, Harvard, Hobbardson, Holden, Lancaster, Leicester, Leominster, Lunenburg, Millbury, Northboro, Notown, Oakham, Oxford, Paxton, Princeton, Rutland, Shrewsbury, Southbridge, Spencer, Sterling, Sutton, Ward, Webster, West Boylston, Westminster, Winchendon, Worcester.
Total, towns 51,983 ---- ---- 943 55.1

Representative	Cong.	Pty.	Address	County
John Davis[r] (Resigned January 14, 1834)	23	NR	Worcester	Worcester
Levi Lincoln (Replaced Davis March 5, 1834)	23	W	Worcester	Worcester
Levi Lincoln	24	W	Worcester	Worcester
Levi Lincoln	25	W	Worcester	Worcester
Levi Lincoln	26	W	Worcester	Worcester
Levi Lincoln[r] (Resigned March 16, 1841)	27	W	Worcester	Worcester
Charles Hudson (Replaced Lincoln May 3, 1841)	27	W	Worcester	Worcester

DISTRICT 6

Towns in Franklin County:
Ashfield, Bernardston, Buckland, Coleraine, Conway, Deerfield, Gill, Greenfield, Heath, Leverett, Leyden, Montague, New Salem, Northfield, Orange, Shelburne, Shutesbury, Sunderland, Warwick, Wendell, Whately.
Total, towns 25,850 ---- ---- ---- ----
Towns in Hampshire County:
Amherst, Chesterfield, Goshen, Greenwhich, Hadley, Pelham, Prescott, Williamsburg.
Total, towns 10,954 ---- ---- ---- ----
Towns in Worcester County:
Athol, Barre, Dana, Enfield, Hardwicke, Petersham, Philipston, Toyalston, Templeton.
Total, towns 13,065 ---- ---- ---- ----
Town of undetermined location:
Plantation
of E. Grant 488 ---- ---- ---- ----
TOTALS 50,437 ---- ---- 1,110 45.4

Representative	Cong.	Pty.	Address	County
George Grennell, Jr.	23	NR	Greenfield	Franklin
George Grennell, Jr.	24	NR	Greenfield	Franklin
George Grennell, Jr.	25	W	Greenfield	Franklin
James C. Alvord† (Died September 27, 1839)	26	W	Greenfield	Franklin
Osmyn Baker (Replaced Alvord January 14, 1840)	26	W	Amherst	Hampshire
Osmyn Baker	27	W	Amherst	Hampshire

DISTRICT 7

County	Aggregate	Slave	%S	sq.mi.	P/sq.mi.
Berkshire	37,835	----	----	----	----
Towns in Franklin County:					
Charlemont	1,065	----	----	----	----
Hawley	1,037	----	----	----	----
Monroe	265	----	----	----	----
Rowe	716	----	----	----	----
Total, towns	3,083	----	----	----	----

Representative	Cong.	Pty.	Address	County
George N. Briggs	23	NR	Lanesboro	Berkshire
George N. Briggs	24	W	Lanesboro	Berkshire
George N. Briggs	25	W	Lanesboro	Berkshire
George N. Briggs	26	W	Lanesboro	Berkshire
George N. Briggs	27	W	Lanesboro	Berkshire

| COUNTIES | | | | | | REPRESENTATIVES | | | | |
| County | Aggregate | Slave | %S | sq.mi. | P/sq.mi. | Representative | Cong. | Pty. | Address | County |

DISTRICT 7 (CONTINUED)

Towns in Hampden County:

Blandford	1,590	----	----	----	----					
Chester	1,407	----	----	----	----					
Norwhich	795	----	----	----	----					
Total, towns	4,515	----	----	----	----					

Towns in Hampshire County:

Cummington	1,261	----	----	----	----					
Middlefield	720	----	----	----	----					
Plainfield	984	----	----	----	----					
Worthington	1,179	----	----	----	----					
Total, towns	4,144	----	----	----	----					
TOTALS	49,577	----	----	1,193	41.6					

DISTRICT 8

Towns in Hampden County:
Brimfield, Granville, Holland, Longmeadow, Ludlow, Monson, Montgomery, Palmer, Russell, Southwick, Springfield, Wales, West Springfield, Westfield, Wilbraham.

| | | | | | | | | | | |
| Total, towns | 27,919 | ---- | ---- | ---- | ---- | | | | | |

Towns in Hampshire County:
Belchertown, Easthampton, Granby, Northampton, South Hadley, Southampton, Ware, Westhampton.

| | | | | | | | | | | |
| Total, towns | 14,005 | ---- | ---- | ---- | ---- | | | | | |

Towns in Worcester County:
Brookfield, New Braintree, North Brookfield, Sturbridge, Warren.

Total, towns	6,161	----	----	----	----					
TOTALS	48,085	----	----	1,075	44.7					

Representatives for District 8:

Representative	Cong.	Pty.	Address	County
Isaac C. Bates	23	NR	Northampton	Hampshire
William B. Calhoun	24	W	Springfield	Hampden
William B. Calhoun	25	W	Springfield	Hampden
William B. Calhoun	26	W	Springfield	Hampden
William B. Calhoun	27	W	Springfield	Hampden

DISTRICT 9

Towns in Middlesex County:
Holliston, Hopkinton, Natick, Newton, Sherburne, Southboro, Westboro.

| | | | | | | | | | | |
| Total, towns | 9,796 | ---- | ---- | ---- | ---- | | | | | |

Towns in Norfolk County:
Bellingham, Brookline, Canton, Dedham, Dover, Foxboro, Franklin, Medfield, Medway, Needham, Roxbury, Sharon, Walpole, Wrentham.

| | | | | | | | | | | |
| Total, towns | 24,502 | ---- | ---- | ---- | ---- | | | | | |

Towns in Worcester County:
Douglas, Mendon, Milford, Northbridge, Upton, Uxbridge.

| | | | | | | | | | | |
| Total, towns | 10,560 | ---- | ---- | ---- | ---- | | | | | |

Town of undetermined location:

Brighton	972	----	----	----	----					
TOTALS	45,830	----	----	911	50.3					

Representatives for District 9:

Representative	Cong.	Pty.	Address	County
William Jackson	23	AM	Newton	Middlesex
William Jackson	24	AM	Newton	Middlesex
William S. Hastings	25	W	Mendon	Worcester
William S. Hastings	26	W	Mendon	Worcester
William S. Hastings†	27	W	Mendon	Worcester

(Died June 17, 1842; not replaced)

| COUNTIES | | | | | | REPRESENTATIVES | | | | |
| County | Aggregate | Slave | %S | sq.mi. | P/sq.mi. | Representative | Cong. | Pty. | Address | County |

DISTRICT 10

COUNTIES						REPRESENTATIVES				
All of Bristol County, except the towns included in District 11,						William Baylies	23	NR	West	Plymouth
						Nathaniel B. Borden	24	D	Bridgewater	
total:	28,340	----	----	----	----	Nathaniel B. Borden	24	D	Fall River	Bristol
Towns in Plymouth County:						Nathaniel B. Borden	25	D	Fall River	Bristol
Bridgewater, East Bridgewater, Middleboro, North						Henry Williams	26	D	Taunton	Bristol
Bridgewater, West Bridgewater.						Nathaniel B. Borden	27	W	Fall River	Bristol
Total, towns	11,511	----	----	----	----					
TOTALS	39,851	----	----	534	74.6					

DISTRICT 11

COUNTIES						REPRESENTATIVES				
Barnstable	28,514	----	----	----	----	John Reed	23	NR	Yarmouth	Barnstable
Towns in Bristol County:						John Reed	24	AM	Yarmouth	Barnstable
Fairhaven	3,034	----	----	----	----	John Reed	25	W	Yarmouth	Barnstable
New						John Reed	26	W	Yarmouth	Barnstable
Bedford	7,592	----	----	----	----	Barker Burnell	27	W	Nantucket	Nentucket
Total, towns	10,626	----	----	----	----					
Duke	3,517	----	----	----	----					
Nantucket	7,202	----	----	----	----					
TOTALS	49,859	----	----	583	85.5					

DISTRICT 12

COUNTIES						REPRESENTATIVES				
Towns in Norfolk County:						John Quincy Adams	23	AM	Quincy	Norfolk
Braintree, Dorchester, Milton, Quincy, Randolph,						John Quincy Adams	24	AM	Quincy	Norfolk
Stoughton, Weymouth.						John Quincy Adams	25	W	Quincy	Norfolk
Total, towns	16,237	----	----	----	----	John Quincy Adams	26	W	Quincy	Norfolk
All of Plymouth County not included in District 10,						John Quincy Adams	27	W	Quincy	Norfolk
total:	44,277	----	----	----	----					
TOTALS	60,514	----	----	710	85.2					

MISSISSIPPI
2 CONGRESSMEN AT LARGE

| COUNTIES | | | | | | REPRESENTATIVES | | | | |
| County | Aggregate | Slave | %S | sq.mi. | P/sq.mi. | Representative | Cong. | Pty. | Address | County |

AT LARGE

COUNTIES						REPRESENTATIVES				
Adams	14,937	10,942	73.2	367	40.7	Franklin E. Plummer	23	W	Westville	Simpson
Amite	7,934	4,089	51.5	616	12.9	Henry Cage	23	D	Woodville	Wilkinson
Claiborne	9,787	6,165	62.9	498	19.7					
Copia	7,001	1,754	25.0	760	9.2	John F. Claiborne	24	D	Madisonville	Madison
Covington	2,551	700	27.4	574	4.4	David Dickson†	24	D	Jackson	Hinds
Franklin	4,622	2,207	47.7	681	6.8	(Died in 1836)				
Greene	1,854	538	29.0	774	2.4	Samuel J. Gholson	24	D	Athens	Monroe
Hancock	1,962	553	28.2	1,963	0.9	(Replaced Dickson January, 1837)				
Hinds	8,645	3,212	37.2	870	9.9					

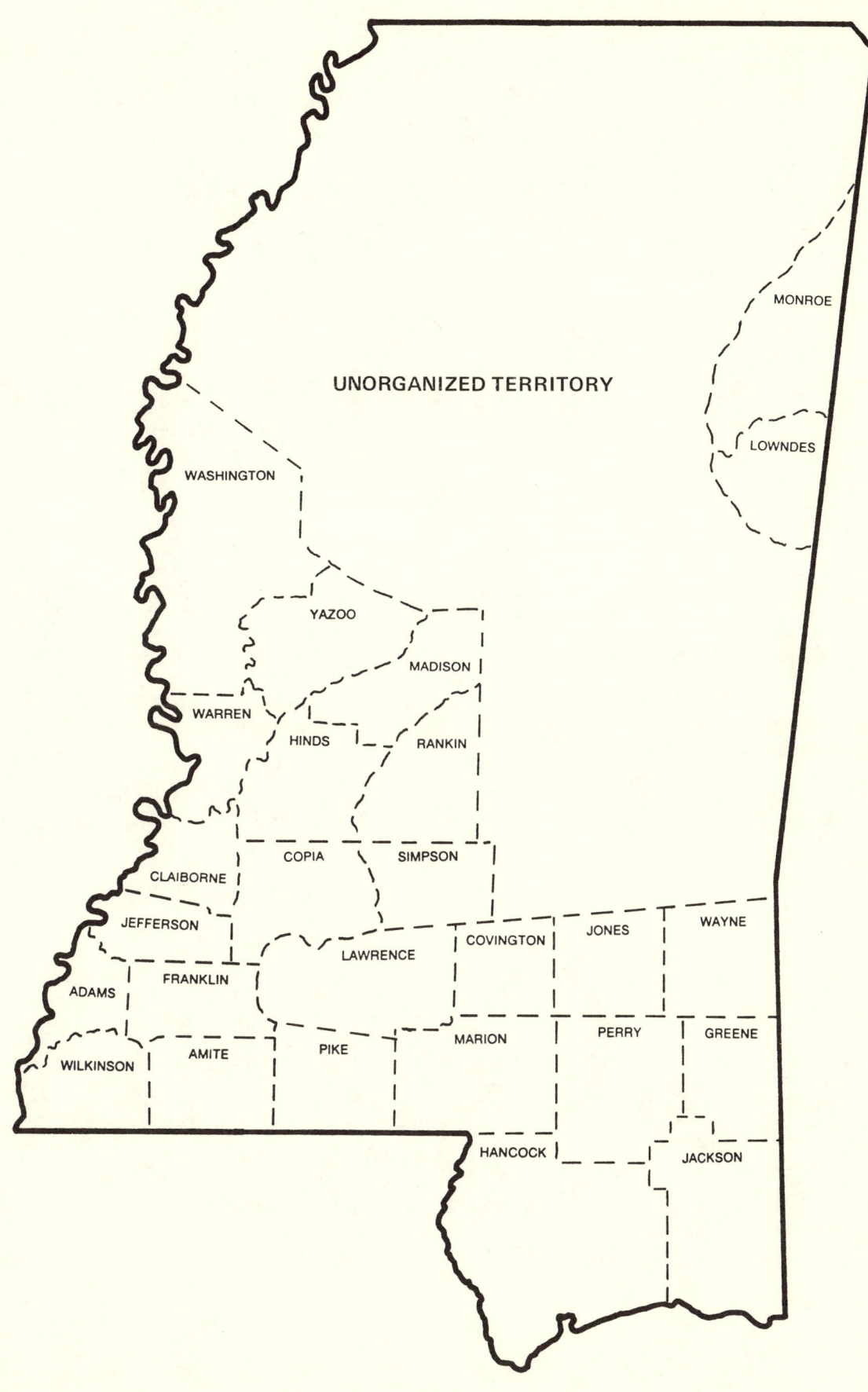

UNORGANIZED TERRITORY

MONROE

LOWNDES

WASHINGTON

YAZOO

MADISON

WARREN

HINDS

RANKIN

COPIA

SIMPSON

CLAIBORNE

JEFFERSON

LAWRENCE

COVINGTON

JONES

WAYNE

FRANKLIN

ADAMS

MARION

PERRY

GREENE

WILKINSON

AMITE

PIKE

HANCOCK

JACKSON

	COUNTIES					REPRESENTATIVES				
County	Aggregate	Slave	%S	sq.mi.	P/sq.mi.	Representative	Cong.	Pty.	Address	County

AT LARGE (CONTINUED)

County	Aggregate	Slave	%S	sq.mi.	P/sq.mi.	Representative	Cong.	Pty.	Address	County
Jackson	1.792	400	22.3	1,132	1.6	John F. H. Claiborne	25a	D	Madisonville	Madison
Jefferson	9,755	6,700	68.7	508	19.2	Samuel Gholson	25	D	Athens	Monroe
Jones	1,471	161	10.9	660	2.2	Sergeant S. Prentiss	25	W	Vicksburg	Warren
Lawrence	5,293	1,807	34.1	969	5.5	Thomas Ward	25	W	Pontotoc	Pontotoc
Lowndes	3,173	964	30.4	550	5.7					(Indian Territory)
Madison	4.973	2,167	43.5	741	6.7					
Marion	3,691	1,715	46.4	988	3.7	Albert G. Brown	26	D	Gallatin	Copia
Monroe	3,861	943	24.4	875	4.4	Jacob Thompson	26	D	Pontotoc	Pontotoc
Perry	2,300	820	35.7	1,134	2.0					(Indian Territory)
Pike	5,402	1,602	29.7	687	7.9					
Rankin	2,083	386	18.5	560	3.7	William L. Gwin	27	D	Vicksburg	Warren
Simpson	2,680	660	24.6	500	5.4	Jacob Thompson	27	D	Oxford	Lafayette
Warren	7,861	4,483	57.0	685	11.5					
Washington	1,976	1,184	59.9	1,975	0.7					
Wayne	2,781	1,076	38.7	890	3.1					
Wilkinson	11,686	7,861	67.3	571	20.5					
Yazoo	6,550	2,470	37.7	650	10.1					
TOTALS	136,621	65,669	47.9	22,178	6.2					

aMississippi elected its representatives in November of odd numbered years (after the beginning of the Congressional term), as Congress had been called to meet in September. The governor issued writs for a special election to fill vacancies until the regular election: John F. Claiborne and Samuel J. Gholson presented credentials and were seated September 4, 1837, when, at their request, the question of the validity of their election was referred to the Committee on Elections. On October 3, 1837, the House decided they had been elected for the full term. Sergeant S. Prentiss and Thomas J. Ward presented credentials on December 27, 1837, and on February 5, 1838, the House rescinded its former decision and declared the seats vacant. Prentiss and Ward were subsequently elected, and took their seats May 30, 1838.

MISSOURI
2 CONGRESSMEN AT LARGE

	COUNTIES					REPRESENTATIVES				
County	Aggregate	Slave	%S	sq.mi.	P/sq.mi.	Representative	Cong.	Pty.	Address	County

AT LARGE

County	Aggregate	Slave	%S	sq.mi.	P/sq.mi.	Representative	Cong.	Pty.	Address	County
Boone	8,859	1,923	21.7	685	12.9	William H. Ashley	23	AB	St. Louis	St. Louis
Callaway	6,159	1,456	23.6	835	7.4	John Bull	23	W	Chariton	Chariton
Cape Girardeau	7,445	1,026	13.8	1,195	6.2	William H. Ashley	24	I	St. Louis	St. Louis
Chariton	1,780	301	16.9	1,534	1.2	Albert G. Harrison	24	D	Fulton	Calloway
Clay	5,338	882	16.5	832	6.4					
Cole	3,023	300	9.9	801	3.8	Albert G. Harrison	25	D	Fulton	Calloway
Cooper	6,904	1,021	14.7	1,284	5.4	John Miller	25	D	Boonville	Cooper
Crawford	1,712	64	3.7	2,783	0.6					
Franklin	3,484	386	11.1	1,796	1.9	Albert G. Harrison†	26	D	Fulton	Calloway
Gasconade	1,545	137	8.9	8,156	0.2	(Died September, 1839)				
Howard	10,854	2,646	24.4	472	23.0	John Jameson	26	D	Fulton	Calloway
Jackson	2,823	193	6.8	2,215	1.3	(Replaced Harrison December, 1839)				

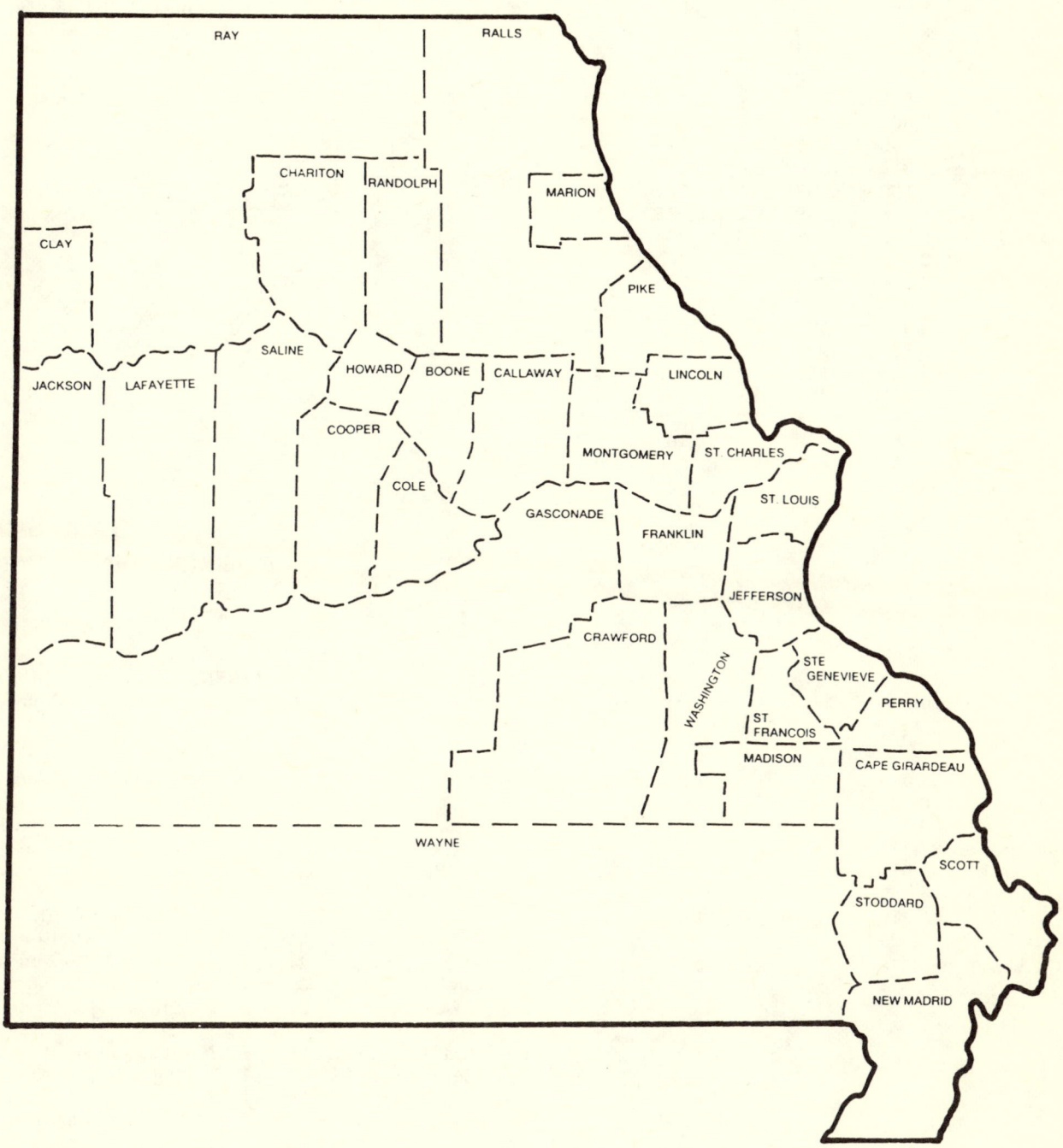

COUNTIES						REPRESENTATIVES				
County	Aggregate	Slave	%S	sq.mi.	P/sq.mi.	Representative	Cong.	Pty.	Address	County

AT LARGE (CONTINUED)

County	Aggregate	Slave	%S	sq.mi.	P/sq.mi.	Representative	Cong.	Pty.	Address	County
Jefferson	2,592	236	9.1	668	3.9	John Miller	26	D	Conners Mills	Cooper
Lafayette	2,912	429	14.7	2,465	1.2					
Lincoln	4,059	745	18.3	625	6.5	John C. Edwards	27	D	Jefferson City	Cole
Madison	2,371	410	17.3	1,105	2.1					
Marion	4,837	1,327	27.4	438	11.0	John Miller	27	D	Conners Mills	Cooper
Montgomery	3,902	605	15.5	960	4.1					
New Madrid	2,350	471	20.0	1,715	1.4					
Perry	3,349	536	16.0	471	7.1					
Pike	6,129	1,193	19.5	681	9.0					
Ralls	4,375	839	19.2	3,985	1.1					
Randolph	2,942	493	16.8	473	6.2					
Ray	2,657	166	6.2	7,058	0.4					
Saline	2,873	706	24.6	2,010	1.4					
Scott	2,136	362	16.9	836	2.5					
St. Charles	4,320	951	22.0	551	7.8					
St. Francois	2,366	959	40.5	457	5.2					
St. Genevieve	2,186	522	23.9	499	4.4					
St. Louis	14,125	2,796	19.8	599	23.6					
Washington	6,784	1,168	17.2	1,295	5.2					
Wayne	3,264	372	11.4	15,167	0.2					
TOTALS	140,455	25,621	18.2	64,646	2.2					

NEW HAMPSHIRE
5 CONGRESSMEN AT LARGE

COUNTIES						REPRESENTATIVES				
County	Aggregate	Slave	%S	sq.mi.	P/sq.mi.	Representative	Cong.	Pty.	Address	County

AT LARGE

County	Aggregate	Slave	%S	sq.mi.	P/sq.mi.	Representative	Cong.	Pty.	Address	County
Cheshire	27,016	----	----	1,254	21.5	Benning M. Bean	23	D	Moultenboro	Strafford
Coos	8,388	----	----	1,820	4.6	Robert Burns	23	D	Hebron	Grafton
Grafton	38,632	----	----	1,732	22.3	Joseph M. Harper	23	D	Canterbury	Merrimack
Hillsborough	37,724	2	----	887	42.5	Henry Hubbard	23	D	Charlestown	Sullivan
Merrimack	34,614	----	----	930	37.2	Franklin Pierce	23	D	Hillsboro	Hillsborough
Rockingham	44,325	3	----	691	64.1					
Strafford	58,910	----	----	1,414	41.7	Benning M. Bean	24	D	Moultenboro	Strafford
Sullivan	19,669	----	----	539	36.5	Robert Burns	24	D	Plymouth	Grafton
TOTALS	269,278	5	----	9,267	29.1	Samuel Cushman	24	D	Portsmouth	Rockingham
						Franklin Pierce	24	D	Hillsboro	Hillsborough
						Joseph Weeks	24	D	Richmond	Cheshire
						Charles G. Atherton	25	D	Nashua	Hillsborough
						Samuel Cushman	25	D	Portsmouth	Rockingham
						James Farrington	25	D	Rochester	Strafford
						Joseph Weeks	25	D	Richmond	Cheshire
						Jared W. Williams	25	D	Lancaster	Coos

COUNTIES

REPRESENTATIVES

County	Aggregate	Slave	%S	sq.mi.	P/sq.mi.	Representative	Cong.	Pty.	Address	County
						AT LARGE (CONTINUED)				
						Charles G. Atherton	26	D	Nashua	Hillsborough
						Edmund Burke	26	D	Newport	Sullivan
						Ira A. Eastman	26	D	Gilmanton	Strafford
						Tristram Shaw	26	D	Exeter	Rockingham
						Jared W. Williams	26	D	Lancaster	Coos
						Charles G. Atherton	27	D	Nashua	Hillsborough
						Edmund Burke	27	D	Newport	Sullivan
						Ira A. Eastman	27	D	Gilmanton	Strafford
						John R. Reding	27	D	Haverhill	Grafton
						Tristram Shaw	27	D	Exeter	Rockingham

[1]Although elections were nominally at large, representatives were spread throughout the state in the same unofficial districts established during the 1820's.

NEW JERSEY
6 CONGRESSMEN AT LARGE

COUNTIES

REPRESENTATIVES

County	Aggregate	Slave	%S	sq.mi.	P/sq.mi.	Representative	Cong.	Pty.	Address	County
						AT LARGE				
Bergen	22,412	584	2.6	420	53.3	Philemon Dickerson	23	D	Paterson	Bergen
Burlington	31,107	23	----	819	37.9	Samuel Fowler	23	D	Hamburg	Sussex
Cape May	4,936	3	----	267	18.4	Thomas Lee	23	D	Port Elizabeth	Cumberland
Cumberland	14,093	2	----	500	28.1					
Essex	41,911	218	0.5	233	179.8	James Parker	23	D	Perty Amboy	Middlesex
Gloucester	28,431	4	----	1,119	25.4	Ferdinand S. Schenck	23	D	Six Mile Run	Middlesex
Hunterdon	31,060	172	0.5	651	47.7	William N. Shinn	23	D	Mount Holly	Burlington
Middlesex	23,157	306	1.3	312	74.2					
Monmouth	29,233	227	0.8	1,118	26.1	Philemon Dickerson	24	D	Paterson	Bergen
Morris	23,666	165	0.7	468	50.5	Samuel Fowler	24	D	Hamburg	Sussex
Salem	14,155	1	----	365	38.7	Thomas Lee	23	D	Port Elizabeth	Cumberland
Somerset	17,689	448	2.5	307	51.6					
Sussex	20,346	51	0.3	527	38.6	James Parker	24	D	Perty Amboy	Middlesex
Warren	18,627	47	0.3	362	51.4	Ferdinand S. Schenck	24	D	Six Mile Run	Middlesex
TOTALS	320,823	2,251	0.7	7,468	43.0	William N. Shinn	24	D	Mount Holly	Burlington
						John B. Aycrigg	25	W	Hackensack	Bergen
						William Halstead	25	W	Trenton	Hunterdon
						John P. P. Maxwell	25	W	Belvidere	Warren
						Joseph F. Randolph	25	W	Freehold	Monmouth
						Charles C. Stratton	25	W	Swedesboro	Gloucester
						Thomas Jones Yorke	25	W	Salem	Salem

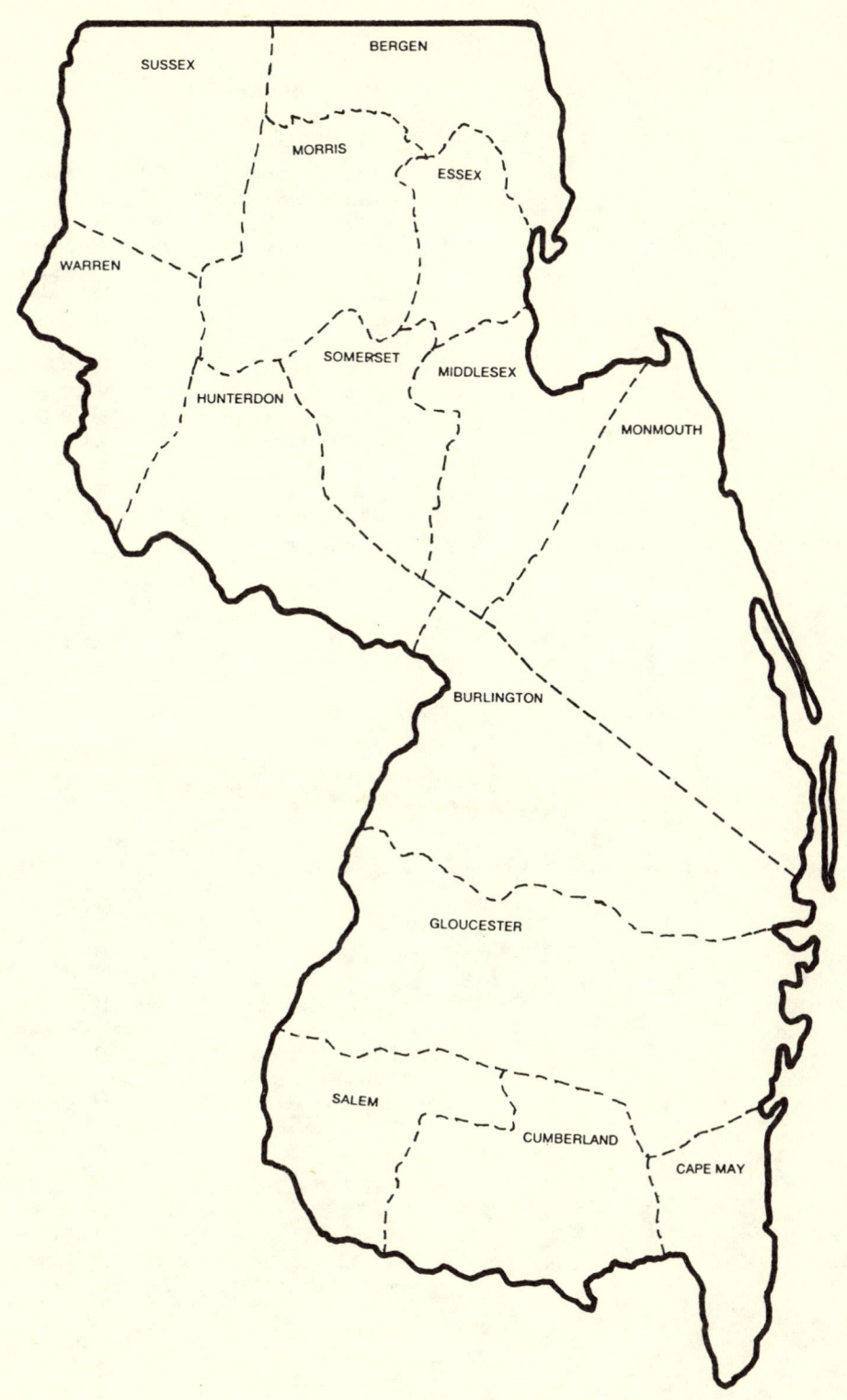

COUNTIES						REPRESENTATIVES				
County	Aggregate	Slave	%S	sq.mi.	P/sq.mi.	Representative	Cong.	Pty.	Address	County

AT LARGE (CONTINUED)

						William R. Cooper[ce]	26[a]	D	Swedesboro	Gloucester
						Philemon Dickerson[ce]	26	D	Paterson	Bergen
						Joseph Kille[ce]	26	D	Salem	Salem
						Joseph F. Randolph	26	W	New Brunswick	Middlesex
						Daniel B. Ryall[ce]	26	D	Freehold	Monmouth
						Peter D. Vroom[ce]	26	D	Somerville	Somerset
						John B. Aycrigg	27	W	Pyramus	Bergen
						William Halstead	27	W	Trenton	Hunterdon
						John P. B. Maxwell	27	W	Belvidere	Warren
						Joseph F. Randolph	27	W	New Brunswick	Middlesex
						Charles C. Stratton	27	W	Swedesboro	Gloucester
						Thomas Jones Yorke	27	W	Salem	Salem

[a] The entire Democratic delegation was unsuccessfully contested by the Whig slate.

NEW YORK

33 DISTRICTS
40 CONGRESSMEN

COUNTIES						REPRESENTATIVES				
County	Aggregate	Slave	%S	sq.mi.	P/sq.mi.	Representative	Cong.	Pty.	Address	County

DISTRICT 1

County	Aggregate	Slave	%S	sq.mi.	P/sq.mi.	Representative	Cong.	Pty.	Address	County
Queens	22,460	----	----	397	56.5	Abel Huntington	23	D	East Hampton	Suffolk
Suffolk	26,780	----	----	929	28.8					
TOTALS	49,240	----	----	1,326	37.1	Abel Huntington	24	D	East Hampton	Suffolk
						Thomas B. Jackson	25	D	Newtown	Suffolk
						Thomas B. Jackson	26	D	Newtown	Suffolk
						Charles A. Floyd	27	D	Commack	Suffolk

DISTRICT 2

County	Aggregate	Slave	%S	sq.mi.	P/sq.mi.	Representative	Cong.	Pty.	Address	County
Kings	20,535	----	----	70	293.3	Isaac B. Van Houten	23	D	Clarkstown	Rockland
Richmond	7,082	----	----	58	122.1	Samuel Barton	24	D	Richmond	Richmond
Rockland	9,888	----	----	176	56.1	Abraham Vanderveer	25	D	Brooklyn	Kings
TOTALS	37,505	----	----	304	123.3	James De La Montanya	26	D	Haverstraw	Rockland
						Joseph Egbert	27	D	Tomkinsville	Richmond

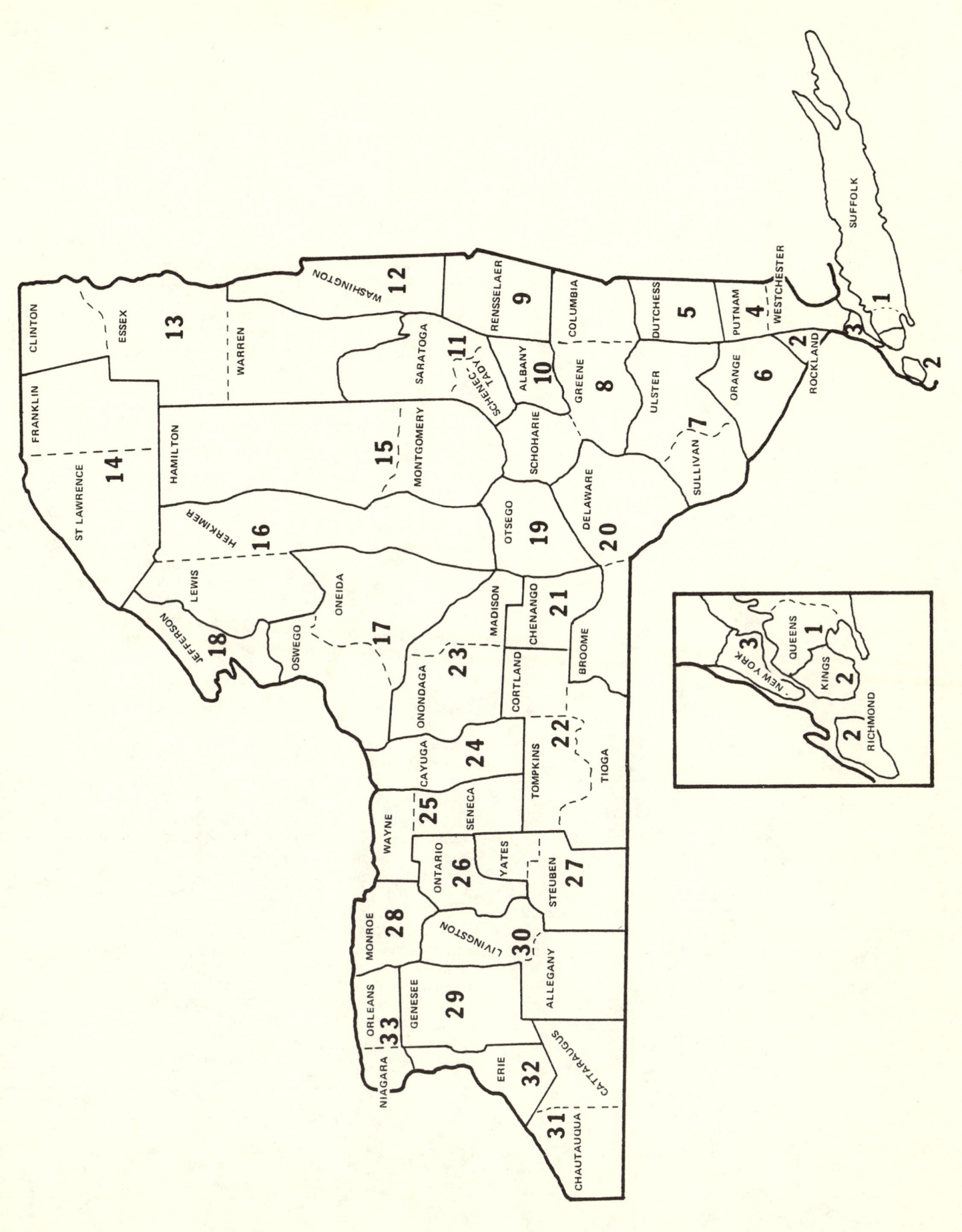

COUNTIES						REPRESENTATIVES				
County	Aggregate	Slave	%S	sq.mi.	P/sq.mi.	Representative	Cong.	Pty.	Address	County

DISTRICT 3

County	Aggregate	Slave	%S	sq.mi.	P/sq.mi.	Representative	Cong.	Pty.	Address	County
Bronx	----	----	----	41	----	Churchill Cambreleng	23	D	New York City	
City and						Cornelius W. Lawrence[r]	23	D	New York City	
County of						(Resigned May, 1834)				
New York	----	----	----	23	----	John J. Morgan	23	D	New York City	
TOTALS	197,112	----	----	64	3079.8	(Replaced Lawrence December, 1834)				
						Dudley Selden[r]	23	D	New York City	
						(Resigned July, 1834)				
						Charles G. Ferris	23	JD	New York City	
						(Replaced Selden December, 1834)				
						Campbell P. White	23	D	New York City	
						Churchill Cambreleng	24	D	New York City	
						John McKeon	24	D	New York City	
						Ely Moore	24	D	New York City	
						Campbell P. White[r]	24	D	New York City	
						(Resigned before Congress assembled)				
						Gideon Lee	24	D	New York City	
						(Replaced White December, 1835)				
						Churchill Cambreleng	25	D	New York City	
						Edward Curtis	25	D	New York City	
						J. Ogden Hoffman	25	W	New York City	
						Ely Moore	25	D	New York City	
						Edward Curtis	26	W	New York City	
						Moses H. Grinnell	26	W	New York City	
						Ogden Hoffman	26	W	New York City	
						James Monroe	26	W	New York City	
						Charles G. Ferris	27	D	New York City	
						John McKeon	27	D	New York City	
						James I. Roosevelt	27	D	New York City	
						Fernando Wood	27	D	New York City	

DISTRICT 4

County	Aggregate	Slave	%S	sq.mi.	P/sq.mi.	Representative	Cong.	Pty.	Address	County
Putnam	12,628	----	----	231	54.6	Aaron Ward	23	D	Mt. Pleasant	Westchester
Westchester	36,456	----	----	443	82.2	Aaron Ward	24	D	Mt. Pleasant	Westchester
TOTALS	49,084	----	----	674	72.8	Gouveneur Kemble	25	D	Cold Spring	Putnam
						Gouveneur Kemble	26	D	Cold Spring	Putnam
						Aaron Ward	27	D	Mt. Pleasant	Westchester

DISTRICT 5

County	Aggregate	Slave	%S	sq.mi.	P/sq.mi.	Representative	Cong.	Pty.	Address	County
Dutchess	50,926	----	----	813	62.6	Abraham Bockee	23	D	Federal Store	Dutchess
						Abraham Bockee	24	D	Federal Store	Dutchess
						Obediah Titus	25	D	Washington	Dutchess
						Charles Johnston	26	W	Pough-keepsie	Dutchess
						Richard D. Davis	27	D	Pough-keepsie	Dutchess

County	Aggregate	Slave	%S	sq.mi.	P/sq.mi.	Representative	Cong.	Pty.	Address	County

COUNTIES / REPRESENTATIVES

DISTRICT 6

County	Aggregate	Slave	%S	sq.mi.	P/sq.mi.	Representative	Cong.	Pty.	Address	County
Orange	45,366	----	----	833	54.5	John W. Brown	23	D	Newburgh	Orange
						John W. Brown	24	D	Newburgh	Orange
						Nathaniel Jones	25	D	Warwick	Orange
						Nathaniel Jones	26	D	Warwick	Orange
						James G. Clinton	27	D	Newburgh	Orange

DISTRICT 7

County	Aggregate	Slave	%S	sq.mi.	P/sq.mi.	Representative	Cong.	Pty.	Address	County
Sullivan	12,864	----	----	980	13.1	Charles Bodle	23	D	Blooming-burg	Sullivan
Ulster	36,425	----	----	1,141	31.9					
TOTALS	49,289	----	----	2,121	23.2	Nicholas Sickles	24	D	Kingston	Ulster
						John C. Brodhead	25	D	Modena	Ulster
						Rufus Palen	26	W	Fallsburg	Sullivan
						John Van Buren	27	D	Kingston	Ulster

DISTRICT 8

County	Aggregate	Slave	%S	sq.mi.	P/sq.mi.	Representative	Cong.	Pty.	Address	County
Columbia	39,907	----	----	645	61.8	John Adams	23	D	Catskill	Greene
Greene	29,525	----	----	653	47.3	Aaron Vanderpoel	23	D	Kinderhook	Columbia
Schoharie	27,902	----	----	624	44.7					
TOTALS	97,334	----	----	1,922	50.6	Valentine Efner	24	D	Jefferson	Delaware
						Aaron Vanderpoel	24	D	Kinderhook	Delaware
						Robert McClellan	25	D	Middleburg	Schoharie
						Zadock Pratt	25	D	Prattsville	Greene
						John Ely	26	D	Coxsackie	Greene
						Aaron Vanderpoel	26	D	Kinderhook	Columbia
						Jacob Houck, Jr.	27	D	Schoharie	Schoharie
						Robert McClellan	27	D	Hudson	Columbia

DISTRICT 9

County	Aggregate	Slave	%S	sq.mi.	P/sq.mi.	Representative	Cong.	Pty.	Address	County
Rensselaer	49,424	----	----	665	74.3	Job Pierson	23	D	Schaghicoke	Rensselaer
						Hiram P. Hunt	24	W	Troy	Rensselaer
						Henry Vail	25	D	Troy	Rensselaer
						Hiram P. Hunt	26	W	Troy	Rensselaer
						Hiram P. Hunt	27	W	Troy	Rensselaer

DISTRICT 10

County	Aggregate	Slave	%S	sq.mi.	P/sq.mi.	Representative	Cong.	Pty.	Address	County
City and County of Albany	53,520	----	----	526	101.7	Gerrit Y. Lansing	23	D	Albany	Albany
						Gerrit Y. Lansing	24	D	Albany	Albany
						Albert Gallup	25	D	East Birne	Albany
						Daniel D. Barnard	26	W	Albany	Albany
						Daniel D. Barnard	27	W	Albany	Albany

DISTRICT 11

County	Aggregate	Slave	%S	sq.mi.	P/sq.mi.	Representative	Cong.	Pty.	Address	County
Saratoga	38,679	----	----	818	47.2	John Cramer	23	D	Waterford	Saratoga
Schenectady	12,347	----	----	207	59.6	John Cramer	24	D	Waterford	Saratoga
TOTALS	51,026	----	----	1,025	49.8	John I. De Graff	25	D	Schenectady	Schenectady
						Anson Brown† (Died June, 1840)	26	W	Ballston	Saratoga
						Nicholas B. Doe (Replaced Brown December, 1840)	26	W	Waterford	Saratoga
						Archibald L. Linn	27	W	Schenectady	Schenectady

County	Aggregate	Slave	%S	sq.mi.	P/sq.mi.	Representative	Cong.	Pty.	Address	County
						DISTRICT 12				
Washington	42,635	8	----	836	50.9	Henry C. Martindale	23	NR	Sandy Hill	Washington
						David A. Russell	24	W	Salem	Washington
						David A. Russell	25	W	Salem	Washington
						David A. Russell	26	W	Salem	Washington
						Barnard Blair	27	W	Salem	Washington
						DISTRICT 13				
Clinton	19,344	----	----	1,059	18.2	Reuben Whallon	23	D	Split Rock	Essex
Essex	19,287	----	----	1,823	10.6	Dudley Farlen	24	D	Warrensburg	Warren
Warren	11,796	----	----	887	13.3	John Palmer	25	D	Plattsburg	Clinton
TOTALS	50,427	----	----	3,769	13.4	Augustus C. Hand	26	D	Elizabeth-town	Essex
						Thomas A. Tomlinson	27	W	Keeseville	Clinton
						DISTRICT 14				
Franklin	11,312	----	----	1,674	6.1	Random H. Gillet	23	D	Ogdensburg	St. Lawrence
St. Lawrence	35,354	----	----	2,768	12.8	Random H. Gillett	24	D	Ogdensburg	St. Lawrence
TOTALS	46,666	----	----	4,442	10.5	James B. Spencer	25	D	Fort Covington	Franklin
						John Fine	26	D	Ogdensburg	St. Lawrence
						Henry B. Van Rensselaer	27	W	Ogdensburg	St. Lawrence
						DISTRICT 15				
Hamilton	1,325	----	----	1,735	0.8	Charles McVean	23	D	Canajoharie	Montgomery
Montgomery	43,715	26	----	906	48.2	Matthias J. Bovee	24	D	Amsterdam	Montgomery
TOTALS	45,040	26	----	2,641	17.0	John Edwards	25	D	Ephratah	Fulton
						Peter J. Wagner	26	W	Fort Plain	Montgomery
						John Sanford	27	D	Amsterdam	Montgomery
						DISTRICT 16				
Herkimer	35,870	----	----	1,435	24.9	Abijah Mann, Jr.	23	D	Fairfield	Herkimer
Lewis	15,239	----	----	1,291	11.8	Abijah Mann, Jr.	24	D	Fairfield	Herkimer
TOTALS	51,109	----	----	2,726	18.7	Aphraxed Loomis	25	D	Little Falls	Herkimer
						Andrew W. Doig	26	D	Lowville	Lewis
						Andrew W. Doig	27	D	Lowville	Lewis
						DISTRICT 17				
Oneida	71,326	15	----	1,223	58.3	Samuel Beardsley	23	D	Utica	Oswego
Oswego	27,119	----	----	964	28.1	Joel Turrill	23	D	Oswego	Oswego
TOTALS	98,445	15	----	2,187	45.0	Samuel Beardsley[r] (Resigned March, 1836)	24	D	Utica	Oneida
						Rutger B. Miller (Replaced Beardsley December, 1836)	24	D	Utica	Oneida
						Joel Turrill	24	D	Oswego	Oswego
						Henry A. Foster	25	D	Rome	Oneida
						Abraham P. Grant	25	D	Oswego	Oswego
						David P. Brewster	26	D	Oswego	Oswego
						John G. Floyd	26	D	Utica	Oneida

COUNTIES						REPRESENTATIVES				
County	Aggregate	Slave	%S	sq.mi.	P/sq.mi.	Representative	Cong.	Pty.	Address	County
						DISTRICT 17 (CONTINUED)				
						David P. Brewster	27	D	Oswego	Oswego
						John G. Floyd	27	D	Utica	Oneida
						DISTRICT 18				
Jefferson	48,493	----	----	1,294	37.5	Daniel Wardwell	23	D	Mannsville	Jefferson
						Daniel Wardwell	24	D	Mannsville	Jefferson
						Isaac H. Bronson	25	D	Watertown	Jefferson
						Thomas C. Chittendon	26	W	Adams	Jefferson
						Thomas C. Chittendon	27	W	Adams	Jefferson
						DISTRICT 19				
Otsego	51,372	----	----	1,013	50.7	Sherman Page	23	D	Unadilla	Otsego
						Sherman Page	24	D	Unadilla	Otsego
						John H. Prentiss	25	D	Cooperstown	Otsego
						John H. Prentiss	26	D	Cooperstown	Otsego
						Samuel S. Browne	27	D	Cooperstown	Otsego
						DISTRICT 20				
Broome	17,579	----	----	714	24.6	Noadiah Johnson	23	D	Delhi	Delaware
Delaware	33,024	----	----	1,443	22.8	William Seymour	24	D	Binghampton	Broome
TOTALS	50,603	----	----	2,157	23.5	Amasa J. Parker	25	D	Delhi	Delaware
						Judson Allen	26	D	Harpersville	Broome
						Samuel Gordon	27	D	Delhi	Delaware
						DISTRICT 21				
Chanango	37,238	3	----	903	41.2	Henry Mitchell	23	D	Norwhich	Chenango
						William Mason	24	D	Preston	Chenango
						John C. Clark	25	D	Bainbridge	Chenango
						John C. Clark	26	W	Bainbridge	Chenango
						John C. Clark	27	W	Bainbridge	Chenango
						DISTRICT 22				
Cortland	23,791	----	----	502	47.3	Nicoll Halsey	23	D	Trumansburg	Tompkins
Tioga	27,690	----	----	524	52.8	Samuel G. Hathaway	23	D	Solon	Courtlandt
Tompkins	36,545	----	----	812	45.0					
TOTALS	88,026	----	----	1,838	47.9	Stephen B. Leonard	24	D	Owego	Tioga
						Joseph Reynolds	24	D	Virgil	Courtlandt
						Andrew D. W. Bruyn† (Died July, 1838)	25	D	Ithaca	Tompkins
						Cyrus Beers (Replaced Bruyn December, 1838)	25	D	Ithaca	Tompkins
						Hiram Gray	25	D	Elmira	Chemung[a]
						Amasa Dana	26	D	Ithaca	Tompkins
						Stephen B. Leonard	26	D	Owego	Tioga
						Samuel Partridge	27	D	Elmira	Chemung[a]
						Lewis Riggs	27	D	Homer	Courtlandt

[a]Created from Tioga County in 1836.

COUNTIES						REPRESENTATIVES				
County	Aggregate	Slave	%S	sq.mi.	P/sq.mi.	Representative	Cong.	Pty.	Address	County

DISTRICT 23

County	Aggregate	Slave	%S	sq.mi.	P/sq.mi.	Representative	Cong.	Pty.	Address	County
Madison	39,038	----	----	661	59.0	William K. Fuller	23	D	Chittenango	Madison
Onondaga	58,973	----	----	794	74.2	William Taylor	23	D	Manlius	Onondaga
TOTALS	98,011	----	----	1,455	67.4					
						William K. Fuller	24	D	Chittenango	Madison
						William Taylor	24	D	Manlius	Onondaga
						Bennet Bicknell	25	D	Morrisville	Madison
						William Taylor	25	D	Manlius	Onondaga
						Nehemiah H. Earll	26	D	Syracuse	Onondaga
						Edward Rogers	26	D	Madison	Madison
						Victory Birdseye	27	W	Pompey	Onondaga
						A. Lawrence Foster	27	W	Morrisville	Madison

DISTRICT 24

County	Aggregate	Slave	%S	sq.mi.	P/sq.mi.	Representative	Cong.	Pty.	Address	County
Cayuga	47,948	----	----	698	68.7	Rowland Day	23	D	Simpronius	Cayuga
						Ulysses F. Doubleday	24	D	Auburn	Cayuga
						William H. Noble	25	D	Cato	Cayuga
						Christopher Morgan	26	W	Aurora	Cayuga
						Christopher Morgan	27	W	Aurora	Cayuga

DISTRICT 25

County	Aggregate	Slave	%S	sq.mi.	P/sq.mi.	Representative	Cong.	Pty.	Address	County
Seneca	21,041	----	----	330	63.7	Samuel Clark	23	D	Waterloo	Seneca
Wayne	33,643	----	----	606	55.5	Graham H. Chapin	24	D	Lyons	Wayne
TOTALS	54,684	----	----	936	58.4	Samuel Birdsall	25	D	Waterloo	Seneca
						Theron R. Strong	26	D	Palmyra	Wayne
						John Maynard	27	W	Seneca Falls	Seneca

DISTRICT 26

County	Aggregate	Slave	%S	sq.mi.	P/sq.mi.	Representative	Cong.	Pty.	Address	County
Ontario	40,288	----	----	651	61.2	John Dickson	23	NR	West Bloomfield	Ontario
						Francis Granger	24	W	Canandaigua	Ontario
						Mark H. Sibley	25	W	Canandaigua	Ontario
						Francis Granger	26	W	Canandaigua	Ontario
						Francis Granger[r] (Resigned March, 1841)	27	W	Canandaigua	Ontario
						John Grieg (Replaced Granger May, 1841)	27	D	Canandaigua	Ontario

DISTRICT 27

County	Aggregate	Slave	%S	sq.mi.	P/sq.mi.	Representative	Cong.	Pty.	Address	County
Steuben	33,851	----	----	1,410	24.0	Edward Howell	23	D	Bath	Steuben
Yates	19,009	----	----	343	55.4	Joshua Lee	24	D	Penn Yan	Yates
TOTALS	52,860	----	----	1,753	30.1	John T. Andrews	25	D	North Reading	Yates
						Meredith Mallory	26	D	Hammondsport	Steuben
						William M. Oliver	27	D	Penn Yan	Yates

	COUNTIES					REPRESENTATIVES				
County	Aggregate	Slave	%S	sq.mi.	P/sq.mi.	Representative	Cong.	Pty.	Address	County

DISTRICT 28

Monroe	49,855	----	----	675	73.8	Frederick Whittlesey	23	NR	Rochester	Monroe
						Timothy Childs	24	W	Rochester	Monroe
						Timothy Childs	25	W	Rochester	Monroe
						Thomas Kempshall	26	W	Rochester	Monroe
						Timothy Childs	27	W	Rochester	Monroe

DISTRICT 29

Genesee	52,147	----	----	1,099	47.4	George W. Lay	23	NR	Batavia	Genesee
						George W. Lay	24	W	Batavia	Genesee
						William Patterson† (Died May, 1838)	25	W	Warsaw	Wyoming[a]
						Harvey Putnam (Replaced Patterson December, 1838)	25	W	Attica	Wyoming[a]
						Seth M. Gates	26	W	Leroy	Genesee
						Seth M. Gates	27	W	Leroy	Genesee

[a]Created from Genesee County in 1841.

DISTRICT 30

Alleghany	26,276	----	----	1,047	25.0	Philo C. Fuller	23	NR	Geneseo	Livingston
Livingston	27,729	----	----	638	43.4	Philo C. Fuller[r] (Resigned September, 1836)	24	W	Geneseo	Livingston
TOTALS	54,005	----	----	1,685	32.0	John Young (Replaced Fuller December, 1836)	24	W	Geneseo	Livingston
						Luther C. Peck	25	W	Pike	Wyoming[a]
						Luther C. Peck	26	W	Pike	Wyoming[a]
						John Young	27	W	Geneseo	Livingston

[a]Pike, Wyoming County, is on the border of Wyoming and Livingston Counties. Representative Peck may have lived or owned property in Livingston County.

DISTRICT 31

Cattaraugus	16,724	----	----	1,318	12.6	Abner Hazeltine	23	NR	Jamestown	Chautauqua
Chautauqua	34,671	1	----	1,081	32.0	Abner Hazeltine	24	W	Jamestown	Chautauqua
TOTALS	51,395	1	----	2,399	21.4	Richard P. Marvin	25	W	Jamestown	Chautauqua
						Richard P. Marvin	26	W	Jamestown	Chautauqua
						Staley N. Clarke	27	W	Ellicottsville	Cattaraugus

DISTRICT 32

Erie	35,719	----	----	1,058	33.7	Millard Fillmore	23	NR	Buffalo	Erie
						Thomas C. Love	24	W	Buffalo	Erie
						Millard Fillmore	25	W	Buffalo	Erie
						Millard Fillmore	26	W	Buffalo	Erie
						Millard Fillmore	27	W	Buffalo	Erie

DISTRICT 33

Niagara	18,482	----	----	532	34.7	Gideon Hard	23	NR	Albion	Orleans
Orleans	17,732	----	----	396	44.7	Gideon Hard	24	W	Albion	Orleans
TOTALS	36,214	----	----	928	39.0	Charles F. Mitchell	25	W	Lockport	Niagara
						Charles F. Mitchell	26	W	Lockport	Niagara
						Alfred Babcock	27	W	Gaines	Orleans

| COUNTIES | | | | | | REPRESENTATIVES | | | | |
County	Aggregate	Slave	%S	sq.mi.	P/sq.mi.	Representative	Cong.	Pty.	Address	County
DISTRICT 1										
Camden	6,733	2,025	30.0	239	28.2	William B. Shepard	23	D	Elizabeth City	Pasquotank
Chowan	6,697	3,768	56.2	173	38.7					
Currituck	7,655	2,320	30.3	246	31.1	William B. Shepard	24	D	Elizabeth City	Pasquotank
Gates	7,866	3,648	46.3	337	23.3					
Hertford	8,537	3,710	43.4	353	24.2	Samuel T. Sawyer	25	D	Edenton	Chowan
Pasquotank	8,641	2,021	30.3	228	37.9	Kenneth Rayner	26	W	Winton	Hertford
Perquimans	7,419	2,749	32.0	246	30.2	Kenneth Rayner	27	W	Winton	Hertford
Tyrrel	4,732	1,391	29.3	781	6.1					
TOTALS	58,280	21,632	37.1	2,603	22.4					
DISTRICT 2										
Bertie	12,262	6,797	55.4	698	17.6	Jesse A. Bynum	23	W	Halifax	Halifax
Halifax	17,739	8,197	46.2	734	24.2	Jesse A. Bynum	24	D	Halifax	Halifax
Martin	8,539	3,279	38.4	455	18.8	Jesse A. Bynum	25	D	Halifax	Halifax
North-ampton	13,391	7,242	54.0	536	25.0	Jesse A. Bynum	26	D	Halifax	Halifax
						John R. J. Daniel	27	D	Halifax	Halifax
TOTALS	51,931	25,515	49.1	2,423	21.4					
DISTRICT 3										
Beaufort	10,969	4,165	37.9	826	13.3	Thomas H. Hall	23	D	Tarboro	Edgecombe
Edgecombe	14,935	6,075	40.6	560	29.3	Ebeneazer Pettigrew	24	W	Coal Springs	Tyrrel
Hyde	6,184	1,943	31.4	613	10.1	Edward Stanley	25	W	Washington	Beaufort
Pitt	12,093	5,365	44.3	655	18.5	Edward Stanley	26	W	Washington	Beaufort
Washington	4,552	1,712	37.6	343	13.3	Edward Stanley	27	W	Washington	Beaufort
TOTALS	48,733	19,260	39.5	2,997	16.3					
DISTRICT 4										
Cateret	6,597	1,593	24.1	536	12.3	Jesse Speight	23	D	Stantonsburg	----
Craven	13,734	6,129	44.6	1,037	12.2	Jesse Speight	24	D	Stantonsburg	----
Green	6,413	2,872	44.7	307	20.9	Charles B. Shepard	25	W	New Bern	Craven
Johnston	10,938	3,639	33.2	872	12.5	Charles B. Shepard	26	D	New Bern	Craven
Jones	5,608	3,075	54.8	467	12.0	William H. Washington	27	W	New Bern	Craven
Lenoir	7,723	3,919	50.7	400	19.3					
Wayne	16,331	3,517	34.0	607	26.9					
TOTALS	67,344	24,744	36.7	4,226	15.9					

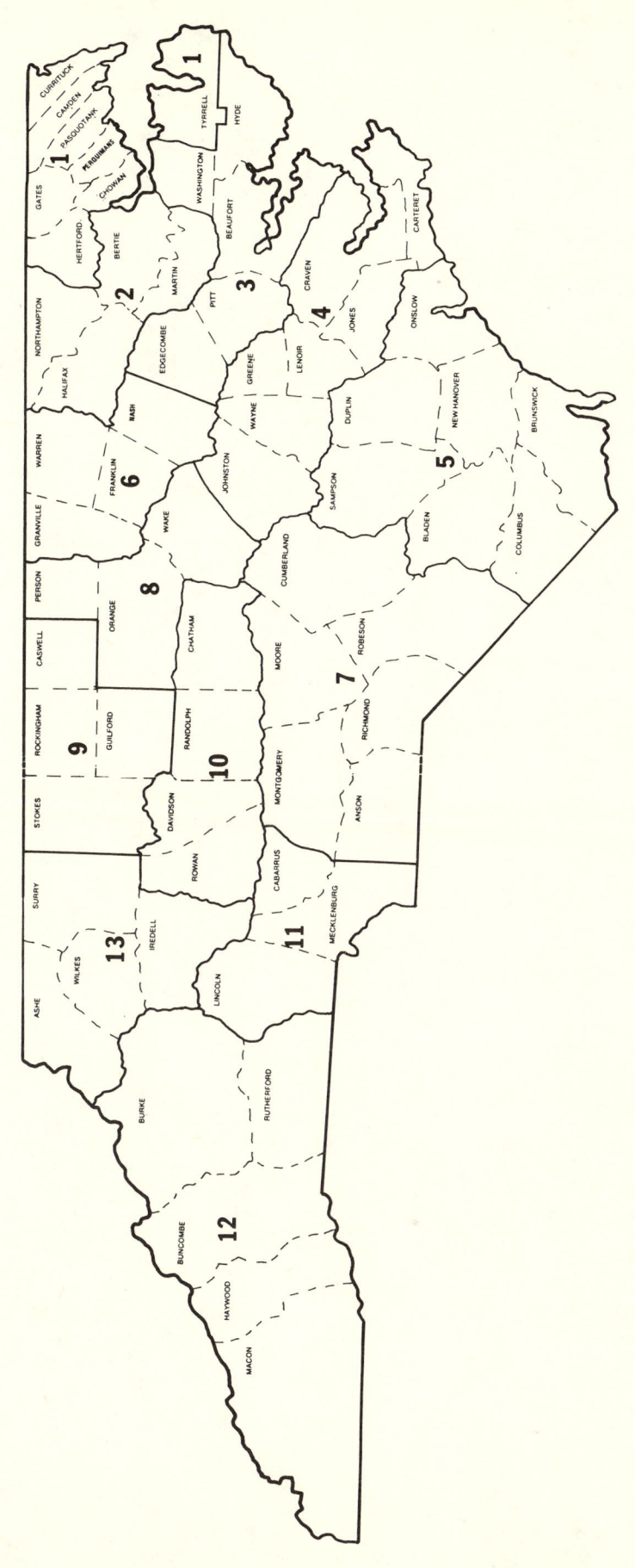

COUNTIES						REPRESENTATIVES				
County	Aggregate	Slave	%S	sq.mi.	P/sq.mi.	Representative	Cong.	Pty.	Address	County

DISTRICT 5

County	Aggregate	Slave	%S	sq.mi.	P/sq.mi.	Representative	Cong.	Pty.	Address	County
Bladen	9,938	3,122	31.4	883	11.3	James I. McKay	23	D	Elizabeth-town	Bladen
Brunswick	5,480	3,107	47.6	856	6.4					
Columbus	4,141	1,079	26.0	945	4.4	James I. McKay	24	D	Elizabeth-town	Bladen
Duplin	11,291	4,434	39.2	815	13.9					
New Hanover	10,959	5,616	51.2	185	59.2	James I. McKay	25	D	Elizabeth-town	Bladen
Onslow	7,814	3,144	40.2	765	10.2	James I. McKay	26	D	Elizabeth-town	Bladen
Sampson	11,634	3,184	27.3	945	12.3					
TOTALS	61,257	23,686	38.7	5,394	11.4	James I. McKay	27	D	Elizabeth-town	Bladen

DISTRICT 6

County	Aggregate	Slave	%S	sq.mi.	P/sq.mi.	Representative	Cong.	Pty.	Address	County
Franklin	10,665	4,960	46.5	540	19.7	Micajah T. Hawkins	23	D	Warrenton	Warren
Granville	19,355	9,166	47.3	686	28.2	Micajah T. Hawkins	24	D	Warrenton	Warren
Nash	8,490	3,006	35.4	644	13.2	Micajah T. Hawkins	25	D	Warrenton	Warren
Warren	11,877	7,327	61.6	474	25.0	Micajah T. Hawkins	26	D	Warrenton	Warren
TOTALS	50,387	24,459	48.5	2,344	21.5	Archibald H. Arrington	27	D	Hilliardston	Nash

DISTRICT 7

County	Aggregate	Slave	%S	sq.mi.	P/sq.mi.	Representative	Cong.	Pty.	Address	County
Anson	14,095	4,778	33.8	633	22.3	Edmund Deberry	23	W	Lawrence-ville	Montgomery
Cumberland	11,966	3,985	33.3	1,257	9.5					
Montgomery	10,919	2,295	21.0	886	12.3	Edmund Deberry	24	W	Lawrence-ville	Montgomery
Moore	7,745	1,673	21.6	959	8.1					
Richmond	9,396	3,512	37.3	794	11.8	Edmund Deberry	25	W	Lawrence-ville	Montgomery
Robeson	9,433	2,499	26.4	1,338	7.1					
TOTALS	63,554	18,742	29.5	5,867	10.8	Edmund Deberry	26	W	Lawrence-ville	Montgomery
						Edmund Deberry	27	W	Lawrence-ville	Montgomery

DISTRICT 8

County	Aggregate	Slave	%S	sq.mi.	P/sq.mi.	Representative	Cong.	Pty.	Address	County
Orange	23,908	7,373	30.8	1,123	21.3	Daniel L. Barringer	23	W	Raleigh	Wake
Person	10,027	4,432	44.2	401	25.0	William Montgomery	24	D	Albrights	Orange
Wake	16,331	3,517	34.0	858	19.0	William Montgomery	25	D	Albrights	Orange
TOTALS	50,266	15,322	30.5	2,382	21.1	William Montgomery	26	D	Germantown	Stokes
						Romulus H. Saunders	27	D	Raleigh	Wake

DISTRICT 9

County	Aggregate	Slave	%S	sq.mi.	P/sq.mi.	Representative	Cong.	Pty.	Address	County
Caswell	15,185	6,434	42.3	428	35.5	Augustine H. Shepperd	23	D	Germantown	Stokes
Guilford	18,737	2,594	13.8	655	28.6	Augustine H. Shepperd	24	D	Germantown	Stokes
Rockingham	12,935	4,126	31.8	569	22.7	Augustine H. Shepperd	25	D	Bethania	Stokes
Stokes	16,196	2,841	17.5	876	18.5	John Hill	26	D	Germantown	Stokes
TOTALS	63,053	13,610	29.1	2,528	24.9	Augustine H. Shepperd	27	W	Salem	Stokes

DISTRICT 10

County	Aggregate	Slave	%S	sq.mi.	P/sq.mi.	Representative	Cong.	Pty.	Address	County
Chatham	15,405	5,056	32.8	709	21.7	Abraham Rencher	23	W	Pittsboro	Chatham
Randolph	12,406	1,462	11.7	798	15.5	Abraham Rencher	24	W	Pittsboro	Chatham
Rowan	20,786	6,189	29.7	1,337	15.5	Abraham Rencher	25	W	Pittsboro	Chatham
TOTALS	48,597	12,707	26.2	2,844	17.1	Charles Fisher	26	D	Salisbury	Rowan

COUNTIES						REPRESENTATIVES				
County	Aggregate	Slave	%S	sq.mi.	P/sq.mi.	Representative	Cong.	Pty.	Address	County

DISTRICT 11

County	Aggregate	Slave	%S	sq.mi.	P/sq.mi.	Representative	Cong.	Pty.	Address	County
Cabarrus	8,810	2,258	25.6	363	24.3	Henry W. Connor	23	D	Sherrill's Ford	Lincoln
Lincoln	22,455	4,882	21.7	1,047	21.4					
Mecklenburg	20,073	7,146	85.6	1,069	37.9	Henry W. Connor	24	D	Sherrill's Ford	Lincoln
TOTALS	51,338	14,286	27.8	2,479	20.7					
						Henry W. Connor	25	D	Sherrill's Ford	Lincoln
						Henry W. Connor	26	D	Sherrill's Ford	Lincoln
						Henry W. Connor	27	D	Sherrill's Ford	Lincoln

DISTRICT 12

County	Aggregate	Slave	%S	sq.mi.	P/sq.mi.	Representative	Cong.	Pty.	Address	County
Buncombe	16,281	1,666	10.2	1,575	10.3	James Graham	23	W	Ruther-fordton	Rutherford
Burke	17,888	3,626	20.0	2,188	8.2					
Haywood	4,578	291	6.3	1,357	3.4	James Graham[ce]	24	W	Ruther-fordton	Rutherford
Macon	5,333	458	8.5	2,057	2.6					
Rutherford	17,557	3,358	19.1	1,180	14.8	(Election successfully contested by David Newlands)				
TOTALS	61,637	9,399	15.2	8,357	7.4	David Newlands	24	(----)	----	----
						(Successfully contested the election of Graham; took seat December, 1836)				
						James Graham	25	W	Ruther-fordton	Rutherford
						James Graham	26	W	Ruther-fordton	Rutherford
						James Graham	27	W	Ruther-fordton	Rutherford

DISTRICT 13

County	Aggregate	Slave	%S	sq.mi.	P/sq.mi.	Representative	Cong.	Pty.	Address	County
Ashe	6,987	492	7.0	968	7.2	Lewis Williams	23	W	Panther Creek	Surry
Iredell	14,918	3,682	24.6	831	18.0					
Surry	14,504	1,945	13.4	862	16.6	Lewis Williams	24	W	Panther Creek	Surry
Wilkes	11,968	1,492	12.4	757	15.8	Lewis Williams	25	W	Panther Creek	Surry
TOTALS	48,377	7,611	15.7	3,418	14.1	Lewis Williams	26	W	Panther Creek	Surry
						Lewis Williams†	27	W	Panther Creek	Surry
						(Died February, 1842)				
						Anderson Mitchell	27	W	Wilkesbro	Wilkes
						(Replaced Williams September 27, 1842)				

COUNTIES						REPRESENTATIVES				
County	Aggregate	Slave	%S	sq.mi.	P/sq.mi.	Representative	Cong.	Pty.	Address	County
DISTRICT 1										
Hamilton	52,317	----	----	487	107.4	Robert T. Lytle	23	D	Cincinnati	Hamilton
						Bellamy Storer	24	W	Cincinnati	Hamilton
						Alexander Duncan	25	D	Cincinnati	Hamilton
						Alexander Duncan	26	D	Cincinnati	Hamilton
						Nathaniel G. Pendleton	27	W	Cincinnati	Hamilton
DISTRICT 2										
Butler	27,142	----	----	484	56.1	Taylor Webster	23	D	Hamilton	Butler
Darke	6,204	----	----	630	9.8	Taylor Webster	24	D	Hamilton	Butler
Preble	16,291	----	----	414	39.4	Taylor Webster	25	D	Hamilton	Butler
TOTALS	49,637	----	----	1,528	32.5	John B. Weller	26	D	Hamilton	Butler
						John B. Weller	27	D	Hamilton	Butler
DISTRICT 3										
Allen	578	----	----	471	1.2	Joseph Crane	23	JD	Dayton	Montgomery
Henry	262	----	----	567	0.5	Joseph Crane	24	D	Dayton	Montgomery
Mercer	1,110	----	----	469	2.4	Patrick G. Goode	25	W	Sidney	Shelby
Miami	12,807	----	----	426	30.1	Patrick G. Goode	26	W	Sidney	Shelby
Montgomery	24,362	----	----	443	55.0	Patrick G. Goode	27	W	Sidney	Shelby
Paulding	161	----	----	396	0.4					
Putnam	230	----	----	462	0.5					
Shelby	3,671	----	----	312	11.8					
Vanwert	49	----	----	396	0.1					
Williams	387	----	----	440	0.9					
Wood	1,102	----	----	621	1.8					
TOTALS	44,719	----	----	5,003	8.9					
DISTRICT 4										
Clinton	11,436	----	----	468	24.4	Thomas Corwin	23	D	Lebanon	Warren
Highland	16,345	----	----	332	49.2	Thomas Corwin	24	D	Lebanon	Warren
Warren	21,468	----	----	400	53.7	Thomas Corwin	25	W	Lebanon	Warren
TOTALS	49,249	----	----	1,200	41.0	Thomas Corwin^r	26	W	Lebanon	Warren
						(Resigned May, 1840)				
						Jeremiah Morrow	26	W	Twenty Mile Stand	Warren
						(Replaced Corwin December,				
						(Replaced Corwin December, 1840)				
						Jeremiah Morrow	27	W	Twenty Mile Stand	Warren

COUNTIES						REPRESENTATIVES				
County	Aggregate	Slave	%S	sq.mi.	P/sq.mi.	Representative	Cong.	Pty.	Address	County

DISTRICT 5

County	Aggregate	Slave	%S	sq.mi.	P/sq.mi.	Representative	Cong.	Pty.	Address	County
Adams	12,281	----	----	383	32.1	Thomas L. Hamer	23	D	Georgetown	Brown
Brown	17,867	----	----	399	44.8	Thomas L. Hamer	24	D	Georgetown	Brown
Clermont	20,466	----	----	506	40.4	Thomas L. Hamer	25	D	Georgetown	Brown
TOTALS	50,614	----	----	1,288	39.3	William Doan	26	D	Withamsville	Clermont
						William Doan	27	D	Withamsville	Clermont

DISTRICT 6

County	Aggregate	Slave	%S	sq.mi.	P/sq.mi.	Representative	Cong.	Pty.	Address	County
Athens	9,787	----	----	606	16.2	Samuel F. Vinton	23	W	Gallipolis	Gallia
Gallia	9,733	----	----	465	20.9	Samuel F. Vinton	24	W	Gallipolis	Gallia
Lawrence	5,367	----	----	387	13.9	Calvary Morris	25	W	Athens	Athens
Meigs	6,158	----	----	390	15.8	Calvary Morris	26	W	Athens	Athens
Monroe	8,768	----	----	468	18.7	Calvary Morris	27	W	Athens	Athens
Washington	11,731	----	----	485	24.2					
TOTALS	51,544	----	----	2,801	18.4					

DISTRICT 7

County	Aggregate	Slave	%S	sq.mi.	P/sq.mi.	Representative	Cong.	Pty.	Address	County
Fayette	8,182	----	----	390	21.0	William Allen	23	D	Chillicothe	Ross
Jackson	5,941	----	----	549	10.8	William K. Bond	24	W	Chillicothe	Ross
Pike	6,024	----	----	450	13.4	William K. Bond	25	W	Chillicothe	Ross
Ross	24,068	----	----	673	35.8	William K. Bond	26	W	Chillicothe	Ross
Scioto	8,740	----	----	558	15.7	William Russell	27	W	Portsmouth	Scioto
TOTALS	52,955	----	----	2,620	20.2					

DISTRICT 8

County	Aggregate	Slave	%S	sq.mi.	P/sq.mi.	Representative	Cong.	Pty.	Address	County
Delaware	11,504	----	----	588	19.6	Jeremiah McLene	23	D	Columbus	Franklin
Franklin	14,741	----	----	506	29.1	Jeremiah McLene	24	D	Columbus	Franklin
Madison	6,190	----	----	470	13.2	Joseph Ridgeway	25	W	Columbus	Franklin
Marion	6,551	----	----	486	13.5	Joseph Ridgeway	26	W	Columbus	Franklin
Pickaway	16,001	----	----	376	42.6	Joseph Ridgeway	27	W	Columbus	Franklin
TOTALS	54,987	----	----	2,426	22.7					

DISTRICT 9

County	Aggregate	Slave	%S	sq.mi.	P/sq.mi.	Representative	Cong.	Pty.	Address	County
Fairfield	24,786	----	----	485	51.1	John Chaney	23	D	Courtwright	Fairfield
Hocking	4,008	----	----	383	10.5	John Chaney	24	D	Courtwright	Fairfield
Morgan	11,800	----	----	498	23.7	John Chaney	25	D	Courtwright	Fairfield
Perry	13,970	----	----	424	32.9	William Medill	26	D	Lancaster	Fairfield
TOTALS	54,564	----	----	1,790	30.5	William Medill	27	D	Lancaster	Fairfield

DISTRICT 10

County	Aggregate	Slave	%S	sq.mi.	P/sq.mi.	Representative	Cong.	Pty.	Address	County
Champaigne	12,131	----	----	352	34.5	Joseph Vance	23	D	Urbana	Champaigne
Clark	13,114	----	----	311	42.2	Samson Mason	24	W	Springfield	Clark
Greene	14,801	----	----	346	42.8	Samson Mason	25	W	Springfield	Clark
Hancock	813	----	----	483	1.7	Samson Mason	26	W	Springfield	Clark
Hardin	210	----	----	462	0.5	Samson Mason	27	W	Springfield	Clark
Logan	6,440	----	----	374	17.2					
Union	3,192	----	----	353	9.0					
TOTALS	50,701	----	----	2,681	18.9					

COUNTIES						REPRESENTATIVES				
County	Aggregate	Slave	%S	sq.mi.	P/sq.mi.	Representative	Cong.	Pty.	Address	County

DISTRICT 11

County	Aggregate	Slave	%S	sq.mi.	P/sq.mi.	Representative	Cong.	Pty.	Address	County
Belmont	28,627	----	----	448	63.9	James M. Bell	23	D	Cambridge	Guernsey
Guernsey	18,036	----	----	610	29.6	William Kennon, Sr.	24	D	St. Clairsville	Belmont
TOTALS	46,663	----	----	1,058	44.1	James Alexander, Jr.	25	W	St. Clairsville	Belmont
						Isaac Parish	26	D	Cambridge	Guernsey
						Benjamin S. Cowan	27	W	St. Clairsville	Guernsey

DISTRICT 12

County	Aggregate	Slave	%S	sq.mi.	P/sq.mi.	Representative	Cong.	Pty.	Address	County
Licking	20,869	----	----	564	37.0	Robert Mitchell	23	D	Zanesville	Muskingum
Muskingum	29,334	----	----	625	46.9	Elias Howell	24	W	Newark	Licking
TOTALS	50,203	----	----	1,189	42.2	Alexander Harper	25	W	Zanesville	Muskingum
						Jonathan Taylor	26	D	Newark	Licking
						Joshua Mathiot	27	W	Newark	Licking

DISTRICT 13

County	Aggregate	Slave	%S	sq.mi.	P/sq.mi.	Representative	Cong.	Pty.	Address	County
Coshocton	11,161	----	----	526	21.2	David Spangler	23	W	Coshocton	Coshocton
Holmes	9,135	----	----	426	21.4	David Spangler	24	W	Coshocton	Coshocton
Knox	17,085	----	----	584	29.3	Daniel P. Leadbetter	25	D	Millersburg	Holmes
Tuscarawas	14,298	----	----	564	23.4	Daniel P. Leadbetter	26	JD	Millersburg	Holmes
TOTALS	51,679	----	----	2,100	24.6	James Mathews	27	D	Coshocton	Coshocton

DISTRICT 14

County	Aggregate	Slave	%S	sq.mi.	P/sq.mi.	Representative	Cong.	Pty.	Address	County
Crawford	4,791	----	----	432	11.1	William Patterson	23	D	Mansfield	Richland
Erie[a]	-----	----	----	----	----	William Patterson	24	D	Mansfield	Richland
Huron	13,341	----	----	780	17.1	William H. Hunter	25	D	Sandusky	Erie[a]
Richland	24,006	----	----	868	27.7	George Sweeney	26	D	Bucyrus	Crawford
Sandusky	2,851	----	----	420	6.8	George Sweeney	27	D	Bucyrus	Crawford
Seneca	5,159	----	----	414	12.5					
TOTALS	50,148	----	----	2,914	17.2					

[a]Created from Huron County in 1838.

DISTRICT 15

County	Aggregate	Slave	%S	sq.mi.	P/sq.mi.	Representative	Cong.	Pty.	Address	County
Cuyahoga	10,373	----	----	560	18.5	Jonathan Sloane	23	W	Ravenna	Portage
Lorain	5,096	----	----	343	14.6	Jonathan Sloane	24	W	Ravenna	Portage
Medina	7,560	----	----	682	11.1	John W. Allen	25	W	Cleveland	Cuyahoga
Portage	18,826	----	----	667	28.2	John W. Allen	26	W	Cleveland	Cuyahoga
TOTALS	41,855	----	----	2,252	18.6	Sherlock J. Andrews	27	W	Cleveland	Cuyahoga

DISTRICT 16

County	Aggregate	Slave	%S	sq.mi.	P/sq.mi.	Representative	Cong.	Pty.	Address	County
Ashtabula	14,584	----	----	767	19.0	Elisha Whittlesey	23	W	Canfield	Trumbull
Geauga	15,813	----	----	560	28.2	Elisha Whittlesey	24	W	Canfield	Trumbull
Trumbull	26,153	----	----	850	30.8	Elisha Whittlesey[r]	25	W	Canfield	Trumbull
TOTALS	56,550	----	----	2,177	26.0	(Resigned July, 1838)				
						Joshua R. Giddings	25	W	Jefferson	Ashtabula
						(Replaced Whittlesey December, 1838)				
						Joshua R. Giddings	26	W	Jefferson	Ashtabula
						Joshua R. Giddings	27	W	Jefferson	Ashtabula

| COUNTIES | | | | | | REPRESENTATIVES | | | | |
County	Aggregate	Slave	%S	sq.mi.	P/sq.mi.	Representative	Cong.	Pty.	Address	County

DISTRICT 17

| COUNTIES | | | | | | REPRESENTATIVES | | | | |
County	Aggregate	Slave	%S	sq.mi.	P/sq.mi.	Representative	Cong.	Pty.	Address	County
Columbiana	35,592	----	----	798	44.6	John Thomson	23	D	New Lisbon	Columbiana
						John Thomson	24	D	New Lisbon	Columbiana
						Andrew Loomis[r]	25	D	New Lisbon	Columbiana
						(Resigned October, 1837)				
						Charles D. Coffin	25	W	New Lisbon	Columbiana
						(Replaced Loomis December, 1837)				
						John Hastings	26	D	Salem	Columbiana
						John Hastings	27	D	Salem	Columbiana

DISTRICT 18

County	Aggregate	Slave	%S	sq.mi.	P/sq.mi.	Representative	Cong.	Pty.	Address	County
Stark	26,588	----	----	609	43.7	Benjamin Jones	23	D	Wooster	Wayne
Wayne	23,333	----	----	620	37.6	Benjamin Jones	24	D	Wooster	Wayne
TOTALS	49,921	----	----	1,229	40.6	Mathias Shepler	25	D	Bethlehem	Stark
						David A. Starkweather	26	D	Canton	Stark
						Ezra Dean	27	D	Wooster	Wayne

DISTRICT 19

County	Aggregate	Slave	%S	sq.mi.	P/sq.mi.	Representative	Cong.	Pty.	Address	County
Harrison	20,916	----	----	378	55.3	Humphrey H. Leavitt[r]	23	D	Steubanville	Jefferson
Jefferson	22,489	----	----	395	56.9	(Resigned July, 1834)				
TOTALS	43,405	----	----	773	56.2	Daniel Kilgore	23	D	Cadiz	Harrison
						(Replaced Leavitt December, 1834)				
						Daniel Kilgore	24	D	Cadiz	Harrison
						Daniel Kilgore[r]	25	D	Cadiz	Harrison
						(Resigned July, 1838)				
						Henry Swearingen	25	D	Smithfield	Jefferson
						(Replaced Kilgore December, 1838)				
						Henry Swearingen	26	D	Smithfield	Jefferson
						Samuel Stokeley	27	W	Steubanville	Jefferson

PENNSYLVANIA
25 DISTRICTS
31 CONGRESSMEN

| COUNTIES | | | | | | REPRESENTATIVES | | | | |
County	Aggregate	Slave	%S	sq.mi.	P/sq.mi.	Representative	Cong.	Pty.	Address	County

DISTRICT 1

County	Aggregate	Slave	%S	sq.mi.	P/sq.mi.	Representative	Cong.	Pty.	Address	County
Towns in Philadelphia County:						Joel B. Sutherland	23	D	City of Philadelphia	
Blockley	3,401	----	----	----	----	Joel B. Sutherland	24	D	City of Philadelphia	
Bristol	1,425	----	----	----	----	Lemuel Paynter	25	D	Southwark	Philadelphia
Germantown	4,634	----	----	----	----	Lemuel Paynter	26	D	Southwark	Philadelphia
Kinnsessing	1,068	----	----	----	----	Charles Brown	27	D	City of Philadelphia	
Moya-mensing	6,822	----	----	----	----					
Passayunk	1,442	----	----	----	----					
Penn Township	2,507	----	----	----	----					

350

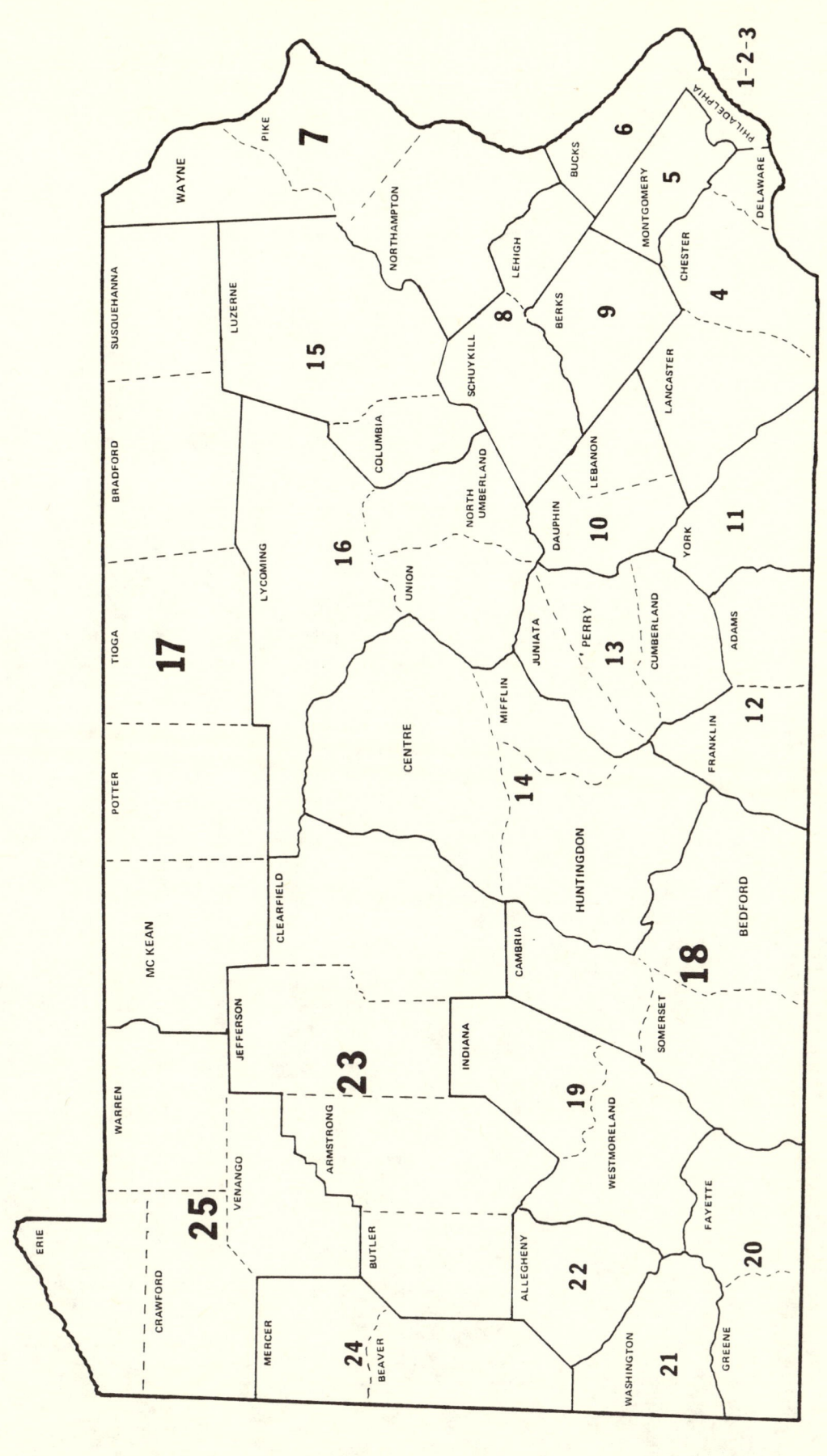

COUNTIES

REPRESENTATIVES

County	Aggregate	Slave	%S	sq.mi.	P/sq.mi.	Representative	Cong.	Pty.	Address	County
						DISTRICT 1 (CONTINUED)				
Rox-borough	3,334	----	----	----	----					
Southwark	20,581	----	----	----	----					
TOTALS	45,214	----	----	20	2260.7					
						DISTRICT 2				
City of Philadelphia	80,462	11	----	15	5364.1	Horace Binney	23	NR	City of Philadelphia	
						James Harper	23	NR	City of Philadelphia	
						James Harper	24	W	City of Philadelphia	
						Joseph B. Ingersoll	24	W	City of Philadelphia	
						John Sergeant	25	W	City of Philadelphia	
						George W. Toland	25	W	City of Philadelphia	
						John Sergeant	26	W	City of Philadelphia	
						George W. Toland	26	W	City of Philadelphia	
						John Sergeant[r] (Resigned September, 1841)	27	W	City of Philadelphia	
						Joseph R. Ingersoll (Replaced Sergeant December, 1841)	27	W	City of Philadelphia	
						George W. Toland	27	W	City of Philadelphia	
						DISTRICT 3				
All of Philadelphia County not included in Districts 1 and 2, total:	59,901	2	----	105	570.5	John G. Watnough	23	NR	City of Philadelphia	
						Michael W. Ash	24	D	City of Philadelphia	
						Francis J. Harper† (Died March, 1841)	25	D	Frankford	Philadelphia
						Charles Naylor (Replaced Harper September, 1841)	26	W	City of Philadelphia	
						Charles Naylor	26	W	City of Philadelphia	
						Charles J. Ingersoll	27	D	City of Philadelphia	
						DISTRICT 4				
Chester	50,910	6	----	761	66.9	Edward Darlington	23	AM	Chester	Delaware
Delaware	17,323	3	----	184	94.1	William Hiester	23	AM	New Holland	Lancaster
Lancaster	76,631	55	0.1	946	81.0	David Potts, Jr.	23	AM	Pottstown	Chester
TOTALS	144,864	64	----	1,891	76.6					
						Edward Darlington	24	W	Chester	Delaware
						William Hiester	24	W	New Holland	Lancaster
						David Potts, Jr.	24	W	Pottstown	Chester
						Edward Darlington	25	W	Chester	Lancaster
						Edward Davies	25	W	Churchtown	Lancaster
						David Potts, Jr.	25	W	Pottstown	Chester
						Edward Davies	26	W	Churchtown	Lancaster
						John Edwards	26	W	Ivy Mills	Delaware
						Francis James	26	W	Westchester	Chester
						Jeremiah Brown	27	W	Goshen	Lancaster
						John Edwards	27	W	Ivy Mills	Delaware
						Francis James	27	W	Westchester	Chester

	COUNTIES					REPRESENTATIVES				
County	Aggregate	Slave	%S	sq.mi.	P/sq.mi.	Representative	Cong.	Pty.	Address	County

DISTRICT 5

Montgomery	39,406	1	----	496	79.4	Joel K. Mann	23	D	Jenkintown	Montgomery
						Jacob Fry, Jr.	24	D	Trappe	Montgomery
						Jacob Fry, Jr.	25	D	Trappe	Montgomery
						Joseph Fornance	26	D	Norristown	Montgomery
						Joseph Fornance	27	D	Norristown	Montgomery

DISTRICT 6

Bucks	45,745	6	----	614	74.5	Robert Ramsey	23	D	Hartsville	Bucks
						Mathias Morris	24	W	Doylestown	Bucks
						Mathias Morris	25	W	Doylestown	Bucks
						John Davis	26	D	Davisville	Bucks
						Robert Ramsey	27	W	Hartsville	Bucks

DISTRICT 7

North-ampton	39,482	----	----	1,478	26.7	David D. Wagener	23	D	Easton	Northampton
						David D. Wagener	24	D	Easton	Northampton
Pike	4,843	1	----	803	6.0	David D. Wagener	25	D	Easton	Northampton
Wayne	7,663	----	----	741	10.3	David D. Wagener	26	D	Easton	Northampton
TOTALS	51,988	1	----	3,022	17.2	John Westbrook	27	D	Dingmans Ferry	Pike

DISTRICT 8

Lehigh	22,256	2	----	348	63.9	Henry King	23	D	Allentown	Lehigh
Schuylkill	20,744	1	----	784	26.4	Edward B. Hubley	24	D	Orwigsburg	Schuylkill
TOTALS	43,000	3	----	1,132	38.0	Edward B. Hubley	25	D	Orwigsburg	Schuylkill
						Peter Newhard	26	D	Allentown	Lehigh
						Peter Newhard	27	D	Allentown	Lehigh

DISTRICT 9

Berks	53,152	7	----	862	61.7	Henry Muhlenberg	23	D	Reading	Berks
						Henry Muhlenberg	24	D	Reading	Berks
						Henry Muhlenberg[r]	25	D	Reading	Berks
						(Resigned February, 1838)				
						George M. Keim	25	D	Reading	Berks
						(Replaced Muhlenberg March, 1838)				
						George M. Keim	26	D	Reading	Berks
						George M. Keim	27	D	Reading	Berks

DISTRICT 10

Dauphin	25,243	18	----	518	48.7	William Clark	23	NR	Dauphin	Dauphin
Lebanon	20,557	5	----	363	56.6	William Clark	24	W	Dauphin	Dauphin
TOTALS	45,800	23	----	881	52.0	Luther Reily	25	D	Harrisburg	Dauphin
						William Simonton	26	W	Hummels-town	Dauphin
						William Simonton	27	W	Hummels-town	Dauphin

DISTRICT 11

York	42,859	28	----	909	47.1	Charles A. Barnitz	23	NR	York	York
						Henry Logan	24	D	Dillsburg	York
						Henry Logan	25	D	Dillsburg	York
						James Gerry	26	D	Shrewsbury	York
						James Gerry	27	D	Shrewsbury	York

COUNTIES						REPRESENTATIVES				
County	Aggregate	Slave	%S	sq.mi.	P/sq.mi.	Representative	Cong.	Pty.	Address	County

DISTRICT 12

County	Aggregate	Slave	%S	sq.mi.	P/sq.mi.	Representative	Cong.	Pty.	Address	County
Adams	21,379	45	0.2	526	40.6	George Chambers	23	NR	Chambersburg	Franklin
Franklin	35,037	11	----	754	46.4					
TOTALS	56,416	56	0.1	1,280	44.1	George Chambers	24	W	Chambersburg	Franklin
						Daniel Sheffer	25	D	York[a]	York
						James Cooper	26	W	Gettysburg	Adams
						James Cooper	27	W	Gettysburg	Adams

[a]Sheffer listed York as his mailing address.

DISTRICT 13

County	Aggregate	Slave	%S	sq.mi.	P/sq.mi.	Representative	Cong.	Pty.	Address	County
Cumberland	29,226	7	----	555	52.6	Jesse Miller	23	D	Landisburg	Perry
Juniata	10,195	----	----	386	26.4	Jesse Miller[r]	24	D	Landisburg	Perry
Perry	14,261	4	----	551	25.8	(Resigned October 30, 1836)				
TOTALS	56,682	11	----	1,492	36.0	James Black	24	D	Newport	Perry
						(Replaced Miller December, 1836)				
						Charles McClure	25	D	Carlisle	Cumberland
						William S. Ramsey[†]	26	D	Carlisle	Cumberland
						(Died October 11, 1840)				
						Charles McClure	26	D	Carlisle	Cumberland
						(Replaced Ramsey December, 1841)				
						Amos Gustine	27	D	Mifflintown	Juniata

DISTRICT 14

County	Aggregate	Slave	%S	sq.mi.	P/sq.mi.	Representative	Cong.	Pty.	Address	County
Centre	18,879	----	----	1,865	10.1	Joseph Henderson	23	D	Brown's Mills	----
Huntingdon	27,145	8	----	1,425	19.0	Joseph Henderson	24	D	Brown's Mills	----
Mifflin	11,495	----	----	431	26.7	William W. Potter	25	D	Bellefonte	Centre
TOTALS	57,519	8	----	3,721	15.5	William W. Potter[†]	26	D	Bellefonte	Centre
						(Died October 28, 1839, before Congress assembled)				
						George McCullough	26	D	Center Line	Centre
						(Replaced Potter December, 1839)				
						James Irvin	27	W	Milesburg	Centre

DISTRICT 15

County	Aggregate	Slave	%S	sq.mi.	P/sq.mi.	Representative	Cong.	Pty.	Address	County
Columbia	20,059	----	----	484	41.4	Andrew Beaumont	23	D	Wilkes-Barre	Luzerne
Luzerne	27,379	----	----	1,738	15.8	Andrew Beaumont	24	D	Wilkes-Barre	Luzerne
TOTALS	47,438	----	----	2,222	21.3	David Petrikin	25	D	Danville	Columbia
						David Petrikin	26	D	Danville	Columbia
						Benjamin A. Bidlack	27	D	Wilkes-Barre	Luzerne

DISTRICT 16

County	Aggregate	Slave	%S	sq.mi.	P/sq.mi.	Representative	Cong.	Pty.	Address	County
Lycoming	17,636	----	----	1,944	9.1	Joseph B. Anthony	23	D	Williamsport	Lycoming
North-						Joseph B. Anthony	24	D	Williamsport	Lycoming
umberland	18,133	----	----	725	25.0	Robert H. Hammond	25	D	Milton	North-umberland
Union	20,795	2	----	645	32.2					
TOTALS	56,564	2	----	3,314	17.1	Robert H. Hammond	26	D	Milton	North-umberland
						John Snyder	27	D	Selingsgrove	Union

County	Aggregate	Slave	%S	sq.mi.	P/sq.mi.	Representative	Cong.	Pty.	Address	County
		COUNTIES						REPRESENTATIVES		

DISTRICT 17

County	Aggregate	Slave	%S	sq.mi.	P/sq.mi.	Representative	Cong.	Pty.	Address	County
Bradford	19,746	13	----	1,148	17.2	John Laporte	23	D	Asylum	Bradford
McKean	1,439	----	----	1,100	1.3	John Laporte	24	D	Asylum	Bradford
Potter	1,265	----	----	992	1.3	Samuel W. Morris	25	D	Wellsboro	Tioga
Susque-						Samuel W. Morris	26	D	Wellsboro	Tioga
hanna	16,787	----	----	833	20.1	Davis Dimock, Jr.†	27	D	Montrose	Susquehanna
Tioga	8,978	----	----	1,146	7.8	(Died January 13, 1842)				
TOTALS	48,215	13	----	5,219	9.2	Almon H. Read	27	D	Montrose	Susquehanna
						(Replaced Dimock March, 1842)				

DISTRICT 18

County	Aggregate	Slave	%S	sq.mi.	P/sq.mi.	Representative	Cong.	Pty.	Address	County
Bedford	24,502	1	----	1,453	16.9	George Burd	23	D	Bedford	Bedford
Cambria	7,076	----	----	692	10.2	Job Mann	24	D	Bedford	Bedford
Somerset	17,762	2	----	1,078	16.5	Charles Ogle	25	W	Somerset	Somerset
TOTALS	49,340	3	----	3,223	15.3	Charles Ogle	26	W	Somerset	Somerset
						Charles Ogle†	27	W	Somerset	Somerset
						(Died May 10, 1841)				
						Henry Black†	27	W	Somerset	Somerset
						(Replaced Ogle. then died November 28, 1841)				
						James Russell	27	W	Bedford	Bedford
						(Replaced Black January, 1842)				

DISTRICT 19

County	Aggregate	Slave	%S	sq.mi.	P/sq.mi.	Representative	Cong.	Pty.	Address	County
Indiana	14,252	----	----	825	17.3	Richard Coulter	23	D	Greensburg	Westmoreland
West-						John Klingensmith, Jr.	24	D	Stewartsville	Westmoreland
moreland	38,400	----	----	1,024	37.5	John Klingensmith, Jr.	25	D	Stewartsville	Westmoreland
TOTALS	52,652	----	----	1,849	28.5	Albert G. Marchand	26	D	Greensburg	Westmoreland
						Albert G. Marchand	27	D	Greensburg	Westmoreland

DISTRICT 20

County	Aggregate	Slave	%S	sq.mi.	P/sq.mi.	Representative	Cong.	Pty.	Address	County
Fayette	29,172	99	0.3	802	364	Andrew Stewart	23	NR	Uniontown	Fayette
Greene	18,028	2	----	578	31.2	Andrew Buchanan	24	D	Waynesburg	Greene
TOTALS	47,200	101	0.2	1,380	34.2	Andrew Buchanan	25	D	Waynesburg	Greene
						Enos Hook	26	D	Waynesburg	Greene
						Enos Hook[r]	27	D	Waynesburg	Greene
						(Resigned April, 1841)				
						Henry W. Beeson	27	D	Uniontown	Fayette
						(Replaced Hook May, 1841)				

DISTRICT 21

County	Aggregate	Slave	%S	sq.mi.	P/sq.mi.	Representative	Cong.	Pty.	Address	County
Washington	42,784	1	----	857	49.9	Thomas M. T. McKenna McKennan	23	NR	Washington	Washington
						Thomas M. T. McKennan	24	W	Washington	Washington
						Thomas M. T. McKennan	25	W	Washington	Washington
						Isaac Leet	26	D	Washington	Washington
						Joseph Lawrence†	27	W	Washington	Washington
						(Died April 17, 1842)				
						Thomas M. T. McKennan	27	W	Washington	Washington
						(Replaced Lawrence May, 1842)				

COUNTIES						REPRESENTATIVES				
County	Aggregate	Slave	%S	sq.mi.	P/sq.mi.	Representative	Cong.	Pty.	Address	County

DISTRICT 22

County	Aggregate	Slave	%S	sq.mi.	P/sq.mi.	Representative	Cong.	Pty.	Address	County
Allegheny	50,552	27	----	857	59.0	Harmar Denney	23	AM	Pittsburgh	Allegheny
						Harmar Denney	24	W	Pittsburgh	Allegheny
						Richard Biddle	25	W	Pittsburgh	Allegheny
						Richard Biddle	26	W	Pittsburgh	Allegheny
						William W. Irwin	27	W	Pittsburgh	Allegheny

DISTRICT 23

County	Aggregate	Slave	%S	sq.mi.	P/sq.mi.	Representative	Cong.	Pty.	Address	County
Armstrong	17,701	----	----	1,249	14.2	Samuel S. Harrison	23	D	Kittannine	Armstrong
Butler	14,581	4	----	794	18.4	Samuel S. Harrison	24	D	Kittannine	Armstrong
Clearfield	4,803	----	----	1,990	2.4	William Beatty	25	D	Butler	Butler
Jefferson	1,441	----	----	652	2.2	William Beatty	26	D	Butler	Butler
TOTALS	38,526	4	----	4,685	8.2	William Jack	26	D	Brookville	Jefferson

DISTRICT 24

County	Aggregate	Slave	%S	sq.mi.	P/sq.mi.	Representative	Cong.	Pty.	Address	County
Beaver	24,183	----	----	807	30.0	John Banks	23	AM	Mercer	Mercer
Mercer	19,729	6	----	670	29.4	John Banks[r]	24	W	Mercer	Mercer
TOTALS	43,912	6	----	1,477	29.7	(Resigned in 1836)				
						John J. Pearson	24	W	Mercer	Mercer
						(Replaced Banks December, 1836)				
						Thomas Henry	25	W	Beaver	Beaver
						Thomas Henry	26	W	Beaver	Beaver
						Thomas Henry	27	W	Beaver	Beaver

DISTRICT 25

County	Aggregate	Slave	%S	sq.mi.	P/sq.mi.	Representative	Cong.	Pty.	Address	County
Crawford	16,030	----	----	1,012	15.8	John Galbraith	23	D	Franklin	Venango
Erie	17,041	1	----	813	21.0	John Galbraith	24	D	Franklin	Venango
Venango	9,470	3	----	878	10.8	Arnold Plumer	25	D	Franklin	Venango
Warren	4,697	----	----	905	5.2	John Galbraith	26	D	Erie	Erie
TOTALS	47,238	4	----	3,608	13.1	Arnold Plumer	27	D	Franklin	Venango

RHODE ISLAND
2 CONGRESSMEN AT LARGE

COUNTIES						REPRESENTATIVES				
County	Aggregate	Slave	%S	sq.mi.	P/sq.mi.	Representative	Cong.	Pty.	Address	County

AT LARGE

County	Aggregate	Slave	%S	sq.mi.	P/sq.mi.	Representative	Cong.	Pty.	Address	County
Bristol	5,446	1	----	25	217.8	Tristram Burges	23	NR	Providence	Providence
Kent	12,789	----	----	202	63.3	Duttee J. Pearce	23	D	Newport	Newport
Newport	16,535	6	----	103	160.5					
Providence	47,018	4	----	413	113.8	Duttee J. Pearce	24	D	Newport	Newport
Washington	15,411	3	----	340	45.3	William Sprague	24	W	Natick	Kent
TOTALS	97,199	14	----	1,083	89.7					
						Robert B. Cranston	25	W	Newport	Newport
						Joseph L. Tillinghast	25	W	Providence	Providence

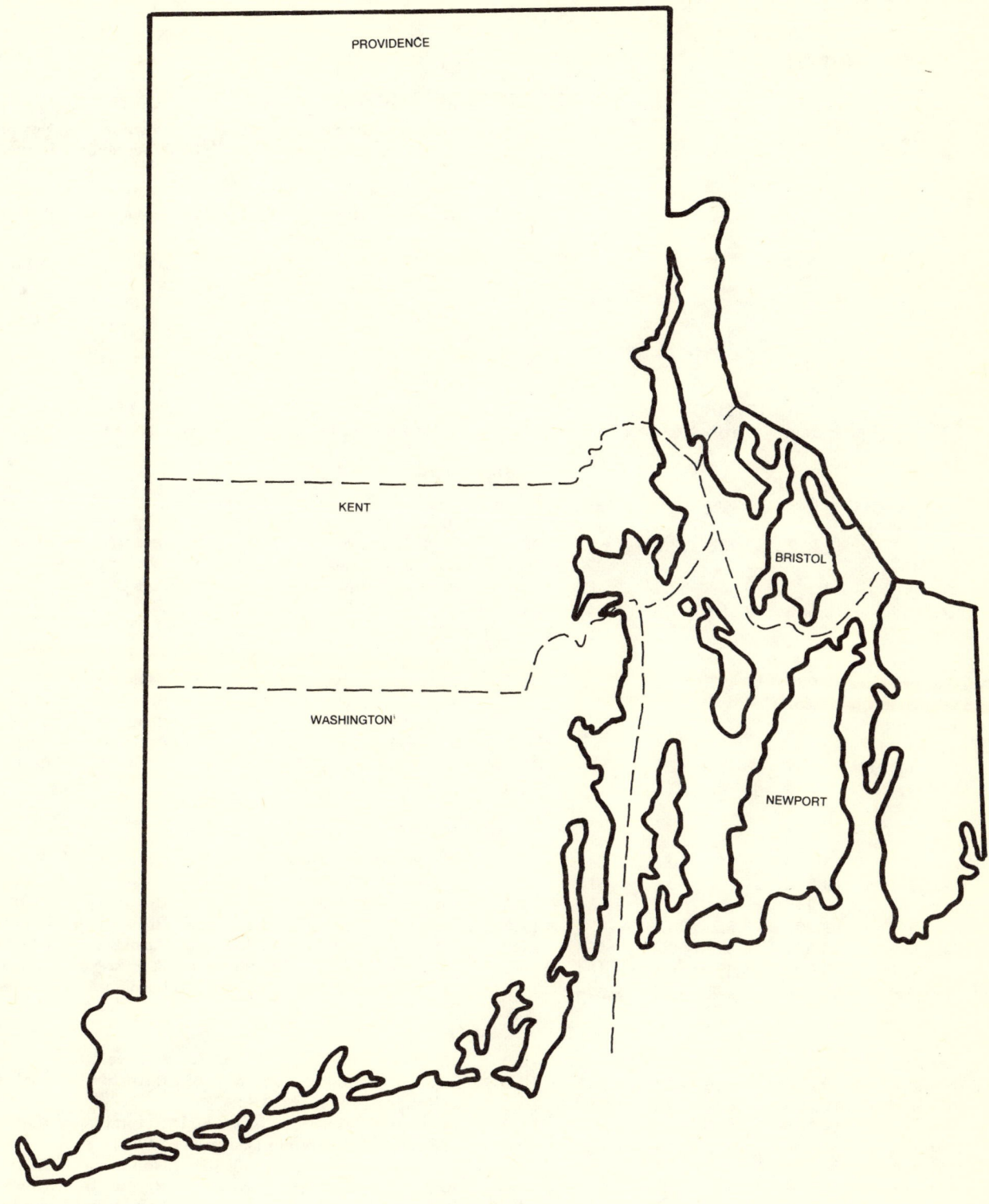

PROVIDENCE

KENT

WASHINGTON

BRISTOL

NEWPORT

	COUNTIES					REPRESENTATIVES				
County	Aggregate	Slave	%S	sq.mi.	P/sq.mi.	Representative	Cong.	Pty.	Address	County

AT LARGE (CONTINUED)

						Robert B. Cranston	26	W	Newport	Newport
						Joseph L. Tillinghast	26	W	Providence	Providence
						Robert B. Cranston	27	W	Newport	Newport
						Joseph L. Tillinghast	27	W	Providence	Providence

SOUTH CAROLINA
9 DISTRICTS
9 CONGRESSMEN

	COUNTIES					REPRESENTATIVES				
County	Aggregate	Slave	%S	sq.mi.	P/sq.mi.	Representative	Cong.	Pty.	Address	County

DISTRICT 1

County	Aggregate	Slave	%S	sq.mi.	P/sq.mi.	Representative	Cong.	Pty.	Address	County
All of Charleston County except those parishes included in District 2,						Henry L. Pinckney	23	D	City of Charleston	
						Henry L. Pinckney	24	SR	City of Charleston	
total:	42,277	33,733	79.8	1,626	26.0	Hugh S. Legare	25	UD	City of Charleston	
City of						Isaac E. Holmes	26	D	City of Charleston	
Charleston	30,289	15,354	50.7	17	1781.0	Isaac E. Holmes	27	D	City of Charleston	
TOTALS	72,566	49,087	67.6	1,643	51.6					

DISTRICT 2

County	Aggregate	Slave	%S	sq.mi.	P/sq.mi.	Representative	Cong.	Pty.	Address	County
Beaufort	37,032	30,861	83.3	1,793	20.7	William J. Grayson	23	W	Beaufort	Beaufort
Parishes in Charleston County:						William J. Grayson	24	SR	Beaufort	Beaufort
Colleton	10,045	9,380	93.4	270	37.2	Robert Barnwell Rhett	25	D	Beaufort	Beaufort
St. Johns						Robert Barnwell Rhett	26	D	Beaufort	Beaufort
St. Andrews	3,727	3,435	92.9	135	27.6	Robert Barnwell Rhett	27	D	Beaufort	Beaufort
TOTALS	78,060	65,160	83.5	3,516	22.2					

DISTRICT 3

County	Aggregate	Slave	%S	sq.mi.	P/sq.mi.	Representative	Cong.	Pty.	Address	County
Darlington	13,728	6,913	50.3	849	16.2	Thomas D. Singleton†	23	SR	Kingtree	Williamsburg
Georgetown	19,943	17,793	89.2	812	24.6	(Died November 25, 1833, before Congress assembled)				
Horry	5,245	1,714	32.6	1,154	4.5	Robert B. Campbell	23	SR	Brownsville	Marlborough
Marion	11,208	3,826	34.1	894	12.5	Robert B. Campbell	24	SR	Brownsville	Marlborough
Marlborough	8,582	4,333	50.4	483	17.8	John Campbell	25	SRD	Parnassas	Marlborough
Williamsburg	9,018	5,362	59.4	1,434	6.3	John Campbell	26	SRD	Parnassas	Marlborough
TOTALS	67,729	39,941	59.0	5,626	12.0	John Campbell	27	SRD	Parnassas	Marlborough

DISTRICT 4

County	Aggregate	Slave	%S	sq.mi.	P/sq.mi.	Representative	Cong.	Pty.	Address	County
Barnwell	19,236	8,497	44.1	1,927	10.0	John M. Felder	23	D	Orangeburg	Orangeburg
Lexington	9,065	3,790	41.8	717	12.6	James H. Hammond[r]	24	SR	Silverton	Richland
Orangeburg	18,453	10,931	59.2	1,701	10.8	(Resigned February, 1836)				
Richland	14,772	8,045	54.4	748	19.7	Franklin H. Elmore	24	SRD	Columbia	Richland
TOTALS	61,526	31,263	50.8	5,093	12.0	(Replaced Hammond December, 1836)				
						Franklin H. Elmore	25	SRD	Columbia	Richland
						Sampson H. Butler	26	D	Barnwell	Barnwell
						Sampson H. Butler	27	D	Barnwell	Barnwell

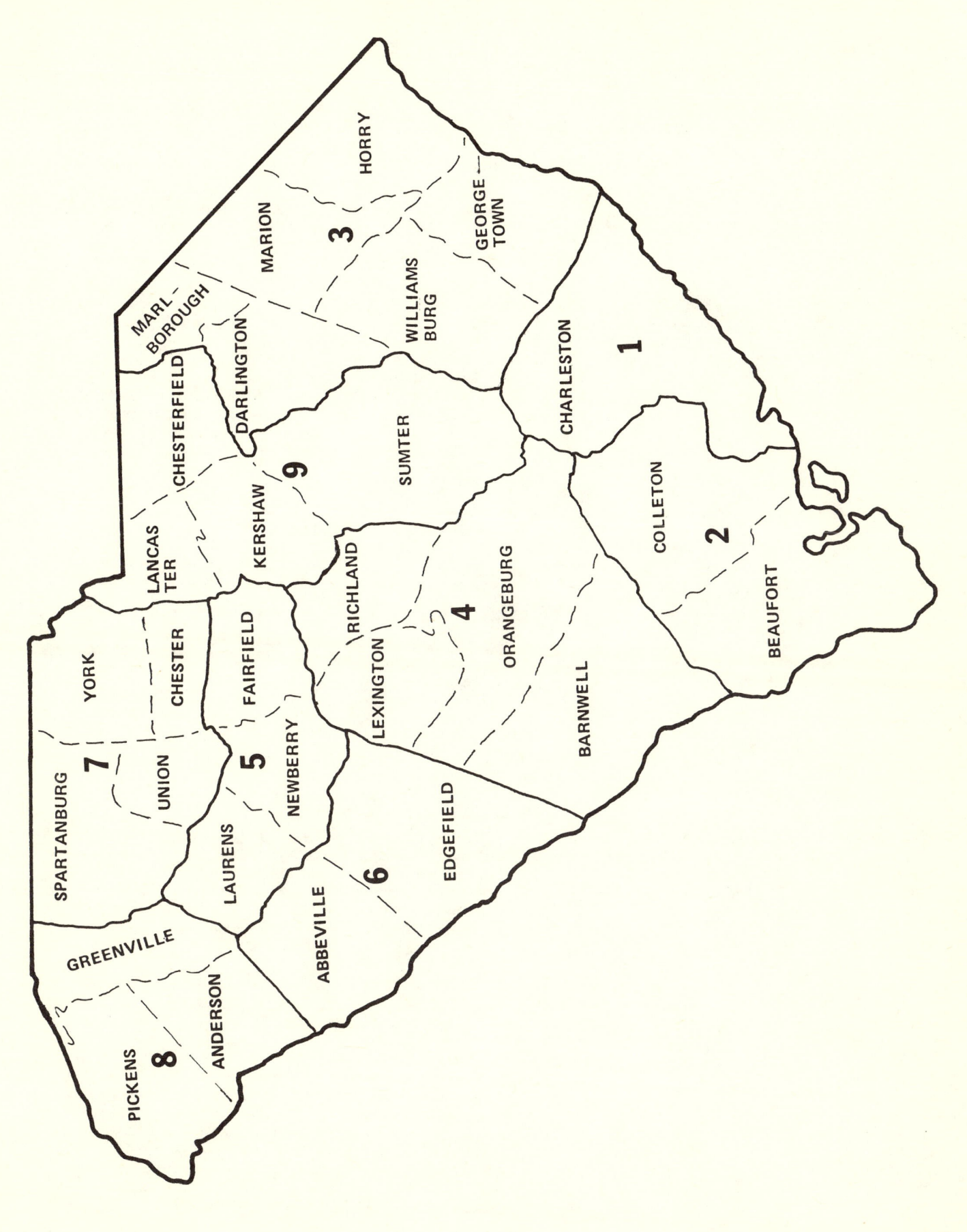

COUNTIES						REPRESENTATIVES				
County	Aggregate	Slave	%S	sq.mi.	P/sq.mi.	Representative	Cong.	Pty.	Address	County

DISTRICT 5

County	Aggregate	Slave	%S	sq.mi.	P/sq.mi.	Representative	Cong.	Pty.	Address	County
Fairfield	21,546	11,746	54.5	696	31.0	John K. Griffin	23	SRW	Milton	Laurens
Laurens	20,863	7,243	34.7	711	29.3	John K. Griffin	24	SRW	Milton	Laurens
Newberry	17,441	8,316	47.6	635	27.5	John K. Griffin	25	SRW	Milton	Laurens
TOTALS	59,850	27,305	45.6	2,042	29.3	John K. Griffin	26	SRW	Newberry	Laurens
						Patrick C. Caldwell	27	D	Newberry	Laurens

DISTRICT 6

County	Aggregate	Slave	%S	sq.mi.	P/sq.mi.	Representative	Cong.	Pty.	Address	County
Abbeville	28,149	13,106	46.5	976	28.8	George McDuffie[r]	23	D	Willington	Abbeville
Edgefield	30,509	15,349	50.3	1,602	19.0	(Resigned in 1834)				
TOTALS	58,658	28,455	48.5	2,578	22.8	Francis W. Pickens	23	SR	Edgefield	Edgefield
						(Replaced McDuffie)				
						Francis W. Pickens	24	SR	Edgefield	Edgefield
						Francis W. Pickens	25	SRN	Edgefield	Edgefield
						Francis W. Pickens	26	N	Edgefield	Edgefield
						Francis W. Pickens	27	ND	Edgefield	Edgefield

DISTRICT 7

County	Aggregate	Slave	%S	sq.mi.	P/sq.mi.	Representative	Cong.	Pty.	Address	County
Chester	17,182	7,142	41.5	584	29.4	William K. Clowney	23	NL	Union	Union
Spartanburgh	21,150	4,927	23.2	1,225	17.3	James Rogers	24	D	Yorkville	York
Union	17,906	7,165	40.0	514	34.8	William K. Clowney	25	SRD	Union	Union
York	17,790	6,633	37.2	684	26.0	James Rogers	26	D	Maybinton	York*
TOTALS	74,028	25,867	34.9	3,007	24.6	James Rogers	27	D	Maybinton	York*

DISTRICT 8

County	Aggregate	Slave	%S	sq.mi.	P/sq.mi.	Representative	Cong.	Pty.	Address	County
Anderson	17,169	4,327	25.2	749	22.9	Warren R. Davis	23	SRD	Pendleton	Anderson
Greenville	16,476	5,064	30.7	792	20.8	Warren R. Davis†	24	SR	Pendleton	Anderson
Pickens	14,473	2,966	20.5	1,146	12.6	(Died January 29, 1835)				
TOTALS	48,118	12,357	25.6	2,687	17.9	Waddy Thompson, Jr.	24	W	Greenville	Greenville
						(Replaced Davis December, 1835)				
						Waddy Thompson, Jr.	25	W	Greenville	Greenville
						Waddy Thompson, Jr.	26	W	Greenville	Greenville
						William Butler	27	W	Greenville	Greenville

DISTRICT 9

County	Aggregate	Slave	%S	sq.mi.	P/sq.mi.	Representative	Cong.	Pty.	Address	County
Chesterfield	8,472	2,992	35.3	790	10.7	James Blair	23	D	Lynchwood	Lancaster
Kershaw	13,545	8,333	61.5	781	17.3	Richard I. Manning	24	UN	Fulton	Sumter
Lancaster	10,361	4,123	39.7	502	20.7	John P. Richardson	25	SRD	Fulton	Sumter
Sumter	28,277	18,721	66.2	1,680	16.8	John P. Richardson[r]	26	SRD	Fulton	Sumter
TOTALS	60,655	34,169	56.3	3,753	16.2	Thomas D. Sumter	26	D	Statsburg	Sumter
						Thomas D. Sumter	27	D	Statsburg	Sumter

	COUNTIES					REPRESENTATIVES				
County	Aggregate	Slave	%S	sq.mi.	P/sq.mi.	Representative	Cong.	Pty.	Address	County

DISTRICT 1

County	Aggregate	Slave	%S	sq.mi.	P/sq.mi.	Representative	Cong.	Pty.	Address	County
Carter	6,414	460	7.1	641	10.0	John Blair	23	D	Jonesboro	Washington
Cocke	6,017	608	10.1	424	14.2	William B. Carter	24	W	Elizabethton	Carter
Greene	14,410	1,070	7.4	613	23.5	William B. Carter	25	W	Elizabethton	Carter
Jefferson	11,801	1,222	10.3	324	36.4	William B. Carter	26	W	Elizabethton	Carter
Washington	10,994	1,040	9.4	508	21.6	Thomas D. Arnold	27	W	Greeneville	Greene
TOTALS	49,636	4,400	8.9	2,510	19.8					

DISTRICT 2

County	Aggregate	Slave	%S	sq.mi.	P/sq.mi.	Representative	Cong.	Pty.	Address	County
Campbell	5,110	245	4.7	451	11.3	Samuel Bunch	23	W	Rutledge	Grainger
Claiborne	8,470	615	7.2	556	15.2	Samuel Bunch	24	W	Rutledge	Grainger
Grainger	10,066	909	9.0	444	22.7	Abraham McClellan	25	D	Blountville	Sullivan
Hawkins	13,683	1,659	12.1	765	17.9	Abraham McClellan	26	D	Blountville	Sullivan
Sullivan	10,073	1,187	11.7	413	24.4	Abraham McClellan	27	D	Blountville	Sullivan
TOTALS	47,402	4,615	9.7	2,629	18.0					

DISTRICT 3

County	Aggregate	Slave	%S	sq.mi.	P/sq.mi.	Representative	Cong.	Pty.	Address	County
Anderson	5,310	471	8.8	335	15.8	Luke Lea	23	UD	Campbell's Station	Knox
Blount	11,028	1,024	9.2	575	19.2					
Knox	14,498	2,033	14.0	508	28.5	Luke Lea	24	UD	Campbell's Station	Knox
Monroe	13,708	1,053	7.6	660	20.8					
Sevier	5,717	382	6.6	597	9.6	Joseph L. Williams	25	W	Knoxville	Knox
TOTALS	50,261	4,963	9.9	2,675	18.8	Joseph L. Williams	26	W	Knoxville	Knox
						Joseph L. Williams	27	W	Knoxville	Knox

DISTRICT 4

County	Aggregate	Slave	%S	sq.mi.	P/sq.mi.	Representative	Cong.	Pty.	Address	County
Bledsoe	4,648	419	9.0	677	6.9	James Standifer	23	W	Mountairy	Bledsoe
Hamilton	2,276	115	5.0	550	4.1	James Standifer	24	W	Mountairy	Bledsoe
Marion	5,508	268	4.8	506	10.9	James Standifer†	25	W	Mountairy	Bledsoe
McMinn	14,460	1,282	8.8	432	33.5	(Died August 20, 1837)				
Morgan	2,582	60	2.3	1,273	2.0	William Stone	25	D	Delphi	Bledsoe
Rhea	8,186	647	7.9	503	16.2	(Replaced Standifer November, 1837)				
Roane	11,341	1,118	9.8	1,629	7.0	Julius W. Blackwell	26	D	Athens	McMinn
TOTALS	49,001	3,909	8.0	5,570	8.8	Thomas J. Campbell	27	W	Athens	McMinn

DISTRICT 5

County	Aggregate	Slave	%S	sq.mi.	P/sq.mi.	Representative	Cong.	Pty.	Address	County
Fentress	2,748	119	4.3	200	13.7	John B. Forester	23	W	McMinnville	Warren
Franklin	15,620	3,547	22.7	627	24.9	John B. Forester	24	W	McMinnville	Warren
Overton	8,242	842	10.2	914	9.0	Hopkins L. Turney	25	D	Winchester	Franklin
Warren	15,210	1,556	10.2	1,151	13.2	Hopkins L. Turney	26	D	Winchester	Franklin
White	9,967	922	9.2	660	15.1	Hopkins L. Turney	27	D	Winchester	Franklin
TOTALS	51,787	6,986	13.5	3,552	14.6					

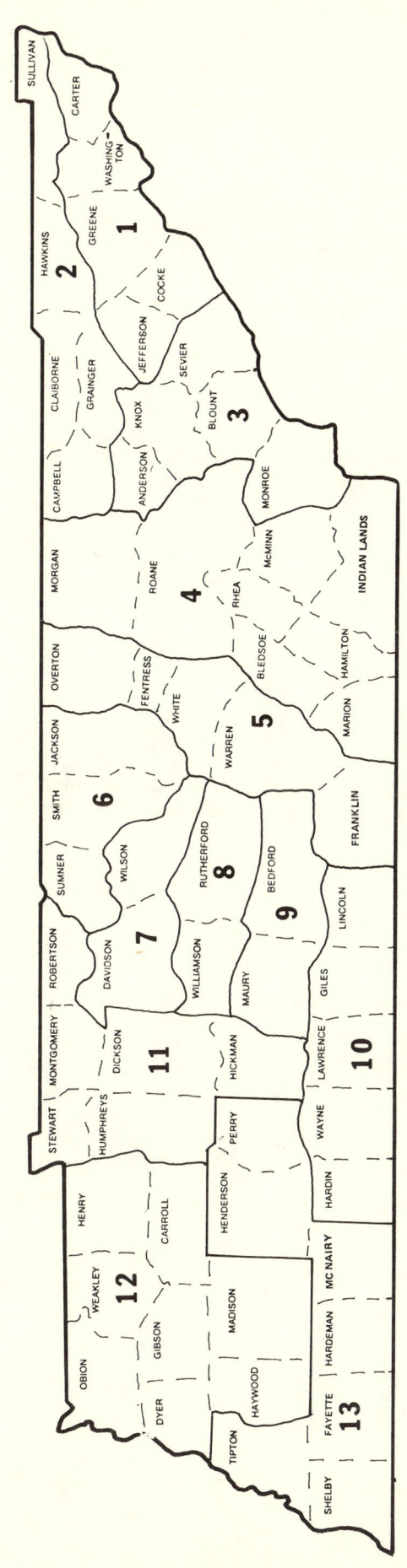

		COUNTIES				REPRESENTATIVES				
County	Aggregate	Slave	%S	sq.mi.	P/sq.mi.	Representative	Cong.	Pty.	Address	County

DISTRICT 6

Jackson	9,698	1,019	10.5	628	15.4	Balie Peyton	23	W	Gallatin	Sumner
Smith	19,906	4,384	22.0	741	26.9	Balie Peyton	24	W	Gallatin	Sumner
Sumner	20,569	7,257	35.2	534	38.5	William B. Campbell	25	W	Carthage	Smith
TOTALS	50,173	12,660	25.2	1,903	26.4	William B. Campbell	26	W	Carthage	Smith
						William B. Campbell	27	W	Carthage	Smith

DISTRICT 7

Davidson	28,122	11,662	41.4	813	34.6	John Bell	23	W	Nashville	Davidson
Wilson	25,472	5,944	23.3	567	44.9	John Bell	24	W	Nashville	Davidson
TOTALS	53,594	17,606	32.8	1,380	38.8	John Bell	25	W	Nashville	Davidson
						John Bell	26	W	Nashville	Davidson
						Robert Caruthers	27	W	Lebanon	Wilson

DISTRICT 8

Rutherford	26,134	8,649	33.0	883	29.6	David Dickinson	23	D	Murfreesboro	Rutherford
Williamson	26,638	10,505	39.4	593	44.9	Abram P. Maury	24	W	Franklin	Williamson
TOTALS	52,772	19,154	36.3	1,476	35.8	Abram P. Maury	25	W	Franklin	Williamson
						Meredith P. Gentry	26	W	Harpeth	Williamson
						Meredith P. Gentry	27	W	Harpeth	Williamson

DISTRICT 9

Bedford	30,396	5,648	18.5	859	35.4	James K. Polk	23	D	Columbia	Maury
Maury	27,665	9,439	34.1	614	45.1	James K. Polk	24	D	Columbia	Maury
TOTALS	58,061	15,087	26.0	1,473	39.4	James K. Polk	25	D	Columbia	Maury
						Harvey M. Watterson	26	D	Shelbyville	Bedford
						Harvey M. Watterson	27	D	Shelbyville	Bedford

DISTRICT 10

Giles	18,703	5,958	31.8	619	30.2	William M. Inge	23	D	Fayetteville	Lincoln
Hardin	4,868	416	8.5	587	8.3	Ebenezer J. Shields	24	W	Pulaski	Giles
Lawrence	5,411	552	10.2	634	8.5	Ebenezer J. Shields	25	W	Pulaski	Giles
Lincoln	22,075	4,091	18.5	640	34.5	Aaron V. Brown	26	D	Pulaski	Giles
Wayne	6,013	279	4.6	739	8.1	Aaron V. Brown	27	D	Pulaski	Giles
TOTALS	57,070	11,296	19.7	3,219	17.7					

DISTRICT 11

Dickson	7,265	1,659	22.8	485	15.0	Cave Johnson	23	D	Clarksville	Montgomery
Hickman	8,119	1,212	14.9	895	9.0	Cave Johnson	24	D	Clarksville	Montgomery
Humphreys	6,187	725	11.7	731	8.5	Richard Cheatham	25	W	Springfield	Robertson
Montgomery	14,349	5,801	40.4	539	26.6	Cave Johnson	26	D	Clarksville	Montgomery
Robertson	13,272	3,601	27.1	476	27.9	Cave Johnson	27	D	Clarksville	Montgomery
Stewart	6,968	1,400	20.1	470	14.8					
TOTALS	56,160	14,398	25.6	3,596	15.6					

| | COUNTIES | | | | | REPRESENTATIVES | | | | |
County	Aggregate	Slave	%S	sq.mi.	P/sq.mi.	Representative	Cong.	Pty.	Address	County
						DISTRICT 12				
Carroll	9,397	1,672	17.7	896	10.4	David Crockett	23	W	Crockett	Gibson
Dyer	1,904	601	31.5	579	3.2	Adam Huntsman	24	D	Jackson	Madison
Gibson	5,801	1,281	22.1	657	8.8	John W. Crockett	25	W	Paris	Henry
Haywood	5,334	1,829	34.2	619	8.6	John W. Crockett	26	W	Trenton	Gibson
Henry	12,249	2,960	24.1	596	20.5	Milton Brown	27	W	Jackson	Madison
Madison	11,594	4,167	35.9	629	18.4					
Obion	2,099	337	16.1	713	2.9					
Weakly	4,797	848	17.6	576	8.3					
TOTALS	53,175	13,695	25.7	5,265	10.1					
						DISTRICT 13				
Fayette	8,652	3,178	36.7	704	12.3	William C. Dunlap	23	D	Bolivar	Hardeman
Hardeman	11,655	3,662	31.4	656	17.7	William C. Dunlap	24	D	Bolivar	Hardeman
Henderson	8,748	1,433	16.3	1,037	8.4	Christopher H. Williams	25	W	Lexington	Henderson
McNairy	5,697	377	6.6	669	8.5	Christopher H. Williams	26	W	Lexington	Henderson
Perry	7,094	408	5.7	411	17.3	Christopher H. Williams	27	W	Lexington	Henderson
Shelby	5,648	2,149	38.0	755	7.5					
Tipton	5,317	1,732	37.5	936	5.7					
TOTALS	52,811	12,939	24.5	5,168	10.2					

County	Aggregate	Slave	%S	sq.mi.	P/sq.mi.	Representative	Cong.	Pty.	Address	County
COUNTIES						REPRESENTATIVES				

DISTRICT 1

County	Aggregate	Slave	%S	sq.mi.	P/sq.mi.	Representative	Cong.	Pty.	Address	County
Bennington	17,468	----	----	672	25.9	Hiland Hall	23	W	Bennington	Bennington
Windham	28,746	----	----	784	36.6	Hiland Hall	24	W	Bennington	Bennington
Towns in Windsor County:						Hiland Hall	25	W	Bennington	Bennington
Andover	975	----	----	----	----	Hiland Hall	26	W	Bennington	Bennington
Baltimore	179	----	----	----	----	Hiland Hall	27	W	Bennington	Bennington
Cavendish	1,493	----	----	----	----					
Chester	2,320	----	----	----	----					
Ludlow	1,227	----	----	----	----					
Springfield	2,749	----	----	----	----					
Windsor	3,134	----	----	----	----					
Total, towns	12,077	----	----	200	59.5					
TOTALS	58,291	----	----	1,656	35.2					

DISTRICT 2

County	Aggregate	Slave	%S	sq.mi.	P/sq.mi.	Representative	Cong.	Pty.	Address	County
Addison	24,940	----	----	784	31.8	William Slade	23	W	Middlebury	Addison
Rutland	31,294	----	----	927	33.7	William Slade	24	AM	Middlebury	Addison
TOTALS	56,234	----	----	1,711	32.9	William Slade	25	W	Middlebury	Addison
						William Slade	26	W	Middlebury	Addison
						William Slade	27	W	Middlebury	Addison

DISTRICT 3

County	Aggregate	Slave	%S	sq.mi.	P/sq.mi.	Representative	Cong.	Pty.	Address	County
Orange	27,285	----	----	690	39.5	Horace Everett	23	W	Windsor	Windsor
All of Windsor County, except those towns included in						Horace Everett	24	W	Windsor	Windsor
District 1,						Horace Everett	25	W	Windsor	Windsor
total:	28,552	----	----	762	37.5	Horace Everett	26	W	Windsor	Windsor
TOTALS	55,837	----	----	1,452	38.5	Horace Everett	27	W	Windsor	Windsor

DISTRICT 4

County	Aggregate	Slave	%S	sq.mi.	P/sq.mi.	Representative	Cong.	Pty.	Address	County
Chittenden	21,765	----	----	520	41.8	Heman Allen	23	W	Burlington	Chittenden
Franklin	24,525	----	----	755	32.4	Heman Allen	24	W	Burlington	Chittenden
Grand Isle	3,696	----	----	83	44.5	Heman Allen	25	W	Burlington	Chittenden
All of Orleans County, except those towns included in						John Smith	26	D	St. Albans	Franklin
District 5,						Augustus Young	27	W	Johnson	Franklin
total:	8,105	----	----	785	10.3					
TOTALS	58,091	----	----	2,143	27.1					

FRANKLIN

ORLEANS

ESSEX

GRAND ISLE

4

CHITTENDEN

CALEDONIA

WASHINGTON

5

ADDISON

ORANGE

3

2

RUTLAND

WINDSOR

BENNINGTON

WINDHAM

1

COUNTIES | REPRESENTATIVES

County	Aggregate	Slave	%S	sq.mi.	P/sq.mi.	Representative	Cong.	Pty.	Address	County

DISTRICT 5

County	Aggregate	Slave	%S	sq.mi.	P/sq.mi.	Representative	Cong.	Pty.	Address	County
Caledonia	20,967	----	----	612	34.2	Benjamin F. Deming†	23	W	Danville	Caledonia
Essex	3,981	----	----	663	6.0	(Died July, 1834)				
Towns in Orleans County:						Henry F. Janes	23	AM	Waterbury	Washington
Barton, Brownington, Charleston, Derby, Glover,						(Replaced Deming December, 1834)				
Greensboro, Holland, Morgan, Salem, Westmore.						Henry F. Janes	24	AM	Waterbury	Washington
Total, towns	5,875	----	----	120	49.0	Isaac Fletcher	25	D	Lyndon	Caledonia
Washington	21,378	----	----	840	25.4	Isaac Fletcher	26	D	Lyndon	Caledonia
TOTALS	52,201	----	----	2,235	23.4	John Mattocks	27	W	Peacham	Caledonia

VIRGINIA
21 DISTRICTS
21 CONGRESSMEN

COUNTIES | REPRESENTATIVES

County	Aggregate	Slave	%S	sq.mi.	P/sq.mi.	Representative	Cong.	Pty.	Address	County

DISTRICT 1

County	Aggregate	Slave	%S	sq.mi.	P/sq.mi.	Representative	Cong.	Pty.	Address	County
Elizabeth						George Loyall	23	D	Borough of Norfolk	
City	5,053	2,218	43.9	69	73.2	George Loyall	24	D	Borough of Norfolk	
Isle of Wight	10,517	4,272	40.6	317	33.2	Francis Mallory	25	W	Hampton	Elizabeth City
Nansemond	11,784	4,943	41.9	408	28.9	Joel Holleman^r	26	D	Burwell Bay	Isle of Wight
Norfolk	14,992	5,838	38.9	394	38.1	(Resigned in 1840)				
Borough of						Francis Mallory	26	W	Hampton	Elizabeth City
Norfolk	9,814	3,756	38.3	53	185.2	(Replaced Holleman January, 1841)				
Princess						Francis Mallory	27	W	Hampton	Elizabeth City
Anne	9,102	3,734	41.0	259	35.1					
TOTALS	61,262	24,761	40.4	1,500	40.8					

DISTRICT 2

County	Aggregate	Slave	%S	sq.mi.	P/sq.mi.	Representative	Cong.	Pty.	Address	County
Greensville	7,117	4,681	65.8	299	23.8	John Y. Mason	23	D	Hicksford	Greensville
Town in Dinwiddie County:						John Y. Mason^r	24	D	Hicksford	Greensville
Petersburg	8,322	2,850	34.2	8	1040.3	(Resigned January 18, 1837; not replaced)				
Prince George	8,367	4,598	55.0	276	30.3	Francis E. Rives	25	D	Littleton	----
Southampton	16,074	7,756	48.2	602	26.7	Francis E. Rives	26	D	Littleton	----
Surry	7,109	3,376	47.5	277	25.7	George B. Cary	27	D	Bethlehem	Southampton
Sussex	12,720	7,736	60.8	494	25.7					
TOTALS	59,709	30,997	51.9	1,956	30.5					

DISTRICT 3

County	Aggregate	Slave	%S	sq.mi.	P/sq.mi.	Representative	Cong.	Pty.	Address	County
Amelia	11,036	8,024	72.7	366	30.2	William S. Archer	23	D	Elkhill	Amelia
Chesterfield	18,637	14,502	77.8	442	42.2	John W. Jones	24	D	Petersburg	Chesterfield
Goochland	10,369	8,082	77.9	289	35.9	John W. Jones	25	D	Petersburg	Chesterfield
Nottoway	10,130	7,352	72.6	308	33.9	John W. Jones	26	D	Petersburg	Chesterfield
Powhatan	8,517	5,472	64.2	269	31.7	John W. Jones	27	D	Petersburg	Chesterfield
TOTALS	58,689	43,432	74.0	1,674	35.1					

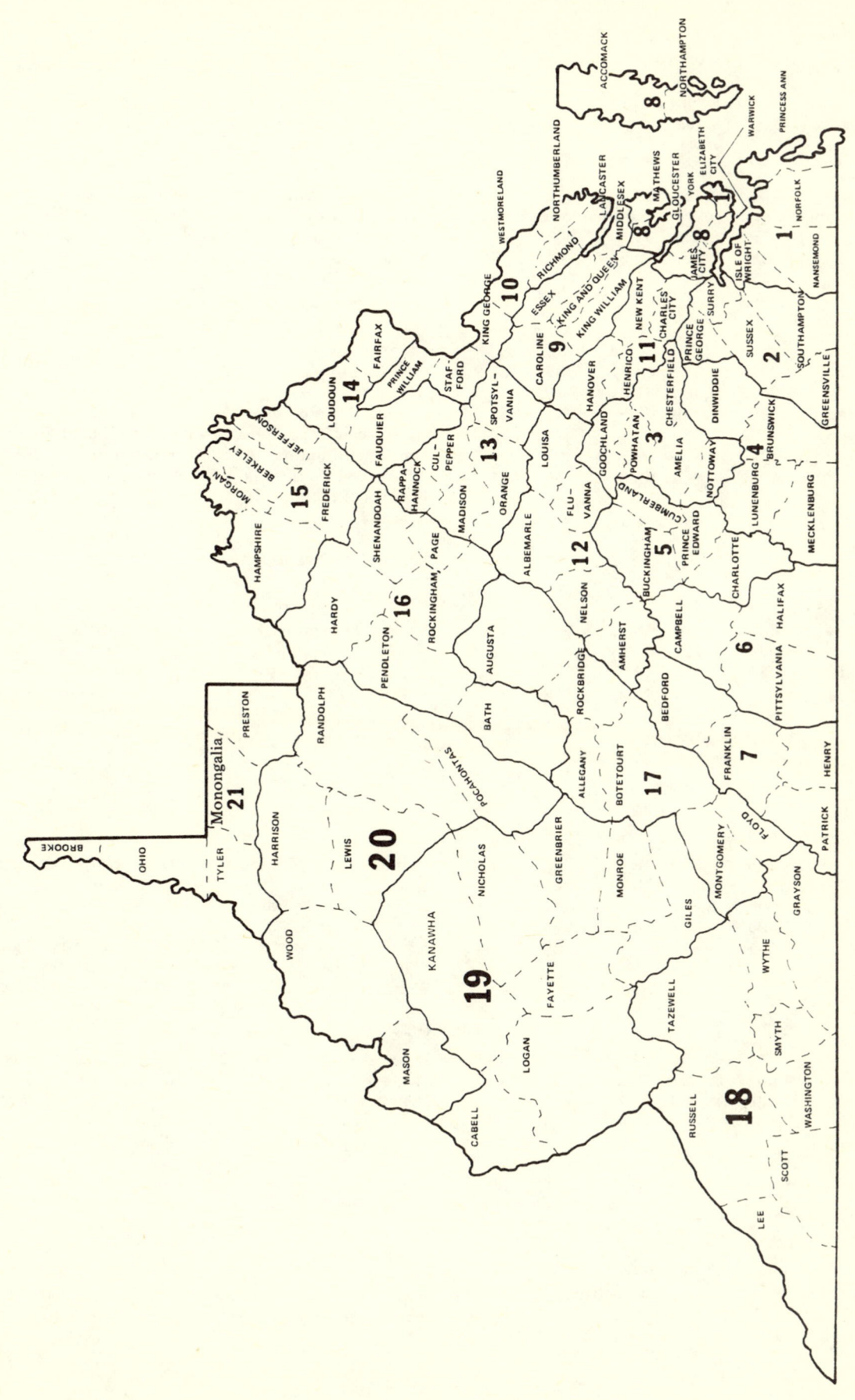

COUNTIES						REPRESENTATIVES				
County	Aggregate	Slave	%S	sq.mi.	P/sq.mi.	Representative	Cong.	Pty.	Address	County

DISTRICT 4

County	Aggregate	Slave	%S	sq.mi.	P/sq.mi.	Representative	Cong.	Pty.	Address	County
Brunswick	15,767	9,758	61.9	579	27.2	James H. Gholson	23	NR	Percivals	Brunswick
All of Dinwiddie County, except the town of Petersburg,						George C. Dromgoole	24	D	Gholsonville	Brunswick
total:	13,579	8,344	61.0	507	26.8	George C. Dromgoole	25	D	Gholsonville	Brunswick
Lunenburg	11,957	7,233	60.5	442	27.1	George C. Dromgoole	26	D	Gholsonville	Brunswick
Mecklenburg	20,477	12,117	59.2	612	33.5	William O. Goode	27	D	Boydton	Mecklenburg
TOTALS	61,780	37,452	60.6	2,140	28.9					

DISTRICT 5

County	Aggregate	Slave	%S	sq.mi.	P/sq.mi.	Representative	Cong.	Pty.	Address	County
Buckingham	18,351	10,929	59.5	737	24.9	John Randolph†	23	NR	Charlotte	Charlotte
Charlotte	15,252	9,433	61.8	470	32.4	(Died May, 1833)				
Cumberland	11,690	7,309	62.5	291	40.2	Thomas T. Bouldin†	23	D	Charlotte	Charlotte
Prince						(Replaced Randolph December, 1833; died February, 1834)				
Edward	14,107	8,593	60.9	407	34.7	James W. Bouldin	23	D	Charlotte	Charlotte
TOTALS	59,400	36,264	61.0	1,905	31.2	(Replaced Thomas Bouldin March, 1834)				
						James W. Bouldin	24	D	Charlotte	Charlotte
						James W. Bouldin	25	D	Charlotte	Charlotte
						John Hill	26	W	Buckingham	Buckingham
						Edmund W. Hubard	27	D	Curdsville	Buckingham

DISTRICT 6

County	Aggregate	Slave	%S	sq.mi.	P/sq.mi.	Representative	Cong.	Pty.	Address	County
Campbell	20,350	9,496	46.7	669	30.4	Thomas Davenport	23	NR	Meadville	Halifax
Halifax	28,034	14,526	51.8	796	35.2	Walter Coles	24	D	Robertson's Store	Halifax
Pittsylvania	26,034	10,999	42.2	1,001	26.0					
TOTALS	74,418	35,021	47.0	2,466	30.2	Walter Coles	25	D	Robertson's Store	Halifax
						Walter Coles	26	D	Robertson's Store	Halifax
						Walter Coles	27	D	Robertson's Store	Halifax

DISTRICT 7

County	Aggregate	Slave	%S	sq.mi.	P/sq.mi.	Representative	Cong.	Pty.	Address	County
Bedford	20,246	8,782	43.4	727	27.8	Nathaniel H. Claiborne	23	D	Rocky Mount	Franklin
Franklin	14,911	4,988	33.4	716	20.8					
Henry	7,100	2,868	40.4	381	18.6	Nathaniel H. Claiborne	24	D	Rocky Mount	Franklin
Patrick	7,395	1,782	24.1	464	15.9					
TOTALS	49,652	18,420	37.1	2,288	21.7	Archibald Stuart	25	D	Mount Airy	Patrick
						William L. Goggin	26	W	Otter Bridge	Bedford
						William L. Goggin	27	W	Otter Bridge	Bedford

DISTRICT 8

County	Aggregate	Slave	%S	sq.mi.	P/sq.mi.	Representative	Cong.	Pty.	Address	County
Accomack	16,656	4,654	27.9	476	35.0	Henry A. Wise	23	D	Accomac	Accomack
Gloucester	10,608	5,691	53.6	228	46.5	Henry A. Wise	24	D	Accomac	Accomack
James City	3,836	1,983	51.7	157	25.2	Henry A. Wise	25	W	Accomac	Accomack
Mathews	7,664	3,481	45.4	89	86.1	Henry A. Wise	26	W	Accomac	Accomack
North-						Henry A. Wise	27	W	Accomac	Accomack
ampton	8,641	3,734	43.2	220	39.3					
Warwick	1,570	910	58.0	75	20.9					
City of Williamsburg[a]										
York	5,354	2,598	48.5	129	41.5					
TOTALS	54,329	23,051	42.4	1,374	39.5					

[a]Included in James City County statistics.

370

COUNTIES					REPRESENTATIVES				
County	Aggregate	Slave	%S	sq.mi.	P/sq.mi.	Representative	Cong.	Pty.	Address	County

DISTRICT 9

County	Aggregate	Slave	%S	sq.mi.	P/sq.mi.	Representative	Cong.	Pty.	Address	County
Caroline	17,760	10,741	60.5	545	32.6	William P. Taylor	23	NR	----	Caroline
Essex	10,521	6,407	60.9	250	42.1	John Roane, Jr.	24	D	Rumford Academy	King William
King and Queen	11,644	6,514	55.9	318	36.6	Robert M. T. Hunter	25	W	Lloyds	Essex
King William	9,812	6,310	64.3	278	35.3	Robert M. T. Hunter	26	W	Lloyds	Essex
Middlesex	4,122	2,138	51.9	130	31.7	Robert M. T. Hunter	27	I	Lloyds	Essex
TOTALS	53,859	32,110	59.6	1,521	35.4					

DISTRICT 10

County	Aggregate	Slave	%S	sq.mi.	P/sq.mi.	Representative	Cong.	Pty.	Address	County
King George	6,397	3,635	56.8	176	36.3	Joseph W. Chinn	23	D	Nuttsville	Lancaster
Lancaster	4,801	2,632	54.8	137	35.0	John Taliaferro	24	W	Fredericksburg	King George
North-umberland	7,953	3,357	42.2	190	41.9	John Taliaferro	25	W	Fredericksburg	King George
Prince William	9,330	3,842	41.2	347	26.9					
Richmond	6,055	2,630	43.4	190	31.9	John Taliaferro	26	W	Fredericksburg	King George
Stafford	9,362	4,164	44.5	270	34.7					
Westmoreland	8,396	3,839	45.7	229	36.7	John Taliaferro	27	W	Fredericksburg	King George
TOTALS	52,294	24,099	46.1	1,539	34.0					

DISTRICT 11

County	Aggregate	Slave	%S	sq.mi.	P/sq.mi.	Representative	Cong.	Pty.	Address	County
Charles City	5,500	2,957	53.8	181	30.4	Andrew Stevenson[r]	23	D	Richmond	Henrico
Hanover	16,253	9,278	57.1	465	34.9	(Resigned June, 1834)				
Henrico	28,797	12,279	42.6	289	99.6	John Robertson	23	W	Richmond	Henrico
New Kent	6,458	3,530	54.7	210	30.8	(Replaced Stevenson December, 1834)				
City of Richmond[a]						John Robertson	24	W	Richmond	Henrico
						John Robertson	25	W	Richmond	Henrico
TOTALS	57,008	28,044	49.2	1,145	49.8	John M. Botts	26	W	Richmond	Henrico
						John M. Botts	27	W	Richmond	Henrico

[a]Included in Henrico County statistics.

DISTRICT 12

County	Aggregate	Slave	%S	sq.mi.	P/sq.mi.	Representative	Cong.	Pty.	Address	County
Albemarle	22,618	11,679	51.6	470	48.1	William F. Gordon	23	NR	Lindsey's Store	Albemarle
Amherst	12,071	5,925	49.1	470	25.7					
Fluvanna	8,221	3,795	46.2	288	28.5	James Garland	24	D	Lovingston	Nelson
Louisa	16,151	9,382	58.1	517	31.2	James Garland	25	D	Lovingston	Nelson
Nelson	11,254	5,946	52.8	471	23.9	James Garland	26	D	Lovingston	Nelson
TOTALS	70,315	36,727	52.2	2,216	31.7	Thomas W. Gilmer	27	W	Chariottes-ville	Albemarle

DISTRICT 13

County	Aggregate	Slave	%S	sq.mi.	P/sq.mi.	Representative	Cong.	Pty.	Address	County
Culpeper	24,027	11,417	47.5	656	36.6	John M. Patton	23	D	Fredericksburg	Spottsylvania
Madison	9,236	4,876	52.8	327	28.2					
Orange	14,637	7,983	54.5	508	28.8	John M. Patton	24	D	Fredericksburg	Spottsylvania
Rappa-hannock[a]						John M. Patton[r]	25	D	Fredericksburg	Spottsylvania
Spott-sylvania	15,134	8,053	53.2	409	37.0	(Resigned in 1838) Linn Banks	25	D	Madison	Culpeper
TOTALS	63,034	32,329	51.3	1,900	33.2	(Replaced Patton June, 1838)				
						Linn Banks	26	D	Madison	Culpeper

[a]Created from Culpeper County.

COUNTIES						REPRESENTATIVES				
County	Aggregate	Slave	%S	sq.mi.	P/sq.mi.	Representative	Cong.	Pty.	Address	County

DISTRICT 13 (CONTINUED)

						Linn Banks[ce]	27	D	Madison	Culpeper
						(Election successfully contested by William Smith; served until December, 1841)				
						William Smith	27	D	Culpeper	Culpeper
						(Successfully contested election of Linn Banks; took seat December, 1841)				

DISTRICT 14

County	Aggregate	Slave	%S	sq.mi.	P/sq.mi.	Representative	Cong.	Pty.	Address	County
Fairfax	9,204	4,001	43.5	399	23.1	Charles F. Mercer	23	NR	Aldie	Loudon
Fauquier	26,086	12,523	48.0	660	39.5	Charles F. Mercer	24	D	Aldie	Loudon
Loudon	21,939	5,363	24.4	517	42.4	Charles F. Mercer	25	W	Aldie	Loudon
TOTALS	57,229	21,887	38.2	1,576	36.3	Charles F. Mercer[r]	26	D	Aldie	Loudon
						(Resigned December, 1839)				
						William McCarty	26	W	Alexandria	Fairfax
						(Replaced Mercer January, 1840)				
						Cuthbert Powell	27	W	Upperville	Fauquier

DISTRICT 15

County	Aggregate	Slave	%S	sq.mi.	P/sq.mi.	Representative	Cong.	Pty.	Address	County
Berkeley[a]	----	----	----	316	----	Edward Lucas	23	D	Charlestown	Jefferson
Frederick	26,046	7,420	28.5	729	35.7	Edward Lucas	24	D	Charlestown	Jefferson
Hampshire	11,279	1,330	11.8	970	11.6	James M. Mason	25	D	Winchester	Frederick
Jefferson	12,927	3,999	30.9	211	61.3	William Lucas	26	D	Charlestown	Jefferson
Morgan	2,694	153	5.7	233	11.6	Richard W. Barton	27	W	Winchester	Frederick
TOTALS	52,946	12,902	24.5	2,459	21.5					

DISTRICT 16

County	Aggregate	Slave	%S	sq.mi.	P/sq.mi.	Representative	Cong.	Pty.	Address	County
Bath	4,002	1,140	28.5	956	4.2	James M. H. Beale	23	D	Mount	Shenandoah
Hardy	6,798	1,167	17.2	1,063	6.4	James M. H. Beale	24	D	Jackson	
Page[a]	----	----	----	----	----	James M. H. Beale	24	D	Mount Jackson	Shenandoah
Pendleton	6,271	496	7.9	695	9.0					
Rockingham	20,683	2,321	11.2	865	23.9	Isaac S. Pennybacker	25	D	Harrisonburg	Rockingham
Shenandoah	19,750	2,423	12.3	823	24.0	Green B. Samuels	26	D	Woodstock	Shenandoah
TOTALS	57,504	7,547	13.1	4,402	13.1	William A. Harris	27	D	Luray	Page

[a]Created from Shenandoah and Rockingham Counties.

DISTRICT 17

County	Aggregate	Slave	%S	sq.mi.	P/sq.mi.	Representative	Cong.	Pty.	Address	County
Alleghany	2,816	571	20.3	444	6.3	Samuel M. Moore	23	NR	Lexington	Rockbridge
Augusta	19,926	4,265	21.4	986	20.2	Robert Craig	24	D	Christiansburg	Montgomery
Botetourt	16,354	4,170	25.5	1,146	14.3					
Floyd[a]	----	----	----	----	----	Robert Craig	25	D	Christiansburg	Montgomery
Montgomery	12,306	2,026	16.5	1,105	11.1					
Rockbridge	14,244	3,398	23.8	601	23.7	Robert Craig	26	D	Christiansburg	Montgomery
Berkeley	10,518	1,919	18.2	316	33.3					
TOTALS	63,464	14,821	23.3	2,459	25.8	Alexander H. H. Stuart	27	W	Staunton	Augusta

[a]Created from Montgomery County.

	COUNTIES					REPRESENTATIVES				
County	Aggregate	Slave	%S	sq.mi.	P/sq.mi.	Representative	Cong.	Pty.	Address	County

DISTRICT 18

County	Aggregate	Slave	%S	sq.mi.	P/sq.mi.	Representative	Cong.	Pty.	Address	County
Grayson	7,675	462	6.0	946	8.1	John H. Fulton	23	D	Adingdon	Washington
Lee	6,461	612	9.5	438	14.7	George W. Hopkins	24	D	Lebanon	Russell
Russell	6,714	679	10.1	1,223	5.5	George W. Hopkins	25	D	Lebanon	Russell
Scott	5,724	330	5.8	950	6.0	George W. Hopkins	26	W	Lebanon	Russell
Smyth[a]	----	----	----	----	----	George W. Hopkins	27	D	Lebanon	Russell
Tazewell	5,749	820	14.3	2,228	2.6					
Washington	15,614	2,562	16.4	949	16.4					
Wythe	12,163	2,094	17.2	460	26.4					
TOTALS	60,100	7,559	12.6	7,194	8.3					

[a]Created from Washington County.

DISTRICT 19

County	Aggregate	Slave	%S	sq.mi.	P/sq.mi.	Representative	Cong.	Pty.	Address	County
Cabell	5,884	561	9.5	300	19.6	William McComas	23	D	Cabell	Cabell
Fayette[a]	----	----	----	----	----	William McComas	24	W	Cabell	Cabell
Giles	5,274	465	8.8	1,330	4.0	Andrew Beirne	25	D	Union	Monroe
Greenbrier	9,006	1,109	12.3	1,026	8.9	Andrew Beirne	26	D	Union	Monroe
Kanawha	9,326	1,717	18.4	3,345	2.8	George W. Summers	27	W	Kanawha	Kanawha
Logan	3,680	163	4.4	3,080	1.2					
Monroe	7,798	682	8.7	473	16.5					
Nicholas	3,346	121	3.6	1,193	2.8					
TOTALS	44,314	4,818	10.9	10,747	4.1					

[a]Created from Kanawha and Logan Counties.

DISTRICT 20

County	Aggregate	Slave	%S	sq.mi.	P/sq.mi.	Representative	Cong.	Pty.	Address	County
Harrison	14,722	771	5.2	1,087	13.5	John J. Allen	23	NR	Clarksburg	Harrison
Jackson[a]	----	----	----	----	----	Joseph Johnson	24	D	Bridgeport	Harrison
Lewis	6,241	172	2.7	835	7.5	Joseph Johnson	25	D	Bridgeport	Harrison
Mason	6,534	713	10.9	1,878	3.5	Joseph Johnson	26	D	Bridgeport	Harrison
Pocahontas	2,542	227	8.9	943	2.7	Samuel L. Hayes	27	D	Stuard's	Lewis
Randolph	5,000	259	5.2	1,457	3.4				Creek	
Wood	6,429	877	13.6	1,184	5.4					
TOTALS	41,468	3,019	7.3	7,384	5.6					

[a]Created from Mason, Kanawha, and Wood.

DISTRICT 21

County	Aggregate	Slave	%S	sq.mi.	P/sq.mi.	Representative	Cong.	Pty.	Address	County
Brooke	7,041	228	3.2	171	4.1	Edgar C. Wilson	23	NR	Morgantown	Monongalia
Monongalia	14,056	362	2.6	755	18.6	William S. Morgan	24	D	White Day	----
Ohio	15,584	360	2.3	106	147.0	William S. Morgan	25	D	White Day	----
Preston	5,144	129	2.5	645	8.0	Lewis Steenrod	26	D	Wheeling	Ohio
Tyler	4,104	108	2.6	619	6.6	Lewis Steenrod	27	D	Wheeling	Ohio
TOTALS	45,929	1,187	2.6	2,296	20.0					

Appendix: County Creations

ALABAMA
(Territory 1817; State 1819)

County Name	Date of Creation	Parent County(ies)	Remarks
Bibb (see Cahawba)			
Butler	1819	Conecuh, Montgomery	
Cahawba	1818		Name changed to Bibb in 1820
Cotaco	1818	Cherokee Turkeytown Cession	Name changed to Morgan in 1821
Covington	1821	Henry	
Dale	1824	Covington, Henry	
Decatur	1821	Jackson	Abolished in 1825
Fayette	1824	Marion, Pickens, Tuskaloosa	
Greene	1819	Marengo, Tuskaloosa	
Henry	1819	Conecuh	
Jackson	1819	Cherokee Cession of 1816	
Jefferson	1819	Blount	
Lowndes	1830	Butler, Dallas, Montgomery	
Morgan (see Cotaco)			
Perry	1819	Montgomery	
Pickens	1820	Tuskaloosa	
Pike	1821	Henry, Montgomery	
Walker	1823	Marion, Tuskaloosa	
Wilcox	1819	Dallas, Monroe	

ARKANSAS
(Territory 1817; State 1836)

See Introduction to County Creations section

CONNECTICUT
(State 1788)

No county creations between these dates.

DELAWARE
(State 1787)

No county creations between these dates.

GEORGIA
(State 1788)

County Name	Date of Creation	Parent County(ies)	Remarks
Appling	1818	Creek Indian Lands	
Baker	1825	Early	
Baldwin	1803	Creek Indian Lands	
Bibb	1822	Houston, Jones, Monroe, Twiggs	
Bryan	1793	Effingham, Liberty	
Bulloch	1796	Bryan, Scriven	
Butts	1825	Henry, Monroe	
Campbell	1828	Correll, Coweta, DeKalb, Fayette	
Carroll	1826	Creek Indian Lands	
Cass	1832	Cherokee	
Cherokee	1831	Carroll, DeKalb, Gwinnett, Habersham, Hall	
Clarke	1801	Jackson	
Cobb	1832	Cherokee	
Columbia	1790	Richmond	
Coweta	1826	Creek Indian Lands	
Crawford	1822	Houston	
Decatur	1823	Early	
DeKalb	1822	Fayette, Gwinnett, Henry, Newton	
Dooly	1821	Indian Lands	
Early	1818	Creek Indian Lands	
Elbert	1790	Madison, Wilkes	
Emanuel	1812	Bulloch, Montgomery	
Fayette	1821	Indian Lands	
Floyd	1832	Cherokee	
Forsyth	1832	Cherokee	
Franklin	1784	Cherokee Lands	
Gilmer	1832	Cherokee	
Gwinnett	1818	Cherokee Lands	
Habersham	1818	Franklin, Cherokee Lands	
Hall	1818	Franklin, Cherokee Lands	
Hancock	1793	Greene, Washington	
Harris	1827	Muscogee, Troup	
Heard	1830	Carroll, Coweta, Troup	
Henry	1821	Walton, Indian Lands	
Houston	1821	Indian Lands	
Irwin	1818	Creek Indian Lands	
Jackson	1796	Franklin	
Jasper (see Randolph)			
Jefferson	1796	Burke, Warren	
Jones	1807	Baldwin	
Laurens	1807	Wilkinson	
Lee	1826	Creek Indian Lands	
Lincoln	1796	Wilkes	
Lowndes	1825	Irwin	
Lumpkin	1832	Cherokee, Habersham, Hall	
McIntosh	1793	Liberty	
Madison	1811	Clarke, Elbert, Franklin, Jackson, Oglethorpe	
Marion	1827	Lee, Muscogee, Stewart	
Meriwether	1827	Troup	
Monroe	1821	Indian Lands	Redefined in 1822
Montgomery	1793	Laurens, Tattnall, Telfair, Washington	

County Name	Date of Creation	Parent County(ies)	Remarks
Morgan	1807	Baldwin, Jasper	
Murray	1832	Cherokee	
Muscogee	1826	Creek Indian Lands	
Newton	1821	Henry, Jasper, Walton	
Oglethorpe	1793	Clarke, Green, Wilkes	
Paulding	1832	Cherokee	
Pike	1822	Monroe	
Pulaski	1808	Laurens	
Putnam	1807	Baldwin	
Rabun	1819	Habersham, Cherokee Lands	
Randolph	1807	Baldwin, Wilkerson	Name changed to Jasper in 1812
Randolph (re-creation)	1828	Lee	
Talbot	1827	Muscogee	
Taliaferro	1825	Green, Hancock, Oglethorpe, Warren, Wilkes	
Tattnall	1801	Montgomery	
Telfair	1807	Wilkinson	
Thomas	1825	Decatur, Irwin	
Troup	1826	Creek Indian Lands	
Twiggs	1809	Wilkinson	
Union	1832	Cherokee	
Upson	1824	Crawford, Pike	
Walton	1818	Cherokee Lands	
Ware	1824	Appling	
Warren	1793	Columbia, Richmond, Wilkes	
Wayne	1803	Creek Cession, Appling, Camden, Glynn	
Wilkinson	1803	Creek Cession	

ILLINOIS
(Territory 1809; State 1818)

County Name	Date of Creation	Parent County(ies)	Remarks
Adams	1825	Pike	
Alexander	1819	Union	
Calhoun	1825	Pike	
Clark	1819	Crawford	
Clay	1824	Crawford, Fayette, Lawrence, Wayne	
Clinton	1824	Bond, Fayette, Washington	
Coles	1830	Clark, Edgar	
Cook	1831	Putnam	
Edgar	1823	Clark	
Effingham	1831	Crawford, Fayette	
Fayette	1821	Bond, Clark, Jefferson, Wayne	
Franklin	1818	Gallatin, White	
Fulton	1823	Pike	
Greene	1821	Madison	
Hamilton	1821	White	
Hancock	1825	Pike, Unorganized Territory	
Henry	1825	Fulton	
Jasper	1831	Clay, Crawford	
Jefferson	1819	Edwards, White	
Jo Daviess	1827	Henry, Mercer, Putnam	
Knox	1825	Fulton	

County Name	Date of Creation	Parent County(ies)	Remarks
La Salle	1831	Putnam, Vermillion	
Lawrence	1821	Crawford, Edwards	
McDonough	1826	Schuyler	
McLean	1830	Tazewell, Unorganized Territory	
Macon	1829	Shelby	
Macoupin	1829	Greene, Madison	
Marion	1823	Fayette, Jefferson	
Mercer	1825	Pike, Unorganized Territory	
Montgomery	1821	Bond	
Morgan	1823	Greene(?)	
Peoria	1825	Fulton	
Perry	1827	Jackson, Randolph	
Pike	1821	Bond, Clark, Madison, Bounty Lands	
Putnam	1825	Fulton	
Rock Island	1831	Jo Daviess	
Sangamon	1821	Bond, Madison	
Schuyler	1825	Fulton, Pike	
Shelby	1827	Fayette	
Tazewell	1827	Sangamon	
Union	1818	Johnson	
Vermilion	1826	Edgar, Unorganized Territory	
Wabash	1824	Edwards	
Warren	1825	Pike	
Washington	1818	St. Clair	
Wayne	1819	Edwards	

INDIANA
(Territory 1800; State 1816)

County Name	Date of Creation	Parent County(ies)	Remarks
Allen	1823	Delaware, Randolph	
Bartholomew	1821	Delaware, Jackson	
Boone	1830	Indian Lands	
Carroll	1828	Indian Lands	
Cass	1828	Allen, Indian Lands	
Clay	1825	Owen, Putnam, Sullivan, Vigo	
Clinton	1830	Indian Lands	
Crawford	1818	Harrison, Orange, Perry	
Daviess	1816	Knox, Orange	
Dearborn	1803	Original County	
Decatur	1823	Delaware	
Delaware	1827	Henry	
Dubois	1817	Pike	
Elkhart	1818	Allen, Indian Lands	
Fayette	1818	Franklin, Wayne	
Floyd	1819	Clarke, Harrison	
Fountain	1825	Montgomery, Wabash	
Grant	1831	Delaware	
Green	1821	Daviess, Sullivan	
Hamilto	1823	Hancock, Marion	
Hancock	1828	Madison	
Hendricks	1823	Wabash	
Henry	1821	Delaware	
Huntington	1832	Indian Lands	
Jennings	1816	Indian Lands	

County Name	Date of Creation	Parent County(ies)	Remarks
Johnson	1822	Delaware, Indian Lands	
La Grange	1832	Indian Lands	
Lawrence	1818	Orange	
La Porte	1832	Indian Lands	
Madison	1832	Fayette	
Marion	1821	Delaware	
Martin	1820	Daviess, Dubois	
Miami	1832	Indian Lands	
Monroe	1818	Orange	
Montgomery	1822	Indian Lands, Wabash	
Morgan	1821	Delaware, Wabash	
Orange	1816	Washington	
Owen	1818	Daviess, Sullivan	
Parke	1821	Vigo	
Pike	1816	Gibson, Knox, Perry	
Putnam	1821	Owen, Vigo, Indian Lands	
Randolph	1818	Wayne	
Ripley	1818	Indian Lands	
Rush	1821	Fayette, Franklin	
St. Joseph	1830	Allen, Indian Lands	
Scott	1820	Clark, Jackson, Jefferson, Jennings, Washington	
Shelby	1821	Delaware, Indian Lands	
Spencer	1818	Perry, Warrick	
Sullivan	1816	Knox	
Tippecanoe	1826	Wabash	
Union	1821	Fayette, Franklin, Wayne	
Vanderburgh	1818	Gibson, Posey, Warrick	
Vermillion	1824	Parke, Wabash	
Vigo	1818	Sullivan	
Wabash	1832	Indian Lands	Wabash was an original territorial county; it was divided into other counties and disappeared, but was recreated in 1832 out of Indian Lands.
Warren	1827	Wabash, Indian Lands	

KENTUCKY
(State 1792)

County Name	Date of Creation	Parent County(ies)	Remarks
Adair	1801	Green	
Allen	1815	Barren, Warren	
Anderson	1827	Franklin, Mercer, Washington	
Barren	1798	Green, Warren	
Bath	1811	Montgomery	
Boone	1798	Campbell	
Bracken	1796	Campbell, Mason	
Breckinridge	1799	Hardin	
Bullitt	1796	Jefferson, Nelson	
Butler	1810	Logan, Ohio	
Caldwell	1809	Livingston	
Calloway	1822	Hickman	
Campbell	1794	Harrison, Mason, Scott	
Casey	1806	Lincoln	

County Name	Date of Creation	Parent County(ies)	Remarks
Christian	1796	Logan	
Clarke	1792	Bourbon, Fayette	
Clay	1806	Floyd, Knox, Madison	
Cumberland	1798	Green	
Daviess	1815	Ohio	
Edmonson	1825	Grayson, Hart, Warren	
Estill	1808	Clarke, Madison	
Fleming	1798	Mason	
Floyd	1799	Fleming, Mason, Montgomery	
Franklin	1794	Mercer, Shelby, Woodford	
Gallatin	1798	Franklin, Shelby	
Garrard	1796	Lincoln, Madison, Mercer	
Grant	1802	Pendleton	
Graves	1821	Hickman	
Grayson	1810	Hardin, Ohio	
Green	1792	Lincoln, Nelson	
Greenup	1803	Mason	
Hancock	1829	Daviess, Breckinridge, Ohio	
Hardin	1792	Nelson	
Harlan	1819	Knox	
Harrison	1793	Bourbon	
Hart	1819	Barren, Hardin	
Henderson	1798	Christian	
Henry	1798	Shelby	
Hickman	1821	Cladwell, Livingston	
Hopkins	1806	Henderson	
Jessamine	1798	Fayette	
Knox	1799	Lincoln	
Laurel	1825	Clay, Knox, Rockcastle, Whitley	
Lawrence	1821	Floyd, Greenup	
Lewis	1806	Mason	
Livingston	1798	Christian	
Logan	1792	Lincoln	
McCracken	1824	Hickman	
Meade	1824	Breckinridge, Hardin	
Monroe	1820	Barren, Cumberland	
Montgomery	1796	Clarke	
Morgan	1822	Bath, Floyd	
Muhlenberg	1798	Christian, Logan	
Nicholas	1799	Bourbon, Mason	
Ohio	1798 & 1799	Hardin	There were two separate statutes of creation, the second revising the first.
Oldham	1823	Henry, Jefferson, Shelby	
Owen	1819	Franklin, Gallatin, Pendleton, Scott	
Pendleton	1798	Bracken, Campbell	
Perry	1820	Clay, Floyd	
Pike	1821	Floyd	
Pulaski	1798	Green, Lincoln	
Rockcastle	1810	Lincoln, Madison, Pulaski	
Russell	1825	Adair, Cumberland, Wayne	
Scott	1792	Woodford	
Shelby	1792	Jefferson	
Simpson	1819	Allen, Logan, Warren	
Spencer	1824	Bullitt, Nelson, Shelby	
Todd	1819	Christian, Logan	

County Name	Date of Creation	Parent County(ies)	Remarks
Trigg	1820	Caldwell, Christian	
Union	1811	Henderson	
Warren	1796	Logan	
Washington	1792	Nelson	
Wayne	1800	Cumberland, Pulaski	
Whitley	1818	Knox	

LOUISIANA
(Territory 1805; State 1812)

County Name	Date of Creation	Parent County(ies)	Remarks
Carroll	1832	Concordia, Ouachita	
Claiborne	1828	Natchitoches	
East Feliciana	1824	Feliciana	
Feliciana	1820	Original Parish	
Jefferson	1825	Orleans	
Lafayette	1823	Attakapas, St. Martin	
Livingston	1832	St. Helena	
Terre Bonne	1822	Lafourche	
Washington	1819	St. Tamany	
West Feliciana	1824	Feliciana	

MAINE[1]
(State 1820)

County Name	Date of Creation	Parent County(ies)	Remarks
Hancock	1789	Lincoln	
Kennebec	1799	Lincoln	
Oxford	1805	Cumberland, York	
Penobscot	1816	Hancock	
Somerset	1809	Kennebec	
Waldo	1827	Hancock, Kennebec, Lincoln	
Washington	1789	Lincoln	

MARYLAND
(State 1788)

County Name	Date of Creation	Parent County(ies)	Remarks
Allegany	1789	Washington	

MASSACHUSETTS
(State 1788)

County Name	Date of Creation	Parent County(ies)	Remarks
Franklin	1811	Hampshire	
Hampden	1812	Hampshire	
Norfolk	1792	Suffolk	

---

[1]County creations before 1820 are noted despite the fact that Maine was not a state before 1820. These counties were a part of Massachusetts until 1820, when Maine became a state. Maine was never a territory of the United States.

MISSISSIPPI
(Territory 1789; State 1817)

County Name	Date of Creation	Parent County(ies)	Remarks
Bainbridge	1823	Covington	Act creating Bainbridge repealed January 24, 1824.
Copiah	1823	Hinds	
Covington	1819	Lawrence, Wayne	
Hinds	1821	Choctaw Cession of 1820	
Jones	1826	Covington, Wayne	
Lowndes	1830	Monroe	
Madison	1828	Yazoo	
Monroe	1821	Chickasaw Cession of 1821	
Perry	1820	Green	
Rankin	1828	Hinds	
Simpson	1824	Copiah	
Washington	1827	Warren, Yazoo	
Yazoo	1823	Hinds	

MISSOURI
(Territory 1812; State 1821)

County Name	Date of Creation	Parent County(ies)	Remarks
Clay	1822	Ray	
Crawford	1829	Gasconade	
Jackson	1826	Lafayette	
Marion	1826	Ralls	
Monroe	1831	Ralls	
Randolph	1829	Chariton	
St. Francois	1821	Jefferson, Ste. Genevieve, Washington	
Scott	1821	New Madrid	

NEW HAMPSHIRE
(State 1788)

County Name	Date of Creation	Parent County(ies)	Remarks
Coos	1803	Grafton	
Merrimac	1823	Hillsborough, Rockingham	
Sullivan	1827	Cheshire	

NEW JERSEY
(State 1787)

County Name	Date of Creation	Parent County(ies)	Remarks
Warren	1824	Sussex	

NEW YORK
(State 1788)

County Name	Date of Creation	Parent County(ies)	Remarks
Allegany	1806	Genesee	
Broome	1806	Tioga	
Cattaraugus	1808	Genesee	
Cayuga	1799	Onondaga	

County Name	Date of Creation	Parent County(ies)	Remarks
Chautauqua	1808	Genesee	
Chenango	1798	Herkimer, Tioga	
Cortland	1808	Onondaga	
Delaware	1797	Otsego, Ulster	
Erie	1821	Niagara	
Essex	1799	Clinton	
Franklin	1808	Clinton	
Genesee	1802	Ontario	
Greene	1800	Albany, Ulster	
Hamilton	1816	Montgomery	
Herkimer	1791	Montgomery	
Jefferson	1805	Oneida	
Lewis	1805	Oneida	
Livingston	1821	Genesee, Ontario	
Madison	1806	Chenango	
Monroe	1821	Genesee, Ontario	
Niagara	1808	Genesee	
Oneida	1798	Herkimer	
Onondaga	1794	Military Lands	
Ontario	1789	Montgomery	
Orleans	1824	Genesee	
Oswego	1816	Oneida, Onondaga	
Otsego	1791	Montgomery	
Putnam	1812	Dutchess	
Rensselaer	1791	Albany	
Rockland	1798	Orange	
St. Lawrence	1802	Clinton, Herkimer, Montgomery	
Saratoga	1791	Albany	
Schenectady	1809	Albany	
Schoharie	1795	Albany, Otsego	
Seneca	1804	Cayuga	
Steuben	1796	Ontario	
Sullivan	1809	Ulster	
Tioga	1791	Montgomery	
Tompkins	1817	Cayuga, Seneca	
Warren	1813	Washington	
Wayne	1823	Ontario, Seneca	
Yates	1823	Ontario, Steuben	

NORTH CAROLINA
(State 1789)

County Name	Date of Creation	Parent County(ies)	Remarks
Ashe	1799	Wilkes	
Avery	1811	Caldwell, Mitchell, Watauga	
Buncombe	1791	Burke, Rutherford	
Cabarrus	1792	Mecklenburg	
Columbus	1808	Bladen, Brunswick	
Davidson	1822	Rowan	
Glasgow	1791	Dobbs	
Greene	1799	Dobbs or Glasgow	
Haywood	1808	Bundombe	
Lenoir	1791	Dobbs	
Macon	1828	Haywood (Cherokee Purchase)	
Person	1791	Caswell	

County Name	Date of Creation	Parent County(ies)	Remarks
Stokes	1789	Surry	
Washington	1799	Tyrrell	

OHIO
(State 1803)

County Name	Date of Creation	Parent County(ies)	Remarks
Allen	1820	Mercer, Indian Territory	
Ashtabula	1807 (1811)	Geauga, Trumbull	Created in 1807; organized in 1811.
Athens	1805	Washington	
Brown	1817	Adams, Clermont	
Butler	1803	Hamilton	
Champaign	1805	Franklin, Greene	
Clark	1817	Champaign, Greene, Madison	
Clinton	1810	Highland, Warren	
Columbiana	1803	Jefferson, Washington	
Coshocton	1810 (1811)	Muskingum, Tuskarawas	Created in 1810; organized in 1811.
Crawford	1820	Old Indian Territory	
Cuyahoga	1808	Geauga	
Darke	1809	Miami	
Delaware	1808	Franklin	
Fayette	1810	Highland, Ross	
Franklin	1803	Ross	
Gallia	1803	Washington	
Geauga	1805	Trumbull	
Green	1803	Hamilton, Ross	
Guernsey	1810	Belmont, Muskingum	
Hancock	1818	Wood, Indian Lands	
Hardin	1820	Indian Lands	
Harrison	1813	Jefferson, Tuscarawas	
Henry	1820	Wood	
Highland	1805	Adams, Clermont, Ross	
Hocking	1818	Athens, Fairfield, Ross	
Holmes	1824	Coshocton, Wayne	
Huron	1809 (1815)	Indian Lands (Firelands?)	Created in 1809; organized in 1815
Jackson	1816	Athens, Gallia, Ross, Scioto	
Knox	1808	Fairfield	
Lawrence	1815	Gallia, Scioto	
Licking	1808	Fairfield	
Logan	1817	Champaign	
Lorain	1822	Cuyahoga, Huron, Medina	
Madison	1810	Franklin	
Marion	1824	Crawford	
Medina	1812	Portage	
Meigs	1819	Athens, Gallia	
Mercer	1820	Dark	
Miami	1807	Montgomery	
Monroe	1813 (1815)	Belmont, Guernsey, Washington	Created in 1813; organized in 1815
Montgomery	1803	Hamilton	
Morgan	1818	Washington	
Muskingum	1804	Fairfield, Washington	
Paulding	1820	Indian Lands	

County Name	Date of Creation	Parent County(ies)	Remarks
Perry	1817	Fairfield, Washington	
Pickaway	1810	Fairfield, Franklin, Ross	
Pike	1815	Adams, Ross, Scioto	
Portage	1807	Trumbull	
Preble	1808	Butler, Montgomery	
Putnam	1820	Old Indian Territory	
Richland	1808 (1813)	Knox	Created in 1808; organized in 1813.
Sandusky	1820	Huron	
Scioto	1803	Adams, Washington	
Seneca	1824	Delaware, Franklin, Wayne	
Shelby	1819	Miami	
Stark	1808	Columbiana	
Tuscarawas	1808	Jefferson, Muskingum	
Union	1820	Delaware, Franklin, Logan, Madison	
Van Wert	1820	Indian Territory	
Warren	1803	Hamilton	
Wayne	1808 (1812)	Columbiana	Created in 1808; organized in 1812.
Williams	1820	Henry	
Wood	1820	Indian Lands	

PENNSYLVANIA
(State 1787)

County Name	Date of Creation	Parent County(ies)	Remarks
Adams	1800	York	
Armstrong	1800	Allegheny, Butler, Clarion, Indiana, Jefferson, Westmoreland	
Beaver	1800	Allegheny, Washington	
Butler	1800	Allegheny	
Cambria	1804	Bedford, Huntingdon, Somerset	
Centre	1800	Huntingdon, Lycoming, Mifflin, Northumberland	
Clearfield	1804	Huntingdon, Lycoming	
Columbia	1813	Northumberland	
Crawford	1800	Allegheny	
Delaware	1789	Chester	
Erie	1800	Allegheny	
Greene	1796	Washington	
Indiana	1803	Lycoming, Westmoreland	
Jefferson	1804	Lycoming	
Juniata	1831	Mifflin	
Lebanon	1813	Dauphin, Lancaster	
Lehigh	1812	Northampton	
Lycoming	1795	Northumberland	
McKean	1804	Lycoming	
Mercer	1800	Allegheny	
Mifflin	1789	Cumberland, Northumberland	
Ontario	1812	Lyzerne, Lycoming	
Perry	1820	Cumberland	
Pike	1814	Northampton	
Potter	1804	Lycoming	
Schuylkill	1811	Berks, Northampton	
Somerset	1795	Bedford	

County Name	Date of Creation	Parent County(ies)	Remarks
Susquehanna	1810	Luzerne	
Tioga	1804	Lycoming	
Union	1813	Northumberland	
Venango	1800	Allegheny, Lycoming	
Warren	1800	Allegheny, Lycoming	
Wayne	1798	Northampton	

RHODE ISLAND
(State 1790)

No county creations between these dates.

SOUTH CAROLINA
(State 1788)

County Name	Date of Creation	Parent County(ies)	Remarks
Anderson	1826	Pendleton District	
Barnwell	1798	Orangeburg	
Chesterfield	1798	Cheraw District	
Colleton	1798	Charleston District	
Darlington	1798	Cheraw District	
Greenville	1798	Washington	
Horry	1801	Kingston	
Kershaw	1798	Claremont, Fairfield, Lancaster, Richland	
Lancaster	1798	Camden District	
Lexington	1804	Orangeburg	
Marion	1798	Georgetown	
Marlboro	1798	Cheraw District	
Richland	1799	Kershaw	
Salem	1792	Claremont, Clarendon	
Sumter	1798	Camden District	
Union	1798	District 96	
Williamsburg	1802	Georgetown	
York	1798	Pinckney	

TENNESSEE
(State 1796)

County Name	Date of Creation	Parent County(ies)	Remarks
Anderson	1801	Knox	
Bedford	1807	Rutherford	
Benton	1835	Henry, Humphreys	
Bledsoe	1807	Roane	
Blount	1795	Knox	
Campbell	1806	Anderson, Claiborne	
Carroll	1821	Western District	
Carter	1796	Washington	
Claiborne	1801	Grainger, Hawkins	
Cocke	1797	Jefferson	
Dickson	1803	Montgomery, Robertson	
Dyer	1823	Western District	
Fayette	1824	Hardeman, Shelby	
Fentress	1823	Morgan, Overton	
Franklin	1807	Bedford, Warren	
Gibson	1823	Western District	

County Name	Date of Creation	Parent County(ies)	Remarks
Giles	1809	Maury	
Grainger	1796	Hawkins, Knox	
Hamilton	1819	Rhea	
Hardeman	1823	Western District	
Hardin	1819	Western District	
Haywood	1823	Western District	
Henderson	1821	Western District	
Henry	1821	Western District	
Hickman	1807	Dickson	
Humphreys	1809	Smith, Stewart	
Jackson	1801	Smith	
Jefferson	1792	Greene, Hawkins	
Knox	1792	Greene, Hawkins	
Lawrence	1817	Hickman, Maury	
Lincoln	1809	Bedford	
McMinn	1819	Indian Lands	
McNairy	1823	Hardin	
Madison	1821	Western District	
Marion	1817	Indian Lands	
Maury	1807	Williamson	
Monroe	1819	Roane	
Montgomery	1796	Tennessee	
Morgan	1817	Roane	
Obion	1823	Western District	
Overton	1806	Jackson	
Perry	1818	Hickman	
Rhea	1807	Roane	
Roane	1801	Blount, Knox	
Robertson	1796	Tennessee	
Rutherford	1803	Davidson	
Sevier	1794	Jefferson	
Shelby	1819	Hardin	
Smith	1799	Sumner	
Stewart	1803	Montgomery	
Tipton	1823	Western District	
Warren	1807	White	
Wayne	1819	Hickman	
Weakley	1823	Western District	
White	1806	Jackson, Overton, Smith	
Williamson	1799	Davidson	
Wilson	1799	Sumner	

VERMONT
(State 1791)

County Name	Date of Creation	Parent County(ies)	Remarks
Caledonia	1792	Newly Organized Territory	
Essex	1792	Unorganized Territory	
Franklin	1792	Chittenden	
Grand Isle	1802	Franklin	
Orleans	1792	Original County	
Washington	1810	Addison, Orgnae	

VIRGINIA
(State 1788)

County Name	Date of Creation	Parent County(ies)	Remarks
Alexandria	1801	Fairfax, Prince William	
Allegheny	1822	Bath, Botetourt, Monroe	
Arlington	1801	Fairfax	
Bath	1790	Augusta, Botetourt, Greenbrier	
Brooke	1796	Ohio	
Cabell	1809	Kanawha	
Fayette	1831	Greenbrier, Kanawha, Logan, Nicholas	
Floyd	1831	Montgomery	
Giles	1806	Monroe, Montgomery, Tazewell	
Jackson	1831	Mason, Kanawha, Wood	
Jefferson	1801	Berkeley	
Kanawha	1788	Greenbrier, Montgomery	
Lee	1792	Russell, Scott	
Madison	1792	Culpeper	
Mason	1804	Kanawha	
Mathews	1790	Gloucester	
Munroe	1799	Greenbrier	
Nelson	1807	Amherst	
Nicholas	1818	Greenbrier, Kanawha, Randolph	
Nottoway	1788	Amelia	
Page	1831	Rockingham, Shenandoah	
Patrick	1790	Henry	
Pocahontas	1821	Bath, Pendleton, Randolph	
Preston	1818	Monongalia	
Scott	1814	Lee, Russell, Washington	
Smyth	1832	Washington, Wythe	
Tazewell	1799	Russell, Wythe	
Tyler	1814	Ohio	
Wythe	1789	Montgomery	

Bibliography

We have divided the bibliography into two parts. The first part lists the statutes we consulted for determining the county composition of the Congressional districts. This listing is by state. The second part lists works used in preparing the demographic, Congressional membership, county creation tables, and the state maps.

PART I

ALABAMA

"An Act to Divide the State into Districts for Electing Representatives to Congress," <u>Acts Passed at the Fourth Annual Session of the General Assembly</u>, no. 58 (December 26, 1822).

"To Divide the State into Districts, for Electing Representatives to Congress," <u>Acts Passed at the Extra and Annual Sessions of the General Assembly</u>, no. 44 (January 10, 1833).

ARKANSAS

"An Act Providing for the Election of a Member of Congress from this State," <u>Acts Passed at the First Session of the General Assembly</u>, p. 152 (November 4, 1836).

CONNECTICUT

"An Act for Regulating the Election of Senators and Representatives, for this State, in the Congress of the United States, <u>Acts and Laws, Made and Passed by the General Court or Assembly of the State of Connecticut, in America</u>, p. 371 (January, 1789).

"An Act in Addition to and Alteration of an Act for Regulating the Election of Senators, and Representatives of this State, in the Congress of the United States," <u>Acts and Laws, Made and Passed by the General Court or Assembly of the State of Connecticut, in America, Holden at Hartford (in Said State) on the Second Thursday of May, Anno Domini, 1792</u>, p. 419 (May, 1792).

"An Act, in Alteration of an Act, entitled, 'Act for Regulating the Election of Senators and Representatives in the Congress of the United States,' " <u>Public Acts Passed by the General Assembly of the State of Connecticut</u>, c. I (October, 1797).

"An Act Relative to the Election of Senators and Representatives, for this State, in the Congress of the United States," <u>Public Acts Passed by the General Assembly of the State of Connecticut</u>, c. XIII (May 28, 1819).

"An Act in Alteration of an Act, Entitled, 'An Act Regulating the Election of Senators and Representatives, for this State, in the Congress of the United States,' " <u>Public Acts Passed by the General Assembly of the State of Connecticut</u>, c. 3 (May 31, 1822).

"An Act Regulating the Election of Senators and Representatives for this State, in the Congress of the United States," <u>Public Acts Passed by the General Assembly of the State of Connecticut</u>, c. 3 (June 5, 1833).

"An Act in Alteration of an Act, Entitled, 'An Act Regulating the Election of Senators and Representatives for this State, in the Congress of the United States,' " <u>Public Acts Passed by the General Assembly of the State of Connecticut</u>, c. 28 (June 5, 1825).

GEORGIA

"An Act Prescribing the Time, Manner, and Places of Holding Elections for Persons to Represent this State in the Congress of the United States," [<u>Acts of the State of Georgia</u>] p. 17 (December 8, 1790).

"An Act Prescribing [the] Times, Manner and Places for Holding Elections for Members to Represent this State, in the Congress of the United States," [<u>Acts of the State of Georgia</u>] p. 36 (December 24, 1791).

"An Act Authorizing the Electors in the Several Counties in this State to Elect Grown Persons to Represent Them in the House of Representatives of the United States," <u>Acts of the General Assembly of the State of Georgia</u>, p. 8 (June 16, 1802).

"An Act to Lay Off the State into Seven Congressional Districts," <u>Acts of the General Assembly of the State of Georgia</u>, p. 89 (December 22, 1824).

ILLINOIS

"An Act to Lay Out the State into Districts, for the Purpose of Electing Representatives to the Congress of the United
    States," Laws of Illinois, p. 70 (February 15, 1831).

INDIANA

"An Act to Provide for the Election of Senators and Representatives from this State to the Congress of the United States,"
    Laws of the State of Indiana, c. XL (January 3, 1817).
"An Act for Dividing this State into Congressional Districts for the Election of Members to the Congress of the United
    States," Laws of the State of Indiana, c. XXVII (January 3, 1822).
"An Act to Amend an Act Entitled, 'An Act for the Formation of Congressional Districts, and for the Election of Senators
    and Representatives to Congress,' Approved, January 30, 1824," Laws of the State of Indiana, c. XXI (January 19,
    1829).
Pence, George, and Armstrong, Nellie G., Indiana Boundaries: Territory, State and County. Indianapolis, 1933.

KENTUCKY

"[An Act for the Election of Representatives to the Congress] of the United States," Acts Passed at the First Session of
    the General Assembly, for the Commonwealth of Kentucky, c. V (April 14, 1792).
"An Act Dividing this State into Congressional Districts," Acts Passed at the First Session of the Eleventh General Assem-
    bly for the Commonwealth of Kentucky, c. XXXIII (December 13, 1802).
"An Act to Divide this State into Congressional Districts," Acts Passed at the First Session of the Twentieth General
    Assembly for the Commonwealth of Kentucky, c. CCCLXXXVIII (February 8, 1812).
"An Act Laying Off the State into Congressional Districts," Acts of the General Assembly, c. CCCXLVI (May 23, 1822).
Littell, William, and Swigert, Jacob (comps.), A Digest of the Statute Law of Kentucky, 2 vols. Frankford: Kendall,
    1822.
"An Act to Divide the State into Congressional Districts," Laws of Kentucky, c. 227 (February 2, 1833).

LOUISIANA

"An Act for Regulating the Election of Representatives of this State in the House of Representatives of the Congress of
    the United States," Acts Passed at the First Session of the First General Assembly of the State of Louisiana, c. XI
    (September 5, 1812).
"An Act to Divide the State of Louisiana into Congressional Districts," Acts Passed at the Second Session of the Fifth
    Legislature of the State of Louisiana, p. 58 (March 21, 1822).

MAINE

"An Act to Divide the State into Districts for the Choice of Representatives in the Congress of the United States, and
    Prescribing the Mode of Election," Laws of the State of Maine, c. CCXXIII (February 8, 1823).
"An Act Providing for the Choice of Representatives to Congress," Laws of the State of Maine, c. 68 (February 28, 1833).

MARYLAND

"An Act Directing the Time, Places and Manner, of Holding Elections for Representatives of this State in the Congress of
    the United States, and for Appointing Electors on the Part of this State for Choosing a President and Vice-President
    of the United States, and for the Regulation of the Said Elections," Laws of Maryland, c. X (December 22, 1788).
"A Supplement to the Act, Entitled, 'An Act Directing the Time, Places and Manner, of Holding Elections for Representa-
    tives of this State in the Congress of the United States, and for Appointing Electors on the Part of this State for
    Choosing a President and Vice-President of the United States, and for the Regulation of Said Elections,' and also to
    Repeal the Act of Assembly therein Mentioned," Laws of Maryland, c. LXII (December 26, 1791).
"An Act to Provide for the Elections of Representatives of this State in the Congress of the United States, and of Electors
    on the Part of this State for Choosing a President and Vice-President of the United States," Laws of Maryland,
    c. LXX (November, 1802).
Dorsey, Clement (ed.), The General Public Statutory Law and Public Law of the State of Maryland. 3 vols. Baltimore:
    John D. Toy, 1840.

MASSACHUSETTS

"An Act for Dividing the Commonwealth into Districts for the Choice of Representatives in the Congress of the United
    States, and Prescribing the Mode of Election," Resolves of the General Court of the Commonwealth of Massachu-
    setts, p. 53 (November 19, 1788).

"Resolve for Districting the Commonwealth, for the Purpose of Choosing Federal Representatives," <u>Resolves of the General Court of the Commonwealth of Massachusetts</u>, p. 23 (June 30, 1792).

"An Act for Dividing the Commonwealth into Districts for the Choice of Representatives in the Congress of the United States, and Prescribing the Mode of Election," <u>Acts and Laws Passed by the General Court of Massachusetts,</u> c. XVIII (June 26, 1794).

"An Act Dividing the Commonwealth into Seventeen Districts, for the Choice of Representatives in the Congress of the United States," <u>Acts and Laws Passed by the General Court of Massachusetts,</u> c. LII (March 10, 1802).

"An Act to Divide the Commonwealth into Districts for the Choice of Representatives in the Congress of the United States, and Prescribing the Mode of Election," <u>Laws of the Commonwealth of Massachusetts</u>, c. CXLV (February 28, 1812).

"An Act to Divide the Commonwealth into Districts for the Choice of Representatives in the Congress of the United States," <u>Public and General Laws of the Commonwealth of Massachusetts</u>, c. LIV (June 14, 1814).

"Resolve Relating to the Election of Members of Congress, After the Separation of the District of Maine," <u>Resolves of the General Court of the Commonwealth of Massachusetts</u>, c. LXII (January 25, 1820).

"An Act to Divide the Commonwealth into Districts, for the Choice of Representatives in the Congress of the United States, and Prescribing the Mode of Election," <u>Laws of the Commonwealth of Massachusetts</u>, c. XXII (June 25, 1822).

"An Act to Divide the Commonwealth into Districts for the Choice of Representatives in the Congress of the United States," <u>Laws of the Commonwealth of Massachusetts</u> (March 5, 1833).

"Of the Election of Representatives in Congress," <u>The Revised Statutes of the Commonwealth of Massachusetts, Passed November 4, 1835</u>, c. 6, sec. 1-2 (February, 1836).

MISSISSIPPI

"An Act to Regulate Elections in this State," <u>Laws of the State of Mississippi. . . .</u>, c. X (March 2, 1833).

MISSOURI

"An Act Providing for the Election of an Additional Representative to the Congress of the United States," <u>Laws of the State of Missouri</u>, c. 45 (January 2, 1833).

NEW HAMPSHIRE

"An Act Directing the Mode of Choosing Representatives to Congress," <u>The Public Acts and Laws of the State of New-Hampshire</u> (June 17, 1790).

"An Act Directing the Mode of Choosing Representatives to the Congress of the United States," <u>The Laws of the State of New-Hampshire. . . .</u>, p. 423 (June 21, 1792).

[Untitled Resolution], <u>Public Laws of New-Hampshire</u>, p. 5 (June 19, 1812).

"An Act to Divide the State into Districts for the Choice of Representatives for this State in the Congress of the United States, and to Prescribe the Mode of Their Election," <u>The Laws of the State of New-Hampshire</u>, c. LX (December 16, 1824).

NEW JERSEY

"An Act to Direct the Time and Mode of Electing Representatives in the Congress of the United States, for this State," <u>Acts of the Fifteenth General Assembly of the State of New-Jersey. . . .</u>, c. CCCXXXVII (of the session beginning October 26, 1790).

"An Act to Direct the Time and Mode of Electing Representatives in the Congress of the United States, for this State," <u>Acts of the Sixteenth General Assembly of the State of New-Jersey</u>, c. CCCLXXIII (May 29, 1792).

"An Act Directing the Time and Mode of Electing Representatives in the House of Representatives of the Congress of the United States," <u>Acts of the Twenty-Second General Assembly of the State of New-Jersey</u>, c. DCCV (March 1, 1798).

"An Act Directing the Time and Mode of Electing Representatives in the House of Representatives of the Congress of the United States for this State," <u>Acts of the Twenty-Eighth General Assembly of the State of New-Jersey</u>, c. XCI (October 29, 1803).

"An Act Directing the Mode of Electing Representatives in the House of Representatives of the Congress of the United States for this State," <u>Acts of the Thirtieth General Assembly of the State of New Jersey</u>, c. C (March 3, 1806).

"An Act Directing the Time and Mode of Electing Electors of the President and Vice-President of the United States, and Representatives in Congress on the Part of this State," <u>Acts of the Thirty-Second General Assembly of the State of New Jersey</u>, c. IX (December 3, 1807).

Bloomfield, Joseph (comp.), <u>Laws of the State of New Jersey</u>. Trenton: J. Wilson, 1811.

"An Act Directing the Time and Mode of Electing Representatives in Congress on the Part of this State, Acts of the <u>Thirty-Seventh General Assembly of the State of New Jersey, p</u>. 5 (November 7, 1812).

"An Act Directing the Time and Mode of Electing Representatives in Congress on the Part of this State," Revised Laws of the State of New Jersey, pp. 434-36 (1821).

"An Act Relative to the Election of Representatives to the Next Congress of the United States," [Acts of the General Assembly of New Jersey], p. 128 (March 2, 1830).

"An Act to Provide for the Appointment of Electors of the Next President and Vice President of the United States, and for the Election of Representatives in the Next Congress," Acts of the Sixty-First General Assembly of the State of New Jersey, p. 1 (October 26, 1836).

NEW YORK

"An Act Directing the Times, Places and Manner of Electing Representatives in this State, for the House of Representatives in this State, for the House of Representatives of the Congress of the United States of America," Laws of the State of New York, c. XI (January 27, 1789).

"An Act for Electing Representatives for this State, in the House of Representatives of the Congress of the United States. . . . ," Laws of the State of New York, c. V (December 18, 1792).

"An Act to Amend the Act for Regulating the Election of Representatives for this State, in the House of Representatives of the Congress of the United States," Laws of the State of New York, c. LXXII (March 30, 1802).

"An Act for Regulating the Election of Representatives for this State in the House of Representatives of the Congress of the United States," Laws of the State of New York, c. XIX (March 20, 1804).

"An Act to Divide the State into Districts for the Election of Representatives to the Congress of the United States," Laws of the State of New York, c. CLXX (April 8, 1808).

"An Act to Divide the State into Districts for the Election of Representatives to the Congress of the United States," Laws of the State of New York, p. 277 (1822).

"An Act to Divide the State into Districts for the Election of Representatives to the Congress of the United States," Laws of the State of New York (1832).

NORTH CAROLINA

"An Act to Amend an Act, Entitled, 'An Act Directing the Manner of Electing Representatives to Represent this State in Congress,' " Laws of North Carolina, c. I (November 1, 1790).

"An Act for Dividing the State into Districts, for the Purpose of Electing Representatives to Congress," Laws of North Carolina, c. XVII (1792).

"An Act for Dividing the State into Districts, for the Purpose of Electing Representatives to Congress," Laws of North Carolina, c. II (November 5, 1802).

"An Act for Dividing the State into Districts for Electing Representatives to Congress," The Laws of the State of North Carolina. . . . , c. VI (November 16, 1812).

OHIO

"An Act to Provide for the Election of a Representative to Congress," Acts of the State of Ohio, c. XXVII (April 16, 1803).

"An Act to District the State of Ohio," Acts of the State of Ohio, c. XXXIII (February 14, 1812).

"An Act, to Divide the State of Ohio into Congressional Districts," Acts Passed at the Second Session of the Twentieth General Assembly of the State of Ohio, c. I (May 23, 1822).

"An Act to Divide the State of Ohio into Congressional Districts," Acts of a General Nature Passed at the Second Session of the Thirtieth General Assembly of the State of Ohio, p. 6 (June 13, 1832).

Downes, Randolph C., Evolution of Ohio County Boundaries. Columbus, 1970.

PENNSYLVANIA

"An Act to Provide for the Election of Representatives of the People of this State in the Congress of the United States," Acts of the General Assembly of the Commonwealth of Pennsylvania, c. XIII (March 16, 1791).

"An Act to Provide for the Election of Representatives of the People of this State in the Congress of the United States," Acts of the General Assembly of the Commonwealth of Pennsylvania, c. CCLVI (April 22, 1794).

"An Act to Provide for the Election of Representatives of the People of this State, in the Congress of the United States," Acts of the General Assembly of the State of Pennsylvania, c. LXXIII (April 2, 1802).

"An Act to Provide for the Election of Representatives of the People of this State, in the Congress of the United States," Acts of the General Assembly of the State of Pennsylvania, c. LXXXII (March 20, 1812).

"An Act to Provide for the Election of Representatives of the People of this State, in the Congress of the United States," Acts of the General Assembly of the State of Pennsylvania, c. CLXXIV (April 2, 1822).

"An Act to Provide for the Election of Representatives of the People of this State, in the Congress of the United States," Acts of the General Assembly of the State of Pennsylvania, no. 227 (June 9, 1832).

RHODE ISLAND

"An Act Directing the Mode of Choosing Representatives to Congress," Public Laws of the State of Rhode Island, p. 25 (June, 1798).

"An Act Explanatory of an Act, Entitled, 'An Act for the Election of a Representative for this State to the Congress of the United States," The Laws of Rhode Island, p. 184 (September 16, 1814).

"An Act to Provide for the Election of a Representative to Represent the People of this State in the House of Representatives of the Nineteenth Congress of the United States," Public Laws of the State of Rhode Island, p. 620 (November 5, 1825).

"An Act in Amendment of the Act Entitled, 'An Act Relative to the Election of Senators and Representatives to Represent this State in Congress, and of Electors for the Election of a President and Vice President of the United States,' " Public Laws of the State of Rhode Island, p. 808 (January 22, 1833).

SOUTH CAROLINA

"An Act Prescribing on the Part of this State, the Times, Places, and Manner of Holding Elections for Representatives in the Congress, and the Manner of Appointing Electors of a President of the United States," Acts and Ordinances of the General Assembly of South Carolina, p. 3 (November 4, 1788).

"An Act Prescribing on the Part of this State, the the [sic.] Times, Places and Manner of Holding Elections for Representatives in the Congress of the United States," Acts and Resolutions of the General Assembly of the State of South Carolina, p. 18 (December 21, 1792).

"An Act Prescribing, on the Part of this State, the Times, Places, and Manner of Holding Elections for Representatives in the Congress of the United states," Acts and Resolutions of the General Assembly of the State of South Carolina, pp. 29-34 (December 18, 1802).

"An Act Prescribing, on the Part of this State, the Times, Places, and Manner of Holding Elections for Representatives in the Congress of the United States," Acts of the General Assembly of South Carolina, pp. 3-7 (August 29, 1812).

"An Act Prescribing, on the Part of this State, the Times, Places and Manner of Holding Elections for Representatives in the Congress of the United States," Acts and Resolutions of the General Assembly of South Carolina, c. 1 (December 21, 1822).

Acts and Resolutions of the General Assembly of the State of South-Carolina, 2 vols. (vol. 1, 1786-1814 and vol. 2, 1814-1839). Columbia, S.C.: 1839.

TENNESSEE

"An Act to Provide for an Election to Elect a Representative or Representatives to Represent this State in the Congress of the United States, and to Supply Vacancies that may hereafter take Place," Acts Passed at the First Session of the Fourth General Assembly of the State of Tennessee, c. XLIII (September 26, 1801).

"An Act to Provide for the Election of Representatives from this State, to the Congress of the United States, and for other Purposes," Acts Passed at the First Session of the Fifth General Assembly of the State of Tennessee, c. LXXIX (November 1, 1803).

"An Act to Provide for the Election of Representatives from this State to the Congress of the United States," Acts Passed at the Second Session of the Ninth General Assembly of the State of Tennessee, c. XXVII (October 12, 1812).

"An Act to Divide the State of Tennessee into Districts for the Election of Representatives in the Congress of the United States," Acts Passed at the Second Session of the Fourteenth General Assembly of the State of Tennessee, c. I (July 31, 1822).

"An Act to Divide the State of Tennessee into Districts, for the Election of Representatives to the Congress of the United States," Public Acts Passed at the Called Session of the Nineteenth General Assembly of the State of Tennessee, c. IV (October 1, 1832).

VERMONT

"An Act Dividing this State into Districts for Electing Representatives to the Congress of the United States," Acts and Laws Passed by the Legislature of the State of Vermont, p. 85 (November 8, 1792).

"An Act Dividing the State into Districts, for Electing Representatives to the Congress of the United States, and Directing the Mode of Their Election," Acts and Laws Passed by the Legislature of the State of Vermont, c. 47 (November 4, 1802).

"An Act for Electing Representatives to the Congress of the United States, and Directing the Mode of Their Election," Acts and Laws Passed by the Legislature of the State of Vermont, c. 100 (November 4, 1812).

"An Act Dividing the State into Districts for Electing Representatives to the Congress of the United States, and Directing the Mode of Their Election," Acts Passed by the Legislature of the State of Vermont, c. 23 (November 11, 1822).

"An Act, Dividing the State into Districts for Electing Representatives to the Congress of the United States, and Directing the Mode of Their Election," Acts Passed by the Legislature of the State of Vermont, c. 11 (November, 1832).

VIRGINIA

"An Act for the Election of Representatives Pursuant to the Constitution of the Government of the United States," Acts Passed at the General Assembly of the Commonwealth of Virginia, c. II (November 20, 1788).

"An Act for Arranging the Counties of this Commonwealth into Districts to Choose Representatives to Congress," Acts of the General Assembly of the Commonwealth of Virginia, c. 1 (December 26, 1792).

"An Act for Arranging the Counties of this State into Districts, to Choose Representatives to Congress," Acts Passed at a General Assembly of the Commonwealth of Virginia, c. XXIV (January 30, 1802).

"An Act for Arranging the Counties of this Commonwealth into Districts to Choose Representatives to Congress," Acts of the General Assembly of the Commonwealth of Virginia, c. XXIII (February 6, 1813).

"An Act to Amend the Act, for Arranging the Counties of this Commonwealth into Districts, to Choose Representatives to Congress," Acts of the Commonwealth of Virginia, c. 40 (January 24, 1823).

"An Act to Amend the Act, Entitled, 'An Act for Arranging the Counties and Towns of this Commonwealth into Districts for the Choice of Representatives to Congress,'" Acts of the General Assembly of the Commonwealth of Virginia c. 37 (February 27, 1833).

PART II

Asseff, Emmitt, Legislative Apportionment in Louisiana. Baton Rouge: Bureau of Government Research, Louisiana State University, 1950.

Bell, Rudolph M., Party and Faction in American Politics: The House of Representatives, 1789-1801. Westport, Conn,: Greenwood Press, 1973.

Biographical Directory of the American Congress, 1774-1971. U.S. Government Printing Office, 1971.

Browne, Gary L., "Baltimore in the Nation, 1789-1861: A Social Economy in Industrial Revolution." Unpublished Ph.D. thesis, Wayne State University, 1973.

Carey, Mathew, Carey's American Atlas. Philadelphia, 1795.

_____, Carey's General Atlas. Philadelphia, 1814.

Congressional Quarterly, Inc., Members of Congress Since 1789. Washington, 1977.

Dauer, Manning J., The Adams Federalists. Baltimore: The Johns Hopkins University Press, 1968.

Diamond, Robert A. (ed.), Guide to U.S. Elections. Washington: Congressional Quarterly, Inc., 1975.

Esarey, Logan, A History of Indiana: From its Exploration to 1850. Indianapolis: W. K. Stewart Co., 1915.

Everton, George B., Handybook for Genealogists. Salt Lake City: Desert Books, 1975.

Finley, Anthony, A New General Atlas. Philadelphia, 1824.

_____, A New General Atlas. Philadelphia, 1831.

Hinton, John Howard, The History and Topography of the United States. Philadelphia, 1832.

Hewes, Fletcher W., Citizen's Atlas of American Politics, 1789-1892. New York, 1892.

Howard, Perry H., to Stanley B. Parsons, 18 February 1977, Personal Files of Stanley B. Parsons, Kansas City, Missouri.

Hughes, Edward J., Counties of Illinois. Illinois State Publications, 1934.

Kane, Joseph Nathan, The American Counties. New York: Scarecrow Press, 1960.

Lucas, Fielding, A General Atlas. Philadelphia, 1824.

Moore, Albert Burton, History of Alabama. University of Alabama Supply Store, 1934.

Pearson, F. B. and Harlor, J. D., Ohio History Sketches. Columbus, Ohio: Fred J. Heer, 1903.

Purcell, Richard J., Connecticut in Transition, 1775-1818. Washington: American Historical Association, 1918.

Records of the States of the United States of America, prepared by the Library of Congress in association with the University of North Carolina under the general editorship of William Sumner Jenkins. Washington, 1949.

Roseboom, Eugene Holloway and Weisenburger, Francis P., A History of Ohio. New York: Prentice-Hall, 1934.

United States Censuses:

Return of the Whole Number of Persons within the Several Districts of the United States. . . . [First Census of the United States, 1791]. Philadelphia, 1791.

Return of the Whole Number of Persons within the Several Districts of the United States. . . . [Second Census of the United States, 1801]. Washington, 1801.

Aggregate Amount of Persons within the United States in the Year 1810 [Third Census of the United States]. Washington, 1811.

Census for 1820. Book One. Washington, 1821.

Fifth Census; or, Enumeration of the Inhabitants of the United States, 1830. Washington, 1832.

United States Department of Commerce, Bureau of the Census, County and City Data Book. Washington, 1973.

Index of Names

(The number in parentheses indicates the Congress with which that name is associated)

ALABAMA

Baylor, Robert E. B. (21)
Chapman, Reuben (24, 25, 26, 27)
Clay, Clement C. (21, 22, 23)
Crabb, George W. (25, 26)
Dellet, James (26)
Houston, George S. (27)
Hubbard, David (26)
Lawler, Joab (24, 25)
Lewis, Dixon H. (21, 22, 23, 24, 25, 26, 27)
Lyon, Francis S. (24, 25)
Mardis, Samuel W. (22, 23)
Martin, Joshua L. (24, 25)
McKee, John (18, 19, 20)
McKinley, John (23)
Moore, Gabriel (18, 19, 20)
Murphy, John (23)
Owen, George W. (18, 19, 20)
Payne, William W. (27)
Shields, Benjamin G. (27)

ARKANSAS

Cross, Edward (26, 27)
Yell, Archibald (24, 25)

CONNECTICUT

Allen, John (5)
Baldwin, John (19, 20)
Baldwin, Simeon (8)
Barber, Noyes (17, 18, 19, 20, 21, 22, 23)
Boardman, William W. (26, 27)
Brace, Jonathan (5, 6)
Brockway, John H. (26, 27)
Burrows, Daniel (17)
Champion, Epaphroditus (10, 11, 12, 13, 14)
Coit, Joshua (3, 4, 5)

(Connecticut, Continued)
Dana, Samuel W. (4, 5, 6, 7, 8, 9, 10, 11)
Davenport, James (4, 5)
Davenport, John (7, 8, 9, 10, 11, 12, 13, 14)
Dwight, Theodore (9)
Edmond, William (5, 6)
Edwards, Henry W. (16, 17)
Ellsworth, William W. (21, 22, 23)
Foote, Samuel A. (16, 18 23)
Gilbert, Sylvester (15)
Goddard, Calvin (7, 8, 9)
Goodrich, Chauncey (4, 5, 6)
Goodrich, Elizur (6)
Griswold, Roger (4, 5, 6, 7, 8, 9)
Haley, Elisha (24, 25)
Hillhouse, James (2, 3, 4)
Holmes, Uriel (15)
Holt, Orrin (24, 25)
Huntington, Benjamin (1)
Huntington, Ebenezer (11, 15)
Huntington, Jabez W. (21, 22, 23)
Ingersoll, Ralph I. (19, 20, 21, 22)
Ingham, Samuel (24, 25)
Jackson, Ebenezer, Jr. (23)
Judson, Andrew T. (24)
Law, Lyman (12, 13, 14)
Learned, Amasa (2, 3)
Merwin, Orange (19, 20)
Miner, Phineas (23)
Moseley, Jonathan O. (9, 10, 11, 12, 13, 14, 15, 16)
Osborne, Thomas B. (26, 27)
Perkins, Elias (7)
Phelps, Elisha (16, 19, 20)
Phelps, Lancelot (24, 25)
Pitkin, Timothy (9, 10, 11, 12, 13, 14, 15)
Plant, David (20)
Russ, John (16, 17)
Sherman, Roger (1)
Sherwood, Samuel B. (15)
Smith, John C. (6, 7, 8, 9)
Smith, Nathaniel (4, 5)

ABOUT THE COMPILERS

Stanley B. Parsons is professor of history at the University of Missouri-Kansas City. He is the author of *The Populist Context: Rural versus Urban Power on a Great Plains Frontier* (Greenwood Press, 1973). William W. Beach is an instructor in history at the University of Missouri-Kansas City. Dan Hermann received his M. A. in history from the University of Missouri-Kansas City.